Community-Based Corrections

Community-Based Corrections

NINTH EDITION

Leanne Fiftal Alarid
University of Texas, San Antonio

 WADSWORTH
CENGAGE Learning·

Australia • Brazil • Japan • Korea • Mexico • Singapore • Spain • United Kingdom • United States

WADSWORTH
CENGAGE Learning·

Community-Based Corrections,
Ninth Edition
Leanne Fiftal Alarid

Editor-in-Chief: Linda Ganster

Senior Acquisitions Editor: Carolyn Henderson Meier

Developmental Editor: Shelley Murphy

Assistant Editor: Virginette Acacio

Media Editor: Andy Yap

Marketing Manager: Michelle Williams

Marketing Program Manager: Jack Ward

Senior Marketing Communications Manager: Heather Baxley

Art and Cover Direction, Production Management, and Composition: PreMediaGlobal

Manufacturing Planner: Judy Inouye

Rights Acquisitions Specialist: Thomas McDonough

Cover Image: *Breathalizer test administered in the work setting to determine alcohol consumption* © Mira/Alamy, *Man having a conversation in a soup kitchen* © JLP/Jose L. Pelaez/Corbis, *Convicted criminals doing painting and decorating in orange tabards with community payback slogan on the back* © Roger Bamber/Alamy, *Adult students listening in classroom* © Hill Street Studios/ Blend Images/Corbis

Cover Designer: Reizebos Holzbaur/Andrei Pasternak

For product information and technology assistance, contact us at **Cengage Learning Customer & Sales Support, 1-800-354-9706.**

For permission to use material from this text or product, submit all requests online at **www.cengage.com/permissions.** Further permissions questions can be e-mailed to **permissionrequest@cengage.com.**

Library of Congress Control Number: 2012930175

Student Edition:

ISBN-13: 978-1-133-04966-1

ISBN-10: 1-133-04966-4

Instructor Edition:

ISBN-13: 978-1-133-31559-9

ISBN-10: 1-133-31559-3

Wadsworth
20 Davis Drive
Belmont, CA 94002-3098
USA

Cengage Learning is a leading provider of customized learning solutions with office locations around the globe, including Singapore, the United Kingdom, Australia, Mexico, Brazil, and Japan. Locate your local office at **www.cengage.com/global.**

Cengage Learning products are represented in Canada by Nelson Education, Ltd.

To learn more about Wadsworth, visit **www.cengage.com/Wadsworth** Purchase any of our products at your local college store or at our preferred online store **www.CengageBrain.com.**

Printed in the United States of America
1 2 3 4 5 6 7 16 15 14 13 12

To my mentor Crazyhorse—the absolute coolest person—to my loving family, and to the Mojos—ride on!
Leanne F. Alarid

Brief Contents

Contents

Preface

Evidence-based practices (EBP) are changing the way that many agencies operate to an acceptance of empirical research and evaluation to determine what improvements can be made for more efficient use of rehabilitation programs and correctional technology. Through the principles of effective correctional intervention, more is known about what works with certain types of offenders. There is also a broader array of choices available as alternatives to incarceration than ever before. EBP has caused a dramatic shift in the way that offenders are supervised in the community and prepared for release from prison.

This book operates on two assumptions. First, most people who are diverted from a conviction or who are convicted of a crime are supervised in the community on a form of community-based corrections and not in jail or prison. A second assumption is that while some people should be incarcerated for their crimes, the reality is that few are kept for the remainder of their natural lives. Between 95–97% of people in jail or prison today will be released at some point and many will undergo a period of community supervision as they transition back to the community. This book examines programs that operate to fit the needs of various types of offenders.

The goal of the ninth edition of *Community-Based Corrections* is to provide students with comprehensive, up-to-date, evidence-based practices and research for probation, release from prison, and other community-based alternatives. We have sought to present community-based correctional programs in their historical, philosophical, social, and legal context and to integrate real-life practice to the greatest extent possible. Because we want this book to be of practical use, we have provided many examples of community-based programs and procedures from various jurisdictions. While we do provide examples from state systems, the federal system is our primary point of reference throughout the text, since local community corrections programs vary so widely.

NEW UPDATES AND ORGANIZATION OF THE NINTH EDITION

The most significant change to note with this edition is a brand new chapter on special needs offenders (Chapter 6), which details the community supervision of offenders who have needs related to substance abuse, mental illness, sex offense conviction, and confirmed gang members. This new chapter brings together information which was previously presented in three different chapters in 8e (Chapters 2, 5, and 8) and updated to the most current and relevant. Information is expanded on problem solving courts and a new topic on veterans courts. One related case study (Case C: Jonas Knight) from Chapter 9 was moved to Chapter 6.

Due to more agencies combining probation and parole supervision together, conditions and modifications have been consolidated into one chapter. Chapter 7 (Probation Modification and Termination) and Chapter 13 (Parole Conditions and Revocation) from the eighth edition were consolidated into one chapter in the current edition as Chapter 7, entitled, *Community Supervision Modification and Revocation*. Prisoner and officer perspectives of release (pp. 298–302 of Chapter 13 from 8e) were moved and updated into Chapter 11 on prisoner reentry in this edition.

Both history chapters now appear earlier in the book: The history of probation (Chapter 4 in 8e) is now Chapter 2 in this edition and the chronology of parole (Chapter 11 in 8e) is now Chapter 3.

Chapter-by-chapter changes from the previous edition include expanded coverage of economic and budgetary issues affecting local, state, and federal jurisdictions in Chapter 1. The first part of Chapter 2 from 8e (on pretrial release, pretrial supervision, and diversion) has been relocated to the beginning of the Sentencing and PSI chapter (now Chapter 4 of this edition). Chapter 4 contains expanded coverage of how different jurisdictions handle sentencing, along with a second presentence investigation report example.

Chapter 5 focuses more coverage on classification, interviewing, and supervision according to evidence-based practices. This chapter also has a brand new case study (Case B: Maria Diaz) on identity theft. The topic of interstate compacts (transfer of supervision to another state) was moved from Chapter 6 (8e) to Chapter 5 in the current edition. The rest of Chapter 6 (from 8e) containing topics relevant to officers, such as salaries, firearms, stress, and private probation, etc. was moved later in the book to become Chapter 12. Chapter 12 is oriented toward careers of community supervision officers and the knowledge, skills, and abilities needed. Chapter 13 on juvenile correctional options contains all new tables and figures throughout, along with expanded material on graduated sanctions and juvenile reentry.

Pedagogical Features and Learning Tools

In the ninth edition, each chapter opens with a human interest story that corresponds to the material pertaining to that particular chapter. Each chapter has learning objectives of noteworthy concepts in a bulleted list format. Key terms are boldfaced in the text, with their accompanying definitions in the margins, and also defined in the glossary at the back of the book. Each chapter contains a new "Fact or Fiction" feature that presents an issue that is perceived in a particular way, and then follows up as to whether that perception is factual or a myth.

The most notable teaching pedagogical teaching tool available in this text allows the student to apply kinesthetic learning and case study methods to examine an arrest report and criminal background check on a created defendant, engage in a mock interview with that client, prepare a presentence report, score the risk/needs assessment, and create an individualized supervision plan for the client. All of these tools are placed in appropriate chapters so students can engage in real-world experience and writing as they read. Each chapter contains the following pedagogical features:

BOXED FEATURES   There are two boxed features running through the text in most chapters. One box theme is "Technology in Corrections" and illustrates how advancements in equipment and knowledge about data systems have impacted the corrections system. The second box theme is "Corrections Up Close" which investigates a particular topic in more detail as it pertains to the chapter material. In six chapters, the "Field Notes" boxed text features different practitioners who write about a different correctional issue from their own perspective.

CHAPTER REVIEW   Each chapter is followed by a bulleted summary list. Internet websites and discussion questions are included to encourage students to critically think about the material in each chapter. Some discussion questions are designed as topics for essay questions or research papers.

CASE STUDIES   Each chapter now has one or two case studies for in-class discussion or to use as a basis for writing assignments. Some of the case studies were revised and instructions were clarified. Brand new case studies were added to five chapters. All of the websites were updated and we added video and podcast links at the end of each chapter.

ANCILLARIES

Instructor Resources

INSTRUCTOR'S RESOURCE MANUAL WITH TEST BANK   by Carly M. Hilinski-Rosick of Grand Valley State University

The manual includes learning objectives, key terms, a detailed chapter outline, a chapter summary, discussion topics, student activities and a test bank. Each chapter's test bank contains questions in multiple-choice, true false, fill-in-the-blank, and essay formats, with a full answer key. The test bank is coded to the learning objectives that appear in the main text, and includes the page numbers in the main text where the answers can be found. Finally, each question in the test bank has been carefully reviewed by experienced criminal justice instructors for quality, accuracy, and content coverage. Our Instructor Approved seal, which appears on the front cover, is our assurance that you are working with an assessment and grading resource of the highest caliber.

The manual is available for download on the password-protected website and can also be obtained by e-mailing your local Cengage Learning representative.

POWERPOINTS   by Barbara Belbot of University of Houston Downtown

These handy Microsoft PowerPoint slides, which outline the chapters of the main text in a classroom-ready presentation, will help you in making your lectures engaging and in reaching your visually oriented students. The presentations are available for download on the password-protected website and can also be obtained by e-mailing your local Cengage Learning representative.

LESSON PLANS   by Deborah Vegh of Central Connecticut State University

The Lesson Plans bring accessible, masterful suggestions to every lesson. This supplement includes a sample syllabus, learning objectives, lecture notes, discussion topics, in-class activities, a detailed lecture outline, assignments, media tools, and "What if . . ." scenarios. Current events and real-life examples in the form of articles, websites and video links are incorporated into the class discussion topics, activities and assignments. The lecture outlines are correlated with PowerPoint slides for ease of classroom use. Lesson Plans are available on the PowerLecture resource and the instructor website.

EXAMVIEW® COMPUTERIZED TESTING   The comprehensive Instructor's Manual described above is backed up by ExamView, a computerized test bank available for PC and Macintosh computers. With ExamView you can create, deliver, and customize tests and study guides (both print and online) in minutes. You can easily edit and import your own questions and graphics, change test layouts, and reorganize questions. And using ExamView's complete word-processing capabilities, you can enter an unlimited number of new questions or edit existing questions.

THE WADSWORTH CRIMINAL JUSTICE VIDEO LIBRARY   So many exciting new videos—so many great ways to enrich your lectures and spark discussion of the material in this text. Your Cengage Learning representative will be happy to provide details on our video policy by adoption size. The library includes these selections and many others.

- *ABC® Videos*. ABC videos feature short, high-interest clips from current news events as well as historic raw footage going back 40 years. Perfect for discussion starters or to enrich your lectures and spark interest in the material in the text, these brief videos provide students with a new lens through which to view the past and present, one that will greatly enhance their knowledge and understanding of significant events and open up to them new dimensions in learning. Clips are drawn from such programs as *World News Tonight, Good Morning America, This Week, PrimeTime Live, 20/20*, and *Nightline*, as well as numerous ABC News specials and material from the Associated Press Television News and British Movietone News collections.
- *Cengage Learning's "Introduction Criminal Justice Video Series"* features videos supplied by the BBC Motion Gallery. These short, high-interest clips from CBS and BBC news programs – everything from nightly news broadcasts and specials to CBS News Special Reports, CBS Sunday Morning, 60 Minutes, and more – are perfect classroom discussion starters. Designed to enrich your lectures and spark interest in the material in the text, these brief videos provide students with a new lens through which to view the past and present, one that will greatly enhance their knowledge and understanding of significant events and open up to them new dimensions in learning. Clips are drawn from BBC Motion Gallery.

CRIMINAL JUSTICE MEDIA LIBRARY   Cengage Learning's Criminal Justice Media Library includes nearly 300 media assets on the topics you cover in your courses. Available to stream from any Web-enabled computer, the Criminal Justice Media Library's assets include such valuable resources as: Career Profile Videos featuring interviews with criminal justice professionals from a range of roles and locations, simulations that allow students to step into various roles and practice their decision-making skills, video clips on current topics from ABC® and other sources, animations that illustrate key concepts, interactive learning modules that help students check their knowledge of important topics, and Reality Check exercises that compare expectations and preconceived notions against the real-life thoughts and experiences of criminal justice professionals. The Criminal Justice Media Library can be uploaded and used within many popular Learning Management Systems. You can also customize it with your own course material. Please contact your Cengage Learning representative for ordering and pricing information.

Student Resources

COURSEMATE   Cengage Learning's Criminal Justice CourseMate brings course concepts to life with interactive learning, study, and exam preparation tools that support the printed textbook. CourseMate includes an integrated eBook, quizzes mapped to chapter Learning Objectives, flashcards, videos, and more, and Engagement-Tracker, a first-of-its-kind tool that monitors student engagement in the course. The accompanying instructor website offers access to password-protected resources such as an electronic version of the instructor's manual and PowerPoint® slides.

CAREERS IN CRIMINAL JUSTICE WEBSITE   *Can be bundled with this text at no additional charge.* Featuring plenty of self-exploration and profiling activities, the interactive Careers in Criminal Justice Website helps students investigate and focus on the criminal justice career choices that are right for them. Includes interest assessment, video testimonials from career professionals, resume and interview tips, and links for reference.

CLEBOOK   Cengage Learning's Criminal Justice ebooks allow students to access our textbooks in an easy-to-use online format. Highlight, take notes, bookmark, search your text, and, for most texts, link directly into multimedia. In short, CLeBooks combine the best features of paper books and ebooks in one package.

CURRENT PERSPECTIVES: READINGS FROM INFOTRAC® COLLEGE EDITION   These readers, designed to give students a closer look at special topics in criminal justice, include free access to InfoTrac College Edition. The timely articles are selected by experts in each topic from within InfoTrac College Edition. They are available free when bundled with the text and include the following titles:

- Introduction to Criminal Justice
- Community Corrections
- Cyber Crime
- Victimology
- Juvenile Justice
- Racial Profiling
- White-Collar Crime
- Terrorism and Homeland Security
- Public Policy and Criminal Justice
- Technology and Criminal Justice
- Ethics in Criminal Justice
- Forensics and Criminal Investigation
- Corrections
- Law and Courts
- Policy in Criminal Justice

ACKNOWLEDGMENTS

This book could not have been written without the generous assistance of many colleagues and corrections professionals. We appreciate the professionals who wrote personal "Field Notes" essays that added more personality to the book: Judge Al Alonso, Eladio Castillo, Ralph Garza, Mark Masterson, Tess Price, and Abel Salinas. Debi Shaffer of the University of Nevada-Las Vegas kindly provided us with information and referrals to use in this edition.

We express our appreciation to Kevin Dooley of Central New Mexico Community College and Debra K. Wicks of Pittsburgh Technical Institute for detailed chapter-by-chapter reviews.

We wish to acknowledge 61 reviewers who provided comments on the 8th edition: Jennifer Cobbina, Michigan State University; Bryn Herrschaft, Rutgers University; Mario Paparozzi, University of North Carolina-Pembroke; Giselle White-Perry, South Carolina State University; Christopher Hensley, University of Tennessee-Chattanooga; Rita Shah, University of California-Irvine; Richard Steinhaus, New Mexico Junior College; Jennifer Prutsman-Pfeiffer, SUNY College-Brockport; Melinda

Schlagerq, Texas A&M University-Commerce; Michael G. Bisciglia, Southeastern Louisiana University; Betsy Witt, Limestone College; Pamela Hart, Iowa Western Community College; Allan Krescent, Los Angeles Valley College; Donna R. Bennett, Trinity Valley Community College; Collin Lau, Chaminade University-Honolulu; Cort Tanner, Cisco College; Diane Sjuts, Metro Community College; James Wright, Chattanooga State Community College; Anne Strouth, North Central State College; James Showers, Pensacola Christian College; Joseph Julian, Broome Community College; Nicholas Fagioli, Kean University; Jim Santor, College of Southern Nevada; Samantha Carlo, Miami Dade College; Henry Meade, University of Texas-San Antonio; Terry Lyons, University of Mississippi; Russell Carlino, Duquesne University; Tracy Grunenfelder, St Martins; William Hitch, University of Mary Hardin-Baylor; Pam Simek, Bossier Parish Community College; Patrick Massaro, Butler County Community College; Doug Devaney, Peru State College; Arnold R. Waggoner, Rose State College; Robert L. Torrisi, Cayuga Community College; David P. Stumpf, Minnesota School of Business; Megan Cole, Brown College; Joyce Dozier, Wilmington College; Tom Destito, Metropolitan State College-Denver; Barry McCrary, Western Illinois University; Jaki Johnson, Okefenokee Technical College; Paul Koch, San Bernardino Valley College; Ann d'Auteuil Bartolo, Fairmont State University; Paul Donnelly, University of Texas-Dallas; Caryl Lynn Segal, University of Texas-Permian Basin; Marianne Hudson, Boise State University; Pierrette R. Ayotte, Thomas College; Teresa McCook, South Georgia Technical College; Mergim Nimani, Southern Connecticut State University; Robert Kelly, Mountain State University; Kelly G. Walls, Bluefield College; Sean Joiner, Augusta Technical College; A.W. Pellicane, Brookdale Community College.; Emran W. Khan, Clayton State University; and Armando Flores, University of Texas-Permian Basin. Their insightful comments and suggestions were invaluable to our continued improvements.

Educators who reviewed earlier editions of the book include Joseph Apiahene, University of Texas-Pan American; Lincoln Chandler, Florida Memorial College; Dana DeWitt, Chadron State University; Teresa Hall, Sandhills Community College; Charles Hinman, Kirtland Community College; G. G. Hunt, Wharton County Junior College; David Jaso, Austin Community College; J. H. Koonce, Edgecombe Community College; Sheri Short, Navarro College; David Stumpf, Central Lakes College; and Ron Walker, Trinity Valley Community College. For the seventh edition we would like to thank Rodney Henningsen, Sam Houston State University; Patrice Morris, Rutgers University-Newark; Gaylene Armstrong, Sam Houston State University; Denny Langston, Central Missouri State University; and Thomas Allen, University of South Dakota. For the eighth edition, we acknowledge Megan Cole, Brown College, 1st Lt. Gary F. Cornelius, George Mason University, Cathryn Lavery, Iona College, Jeffrey O'Donnell, Point Park University, and George Alexander, Buffalo State University. Finally, we would like to thank the following individuals for their pictorial contributions to the text: Ray Alarid, Bob Goodson, Mike Hicks, Alex Holsinger, Kristi Holsinger, LaShaun Lars, Wayne Lucas, Eric Myers, Dolly Owen, Donnie Turner, the Choppers, and Jim Wuster. This text is more interesting because of you.

Leanne Fiftal Alarid

PART I

Overview and Evolution of Community Corrections

The idea behind community corrections programs is that most offenders can be effectively held accountable for their crimes at the same time that they fulfill legitimate living standards in the community. Most offenders do not pose an imminent danger to themselves or to others and can therefore remain in the community to maintain relationships. Punishing offenders living in the community confers several benefits.

First, the offender remains in the community in which he or she has responsibilities. With legitimate employment, offenders can support themselves and their family of origin, and they will pay taxes. Second, offenders living in the community are more likely than prison-bound offenders to compensate their victim through restitution or to pay back the community through community service. Finally, community corrections programs do not expose offenders to the subculture of violence that exists in many jails and prisons.

Chapter 1 introduces the array of community corrections programs and explains why the study of community corrections is important, including the movement of the field toward evidence-based practices. Chapter 2 chronicles the history of probation from the early 1800s to the present, including a section discussing how supervision philosophy has changed over time, and ends with a description of who is on probation. Chapter 3 examines the history of reentry that began as discretionary parole, which for violent and habitual offenders has been replaced by mandatory release. Discretionary parole remains an important decision point in the correctional process.

An Overview of Community Corrections: Goals and Evidence-Based Practices

CHAPTER LEARNING OBJECTIVES

1. Describe how correctional agencies and programs carry out the conditions or sentence imposed by the court judge.
2. Define corrections and its purpose.

3. Examine sentencing policies and how they have contributed to correctional growth in institutional and community-based corrections.
4. Identify various types of community corrections programs.

Casey Anthony walks out of jail with her attorney in July 2011, where she had been for nearly three years during her trial for which she was acquitted on charges of killing her daughter Caylee. Anthony was found guilty of lying to police and sentenced to time served. She began serving one year of probation in August for felony check charges.

CHAPTER OUTLINE

KEY TERMS

community corrections
post-adjudication
pre-adjudication
probation
indeterminate sentencing
presumptive sentence

determinate sentencing
bail
pretrial supervision
intermediate sanctions
prisoner reentry
prerelease program

parole
restorative justice
evidence-based practices
net widening
recidivism

On July 3, 2010, Walter Phelps was shot during an armed robbery of his hardware store in a small town in southern Georgia. One month later, he died from gunshot wound complications. The perpetrator, Jordan Harris, was out of jail on pretrial release for other pending armed robberies. At the time, Harris was wearing an ankle device hooked to an electronic monitor that was court-ordered to be tracked by an outside company. The problem was that although the ankle device was provided, the company was not tracking Harris at the time of the hardware store robbery, and too much time elapsed between the point at which Harris was supposed to be monitored and the time the arrest warrant was issued. The company claimed it was confused by the court order, and there were multiple contractors that provided services, so it was unclear who was to provide the electronic monitoring service or issue the warrant. Georgia lawmakers recently authorized bail bond companies to provide electronic monitoring to offenders on pretrial release because these companies, without having to obtain a warrant, are already authorized to pick up offenders who violate their bond conditions (Wallace, 2011).

Is bail company-sponsored electronic monitoring for pretrial defendants on bond a good idea?

THE CORRECTIONAL DILEMMA

In the United States approximately 7.4 million people, equivalent to about 3% of the total adult population, are currently under some form of correctional supervision. Our nation's crime control policies over the past three decades have resulted in a steady increase of convicted misdemeanants and felons in the correctional system. However, in 2009 the overall state prison population declined

community corrections
A nonincarcerative sanction in which offenders serve all or a portion of their sentence in the community.

post-adjudication
The defendant has either pleaded guilty or been found guilty by a judge or jury.

pre-adjudication
Treatment with supervision occurs in the community prior to a finding of guilt.

slightly for the first time in 40 years. Our country's recent economic troubles have required that we rethink correctional punishment—that is, both the goals and the means we use to achieve those goals (VERA Institute of Justice, 2010). The days of new prison expansion for *state* departments of corrections seem to be over, at least for now. (Note that the only increases in prison population are for *federal* prisoners.) Some states are actively taking steps to reduce the number of people in the corrections system while others are reallocating resources from the most costly form of punishment (jails and prisons) to a less costly but effective approach right in the community.

This text focuses exclusively on community-based corrections. **Community corrections** refers to any sanctions in which offenders serve all or a portion of their entire sentence in the community. Most community corrections options are **post-adjudication**, which means that the defendant has either pleaded guilty or been found guilty by a judge or jury. After a finding of guilt, the court sentences the defendant, and the corrections system carries out that sentence. Some types of community correctional supervision, however, are **pre-adjudication**, which means that treatment with supervision occurs in the community prior to a finding of guilt. Table 1.1 distinguishes these differences.

TABLE 1.1   Pre-Adjudication vs. Post-Adjudication Corrections

PRE-ADJUDICATION	
Community Corrections	**Institutional Corrections**
Pre-trial release	Jail
Pre-trial supervision/house arrest	Jail-based work release
Victim offender mediation	
Diversion/deferred adjudication	
Pre-sentence investigation	
Circle sentencing	
POST-ADJUDICATION	
Community Corrections	**Institutional Corrections**
Probation supervision (regular)	Jail
Probation supervision (intensive/specialized)	Prison
Parole (mandatory release or discretionary parole)	
Add-On Sanctions/Treatment to Probation or Parole	**Treatment While Incarcerated**
Residential halfway house	Substance abuse
Residential substance abuse facility	Battering/assault/child abuse
Residential boot camp	Sexual victimization/perpetration
Prerelease facility/work release	Education or vocation classes
House arrest/electronic monitoring	Reentry preparation
Day reporting center	
Community service	
Restitution, fines, fees	

(Continues)

TABLE 1.1 Pre-Adjudication vs. Post-Adjudication Corrections (*Continued*)

Add-On Sanctions/Treatment to Probation or Parole	Treatment While Incarcerated
Outpatient treatment/therapy (substance abuse, parenting, battering/assault, sexual victimization, sex offender)	
Weekly education/classes (school, life skills, vocational, theft prevention, financial/credit counseling)	
Community reparation boards	

A community sentence seeks to repair the harm the offender has caused the victim or the community and to reduce the risk of reoffending in the future. Figure 1.1 shows the wide variety of community-based sanctions available, ranging from residential programs (halfway houses and prerelease and therapeutic communities) to economic sanctions (restitution, fines, and forfeitures) to nonresidential or outpatient options (probation, parole, and electronic monitoring).

The most common form of community supervision is **probation.** Probation is defined as the release of a convicted offender under conditions imposed by a court for a specified period, during which time that court retains authority to modify those conditions or to resentence the offender if he or she violates those conditions. Probation forms the basis of community supervision, and most of the other sanctions introduced in Figure 1.1 are programs or conditions of probation.

probation
The community supervision of a convicted offender in lieu of incarceration under conditions imposed by the court for a specified period during which the court retains authority to modify the conditions or to resentence the offender if he or she violates the conditions.

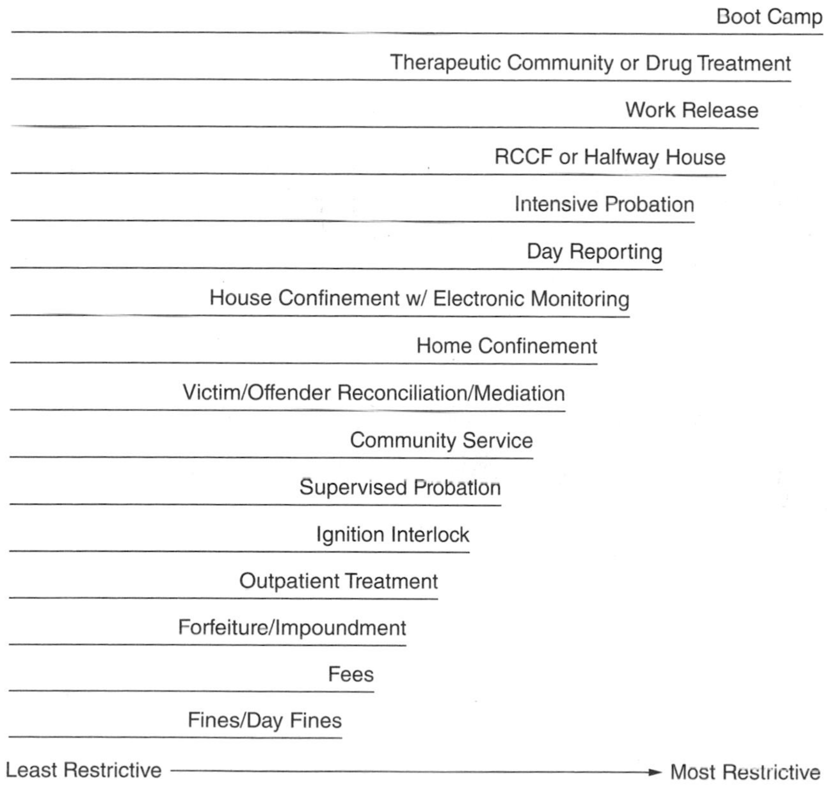

```
                                              Boot Camp
            Therapeutic Community or Drug Treatment
                                          Work Release
                          RCCF or Halfway House
                            Intensive Probation
                               Day Reporting
        House Confinement w/ Electronic Monitoring
                          Home Confinement
        Victim/Offender Reconciliation/Mediation
                        Community Service
                     Supervised Probation
                      Ignition Interlock
                   Outpatient Treatment
               Forfeiture/Impoundment
                             Fees
                      Fines/Day Fines

Least Restrictive ——————————————————→ Most Restrictive
```

FIGURE 1.1 Community Corrections by Restrictiveness.

Adapted From: Center for Community Corrections (1997). *A Call for Punishments that Make Sense*, p. 37 Washington, DC: Bureau of Justice Assistance. Retrieved From: www. communitycorrectionsworks.org/ steve/nccc/punishments.pdf

It is helpful to understand community corrections as involving many alternatives, whereby combinations of sanctions can be applied to different offenders to achieve individualized results. The American Probation and Parole Association (APPA) was created to bridge these alternatives. As an international policy and educational organization for practitioners who work with adults and juveniles in the field of community corrections, the APPA serves to educate and train members and to develop standards for the discipline. The purpose of probation is explained in Box 1.1 APPA's policy statement, which is applicable to all programs and agencies in community corrections.

BOX 1.1   COMMUNITY CORRECTIONS UP CLOSE

What Is the Purpose of Probation?

The purpose of probation is to assist in reducing the incidence and impact of crime by probationers in the community. The core services of probation are to provide pre-sentence investigation and reports to the court, to help develop appropriate court dispositions for adult offenders and juvenile delinquents, and to supervise those people placed on probation. Probation departments in fulfilling their purpose may also provide a broad range of services including, but not limited to, crime and delinquency prevention, victim restitution programs, and intern or volunteer programs.

Position

The mission of probation is to protect the public interest and safety by reducing the incidence and impact of crime by probationers. This role is accomplished by:

- assisting the courts in decision making through the probation report and in the enforcement of court orders;
- providing services and programs that afford opportunities for offenders to become more law-abiding;
- providing and cooperating in programs and activities for the prevention of crime and delinquency;
- furthering the administration of fair and individualized justice.

Probation is premised upon the following beliefs:

- *Society has a right to be protected from persons who cause its members harm, regardless of the reasons for such harm.* It is the right of every citizen to be free from fear of harm to person and property. Belief in the necessity of law to an orderly society demands commitment to support it. Probation accepts this responsibility and views itself as an instrument for both control and treatment, appropriate to some, but not all, offenders. The wise use of authority derived from law adds strength and stability to its efforts.
- *Offenders have rights deserving of protection.* Freedom and democracy require fair and individualized due process of law in adjudicating and sentencing the offender.

- *Victims of crime have rights deserving of protection.* In its humanitarian tradition, probation recognizes that prosecution of the offender is but a part of the responsibility of the criminal justice system. The victim of criminal activity may suffer loss of property, emotional problems, or physical disability. Probation thus commits itself to advocacy for the needs and interests of crime victims.
- *Human beings are capable of change.* Belief in the individual's capability for behavioral change leads probation practitioners to a commitment to the reintegration of the offender into the community. The possibility for constructive change of behavior is based on the recognition and acceptance of the principle of individual responsibility. Much of probation practice focuses on identifying and making available those services and programs that will best afford offenders an opportunity to become responsible, law-abiding citizens.
- *Not all offenders have the same capacity or willingness to benefit from measures designed to produce law-abiding citizens.* Probation practitioners recognize the variations among individuals. The present offense, the degree of risk to the community, and the potential for change can be assessed only in the context of the offender's individual history and experience.
- *Intervention in an offender's life should be the minimal amount needed to protect society and promote law-abiding behavior.* Probation subscribes to the principle of intervening in an offender's life only to the extent necessary. Where further intervention appears unwarranted, criminal justice system involvement should be terminated. Where needed intervention can best be provided by an agency outside the system, the offender should be diverted from the system to that agency.
- *Punishment.* Probation philosophy does not accept the concept of retributive punishment. Punishment

(Continues)

| BOX 1.1 | COMMUNITY CORRECTIONS UP CLOSE (*Continued*) |

What Is the Purpose of Probation?

as a corrective measure is supported and used in those instances in which it is felt that aversive measures may positively alter the offender's behavior when other measures may not. Even corrective punishment, however, should be used cautiously and judiciously in view of its highly unpredictable impact. It can be recognized that a conditional sentence in the community is, in and of itself, a punishment. It is less harsh and drastic than a prison term but more controlling and punitive than release without supervision.

- *Incarceration may be destructive and should be imposed only when necessary.* Probation practitioners acknowledge society's right to protect itself and support the incarceration of offenders whose behavior constitutes a danger to the public through rejection of social or court mandates. Incarceration can also be an appropriate element of a probation program to emphasize

the consequences of criminal behavior and thus effect constructive behavioral change. However, institutions should be humane and required to adhere to the highest standards.

- *Where public safety is not compromised, society and most offenders are best served through community correctional programs.* Most offenders should be provided services within the community in which they are expected to demonstrate acceptable behavior. Community correctional programs generally are cost effective, and they allow offenders to remain with their families while paying taxes and, where applicable, restitution to victims.

For Debate: Is the APPA's position on the purpose of probation still pertinent today?
Source: American Probation and Parole Association (1997). "APPA Position Statement: Probation." Available at: http://www.appa-net.org/eweb/DynamicPage.aspx?Site=APPA_2&WebCode=IB_PositionStatements Reprinted with permission.

Table 1.2 shows the latest government statistics on the number of people currently under some form of correctional supervision. As of 2010 there were 4.2 million offenders on probation and over 819,000 on parole, for a total community corrections population of 5 million (Glaze, Bonczar, and Zhang 2010). Women comprise 24% of probationers, 12% of parolees, and 7% of all prisoners. Although men account for a disproportionately greater percentage of offenders than women, most women are eligible for a community corrections sentence because they tend to have shorter criminal records and commit less violent crimes by comparison.

There are considerably more male and female offenders under community supervision than the 2.4 million offenders incarcerated in jail and prison. The correctional system carries out the order of the courts, but the variance in the *rate* per 100,000 people is derived from a number of factors that include the nature of each state's sentencing laws, police discretion in responding to criminal behavior, the rate of release from prison, and each agency's probation and parole violation policy. We begin by describing the nature of sentencing, which is distinguished by two basic philosophies: indeterminate and determinate.

FACT OR FICTION?

The U.S. has the highest incarceration rate in the world when compared to other countries, but probation is still the most common correctional sentence in the U.S.

Fact.

There are more than twice the number of Americans on probation than in all jails and prisons combined. This is because probation includes deferred adjudication, diversion, and post-conviction community sentences.

Indeterminate Sentencing

From the 1930s to the mid-1970s, **indeterminate sentencing** was the primary sentencing philosophy in the United States. Under this model, judges decided who went to prison, and parole boards decided when offenders were rehabilitated and ready for release on parole (Forst, 1995). The release date was unknown by an offender and subject to a majority decision of the parole board, which determined whether that offender was making sufficient progress toward rehabilitation and was ready to rejoin the larger society. While incarcerated, offenders were able to enroll in a variety of programs aimed at self-improvement and skill building to demonstrate readiness for the parole board.

indeterminate sentencing
A sentencing philosophy that encourages rehabilitation and incorporates a broad sentencing range where discretionary release is determined by a parole board based on the offender's remorse, insight into his or her mistakes, involvement in rehabilitation, and readiness to return to society.

TABLE 1.2   Adults on Probation, Parole, in Jail and in Prison: 1980–2010

Year	Total Estimate in Millions	COMMUNITY SUPERVISION		INCARCERATION	
		Probation	Parole	County Jail	State & Fed Prison
1980	1.84	1,118,097	220,438	182,288	319,598
1981	2.01	1,225,934	225,539	195,085	360,029
1982	2.19	1,357,264	224,604	207,853	402,914
1983	2.48	1,582,947	246,440	221,815	423,898
1984	2.69	1,740,948	266,992	233,018	448,264
1985	3.01	1,968,712	300,203	254,986	487,593
1986	3.24	2,114,621	325,638	272,735	526,436
1987	3.46	2,247,158	355,505	294,092	562,814
1988	3.74	2,356,483	407,977	341,893	607,766
1989	4.06	2,522,125	456,803	393,303	683,367
1990	4.35	2,670,234	531,407	403,019	743,382
1991	4.54	2,728,472	590,442	424,129	792,535
1992	4.76	2,811,611	658,601	441,781	850,566
1993	4.94	2,903,061	676,100	455,500	909,381
1994	5.14	2,981,022	690,371	479,800	990,147
1995	5.34	3,077,861	679,421	507,044	1,078,542
1996	5.49	3,164,996	679,733	518,492	1,127,528
1997	5.73	3,296,513	694,787	567,079	1,176,564
1998	6.13	3,670,441	696,385	592,462	1,224,469
1999	6.34	3,779,922	714,457	605,943	1,287,172
2000	6.44	3,826,209	723,898	621,149	1,316,333
2001	6.58	3,931,731	732,333	631,240	1,330,007
2002	6.76	4,024,067	750,934	665,475	1,367,547
2003	6.92	4,144,782	745,125	691,301	1,392,796
2004	7.00	4,151,125	765,819	713,990	1,421,911
2005	7.05	4,189,456	772,967	747,529	1,496,013
2006	7.37	4,237,023	798,202	765,819	1,570,115
2007	7.39	4,215,361	799,058	780,174	1,595,034
2008	7.45	4,234,471	821,177	785,536	1,609,759
2009	7.45	4,244,046	824,834	767,434	1,613,656
2010	7.38	4,203,967	819,308	748,728	1,613,656

Notes: Counts for probation, prison, and parole populations are for December 31 of each year; jail population counts are for June 30 of each year. Counts of adults held in facilities for 1993–1996 were estimated and rounded to the nearest 100. Totals in 1998 through 2002 exclude probationers held in jail or prison. Data for jail and prison are for inmates under custody under public and private facilities. Some data have been revised based on the most recently reported counts and may differ from previous editions of Sourcebook.

Sources: All sources for this table were published by either Sourcebook or by the Bureau of Justice Statistics, U.S. Department of Justice in Washington, DC. For probation and parole between 2000–2010: L. E. Glaze, T. P. Bonczar, and F. Zhang. 2010. *Probation and Parole in the United States, 2009*; L. E. Glaze and S. Palla. 2005. *Probation and Parole in the United States, 2004*; L. E. Glaze and T. P. Bonczar. 2008. *Probation and Parole in the United States, 2007*. L. E. Glaze and T. P. Bonczar. 2009. *Probation and Parole in the United States, 2008*; For jails between 2000–2010: Minton, T. D. (2010). *Jail Inmates at Mid-year 2010—Statistical Tables*. For prisons: Sabol, W. J., H. C. West, and M. Cooper (2009). *Prisoners in 2008. Correctional Populations in the United States* 1990–2003.

Parole was also used as a backdoor strategy for controlling the prison population. When prisons became too crowded, the parole rate increased to make room for incoming prisoners. Under indeterminate sentencing, offenders who did not go to prison were, for the most part, placed on probation. Few intermediate sentencing options existed other than prison or probation, and those that did, such as halfway houses and intensive probation, were used infrequently (Tonry, 1997).

Support for indeterminate sentencing declined as people questioned whether prison rehabilitation worked and whether parole boards could accurately determine when offenders were ready for release. This lack of confidence in correctional programming peaked in 1974 with Robert Martinson's publication concluding that "with few and isolated exceptions, the rehabilitative efforts that have been reported so far had no appreciable effect on recidivism" (p. 25). Martinson's findings were poorly stated, criticisms were lodged against the methodology used, and Martinson later recanted those statements. In the complete report published the next year, Douglas Lipton, Robert Martinson, and Judith Wilks (1975) concluded:

> While some treatment programs have had modest successes, it still must be concluded that the field of corrections has not as yet found satisfactory ways to reduce recidivism by significant amounts. (p. 627)

Both of these publications began a national debate about the efficacy of treatment programs. Ironically, the original intent of Martinson's article was an attempt to decrease the use of *prisons* rather than of treatment programs, so unbeknownst to his coauthors, Martinson published the solo piece and was ill prepared for the catastrophe that followed. His study was a prelude to one of the most conservative eras in American politics, wherein policy makers in many political jurisdictions were looking for reasons to repudiate the putative liberal policies of previous decades. The study confirmed what a cadre of reactionary policy makers wanted to hear at a time when sentiments within the professional corrections community still ran toward a philosophy of rehabilitation rather than retribution (Locke, 1998, p. 257).

In addition to raising questions about rehabilitation, indeterminate sentences created another problem. Most indeterminate sentences were structured with no maximum ending date. With an unknown or ambiguous release date, some offenders spent many more years behind bars than their crimes warranted, whereas others—who may have convinced the parole board they were "cured"—were released after only a few years. This issue became a question of fairness.

Origins of Modern Determinate Sentencing

A working group, the American Friends Service Committee, called for repealing all indeterminate sentencing laws. The main premise of the committee's final report, published under the title *Doing Justice: The Choice of Punishments* (von Hirsch, 1976), was that offenders convicted of similar crimes should serve roughly equal terms in prison. The committee recommended an adoption of a **presumptive sentence** for each crime or category of crimes, with presumptive sentences graded according to severity of crime based on two scales: the harm done by an offense and an offender's culpability. Judgment of the degree of culpability would be based partly on an offender's prior record. Having proposed punishment as the main goal of sentencing, the committee then ruled out prison as punishment for all but the most serious offenses—those in which bodily harm was threatened or done to a victim. The committee proposed alternatives such as periodic imprisonment, increased use of fines, and other lesser sanctions.

At about the same time, a **determinate sentencing** model emerged. David Fogel (1979), author of *We Are the Living Proof: The Justice Model for Corrections*, is

presumptive sentence
A statutorily determined sentence that offenders will presumably receive if convicted. Offenders convicted in a jurisdiction with presumptive sentences will be assessed this sentence unless mitigating or aggravating circumstances are found to exist.

determinate sentencing
A sentencing philosophy that focuses on consistency for the crime committed, specifying by statute or sentencing guidelines an exact amount or narrow range of time to be served in prison or in the community, which mandates the minimum amount of time before the offender is eligible (if at all) for release. Also known as a presumptive, fixed, or mandatory sentence.

considered by many to be the father of determinate sentencing. As early as 1970 he actively urged a narrowing of sentencing and parole discretion. His work was influential in helping to draft legislative change in various states. One of his goals was to disconnect release date from prison program participation. He advocated abolishing parole boards and establishing "flat-time" sentencing for each class of felonies.

Maine became the first state to return to a determinate sentencing in which minimum and maximum sentence range is predefined and release is determined by legislative statute (Forst, 1995). Sentence length is therefore determined by criminal behavior rather than by how long it takes for an offender to become rehabilitated behind bars. With fewer sentencing options for judges, personal and social variables have played less of a role in the sentencing process. The slogan "You do the crime, you do the time" became popular, and funding for prison treatment programs diminished. In determinate sentencing, judges have less discretion, and though they are able to deviate slightly (higher or lower) from prescribed sentencing guidelines, they must provide justification for doing so. Parole board decision making has also been limited in many states to only certain types of offenders or has been abolished altogether (Petersilia, 2003).

Examples of determinate sentencing policies have included mandatory minimums, truth-in-sentencing, three strikes laws, and sentencing guidelines. All states have adopted mandatory minimum sentencing laws requiring certain types of offenders, such as violent or repeat offenders, to serve a certain amount of time before release can be considered. Truth-in-sentencing laws are a type of mandatory minimum requiring that offenders serve at least 85% of an original sentence length before becoming eligible for release (Petersilia, 2003). Three strikes laws mandate long prison terms for a third felony conviction. Some states require a life sentence for violent third-time felons, while other states might count any third felony, whether it is violent or nonviolent.

Sentencing guidelines form a matrix based on an offender's prior criminal record and current conviction, which a judge must follow at the federal level and also in those states where guidelines are mandatory. Some states have guidelines that are only suggestive, although others still have never developed sentencing guidelines. Even though guidelines have decreased sentencing disparity and created accountability for sentencing decisions, most judges have disliked limits on their discretion. Although probation is still allowed at the federal level, federal parole has been abolished, and prisoners are now mandatorily released for one year. Federal guidelines have been continually revised and now allow judges to consider more mitigating and aggravating circumstances in adjusting a sentence. Most states, however, have retained aspects of both indeterminate and determinate sentencing structures, examples of which are given in Chapter 4.

THE PARADOX

We are used to thinking of community safety as contingent upon who is allowed to live in the community. Justice seems separationist because formal justice processes remove offenders from everyday life for accusation and conviction ceremonies, and they often result in penal removal, as well. The idea that communities are made safe by eliminating unsafe residents is equally an ingrained idea in American traditions. (Clear & Corbett, 1997, p. 2)

Correctional policy is in many ways a paradox between economic constraints on what we can afford and shifts in the tide of public perception—that is, in what is important to vocal constituents and to public interest groups. Maruna and King (2008) note a shift away from expert-driven decisions in penal policy to one characterized "more explicitly by symbolic and expressive concerns . . . [and]

emotionalization of public discourse about crime and law" (p. 338). They argue that correctional policy is driven by politics rather than by rationality, and that public opinion is influenced by the media. The media has long been criticized for sensationalizing violence and atypical crimes while downplaying average or common crimes that never result in a prison sentence. The average American citizen as a result is only exposed to a very small percentage of the overall crime picture and is less informed than are experts about what should be done in response to crime.

Public Attitudes About Community Corrections

When it comes to discussing alternatives to incarceration for nonviolent offenders, a recent national public opinion poll indicated that the most well known of these were probation, house arrest, and electronic monitoring. Less familiar options were restorative justice, day reporting, and drug court. The majority of adults thought that alternatives to incarceration such as probation, restitution, community service, and/or rehabilitation services:

- were appropriate for nonviolent offenders;
- were appropriate when a theft was less than $400; and
- did not necessarily decrease public safety.

Nearly half (45%) thought that probation and rehabilitation were likely to reduce recidivism for nonserious offenders over prison or jail (Hartney & Marchionna, 2009).

Proposed strategies to increase the level of public support for community corrections include appealing to the public on an emotional level. The emotions of fear and anger tend to recommend punitiveness for some offenders while compassion and forgiveness, which are considerably much harder to accomplish, require a process to work toward as individuals and communities heal. Another notion with emotional appeal is that of "redeemability"—that is, convincing the public that offenders can change their ways if given the tools and the means to do so (Maruna & King, 2008, p. 345). But these are only half of the solution. Experts also suggest that the media should present a broader view of issues than just atypical cases. Public opinion research on sentencing preferences demonstrated higher validity when the public was given diverse sentencing options and adequate information, such as program descriptions and detailed knowledge about an offense or an offender.

Prison Is Expensive

The other side of the correctional paradox is that corrections' funding source is driven almost completely by public tax dollars. Correctional budgets have been hit hard these last few years, due in part to the most recent economic recession that forced states to cut social programs, initiate hiring freezes, and lay off employees. Even with federal aid given to states via the Recovery Act, economic recovery has been slower than expected (through fewer taxes paid and a higher unemployment rate), which has significantly affected all levels of government (VERA Inst. Just., 2010). In response to the fiscal crisis, state legislators and correctional administrators have considered the following options:

- decriminalizing lower-level nonviolent and/or drug felony offenses down to Class A misdemeanors;
- repealing mandatory minimums;
- using more graduated sanctions in the community;
- increasing parole rates;
- changing probation and parole policies for responding to violations;

- denying requests to incarcerate for anything but new crimes;
- closing existing housing units within a prison; and
- closing existing prisons altogether.

There is growing consensus that the use of jail and prison facilities, which are the most expensive option, should be reserved for the most dangerous offenders. At the same time, community-based correctional options should be expanded.

In comparison to prisons, probation and parole agencies garnered about 18 cents of every correctional dollar to supervise the 70% of all people under correctional supervision. Table 1.3 shows annual costs per person for selected forms of correctional supervision in the federal system and in a sampling of states with moderate living costs. Incarceration is significantly more expensive than community supervision, especially considering that for the latter, the offender shares some of the costs. For example, probationers subsidize annual costs with monthly fees on a sliding scale ranging between $25 and $60. Parole, electronic monitoring, day reporting, and residential community correction facilities are all partially subsidized by the offender.

TABLE 1.3   Daily Cost per Person for Selected Forms of Correctional Supervision

Supervision Type	Federal (FY 09-10)	North Carolina (FY 10-11)
Prison[a]	$74.66	$74.34
Pretrial detention[a]	$67.79	$57.30
Pretrial community supervision	$6.38	$6.04
Residential community facility[b] or residential substance abuse facility	$60.27	$47.34
Probation	$10.43	$3.44
Intensive probation	$12.10	$15.27
Parole	$8.10	$3.44
Additional community services		
Community service work program	N/R	$0.97
Day reporting	N/R	$24.70
Electronic monitoring using:		
Radio frequency	$5.25[c]	$7.71
Global positioning systems	$10.50[c]	$11.07

Notes:

N/R = Cost not reported

[a] = These costs are averaged for supervision of general population offenders. Costs for special needs offenders and those in maximum security institutions are significantly higher.

[b] = The cost of *all* RCCFs to taxpayers are actually lower.

[c] = This is the reported cost in 2007 and adjusted by 16% increase to reflect 2009–2010 rates.

Sources: North Carolina Department of Corrections (2010). Cost of supervision ending June 30, 2010. Retrieved from: http://www.doc.state.nc.us/dop/cost/ North Carolina pretrial detention and supervision 2008 costs retrieved from http://www.ncgccd.org/pdfs/pubs/ncincarceration.pdf and http://www.jrsa.org/events/conference/presentations-08/Douglas_Yearwood.pdf NC radio frequency electronic monitoring from: http://www.doc.state.nc.us/dcc/dccBrochures/ehaBrochure.pdf Bureau of Prison and U.S. Probation and Pretrial Services costs retrieved from: www.bop.gov Federal electronic monitoring costs retrieved from: http://www.uscourts.gov/news/TheThirdBranch/07-04-01/GPS_Your_Supervising_Officer_is_Watching.aspx Federal probation and parole costs estimated from: http://www.csosa.gov/about/financial/budget/2012/FY12-CSP-Budget-Submission.pdf

THE ROLE OF CORRECTIONS AT THREE MAJOR DECISION POINTS

The three major decision points in the corrections system—bail, sentencing, and reentry—are guided by formal written laws, codes, and statutes as well as by informal discretion. Discretion is a form of subjective decision making that begins when a victim or witness decides whether or not to report a crime to the police. Some argue that discretion plays at least as important a role as formal law. Another decision point early in the process is the arresting decision made by a law enforcement officer. As seen in Figure 1.2, community corrections plays a pivotal role at three major decision points that follow an arrest.

Pretrial and the Bail Decision

After a police officer makes an arrest, the suspect is booked in jail and the prosecutor's office decides whether to charge the suspect with a crime. If the prosecutor chooses not to charge, the suspect is automatically released. If the prosecutor opts to charge, the suspect officially becomes a defendant and goes before a judge, magistrate, or other official authorized to inform the defendant of the charges, determine whether the defendant is requesting appointed counsel, and ascertain whether the defendant is eligible for release from jail. Although most defendants are released on their own recognizance with the promise to appear at their next court date, some defendants must secure their next appearance with **bail,** or monetary payment deposited with the court to ensure their return. When the conditions of the bond have been satisfied, the defendant is released on a bond. Many times, particularly in the

bail
Monetary payment deposited with the court to ensure the defendant's return for the next court date in exchange for the defendant's release.

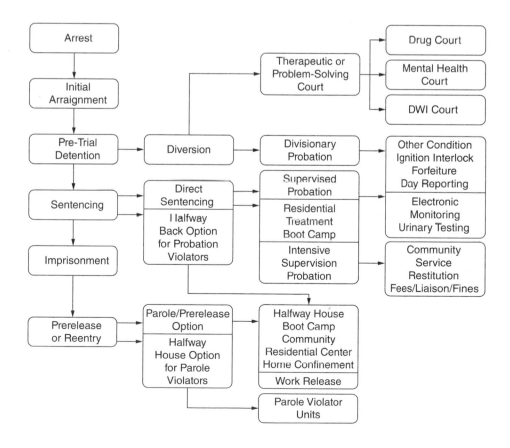

FIGURE 1.2 The Three Main Decision Points: How Cases Are Referred to Community Corrections.

Adapted From: Center for Community Corrections (1997). *A Call for Punishments that Make Sense*, p. 35 Washington, DC: Bureau of Justice Assistance.

federal system, the defendant is released on **pretrial supervision,** which is a form of correctional supervision of a defendant who has not yet been convicted. Forms of pretrial supervision can include client reporting, house arrest, and electronic monitoring. Pretrial supervision has four functions. It:

1. accounts for a defendant's whereabouts to keep the community safe;
2. allows a defendant to prepare for upcoming court appearances;
3. allows a defendant to continue working and supporting dependents; and
4. keeps bed space in a jail available for defendants who may not be eligible for release.

Sentencing Decision

Community corrections agencies and programs perform the important function of implementing the sentence imposed by a judge. At a basic level, a correctional sentence is a social control mechanism for convicted offenders, and it also keeps citizens law abiding through general deterrence. We recognize the importance of incarcerating offenders who are dangerous to the public or who have committed violent crimes so heinous that incarceration is a deserved punishment. However, the vast majority of people who commit a crime can be punished in ways that do not warrant imprisonment. Judges and prosecutors need a variety of "front-end" punishments from which to choose, and community corrections offers a diversity of sentencing options.

The community-based punishments shown earlier in Figure 1.1 are known as **intermediate sanctions** because they offer graduated levels of supervision. They provide rewards for positive behavior, with gradually less supervision when offenders achieve and maintain desired program outcomes. Intermediate sanctions can also impose higher levels of surveillance, supervision, and monitoring than probation alone, but they provide less supervision than jail or prison. A full range of sentencing options gives judges greater latitude to select punishments that closely fit the circumstances of a crime and the offender (DiMascio, 1997). We discuss the sentencing decision in chapter 4 and then devote six chapters to the forms community corrections takes, beginning with probation and the various graduated residential, monetary, and nonresidential sanctions.

Reentry Decision

Over 40 years ago, the President's Commission on Law Enforcement and Administration of Justice (1967) introduced the term *reintegration*. The commission's report stated that

> institutions tend to isolate offenders from society, both physically and psychologically, cutting them off from schools, jobs, families, and other supportive influences and increasing the probability that the label of criminal will be indelibly impressed upon them. The goal of reintegration is likely to be furthered much more readily by working with offenders in the community than by incarceration. (p. 165)

The commission called on the community to provide needed employment and educational opportunities while community correctional workers act as advocates to link offenders to programs and monitor their progress. This goal still holds true today, though instead of *reintegration* we use the term *reentry*. Reentry requires an offender in adapting to a community setting to participate in programs that develop legitimate accomplishments and opportunities, although there seems to be less emphasis today on the role of the community in assisting in the offender's return—an issue discussed in greater detail in chapter 11.)

Approximately 95–97% of prisoners incarcerated today will one day leave prison and rejoin the larger society. A community correction serves an important purpose by assisting prisoners in community reentry after having spent time in prison. **Prisoner reentry** is any activity or program "conducted to prepare ex-convicts to return safely to the community and to live as law-abiding citizens" (Petersilia, 2003, p. 3). Prisoner reentry applies to prisoners released automatically based on mandatory statutes as well as to prisoners released early at a parole board's discretion.

PRERELEASE PROGRAM   A **prerelease program** is a minimum-security institutional setting for imprisoned offenders who have already done some time in prison and are nearing release. Prerelease offenders are chosen by corrections officials and transferred to a different type of residential program that offenders can complete in a shorter duration than if they had served their full prison sentence. Prerelease programs are considered more treatment-oriented than is prison. Examples of these programs are halfway houses, boot camps, and therapeutic communities that are located inside a prison, separate from the general prisoner population. The purpose of back-end programs is to save money and prison space while also providing program participants with a specialized treatment regimen. Examples of prerelease programs are discussed in chapter 8.

PAROLE   **Parole** is the discretionary release of an offender, under conditions established by the paroling authority, before the expiration of the offender's sentence. Parole is in many ways similar to probation. Both involve supervised release in a community and the possibility of revocation should the parolee or probationer violate the conditions of release. Although some technical differences do exist, the primary difference is that probation is supervision in the community instead of incarceration, whereas parole is supervised release after a portion of the prison sentence has been served. (See chapters 3 and 11 for more coverage of parole.)

prisoner reentry
Any activity or program conducted to prepare ex-convicts to return safely to the community and to live as law-abiding citizens.

prerelease program
A minimum-security community-based or institutional setting for offenders who have spent time in prison and are nearing release. The focus of these programs includes transitioning, securing a job, and reestablishing family connections.

parole
Early privileged release of a convicted offender from a penal or correctional institution, under the continual custody of the state, to serve the remainder of his or her sentence in the community under supervision.

THEORIES BEHIND COMMUNITY CORRECTIONAL GOALS

The primary responsibility of community corrections supervision is to carry out the sentence of a court. In carrying out this responsibility, community corrections programs must be concerned with protecting the public, addressing victims' needs, and changing an offender's attitudes and behaviors through treatment and deterrence. A number of theories pertain to meeting these goals, such as: principles of correctional intervention, restorative justice, and shaming.

Protection of the Public Through Offender Supervision According to Risk Level

Most offenders have shown by their offenses that they cannot easily conform to the norms of society. One of the goals of community-based corrections, therefore, is to help offenders conform to behavioral expectations and to monitor their progress toward that goal. Perhaps the major criticism of traditional probation and parole has been their perceived failure to protect the public from further criminal attacks by individuals under supervision in the community. For probation or any other community-based program to be effective and accepted by policy makers and the public, it must first demonstrate that the offenders under supervision are adequately monitored and that the public has nothing to fear from their actions.

Protection of the public can be accomplished in a variety of ways. First, as discussed in chapter 5, offenders are assessed to determine the degree of risk posed by their projected participation in community programs. Second, those who supervise offenders in community-based programs must accept responsibility to protect the public by monitoring compliance with court orders and conditions of release. Finally, violations of supervised conditions must be taken seriously. If the programs are to become credible sanctions, courts and paroling authorities must be willing to revoke probation or parole for those who commit new crimes while on supervision. (Reasons for violating probation and parole are covered in Chapter 7.)

Addressing Victims through Restorative Justice

restorative justice
Various sentencing philosophies and practices that emphasize the offender taking responsibility to repair the harm done to the victim and to the surrounding community. Includes forms of victim offender mediation, reparation panels, circle sentencing, and monetary sanctions.

Community-based sanctions provide offenders opportunities to repay their victims and their communities. A different philosophy of justice has emerged in recent years known as **restorative justice,** or community justice. Restorative justice is centered on the victims of crimes throughout the criminal process and emphasizes the responsibility of offenders to repair the injustice they have caused their victims (Karp, 1998; Van Ness & Strong, 1997; Wright, 1996).

When a crime is committed, the offender harms both the individual victim and the community at large. Through a variety of techniques such as community boards, mediation, and face-to-face meetings with victims, restorative justice attempts to strengthen community life by drawing on the strengths of victims instead of focusing on their deficits (Umbreit, 1999). Local volunteers and the faith community agree to mentor or assist in the supervision of an offender's reparation. The offender must repair the damage by remaining in the community and performing community service, providing victim restitution, and participating in victim impact panels and other educational programs.

Restorative justice is most effective for nonviolent crimes, particularly those committed by juveniles or first-time adult felony offenders, because the victim is compensated for property losses. What many victims may not realize is that although incarcerating offenders for property crime will provide a loss of temporary freedom, the victim will rarely, if ever, be compensated. When given a choice between compensation and incarceration, 75% of respondents to a study conducted in Minnesota indicated they would rather be compensated for a property crime than demand the offender be incarcerated (Umbreit, 1999). Thus community-based corrections programs are necessary and important for guiding the restorative justice process. At this time, however, restorative justice is less likely to be endorsed for violent crimes. (Reparations based on the restorative justice model are discussed in chapter 10.)

Rehabilitating Offenders Through the Principles of Correctional Intervention

A third goal of community corrections programs is to correct some of the inadequacies of offenders linked to their criminal behavior and continued involvement in the criminal justice system. Some of these problems include, but are not limited to, drug or alcohol addiction, lack of emotional control, inadequate education or vocational training, lack of parenting skills, and mental illness or developmental disability. Correctional treatment, or "programming," is the means by which offenders can receive assistance for their problems to reduce further criminal behavior.

The basis of effective rehabilitation theory is that behavioral change is possible. Offenders should have an *opportunity* to change, and they must have a genuine *desire* to change—to complete the mental, emotional, and sometimes spiritual work to promote a personal transformation. Individual motivation is an important point, because some offenders are not ready to change or do not respond to treatment.

Different treatment approaches must be used to address the unique problems and personalities of offenders. Many advances have been made, such that more is now known about which correctional interventions work most effectively with offender populations. These principles include:

- early risk assessment;
- focus on the highest risk offenders;
- use of cognitive-behavioral treatment for at least three to nine months; and
- linkage of treatment interventions to criminal behavior problems and needs (Gendreau, 1996).

Proponents of rehabilitation believe that for certain types of offenders, if the issues related to recidivism are addressed, the likelihood of future criminal behavior can be reduced between 10–60%. Gendreau (1998) estimates that only 10–20% of all correctional rehabilitation programs are of "high quality." A high-quality treatment program is one that provides an effective correctional service.

A final point is that oftentimes offenders receive more treatment under a community corrections sentence than they do in prison. This results in part because programs in prison are 100% taxpayer-funded while community-based programs are driven partially by taxpayers but also subsidized by offenders who pay for services as clients. Even as correctional budgets have tightened and in-prison treatment programs have been trimmed, taxpayers are bearing less of the cost for offender treatment in the community.

Deterrence through Shaming

Deterrence of offenders entails using shaming, or scarlet-letter sanctions, to *briefly* stigmatize offenders publicly. The theory of shaming is that punishment should affect an offender's dignity. Examples of shaming sentences include forcing offenders to issue public apologies, obligating offenders to place a bumper sticker on their car or a sign on their front yard acknowledging their crime, or forcing a slumlord to live in one of his rat-infested apartments (Reske, 1996). According to Kelly (1999), for shaming to be effective, five conditions must be present:

1. The offender must belong to an identifiable group, like a religious or an ethnic community.
2. The shaming penalty must be sufficient to compromise the offender's social standing in this group.
3. The punishment must be communicated to the offender's community, which must in fact withdraw from or shun him or her.
4. The offender must actually fear being shunned.
5. There must be some method of regaining social status by bringing the offender back into the community, unless the offense is so grave that the offender must be permanently shunned. (pp. 806–807)

Although used only rarely by a small number of judges, shaming is quite controversial as commentators question whether it violates the Eighth Amendment of the Constitution. In an analysis of the constitutionality of scarlet-letter sanctions, one researcher recommended that their duration be short and that they not endanger an offender's safety in any way. Kelly (1999) suggested that we need "to create a more objective test that asks whether a reasonable person would consider the particular scarlet-letter probation condition severely humiliating and shameful" (p. 860). Currently, very little empirical evidence exists on the effectiveness of shaming punishments (Reske, 1996).

In sum, community corrections is important because its sanctions provide options for individuals who have committed a crime but do not pose a serious threat to community safety. Community-based corrections seeks to sanction offenders through punishment while also attempting to improve individual life circumstances. Decreasing risk, increasing rehabilitation, and restoring justice are important aspects of changing offenders' attitudes and behaviors, leading to the prevention of criminal behavior. Community corrections also serves to ease institutional crowding in jails and prisons by drawing from the population of convicted offenders those predicted to be less risk to the outside community.

EVIDENCE-BASED PRACTICES IN COMMUNITY CORRECTIONS

evidence-based practices Integrating into everyday practice the correctional programs and techniques that have been shown to be the most effective with offenders using evaluation results from systematically evaluated research studies.

Insofar as community corrections serves to increase public safety and multiplies possibilities of choice for those who break the law, fostering public recognition of its importance is a challenge. One of the ways to accomplish such an image change is through evidence-based practices.

Evidence-based practices (EBP) involves using current best practices or interventions for which there is consistent and solid scientific evidence of success. Assessment must show that such practices work to meet intended outcomes and are open to periodic measurement, evaluation, and dissemination of interventions. EBP is used in a number of fields, including medicine, education, social work, mental health, and criminal justice. Within the criminal justice system, EBP is used in police departments, courts, and correctional departments.

EBP is not based on intuition, speculation, anecdotal evidence, or tradition (e.g., "that's the way we've always done it around here"). Rather, EBP is grounded in empirical data and research in studying what works. The idea behind EBP in corrections is that agencies use only the most successful programs. The best programs are those that are effective in changing offender behavior—whether that behavior is reducing technical violations or rearrest, increasing the number of drug-free days, or increasing the number of days an offender is employed while on supervision. Each goal must be measured empirically—meaning that accurate data needs to be recorded electronically for later evaluation.

Evaluating Effectiveness

For citizens to view community corrections as the preferred punishment option, agency leaders need to be open about research and program evaluations. To measure both the process of going through a program and the impact a program has had after its completion, it is necessary to conduct and report empirical research in a way that makes sense to the average citizen (MacKenzie, 2000).

It is important to determine the methodological rigor and sophistication of the research to know what does and does not work. The research must be able to identify for which type of offenders and under what conditions the treatment best works. Although more is now known about this, continuing to evaluate community-based programs and other offender treatment efforts is worthwhile (Latessa & Holsinger, 1998).

When evaluating the effectiveness of a program, it would be ideal to compare offenders who are randomly selected to receive a *treatment* (for example, the community corrections program) with matched *control* groups (those on regular probation, in prison, or both). Then the groups could be compared on a number of outcome measures. This ideal situation is hard to come by in reality because sentencing guidelines prevent such comparison groups, and many judges cannot be persuaded to randomly assign offenders to programs.

Furthermore, many offenders are sentenced to multiple types of programs. Thus it is difficult to isolate one treatment effect from another and to evaluate which program has had the intended effect. It is also difficult to assess which program element is responsible for positive or negative effects.

In particular, a final difficulty with evaluating the effectiveness of intermediate sanctions is determining whether participants were diverted from probation (a front-end strategy) or from prison (a back-end strategy). In other words, suppose the only two sentencing choices were probation or prison (the control group). The intermediate sanction (the program to be measured)—which targets criminals who would have gone to prison anyway but are being given one last chance—takes on more serious offenders than if it had recruited offenders who were not prison-bound. Intermediate sanctions would be an increased penalty for offenders who would otherwise have been sentenced to probation had that intermediate sanction not existed. This is called **net widening,** or "widening the net," and it usually results in a cost increase instead of a cost savings. We revisit the net-widening issue throughout the book when we apply this term to diversion, boot camps, and intensive supervision probation.

Outcome Measures in Evaluation

The most commonly used measure of program or treatment effectiveness is the rate of **recidivism.** Recidivism is defined as a repetition of or return to criminal behavior, measured in one of three ways: rearrest, reconviction, or reincarceration. Some studies differentiate a return to criminal behavior from technical violations committed while under community supervision. Other studies lump violations together as a single category. The way recidivism is defined is determined by agency access and methods of data collection. Determining success or failure is difficult because researchers define recidivism in a variety of ways; hence there are no universally accepted means by which to measure it.

Recidivism as the primary (or sometimes the only) outcome measure has caused concern among criminal justice researchers. Reasons for not including other outcome measures are that programs keep poor records of those or that available measures are buried within an officer's handwritten notes deep within offender files. As more programs go paperless, data becomes easier to collect and measure.

Other variables of importance will, of course, depend on the type of program being evaluated. Variables that can be measured during supervision include: the number of days employed; the amount of restitution collected compared to the amount ordered; the percent of fines and/or fees collected; the number of community service hours performed; the number of clients enrolled in school; the number of drug-free days; the types of treatment programs completed; and the number of times clients attended each treatment program. The type of termination—that is, whether a client completed supervision successfully or unsuccessfully—is critical. The number and types of technical violations and/or new arrests are vital measures, particularly for unsuccessful clients. Finally, effectiveness can also be measured based on the

net widening
Using stiffer punishment or excessive control for offenders who would have ordinarily been sentenced to a lesser sanction.

recidivism
The repetition of or return to criminal behavior, variously defined in one of three ways: rearrest, reconviction, or reincarceration.

impacts that community corrections programs have in reducing institutional crowding and on incurring total cost savings.

Community corrections programs have been encouraged to develop evidence-based practices that incorporate sound diagnostic and classification testing of risks and needs as well as cognitive-behavioral treatment paired with community supervision techniques, all of which we discuss later in the text.

SUMMARY

- Community corrections provides many options for individuals who have committed a crime but do not pose a serious threat to community safety.

- Community-based corrections seeks to sanction offenders through punishment while also attempting to improve individual life circumstances. Reintegration, rehabilitation, and restorative justice are important components in changing offenders' attitudes and behaviors, leading to the prevention of criminal behavior.

- Community corrections also serves to ease institutional crowding in jails and prisons by drawing from the population of convicted offenders those predicted to be less risk to the outside community.

- Providing a range of community-based sanctions allows a rewarding of positive behavior by increasing freedom and a punishing of negative behavior by increasing the sanction.

- The public demands correctional programs that satisfy both punishment and public safety objectives. Evidence-based practices offer steps to further professionalize and transform the image of community-based corrections as the method of choice for lasting offender change.

- The effectiveness of community supervision programs depends on the following factors: how recidivism is defined and how long after supervision it is measured; how other outcome variables are measured during supervision; whether there is a comparison group; how the groups are selected; and whether net widening has occurred.

DISCUSSION QUESTIONS

1. What do you believe is the primary purpose of community-based corrections?

2. Other than the factors mentioned in the book, what other factors may have contributed to growth in the correctional system?

3. What does a *continuum of sanctions* mean in the sentencing process? If you were a judge, how would you apply this continuum?

4. Will evidence-based practices be just another passing fad?

5. To measure the effectiveness of community corrections, are there any other outcome measures (other than those discussed) that could be used?

WEBSITES, VIDEOS, AND PODCASTS

Websites

National Center on Institutions and Alternatives
www.ncianet.org

Community-Based Corrections in Clark County, Washington
www.co.clark.wa.us/corrections/index.html

The Corrections Connection
www.corrections.com

Fortune Society
www.fortunesociety.org

Doble Research Company
http://www.dobleresearch.com

What Works in Community Corrections—An Interview with Joan Petersilia

> http://www.pewcenteronthestates.org/uploaded Files/Petersilia-Community-Corrections-QandA.pdf

Videos/Podcasts

Adult Community Correction: Monroe County—Part 1

> http://www.youtube.com/watch?v=HJnHy9BFKhk

Adult Community Correction: Monroe County—Part 2

> http://www.youtube.com/watch?v=w5pIo9P9o5o& feature=related

The links above connect you to YouTube videos that cover the goals, objectives, success, and functioning of an Adult Community Correction program in Monroe County.

Evidence-Based Practices in Community Corrections—DC Public Safety (2009)

> http://www.corrections.com/system/podcast/ file/114/CSOSA78.mp3

This podcast is an interview with a former probation officer that focuses on evidence-based practices in regard to parole and probation, reentry programs, and community-based programs. The interview questions whether evidence-based practices really exists in community corrections.

CASE STUDY EXERCISES

Organizations and Associations Related to Community Corrections

In this chapter, you became familiar with the American Probation and Parole Association's (APPA) position on probation. Assume you are a staff member who works for a state legislator and you have been assigned to examine organizations and interest groups affiliated with community-based corrections. Report back to the legislator the APPA's position on the expansion of various community-based alternatives.

CASE A: Looking Further into the APPA

The APPA is an international organization that provides education and training for community corrections practitioners and supervisors. APPA establishes standards in all areas of community supervision, including restitution, electronic monitoring, pretrial, conditional early release, and issues related to prisons. Go to http://www.appa-net.org and click on *About APPA* and then on *Where we stand*—this area shows position statements, resolutions, and position papers. Research three different topics and the position the APPA has taken

on these issues. Report your findings to the legislator and discuss whether they are politically feasible in today's economic climate.

CASE B: Researching Other Community Corrections Advocacy Groups

The APPA is only one of several organizations that serve a similar purpose for community corrections advocacy. Other organizations include:

- American Correctional Association **(http://www.aca.org)**;
- National Association of Pretrial Services Agencies **(http://www.napsa.org/)**;
- International Community Correctional Association **(http://www.iccaweb.org)**; and
- International Association of Reentry **(http://www.iarreentry.org/)**.

Look up one of the four organizations above and compare and contrast it to the APPA from Case A. Which organization—the APPA or another organization—would you most likely recommend to the legislator for its practicality in its approach to the problem, and why?

How Probation Developed: Chronicling Its Past and Present

CHAPTER LEARNING OBJECTIVES

1. Recall the social and legal history of probation in England and the United States.
2. Discuss the founders of probation.
3. Restate how supervision philosophies have changed in the United States.
4. Describe how probation is organized and operates.
5. Examine how community corrections acts help implement community supervision programs.
6. Characterize how probation supervision has changed over time.

Probation officers spend a significant amount of time in court. When probation first began, many probation departments were located inside the courthouse itself.

© Richard Cummins/Getty Images

CHAPTER OUTLINE

KEY TERMS

amercement
security for good behavior
filing
motion to quash
surety
recognizance

suspended sentence
conviction
John Augustus
parens patriae
community corrections acts
casework

brokerage of services
community resource management
    team model
justice model
neighborhood-based supervision

The kind efforts of one person can indeed make a difference. Take a look at John Augustus (1785–1859), who owned a shoe manufacturing company on the west side of Boston. His business prospered, and he owned a number of residences, one of which is now the Jonathan Harrington House, which faces the Lexington Common. Augustus was a member of the Washington Total Abstinence Society; its members pledged to abstain from alcohol and to assist alcoholics. Discovering that people were being arrested and detained in jail for public intoxication, Augustus decided to bail out complete strangers who he thought would most likely change their habits and return to court. His home became a refuge for the defendants he had bailed out until he accompanied them to their next court appearance. Augustus described the scene in his own words:

> In the month of August 1841, I was in court one morning when the door communicating with the lock-room was opened and an officer entered, followed by a ragged and wretched looking man, who took his seat upon the bench allotted to prisoners. I imagined from the man's appearance that his offence was that of yielding to his appetite for intoxicating drinks, and in a few moments I found that my suspicions were correct, for the clerk read the complaint, in which the man was charged with being a common drunkard. The case was clearly made out, but before sentence had been passed, I conversed with him a few moments, and found that he was not yet past all hope and reformation, although his appearance and his looks precluded a belief in the minds of others that he would ever become a man again. He told me that if he could be saved from the House of Correction, he never again would taste intoxicating liquors; there was such an earnestness in that tone, and a look expressive of firm resolve, that I determined to aid him; I bailed him, by permission of the Court. He was ordered to appear for sentence in three weeks from that time. He signed the pledge and became a sober man; at the expiration of this period of probation, I accompanied him into the courtroom; his whole appearance was changed and no one, not

even the scrutinizing officers, could have believed that he was the same person who less than a month before, had stood trembling on the prisoner's stand. The Judge expressed himself much pleased with the account we gave of the man, and instead of the usual penalty—imprisonment in the House of Correction—he fined him one cent and costs, amounting in all to $3.76, which was immediately paid. The man continued industrious and sober, and without doubt has been, by this treatment, saved from a drunkard's grave. (1852, pp. 4–5).

Within a year, Augustus' efforts became well known to private philanthropists who donated money so he and his volunteers could continue. For the next 15 years until his death in 1859, Augustus was dedicated to helping men, women, and children accused of different types of offenses, despite great opposition from jailers who lost money on every defendant he bailed and from people in the community who thought that the accused deserved jail. In total, he assisted 1,946 people, spent $19,464 for bail, and paid $2,418 in fines and court costs. He felt his strategies were more effective than jail, and today John Augustus is known as the father of probation.

PRECURSORS TO AMERICAN PROBATION

Probation, as it is known and practiced today, evolved out of ancient precedents in England and the United States devised to avoid the mechanical application of the harsh penal codes of the day (Rotman, 1995). Early British criminal law, which was dominated by the objectives of retribution and punishment, imposed rigid and severe penalties on offenders. The usual punishments were corporal: branding, flogging, mutilation, and execution. Capital punishment was commonly inflicted on children and animals as well as men and women. At the time of Henry VIII, for instance, more than 200 crimes were punishable by death, many of them relatively minor offenses against property.

Methods used to determine guilt—what today is called *criminal procedure*—also put the accused in danger. Trial might be by combat between the accused and the accuser, or a person's innocence might be determined by whether he or she sank when bound and thrown into a deep pond—the theory being that the pure water would reject wrongdoers. Thus, the choice was to drown as an innocent person or to survive the drowning only to be otherwise executed. Sometimes the offender could elect to be tried "by God," which involved undergoing some painful and frequently life-threatening ordeal, or "by country," a form of trial by jury for which the accused first had to pay an **amercement** to the king. The accepted premise was that the purpose of criminal law was not to deter or rehabilitate but to bring about justice for a past act deemed harmful to the society.

Early legal practices in the United States were distinct from British common law in a number of ways. First, **security for good behavior,** also known as *good abearance,* was a fee paid to the state as collateral for a promise of good behavior. Much like the modern practice of bail, security for good behavior allowed the accused to go free in certain cases either before or after conviction. Under **filing,** the indictment was "laid on file" in cases in which justice did not require an immediate sentence. However, the court could impose certain conditions on the defendant. The effect was that the case was laid at rest without either dismissal or final judgment and without the necessity of asking for final continuances.

amercement
A monetary penalty imposed arbitrarily at the discretion of the court for an offense.

security for good behavior
A recognizance or bond given the court by a defendant before or after conviction conditioned on his or her being "on good behavior" or keeping the peace for a prescribed period.

filing
A procedure under which an indictment was "laid on file," or held in abeyance, without either dismissal or final judgment in cases in which justice did not require an immediate sentence.

motion to quash
An oral or written request that the court repeal, nullify, or overturn a decision, usually made during or after the trial.

surety
An individual who agrees to become responsible for the debt of a defendant or who answers for the performance of the defendant should the defendant fail to attend the next court appearance.

Massachusetts's judges also often granted a **motion to quash** after judgment, using any minor technicality or the slightest error in the proceedings to free the defendant in cases in which they thought the statutory penalties inhumane. Some early forms of bail had the effect of suspending final action on a case, although the chief use of bail then (as now) was for the purpose of ensuring appearance for trial, such as using the assistance of **sureties.**

All of these methods had the common objective of mitigating punishment by relieving selected offenders from the full effects of the legally prescribed penalties that substantial segments of the community, including many judges, viewed as excessive and inappropriate to their offenses. They were precursors to probation as it is known today. The procedures most closely related to modern probation, however, are recognizance and the suspended sentence.

Procedures Related to Modern Probation

recognizance
Originally a device of preventive justice that obliged people suspected of future misbehavior to stipulate with and give full assurance to the court and the public that the apprehended offense would not occur. Recognizance was later used with convicted or arraigned offenders with conditions of release set.

suspended sentence
An order of the court after a verdict, finding, or plea of guilty that suspends or postpones the imposition or execution of sentence during a period of good behavior.

In the 1830 case of *Commonwealth v. Chase,* often cited as an example of the early use of release on **recognizance,** Judge Peter Oxenbridge Thacher found the defendant (Jerusha Chase) guilty on her plea, suspended the imposition of sentence, and ruled that the defendant was permitted to be released upon her word that she would reappear at a later date for her next court appearance. Recognizance came to be used in Massachusetts as a means of avoiding a final conviction of young and minor offenders in the hope that they would avoid further criminal behavior. The main thrust of recognizance was to humanize criminal law and to mitigate its harshness. While recognizance was illegal in 1830, it is used today to ensure a defendant's presence at court and is *neither* a disposition nor a form of supervision in itself.

A **suspended sentence** is a court order, entered after a verdict, finding, or plea of guilty, that suspends or postpones the filing, imposition, or execution of sentence contingent on the good behavior of the offender. Suspended sentences grew out of efforts to mitigate the harsh punishments demanded by early English law.

There are two kinds of suspended sentence—suspension of *imposition* of sentence and suspension of *execution* of sentence. In the case of suspension of imposition of sentence, a verdict or plea may be reached but no sentence is pronounced, and there is no conviction. This means that there is no criminal record and no loss of civil rights provided law-abiding behavior continues for a specified period of time (for example, for three years). The withholding or postponement of sentence is revoked or terminated if the offender commits a new crime.

conviction
A judgment of the court, based on a defendant's plea of guilty *or nolo contendere,* or on the verdict of a judge or jury, that the defendant is guilty of the offense(s) with which he or she has been charged.

In the case of suspension of execution of sentence, a defendant is placed on probation and the **conviction** remains on record. A conviction is followed by the execution of criminal sanctions and loss of civil rights and privileges. The suspended sentence can thus be either a separate disposition or a sentencing alternative connected with probation.

THE POWER TO SUSPEND SENTENCE   English common law courts had the power to suspend sentence for a limited period or for a specified purpose. Handing down suspended sentences and calling it "probation" was a common practice in the federal courts. In a case known as the "Killits" case, Judge Killits refused to vacate a suspended sentence even when the victim did not wish to prosecute. This case went all the way to the U.S. Supreme Court, and in 1916 the Court held that federal courts had no power to suspend indefinitely the imposition or execution of a sentence (*Ex parte United States* 242 U.S. 27, 1916). This aspect—the recognition of legislative authority to grant the power of indefinite suspension to the courts—made probation as now defined and practiced in the United States largely statutory.

As a result of the Killits case, the president pardoned approximately 2,000 people. The Supreme Court, as a remedy to an indefinite suspension, suggested probation legislation.

The early controversy about the court's authority to suspend sentence has also resulted in differing ideas about the relationship between probation and suspended sentence. In some jurisdictions, probation was not a sentence in itself but was a form of suspended execution of sentence. In 1984 the Federal Sentencing Reform Act recognized probation as a bona fide sentence (18 U.S.C.A. 3561).

The Founders of Probation

Volunteers and philanthropists were instrumental in the development and acceptance of probation in practice long before probation became law. The development of the probation idea can be credited to two cofounding individuals: John Augustus and Matthew Davenport Hill.

JOHN AUGUSTUS The credit for founding probation in the United States is reserved for **John Augustus,** a Boston boot maker whose life and efforts were detailed at the beginning of this chapter. Followers of John Augustus included John Murray Spear, who served as a "voluntary public defender, lecturer, and traveler, a tract distributor, and a worker with discharged prisoners" (Lindner & Savarese, 1984b, p. 5). The settlement movement, a group of university students and professors, was also prominent in the establishment of probation in New York. The University Settlement was a grassroots social reform organization that advocated for the poor people of the community, including those on probation. In protest of materialism, industrialization, and widening gaps between social classes, settlement residents lived and worked in the poorest sections of the city and resolved to teach and learn from the local residents (Lindner & Savarese, 1984c, 1984d).

> **John Augustus**
> A Boston bootmaker who was the founder of probation in the United States.

In 1878, almost 20 years after the death of John Augustus, adult probation in Massachusetts was sanctified by statute. A law was passed authorizing the mayor of Boston to appoint a paid probation officer to serve in the Boston criminal courts as a member of the police force. Three years later this law was changed so the probation officer reported to the prison commissioner. Due to corruption, the law was revised again to disallow police officers from becoming probation officers (Panzarella, 2002). Statewide probation did not begin until 1891 when a statute transferred the power of appointment from the municipalities to the courts and made such appointment mandatory instead of permissive. For the first time, the probation officer was recognized as an official salaried agent of the court.

MATTHEW DAVENPORT HILL Matthew Davenport Hill was less known in the United States, but he deserves equal credit alongside John Augustus as a cofounder of probation. Hill laid the foundation for probation in England, where he lived and worked. Born to Reverend Thomas Wright Hill in 1792 and the eldest of eight children, Matthew Davenport Hill was a member of a family intimately involved in politics and the movement for social change (Lindner, 2007). While in Parliament, Hill was deeply concerned with equality for all people and worked toward ending the transportation of English convicts, among other causes. According to criminal justice historian Charles Lindner:

> His contribution to helping develop a probation system may have evolved from his early experiences as a lawyer, during which time he witnessed a number of cases in which young offenders were sentenced to a term of imprisonment of only one day… [Hill] also required that there be persons willing to act as guardians of the young offender. (Lindner, 2007, p. 40).

John Augustus owned a shoe factory similar to this one, in which he employed pretrial defendants to work until their next court date.

The guardians would be required to report back to Hill's court on the juveniles' behavior. Police had the power to enforce the court reporting process and to provide social service assistance. Hill kept court records of offenders' behavior, which included early accounts of recidivism measured by reconviction rates. Apparently, over a 12-year period, 80 offenders out of 417 were reconvicted, many because they returned to similar circumstances that contributed to crimes in the first place (Lindner, 2007, p. 40). Hill was a close personal friend of a number of other justice reformers, including Jeremy Bentham; Sir Robert Peel; Dr. Enoch Wines, a prison reformer; and Captain Alexander Maconochie (discussed in the next chapter as influential in the development of parole). Matthew Davenport Hill died in 1872 at the age of 80.

Development of Federal Probation

Historical accounts of federal probation suggest that federal judges were extremely resistant to enacting probation legislation. Between 1909 and 1925, 34 unsuccessful attempts were made to pass a law authorizing federal judges to grant probation. Because prohibitionists were afraid that judges would place violators of the Volstead Act (the Prohibition Amendment) on probation (Evjen, 1975), through their intense lobbying they convinced judges not to support probation. The bill was finally passed in 1925 and sent to President Coolidge, who as former governor of Massachusetts, understood how probation worked. Because probation in Massachusetts had been successful for nearly five decades, Coolidge had no problem signing the National Probation Act. The act authorized each federal district court to appoint one salaried probation officer with an annual income of $2,600.

Between 1927 and 1930, eight probation officers were required to pass the civil service examination. In 1930 the original law was amended to empower judges to appoint without reference to the civil service list, and the limitation of one officer to each district was removed. At the same time, the Parole Act was amended to give probation officers field supervision responsibility for federal parolees and probationers. Thus the average caseload was 400 probationers per probation officer. Officers relied heavily on as many as 700 volunteers (Evjen, 1975).

Between 1930 and 1940, the Federal Bureau of Prisons (FBP) administered the federal probation system, and Colonel Joel R. Moore became the first federal probation supervisor. The number of officers increased from eight to 233, but the appointments remained largely political.

By 1940 the U.S. probation system had increased so dramatically that the administration of probation was moved from the FBP to the Administrative Office of the U.S. Courts. The era from 1940 to 1950 was concentrated on initial qualifications, standardized manuals, and in-service training. Initial qualifications for federal probation officers stipulated that they be at least 25 years old but preferably 30–45 years of age, have a baccalaureate degree, possess two years of experience in social work, and be mature, intelligent, of good moral character, patient, and energetic (Evjen, 1975).

In 1984 the Comprehensive Crime Control Act abolished federal parole and brought all supervised prison releasees under the auspices of federal probation. Federal probation was administered as an appendage of the federal courts, where it remains today.

History of Juvenile Probation and the Juvenile Court

From the 1700s to the early 1800s, children were disciplined and punished for crimes informally by parents and other adults in the community. Most children contributed to the family income, but there were no formal mechanisms to care for children who were left homeless or whose parents had died. Between 1817 and the mid-1840s, middle-class female reformers, or "child savers," institutionalized runaway or neglected children in houses of refuge to provide them with a family environment, but the good intentions of the child savers were not fully realized in practice. Although some institutions were humane, most children were further exploited for labor, abused, and victimized.

To protect children from this exploitation, the New York Children's Aid Society shipped children to farmers in the West to keep them from being committed to a house of refuge. In 1890 the Children's Aid Society of Pennsylvania offered to place in foster homes delinquents who would otherwise be sent to reform school. Known as *placing out,* this practice was an early form of juvenile probation (Binder, Geis, and Bruce, 1997).

The Illinois Juvenile Court Act of 1899 legally established a juvenile system that was different from the adult system to stop the exploitation of children. The court was anchored in the belief that a child's behavior was the product of poor family background and surroundings. It operated informally, was civil in nature, and was geared toward rehabilitation. Initially there were those who believed that juvenile courts were created to coddle young criminals (Butts and Harrell, 2003). This is likely an oversimplification. Indeed, although "some reformers were motivated by a desire to save growing numbers of poor and homeless children from the streets of America's cities, [others such as judges, prosecutors, and police were] mainly interested in removing the legal obstacles that prevented criminal courts from dealing effectively with young hoodlums" (p. 4). Before the advent of the juvenile court, intervention did not occur until after youths were convicted of a crime, so the thinking was that the juvenile system could intervene at an earlier point in time, well before a conviction. "The trick was to create a new type of court that would have the power to intervene but would not have to abide by the restrictions of criminal procedure and due process rights" (Butts and Mears, 2001, p. 172).

In creating this, the state could intervene in cases in which a juvenile needed protection from an abusive home or from neglect.

Another observer said that "the 1899 Illinois Juvenile Court Act was, in part, yet another response to the growing incidence of jury nullification, concern about the dominance of sectarian industrial schools in Chicago filling with immigrants, and reform-based opposition to confining youth with adults" (Shepherd, 1999, p. 16). Whatever the motivation, the idea of a separate court for juvenile offenders caught on and spread quickly. By 1925, 46 states, three territories, and the District of Columbia had juvenile courts (Shepherd, 1999). Two concepts that formed the backbone of the original juvenile justice system were a recognition that level of mental intent over one's actions for youth is different than that for adults, and that the state might have to intervene as a protector in the best interest of a child.

Volunteer successors to John Augustus were influential in the development of juvenile probation in the United States. These volunteers included Rufus R. Cook, Miss L. P. Burnham, and Lucy L. Flower, among others. Rufus "Uncle" Cook provided supervision to juveniles while he also served as chaplain of the Suffolk County jail in Boston. Miss L. P. Burnham was credited with being "the first career woman in the probation field" (Lindner and Savarese, 1984b, p. 5). Lucy Flower, wife of a prominent Chicago attorney, was responsible for the creation of juvenile probation services in Illinois. She obtained support from the Chicago Bar Association to draft and pass the necessary legislation to provide a separate court and detention system that was different from the adult system (Lindner and Savarese, 1984b).

Juvenile probation was formed under English common law and the doctrine of **parens patriae,** which is a Latin term for the doctrine that "the state is parent" and therefore serves as guardian of juveniles who might not be able to fend for themselves. The state intervened as a substitute parent in an attempt to act in the best interests of a child by using four principles. First, the court appointed a guardian to care for a child. The second principle was that parents of offenders must be held responsible for their children's wrongdoing. Third, no matter what offense children had committed, placing them in jail was an unsuitable penalty. The fourth principle stated that removing children from their parents and sending them even to an industrial school should be avoided, and

parens patriae
Latin term meaning that the government acts as a "substitute parent" and allows the courts to intervene in cases in which it is in the child's best interest that a guardian be appointed for children who, through no fault of their own, have been neglected and/or are dependent.

> that when it [a child] is allowed to return home it should be under probation, subject to the guidance and friendly interest of the probation officer, the representative of the court. To raise the age of criminal responsibility from seven or ten to sixteen or eighteen without providing for an efficient system of probation, would indeed be disastrous. Probation is, in fact, the keynote of juvenile court legislation. (Mack, 1909, p. 162)

Mack further related:

> Whenever juvenile courts have been established, a system of probation has been provided for, and even where as yet the juvenile court system has not been fully developed, some steps have been taken to substitute probation for imprisonment of the juvenile offender. What they need, more than anything else, is kindly assistance; and the aim of the court, appointing a probation officer for the child, is to have the child and the parents feel, not so much the power, as the friendly interest of the state; to show them that the object of the court is to help them to train the child right, and therefore the probation officers must be men and women fitted for these tasks. (p. 163)

A detailed discussion of the contemporary juvenile court and other types of community corrections for juveniles is found in chapter 14. For now, we return to a discussion of early probation laws in the adult system at the time when probation first began in the northeastern region of the United States.

Early Probation Legislation in Other States

New York's probation law allowed police officers to be probation officers, but one of the two positions was occupied by three different University Settlement members (Lindner and Savarese, 1984d). Later probation legislation in other states included a provision that the probation officer not be an active member of the regular police force. Although this early legislation provided for the appointment of probation officers, most legislation did not provide money for salaried positions. According to Lindner and Savarese (1984a), this omission was deliberate because there was a feeling that probation legislation would not have passed at all if there were appropriations and costs attached. Thus probation workers in many areas were volunteers, paid from private donations, or they were municipal workers and other court officers who supervised probationers in addition to their regular jobs.

ORGANIZATION OF PROBATION DEPARTMENTS

After Massachusetts, Vermont was the second state to pass a probation statute, adopting a *county* plan of organization in 1898. Each county judge was given the power to appoint a probation officer to serve all the courts in the county. California enacted a probation statute in 1903 following the Vermont pattern of county-based probation administration. The California law provided for adult as well as juvenile probation (U.S. Department of Justice, 1974).

On the other hand, Rhode Island in 1899 adopted a *statewide* and state-controlled probation system. A state agency, the Board of Charities and Correction, was given the power to appoint a probation officer and assistants. States such as New York ultimately followed a state-controlled system (U.S. Department of Justice, 1974). As various states enacted probation legislation, they did not do so uniformly. Initial probation legislation followed either Vermont's local organizational pattern or Rhode Island's state organizational pattern. Initial probation development in the U.S. resembled a patchwork quilt in many ways.

Over time, changes have occurred in the way that probation departments are structured. Smaller, more localized departments have found themselves at a disadvantage when trying to compete fiscally with larger agencies, such as state prisons and county jails, that may send representatives to the state capitol during key budget times. For that reason, many probation and parole departments have merged. It has been only recently that some probation departments have combined adult and juvenile probation services. The three main structural differences among probation agencies pertain to:

- branch of government: this may be executive/state or judicial/local;
- autonomy: these may be combined with parole or can each be stand-alone departments; and
- age factors: agencies may combine their adult and juvenile supervision together or be separate.

Table 2.1 shows how probation and parole agencies are currently structured. About half of all states administer adult and juvenile systems very differently. However, juvenile and adult probation services are fully integrated in at least 10 states and are partially integrated in select jurisdictions in another six states (Krauth and Linke, 1999).

TABLE 2.1 Organizational Structure of Adult and Juvenile Probation/Parole Services

	ADULT		JUVENILE	
STATE	Level/Branch	Combined or Separate Adult Probation & Parole	Level/Branch	Combined or Separate Juvenile w/Adult
Alabama	State/Executive	Combined	County/Judicial	Separate
Alaska	State/Executive	Combined	State/Executive	Separate
Arizona	County/Judicial	Both	County/Judicial	Both
Arkansas	State/Executive	Combined	County/Judicial	Separate
California	County/Judicial	Separate	County/Judicial	Combined
Colorado	State/Judicial	Separate	County/Judicial	Combined
Connecticut	State/Judicial	Separate	State/Judicial	Separate
Delaware	State/Executive	Combined	State/Executive	Separate
Florida	State/Executive	Combined	State/Executive	Separate
Georgia	State/Executive	Separate	Mixed/Exec. & Judicial	Separate
Hawaii	State/Judicial	Separate	State/Judicial	Separate
Idaho	State/Executive	Combined	County/Judicial	Separate
Illinois	County/Judicial	Separate	County/Judicial	Combined
Indiana	County/Judicial	Separate	County/Judicial	Combined
Iowa	County/Executive	Combined	State/Judicial	Separate
Kansas	State/Judicial	Separate	County/Judicial	Combined
Kentucky	State/Executive	Combined	State/Executive	Separate
Louisiana	State/Executive	Combined	Mixed/Exec. & Judicial	Separate
Maine	State/Executive	Separate	State/Executive	Separate
Maryland	State/Executive	Combined	State/Executive	Separate
Massachusetts	State/Judicial	Separate	State/Judicial	Separate
Michigan	State/Executive	Combined	County/Judicial	Both
Minnesota	Mixed/Exec. &Judicial	Both	Mixed/Exec & Judicial	Separate
Mississippi	State/Executive	Combined	Mixed/Exec. & Judicial	Separate
Missouri	State/Executive	Combined	Mixed/Exec. & Judicial	Separate
Montana	State/Executive	Combined	State/Judicial	Separate
Nebraska	State/Judicial	Separate	State/Judicial	Combined
Nevada	State/Executive	Combined	County/Judicial	Separate
New Hampshire	State/Executive	Combined	State/Executive	Separate
New Jersey	State/Judicial	Separate	State/Judicial	Combined
New Mexico	State/Executive	Combined	State/Executive	Separate
New York	County/Executive	Separate	County/Executive	Combined
North Carolina	State/Executive	Combined	State/Executive	Separate
North Dakota	State/Executive	Combined	State/Exec. &Judicial	Separate
Ohio	Mixed/Exec. &Judicial	Both	County/Exec. & Judicial	Both
Oklahoma	State/Executive	Combined	Mixed/Exec. & Judicial	Separate
Oregon	County/Executive	Combined	Mixed/Executive	Both
Pennsylvania	Mixed/Exec. &Judicial	Both	County/Judicial	Both
Rhode Island	State/Executive	Combined	State/Executive	Separate

(*Continues*)

TABLE 2.1 Organizational Structure of Adult and Juvenile Probation/Parole Services (*Continued*)

STATE	ADULT			JUVENILE	
	Level/Branch	Combined or Separate Adult Probation & Parole	Level/Branch	Combined or Separate Juvenile w/Adult
South Carolina	State/Executive	Combined	State/Executive	Separate
South Dakota	State/Judicial	Separate	State/Judicial	Combined
Tennessee	State/Executive	Separate	Mixed/Exec. & Judicial	Separate
Texas	County/Judicial	Combined	County/Judicial	Both
Utah	State/Executive	Combined	State/Judicial	Separate
Vermont	State/Executive	Combined	State/Executive	Separate
Virginia	State/Executive	Combined	Mixed/Exec. & Judicial	Separate
Washington	State/Executive	Combined	County/Exec. & Judicial	Separate
West Virginia	County/Judicial	Separate	State/Judicial	Combined
Wisconsin	State/Executive	Combined	County/Exec. & Judicial	Separate
Wyoming	State/Executive	Combined	Mixed/Exec. & Judicial	Separate

Executive = Administered under the executive branch of government.
Judicial = Administered under the courts/judicial branch.

Source: Barbara Krauth and Larry Linke. 1999. *State Organizational Structures for Delivering Adult Probation Services.* Longmont, CO: LIS, Inc. for the National Institute of Corrections, U.S. Department of Justice.

Community Corrections Acts

To address concerns about local community differences and the lesser political pull of local government, community corrections acts were developed to expand local sentencing options in lieu of imprisonment. **Community corrections acts** (CCAs) are statewide agreements through which funds are granted to local governments to develop and deliver community correctional sanctions and services (McManus and Barclay, 1994). CCAs decentralize correctional sanctions so that they more closely reflect community values and attitudes. The first community corrections act was enacted in Minnesota in 1973, and CCAs now exist in 28 states.

> **community corrections act**
> Formal written agreement between the state government and local entities for the state to fund counties to implement and operate community corrections programs on a local level.

State-run programs do not qualify as CCAs—only those that are operated locally or through private agencies do. In this way, local governments benefit from the greater revenue-generating capacity of state government. Oregon is a good example of a CCA that shares characteristics found in other state agreements (see Box 2.1). Harris (1996) found that most CCAs are legislatively authorized statewide to provide state funding for local initiatives, decentralization of program design and delivery, and citizen participation and/or privatization. This is important because local communities are allowed an opportunity to develop programs to fit their needs. For example, Ohio and North Carolina developed day reporting centers, whereas Iowa and Indiana developed victim-offender dialogue meetings. Jurisdictions that want to initiate a new program, such as a drug court or mental health court, must agree to contribute matching funds (Center for Community Corrections, 1997). Note that Oregon's act includes a provision for a monthly fee while under supervision, so that offenders help subsidize their own costs to taxpayers.

States that do not have CCAs (e.g., Arkansas, Idaho, Illinois, Louisiana, Nevada, New Hampshire, North Dakota, Rhode Island, Utah, and Vermont) still subsidize and contract with public and private agencies, but the funding mechanism is not formalized and appears less consistent than in states that have CCAs in place.

BOX 2.1   OREGON COMMUNITY CORRECTIONS ACT

423.475. The Legislative Assembly finds and declares that:

(1) Passage by the voters of chapter 2, Oregon Laws 1995, has created mandatory minimum penalties for certain violent offenses, and the probable effect thereof will be a significant increase in the demands placed on state secure facilities.

(2) The state recognizes that it is in a better position than counties to assume responsibility for serious violent offenders and career property offenders.

(3) Counties are willing, in the context of a partnership with the state, to assume responsibility for felony offenders sentenced to a term of incarceration of 12 months or less.

(4) Under the terms of the partnership agreement, the state agrees to provide adequate funding to the counties if the counties agree to assume responsibility of those offenders.

423.505 Legislative policy on program funding. Because counties are in the best position for the management, oversight and administration of local criminal justice matters and for determining local resource priorities, it is the legislative policy of this state to establish an ongoing partnership between the state and counties and to finance with appropriations from the General Fund statewide community correction programs on a continuing basis. The intended purposes of this program are to:

(1) Provide appropriate sentencing and sanctioning options including incarceration, community supervision and services;

(2) Provide improved local services for persons charged with criminal offenses with the goal of reducing the occurrence of repeat criminal offenses;

(3) Promote local control and management of community corrections programs;

(4) Promote the use of the most effective criminal sanctions necessary to protect public safety, administer punishment to the offender and rehabilitate

the offender [1977 c.412 §1; 1989 c.607 §1; 1995 c.423 §2]

423.520. The Department of Corrections shall make grants to assist counties in the implementation and operation of community corrections programs. The department shall require recipients of the grants to cooperate in the collection and sharing of data necessary to evaluate the effect of community corrections programs on future criminal conduct. [1977 c.412 §5; 1987 c.320 §221; 1995 c.423 §3; 1997 c.433 §10]

(1) The county may contract with public or private agencies including, but not limited to, other counties, cities, special districts and public or private agencies for the provision of services to offenders. [1977 c.412 §13; 1987 c.320 §224; 1989 c.613 §2; 1995 c.423 §7]

423.570 Monthly fee payable by person on supervised release; use; payment as condition of release; waiver. (1) A person sentenced to probation or placed by an authority on parole, post-prison supervision or other form of release, subject to supervision by a community corrections program established under ORS 423.500 to 423.560, shall be required to pay a monthly fee to offset costs of supervising.

(3) The fee shall be determined and fixed by the releasing authority but shall be at least $25.

(4) Fees are payable one month following the commencement of supervision and at one-month intervals thereafter. Each county shall retain the fee to be used for funding of its community corrections programs.

Question: What are the main parts of Oregon's community corrections act that allow county probation departments to function?
Source: Oregon Legislative Assembly, Legislative Counsel Committee. Adapted from the 2009 Oregon Revised Statutes, Chapter 423—Corrections and Crime Control Administration and Programs. Retrieved from: http://www.oregon.gov/DOC/TRANS/CC/docs/pdf/Community_Corrections_Act.pdf

Community Supervision Models Over Time

As community corrections acts were established, they helped create stability for the notion of correctional supervision in the community as a primary mode of social control. In this section, we review how probation supervision styles have changed over the last 100 years.

CASEWORK MODEL: 1900–1970 When probation began, the supervision process was oriented toward **casework,** providing therapeutic services to probationers or parolees (often referred to as clients) to assist them in living productively in the community. Probation and parole officers frequently viewed themselves as "caseworkers," or social workers, and the term "agent of change" was a popular description of their role. The literature on probation and parole supervision during this period was replete with medical and psychiatric terminology, such as *treatment* and *diagnosis*. Casework placed stress on creating therapeutic relationships with clients through counseling and directly assisting in behavior modification (National Advisory Commission on Criminal Justice Standards and Goals, 1973). The probation officer was thus viewed as a social worker engaged in a therapeutic relationship with the probationer "client."

casework
A community supervision philosophy that allowed the officer to create therapeutic relationships with clients through counseling and directly assisting in behavior modification to assist them in living productively in the community.

BROKERAGE OF SERVICES MODEL: 1971–1980 In the early 1970s the casework approach began to break down. Many services needed by probationers and parolees could be more readily and effectively provided by specialized community agencies that handled mental health, employment, housing, education, private welfare, and other services. The National Advisory Commission on Criminal Justice Standards and Goals (1973) reported: "Probation also has attempted to deal directly with such problems as alcoholism, drug addiction, and mental illness, which ought to be handled through community mental health and other specialized programs" (pp. 107–108). This alternative strategy for delivering probation and parole services was referred to as the **brokerage of services** approach. The "service broker" type of probation or parole officer did not consider himself or herself the primary agent of change as in the casework approach. Instead, the officer attempted to determine the needs of a probationer or parolee and located the appropriate community agency to which the client was referred. Thus an unemployed parolee might be referred to vocational rehabilitation services, employment counseling, or the state employment office. Instead of attempting to counsel a probationer with emotional problems, the service-broker officer would locate agencies and refer the probationer to staff skilled in working with problems faced by the client. In this supervision strategy, developing linkages between clients and appropriate agencies was considered one of the probation or parole officer's most important tasks.

brokerage of services
Supervision that involves identifying the needs of probationers or parolees and referring them to an appropriate community agency.

Closely allied to the brokerage approach was the **community resource management team model.** Individual probation and parole officers became specialists by developing skills and linkages with community agencies in one or two areas. For example, one officer might be designated a drug abuse specialist and another an employment specialist, whereas a third developed expertise with female offenders. This approach recognized that the diverse needs of the probation or parole caseload could not be adequately satisfied by one individual. Thus the caseload was "pooled," and the probationer might be assisted not by one officer but by several.

community resource management team model (CRMT)
A supervision model in which probation or parole officers develop skills and linkages with community agencies in one or two areas only. Supervision under this model is a team effort, each officer utilizing his or her skills and linkages to assist the offender.

JUSTICE MODEL: 1981–2000 By the mid-1980s, the **justice model** dominated probation and parole supervision. The justice model advocated an escalated system of sanctions corresponding to the social harm resulting from an offense and an offender's culpability. The justice model regarded a sentence of probation not as an alternative to imprisonment but as a valid sanction in itself. The public tends to regard probation established as an alternative to incarceration as an expression of leniency. The justice philosophy regarded probation as a separate, distinct sanction requiring penalties that are graduated in severity and duration according to the seriousness of a crime.

Advocates of the justice model considered practices of counseling, surveillance, and reporting to accomplish very little and to have minimal impact on

justice model
The correctional practice based on the concept of just deserts and even-handed punishment. The justice model calls for fairness in criminal sentencing, in that all people convicted of a similar offense will receive a like sentence. This model of corrections relies on determinate sentencing and/or abolition of parole.

neighborhood-based supervision
A supervision strategy that emphasizes public safety, accountability, partnerships with other community agencies, and beat supervision.

recidivism. They favored probation that consists of monitoring court orders for victim restitution or community service and that ensures an imposed deprivation of liberty is carried out. Thus, this model primarily assisted offenders in complying with supervision conditions. Other services such as mental health counseling and alcohol and drug treatment are available but are brokered through social agencies in the community.

NEIGHBORHOOD-BASED SUPERVISION: 2001–PRESENT   A philosophical change has unfolded yet again as probation supervision has been rethought to encompass both offenders and the communities in which they reside. This supervision strategy, which emphasizes the community more than previous models, is known by a variety of terms, such as **neighborhood-based supervision** (the term we use in this text), "community justice," and "broken windows probation" (Beto, 2000).

In neighborhood-based supervision (NBS), the probation officers are in the community more than an office, engaging community groups as partners in offender supervision. By making probation more visible and establishing leverage with community groups, NBS aims to transform probation into a more respected punishment in the community. The strategies of NBS would in turn improve the overall quality of life in the community and contribute to decreased crime. NBS holds probation administrators and line officers accountable for achieving specific outcomes through such elements as:

- emphasis on public safety;
- partnerships with police, treatment providers, and faith-based practitioners;
- supervision in field beats;
- strong and consistent enforcement of probation conditions;
- use of satellite tracking and geographic information systems technology;
- rational allocation of resources using offender assessments; and
- measuring program effectiveness by establishing performance-based initiatives (Beto, 2000, p. 12).

This philosophy has required a paradigm shift in how probation officers and supervisors currently think and operate. In light of these changes, serving a dual role as therapeutic change agents and enforcers who see to it that their clients do not threaten public safety is a constant challenge. In chapter 5, we discuss how neighborhood-based community supervision is implemented.

WHO IS ON PROBATION?

Table 2.2 shows that probationer demographics have stayed fairly stable over time. About 60 percent of probationers nationwide have a direct sentence of probation, 30 percent have some type of suspended sentence (such as diversion), and 9 percent have a split sentence (a short time in jail, followed by a longer period of probation). The vast majority of probationers have been sentenced for a drug or alcohol violation, secondarily for property offenses, with less than 20 percent of probationers sentenced for a violent offense. About 76 percent of all adult probationers are men, and 24 percent are women. The race/ethnic group composition for probationers varies by region of the country, but on a nationwide scale more than half (56 percent) of probationers are white, 30 percent are African-American, 12 percent are of Hispanic origin, and 2 percent are either Native American or Asian/Pacific Islander.

TABLE 2.2 Characteristics of Adults on Probation Over Time: 1995, 2000, and 2009

	1995	2000	2009
Gender			
Male	79%	78%	76%
Female	21	22	24
Race/Origin			
White	53	54	55
Black	31	31	30
Hispanic	14	13	13
American Indian/Alaska Native	1	1	1
Asian/Pacific Islander[a]	1	1	1
Status of Probation			
Direct imposition	48	56	54
Split sentence	15	11	9
Sentence suspended	26	25	27
Imposition suspended	6	7	8
Other	4	1	2
Status of Supervision			
Active	79	76	72
Inactive	8	9	6
Absconded	9	9	8
Supervised out of state	2	3	3
Warrant status	*	*	6
Residential program	*	*	1
Financial conditions remaining	*	*	1
Other	2	3	2
Type of Offense			
Felony	54	52	51
Misdemeanor	44	46	47
Other infractions	2	2	2
Most Serious Offense			
Violent	*	*	19
Property	*	*	26
Drug law violation	*	24	26
Public order/DWI	16	18	19
Other	84	52	10
Adults Entering Probation			
Without incarceration	72	79	65
With incarceration	13	16	21
Other types	15	5	14

(*Continues*)

TABLE 2.2   Characteristics of Adults on Probation Over Time: 1995, 2000, and 2009 (*Continued*)

	1995	2000	2009
Adults Leaving Probation			
Successful completions	62	60	65
Returned to incarceration	21	15	17
With new sentence	5	3	4
With the same sentence	13	8	8
Treatment or unknown	3	4	5
Absconder[b]	*	3	3
Technical violators[b]	*	11	10.5
Death	1	1	0.5
Other	16	11	4

Notes: *Not measured. [a]Includes Native Hawaiians. [b]In 1995 absconder and others unsuccessful were reported as "other."

Sources: Lauren E. Glaze and Seri Palla. 2005. *Probation and Parole in the United States, 2004.* Washington, DC: U.S. Department of Justice, Bureau of Justice Statistics; Lauren E. Glaze and Thomas P. Bonczar, and Fan Zhang. 2010. *Probation and Parole in the United States, 2009.* Washington, DC: U.S. Department of Justice, Bureau of Justice Statistics.

SUMMARY

- In the American colonies where English law prevailed, distinct American practices developed. Precursors to American probation included filing, security for good behavior, recognizance, and suspension of imposition of sentence. American judges exercised discretion to reduce the severity of punishment in cases in which the circumstances of the crime or characteristics of the offender warranted leniency.

- An increasing awareness that prisons were not accomplishing their stated purpose of reforming the offender and that suspension of sentence without supervision was not a satisfactory alternative brought about the development of probation as it is known today.

- Upon the foundation laid by judges, volunteers, and the University Settlement movement, John Augustus brought about the practice of probation as it is known today.

- The concept that crimes committed by children should be dealt with differently than with adults, with special courts and special facilities for juveniles, was formalized by the creation of the first juvenile court in Illinois in 1899.

- There are two kinds of suspended sentence—suspension of *imposition* of sentence and suspension of *execution* of sentence. Suspension of imposition of sentence means there is no conviction, and the sentence will be dropped if the defendant completes probation successfully. Suspension of execution of sentence means the defendant is placed on probation and the conviction remains on record.

- Probation organizational patterns have little uniformity throughout the United States.
  - Probation services may be combined with parole or kept separate.
  - Adult and juvenile probation may be combined or kept entirely separate.
  - Probation may be administered by the executive branch of government or by the judiciary.

- Community corrections acts provide state funding to local probation agencies for development of a wide range of community supervision and treatment programs.

- The varied approaches to community supervision that characterize the four eras of probation are: case work, brokerage of services, the justice model, and neighborhood probation.

DISCUSSION QUESTIONS

1. What was the significance of the decision in *Commonwealth v. Chase?*

2. What are the two kinds of suspended sentences? Why is the distinction critical to an understanding of modern probation?

3. What was the *Killits* case? What was its impact on modern probation?

4. How did John Augustus and Matthew Davenport Hill create support for probation as we know it today?

5. Why are community corrections acts necessary to local-level supervision?

6. How has the concept of supervision changed over the past century? What factors have brought about these changes?

7. Which model of supervision do you view as most effective for use today?

WEBSITES, VIDEOS, AND PODCASTS

Websites

History of New York Corrections, N.Y. Corrections Society
http://www.correctionhistory.org/

History of U.S. Probation Office
http://www.nmcourt.fed.us/web/PBDOCS/Files/history.html

Hampshire Probation Service, United Kingdom
http://www.hampshire-probation.gov.uk

American Probation and Parole Association
http://www.appa-net.org/

Federal Probation
http://www.uscourts.gov/library/fpcontents.html

Learn about the basic assumptions of community corrections, outline the arguments favoring community corrections, and test your knowledge.

Juvenile Delinquency Court Orientation Video
http://www.youtube.com/watch?v=rRXKIZTKJ-w

This step-by-step video familiarizes youth and their families with how Juvenile Court works.

CASE STUDY EXERCISES

The Diversion Decision

This chapter has discussed factors that affect the decision to grant diversion sentences. The following case examples are before the court, and you are tasked with deciding whether a case should or should not be diverted. You must justify your decision in writing.

CASE A: Defendant Smith, Possession of Ecstasy

Defendant Smith has been arrested for possession of Ecstasy—enough for two hits. Smith has no criminal history and has been employed as a laborer with a construction company for two years, excluding a brief layoff period. He has a good work record with the company. He admits that he uses alcohol and had been drinking and using Ecstasy the night of the offense. Smith has used marijuana and cocaine but indicates that all usage was in the past rather than recent. He lives by himself; he has never been married and has one child from a previous relationship. He is two months behind on his child-support payments and does not see his child very often. Smith's defense attorney argues that his client has never been in any form of mental-health counseling, substance-abuse treatment, or counseling, and that he would agree to go to drug court as a diversionary measure. The state's attorney is opposed to drug court for Defendant Smith because of the type of drug—Ecstasy. The police have recently been trying to rid the streets of the supply of Ecstasy and believe that Smith may be somehow tied to a major Ecstasy drug ring in the area, but they need more time to prove the allegations, which right now are "shaky" at best.

CASE B: Defendant Thompson, Reckless Injury to a Person

Defendant Thompson has been arrested for a felony crime—"throwing objects from an overpass"—that resulted in injury to a passenger of a vehicle. Thompson is a 19-year-old college freshman. He and another college friend had prepared shredded paper in their school colors for a homecoming football game. While walking across an overpass over the interstate highway, he and another student decided to throw some of the shredded paper, which was held in black plastic trash bags. They proceeded to cut open a bag and pour the paper down on the vehicles. When they cut into a second bag and poured the contents onto the passing vehicles, they were unaware that a brick had been put into the bag for weight. The brick struck the windshield of a vehicle, causing the windshield to break and chip; a piece of the glass flew into the eye of the victim, causing permanent loss of vision.

Defendant Thompson has a prior misdemeanor for theft when he was 17, for which he received a one-year diversionary sentence, which he completed just six months ago. He is not employed and is a full-time college student. He makes passing grades and has not had any student violations at the university. He denies any illegal drug usage and admitted to drinking in the past, but he denies drinking at all since his prior misdemeanor arrest. Thompson's attorney proposes to the court diversion once again: Thompson will continue to attend school, and he will participate in community service by helping the victim and her family at their farm without pay. The state's attorney is adamantly opposed to diversion insofar as this is Thompson's second arrest in less than two years. Due to the seriousness of the victim's injuries, the state's attorney feels this offense should become part of the court record. The district attorney believes that diversion would trivialize the victim's injuries and appeals to you not to grant diversion.

History of Parole and Mandatory Release

CHAPTER LEARNING OBJECTIVES

1. Explain how transport and ticket-of-leave influenced the development of parole.
2. Describe how parole was inspired by the work of Alexander Maconochie on Norfolk Island.
3. Discuss how parole was subsequently implemented by Walter Crofton in Ireland and Zebulon R. Brockway in New York's Elmira Reformatory.
4. Identify the reasons why discretionary parole was replaced by mandatory release.
5. Argue the pros and cons of medical parole.

Norfolk Island was the destination where English convicts who were disciplinary problems were sent. This view is the way the former penal colony now looks.

© Michael S. Yamashita/CORBIS

CHAPTER OUTLINE

KEY TERMS

parole
mandatory release
discretionary release
parole d'honneur
Alexander Maconochie
transportation

ticket-of-leave
marks system
Norfolk Island
Sir Walter Crofton
Irish system
Zebulon R. Brockway

medical model
just deserts
justice model
medical parole

Raymond Palen has served 17 years on a 20-year prison sentence for sexual assault. He has been confined to a geriatric prison unit for the last four years due to his ailing health and his age. He is now 79 years old and has heart problems, diabetes, arthritis, and uses a walker. He was transferred to a geriatric unit so he could be in closer proximity to a hospital and so he would no longer be victimized by younger prisoners. Palen is one of thousands of elderly prisoners who are eligible for release but do not receive it because of the political consequences of paroling a sex offender. Prisoners over 55 years comprise 8 percent of all prisoners, but their medical conditions absorb nearly one third of the entire medical budget for prisoners of all ages. If Palen were released, he would qualify for Medicaid, a federal program, rather than using dwindling state funds. Compassionate release is being reconsidered in today's tough economic climate (Lee, 2011).

mandatory release
Conditional release to the community under a determinate sentence that is automatic at the expiration of the minimum term of sentence minus any credited time off for good behavior.

discretionary release
Conditional release because members of a parole board have decided that the prisoner has earned the privilege while still remaining under supervision of an indeterminate sentence.

INTRODUCTION

Most prisoners who reenter the community do so under some type of supervised release. With over 800,000 state and federal prisoners currently under supervision across the country, most will be off supervision completely within one to two years (Bonczar, 2008). There are two types of post-prison supervision: discretionary and mandatory release. Individuals on **mandatory release** enter the community automatically at the expiration of their maximum term minus credited time off for good behavior. Mandatory release is decided by legislative statute or good time laws. In contrast to mandatory release, individuals released on **discretionary release** enter the community because members of a parole board have decided that the prisoner has earned the privilege of being

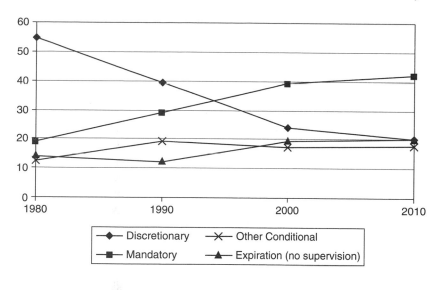

FIGURE 3.1   Four Types of State Prisoner Releases (% of each type of release), 1980–2010

Source: Glaze, Lauren E. & Palla, Seri. 2005. Probation and parole in the United States, 2004. (NCJ 210676). Washington, DC: U.S. Department of Justice, Bureau of Justice Statistics. Numbers for 2010 estimated based on BJS statistical trends between 2001 and 2010.

released from prison while still remaining under supervision of an indeterminate sentence.

Parole entails the conditional release of a convicted offender from a correctional institution, under the continued custody of the state, to serve the remainder of his or her sentence under supervision in the community. Historically, parole referred only to discretionary release. But as you will see in this chapter, as laws and release methods have changed, parole has become a broader concept incorporating mandatory supervision. *Parole in this text refers to post-prison supervision of both mandatory and discretionary released offenders.* Parolees on both mandatory release and discretionary release are supervised by a parole officer and adhere to similar conditions. If these conditions are not followed, either the mandatory or discretionary type of parolee can be returned to prison for the remainder of a sentence. Figure 3.1 shows the types of release and how their numbers have changed over the years. You can see that mandatory release has increased, whereas prisoners leaving prison on discretionary release have decreased.

parole
Release of a convicted offender from a penal or correctional institution, under the continual custody of the state, to serve the remainder of his or her sentence in the community under supervision, either by discretionary or mandatory release stipulations.

THE ORIGINS OF PAROLE

The English word *parole* is derived from the French **parole d'honneur,** meaning "word of honor." The French seem to prefer the term *conditional liberation* to the one borrowed from their language. In 1791 during the French Revolution, the Comte de Mirabeau (Honoré-Gabriel Rigueti) published a report based on the concept of reformation, which emphasized the principles of labor, segregation, rewards under a mark system, conditional liberation, and aid on discharge. Another Frenchman, Bonneville de Marsangy, public prosecutor of Versailles, published a book in 1847 in which he discussed conditional liberation, police supervision of discharged convicts, aid upon discharge, and rehabilitation. This book was distributed by the government to the members of both chambers of Parliament (Wines, 1919).

parole d'honneur
French for "word of honor," from which the English word parole is derived.

The credit for putting parole into *practice* originated simultaneously with three European prison administrators: a Spaniard, Manuel Montesinos; a German, Georg Michael Obermaier; and an Englishman, Alexander Maconochie.

Manuel Montesinos

In 1835 Colonel Manuel Montesinos was appointed governor of the prison at Valencia, Spain, which held about 1,500 convicts. He organized the institution using military-type discipline, and he encouraged prisoner vocational training and education. The novelty of his plan was that although there were practically no officers to watch the prisoners, they nevertheless made few, if any, attempts to escape. Each prisoner could earn a one-third reduction in the term of his sentence by good behavior and positive accomplishments. The number of prisoner recommitments while Montesinos was governor was significantly reduced. Despite all his efforts, the law that allowed this program was subsequently repealed, and Montesinos ultimately resigned. He drew the following conclusions from his experiment:

> Self-respect is one of the most powerful sentiments of the human mind, since it is the most personal; and he who will not condescend, in some degree, according to circumstances, to flattery of it, will never attain his object by any amount of chastisement; the effect of ill treatment being to irritate rather than to correct, and thus turn from reform instead of attracting to it. The moral object of penal establishments should not be so much to inflict punishment as to correct, to receive men idle and ill-intentioned and return them to society, if possible, honest and industrious citizens. (as quoted in Wines, 1919, p. 194)

Georg Michael Obermaier

When Georg Michael Obermaier became governor of a prison in Munich, Germany, in 1842, he found approximately 700 rebellious prisoners kept in order by more than 100 soldiers (Wines, 1919). In a short time he gained the men's confidence, removed their chains, discharged nearly all of their guards, and appointed some of the guards superintendents of each of the industrial shops. Obermaier's success in reforming prisoners was so great that reportedly only 10 percent of prisoners relapsed into crime after their discharge. He was aided by two favorable circumstances: Many of the men had no fixed term of imprisonment, and discharged inmates were supervised by prison aid societies.

Alexander Maconochie

Alexander Maconochie
A British naval captain who served as governor of the penal colony on Norfolk Island, who instituted a system of early release that was the forerunner of modern parole. Maconochie is known as the "father of parole."

marks system
A theory of human motivation organized by Maconochie that granted credits for good behavior and hard work, or took away marks for negative behavior. Convicts used the credits or marks to purchase either goods or time (reduction in sentence).

Chief credit for developing early parole systems, however, goes to **Alexander Maconochie,** who was in charge of the English penal colony on Norfolk Island. In 1837 Maconochie, a retired British naval captain and professor of geography, proposed a **marks system** whereby the duration of a sentence would be determined not by time but by a prisoner's industry and good conduct. Daily tallies or "marks" would be credited to prisoners in accordance with their behavior and the amount of labor they performed. As prisoners evidenced good behavior and work ethics, their freedom and privileges gradually increased. Marks were deducted for negative behavior. Maconochie's system allowed prisoners to move from strict imprisonment, to labor in work gangs, through

Courtesy Michael Maconochie, London

Alexander Maconochie served as superintendent of the penal colony on Norfolk Island, where he and his family lived with 2,000 incorrigible convicts. Maconochie was best known for his early "marks system" and as a champion of prisoner rights and privileges to encourage good behavior. Although he was successful at transforming the lives of many convicts, his humane treatment of prisoners was politically unfavorable, and he was subsequently replaced.

conditional release around the island, and finally to complete restoration of liberty (Morris, 2002).

NORFOLK ISLAND   Maconochie was given an opportunity to test his marks system in 1840 when he was appointed superintendent of the notorious penal colony on **Norfolk Island,** 1,000 miles off the eastern coast of Australia. Norfolk Island was known to have 2,000 of the most incorrigible convicts; they had been sent there from other prisons in Britain and Ireland because they had committed crimes of violence while incarcerated. Within a span of four years, Maconochie's humane system transformed prisoners' horrific lives into ones of peaceful, orderly existence. Maconochie discontinued flogging and chain gangs and introduced adequate food, health care, disciplinary hearings, and reading material (Morris, 2002).

Despite his successes, many influential colonists in Australia who believed that convicts should be kept in irons and flogged saw Maconochie's treatment of prisoners as radical and lobbied the governor for the reformer's dismissal. The governor was torn between his hope that Maconochie's experiment would succeed and his fear of the political power of the colonists who opposed the project. Maconochie was dismissed in 1844, and his experiment came to an abrupt end. As free settlers in Australia increased in number, they protested the use of the country as a dumping ground for prisoners. In 1867, transport of prisoners from England to Australia was terminated (Morris, 2002).

Norfolk Island
The notorious British super-max penal colony 1,000 miles off the coast of Australia that housed the most incorrigible prisoners.

BOX 3.1   COMMUNITY CORRECTIONS UP CLOSE

Early Settlers in America Were Sometimes, as in Australia, Convicts: England's Experience in Banishing Prisoners to the U.S. and Australia

Transportation of English criminals to North America began with a 1597 law that allowed the banishment of dangerous criminals as a partial solution to the poor economic conditions and widespread unemployment in England. Felons who could physically work were transported by private contractors to distant lands to help grow food, some of which was transported back to England. The government paid private contractors a fee for each prisoner who arrived alive. Upon arrival, prisoners were sold as indentured servants to the highest bidder. In exchange, transported convicts were granted a stay of execution for as long as they remained out of trouble.

The Revolutionary War of 1776 brought an end to the practice of transporting criminals to America, but the public demand in England for the transportation of convicts rose. England turned its attention to transporting its prisoners to mainland Australia and Norfolk Island, with the first shipload arriving in 1788. In contrast with the transport of prisoners to the American colonies, the British government incurred all expenses of transportation to and maintenance in Australia, and the prisoners remained under government control instead of being indentured. As of 1811, prisoners were eligible to receive a **ticket-of-leave** after they had served a specified amount of time. (For example, those serving a seven-year sentence became eligible for a ticket-of-leave after four years, and those serving life sentences became eligible for such after eight years.)

Other than England, what other countries were involved in the transport of prisoners?

---

transportation
The forced exile of convicted criminals. England transported convicted criminals to the American colonies until the Revolutionary War and afterward to Australia.

ticket-of-leave
A license or permit given to a convict as a reward for good conduct, which allowed him to go at large and work for himself before his sentence expired, subject to certain restrictions and revocable upon subsequent misconduct. A forerunner of parole.

Sir Walter Crofton
An Irish prison reformer who established an early system of parole based on Alexander Maconochie's experiments with the mark system.

Irish System
Developed in Ireland by Sir Walter Crofton, the Irish system involved graduated levels of institutional control leading up to release under conditions similar to modern parole. The American penitentiaries were partially based on the Irish system.

The years following saw an outbreak of crime and prison riots in England, conditions that were attributed to poor prison administration and a lack of supervision of recently released prisoners. The British public thus came to regard prison releasees as a menace to public safety. A royal commission was appointed to investigate the situation, and a report resulted in policemen becoming responsible for supervising released prisoners. Later a number of prisoner aid societies, supported in part by the government, were established.

Sir Walter Crofton and the Irish System

Sir Walter Crofton, who studied Maconochie's innovations on Norfolk Island, became the administrator of the Irish prison system in 1854. Crofton adopted the use of the marks system inside prison. Under his administration, the **Irish system** became renowned for its three levels: strict imprisonment, indeterminate sentence, and ticket-of-leave. Each prisoner's classification was determined by the marks he or she had earned for good conduct and achievement in industry and education, a concept borrowed from Maconochie's experience on Norfolk Island.

The ticket-of-leave system was different from the one in England. The general written conditions of the Irish ticket-of-leave were supplemented with instructions designed for closer supervision and control and thus resembled the conditions of parole in the United States today. Ticket-of-leave men and women residing in rural areas were under police supervision, but a civilian employee called the "inspector of released prisoners" supervised those living in Dublin. The inspector had the responsibility of securing employment for the ticket-of-leave person, visiting his or her residence, and verifying employment. The Irish system of ticket-of-leave had the confidence and support of the public and of convicted criminals.

Parole was later applied to prisoners of war as part of Articles 10, 11, and 12 of the 1949 Geneva Convention. A parole agreement in this context is a promise that prisoners of war give their captors that they will not escape or bear arms. If a country authorizes military members to use parole, captors may choose to free a prisoner of war under certain conditions bound by the POW's word of honor. Although parole is authorized by some countries in the world, the United States does not allow any member of the armed services to enter into a parole agreement.

THE DEVELOPMENT OF PAROLE IN THE UNITED STATES

In the United States, parole was first tried in New York at Elmira Reformatory in 1876. Federal parole began in June 1910 as a result of legislation that established the first three federal penitentiaries. In 1930 a formalized federal parole board was created under the U.S. attorney general's office. In 1950, because of an increased prison population in the federal system, the parole board expanded and was placed under the Justice Department.

Four Justifications of Parole

Four rationales justified the development of parole in the United States: (1) reduction in the length of incarceration as a reward for good conduct; (2) supervision of the parolee; (3) imposition of the indeterminate sentence; and (4) reduction in the rising cost of incarceration.

REWARD FOR GOOD PRISON CONDUCT   The first legal recognition in the United States of shortening a term of imprisonment as a reward for good conduct was by way of an 1817 good time law in New York. Good time was rewarded with one day subtracted off a prisoner's sentence for each day in which there were no reports of misconduct.

POST-RELEASE SUPERVISION   Volunteers and prison society members originally supervised those released from prison. The Philadelphia Society for Alleviating the Miseries of Public Prisons recognized the importance of caring for released prisoners as early as 1822. In 1851 the society appointed two agents to assist prisoners discharged from the Philadelphia County prison and the penitentiary. The first public employees paid to assist released prisoners were appointed by the state of Massachusetts in 1845.

RELEASE FROM AN INDETERMINATE SENTENCE   By 1865, American penal reformers were well aware of the reforms achieved by the conditional release programs of the Irish system. As a result, an indeterminate sentence law was adopted in 1876 in New York with the help of prison superintendent **Zebulon R. Brockway.** The system established at Elmira included grading inmates on their conduct and achievement, compulsory education, and careful selection for parole. Volunteer citizens, known as guardians, supervised the parolees. A condition of parole was that parolees report to their guardian on the first day of each month. Written reports were submitted to the prison institution after being signed by a parolee's employer and guardian. By 1944 every U.S. jurisdiction had adopted some form of parole release and indeterminate sentencing.

REDUCING THE COST OF INCARCERATION   Parole may have been initiated in the U.S. primarily for economic reasons. For about one century between the 1840s and 1940s, American prisons were self-supported entirely by convict labor. Many southern penitentiaries turned a huge profit from convict labor by leasing their convicts to private companies. The private companies benefited because they paid the prison less than they otherwise would have had to pay nonincarcerated workers for hard labor such as building railroads, manufacturing goods to sell on the open market, and growing crops. Prison administrators pocketed the money, given that

FACT OR FICTION?

Reducing a prisoner's sentence for good behavior is unnecessary and shortens the length of stay too much.

Fiction.
Fact: The use of "good time" is a necessary behavioral management tool favored by correctional administrators as a way to regulate behavior of prisoners while incarcerated. Without good time, there is no privilege with which to reward an offender for positive behavior and to withhold for negative behavior. It is also useful to increase good time for all prisoners across the board when institutions become too crowded, which means that good time can be earned faster in crowded prisons.

Zebulon R. Brockway
The American prison reformer who introduced modern correctional methods, including parole, to the Elmira Reformatory in New York in 1876.

the prisoners did not get paid. Most prisoners worked long hours "under the gun" in remote prison camps miles away from the main prison unit (Walker, 1988).

Private companies liked the idea of using convict labor so much that its use began to affect the employment rate of "free world" people (i.e., those who were not prisoners). Organized labor unions outside of prison began to apply pressure to limit private companies' use of convict labor. Due to the high unemployment rate during the Great Depression, legislation was passed to limit convict labor only to goods that could be sold to other government entities. Because of this legislation, prisoners in remote prison camps had to be relocated to a prison unit where they would be behind bars and work within the walls. More prisons had to be constructed to make space for these incoming prisoners. The profits decreased, and for the first time taxpayers began to bear some of the cost of incarceration (Walker, 1988). Not long after legislation was passed that limited convict labor to prison walls, the notion of parole became more accepted.

The Medical Model: 1930–1960

medical model
The concept that, given proper care and treatment, criminals can be cured into productive, law-abiding citizens. This approach suggests that people commit crimes because of influences beyond their control, such as poverty, injustice, and racism.

Parole was seen as a major adjunct to the rehabilitation philosophy that dominated American corrections from the 1930s through the 1960s. This rehabilitative ideal, called the **medical model,** assumed that criminal behavior had its roots in environmental and psychosocial aspects of an offender's life and that these behaviors could be corrected. This meant that every offender must be dealt with on an individual basis to determine the causes of his or her criminal behavior.

Under the old punitive model of corrections, the question was "What did he do?" The medical model was more concerned with why criminals commit crime and what could be done to improve a convict's situation. According to this model, if prison staff could diagnose and treat "badness," then a lawbreaker should be released when "cured." The mechanisms for accomplishing this release were the indeterminate sentence and parole. The release decision was thus shared between the court, which set a minimum and a maximum period of incarceration, and the correctional system. The parole board's responsibility was to determine the optimal release time at which an inmate was ready to reenter the community as a responsible citizen.

The medical model assumed that correctional specialists had the ability to diagnose an offender's problems and to develop a means of curing those problems. Because one cannot know at the time of diagnosis how long it will take to effect a cure, the indeterminate sentence made it possible, in theory at least, to confine an offender only as long as necessary and to follow up that confinement with community supervision.

Various parole boards came under attack by critics who claimed that parole release failed to produce the desired lasting changes in offenders' behavior and attitudes. Other critics pointed out that future behavior was difficult to accurately predict.

From Discretionary Parole to Mandatory Release

just deserts
The concept that the goal of corrections should be to punish offenders because they deserve to be punished and that punishment should be commensurate with the seriousness of the offense.

justice model
The correctional practice based on the concept of just deserts and even-handed punishment. The justice model calls for fairness in criminal sentencing, in that all people convicted of a similar offense will receive a like sentence. This model of corrections relies on determinate sentencing and/or abolition of parole.

The correctional system's inability to reduce recidivism, rehabilitate offenders, or make predictive judgments about offenders' future behavior brought about public disillusionment, disappointment, and resentment. Concern also arose that wide and unfair disparities existed in sentencing based on an offender's race/ethnicity, socioeconomic status, and place of conviction (Petersilia, 2000b). As you read in Chapter 1, the pendulum shifted in the 1970s from a rehabilitative focus on the offender (via indeterminate sentencing), to the **"just deserts"** or **justice model's** emphasis on severity of the crime (inherent in determinate sentencing).

With parole boards abolished in 15 states for *all* offenses and another five states abolishing discretionary release for violent offenses (Hughes, Wilson, & Beck, 2001), "parole" is now split into either "discretionary release" or "mandatory release." Because of determinate sentencing and an increased abolishing of discretionary release, only between 24–39% of prisoners are now released via discretionary release, whereas mandatory release numbers have increased (Petersilia, 2003).

Under discretionary release, offenders reentered society when correctional authorities and board members believed they were ready or thought they had improved their lives enough to earn the privilege to be released. This meant that offenders had to show they had a reentry plan and that they knew how they were going to stay out of trouble. Under mandatory release, offenders are released no matter how many disciplinary reports they have had or how they acted while incarcerated. Thus, many offenders under mandatory release are ill prepared for the transition and may not have the right kind of social support when they go home (Petersilia, 2003). "In the long run, no one is more dangerous than a criminal who has no incentive to straighten himself out while in prison and who returns to society without a structured and a supervised release plan" (p. 18).

PAROLE TODAY

Table 3.1 lists by state the current discretionary capability of parole boards to release prisoners. "Full" discretion means that a parole board has the discretion to release all inmates, although in most states prisoners must still serve a minimum percentage of their sentence. "Limited" discretion means a parole board has the discretion to release only certain kinds of offenders and that parole release is completely denied to recidivists or offenders convicted of violent crimes. States that no longer have discretionary release for anyone still honor the few cases that were committed in the past under the old law. These states are labeled "old cases." This table also classifies the current sentencing philosophies of each state as "indeterminate," "determinate," or a combination of both, depending on the type of offense.

States that limit parole boards' power of release require that prisoners serve a flat minimum or some proportion of their maximum sentence before becoming eligible for parole. Other jurisdictions that retained discretionary release have established guidelines to reduce and structure release decision making. Both the American Probation and Parole Association and the Association of Paroling Authorities favor retaining parole boards as an important correctional institution tool. Arguments in favor of discretionary release include:

- Parole boards can impose prisoner participation in treatment programs as incentives for release; with automatic release, however, there are no incentives for prisoners to better themselves while behind bars.
- Parole boards have improved their techniques for more objective and open decision making through parole guidelines.
- Victims can attend parole board hearings to convince the board not to release their offender, but victims have no say in mandatory or automatic release situations.
- Release decisions are made by computer under automatic release, not by a human parole board that can keep prisoners in prison if it feels they remain a danger to society.
- Abolishing discretionary release does not mean that prisoners will serve their full sentence; it does not prevent prisoners from release, and it does not necessarily increase public safety (Burke, 1995).

FACT OR FICTION?

First-time felons given determinate sentencing and mandatory release serve *more* time on average in prison than do first-timers given indeterminate sentencing and discretionary release for the same crime.

Fiction.

Fact: First-time offenders on mandatory release serve on average *less* time in prison than do first-timers on discretionary release (except for DWI offenders). However, offenders convicted of two or more felonies do serve longer sentences now than repeat offenders did in the 1990s (Hughes, Wilson, & Beck, 2001).

TABLE 3.1   Release Authority of Parole Boards by State

State	Discretion to Release	Indeterminate or Determinate	Comments: Who Is Eligible for Discretionary Release?
Alabama	Full	I	
Alaska	Full	I, D	
Arizona	Old cases	D	Offenses prior to 1994
Arkansas	Old cases	D	Offenses prior to 1994
California	Limited	I, D	Lifers only with concurrence of governor
Colorado	Full	I, D	
Connecticut	Full	I, D	Violent offenders have face-to-face hearings
Delaware	Old cases	D	Offenses prior to 6/30/90
Florida	Old cases	D	Capital murder/sexual battery prior to 10/1/94
Georgia	Limited	I, D	All nonviolent offenders
Hawaii	Full	I, D	Violent offenders meet mandatory minimum
Idaho	Full	I, D	Violent offenders meet mandatory minimum
Illinois	Limited	D	Juveniles only
Indiana	None	D	
Iowa	Full	I	
Kansas	Old cases	D	Offenses prior to 7/1/93
Kentucky	Full	I, D	Violent offenders meet mandatory minimum
Louisiana	Limited	I, D	All nonviolent offenders
Maine	None	D	
Maryland	Limited	I, D	All offenders eligible except lifers
Massachusetts	Full	I	
Michigan	Full	D	All must meet minimum time first
Minnesota	Limited	I, D	Strictly controlled Hearing/Release Unit
Mississippi	Old cases	D	Offenses prior to 7/1/95
Missouri	Full	I, D	Violent must meet minimum first
Montana	Full	D	All must meet minimum time first
Nebraska	Full	D	All must meet minimum time first
Nevada	Full	I	
New Hampshire	Full	I	
New Jersey	Full	I	
New Mexico	Old cases	D	Offenses prior to 1979
New York	Full	I, D	All must meet minimum time first
North Carolina	Old cases	D	Offenses prior to 1994
North Dakota	Full	I, D	Violent must meet minimum first
Ohio	Old cases	D	Offenses prior to 7/1/96
Oklahoma	Limited	D	Governor has releasing authority
Oregon	Old cases	D	Offenses prior to 11/1/89
Pennsylvania	Full	I	With sentences of two years or more
Rhode Island	Full	D	All must meet minimum time first
South Carolina	Limited	I, D	Sentences must be below 20 years
South Dakota	Old cases	D	Offenses prior to 7/1/96
Tennessee	Limited	I, D	Nonviolent offenders eligible only

(Continues)

TABLE 3.1 Release Authority of Parole Boards by State (*Continued*)

State	Discretion to Release	Indeterminate or Determinate	Comments: Who Is Eligible for Discretionary Release?
Tennessee	Limited	I, D	Nonviolent offenders eligible only
Texas	Full	I, D	
Utah	Full	I	
Vermont	Full	I	
Virginia	Old cases	D	Offense prior to 1995
Washington	Limited	I, D	
West Virginia	Full	D	All must meet minimum time first
Wisconsin	Old cases	D	Offenses prior to 2000
Wyoming	Full	D	All must meet minimum time first

Full: Parole board has discretion to release all inmates (though some must still serve a minimum percent of their sentence).

Limited: Parole board has discretion to release only certain kinds of offenders, whereas parole release is denied to others.

Old Cases: No parole discretionary release exists on current cases—only on the few cases left that were committed in the past under the old law.

Indeterminate/Determinate Sentence: The philosophy of sentencing currently practiced. (If both are listed, determinate sentencing is typically reserved for violent/repeat offenders.)

Adapted from: Association of Paroling Authorities International, Paroling Authorities Survey, 2005. Retrieved from: http://www.apaintl.org/documents/surveys/2005.pdf

Joan Petersilia agrees: "While abolishing parole [discretionary release] may make good politics, it contributes to bad correctional practices—and ultimately, less public safety. . . . The public doesn't understand the tremendous power that is lost when parole is abandoned" (Petersilia, 2000a, p. 32). Parole is far from completely disappearing from the correctional scene. Growth in the sheer number of releasees is expected in the future when prisoners complete the minimum terms of their sentences.

Characteristics of Parolees

Nearly 820,000 people are on parole (Glaze, Bonczar, & Zhang, 2010). Generally, the southern region of the U.S. has the highest incarceration rates, yet the lowest parole rates. The northeastern region shows the opposite situation—a higher rate of parole and a lower rate of incarceration per 100,000 residents.

Table 3.2 shows how parolee characteristics have changed over time. Most parolees formerly were men, but since 2000, 12 percent of offenders on parole are women. Parolees typically serve between one and two years of time under post-prison supervision, with about 6 percent serving parole in another state than the one in which the crime was committed. Parole success rates are lower than those for probation, with about 44 percent of all parolees successfully completing their parole term. About three out of 10 parolees are removed from parole for too many rule violations, and one out of 10 for commission of a new crime, attesting to how difficult it is for parolees to transition once they have been imprisoned (Bonczar, 1997; Glaze, 2001; Glaze, Bonczar, & Zhang, 2010). Figure 3.2 shows the original offense for which offenders on parole were sentenced to prison and for which they continue to serve this sentence out in the community.

Contemporary Functions of Parole

In offering a gradual transition from prison to the community, parole continues to aid in reintegration and to reduce recidivism by helping ex-offenders become gainfully employed so they can later support themselves. However, parole officers

TABLE 3.2   Characteristics of Adult Parolees Over Time

	1995	2000	2009
Gender			
Male	90%	88%	88%
Female	10	12	12
Race/Ethnicity			
White	34	38	41
Black	45	40	39
Hispanic	21	21	18
American Indian/Alaska Native	1	1	1
Asian/Pacific Islander/Hawaiian	**	**	1
Status of Supervision			
Active	78	83	85
Inactive	11	4	4
Absconded	6	7	5
Supervised out of state/other	4	6	6
Sentence Length			
Less than one year	6	3	5
One year or more	94	97	95
Adults Leaving Parole			
Successful completion	45	43	44
Returned to incarceration	41	42	39
With new sentence	12	11	11
Other	29	31	28
Absconder[a]	*	9	11
Other unsuccessful[a]	*	2	2
Death	**	**	1
Other	10	2	3

Note: *Not available. **Less than 0.5 percent. [a]In 1995 absconder and other unsuccessful were reported among "other."

Sources: Bonczar, Thomas P. 1997. Characteristics of Adults on Probation, 1995 (NCJ 164267). Washington, DC: U.S. Department of Justice, Bureau of Justice Statistics; Glaze, Lauren E. 2001. *Probation and Parole in the United States, 2000* (NCJ 188208)**.** Washington, DC: U.S. Department of Justice, Bureau of Justice Statistics; Glaze, Lauren E., Thomas P. Bonczar, & Fan Zhang. 2010. *Probation and Parole in the United States, 2009.* Washington, DC: U.S. Department of Justice, Bureau of Justice Statistics.

are under greater scrutiny than previously to protect the public from released offenders by:

1. enforcing restrictions and controls on parolees in the community;
2. providing services that help parolees integrate into a noncriminal lifestyle; and
3. increasing the public's level of confidence in the effectiveness and responsiveness of parole services (Williams, McShane, & Dolny, 2000a).

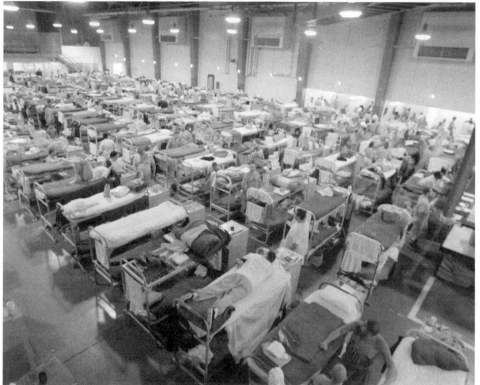

One contemporary function of community corrections is population control of crowded prisons so they don't become like this gymnasium in San Quentin State Prison, California.

© AP Images/Eric Risberg

Some argue that parole has changed essentially from being a tolerant force for reintegration to merely an enforcement of the law with a low tolerance for mistakes. This shift in focus may be one reason why revocation rates remain so high.

PRISON POPULATION CONTROL   Parole has served as the "back doorkeeper" of America's prisons, often operating as a safety valve to relieve crowded institutions. Some states have given legislative authority and directives to their parole boards to control prison population. Others have done so through informal agreements among the governor, the director of corrections, and the parole board. Boards in states such as Georgia, Michigan, and Texas have become actively involved in prison population management out of necessity. Prison populations in those states had risen to levels that threatened correctional authorities' ability to maintain control of their institutions. Federal court orders have established limits on the prison population in various states.

SAVING MEDICAL COSTS   With the high cost of health care and the increased graying of America's prisoners, discussion has centered on the necessity for increasing the rate of **medical parole,** or compassionate release, as an option for elderly and/or terminally ill prisoners no longer a risk to public safety. Each prisoner on medical parole is required to have either a medical condition that is terminal, that permanently limits them from movement, or that could be treated less expensively in a community treatment facility than in a prison.

medical parole
The conditional release from prison to the community of a prisoner with a terminal illness who does not pose an undue risk to public safety.

Releasing terminally ill prisoners to a community hospice to live out their remaining months is not that widely implemented despite repeated arguments showing hospice care to be a cost-effective and humane treatment for inmates and their families (Berry, 2009; Rikard & Rosenberg, 2007). Medical parole seems to be a politically unpopular measure in high-profile cases, as indicated by Susan Atkins' denial for medical parole in 2009. Atkins, a follower of Charles Manson, was convicted over 40 years ago for her role in the highly publicized murders. Bedridden with brain cancer, she was denied transfer to live out her last days in a community hospice due to the wishes of victims' family that she remain incarcerated.

Roughly two thirds of prison systems and nearly half of all city or county jails have a medical parole policy, but only about 300 people are released nationwide on medical parole (Hammett, Harmon, & Maruschak, 1999). The use of medical parole has recently attracted new interest as states examine ways to cut medical costs and decrease the number of prisoners. The case study at the end of this chapter allows you to consider the issue of compassionate release.

SUMMARY

- Parole has its origins in the work of penal reformers in Germany, Spain, and France as well as that of Alexander Maconochie on Norfolk Island. Prison reformer Zebulon R. Brockway studied Maconochie's work and implemented his ideas in the U.S.

- Steadily increasing crime rates, a perceived failure of rehabilitation programs, and the perception that parole boards were incapable of making predictive judgments about offenders' future behavior caused the replacement of the medical rehabilitation model and indeterminate sentencing philosophies of the 1930s with the justice model and determinate sentencing in the 1970s.

- Parole is now divided into discretionary release and mandatory release. Under discretionary release, when correctional authorities believe offenders have improved their lives enough to earn the privilege to be released, they reenter society. Under mandatory release, which has steadily increased, offenders are released regardless of disciplinary reports or their behavior while incarcerated.

- Currently, 20 percent of all people released from prison do not receive any post-prison supervision.

- The purpose of parole is to ease crowded facilities, to save money, and to reintegrate offenders. In this era of economic instability, medical parole as a way to control medical costs is being reconsidered as an option.

DISCUSSION QUESTIONS

1. Discuss the founders of parole and their contributions.

2. What was the English ticket-of-leave, and how did that compare with the marks system?

3. Why did England transport convicts to America and Australia? What was the connection between transport and parole?

4. What was the significance of Alexander Maconochie's approach to prison administration upon the behavior of the convicts?

5. Why was Maconochie dismissed from Norfolk Island despite his success?

6. How did parole develop in the United States? Be sure to include in your explanation discussions of the Irish system and the indeterminate sentence.

7. What role does parole play in the twenty-first century?

8. What are the pros and cons of abolishing parole?

9. How do you feel about the use of medical parole?

WEBSITES, VIDEOS, AND PODCASTS

Websites

History of parole in Alabama
   http://www.pardons.state.al.us

History of parole in Delaware
   http://www.state.de.us/parole/default.shtml

History of parole in Texas
   http://www.tdcj.state.tx.us/parole/parole-history.htm

History of parole in Utah
   http://bop.utah.gov/history.html

Videos/Podcasts

History of women in prison and parole:
   http://www.youtube.com/watch?v=Z9c1IrD2N8s

A 1956 movie about the history of women in prison and parole in Corona, CA.

A 100-year-old sex offender on post-prison supervision:
   http://www.youtube.com/watch?v=9pXsMcGqrX0

News coverage of 100-year-old sex offender who has been released from jail but will be under post-supervision in a halfway house.

Medical Parole
   http://www.corrections.com/system/podcast/file/34/media_20021217.mp3

This is an interview with Bob, who has coordinated medical parole. The podcast defines, explains, and discusses medical parole and compares it to compassionate parole.

CASE STUDY EXERCISES

Should Terminally Ill and/or Elderly Prisoners Be Medically Paroled?

Assume that you are part of a committee that evaluates medical parole prisoners with various documented medical diagnoses. A prisoner has met the minimum requirements on time served for parole, but your job is to determine, based on two factors, whether he or she should be released early on medical parole while still remaining under community supervision:

1. That he or she is no longer a risk to public safety if released into the community.
2. That he or she has a verifiable terminal medical condition OR a permanent medical condition that limits movement OR a medical condition that could be treated less expensively in a community treatment facility instead of a prison.

Case A: Tony, Terminally Ill and in for Murder

Tony has served 40 years in prison for a highly publicized murder case that he committed when he was 20 years old. He has been a model inmate, compiling few disciplinary reports while incarcerated. He was a clerk in the law library until about five years ago, when he had to quit his job because he was diagnosed with a brain tumor. The tumor was cancerous, so he received chemotherapy and radiation for two years, but that did not completely stop the cancer from spreading throughout his body. Now at age 62 Tony is bedridden, breathes and eats through a tube, and takes pain medication to ease his suffering. He has been deemed not to be a danger to anyone. It costs the state $1,000 per day just to keep Tony locked up, whereas a community hospice could provide the same medical care for $500 per day. However, his case was a high-profile murder case, and the victim's survivors said they will never forgive Tony, nor will they give up fighting for him to stay in prison until he dies, no matter what the cost.

Case B: William, Elderly and in Prison for Motor Vehicle Theft and Reckless Endangerment

William, a career criminal, has a long rap sheet consisting of at least five felony crimes and over two dozen misdemeanors, mostly drug-related and property offenses. In his life, he has spent more time institutionalized than out in the free world. He was arrested on his latest felony when he was 60 years old. Although he pleaded guilty to motor vehicle theft, he said that he mistook the car for his own and didn't mean to steal it—his eyesight was bad. Now at age 75, he has served 15 years out of his 20-year sentence, and is ready to turn over a new leaf. William is tired of institutions—his health is not what it used to be. He does not have a terminal illness, but he is diabetic and has heart problems. Due to diabetes, William's left foot was amputated and he is blind in one eye. He is not capable of working, but he can get around pretty well in a wheelchair. Given that he was insured and suffered no serious losses, the victim in the case has no problem with William's release.

PART II

Techniques of Evidence-Based Community Correctional Supervision

This section focuses on the techniques of evidence-based correctional practice that are important in community supervision. In explaining these practices, two other decision points are discussed in this section: the bail or pretrial release decision and the sentencing decision. Chapter 4 explains how the presentence investigation report aids judges and explains how to conduct an interview and assemble a presentence report.

Chapter 5 is the foundation chapter in evidence-based practice in the community supervision of probationers and parolees. Some of these techniques include the assessment of risk and needs, targeting high-risk offenders for the bulk of treatment, focusing on criminogenic needs, and cognitive behavioral treatment. As caseloads have become larger, the time spent per low-risk client has diminished, and face-to-face contacts have been replaced by correctional technology. Face-to-face contact is still important for high-risk clients and those special needs. Chapter 6 discusses various types of unique needs, such as clients with substance abuse problems, mental health problems, and sex offenders. Chapter 7 discusses what happens when community conditions need to be modified or terminated. Both probation and parole conditions are discussed when these conditions are not followed.

4

Pretrial Supervision, Sentencing, and the Presentence Investigation Report

CHAPTER LEARNING OBJECTIVES

1. Distinguish the differences among pretrial release, pretrial supervision, and diversion.
2. Explain the factors involved in a decision to release pretrial defendants from detention.
3. Define the legal factors in granting community sentences.
4. Explain the purpose and contents of a presentence investigation report.
5. Summarize the legal issues and criticisms regarding the presentence investigation report.

Spider Dan makes his way to the top of the Millennium Tower in San Francisco. Goodwin used suction cups without any ropes to scale the 645-foot residential building. He was arrested and received probation.

© Mike Kepka/San Francisco Chronicle/AP/dapd

KEY TERMS

pretrial release
delegated release authority
pretrial supervision
surety bond
failure to appear
diversion
sentencing
reflective justice
presumptive sentencing grids

sentencing commission
standard conditions
special conditions
clear conditions
reasonable conditions
presentence investigation
        report (PSI)
post-sentence report
offender-based presentence report

presentence investigation
offense-based presentence
        report
victim impact statement
disclosure
harmless error
hearsay evidence
exclusionary rule

Dan Goodwin was convicted of delaying and obstructing arrest and of being a public nuisance. In September, 2010, "SpiderDan" climbed up the *outside* of the Millennium Tower glass building using suction cups to support his body. He made it to the 59th floor before he was arrested and removed from the residential high-rise building on the south side of San Francisco. SpiderDan said he was only trying to draw attention to the continuing vulnerability of high-rise buildings, but the judge was not so easily amused. In January, 2011, the judge sentenced Goodwin to two years of probation, 100 hours of community service, and payment of nearly $3,600 that it had cost firefighters to respond to the scene. Goodwin planned to appeal his sentence (*Bay City News*, 2011).

Many misdemeanor offenders and some low-level felony offenders are issued a citation or summons for their next court appearance. Offenders who are arrested typically spend a night in a city jail or holding cell and are released the next day. If a suspect is expected to stay longer in a local jail, he or she is interviewed by a bail commissioner or magistrate who will make decisions about the bond or the terms on which the defendant will be released from jail, if at all. A release decision takes place between 24 and 72 hours following arrest. Most people who are accused of a crime do not need to be held in jail while waiting for their next court date, insofar as holding them disrupts their employment, their family life, and their ability to prepare for and aid in their own defense (Miyashiro, 2008). Still, about 38% of felony defendants were held in confinement until their case was completed (Bureau of Justice Statistics, 2006).

PRETRIAL SERVICES

Pretrial services is an agency that assists a court in deciding whom to release and whom to detain (the release decision). Further, as part of the release decision for some defendants, pretrial services is also involved in supervision of community safety and court efficiency by ensuring that defendants appear at their next court date (VanNostrand & Crime & Justice Institute, 2007). Ultimately, a pretrial defendant's case will likely result in one of four options: dismissal; diversion; conviction as a result of a plea agreement; or the defendant requesting to go to trial. We discuss pretrial release and pretrial supervision more closely below.

Pretrial release is defined as a defendant's release from jail while awaiting his or her next court appearance. The pretrial release decision is one of the first decisions made following an arrest in order that defendants who qualify can be effectively released to the community prior to their next court date. Pretrial release allows defendants who have not yet been convicted an opportunity to live and work as productive citizens until their next scheduled court date.

pretrial release
A defendant's release in the community following arrest as an alternative to detention while the defendant prepares for the next scheduled court appearance.

History of Pretrial Release

Early research indicated that being detained during the pretrial process was a disadvantage to a defendant's sentencing outcome. Consequently, bail was offered as a way to guarantee a defendant's return to court. However, people most likely to be detained at the time could not afford bail because they were impoverished. The situation inspired the Manhattan Bail Project as the first opportunity for defendants to be released on their own recognizance (ROR) before their next scheduled court

Judge Hutson listens to a recently arrested defendant before rendering a pre-release decision.

ROBERT B. HUTSON
JUDGE

© Spencer Grant/PhotoEdit

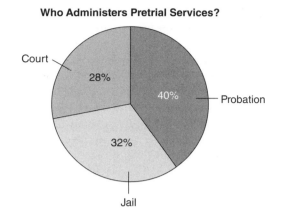

Who Administers Pretrial Services?

Court 28%

Probation 40%

Jail 32%

FIGURE 4.1   Agencies that administer pretrial services to defendants.

date. This in turn led to the Federal Bail Reform Act of 1966, which established guidelines on appropriate bail amounts and alternatives to detention for those unable to afford bail. The act was a reminder that the law favors *release*, unless there is a substantial risk that a defendant may not appear at the next court hearing. Pretrial programs became so successful that within two decades more than 200 cities had developed such programs. Growing concern about the risks posed by some pretrial defendants led to the passage of a second Bail Reform Act in 1984 that included the safety of the public as an important criterion in a decision to detain a pretrial defendant. When this act was challenged in the courts, the U.S. Supreme Court reaffirmed that pretrial detention served not for punishment but for defendants who posed a threat to themselves or to others (*U.S. v. Salerno,* 1987). As a result, community safety and the risk of flight are still the two most influential factors in bail decisions, with an interest in public safety outweighing a concern for individual liberties (VanNostrand & Keebler, 2007). Today, prerelease programs are managed by one of three agencies—probation, jails, or the courts—so that they are a compilation of court and correctional functions (see Figure 4.1).

The Pretrial Release Decision

In both state and federal systems, pretrial services recommends the "least restrictive option" available to a court, taking into consideration the safety of a community and a defendant's likelihood of reappearance in court. This approach requires judges to consider all possible alternatives and to detain only if none is appropriate. The pretrial release decision typically consists of a quantitative nine-point assessment of the potential risk posed, such as on the basis of the Risk Prediction Index (RPI). Factors that predict **failure to appear** and risk of community safety include (VanNostrand & Crime & Justice Institute, 2007, p. 16):

failure to appear
A situation in which a defendant does not attend a scheduled court hearing.

- current charges;
- outstanding warrants and pending charges at time of arrest;
- active community supervision at time of arrest;
- previous criminal convictions;
- history of failure to appear;
- history of violence;
- residence stability;
- employment stability;
- community ties; and
- substance abuse history.

Defendants on supervised pretrial release in the federal system may remain in this condition for one to two years to better prepare for their defense, and may return to work or school while their case is pending. However, not every defendant placed on pretrial release is supervised by a pretrial program.

When recommending the least restrictive measure and the possible release of a suspect from custody, pretrial services officers interview a defendant to see whether he or she poses a danger to the community and to determine the likelihood that said defendant will appear for the next court date (Newville, 2001). The defendant is not required to answer any questions about the pending crime, nor does the pretrial services officer consider the weight of the evidence against the defendant.

Most pretrial services officers made a release or detain recommendation to the court (88%), but 21% of these programs **delegated release authority**, which allowed a pretrial services officer to release a defendant before an initial court appearance (Clark & Henry, 2003). An eight-question pretrial assessment has been approved to predict new arrests and future incidents of failure to appear in court. Its items include defendant's age at first arrest, any previous times the defendant has failed to appear in court, number of jail incarcerations, employment status, self-reported use of illegal drugs, and stability of residence (Lowenkamp, Lemke, & Latessa, 2008).

TYPES OF BONDS   A judge ultimately makes both a release (in/out) decision and sets the type of bond or bail. Table 4.1 identifies and defines the ways a defendant can be released. Secured bonds require cash or property assets deposited directly with a court, such as when a defendant uses the services of a bail company. Unsecured bonds do not require any money up front and only require the full bond amount if a defendant refuses to appear. Release on Recognizance (ROR) requires only a signed agreement by a defendant that he or she will appear, and is also known as a "personal recognizance" or "PR bond." If a defendant with a ROR fails to attend the next hearing, there is no bond amount to pay, but a warrant is still issued for that

Bail bond companies help provide the means of release for pretrial detainees who do not have the money to pay the full bail amount.

© Marmaduke St. John/Alamy

TABLE 4.1   Types of Federal Pretrial Release

Release Type	Percent of Released Defendants*	Definition
Unsecured Bond	42%	Defendant pays no money to the court but is liable for the full bail amount if fails to appear (FTA).
Release on recognizance	34%	Defendant signs an agreement to appear; no money is paid or owed to the court for FTA.
Surety bond	10%	Use of a bail bond company wherein the bail company is liable if the defendant FTA; bail company charges a 10%–15% fee for taking the risk.
Deposit/ Collateral	9%	Defendant deposits bail amount in cash or property collateral with court; money is returned after court dates; bond is forfeited for FTA.
Conditional release	5%	Defendant is released with specific court-ordered conditions (third party, elec. monit.).

*Percentages include released defendants only and do not include defendants who were denied bail or who could not afford their set bail amount.

Source: Compendium of Federal Justice Statistics. 2007. Type of pretrial release for cases terminated October 2003 to September 2004, Table 3.2. Washington, DC: U.S. Department of Justice.

defendant's arrest. The table percentages do not include defendants who were denied bail (about 6%) or those who could not afford their bail amount.

WHY ARE MORE DEFENDANTS BEING DETAINED?   Pretrial detention rates have been steadily *increasing* in the federal system and now comprise over 60% of defendants. In contrast, state courts' average detention rates have remained consistent at 34%–38% of defendants (VanNostrand & Keebler, 2007). One explanation might be an increase in immigration cases that necessitate detention if a defendant cannot show community ties and might be a flight risk. However, no evidence has existed for detaining defendants based on their offense, particularly for drug offenses and weapons charges. With immigration cases, the failure to appear rate is a little bit higher than that for other crimes (4.3% for immigration offenses vs. 2.8% for violent crimes), but the likelihood of committing a new crime on release is less (2.3% for immigration offenses vs. 6.9% for weapons-related offenses). Researchers are hinting at a possibility of racial disparity in federal pretrial decision making (Byrne & Stowell, 2007). When immigration cases were excluded, less than half of defendants were released on average (47%) nationwide—with districts varying widely, from a low of 24% to a high of 76% of arrested defendants released. If immigration cases were included, then the most recent numbers show that 61% of all federal defendants were detained prior to sentencing or trial (VanNostrand & Keebler, 2007).

Another explanation of rising pretrial detention rates is that as individual situations have changed, that has increased the measure defendants received. For example, fewer defendants are employed—31% of defendants today compared with 57% in 1987. Also, more defendants are transient. For example, in 1987, two-thirds of defendants lived in the same area for five years or more. Today that rate has diminished to one third of defendants, leading one to question whether the pretrial decision favors release (Cadigan, 2007). One consistent trend is that most pretrial defendants, whether they are supervised or not, appear in court and do not commit new offenses, suggesting an overuse of pretrial supervision in the federal system (Byrne & Stowell, 2007). With approval of a new risk prediction instrument, it is estimated that this trend should decrease and become more precise in the future.

Pretrial Supervision

pretrial supervision
Court-ordered correctional supervision of a defendant who has not yet been convicted whereby the defendant participates in activities such as reporting, house arrest, and electronic monitoring to ensure appearance at the next court date.

surety bond
A certificate signed by the principal and a third party, promising to pay in the event the assured suffers damages or losses because the employee fails to perform as agreed.

Once a decision has been made to release a defendant, **pretrial supervision** can be ordered as a condition of bail. Pretrial supervision is also known as a **surety bond** in some jurisdictions because a third party (a pretrial services officer) is designated by the courts to assume supervision until a case has been resolved. Most felons in the federal system are on some form of pretrial supervision for between six to seven months, or an overall average of 203 days until sentencing. If a defendant requests a trial, he or she remains on pretrial supervision until the trial's conclusion, which reportedly takes twenty months from arrest (Cadigan, 2003). In the state system, for every 100 defendants evaluated, only 20% received pretrial supervision. Clients on pretrial supervision were required to call in weekly until their scheduled court date, comply with curfew, submit to drug testing, maintain employment, and avoid contact with victims and any witnesses who might have to testify.

When a defendant is not in compliance with pretrial supervision conditions, 89% of programs will give that defendant a warning the first time. Most programs will report the second act of noncompliance to a court with a recommendation for specific action, such as increasing telephone contact with said defendant (Clark & Henry, 2003). More serious acts of noncompliance, such as absconding or a rearrest, can result in a court's issuance of a bench warrant, the detention of a suspect, or bail revocation.

One thing is certain—random drug testing and providing services during the pretrial process do not increase the likelihood of court appearances nor do they affect the likelihood of new offenses at pretrial (VanNostrand & Crime & Justice Institute, 2007). Type of offense seems to be related more to court appearances and risk of committing crime. Offenders on bond for murder, burglary, or motor vehicle theft were more likely than other types of felony offenders to appear for court but were also more likely to commit new felony crimes while on pretrial release (Cohen & Reaves, 2006). On the other hand, Byrne and Stowell (2007) found that in the federal system even though technical rule violations increased, there was no overall change in new crimes committed. They conclude, "This certainly suggests that setting multiple release conditions and identifying technical violators of these release conditions does not improve community safety and the appearance of defendants at subsequent court dates" (p. 32).

FACT OR FICTION?

Defendants who are released on their own recognizance tend not to show up for their next court date.

Fiction.
Fact: Of the federal offenders who were released pretrial, those who had used a bail company (surety bond) had a failure-to-appear rate that was nearly twice that of release on recognizance (Cooprider, Gray, and Dunne, 2003).

FAILURE TO APPEAR   The purpose of pretrial supervision is to ensure that a defendant appears for court and that the public is safe while that defendant is out on bond. Defendants who failed to appear (FTA) did not attend their scheduled court date and seemed most likely to flee the day before their trial or sentencing hearing, or just prior to surrendering themselves for incarceration (Henry, 2007). Clark and Henry (2003) found that the number of jurisdictions nationwide that issues warrants and conducts other forms of follow-up for failure to appear has actually decreased in recent years.

Diversion

Thus far we have talked about pretrial release and supervision under the assumption that an offender has been released on bond under a certain set of supervisory conditions. Another option during the pretrial process is that a prosecutor or defense attorney can suggest **diversion**, which is a suspension or removal of a case from further court action provided a defendant successfully completes the terms of community supervision. Upon a defendant's successful completion of diversion and so long as said defendant stays out of trouble for two to five years following diversion, the charges are dismissed and there is no official conviction. For this reason, diversion is a type of pretrial supervision. However, the main difference between the two is that diversion completion results in no criminal record because a person is considered low-risk, whereas pretrial supervision as part of a surety bond will still result in a criminal conviction (given that supervision was necessary before conviction insofar as a defendant was considered high-risk).

Prosecutors and defense attorneys in many jurisdictions are able to recommend defendants for diversion programs before an arraignment or plea. In considering which factors were important in their decision, a defendant's probation or parole history, mental health, substance abuse history, community ties, and evaluative needs were all viewed as relevant by both prosecutor and defense. A defendant's adult criminal record, gang affiliation, official version of offense, and pending cases were all ranked significantly higher in a diversion decision by prosecutors than by defense attorneys (Alarid & Montemayor, 2010b).

CANDIDATES FOR DIVERSION A defendant's situation and offense must qualify for this alternative to traditional criminal sentencing. Defendants whose situations qualify for diversion might be juveniles or first-time felons, persons charged with certain offenses, or offenders with mental health problems. Diversion enables offenders to avoid the criminal label or deviant stigma that results from having a conviction. It can help first-time offenders who do not pose a risk to public safety and who, upon completion of its program, are unlikely to return to criminal behavior. Persons with special needs, such as mental illness, who have also committed minor offenses are better suited for rehabilitative functions like medication stabilization and counseling (Castillo & Alarid, 2009). Offenses that qualify for diversion typically include theft, possession of controlled substances, driving while intoxicated, domestic assault, and prostitution. (Alarid & Montemayor, 2010b). In the federal system, white-collar criminals such as those accused of fraud, larceny theft, and embezzlement are eligible for pretrial diversion. Offenders who are ineligible include those with two or more prior felony convictions, addicts, public officials, and those accused of a crime violating national security (Ulrich, 2002).

SENTENCING

Sentencing has long been considered the most difficult decision in the criminal justice process. **Sentencing** can be defined as a post-conviction stage in which a defendant is brought before a court for formal judgment pronounced by a judge. The judge is influenced by a presentence investigator's report as well as by the wishes of prosecutor and defense attorney. Sentencing demands choosing among a number of alternatives and considering issues of public safety, rehabilitation, deterrence, and retribution. The philosophy behind community sentences argues that an offender can better learn how to live productively in a community by remaining in free society under supervision than in being transferred to the setting of a jail or prison.

diversion
An alternative program to traditional criminal sentencing or juvenile justice adjudication that provides first-time offenders with a chance or addresses unique treatment needs, with the successful completion resulting in the dismissal of the current charges.

sentencing
The postconviction stage, in which the defendant is brought before the court for formal judgment pronounced by a judge.

Factors That Affect Granting a Community Sentence

A judge's decision to allow a defendant to serve a community corrections sentence depends on the offender's eligibility by law for a community corrections sentence and ability to meet those conditions, the availability of community-based services, and the factors contained in a presentence investigation report. Judges engage in a process of **reflective justice**, which means that each individual case is considered in terms of "its subjectivities, harms, wrongs, and contexts, and then measured against concepts such as oppression, freedom, dignity, and equality" (Hudson, 2006, p. 39). In reflective justice, judges use a presentence investigation report (discussed later in the chapter) to examine the stability of a defendant, family ties, marital status, employment length, and drug abuse history. Judges also take into account whether a case was plea bargained or brought to trial and the amount of media attention generated that may affect public opinion.

Determinate Sentencing Examples

Among the goals of sentencing guidelines and the determinate sentencing movement are to reduce or eliminate perceived sentencing disparity, increase judicial accountability for sentences, increase punishments for violent offenders, and provide a basis for population projections and resource allocation (Lubitz & Ross, 2001). About half of all states have adopted some form of sentencing guidelines. Although these guidelines vary greatly from jurisdiction to jurisdiction, they generally establish a sentence based on severity of offense and offender's prior criminal history.

With **presumptive sentencing grids**, judges are obligated to use guidelines that they must provide written reasons for any deviation from. **Sentencing commissions** monitor how sentencing guidelines and judicial departures are used and make sentencing recommendations to a legislature. These departures may also be subject to appellate court review. North Carolina and Pennsylvania have "structured presumptive sentencing zones"; that is, they have integrated intermediate sanctions directly into both their felony and misdemeanor sentencing guidelines. Violent offenders in these states receive lengthier prison sentences than do nonviolent offenders, who can receive intermediate sanctions or other forms of community-based or even restorative justice sanctions (Lubitz & Ross, 2001). We present two different sentencing guidelines—the federal sentencing table and the North Carolina sentencing guidelines.

UNITED STATES SENTENCING GUIDELINES   The original United States Sentencing Guidelines set narrow, mandatory ranges of punishment based on the current offense or plea, an offender's prior criminal history, and the established facts that, if proven by a preponderance of evidence, could potentially increase an offender's sentence above the range in the Guidelines. If a prosecutor could show aggravating facts to a sentencing judge, a court would be obligated to enhance a punishment even further. *U.S. v. Booker* (2005) ruled this practice unconstitutional, but two distinct majority opinions followed. One said that to enhance a punishment, a defendant had to admit to aggravating circumstances or a prosecutor had to prove guilt to a jury beyond a reasonable doubt. The second majority opinion said the Guidelines should be advisory rather than mandatory. This served once again to give federal judges discretion in sentencing.

The federal sentencing guidelines were most recently updated in 2010 and are shown in Figure 4.2.

There are 43 offense levels listed in the first column pertaining to a current offense, each of which has its own row. The criminal history score ranges between

reflective justice
Each defendant's case is considered in total according to its subjectivities, harms, wrongs, and contexts, and then measured against concepts such as oppression, freedom, dignity, and equality.

presumptive sentencing grids
A narrow range of sentencing guidelines that judges are obligated to use. Any deviations must be provided in writing and may also be subject to appellate court review.

sentencing commission
A governing body that monitors the use of the sentencing guidelines and departures from the recommended sentences.

FIGURE 4.2   FEDERAL SENTENCING TABLE (in months of imprisonment)

Criminal History Category (Criminal History Points)

Zone	Offense Level	I (0 or 1)	II (2 or 3)	III (4, 5, 6)	IV (7, 8, 9)	V (10, 11, 12)	VI (13 or more)
	Abuse; Animals, Crimes Against	0–6	0–6	0–6	0–6	0–6	0–6
	Arson & Burning; Assault	0–6	0–6	0–6	0–6	0–6	1–7
		0–6	0–6	0–6	0–6	2–8	3–9
	Assisted Suicide	0–6	0–6	0–6	2–8	4–10	6–12
Zone A	Bad Check; Bribery; Burglary	0–6	0–6	1–7	4–10	6–12	9–15
		0–6	1–7	2–8	6–12	9–15	12–18
		0–6	2–8	4–10	8–14	12–18	15–21
		0–6	4–10	6–12	10–16	15–21	18–24
	Cemeteries & Funerary Objects	4–10	6–12	8–14	12–18	18–24	21–27
Zone B	Commercial Fraud	6–12	8–14	10–16	15–21	21–27	24–30
		8–14	10–16	12–18	18–24	24–30	27–33
Zone C	Consumer Protection Laws; Counterfeiting	10–16	12–18	15–21	21–27	27–33	30–37
	Credit Card Crimes	12–18	15–21	18–24	24–30	30–37	33–41
	Criminal Gang Offenses	15–21	18–24	21–27	27–33	33–41	37–46
	Destructive Devices; Disturbing the Peace	18–24	21–27	24–30	30–37	37–46	41–51
	Election Offenses; Extortion & Other Threats	21–27	24–30	27–33	33–41	41–51	46–57
	False Statements, Other	24–30	27–33	30–37	37–46	46–57	51–63
	Fraud, Financial Crimes Against Vulnerable Adults; Fraud	27–33	30–37	33–41	41–51	51–63	57–71
	Fraud, Telecommunication Service Providers; Gambling	30–37	33–41	37–46	46–57	57–71	63–78
	Handguns	33–41	37–46	41–51	51–63	63–78	70–87
	Harboring, Escape, & Contraband	37–46	41–51	46–57	57–71	70–87	77–96
	Hate Crimes; Identity Fraud	41–51	46–57	51–63	63–78	77–96	84–105
	Influencing or Intimidating Judicial Process	46–57	51–63	57–71	70–87	84–105	92–115
	Interference with Government Operations; Kidnapping	51–63	57–71	63–78	77–96	92–115	100–125
	Lotteries; Machine Guns; Malicious Destruction; Manslaughter	57–71	63–78	70–87	84–105	100–125	110–137
	Marriage, Crimes Against; Motor Vehicle Offenses	63–78	70–87	78–97	92–115	110–137	120–150
Zone D		70–87	78–97	87–108	100–125	120–150	130–162
		78–97	87–108	97–121	110–137	130–162	140–175
		87–108	97–121	108–135	121–151	140–175	151–188
	Murder; Nudity & Related Sexual Displays; Obscene Matter	97–121	108–135	121–151	135–168	151–188	168–210
		108–135	121–151	135–168	151–188	168–210	188–235
	Perjury; Prescription Drugs; Prostitution	121–151	135–168	151–188	168–210	188–235	210–262
	Public Fraud	135–168	151–188	168–210	188–235	210–262	235–293
		151–188	168–210	188–235	210–262	235–293	262–327
		168–210	188–235	210–262	235–293	262–327	292–365
	Public Health & Safety, Crimes Against	188–235	210–262	235–293	262–327	292–365	324–405
		210–262	235–293	262–327	292–365	324–405	360–life
	Railroads, Crimes Involving; Robbery; Sabotage & Related Crimes; Sexual Crimes	235–293	262–327	292–365	324–405	360–life	360–life
		262–327	292–365	324–405	360–life	360–life	360–life
		292–365	324–405	360–life	360–life	360–life	360–life
	Stalking & Harassment; Statewide DNA Data Base System; Surveillance & Other Crimes Against Privacy	324–405	360–life	360–life	360–life	360–life	360–life
	Telecommunications & Electronics	360–life	360–life	360–life	360–life	360–life	360–life
	Theft Trespass; Unlawful Use of Goods; Weapons Crimes	life	life	life	life	life	life

Source: U.S. Sentencing Commission. 2010. *Federal Sentencing Guidelines Manual* Chapter 5, Part A, Updated November 1, 2010, p. 401.

1 and 6 and is listed in its own column. The intersection between the current offense row and the criminal history score determines the range in months of imprisonment. The criminal history score is determined by adding together three subsections:

Subsection 1: Add (a) **3** points for each prior sentence of imprisonment exceeding one year and one month; (b) **2** points for each prior sentence of imprisonment of at least sixty days not counted in (a); (c) and **1** point for each prior sentence not counted in (a) or (b), up to a total of **4** points for this subsection.

Subsection 2: Add (d) **2** points if a defendant committed the instance of offense while under any criminal justice sentence, including probation, parole, supervised release, imprisonment, work release, or escape status.

Subsection 3: Add (e) **1** point for each prior sentence resulting from conviction of a crime of violence that did not receive any points under (a), (b), or (c) above because such sentence was counted as a single sentence, up to a total of **3** points for this subsection.

There are countless exceptions to the point system, so for full instructions visit chapter 4, part A of the Sentencing Guidelines Manual at: http://www.ussc.gov/Guidelines/2010_guidelines/Manual_HTML/Chapter_4.htm

NORTH CAROLINA SENTENCING GUIDELINES   How do you increase sentence lengths for only the most serious offenses *without* building new prisons? North Carolina has done so by incarcerating only the most serious offenders—so that violent prisoners must serve 100% of their time in prison without early release. Violent offenders must also serve an automatic nine month post-release community supervision, whereas sex offenders serve five years of community supervision after prison. So far this sounds like what many states did, except that sentencing guidelines in many states did not authorize community options. The difference between North Carolina and other states can be seen in the former's sentencing grid, which allows more classes of crimes to be eligible for community-based corrections and builds that expectation right into the grid (see Figure 4.3). As a result, sentence lengths for violent offenders increased, but the *percent of sentenced offenders going to prison decreased*. The state instead increased its use of pretrial release programs, work release, day-reporting centers, and community substance abuse treatment programs for drug and nonviolent offenders.

Sentence type is listed for each class of crimes. North Carolina's sentencing grid (see Figure 4.3) has three types of sentences: (1) jail or prison *(prison)*; (2) residential intermediate sanctions or intensive supervision such as boot camps and day reporting *(CC);* and (3) nonresidential community options *(probation),* which can include probation, community drug treatment, community service, restitution, and fines. Prior record points are calculated as follows: 1 point per Class 1 or A1 misdemeanor; 2 points per property or drug felony; 4 points for each voluntary or involuntary manslaughter; 6 points for kidnapping or robbery or second-degree murder; 9 points for each rape; and 10 points for each first-degree murder (Wright, 1998).

Within each class of crimes, you will also see an *aggravating* sentence, a *presumptive* sentence, and a *mitigating* sentence. A sentence may not deviate from a presumptive one except in a predefined list of aggravating and mitigating circumstances. For example, if there was a firearm used in a crime (an aggravating circumstance), 60 months are added to the minimum. If "substantial assistance" is rendered for helping a prosecutor arrest or prosecute other criminals, judges may reduce

FIGURE 4.3 North Carolina Felony Sentencing Grid (Numbers Represent Months)

CURRENT FELONY CRIME CLASS		I 0 Pts	II 1–4 Pts	III 5–8 Pts	IV 9–14 Pts	V 15–18 Pts	VI 19+ Points
				PRIOR RECORD LEVEL			
Class A: Murder				Death or Life Without Parole ONLY			
Class B1: Agg Sexual Battery	Sentence Type Aggravating	Prison 240–300	Prison 288–360	Prison 336–420	Prison 384–480	Prison Life Without Parole	Prison Life without Parole
Agg Child Molestation Rape, Agg Sodomy	Presumptive Mitigating	192–240 144–192	230–288 173–230	269–336 202–269	307–384 230–307	346–433 260–346	384–480 288–384
Class B2: Second deg. Murder	Sentence Type Aggravating Presumptive Mitigating	Prison 135–169 108–135 81–108	Prison 163–204 130–163 98–130	Prison 193–238 152–190 114–152	Prison 216–270 173–216 130–173	Prison 243–304 194–243 146–194	Prison 270–338 216–270 162–216
Class C: Kidnapping Second deg. Rape Agg Assault	Sentence Type Aggravating Presumptive Mitigating	Prison 63–79 50–63 38–50	Prison 86–108 69–86 52–69	Prison 100–125 80–100 60–80	Prison 115–144 92–115 69–92	Prison 130–162 104–130 78–104	Prison 145–181 116–145 87–116
Class D: Armed Robbery Burglary First Degree Arson	Sentence Type Aggravating Presumptive Mitigating	Prison 55–69 44–55 33–44	Prison 66–82 53–66 40–53	Prison 89–111 71–89 53–71	Prison 101–126 81–101 61–81	Prison 115–144 92–115 69–92	Prison 126–158 101–126 76–101
Class E: Child Molestation Drug Trafficking Drug Manuf/Selling	Sentence Type Aggravating Presumptive Mitigating	CC or Prison 25–31 20–25 15–20	CC or Prison 29–36 23–29 17–23	Prison 34–42 27–34 20–27	Prison 46–58 37–46 28–37	Prison 53–66 42–53 32–42	Prison 59–74 47–59 35–47
Class F: Involun. Manslaughter Att Rape, Incest, Cocaine 200–400 g	Sentence Type Aggravating Presumptive Mitigating	CC or Prison 16–20 13–16 10–13	CC or Prison 19–24 15–19 11–15	Res CC or Prison 21–26 17–21 13–17	Prison 25–31 20–25 15–20	Prison 34–42 27–34 20–27	Prison 39–49 31–39 23–31
Class G: Sec Degree Arson Robbery; Unlawful Carrying of a Weapon	Sentence Type Aggravating Presumptive Mitigating	CC or Prison 13–16 10–13 8–10	CC or Prison 15–19 12–15 9–12	CC or Prison 16–20 13–16 10–13	CC or Prison 20–25 16–20 12–16	Prison 21–26 17–21 13–17	Prison 29–36 23–29 17–23
Class H: Forgery, Theft Sale/Distribution LSD or Cocaine	Sentence Type Aggravating Presumptive Mitigating	Probation or CC 6–8 5–6 4–6	CC 8–10 6–8 4–6	CC or Prison 10–12 8–10 6–8	CC or Prison 11–14 9–11 7–9	CC or Prison 15–19 12–15 9–12	Prison 20–25 16–20 12–16
Class I: Poss Control. Sub Bad Checks Agg Stalking	Sentence Type Aggravating Presumptive Mitigating	Probation 6–8 4–6 3–4	Probation CC 6–8 4–6 3–4	CC 6–8 5–6 4–5	CC or Prison 8–10 6–8 4–6	CC or Prison 9–11 7–9 5–7	CC or Prison 10–12 8–10 6–8

Source: North Carolina Sentencing and Policy Advisory Commission, Structured Sentencing for Felonies—Training and Reference Manual. (Raleigh: North Source: North Carolina Sentencing and Policy Advisory Commission, 1994).

Note: For each Crime class, a "sentence type" directs the judge to: "prison" (Jail or prison); "CC" (any residential community correction program, or "probation" (which includes nonresidential and economic options). Then the judge selects the presumptive row, unless aggravating or mitigating circumstances warrant a deviation.

or even suspend a mandatory sentence for drug defendants (a mitigating situation). Only sentences may be appealed in which a deviation occurred based on an aggravating or mitigating circumstance, or if a prior record score was miscalculated. Research shows that North Carolina has been effective in differentiating the type of offenders sent to prison from those who serve time in the community (Wright, 1998). Any modifications of the grid must also show how such changes would impact the current number of prison beds or community resources.

Indeterminate Sentencing Example

Many states continue to use an indeterminate sentencing structure that provides for more judicial discretion on type of sentence (prison vs. community-based options). Such sentencing also allows for consideration of early release by a parole board after a minimum term has been met. In Figure 4.4, you will see the punishments determined for each category of crimes listed in the very first column. The first column begins with misdemeanors and then graduates to felony crimes, ending with capital felonies at the bottom. In each instance, there is a sentence length and a fine listed, but judges are not limited to incarceration only—community options are available in most every crime class except for offenders who have repeated a felony and in death penalty or capital crime cases.

THE PRESENTENCE INVESTIGATION REPORT

presentence investigation report (PSI)
A report submitted to the court before sentencing describing the nature of the offense, offender characteristics, criminal history, loss to the victim, and sentencing recommendations.

Prior to a judicial sentencing decision, many probation departments provide a judge with a **presentence investigation report (PSI)**. The PSI is a document prepared by a probation officer to aid judges in a felony sentencing decision or in a case of offenders who have violated probation and are facing a potential incarceration sentence. The PSI is also used by prosecutors, defense attorneys, parole boards, and probation or parole officers in carrying out their tasks and making decisions. Although U.S. probation officers are involved in both case supervision and in conducting five or six presentence investigations per month (Quinn, 2002), most state and local probation agencies separate investigative from supervision duties, such as by designating some probation officers to only conduct presentence investigations and write PSI reports whereas other officers to supervise cases.

Purposes of the PSI Report

The primary purpose of a presentence investigation report is for a probation officer to provide a judge with timely, relevant, and accurate information in order to make a rational sentencing decision. Probation officers are not seeking to change a judge's mind—they are merely attempting to summarize a case and to provide supporting evidence (Kittrie, Zenoff, & Eng, 2002).

The PSI report describes the nature of an offense, offender characteristics, criminal history, loss to a victim, and sentencing recommendations. In juvenile court, a judge is furnished with a social history, or predispositional report, prior to a disposition hearing. Presentence reports are seldom used in sentencing for misdemeanor crimes. The PSI has been used for felony sentencing since the early 1900s and was

FIGURE 4.4 Indeterminate Sentencing Example

FIRST OFFENSE EXAMPLES			
MISDEMEANORS	AGAINST PERSON	PROPERTY	ALCOHOL/DRUG
Class C **No jail** **$500 fine**	Leaving child in a vehicle	Less than $50 loss Criminal trespass	Accessible firearm to child Public intoxication Alcohol in vehicle
Class B **0–180 days** **$2,000 fine**	Indecent exposure Enticing a child	$50–$500 losses Disorderly conduct	< 2 oz. marijuana possession
Class A **0–365 days; $4,000 fine**	Assault Terroristic threat Harboring runaway child	$500–$1,500 losses FTA/jumping bail Animal cruelty	Driving While Intoxicated 2–4 oz. marijuana possession
FELONIES	AGAINST PERSON	PROPERTY	ALCOHOL/DRUG
State Jail **180 days–2 yrs.** **$10,000 fine**	Negligent homicide Reckless/negligent injury Placing child in danger Aiding suicide Interfering w/child custody	$1,500–$20,000 Credit card abuse Check fraud Computer crime Dog fighting	DUI w/child passenger > 4 oz. marijuana possession Manufacturing Delivery Possession (Amt. depends on drug class/schedules)
3rd Degree **2–10 yrs.** **$10,000 fine**	Terroristic threat Kidnapping Indecency w/child Assault/stalking Unlaw. Carrying Weapon	$20,000–$100,000 in losses Burglary, forgery Theft, counterfeiting Fraud, computer Property destruction	Third time DUI Manufacturing Delivery Possession (Amt. depends on drug class/schedules)
2nd Degree **2–20 yrs.** **$10,000 fine**	Sec. degree murder Manslaughter Trafficking 14 and older Agg. kidnapping Indecency with child/incest Agg. assault	$100,000–$200,000 in losses Arson (no death) Robbery Burglary, forgery Theft, counterfeiting Fraud, computer	Manufacturing Delivery Possession (Amt. depends on drug class/schedules)
1st Degree **5–99 yrs.** **$10,000 fine**	Trafficking children <14 Agg. kidnapping Murder Injury to a child Agg. sexual assault Agg. assault (victim-specific)	Arson (death/injury) $200,000 and above in total losses Agg. robbery Burglary Theft, mischief Insurance fraud	Manufacturing Delivery Possession (Amt. depends on drug class/schedules)
Capital **Life without parole** **Death**	Capital murder	_____	_____

(Continues)

FIGURE 4.4   Indeterminate Sentencing Example (*Continued*)

SENTENCING ENHANCEMENTS FOR REPEAT/HABITUAL OFFENSES

IF INSTANT OFFENSE IS:	AND PREVIOUS CONVICTIONS ARE:	THEN PUNISHMENT IS:
Class C Misd	Three Class A, B or ANY felony*	0–180 days / $2,000 fine
Class B Misd	One Class A, B or ANY felony*	30–180 days / $2,000 fine
Class A Misd	One Class A or ANY felony*	90–365 days / $4,000 fine

INSTANT OFFENSE	PREVIOUS CONVICTIONS:	THEN OFFENSE BECOMES:
State jail felony	Two state jail felonies	3rd degree felony
State jail felony	Two felonies	2nd degree felony
3rd degree felony	One felony	2nd degree felony
2nd degree felony	One felony	1st degree felony
1st degree felony	One felony	15–99 years or life
1st, 2nd, or 3rd degree	Two felonies (2nd one occurred prior to the 1st one becoming final)	25–99 years or life

NOTES:

⁺ A state jail felony may be prosecuted as a Class A misdemeanor if the circumstances warrant and the character and rehabilitative needs of the defendant would best serve the interests of justice.

* The following situations count as one previous adult felony:

Juvenile felony adjudication after 1995

Deferred adjudication

Felony in another state

Drug-Free Zones (If drug offense is committed within 1,000 feet of school, a youth center or on a school bus, minimum sentence is increased by five years and maximum fine is doubled.)

Source: Office of the Attorney General. 2007. *Texas Penal Code Offenses by Punishment Range.* Austin, Texas.

FACT OR FICTION?

With the greater use of sentencing guidelines that are based on current crime and prior criminal record, the PSI report becomes less important to a judge's sentencing decision.

Fiction.

Fact: Although sentencing guidelines restrict judicial discretion compared with indeterminate sentencing, a PSI report is particularly important in the federal system for identifying mitigating and aggravating circumstances that legally allow a judge to deviate from those guidelines.

declared by the U.S. Supreme Court to be a valid instrument in 1949 (*Williams v. New York*). Other than for sentencing recommendations, the PSI report has other uses (Petersilia, 2002; Norman & Wadman, 2000):

- It assists jails and prisons in suggesting types of institutional programming that would fit an offender's needs while incarcerated.
- Paroling authorities can compare a defendant's version of an offense at the time of arrest to that determined by a parole board hearing.
- It assists in making community supervision caseload assignments.
- It serves a basis for writing a client treatment or program plan.

About 64% of all felony cases nationwide included a PSI prior to sentencing. About half of all states require a presentence investigation in all felony cases, whereas a PSI is discretionary in 16 states and nonexistent in about 10 states (Petersilia, 2002). In the federal system, PSIs have increased in significance because federal probation officers are considered experts on federal sentencing guidelines. In one year alone in the federal system, federal probation officers wrote 65,156 presentence and post-sentence reports and completed 52,047 collateral presentence investigations and an additional 27,117 prerelease investigations of military defendants (U.S. Department of Justice, 2005a).

A **post-sentence report** may be written after a defendant has pleaded guilty and waived a presentence report, when a court proceeds directly to sentencing. In such cases, the post-sentence report serves to aid a probation or parole officer in supervision efforts during probation, parole, or release and to assist a prison system in classification, programming, and release planning (Stinchcomb & Hippensteel, 2001). It is estimated that half of all investigation reports written at the state level are post-sentence reports.

With the introduction of sentencing guidelines, sentencing has become less discretionary, with the result that the importance of the PSI has declined in some states. For example, in some jurisdictions in which sentencing guidelines are used, probation officers no longer write presentence reports. Instead they complete a *guidelines worksheet* and calculate a presumptive sentence. This short form deprives other agencies in the criminal justice system of valuable information about an offender.

post-sentence report
A report written by a probation officer after the defendant has pled guilty and been sentenced in order to aid probation and parole officers in supervision, classification, and program plans.

Contents of the PSI Report

For jurisdictions that do conduct a PSI, what are the essentials of a presentence report? The philosophy guiding the preparation of presentence reports can be characterized as either offender-based or offense-based.

OFFENDER-BASED PSI REPORTS: 1920S–1980S During the era of indeterminate sentencing, presentence investigation reports were **offender-based** and focused on rehabilitation. That is, probation officers were guided in their **presentence investigation** by a philosophy that attempted to understand the causes of an offender's antisocial behavior and to clinically evaluate his or her potential for change. By learning about the character of the person under consideration and the external influences that surrounded him or her, an offender-based PSI suggested alternatives for sentencing beyond incarceration that were specific to that offender.

presentence investigation
An investigation undertaken by a probation officer for the purpose of gathering and analyzing information to complete a report for the court.

OFFENSE-BASED PSI REPORTS: 1980S–PRESENT The content of presentence investigation reports changed to reflect the turn to determinate sentencing. An **offense-based presentence report** focuses primarily on the crime committed. The sentencing court is concerned with an offender's culpability in an offense, whether anyone was injured, whether a firearm was used, the extent of loss to victim(s), and other aspects of an offense. Secondary information about an offender is considered relevant, such as prior criminal record, employment history, family ties, health, and drug use. Instruction on how to conduct and write an offense-based presentence report for a client is provided in Case Study 3 at the end of this chapter.

offense-based presentence report
A presentence investigation report that focuses primarily on the offense committed, the offender's culpability, and prior criminal history.

In jurisdictions in which a court uses sentencing guidelines to determine appropriate sentences, the emphasis of a PSI report is on applying particular guidelines to the facts of a case. This means that all presentence reports should be factually accurate, objective, nonjudgmental, and ideally verified by a presentence officer. The report's length and content should be appropriate to the seriousness of an offense. The greater the consequences of a judgment, the more likely a court or a subsequent decision-making body will need more information.

Probation officers have often noted that judges frequently only skimmed their lengthy reports and skipped to the end where a sentence was recommended. In response to this reality, some jurisdictions have moved to shortened versions that focus only on certain relevant variables. In some cases, such brief versions of a PSI report are presented to a court in a fill-in-the blanks format. This practice places a duty on a probation officer to present the most critical information in a concise yet complete manner. Other reports are open-ended and in paragraph format, analogous to an essay.

Federal and some state presentence reports also require a **victim impact statement**. The use of victim impact statements stems from a renewed interest in victims' rights and in mitigating the harm an offender has caused. A victim impact statement identifies the name of a victim and his or her relationship to the offender. This statement informs a judge about any physical injury the victim may have suffered, whether the victim sought medical attention, whether he or she endured physical rehabilitation, and the permanency of the injuries. A victim impact statement specifies the emotional and psychological toll that an offense has taken on a victim and that victim's family. A breakdown of the victim's financial costs not covered by a victim compensation fund is also provided. An example of a victim impact statement is shown in Box 4.1.

victim impact statement
A written account by the victim(s) as to how the crime has taken a toll physically, emotionally, financially, or psychologically on the victim and the victim's family. Victim impact statements are considered by many states at time of sentencing and at parole board hearings.

BOX 4.1   A SAMPLE VICTIM IMPACT STATEMENT

A male defendant, age 34, was charged with Assault First Degree, two counts of Assault Second Degree, Armed Criminal Action, Kidnapping, two counts of Burglary, and Felonious Restraint. The male defendant followed the female victim when she moved from South Carolina to Missouri. They had two boys together, now ages 8 and 10. Based on the defendant's previous arrests for domestic violence in South Carolina, the victim obtained a full order of protection upon arriving in Missouri, with the court giving her full custody of their children and prohibiting defendant from having any contact with her. She chose not to list her residence because she was attempting to keep that information confidential. She did allow for defendant to call their sons on weekends; however, she indicated that he never called to speak to their children.

On Valentine's Day, defendant broke into victim's apartment, ripped out the lining of her couch, and hid inside of it. Upon her arrival home with their sons, he woke up (he had fallen asleep waiting for her). When she sat on the couch, he popped out of it and began to assault her. She was beaten severely around her face, arms, and stomach area. The entire assault was in front of their two sons. Finally, she was able to get to a gun, which she kept loaded in her bedroom closet. He managed to rip the gun from her hands, and he shot her point blank in the forehead. The victim survived the attack and attempted murder.

She gave the following victim impact statement at the sentencing hearing:

> In front of our boys, you tried to kill their mother. It has always been about you. I had to move six states away from you, to another time zone, and it wasn't far enough. You have cost me two jobs and a lifetime of self-esteem. The bullet is lodged in my forehead. Would you like to feel it? You put it there. I know that it wasn't smart of me to have a loaded gun in my house with two young children. Does everyone see now what choice I had? I didn't have any choices. You made all of my decisions for me. I told you that I wanted to live near my family again someday. I did not take the children away from you, and I did not move for any man. Although, that is what you want to believe. Even though I have $100,000 dollars in medical expenses to pay, the state was only able to cover $15,000, I would rather be stuck with that debt, than stuck with you. Tell me again that you will pay for my hospital bills as long as I don't testify against you. Well, you always said that you wanted to live in Missouri, congratulations, now you have your chance.

Source: State of Missouri v. Anthony Williams CR2000-00704.

Preparing the PSI Report

Preparing the PSI report requires many important skills, including interviewing, investigating, and writing. A probation officer's responsibility is to gather the facts about an offense and offender, verify the information received, and present it in an organized and objective format.

Preferred practice is to conduct a presentence investigation and prepare a presentence report after adjudication of guilt but before a sentencing hearing. A presentence investigation should not be undertaken until after a finding of guilt because none of the material in a presentence report is admissible at trial or during plea negotiation, and an investigation represents an invasion of privacy. Exceptions to this rule are allowed when a defendant's attorney consents to preparation of a report before conviction and plea. When this happens, it is called a *pre-plea report*. Attorneys are generally not open to receiving a pre-plea or pre-arraignment document instead of a regular PSI (Alarid & Montemayor, 2010a).

Presentence Interview and Verification

The first task in preparing any type of PSI report is to interview a newly convicted offender regarding his or her criminal history, education, employment, physical and emotional health, family, and other relevant data. An officer also uses this time to develop an initial sense of the offender's character, personality, needs, and problems. This meeting usually occurs in the probation officer's office or, if the defendant has not been released on bail, in jail. In some cases the initial interview takes place at the defendant's home, which provides the officer an opportunity to observe the offender's home environment and thus offers an additional dimension to his or her

A probation officer interviews an offender to prepare a presentence investigation report before the sentencing hearing.

© Catchlight Visual Services/Alamy

understanding of the defendant. The officer interviews the defendant's family and friends, the arresting police officer, the victim and/or victim's family, and the defendant's present employer or school officials, all of whom are known as **collateral contacts**.

Following the initial interview, the probation officer verifies information supplied by the offender and obtains "court dockets, plea agreements, investigative reports from numerous agencies, previous probation or parole records, pretrial services records, criminal history transcripts, vital statistics records, medical records, counseling and substance abuse treatment records, scholastic records, employment records, financial records, and others" (Storm, 1997, p. 13). Many of these records are protected by state and federal privacy laws and obtaining them may require the defendant's written permission for release.

The probation officer is interested in information that might influence the sentencing decision but that is omitted during the trial, particularly any aggravating or mitigating circumstances. When obtaining information from any source—particularly from relatives, friends, acquaintances, and employers—the probation officer must be careful to distinguish facts from conclusions. As a general rule, the report should contain only information the probation officer knows to be accurate. In some cases, information may be presented that the officer has been unable to verify. When that is necessary, the officer should clearly denote the information as "unconfirmed" or "unverified."

In writing the evaluative summary, probation officers must practice their analytical ability, diagnostic skills, and understanding of human behavior. They must bring into focus the kind of person that is before the court, the basic factors that landed the person in trouble, and the special assistance the defendant needs for resolving those difficulties. Part of the evaluative summary should discuss the defendant's probability of risk to the community, the amount of harm the defendant caused the victim and/or community, the defendant's ability to pay restitution and court fines, and the defendant's need for treatment (Storm, 1997). Writing the presentence report can actually be conducted while telecommuting from home (see Box 4.2).

BOX 4.2   TECHNOLOGY IN CORRECTIONS

Telecommuting for Presentence Officers

Probation office budgets have not kept pace with the increased numbers of probationers being supervised in the community. Many probation officers across the country must share office space, which makes officer rapport and confidentiality difficult to maintain. As a result, many federal probation offices have experimented with telecommuting. Telecommuting allows presentence officers to complete a presentence investigation report from home using laptops, telephone calling cards, electronic computer access, and remote system linkages. Telecommuters are home two or three days out of every work week and reportedly are more satisfied with their jobs than when they were working strictly out of an office. In addition, presentence officers who telecommuted were more productive from home than they were before the telecommuting program began. One federal probation office in Florida found that telecommuting was more successful for officers who wrote presentence investigation reports than for officers who supervised a caseload full of clients. Telecommuting was so successful that the Middle District of Florida now allows officers with at least two years of presentence experience and "above average performance evaluations" to apply.

Source: Christopher Hansen. 2001. The Cutting Edge: A Survey of Technological Innovation: Where Have All the Probation Officers Gone? *Federal Probation* 65(1): 51–53.

The Sentence Recommendation

A probation officer's recommended sentence to a judge largely depends on the sentencing guideline system or statutory equivalent. It is important to note that officers recommend a sentence type but *not* a sentence length. Probation officers were consistent in their sentence recommendations in about 70% of cases that advocated for intermediate sanctions. However, probation officers in the jurisdiction studied more often recommended intermediate sanctions for reasons of "net widening" (that is, imposing a harsher sentence than probation) than as an actual alternative to prison (Homant & DeMercurio, 2009). The researchers buttressed this evidence by finding that, in cases in which intermediate sanctions were recommended first, if a judge did not agree with this course, then an officer would recommend probation as a second choice. If intermediate sanctions were truly an alternative to prison, then prison would have been the second choice over probation.

The sentencing judge adopted the probation officer's recommendation in 66% of cases when prison was recommended and in 85% of cases when probation was recommended. Another study in Utah found that the court agreed with the probation officer's recommendation about 91% of the time in felony and misdemeanor cases (Norman & Wadman, 2000). An appropriate use of sentencing guidelines reduced sentencing disparity such that prior criminal record and offense severity were the most important predictors of sentencing outcomes, but courtroom work group (attorneys and judge) collectively affected the sentence a defendant received (Haynes, Ruback, & Cusick, 2010). Alarid and Montemayor (2010a) found that legal factors such as a defendant's criminal history, previous times on probation and parole, pending cases, and police version of an offense were more important to attorneys than extra-legal factors. Important extra-legal factors for both prosecutors and defense attorneys included social support system, mental health issues, and substance abuses. Although legal factors can be used to control sentencing disparity, practitioners also found that extra-legal factors were valuable aids in identifying treatment intervention services.

Legal Issues Concerning the Presentence Report

Various legal concerns about the PSI report have been raised on appeal in the courts and are each briefly addressed.

DOES A DEFENDANT HAVE A CONSTITUTIONAL RIGHT TO DISCLOSURE OF THE PSI REPORT?   **Disclosure** is an opportunity for a defendant (and/or a defendant's attorney) to view a draft of the presentence report. The U.S. Supreme Court held that there is no denial of due process when a court does not disclose a report's contents to a defendant or give a defendant an opportunity to rebut them (*Williams v. Oklahoma*, 1959; *Williams v. New York*, 1949). A defendant may have such a right, however, if disclosure is required by state law. Despite the Supreme Court ruling, federal defendants are provided an opportunity to view a PSI draft at least 35 days prior to sentencing, and then are given 14 days to refute any statements prior to final report submission to federal court. A PSI is not, however, a public document, so disclosure is limited to the defendant, the defendant's attorney, and the prosecutor. To safeguard information that victims and witnesses provide that they fear might be used by an offender to retaliate, the federal system requires withholding various parts of a PSI from a defendant when:

disclosure
The right of a defendant to read and refute information in the presentence investigation report prior to sentencing.

- disclosure might disrupt rehabilitation of that defendant (such as psychiatric reports addressing future dangerousness);
- information was obtained on a promise of confidentiality; and
- harm might result to that defendant or to any other person from such disclosure.

In sum, federal rules represent an intermediate position between complete disclosure and complete secrecy.

ARE INACCURACIES IN A PSI REPORT LEGAL GROUNDS FOR RESENTENCING?   Disclosure policies attempt to minimize errors in the final PSI report submitted to a court. Two federal circuit courts ruled that detected inaccuracies in a PSI report are not grounds for automatic revocation of the sentence imposed (*United States v. Lockhart,* 1995; *United States v. Riviera,* 1996), provided the error is **harmless**—meaning the error would not have affected the sentencing outcome. If the inaccuracies would have changed a sentencing outcome, a defendant has the burden of establishing that an error was harmful. The remedy entails vacating an original sentence and remanding a harmful error case to a trial court to prepare a new PSI report prior to resentencing.

IS HEARSAY ALLOWABLE IN A PSI?   **Hearsay evidence** is information that does not come from direct knowledge but that is received from a third party. Although hearsay is not admissible in trial, it is not in and of itself constitutionally objectionable in a PSI report. It is important that a judge be given every opportunity to obtain relevant information during sentencing without rigid adherence to rules of evidence.

DOES THE EXCLUSIONARY RULE APPLY?   The **exclusionary rule** establishes that evidence seized by police in violation of the Fourth Amendment is not admissible in court, so illegally obtained evidence cannot be used to convict. Once a defendant has been convicted, evidence obtained or seized illegally *can* be included within a PSI report.

MUST MIRANDA WARNINGS BE GIVEN DURING A PRESENTENCE INTERVIEW?   *Miranda v. Arizona* (1966) held that defendants must be reminded of their Fifth and Sixth Amendment rights whenever they are in a "custodial interrogation" situation. Appellate courts held that *Miranda* warnings do not need to be given by a probation officer when interviewing a defendant in connection with a PSI report. A presentence investigation does not trigger a defendant's right to be free from self-incrimination even if that defendant is in custody and facing serious punishment (*United States v. Allen,* 1993; *United States v. Washington,* 1993).

DOES A DEFENDANT HAVE A RIGHT TO COUNSEL DURING A PRESENTENCE INTERVIEW? A defendant does not possess a Sixth Amendment right to have an attorney present during a PSI report interview, according to the Tenth Circuit Court (*United States v. Gordon,* 1993; *United States v. Washington,* 1993). The rationale is that guilt has already been determined; hence, an adversarial situation that requires the assistance of a lawyer is absent. However, a Massachusetts court disagreed, saying that a defendant has a right to counsel at a presentence interview because this interview has "due process implications with respect to a defendant's interest in a fair and even-handed sentence proceeding" (*Commonwealth of Massachusetts v. Talbot,* 2005). The legal issues of a PSI continue to be clarified over time.

COMMUNITY CORRECTION CONDITIONS

An authority to impose conditions of a community corrections sentence is vested with the courts. Although conditions may be recommended by a presentence investigator or probation officer, a judge has final say regarding conditions imposed on an offender. Box 4.3 shows the conditions of federal probation.

harmless error
An error that occurs prior to conviction that does *not* affect the sentencing outcome of the case.

hearsay evidence
Information offered as a truthful assertion that does not come from the personal knowledge of the person giving the information but from knowledge that person received from a third party.

exclusionary rule
A rule of evidence that enforces the Fourth Amendment's prohibition against unreasonable search and seizure, whereby illegal police searches are not admissible in a court of law. The purpose is to deter police misconduct.

BOX 4.3 CONDITIONS OF FEDERAL PROBATION

Mandatory Conditions

The court shall provide, as an *explicit condition* of a sentence of probation, that the defendant:

1. not commit another Federal, State, or local crime during the term of probation;
2. not unlawfully possess a controlled substance, refrain from any unlawful use of a controlled substance and submit to one drug test within 15 days of release on probation and at least 2 periodic drug tests thereafter;
3. will make restitution;
4. will pay the assessment imposed;
5. will notify the court of any material change in economic circumstances that might affect ability to pay restitution, fines, or special assessments;
6. will report the address where the person will reside and any subsequent change of residence to the probation officer;
7. if the court has imposed and ordered execution of a fine and placed the defendant on probation, payment of the fine.
8. only for a domestic violence crime)—attend a rehabilitation program that has been approved by the court, in consultation with a State Coalition Against Domestic Violence or other appropriate experts.

Discretionary Probation Conditions

The court may provide, as further conditions of a sentence of probation, to the extent that such conditions are reasonably related, that the defendant:

1. support his dependents and meet other family responsibilities;
2. make restitution to a victim of the offense;
3. work conscientiously at suitable employment or pursue conscientiously a course of study or vocational training that will equip him for suitable employment;
4. refrain from engaging in a specified occupation, business, or profession bearing a reasonably direct relationship to the conduct constituting the offense;
5. refrain from frequenting specified kinds of places or from associating unnecessarily with specified persons;
6. refrain from excessive use of alcohol, or any use of a narcotic drug or other controlled substance without a prescription by a licensed medical practitioner;
7. refrain from possessing a firearm, destructive device, or other dangerous weapon;

8. undergo available medical, psychiatric, or psychological treatment, including treatment for drug or alcohol dependency, as specified by the court, and remain in a specified institution if required for that purpose;
9. remain in the custody of the Bureau of Prisons during nights, weekends, or other intervals of time, totaling no more than the lesser of one year or the term of imprisonment authorized for the offense, during the first year of the term of probation;
10. reside at, or participate in the program of, a corrections facility (including a facility maintained contract to the Bureau of Prisons) for all or part of probation;
11. work in community service as directed by the court;
12. reside in a specified place or area, or refrain from residing in a specified place or area;
13. remain within the jurisdiction of the court, unless granted permission to leave by the court or a probation officer;
14. report to a probation officer as directed by the court or the probation officer;
15. permit a probation officer to visit him at his home or elsewhere as specified by the court;
16. answer inquiries by a probation officer and notify the probation officer promptly of any change in address or employment;
17. notify the probation officer promptly if arrested or if questioned by a law enforcement officer;
18. remain at his place of residence during nonworking hours and, if the court finds it appropriate, that compliance with this condition be monitored by telephonic or electronic signaling devices;
19. comply with the terms of any court order requiring payments by the defendant for the support and maintenance of a child or of a child and the parent with whom the child is living;
20. be ordered deported by a United States district court, if, after notice and hearing, the Attorney General demonstrates by clear and convincing evidence that the alien is deportable;
21. satisfy such other conditions as the court may impose.

U.S. Code, Title 18, Part II, Chapter 227, Subchapter B, Sec. 3563. *Conditions of Federal Probation.*

Standard Conditions

Standard conditions are imposed on all community sentences in a jurisdiction, regardless of the nature of offense committed. Standard conditions (also called *mandatory* conditions in the federal system) are either prescribed by law or set by court or agency practice and require any offender sentenced to a community corrections sanction to:

- obey all federal and state laws and municipal ordinances;
- follow all directives of a supervising officer;
- not lie or misrepresent the truth to a supervising officer;
- work and/or attend school regularly;
- refrain from use of all controlled substances except those prescribed by a licensed medical practitioner;
- submit to drug testing;
- obtain permission from an officer before changing residence or employment or leaving a jurisdiction;
- report regularly to a supervising officer;
- keep current on monthly supervision fees;
- agree that vehicle and any property under offender's control are subject to search at any time by a community supervision officer; and
- refrain from associating with people who have criminal records unless permission is granted by a supervising officer.

Special Conditions

Special conditions (also known as discretionary conditions in the federal system) are additional stipulations tailored to fit the problems and needs of an offender. As such, a judge imposes them consistent with the crime committed or the offender's deficits in skill or ability. For example, a defendant may be required to:

- attend literacy classes if he or she does not know how to read or write;
- obtain a GED if he or she did not finish high school;
- participate in drug or alcohol treatment if he or she is addicted;
- attend parenting classes if there are issues with dependent children;
- pay victim restitution if damage was caused;
- refrain from entering designated areas if the offense involves crimes against children; and
- seek mental health treatment if he or she suffers from mental dysfunction.

LIMITATIONS OF SPECIAL CONDITIONS Special conditions of community supervision must be related to an offense of conviction, be **clearly** stated without ambiguity, be **reasonable** so that a probationer can comply, and must either protect society or rehabilitate an offender. The definition of clear and reasonable and relationship to offense of conviction depends on an offender's circumstances and is decided on a case-by-case basis. For example, requiring an employed offender with a good salary to pay $500 each month in restitution may be reasonable, but the same condition would be unreasonable if imposed on an indigent probationer with a sixth-grade education. Another example is that a probationer cannot be ordered to attend sex offender treatment for a nonsexual offense (*State v. Bourrie*, 2003). In an interesting twist, a probationer who has never had a drinking problem and whose crime is unrelated to use of alcohol can still be ordered to refrain from the use of alcohol. The Federal Court of Appeals held that a trial court could require that a defendant totally abstain

BOX 4.4	COMMUNITY CORRECTIONS UP CLOSE

Are Scarlet Letter Probation Conditions Constitutional?

Appellate courts in the country are sharply divided on the validity of scarlet letter conditions. For example, in *Ballenger v. State* (1993), a Georgia appellate court upheld the imposition of a condition requiring a probationer to wear a plastic fluorescent pink bracelet imprinted with the words "D.U.I. CONVICT." A number of jurisdictions, however, have rejected scarlet letter conditions based on their *state* constitution or because these are not reasonably related to a defendant's rehabilitation. For example, a court required a probationer convicted of shoplifting to wear a T-shirt bearing the words "I am a convicted shoplifter" whenever he was outside his living quarters (*People v. Heckler,* 1993). The appellate court found this condition impinged on the probationer's inalienable right to privacy

and also determined that procuring employment would be difficult while wearing the shirt.

In *People v. Meyer* (1997), a trial court ordered a defendant to erect at his home a 4′ × 8′ sign with 8″ high lettering that read "Warning! A Violent Felon Lives Here. Enter at Your Own Risk!" The Illinois Supreme Court found the purpose of this sign was to inflict humiliation on the probationer. The court further noted that the statutory provisions for probation in Illinois did not include humiliation as a punishment. Thus, the court disallowed this condition. These cases indicate a split in court decisions and thus leave open the question to the U.S. Supreme Court as to whether a state legislature can amend its laws and authorize a trial court to impose a scarlet letter condition.

---

from using alcohol during probation because in this case the defendant's *family* living at the same residence had an active history of alcohol abuse and the defendant had a serious problem with illegal drugs (*United States v. Thurlow,* 1995).

Scarlet letter conditions of community supervision involve shaming an offender by requiring him or her to publicly proclaim guilt. Jurisdictions that have upheld scarlet letter or shaming conditions have done so on grounds of furthering the aims of probation by deterring an offender from committing similar crimes in the future. In addition, these courts have held that shaming conditions do not violate the Eighth Amendment prohibition against cruel and unusual punishment. Courts are in disagreement as to whether scarlet letter conditions serve a legitimate purpose for probation (see Box 4.4).

Supervision Conditions and the Constitution

By virtue of having a criminal conviction, offenders have limited constitutional rights, but they nonetheless retain rights considered basic and fundamental. We discuss two different amendments below.

FIRST AMENDMENT RIGHTS   First Amendment rights of religion, speech, assembly, press, and of petitioning the government for redress of grievances are considered basic, fundamental rights that deserve protection by the courts. For example, much of the literature of Alcoholics Anonymous (A.A.) refers to monotheistic principles and encourages prayer, leading a court to conclude that, although A.A. was not a religion per se, its practices infringed on a person's First Amendment rights of religion. Therefore, requiring A.A. meeting attendance as a condition of probation was ruled unconstitutional (*Warner v. Orange County Department of Probation,* 1997). Multiple courts have reaffirmed this ruling, with the most recent Federal Appellate ruling allowing a parolee to sue a parole officer or department for ordering said parolee (who was a Buddhist) to attend A.A. and recommending revocation for failure to attend (*Inouye v. Kemna,* 2007).

SEARCHES AND SEIZURES   The Fourth Amendment right against unreasonable search and seizure is not as highly protected for probationers as are other constitutional rights. In *Griffin v. Wisconsin* (1987), the U.S. Supreme Court ruled that a warrantless search of a probationer's home is valid as long as reasonable grounds exist to believe contraband is present in violation of the conditions of probation. The Court also found that a departmental policy regulation permitting the search, on which a probation officer had relied, was consistent with the Fourth Amendment's "reasonableness" requirement and was therefore valid.

When a police officer or a probation officer has reasonable suspicion that a probationer has violated one or more probation conditions, or when a search may yield evidence that a probationer has engaged in criminal activity, the Supreme Court ruled that such an officer can conduct a warrantless search of a probationer's home (*United States v. Knights*, 2001). In conclusion, when fundamental constitutional rights are limited or infringed upon by a condition of probation, the government must establish a "compelling state interest" that would justify keeping that condition; otherwise, the condition must be withdrawn.

SUMMARY

- Pretrial services consist of a pretrial release from jail and pretrial supervision of defendants as a condition of their release.

- Pretrial release can consist of either a quantitative point system (as in state and local cases) or professional subjective assessment (for the federal system) to determine risk of flight.

- The purpose of pretrial supervision is to ensure that a defendant appears in court and the public is safe while that defendant is out on bond.

- Diversion focuses on offenders who voluntarily agree to enter a contractual agreement with the courts, jail, or probation office whereby they are supervised in the community.

- Upon completion of a period of diversion supervision, an offender will not have a formal record of conviction. If an offender on diversion supervision does not comply with the conditions, a formal execution of sentence ensues.

- Granting a community sentence to an individual offender depends primarily on severity of current offense and prior criminal history. The needs of the offender, the risk the offender poses in the protection of society, and the maintenance of social order must all be carefully weighed. Balancing of the best interests of both offender and society is the crux of sentencing.

- Community values and an individual judge's philosophy of sentencing contribute to a decision. Sentencing philosophy is based on one or more of the following: retribution, incapacitation, deterrence, rehabilitation, and "just deserts."

- The use of sentencing guidelines has reduced some sentencing inequality at the expense of reducing judicial discretion to sentence on a case-by-case basis.

- The presentence investigation report is a confidential document written by a person with a social science background rather than a strictly legal background.

- The primary purpose of a presentence report is to examine and expose the factors that will mitigate for or against successful community supervision.

- Legal issues in a PSI include: an offender has an opportunity to refute information contained in the PSI, hearsay evidence is allowed, and the presentence interview does not require Miranda warnings nor the presence of an attorney.

- Supervision conditions are both standard conditions (imposed on all probationers) and special conditions (tailored to fit an offender and offense).

- Each community condition must be related to an offense, be clear and reasonable, and serve a legitimate purpose for probation.

DISCUSSION QUESTIONS

1. What kinds of individuals do you think are best suited for pretrial release?

2. What rate of failure to appear is acceptable to you? How can FTAs be further reduced?

3. How can bail be made more affordable for indigent offenders who cannot afford to bond out of jail?

4. What should be the purpose of sentencing for first-time felony offenders—rehabilitation, deterrence, incapacitation, or retribution? What about for repeat offenders?

5. Is it more important that sentences be consistent for all offenders of a similar class of crimes or that

sentences be adapted to the characteristics and needs of each offender?

6. Argue for or against the proposition that probation conditions should be left solely to the discretion of judges and should not be prescribed by law.

7. What are the limitations on the power of courts to impose conditions? Why are these limitations important?

8. Argue for or against scarlet letter conditions for a person convicted of "Driving While Intoxicated" for the first time.

9. Given the time and effort it takes to complete a PSI interview and report, is the effort worth it? Why or why not?

10. How have sentencing guidelines affected the content of a PSI report?

11. What is the purpose of a victim impact statement in a PSI report? What factors have brought about the use of this statement?

12. What factor(s) might explain why probation officers' recommendations are so highly correlated with actual sentences imposed by judges?

 ## WEBSITES, VIDEOS, AND PODCASTS

Websites

San Francisco Pretrial Diversion Project, Inc.
http://www.sfpretrial.com/community.html

Minnesota (Clay County) Pretrial Diversion Programs for Juveniles
http://www.co.clay.mn.us/Depts/Attorney/PJDivPro.htm

Louisiana (Baton Rouge) Parish Attorney Pretrial Diversion Division
http://brgov.com/dept/parishattorney/pretrial.htm

Families Against Mandatory Minimums
http://www.famm.org

Executive Summary of the Risk Assessment Used in Virginia Sentencing
http://www.ncsconline.org/WC/Publications/Res_Senten_RiskAssessExecSumPub.pdf

U.S. Sentencing Commission
http://www.ussc.gov

History of the Presentence Investigation Report
http://www.cjcj.org/files/the_history.pdf

Kansas Guidelines for the Presentence Investigation Report
http://www.Kywp.uscourts.gov/prob.html

California Court Guidelines for the Presentence Investigation Report
www.courtinfo.ca.gov/rules

Colorado Attorney Advice for Offenders Regarding the PSI
http://www.hmichaelsteinberg.com/thepresentencereport.htm

Conditions of Probation in Alaska
http://touchngo.com/lglcntr/akstats/Statutes/Title12/Chapter55/Section100.htm

Intensive Probation Conditions in Arizona
http://www.superiorcourt.maricopa.gov/AdultProbation/AdultProbationInformation/Supervision/

Terms and Conditions of Probation in Benton County, Indiana
http://www.in-map.net/counties/BENTON/probation/terms.html

Videos/Podcasts

Presentencing in Ohio
http://www.youtube.com/watch?v=O6yVkj9gf2g

This video is a brief explanation of how presentencing is used in Ohio.

Presentence investigation report discussed by DWI lawyer
http://www.youtube.com/watch?v=8-vSySwLJLs

In this video a lawyer discusses what PSI is and why it is important in court.

Federal Judicial Center presents a panel discussion of PSI issues related to two different case studies. The video is entitled: *Special Needs Offenders: Women Offenders and Their Children.*

Part 1 of *Special Needs Offenders: Women Offenders and Their Children* addresses U.S. v. Jones.
http://www.youtube.com/watch?v=yXZkfH8ypbU

Part 2 of *Special Needs Offenders: Women Offenders and Their Children* addresses U.S. v. Thomas.
http://www.youtube.com/watch?v=UDkBd1O3fuw&feature=relmfu

CASE STUDY EXERCISE NO. I

The Sentencing Decision

*The following two cases assume that a judge has granted proba-
tion. Discuss which probation conditions would be appropriate
and an appropriate length for the term of probation supervision.*

CASE A

Defendant Green devised a scheme to pass fictitious payroll
checks. He recruited other individuals to pass the fictitious checks
in exchange for money. Mr. Green opened a bank account using
a fictitious check he had produced. He then produced additional
fictitious payroll checks using the bank's logo, routing number,
and account number. He recruited individuals from homeless
shelters who had valid identification. Upon receiving checks from
Mr. Green, the individuals went to area stores to pass the fictitious payroll checks. Mr. Green gave a portion of the money to
the individual passing the check and kept the remainder. When
his residence was searched subsequent to his arrest for the offense, an electronic typewriter, 29 payroll checks matching those
previously passed, a computer, marijuana, and drug paraphernalia
lia were confiscated. Upon further examination of the computer,
evidence of payroll check counterfeiting was discovered on it.
Nine retail stores were victimized in the offense because they had
cashed the payroll checks. A total loss of $14,503 was determined
through documentation and investigation.

Mr. Green's prior criminal history includes a conviction for misdemeanor possession of marijuana and disorderly conduct. He was
raised in a two-parent home. Neither of his parents has a criminal
record, and it appears they provided their son with appropriate
structure and discipline. Mr. Green revealed he has used marijuana
for the past 12 years. He is currently 28 years of age. He has a high
school diploma and a sporadic work history. His personal finances
reveal his only asset to be an automobile valued at $4,500. He has
four credit card accounts. Two of the accounts are current with
combined balances of $670. The other two accounts are in collec-
tion status and their balances total $6,210. The defendant is eligible
for not less than one nor more than five years probation by statute.

CASE B

Police officers stopped Defendant Tuff after they observed his vehicle stopping and starting at an accelerated speed. They subsequently arrested him on several charges.

Police observed Mr. Tuff's vehicle accelerate at an unsafe
speed after stopping at a yield sign. Mr. Tuff's vehicle had come to
a stop at the yield sign, although there was no traffic requiring a
stop. Police stopped Mr. Tuff. They smelled an odor of alcohol on
Mr. Tuff, and a breath test showed he had a blood alcohol content
of 0.162. Mr. Tuff was arrested. Found on his person were a .38
caliber handgun and a small amount of marijuana. An open container of beer was inside the vehicle. Police reports reveal Mr. Tuff

became angry and violent during the arrest. He had to be placed
in restraints.

Mr. Tuff was convicted of Driving Under the Influence, Transporting an Open Container, and Carrying a Concealed Weapon.
All were misdemeanor charges. Mr. Tuff has a prior arrest for Disorderly Conduct. The prior offense involved police responding to
a disturbance at which shots had been fired. Upon arrival, officers
saw the defendant throw a pistol up onto a roof. He was chased
and appeared to be intoxicated when apprehended. Mr. Tuff told
officers he had called police because someone had shot at his
home. Mr. Tuff was irate, shouting profanities and screaming that
he was going to kill someone. When attempts to calm him were
unsuccessful, Mr. Tuff was taken into custody and charged with
Disorderly Conduct.

Defendant Tuff is 21 years of age. His parents were divorced
when he was born. At the age of six, he began living with his maternal grandparents because his mother worked nights at a tav-
ern. Mr. Tuff reports going to a Job Corps when he was 16 years
old. He was terminated early from the two-year program with the
Job Corps after assaulting a security guard for not being allowed
a pass into town. Mr. Tuff has been employed as a laborer for
three different firms. The longest term of employment in any of
the positions was eight months. He was terminated from two of
the positions due to absenteeism. He states he resigned from the
third job due to personal problems with his spouse and a dispute
with his employer over pay. Mr. Tuff completed one year of high
school before the Job Corps. He completed his GED as a condition of a previous term of probation.

Mr. Tuff states he was referred for anger management classes
when in junior high school. He acknowledged he has had prior
thoughts of suicide and on one occasion played Russian roulette.
On another occasion he tried to shoot himself in the head and
pulled the trigger; however, a friend pulled the gun away, causing
the bullet to miss him. He states he was "depressed with life" at
the time. He explains he does not currently feel a desire to commit suicide and does not desire counseling. Mr. Tuff began using
marijuana when he was in high school. He has also reported use
of crack cocaine and methamphetamine. A urine specimen submitted by him during the presentence phase revealed the use of
marijuana.

The defendant was married two years ago. He has a daughter.
The marriage lasted only a short period of time, and Mr. Tuff states
the couple has been separated for more than a year. He does
not have contact with his wife or child and is court-ordered to
pay $250 monthly in child support. His personal finances reveal
his only reported asset to be a pickup he estimates as valued at
$8,000. His only outstanding debt is $3,600 in child support owed
to the county in which his daughter resides. The defendant is eligible for not more than five years probation by statute.

CASE STUDY EXERCISE NO. 2

Sample Federal Presentence Investigation Report

Below you will find an example of a federal presentence investigation report in which all names and places are fictitious. After reading the report, you may wish to discuss the case in class or use the sample PSI to construct your own.

IN THE UNITED STATES DISTRICT COURT
FOR THE WESTERN DISTRICT OF ATLANTIS

UNITED STATES OF AMERICA)
vs.   ) PRESENTENCE INVESTIGATION REPORT)
Docket No. CR 09-002-01-KGG
Frank Jones)

Prepared for:	The Honorable Kelly G. Green
	U.S. District Judge
Prepared by:	Craig T. Doe
	U.S. Probation Officer
	Breaker Bay, Atlantis
	(123) 111-1111
Assistant U.S. Attorney	Mrs. Sharon Duncan
Defense Counsel	Mr. Arthur Goodfellow
Sentence Date:	June 5, 2009
Offense:	Count One: Tax Evasion (26 U.S.C. § 7201)
Release Status:	At liberty on a $50,000 personal recognizance bond with pretrial supervision (no pretrial custody)
Detainers:	None
Codefendants:	None
Related Cases:	Nancy Oscar CR 09-002-01; Vincent St. James CR 09-005-01
Date Report Prepared:	5/15/09
Date Revised:	5/25/09

Identifying Data:

Date of Birth:	3/19/78
Race:	White
Sex:	Male
S. S. #:	222-22-2222
FBI #:	222-22-22B
USM #:	22222-222
Education:	11th grade
Dependents:	two
Citizenship:	U.S.
Legal Address:	1430 Bird Avenue, Breaker Bay, AT 10101
Aliases:	None
Tattoos:	None
Gang Affiliation:	None known

PART A. THE OFFENSE

Charge(s) and Conviction(s)

1. Frank Jones was named in a three-count indictment filed by a Western District of Atlantis grand jury on November 1, 2008. Counts one through three charge that the defendant attempted to evade income tax due and owed by him and his wife for calendar years 2005, 2006, and 2007, in violation of 26 U.S.C. § 7201. On November 15, 2008, a superseding information was filed by the United States Attorney's Office in the Western District of Atlantis. The information charges that on October 15, 2007, Mr. Jones evaded income tax due and owed by him and his wife for the calendar year 2007 by writing a check to the American Medisearch Organization in the amount of $20,000, for which he received 90% back in cash, and by filing a false tax return in which he deducted as a charitable contribution the entire amount of $20,000, in violation of 26 U.S.C. § 7201.

2. On November 21, 2008, Mr. Jones appeared before a U.S. magistrate judge and pleaded not guilty to all of the charges. He was released after posting bond and was ordered to report to the Pretrial Services Agency. On December 1, 2008, in accordance with the terms of a written plea agreement, the defendant pleaded guilty as charged in the superseding information. The parties entered into a plea agreement per F.R.Crim.P. 11(c)(1)(A), which calls for the dismissal of the original indictment. Mr. Jones is scheduled to be sentenced on June 5, 2009.

3. According to his supervising pretrial services officer, Mr. Jones made satisfactory adjustment while under pretrial services supervision and reported as directed. Additionally, Mr. Jones maintained employment, and there were no substance-related issues with the defendant.

The Official Version

1. The American Medisearch Organization (AMO) is a not-for-profit national corporation that supervises fungus research. Across the country, the AMO derives its funds from 50 charter divisions, which are separately incorporated not-for-profit organizations. Atlantis Division, Inc. of the AMO is located in Breaker Bay, Atlantis. In late 2007 the AMO began to raise funds through an annual fall dinner-dance called Casino Night.

2. Nancy Oscar began employment with the AMO in 1999 as a field services representative. Ms. Oscar, who created the dinner-dance fund-raising event, was responsible for the fund-raising activities of the AMO. Three schemes developed from the dinner-dance, all of which were aimed at enabling various "contributors" to inflate or falsify their "charitable" donations that they would then report and deduct on personal, corporate, partnership, or private foundation federal income tax returns.

3. At the dinner-dance, which was usually held in October, guests were permitted to write checks, payable to the AMO,

to purchase gambling chips. Ten percent of the value of each check was retained by the AMO as a donation, but 90% was returned to the contributor in the form of gambling chips.

4. Although the AMO raised money from other fund-raising events, its major source of income was from the annual dinner-dance. Over the years the number of people attending the dinner-dance increased, the amount of advance check cashing increased, the amount of checks written for gambling chips increased, and the amount of money raised for the AMO increased. In 2004 the organization raised $73,000, whereas in 2007 the organization raised $360,000.

5. This scheme was in essence a check-cashing operation, allowing contributors to draw on checks to the AMO several weeks before the dinner-dance affair.

6. After the checks cleared the account, Ms. Oscar and other employees at her direction arranged for the bank to ship cash to the dinner-dance site. Ms. Oscar and some of the officers and members of the AMO then met in rooms at the dinner-dance site where they placed the cash in envelopes in amounts corresponding to 90% of the face value of the checks sent in advance of the dinner-dance by the contributors. Ms. Oscar also arranged for additional cash to be available at the dinner-dance for those members who chose to redeem their chips for cash. The scheme was able to continue and flourish not only because of the greed of the so-called contributors but also due to Ms. Oscar's bookkeeping methods.

7. In support of their income tax submissions, contributors often attached to their tax returns copies of the fraudulent checks they had written to the AMO, and during routine audits they furnished original copies of these fraudulent checks to agents of the Internal Revenue Service, thus directly or indirectly misrepresenting the full amount of the checks as charitable contributions to the AMO.

8. Over the years the number of participants in this scheme substantially increased. Although the dinner-dance attendees increased from approximately 65 in 2000 to approximately 650 in 2004, according to available records, the federal government has sought prosecution of only those contributors who participated in the various kickback schemes and filed fraudulent tax returns when the total amount of their checks written to the AMO was $30,000 or more over several years, or $20,000 in one given year. To date, the government has prosecuted Nancy Oscar, who was the organizer and creator of this scheme. She has recently pleaded guilty to a three-count indictment charging her with mail fraud, income tax evasion, and wire fraud along with five "contributors"—namely, the defendant Frank Jones together with Samuel James, Brian McDonald, Vincent St. James, and Donald Goodman. In total, the government expects to obtain indictments of approximately 37 additional contributors. Although the value of the checks written to the AMO varied from contributor to contributor, the check writers are equally culpable.

9. Frank Jones participated in this false deduction scheme involving the Atlantis division of the AMO and filed fraudulent income tax returns for the years 2005, 2006, and 2007. During each of these years Mr. Jones made contributions of $20,000,

but he received 90% of the contribution (or $18,000) back in cash or in gambling chips, some of which he gambled with but the majority of which he redeemed for cash. However, on each of his individual income tax returns, filed jointly with his wife, Mr. Jones deducted the full amount of $20,000 as a charitable contribution, even though he was only entitled to deduct $2,000 in each tax year, which represents the 10% retained by the Atlantis Medisearch Organization as a contribution.

Victim Impact Statement

The Internal Revenue Service is the victim. In each tax year of 2005, 2006, and 2007, Frank Jones deducted $20,000 as a charitable contribution from his taxable income, when in fact he was only entitled to deduct a total of $2,000 as a charitable contribution during each tax year. As a result, Mr. Jones underreported his taxable income by $54,000. According to the results of an Internal Revenue Service audit, Mr. Jones had outstanding tax liabilities, not including interest and penalties, in the amount of $27,000, which he has paid in full.

Adjustment for Defendant's Acceptance of Responsibility

1. During an interview with Internal Revenue Service agents and later during an interview with a probation officer, Mr. Jones readily admitted his involvement in this offense. He explained that he had falsely claimed the charitable deductions on his personal tax returns because everyone else who attended the dinner-dance was claiming the deductions.

2. Mr. Jones added that his involvement in this offense has had an adverse effect on his career and in retrospect he never envisioned the potential impact such wrongdoing would have on his life. He expressed feelings of both embarrassment and regret, and assumes full responsibility for his criminal conduct, as supported by his recent tax payment to the Internal Revenue Service in the amount of $27,000. Mr. Jones indicates that he will immediately pay the balance of his tax liabilities once the IRS has assessed interest and penalties.

Offense Level Computation

The 2005 edition of the *Guidelines Manual* has been used in this case.

1. **Base Offense Level:** In this offense, the total amount of evaded taxes is $27,000. According to USSG. §2T4.1(D), the base offense level for tax losses of more than $12,500 but less than $30,000 is twelve.   12

2. **Specific Offense Characteristics:** Pursuant to the provision found in USSG. §2T1.1(b)(1), since the defendant failed to report or to correctly identify the source of income exceeding $10,000 in any year from criminal activity, the offense level is increased by two levels.   +2

3. **Adjustment for Role in the Offense:** None.   0

4. **Adjusted Offense Level (Subtotal):**   14

5. **Adjustment for Acceptance of Responsibility:** The defendant has shown recognition of responsibility for his conduct and a reduction of two levels for acceptance of responsibility is applicable under USSG. §3E1.1(a).   −2

6. **Total Offense Level:**   12

PART B. THE DEFENDANT'S CRIMINAL HISTORY
Juvenile Adjudications
None

Criminal History Computation
A check with the FBI and local police authorities reveals no prior convictions for Frank Jones. Therefore, Mr. Jones has a criminal history score of zero. According to the sentencing table (chapter five, part A), 0 to 1 criminal history points establish a criminal history category of I.

PART C. OFFENDER CHARACTERISTICS
Personal and Family Data
Frank Samuel Jones was born on March 19, 1978, in Breaker Bay, Atlantis, to the union of Samuel and Patricia Jones. Mr. Jones is an only child and was raised by his parents in the Upper River section of Breaker Bay in an upper middle-class socioeconomic setting. Mr. Jones has fond memories of his developmental years, indicating that he was reared according to Roman Catholic traditions by concerned, loving parents who emphasized hard work, respect, and honesty.

The defendant's father was a partner in the Atlantis Tallow Company, a refinery and exporting company that manufactured tallow, the main ingredient in soap. When the defendant was 17 years old, his father became critically ill with tuberculosis and was not expected to recover. Mr. Jones withdrew from school and worked at his father's company. According to the defendant, his father died following a massive heart attack. While reporting a positive relationship with his father, Mr. Jones advised us that he had felt much closer to his mother, who died of natural causes at the age of 80.

Mr. Jones married Nancy Lipson Smith. This union produced two children—Frank, Jr., and Melissa, ages 13 and 15, respectively, For the past 13 years, the defendant and his family have resided at 1701 Seagull Lane, in a rather reclusive, wooded, upper-class area in Breaker Bay. A home investigation found this five-bedroom bi-level, ranch-style home to be impeccably maintained.

Mrs. Jones describes her marriage in harmonious terms and states that the defendant is a kind, considerate, and devoted husband and father. Mr. Jones, for the most part, is a private person and has suffered embarrassment as a result of the publicity in this case. The defendant's wife believes that her husband's actions "were not very well thought out," adding that "he never thinks about the impact his actions may have on his life or family." Mrs. Jones considers the defendant's conduct in this offense as an isolated incident contrary to his otherwise "law-abiding lifestyle." According to Mrs. Jones, her husband has been described by his children as a "workaholic," but he never allows himself to neglect the needs or concerns of his family.

Physical Condition
The defendant is 5'10" tall and weighs 180 pounds. He has brown eyes and slightly graying short brown hair. At our request, the defendant's private physician, John W. Brown, M.D., provided a summary of Mr. Jones' overall health, which was described as excellent and free from hospitalizations.

Mental and Emotional Health
The defendant states that he has never been seen by a psychiatrist and describes his overall mental and emotional health as good. We have no information to suggest otherwise. Mr. Jones was polite and cooperative during the presentence process and presented himself as a professional and soft-spoken businessman, voicing normal stress and concerns affiliated with pending legal difficulties.

Substance Abuse
Mr. Jones states that he rarely drinks alcohol and has never used narcotics. A urine specimen collected by the probation officer tested negative for illicit drug use.

Education and Vocational Skills
The defendant later received his GED and continued his education at Atlantis University, where he received a Bachelor of Science degree in marketing. This was confirmed by the registrar's office at Atlantis University

Employment Record
For the last five years, Mr. Jones has been employed by Greater Life Securities, Inc., in Breaker Bay, where he earns approximately $80,000 a year. Prior to that he was employed by Marshall, Jones, and LaBelle Securities. Mr. Jones also worked at his father's business for several years.

Financial Condition: Ability to Pay
A review of the defendant's amended personal income tax returns for 2005 through 2007 (which now reflect the $57,000 in additional income previously reported as charitable deductions) reveals that he earned approximately $121,000 adjusted gross income.

Equity in Other Assets: 1701 Seagull Lane, Breaker Bay, Atlantis (family residence), $ 280,000

Unsecured Debts: Auto Loan, $17,000; Credit cards, −$ 3,000
Monthly Cash Flow: $4,500

Based on the defendant's financial condition, he has the ability to pay a fine within the guideline range.

PART D. SENTENCING OPTIONS
Guideline Provisions: Based on an offense level of 12 and a criminal history category of I, the guideline range of imprisonment is 10 to 16 months.

Statutory Provisions: The defendant is eligible for a term of probation in this offense, pursuant to 18 U.S.C. § 3561(a). The authorized term for a felony is not less than one nor more than five years, pursuant to 18 U.S.C. § 3561(c)(1).

Impact of Plea Agreement
Under the plea agreement, Mr. Jones has entered a plea to one count of tax evasion, in return for the dismissal of two other tax evasion counts.

Fine
According to USSG §5E1.2(c)(3), the minimum fine for this offense is $3,000 and the maximum fine for this offense is $30,000.

Restitution

Pursuant to 18 U.S.C. § 3663, restitution may be ordered. In this case, the $57,000 + interest and penalties = $62,500 are outstanding to the Internal Revenue Service, and can be forwarded to the following address:

Internal Revenue Service

Attention: Mr. Sam Claim

111 IRS Tower

Breaker Bay, Atlantis 11111

In accordance with the provisions of USSG §5E1.1, restitution of $62,500 shall be ordered.

PART E: FACTORS THAT MAY WARRANT DEPARTURE

The probation officer has no information concerning the offense or the offender that would warrant a departure from the prescribed sentencing guidelines.

PART F: SENTENCING RECOMMENDATION
U.S. DISTRICT COURT FOR THE WESTERN DISTRICT OF ATLANTIS
DOCKET. # CR 05-002-01-KGG

Total Offense Level	**12**
Criminal History Category: I	

Frank Jones is a successful businessman who appears to be a situational offender, having been motivated by opportunistic greed. Although his acceptance of responsibility and remorse are reflected in the guideline calculation, a sentence within the guideline range is recommended. As such, a split sentence of five months in a federal community correctional facility followed by five months of home confinement as a condition of supervised release is the recommended sentence in order to reflect the seriousness of the defendant's conduct and to provide just punishment. The defendant earns a considerable income and is employed with a reputable commodities firm. In view of Mr. Jones' financial profile, restitution of $62,500 and a fine of $20,000 in addition to the $100 penalty assessment are also recommended to be paid immediately. Inasmuch as he does not appear to pose a risk to the community nor to be in need of correctional treatment, the minimum term of supervised release of two years will be sufficient. Since the defendant will owe interest and penalties to the Internal Revenue Service as soon as they are calculated, it is recommended that collection of these monies be a condition of supervised release. A restriction against incurring any new debts until the criminal sanctions are paid is an additional recommended condition. Disclosure of financial information is also recommended. As this is a felony conviction, Mr. Jones must submit to DNA testing. Within 72 hours of sentencing, the defendant shall report in person to the Atlantis Federal Community Corrections Center, 123 Willow Lane. While on supervised release the defendant shall not commit any federal, state, or local crimes, and he shall be prohibited from possessing a firearm or other dangerous device. The defendant shall not possess a controlled substance, and he shall comply with the standard conditions of supervised release as recommended by the United States Sentencing Commission.

Respectfully submitted,

Craig T. Doe

U.S. Probation Officer

Instructions on How to Conduct a Presentence Interview and Write a Presentence Investigation Report

Create a client named Sue Steel OR your instructor can create a mock interview in which the class interviews a client named Sue Steel. The 10-part section below is a bit different from that of the federal PSI, but it includes all the necessary information that you would find representing a state-level PSI.

Before the PSI Interview

You can prepare your own questions to ask the client or use the sample assessment interview at the back of chapter 5. Read the instructions on how to complete and score the interview questions. Most of the questions you'll need to complete the PSI are already addressed, except for:

"How many times have you moved around in the last 12 months?"

"What percentage of the time have you been employed in the last 12 months?"

Tips on Conducting a Presentence Interview

You have one class period to ask questions of the defendant. The goal of a PSI is to gain a breadth of information from the defendant on behalf of the judge. To meet this goal, here are five tips:

1. Ask questions in a clear and objective way—you may need to restate a question if the defendant does not understand jargon or certain words.
2. Avoid showing bias or judgment about the defendant's responses. Your job is to get the defendant's point of view—not to point fingers, criticize, nor to seek what you think is the truth.
3. Pay attention to your own emotions and/or reactions and try not to let those show—that is the mark of a true professional.
4. If the defendant provides a response that you question or if the response directly conflicts with other information you already have, make note of this difference (e.g., the defendant self-reports that he is not in a gang, but PO notices that defendant had a tattoo on his forearm that "seems to resemble a tattoo of the Mexican Mafia or that is commonly thought of as a gang tattoo."). Document both of these differences in your PSI.
5. For every section of your PSI, make note of the information SOURCE—it will be primarily an *official report* (arrest/conviction data), a *self-report* (from the defendant), or a *collateral report* (from a third party other than the defendant).

After the Presentence Interview, Complete the PSI Report

Use the interview of the defendant, along with the following information, to assemble the PSI report: the arrest report, prosecutor information, criminal background check, and interviews with victims, witnesses, and others who know the defendant (collateral interviews).

Construct the PSI in outline or bulleted format using the same 10-part headings and subheadings—*the more detailed and complete, the better*. Be sure to include everything asked for and include HOW you received the information (e.g., Self-report during the PSI interview? Official records? Collateral interview? Your direct observations?). If information is not readily available for an area, you need to say so—do not leave blank.

PSI Format

TO: Judge Name (Your instructor)
FROM: Probation Officer Name (Your name)
RE: Defendant's Name, Case Numbers

1. Defendant's Personal Characteristics
   - Name and aliases
   - Case numbers
   - Gender
   - Date of birth
   - Education level
   - Employment history and skills
   - Vocational skills
   - Military service
   - Mental health history (any psychotropic medications?)
   - Physical health (major illnesses, current prescription meds)
   - Drug history, dependency, and/or current addiction
   - Known gang affiliation
2. Current Offense
   - Facts of the crime from the police report
   - Initial charge(s) and final plea agreement or conviction(s)
   - Defendant's version of the offense and circumstances leading up to it
   - Accomplices and/or role in current offense
   - Defendant's acceptance of responsibility for crime
   - Level of cooperation or terms of the agreement upon which a plea of guilty was based
3. Defendant's Prior Criminal History
   - Juvenile adjudications (case numbers, offense type, dates, and dispositions)
   - Adult diversions or convictions (case numbers, offense type, dates, and dispositions)
   - Previous time spent in custody
   - Pending charges or outstanding warrants
4. Family History and Background
   - Family of origin (parents, upbringing, siblings)
   - Criminal history of family members
   - Marital status (evidence of domestic violence or abuse?)
   - Dependent children
   - Current family ties and responsibilities (e.g., child support?)
   - Stable living arrangements

5. Victim Impact Statement: Use the victim impact statement and the collateral interviews provided (verbatim) in this book OR (if your instructor says) contact victims and request statements or interviews.
   - Any statements made by the victim to police or the probation officer
   - The type of harm done to the victim as a result of the offense (physical, emotional, psychological, financial, property)
   - The monetary amount of the victim's loss
6. Collateral Information from People Who Knew the Defendant
   - Former employers
   - Former educators and teachers
   - Former probation or parole officers
   - Former neighbors
   - Interviews with family members
7. Fines and Restitution: Use the victim impact statement to estimate loss and use the defendant's monthly bills and/or what he or she makes in wages to estimate what could be paid each month.
   - Mandatory and recommended restitution and/or fines to be assessed against the defendant
   - Defendant's ability to pay restitution and fines
   - Does defendant have any other debts (credit card debt, auto loans, mortgage, etc.)?
8. Determinate Sentencing Options
   - *Using Figure 4.3 (North Carolina sentencing grid):* Figure the prior criminal history score. Then figure the presumptive sentence for EACH charge separately. State the *sentencing type* (jail/prison, CC [community corrections], or probation) and what is most suitable for this defendant.
   - *Using Figure 4.3 (North Carolina sentencing grid):* Decide whether there are mitigating or aggravating circumstances that warrant departure from the presumptive sentence. In other words, are there any situations, characteristics of the defendant, or things you want the judge to know about prior to sentencing to either mitigate (go easier) or aggravate (go tougher) what the sentencing grid says (in your part 8)?
9. Indeterminate Sentencing Options
   - *Using Figure 4.4 (the indeterminate sentencing table):* Figure the client's sentence and compare with your results from the North Carolina sentencing grid.
10. Summary Sentencing Recommendation to the Court
   - Summarize the main points from Sections 1–9. Do not present any new information—just the highlights should be used as a justification.

ENCLOSED DOCUMENTS YOU WILL NEED TO COMPLETE THE PSI:

Police Arrest Report:

Officer Briggs responded to a disturbance call at JC Penney at Anytown Mall at 3:15 PM on April 12, 2011. The call was placed by Mall Security Officer Washington at 2:53 PM. Officer Briggs interviewed the JC Penney clerk who had notified mall security. The clerk said that Defendant Steel became agitated and irate because the clerk refused to accept her check without proper identification. As Steel angrily tried to leave the mall, she was approached for questioning by private security. One of the private security officers happened to notice a "shiny metal object" in her waistband that appeared to be a weapon of some sort. Private security conducted a frisk and recovered a .38 caliber weapon from her waistband and a book of checks for "Lisa L. Griswald" when she was arrested. Private security detained Steel at the mall until police arrived. Defendant booked in county jail at 4:25 PM.

Officer Briggs phoned the bank and the victim. Bank research conducted the next business day on this account revealed that four checks were written to retail stores that totaled $975 over a period of three days. The signature of all four checks did not match the signature on file at the bank. The four checks were written out of order—in different numerical sequence from the rest of the checks in the account.

Victim Lisa Griswald confirms never receiving said checks in the mail, and confirms that she did not write these checks nor authorize anyone else to sign checks on her account.

NCIC Criminal Background Check

NAME: Steel   Sue   M.   White   Female
DOB: 01/05/85   SS# 123-45-6789   FBI: 98765US43
Aliases: Harris, Cherlyn   DOB: 6/30/85
             Steel, Suzanne   DOB: 3/20/81
1679   S. Madison   Anytown, TX 78999
Prints on file
Finger Print Class: PO   PI   09   CO   18
                              15   PM   12   23   19
Adult Arrest Record:
2010 MISD 123—Theft by Deception. Bench warrant issued.
2008CV 5967422496—Credit Card Abuse. Disposition unknown.
2004CV 283845067—Simple Felony Fraud. Probation completed after 14 months.
Juvenile Arrest Record:
2002JV 16412345—Juvenile records sealed.

Information from the Prosecutor

The prosecutor has reviewed the case and has decided that enough evidence exists in the police report to charge Defendant Steel with two felonies, and those felonies fall under the North Carolina Sentencing Grid:

Forgery   Class "I" Felony   Case #: 2011CV 993564
(pled down from a Class "H" felony)
Unlawful Carrying of a Firearm During Commission of a Felony
                    Class "G" Felony   Case #: 2011CV 993565

Court Fee Schedule

Fees that the offender might be asked to pay, depending on the sentence imposed:

$40–$75 per month	Outpatient Treatment (assuming once per week)
$60 per month	Probation
$400 per month	Residential Community Corrections Facility (work release or halfway house)
No charge	Inpatient Substance Abuse Treatment
$8 per test	Drug and/or Alcohol Tests (urinalysis)

$75 per session	Diagnostic Testing (severity of mental illness, substance abuse)
$15 per month	Electronic Monitoring (radio frequency land-line)
$100 per month	Electronic Monitoring (global positioning system)

Fines (Court Costs)

$40 per offense	General State Victim Compensation Fund
$100–$500	Court Operations (depending on complexity of investigations and hearings)
$20 per sample	Provide a DNA Sample

Victim Impact Statement

Lisa Griswald made the following statement to the prosecutor: "Ms. Steel is a neighbor that lives down my street. I have said "hi" to her once or twice but never expected that she would be the kind of person to do anything like this. I was just shocked when the police called me. Although the Bank knows that I didn't write the checks, my checking account is still short $975.00 which is a lot of money for me to lose in one month. That is nearly all I have—now I am unable to cover my rent and pay my utility bills. I may be able to work something out with some of the companies under the circumstances, but I am not sure if my landlord will go for it. If I could just get my money back, that's all I want. I don't know what I'm going to do."

Interview with former employers:

Mrs. Juanita Medina, the defendant's most recent employer, was contacted by phone to verify that Sue Steel was employed at a janitorial service cleaning office buildings. Steel worked at this firm prior to detention in this case. Mrs. Medina was willing to re-hire Steel upon her release from custody because her "work habits were good." Her employer is aware of her conviction and supervision. No other job history could be verified.

Interview with neighbors:

One neighbor, who wishes to remain anonymous, says he remembered the defendant as "quiet and kept to herself."

Interviews with family members:

Defendant's sister (Mary Sparks) has one child of her own and has agreed for Steel to reside with her if Steel is granted community supervision. The home was checked, and it seems to be acceptable and close to a bus route. Defendant Steel has one dependent child, who is currently in the temporary custody of her mother. Steel's mother could not be reached despite repeated calls. Defendant's father is reportedly deceased.

5

Classification and Supervision

CHAPTER LEARNING OBJECTIVES

1. Identify the importance of caseload classification in identifying risk and needs.
2. Describe classification techniques that lead to defining the level of supervision and development of a treatment plan.
3. List the principles of effective correctional intervention in offender treatment.
4. Recall how workload allocation is important to keep caseloads manageable.
5. Explain how neighborhood-based supervision probation officers are involved with a community.
6. Understand how offenders are supervised when they want to go to a different jurisdiction than where a crime was committed.

Snoop Dogg can rest more easily now, knowing that he successfully completed probation in 2011.

CHAPTER OUTLINE

KEY TERMS

classification
risk assessment
static factors
dynamic factors
supervision
surveillance

field contact
caseload
principles of effective intervention
cognitive-behavioral therapy
motivational interviewing
chronos

Interstate Compact
sending state
receiving state
Interstate Compact for Adult
    Offender Supervision

In 2011, hip-hop artist Snoop Dogg is finally off paper—having successfully completed over four years on probation. Snoop was released from supervision nearly one year early for good behavior. The probation sentence stemmed from a 2006 arrest at a California airport passenger pick-up zone for suspicion of transporting marijuana and possession of a weapon. A firearm was later found in a separate search at his home. While on probation, Snoop Dogg was required to complete 800 hours of community service, of which half of those hours involved a youth football league he started (Morgan, 2011). Prior to this charge, Snoop Dogg was convicted in 1990 of possession of cocaine, for which he served three years on probation. Six years later, he was acquitted of murder after an alleged street-gang member was killed by gunfire from the same vehicle in which Snoop Dogg was riding.

INTRODUCTION

Probation departments provide both an investigatory and a supervisory function in the criminal justice system. Earlier we addressed the presentence investigatory function, and in this chapter we discuss the classification and supervisory functions of post-sentence probation and parole officers. Much of this chapter applies to both probation and parole supervision insofar as the mechanics of the supervision process and the conditions are similar. In many states and in the federal system, officers supervise a mix of both probationers and parolees on the same caseload. Community officers are involved in the following evidence-based correctional practices (EBP) to improve the supervision of offenders: classification assessments, case planning, motivational interviewing, cognitive-behavioral treatments, and correctional intervention principles.

CLASSIFICATION: THE FIRST STEP IN SUPERVISION

classification
A procedure consisting of assessing the risks posed by the offender, identifying the supervision issues, and selecting the appropriate supervision strategy.

Each new client under community supervision must first be classified. **Classification** consists of the use of an objective assessment scale by a supervising officer to compute the risks posed by an offender, identification of offender needs requiring intervention, and selection of appropriate supervision and treatment strategies. Research indicates that objective actuarial prediction models, if used by a trained officer, are more reliable and efficient than subjective methods. The highest priority is placed on identifying risks that would likely jeopardize public safety if not addressed. Risk variables also determine the level of supervision required by an offender. At the same time, a priority is placed on identifying needs that, if not addressed, will likely lead to a return to criminal behavior (Lowenkamp, Latessa, & Holsinger, 2006).

Risk Assessments

risk assessment
A procedure that provides a measure of the offender's propensity to further criminal activity and indicates the level of officer intervention that will be required.

Risk assessment provides a measure of a probationer's or parolee's propensity for violence (Davies & Dedel, 2006) and dangers to the public as well as propensity to engage in future criminal activity. The earliest assessments relied on interviewing an offender and using case-by-case anecdotal information to make decisions. Although professional judgment and intuition can be accurate, questions were inconsistent and comparisons among cases were difficult.

Probation and parole jurisdictions developed some form of risk prediction scale to assist them in supervision planning and in caseload classification. These

© Andrew Ramey/PhotoEdit

The foundation of supervision is getting into the field to meet with clients in their own neighborhoods.

instruments differ in some respects, but all of them group offenders according to known statistical probability of committing new crimes or of violating the conditions of supervision. Some of these instruments include the Wisconsin Risk Assessment, the Correctional Offender Management Profiles for Alternative Sentences (COMPAS), the Salient Factor Score (developed for the federal system), and the Risk Management System (Dow, Jones, & Mott, 2005). The better assessments seem to include both static and dynamic factors. **Static** factors are variables that have already occurred in the past and will not change, such as number of arrests and convictions. **Dynamic** factors, on the other hand, are variables that do change and are the most valuable in measuring both negative and positive offender change over time. Dynamic factors include family relations, friendships, emotional health, housing situation, leisure activities, and financial situation.

Given that the purpose of a risk assessment instrument is to differentiate offenders by low, medium, and high risk, a good assessment instrument can correctly do this significantly better than chance. The Wisconsin Risk Assessment instrument has been criticized as classifying 80% of offenders as high risk (Eisenberg, Bryl, & Fabelo, 2009), whereas the Risk Management System has the opposite problem: It seems to identify too many offenders as low risk (Shaffer et al., 2011). Two different instruments, the Ohio Risk Assessment System (Latessa et al., 2010), and the Level of Service Inventory-Revised (LSI-R) seem better able to distinguish levels of risk.

The LSI-R is a 54-item scale that assigns a numerical value to many of the same factors identified in a presentence report. An officer completes the LSI-R by interviewing an offender and scoring one point for every affirmative answer. The LSI-R has been validated for use with male and female adult offenders and some juvenile offender populations (Manchak, Skeem, Douglas, & Siranosian, 2009; Vose, Lowenkamp, Smith & Cullen, 2009). The risk score of the LSI-R can accurately predict future criminal activity to the extent that the higher a risk score, the more likely an offender will recidivate (Lowenkamp & Bechtel, 2007). For this reason, high-risk offenders should receive the bulk of treatment services to counteract that risk. A meta-analysis of 47 different studies of the LSI-R shows that it accurately targets high-risk clients who are at greatest need of intervention, but that it more accurately predicts adult men and is less accurate at predicting recidivism for female offenders (Vose, Cullen, & Smith, 2008). There is a fourth generation risk and needs assessment called the LSI Case Management Inventory that integrates assessment with case planning (VanBenschoten, 2008) to better link risk and needs to a treatment plan.

No matter whether programs were treatment-oriented or supervision-oriented, mixing low-risk offenders with high-risk offenders in the same program *increased* recidivism later. These findings have led to is the idea that the most intensive treatment programs should be reserved for the highest-risk offenders, in part because this target population will benefit exponentially more from intervention than will low-risk offenders (Hanley, 2002). Figure 5.1 shows a typical risk and needs assessment.

Identifying Treatment Needs

An officer must also identify those characteristics, conditions, or behavioral problems that limit an offender's motivation or that might lead to a return to criminal behavior. Such treatment needs include drug or alcohol abuse, mental illness, anger management issues, and deficiencies in education and vocational skills. Treatment activities are defined as actions taken by a supervising officer intended to bring about a change in an offender's conduct or condition for the purpose of rehabilitation and reintegration into a law-abiding community. Together both risk and needs

static factors
Correlates of the likelihood of recidivism that (once they occur) cannot be changed (age at first arrest, number of convictions, and so forth).

dynamic factors
Correlates of the likelihood of recidivism that can be changed through treatment and rehabilitation (drug and alcohol abuse, anger management, quality of family relationships, and so forth).

FIGURE 5.1

RISK ASSESSMENT

Defendant:_____   DATE:_____

Enter one number for each question on the corresponding line to the right of that question that best describes this defendant

Q1. Number of address changes in the last 12 months.................
- **0** None
- **2** One
- **3** Two or More

Risk Score

_____ Q1

Q2. Percentage of time employed in the last 12 months..............
(If not working because of disability, score N/A)
- **0** 60%–100% (or disabled)
- **1** 40%–59%
- **2** Under 40%

_____ Q2

Q3. Is alcohol usage related to criminal activity?.........................
- **0** Alcohol use unrelated to activity (no evidence of use during offense).
- **1** <u>Probable</u> relationship
- **2** <u>Definite</u> relationship/pattern of committing offenses while using alcohol

_____ Q3

Q4. Is drug use related to criminal activity?.......................... ....
- **0** No use or abuse of drugs
- **1** <u>Probable</u> relationship.
- **2** <u>Definite</u> relationship/pattern of offenses while using drugs, sale or manufacture of illegal drugs.

_____ Q4

Q5. Attitude/Motivation...
- **0** Motivated to change; receptive to assistance
- **2** Somewhat motivated but dependent or unwilling to accept responsibility
- **5** Not motivated to change.

_____ Q5

Q6. Age at first adjudication of guilt...
- **0** 24 or older
- **1** 20–23 yrs
- **2** 19 yrs or younger

_____ Q6

Q7. Number of prior periods of probation / Parole supervision......
(as an adult or juvenile)
- **0** None
- **4** One or more

_____ Q7

Q8. Number of prior Probation / Parole <u>revocations</u>....................
(adult or juvenile)
- **0** None
- **4** One or more

_____ Q8

Q9. Number of prior <u>felony</u> adjudications of guilt........................
(include all juvenile commitments and deferrals)
- **0** None
- **2** One
- **4** Two or more

_____ Q9

Q10. Adult or juvenile adjudications for....................................
(Select applicable answer and add for score Robbery include current offense, <u>Maximum score: 5</u>)
- **0** None
- **2** Burglary, Theft, Auto Theft or
- **3** Worthless Checks or Forgery

_____ Q10

Q11. Adult or juvenile adjudications for....................................
Assaultive offense within the last FIVE years (one that involves use of a weapon, physical force, or the threat of force)
- **0** No
- **8** Yes

_____ Q11

SUM Questions 1–11: _____

Circle one RISK Level based on the SUM of questions 1-11:

Minimum Risk   0–11
Medium Risk   12–24
Maximum Risk   25–40

(Continues)

FIGURE 5.1 (*Continued*)

NEEDS ASSESSMENT

Defendant:_____   DATE:_____

Enter one number for each question on the corresponding line to the right of that question that best describes this defendant. Please note that all numbers in the first column are negative and are subtracted from the total.

Q1. ACADEMIC/VOCATIONAL SKILLS

−1 High school or above skill level   0 Adequate skills, able to handle everyday requirements   +2 Low level causing minor adjustment problems   +4 Minimal skill level causing erious adjustment problems   _____ Q1

Q2. EMPLOYMENT

−1 Satisfactory employment for one year or longer   0 No difficulties reported; or homemaker, student or retired   +3 Unsatisfactory employment or unemployed but has adequate job skills   +6 Unemployed; needs training   _____ Q2

Q3. FINANCIAL MANAGEMENT

−1 Long-standing pattern of self-sufficiency e.g., good credit   0 No current difficulties   +3 Situational monetary difficulties   +5 Severe difficulties; may include overdrafts, bad checks or bankruptcy   _____ Q3

Q4. MARITAL/FAMILY RELATIONSHIPS

−1 Relationships and support exceptionally strong   0 Relatively stable relationship   +3 Some disorganization or stress but potential for improvement   +5 Major disorganization or stress   _____ Q4

Q5. COMPANIONS

−1 Good support and influence   0 No adverse relationships   +2 Associations with occasional negative results   +4 Associations almost completely negative   _____ Q5

Q6. EMOTIONAL STABILITY/MENTALLY ILL

−2 Exceptionally well adjusted;   0 No symptoms of emotional instability; appropriate emotional responses   +4 Some emotional instability e.g. anxiety, depression   +7 Mentally ill; needs meds e.g., lashes out or retreats into self   _____ Q6

Q7. ALCOHOL USAGE PROBLEM

0 No use; use with no abuse no disruption of functioning   +3 Occasional abuse; some disruption of functioning   +6 Frequent abuse; serious disruption of functioning   _____ Q7

Q8. OTHER DRUG USAGE PROBLEM

0 No disruption of functioning   +3 Occasional abuse; some disruption of functioning   +5 Frequent abuse; serious disruption of functioning   _____ Q8

Q9. ABILITY TO FUNCTION INDEPENDENTLY

0 Able to function independently   +3 Some need for assistance; Recommend assessment   +6 Deficiencies severely limit independent functioning; Disability   _____ Q9

Q10. PHYSICAL HEALTH

0 Sound physical health; seldom ill   +1 Illness interferes with some functioning   +2 Serious handicap or chronic illness; needs frequent medical care   _____ Q10

Q11. SEXUAL BEHAVIOR (Victim of sexual abuse, evidence of prostitution, etc.)

0 No apparent dysfunction   +3 Real or perceived situational or minor problems   +5 Chronic or severe problems needing treatment   _____ Q11

Sum of Questions 1–11: _____

Circle one NEEDS level based on the SUM of questions 1–12

Minimum Needs   0–14
Medium Needs   15–29
Maximum Needs   30 and above

assessments can (and should) define the types of correctional services that are made available to offenders (Andrews, Bonta, & Wormith, 2006).

Sources of information that can be used to identify treatment needs include a presentence report, prison disciplinary records, a prerelease plan, physical or medical health evaluations, records of drug or alcohol abuse and other related criminal conduct, financial history, and residential history. Because federal PSIs are so detailed, they capture most of the information in the risk and needs assessment of the LSI-R. In these cases, case managers use the LSI-R to gauge honesty (or consistency) by comparing client responses to the PSI and the LSI-R. The importance of carefully gathering and evaluating an offender's history cannot be overstated, for past behavior is at present the best predictor we have of future behavior. Box 5.1 provides examples of questions that are important during an initial client interview.

THE SUPERVISION CASE PLAN

After reviewing court-ordered conditions of probation, assessing an offender's risk by calculating a risk score, and determining treatment concerns, an officer identifies specific supervision issues and selects appropriate strategies for addressing them (Storm, 1997). In other words, an officer develops a case plan, which is an individualized written document that clarifies how each court-ordered condition is to be fulfilled by offender and supervising officer in the context of the risks and needs posed. A case plan is negotiated and signed by both parties. Progress on the case plan is reviewed during each appointment and can be modified as circumstances change.

A **supervision** issue is an identified problem, offender characteristic, or pattern of conduct that requires intervention to overcome or change. An issue is identified

supervision
The oversight that a probation or parole officer exercises over those in his or her custody.

Case management involves a balance between helping offenders get through their supervision, and communicating consequences of their actions.

© Spencer Grant/Stock, Boston Inc.

BOX 5.1   SAMPLE COMMUNITY SUPERVISION INTAKE INTERVIEW

- Full name, including any aliases
- Address/phone/e-mail
- Number of address changes in the past year
- Religious denomination preference
- Are you a military veteran?

Current/Instant Offense

- What was/were your offense(s) of conviction?
- What is the length of your sentence? Is it deferred or regular?

Prior Record

- Do you have a juvenile record?
- How old were you at the time of your first offense?
- What previous convictions do you have on your adult record?
- Do you have any pending charges or court dates?

Education and Training

- What is your education level?
- Did you finish high school? If not, do you have a GED?
- Do you have any certificates or special vocational training?

Employment

- What was your last job? Rate of pay? Reason for leaving?
- What was your longest period of employment?
- What was your longest period of unemployment?

Marital Status and Children

- Have you ever been married? Legally married or common law? To whom?
- Names/ages/father or mother of children?
- Do you retain custody? If not, who does?

- With whom do your children live?
- Are your children involved with juvenile probation or protective services?

Family of Origin

- Describe your relationship with your parents/in-laws/siblings.
- Do you have other relatives involved with the criminal justice system?

Finances

- Describe your credit history/finances/current debts.
- Are you receiving Aid to Families with Dependent Children/food stamps/social security/Medicare/child support?

Medical and Mental Health

- Do you have a history of medical conditions (including pregnancies, surgeries, miscarriages, and abortions)?
- Are you having any medical problems right now?
- Are you taking any medications?
- Have you ever experimented with any illegal drugs?
- When was the last time you used any illegal drug? What was it and how often?
- Do you use alcohol? How recently? How often?
- Did you ever seek treatment for substance abuse?
- Have you ever suffered from depression?
- Have you ever tried to commit suicide? Were you hospitalized?
- Have you ever sought mental health treatment or been diagnosed with a mental illness?
- Have you ever been physically or sexually abused or involved in an abusive relationship?
- Have you ever received treatment or rehabilitation for anything else? If so, for what?

and an officer develops strategies to deal with or monitor that issue. Interviewing an offender can be done using a structured assessment interview, which can be found at the back of this chapter following the case study. The interview contains 55 questions to ask an offender. The risk and needs assessments and the interview are used to identify strengths and weaknesses of various life issues. The weaknesses are linked to the current offense or else have occurred so often that they are serious problems that need to be changed or addressed. Implementation of this case plan occurs through surveillance and the development of prosocial behaviors.

Implementing the Case Plan: Surveillance

surveillance
Community monitoring methods of ascertaining offender compliance through one or more of the following means: face-to-face home visits, curfew, electronic monitoring, phone verification, and drug testing.

field contact
An officer's personal visit to an offender's home or place of employment for the purpose of monitoring progress under supervision.

Surveillance is an important element of supervision that provides a means of ascertaining whether probationers and parolees are continuing to meet the conditions imposed by a court or parole board. Surveillance can be a good tool for reducing an offender's access to crime opportunities (Cullen, Eck, & Lowenkamp. 2002). The most common form of surveillance is maintaining contact through face-to-face meetings with each client in an office setting. Offenders also check in through phone and/or mail verification. A **field contact** is considered to be the most time consuming but is also the most valuable type of contact. In a field contact, an officer visits an offender's home or place of employment to monitor progress.

On a quarterly basis, supervision officers make at least one collateral contact, which means that an officer contacts employers, teachers, and/or relatives to verify that each offender is adhering to probation conditions. Few offices, however, specify the quality of the contact. Other ways that probationers have to contact their probation officer include kiosk machines in the community (see Box 5.2).

Methods of surveillance include unannounced and announced home visits, curfew, electronic monitoring, and collection of urine samples for drug testing (Taxman, 2002).

In addition to surveillance by probation officers, police watch probationers and parolees and can conduct warrantless searches of probationers' homes based on a "reasonable suspicion" of criminal activity (*United States v. Knights,* 2001). Reasonable

---

BOX 5.2   TECHNOLOGY IN CORRECTIONS

Virtual and Mobile Community Supervision Techniques

Technological advances have enabled community supervision officers to rethink day-to-day supervision methods. In the past officers used to spend most of their day in their offices responding to calls and receiving visits from probationers. Now technology has afforded low-risk probationers an opportunity to check in with their officers using centrally located kiosk machines. A kiosk machine has an interactive, computerized touch screen that allows offenders on probation or parole to receive and send personal messages back and forth to their supervising officer at any time of day. The machine can be set up anywhere that is monitored, such as in a lobby of a police station or in a grocery store that is open 24 hours a day. Each probationer's password to a touch screen is his or her fingerprints. Offenders can use kiosk machines to notify their probation officer of a change of address or employment and be asked questions in turn, to which they can type a response. Kiosks also store information on bus routes, job postings, and schedules for services such as treatment programs, employment offices, and driver's license bureaus. In some jurisdictions, kiosks have replaced face-to-face meetings.

For offenders in remote areas or probationers who cannot afford telephones, special pagers are provided in lieu of a kiosk that allow a supervision officer to beep a client with a directive, such as to call the officer immediately or to submit a urine sample within a designated period of time. Clients do not know the number to their personal pagers, so no one else can beep them with personal calls.

With less time spent on low-risk clients, probation and parole officers can then spend more time out in the field meeting their higher-risk clients in person. To document their visits while in the field, probation officers carry a portable office that consists of a cell phone, pager, and laptop computer. Some jurisdictions have already replaced laptop computers with tablet PCs, Blackberrys, or PDAs equipped with wireless Internet capabilities. All of these devices are handheld so they are lightweight and allow an officer mobility. Most tablet PCs have either a handwriting or voice recognition feature, so there is no keyboard. Internet access allows officers to retrieve GPS coordinates of offenders, retrieve client information from protected databases, and check public record databases through SmartLinx with the same level of security they enjoy at their physical office.

suspicion is a lower standard of proof than "probable cause," which is needed for most residence searches. However, the U.S. Supreme Court has held that a probationer has a diminished expectation of privacy while on probation and is more likely to violate the law than a citizen not on probation. Public support and cooperation are difficult to obtain for any probation or parole system that does not assure a community of at least minimum protection against potential criminal activities by those under supervision.

Levels of Supervision

One of the principles of effective supervision entails developing various levels of supervision to differentiate offenders who need closer supervision from those who require less. Although various names are used, there are typically three or four levels of supervision. A three-level supervision refers to maximum, medium, and minimum supervision, while a four-level probation system like that found in Table 5.1 refers to maximum (sex offenders), high, standard, and administrative supervision.

At the lowest level of supervision, there may be no requirement that a probationer personally visit or contact a probation officer. Rather, the probationer may be required to call in and leave a message on a voice-recorded line, or mail-in a verification of address and employment. This level of supervision is known as *administrative supervision* and in California as *banked probation*. Over 60% of all Los Angeles probationers were tracked solely by computer and had no contact with an officer. Administrative probation is for offenders who have committed minor crimes, who have satisfied their financial obligations, or have been in compliance for two years and can be transferred down to this level.

Regular or standard probation supervision includes a wide variety of contact types. For example, Offender A on medium supervision may expect two face-to-face contacts per month and verification of residence and employment once every 12 months. Offender B on medium supervision may only have one quarterly face-to-face contact but weekly mail-in and quarterly home visits. The frequency and intensity of contacts increase with the supervision level, such that an offender on the highest level can expect one weekly face-to-face or field contact, one monthly collateral contact, verification of residence and employment every three months, and a criminal history check every 12 months.

Caseload and Workload Standards

Central to the enactment of evidence-based practices is handling a manageable caseload. A **caseload** is defined as the number of individuals or cases one probation or parole officer can supervise effectively. In practice, caseloads vary widely because

caseload
The number of individuals or cases for which one probation or parole officer is responsible.

TABLE 5.1 Differences for Each Supervision Level

Supervision Level	Minimum Monthly Contacts	Maximum Caseload Cap	Percent on Each Level
Max	4	40	3.3%
High	2	80	8.3%
Standard	1	250	46.5%
Administrative	0	No Cap	41.8%

Source: Georgia Department of Corrections. 2009. Retrieved from: http://www.dcor.state.ga.us/

Reporting kiosks, such as this one in New York, are more common in public areas or in police stations to allow non–violent and low-risk offenders the convenience of checking in with their probation officer.

© Joel Gordon

not every offender requires the same amount of supervision. The more intensive the supervision, the lower the caseload number. U.S. probation officers supervise 50 to 60 cases and conduct five or six presentence investigations per month, so they are involved in both supervision and investigation (Quinn, 2002). For stand-alone local probation departments in which an investigation function is separated from a supervision function, the average caseload of regular probationers consists of 127 adults, with a high of 239 in Rhode Island. In contrast, a single caseload of parolees on regular supervision consists of 70 per officer. Intensive supervision probation and parole caseloads average 18 to 29 offenders, and offenders with special needs average 35 to 55 offenders per officer nationwide (Camp, Camp, & May, 2003).

It appears that concerns about increased caseload size have led some states to place statutory limits on the number of people that one officer should supervise. For example, the New Jersey Supreme Court limited specialized (or maximum level) caseloads to no more than 50 offenders per officer, but placed no limits on standard supervision. In contrast, Maryland does not cap any caseloads, so the state can (in theory) continue to increase the number of offenders supervised.

The American Probation and Parole Association has long recommended a "workload standard" of about 120 hours per month. The workload standard is more accurate, particularly if an officer supervises offenders of varying levels. Workload is calculated by first assuming the number of hours required to supervise each client based on his or her level of supervision (maximum, medium, or minimum). A maximum supervision case may require, for example, four hours of an officer's time per month. A medium supervision case may require two hours per month, whereas a minimum supervision case may only require one hour or less per month of an officer's time. Given these calculations, one officer could effectively supervise 30 maximum supervision cases, 60 medium cases, and as many as 120 minimum cases. Development of a workload standard would allow comparison between jurisdictions and improve the next step of case planning.

Implementing the Case Plan: Treatment

Thus far we have discussed how implementing a case plan is achieved through contact and surveillance, and how the form each takes depends on the level of supervision. Along with reducing opportunities for crime, implementing a case plan must also be directed toward removing or reducing barriers that could result in recidivism as well as assisting an offender in positive behavioral change, which may involve placement in a treatment program (Cullen, Eck, & Lowenkamp, 2002).

THE PRINCIPLES OF EFFECTIVE CORRECTIONAL INTERVENTION For the last few decades, researchers and treatment specialists have sought to figure out what type of treatment is most effective with which types of offenders. Paul Gendreau (1996) published the **principles of effective intervention**, a theoretical perspective of evidence-based correctional practices that is currently considered the basis by which correctional treatment programs should operate. There are a total of eight principles, which indicate that treatment services should:

> **principles of effective intervention**
> Eight treatment standards that, if practiced, have been shown to reduce recidivism above that of other methods and constitute a theory behind evidence-based correctional practices.

1. be intensive, occupying 40%–70% of each day for three to nine months;
2. contain cognitive-behavioral components to prepare the mind for behavioral change;
3. match program level with client aptitudes or propensities according to gender, age, cultural background, and risk level, so that higher-risk clients make greater strides;
4. offer positive reinforcements that exceed punishments by a ratio of 4:1;
5. require minimum education and experience levels for staff;
6. teach clients to replace criminal networks with prosocial ones;
7. provide relapse prevention and aftercare; and
8. evaluate the program and assess its compliance to the previous seven principles by using the Correctional Program Assessment Inventory (CPAI). The CPAI examines each program in terms of its implementation, leadership, staff quality, and level of available funding.

Many agencies, such as the Federal Probation District in Hawaii and jurisdictions in Maryland, embrace these principles as they discover the true meaning of evidence-based practices (see Davidson, Crawford, & Kerwood, 2008; Taxman, 2008), which in turn see the value in collecting data that will later be important to an evaluation.

COGNITIVE-BEHAVIORAL THERAPY One of the principles of correctional intervention is the use of **cognitive-behavioral therapy** (CBT) with offenders. CBT, an effective method for helping a person to change, is a blend of cognitive therapy, which focuses on self-defeating thought patterns, and behavioral therapy, which works on

> **cognitive-behavioral therapy**
> A therapeutic intervention of helping a person change, that is a blend of two different types of therapies: cognitive therapy which prepares the mind, and behavioral change which conditions the body.

BOX 5.3   COMMUNITY CORRECTIONS UP CLOSE

Six Examples of Cognitive-Behavioral Therapy for Offenders

Cognitive-behavioral programs are a general category of therapy programs that are effective for people who are resistant to change. The cognitive component focuses on reducing narcissistic traits of self-hatred and self-centeredness and preparing the mind for behavioral change. The behavioral component links self-destructive mental processes to harmful acting out. These therapy modules are delivered in group sessions for six to twelve offenders by a trained group facilitator. We briefly discuss six examples below:

1. *Moral Reconation Therapy (MRT)*. Developed by Little and Robinson in the mid-1980s, this therapy program, which is 32 hours long, is based on an assumption that people who have moral development skills are less likely to repeat criminal behavior. MRT is useful for offenders during residential treatment and particularly for offenders who need to learn how to think more abstractly and to share another person's perspective. When used with probationers and parolees, MRT reduced recidivism by nearly two thirds over a time frame between 6–24 months (Little, 2005).

2. *Reasoning and Rehabilitation* (R&R). Developed in the mid-1980s by Ross and Fabiano, this therapy assumes that offenders are egocentric and lack cognitive skills of self-control and interpersonal problem solving. It is similar to MRT but with less focus on morals.

3. *Thinking for a Change* (T4C). Developed in the mid-1990s by Bush, Glick, and Taymans and adopted for use and dissemination by the National Institute of Corrections,

this program consists of 22 lessons lasting one to two hours each. It is classified as a *cognitive restructuring* program in which offenders examine their attitudes, beliefs, and thinking patterns so they can more fully consider the consequences of their actions. Change is sought through social skills and problem-solving techniques, and two sessions per week is considered an optimal dosage.

4. *Strategies for Self-Improvement and Change* (SSC). This year-long program was developed by Wanberg and Milkman for adult substance abusers engaged in a long-term community treatment program. The therapy examines thoughts and behavior patterns that contribute to substance abuse, emphasizing commitment to change and taking responsibility for oneself.

5. *Relapse Prevention Therapy* (RPT). After intensive residential treatment, RPT is a good aftercare program that follows the SSC program discussed above. RPT is also good for relapse prevention of any obsessive thoughts and/or compulsive or habitual behavior. RPT, developed in 2000 by Parks and Marlatt, teaches coping skills when habitual thoughts resurface.

6. *Aggression Replacement Training* (ART). For youth and adult offenders with anger management problems, this therapy uses cognitive-behavioral techniques to recognize and appropriately handle anger. Developed by Goldstein and Glick in the mid-1990s, this is a 30-hour program.

Source: Hansen, Chris. 2008. Cognitive-behavioral interventions: Where they come from and what they do. *Federal Probation* 72 (2): 43–49.

---

inappropriate acting out. CBT is used to overcome phobias, quit habitual behaviors such as smoking, drinking, or drug use, and to change harmful thinking patterns such as those linked to criminality. Box 5.3 discusses six different types of cognitive-behavioral therapy used with offenders.

CBT helps an offender replace both unhealthy thinking processes and criminal behavior with a sense of responsibility, empathy, and prosocial behavior. One CBT program called *Thinking for a Change* was evaluated over one year using treatment and control groups of medium- to high-risk offenders in stable mental health who were neither substance abusers nor sex offenders. Although technical violation rates and rates of rearrest were not significantly different between the two groups, the treatment group had better interpersonal problem-solving skills compared to the control group (those not involved in the treatment regimen) (Golden, Gatchel, & Cahill, 2006). Cullen and Gendreau (2000), who had more positive results, were able to show, through examining multiple studies, that cognitive-behavioral treatment programs following Gendreau's principles reduced recidivism by 25% for the treatment group compared to the control group. Correctional treatment programs that did not follow these principles either had no effect or were able to reduce recidivism by only about 10%.

MOTIVATIONAL INTERVIEWING Think of community supervision as a two-way relationship between an offender with the motivation to change and an officer who responds to and encourages that change. A *strength-based* or *asset-building* approach to offender change would reward offenders with oral or written praise, certificates of completion, vouchers with small monetary rewards, or special privileges that encourage certain positive behaviors. Although removing privileges for negative behavior would be expected, simultaneously incorporating a reward system can motivate a probationer to change (Alexander, VanBenschoten, & Walters, 2008).

This communication style, in which a community supervision officer creates a positive climate of sincerity and understanding that assists an offender in changing, has also been called **motivational interviewing** (Clark, 2005). Developing an honest, direct relationship along with good communication skills is an effective means of promoting change and of ensuring successful completion of a term of probation. The key in motivational interviewing is to get an offender to recognize the cognitive-behavioral problem rather than to argue why he or she hasn't made the strides toward change pointed out by others. Effective techniques include asking open-ended questions of an offender, demonstrating empathy, and taking a genuine interest by way of follow-up statements and positive recognition (Taxman, 2008). Statements such as "How can we come together on this?" and "It's your choice, but is there anything we can do to help you avoid those consequences?" (Clark, 2005, p. 26) are less confrontational than assuming a *deficit-focused* approach that responds to negative rule-breaking behavior with officer punitiveness, mandates, threats, and graduated sanctions. Recent research has shown the effectiveness of motivational interviewing techniques for offenders finding employment, paying probation fees, recognizing drinking behavior, and preparing for substance abuse treatment (Alexander, VanBenschoten, & Walters, 2008). Similar techniques have even been shown to reduce arrests and technical violations (Taxman, 2008).

motivational interviewing
A communication style in which the community supervision officer creates a positive climate of sincerity and understanding that assists the offender in the change process

EMPLOYMENT ASSISTANCE Employment is likely the single most important element in preventing recidivism for probationers and parolees (Petersilia, 2003). Not only does employment provide financial support for an offender and his or her family, but it is also crucial for establishing and maintaining self-esteem and personal dignity—qualities seen by most authorities as essential for successful reintegration into a community. Experienced probation and parole officers know this to be true, and consequently most probation and parole conditions require an offender to maintain employment during the period of supervision. However, finding and maintaining employment is not simple. Offenders are often the last to be hired and the first to be terminated. Many of them are unskilled, and many have poor work habits. Some are barred from employment in their chosen fields as a result of regulatory and licensing laws that preclude people with a criminal conviction. (We discuss these issues in chapter 14.)

Because of the critical relationship between success under parole or probation supervision and meaningful employment, probation and parole officers must assess the employment status of each person under their supervision and work with him or her to land a job. Many require vocational or job-readiness training before they can seek a job. Ideally these services are obtained from external agencies and organizations such as state employment offices and vocational rehabilitation services. For example, a workforce development program in Delaware offered paid vocational training, job counseling, and job referrals to agencies with pre-established relationships. Involvement in this workforce program significantly reduced recidivism for offenders who participated (15% revocation or rearrest rate) compared with a matched group of probationers from other districts (26% revocation or rearrest) who did not participate (Visher, Smolter, & O'Connell, 2010).

APPEALING TO INFORMAL SOCIAL CONTROLS   Informal social controls such as provided by family members and community agencies are also significant resources that officers can access to help probationers develop prosocial behaviors. Probationers were significantly more likely to succeed under probation if they had the support of family or friends than if they did not have such support (Taxman, 2002). Neighborhood-based supervision uses these techniques to aid in supervision.

Read one federal probation officer's view (see Box 5.4) about a typical day on the job, and see whether you are able to determine which activities are surveillance functions and which are oriented toward treatment.

chronos
A chronological account of detailed notes written by a probation or parole officer and organized by date, about any client contact and/or case information that becomes a permanent part of the offender's case file.

BOX 5.4   COMMUNITY CORRECTIONS UP CLOSE

A Day in the Life of a Federal Probation Officer

It's Tuesday, and I've got my work cut out for me on this cold January day in West Texas. On the way in to work I mentally review the upcoming scheduled events for the day: 8:30 A.M. meet with assistant U.S. attorney regarding a probation revocation hearing on John D.; 9:00 A.M. revocation hearing in Judge B's court—contested; thereafter, head for the counties to do field supervision and collateral work. This will be an overnighter, so I'll be back in the office on Thursday—another court day.

I'm almost at the office, but I need to make a quick stop at Joe R.['s] to collect a random urinalysis (UA). He's been out a month now and seems to be doing all right. He's working, home is stable, and the UA will address the primary supervision issue in this case—history of drug abuse. I'm almost ready to complete an initial supervision plan in this case. Although he participated in drug treatment in the institution, he may need treatment in the community. Time will tell; but for right now random UAs will do.

Well, I caught him before he left for work, and things seem solid. The wife seemed happy, the job is stable, and there was no problem with the UA. It's going to be a great day! I love this job! On to the office.

Oops, I spoke too soon. Telephone voice mail: David S. got arrested for DWI [driving while intoxicated]—he's still locked up at County. I'll swing by the county jail on the way out of town. Other than that, no other emergencies.

The assistant U.S. attorney is ready for a contested hearing. That's fine; five dirty UAs and failure to participate in drug treatment will get you every time. The supervision file is well documented, and I'm prepared to testify as to chain of custody on the dirty UAs. Our contract provider was subpoenaed and will testify on the failure to participate violation. We're in Judge B's court, and the AUSA [assistant U.S. attorney] tells me the defendant has decided to plead true and throw himself on the mercy of the court—good luck. Sure enough, the judge revokes John D.'s probation and sentences him to twenty-four months' custody. John takes it all right, but his mother doesn't. If he had taken the judge's advice and "lived at the foot of the cross," he'd still be on probation—instead, he's locked up, and his mother is crying in court. It's always harder on the family. I'll talk to her—maybe it will help. John couldn't do it on the street, so maybe he will get the help he needs inside. [The federal correctional institution in] Fort Worth has an excellent treatment program—I'll tell her that and maybe she will feel better. I hate this job!

Well, it's midmorning and time to hit the road. Fort Stockton is 100 miles down the road, but I've got to stop at the county jail on the way out of town. I'll check out the government vehicle with the four-wheel drive in case the roads get bad; cellular phone; pepper spray; sidearm; and laptop in case I have time to do **chronos**. Gosh times have changed; in the good old days I'd be leaving town in my personal vehicle with a smile on my face.

At the county lockup David S. advises he was arrested by the P.D. [police department] for DWI—but he really only "had a couple." Of course, he forgot he was supposed to abstain completely from alcohol. When I get back in

(Continues)

BOX 5.4   **COMMUNITY CORRECTIONS UP CLOSE** (*Continued*)

town I'll get the offense report, staff the case with the boss, and decide what type of action to take. David has been on supervision for over a year and has done exceptionally well. Graduated sanctions may be in order, and if so, I'll ask the court to place him in the halfway house with a required treatment condition.

On the road again. This is what I've got to do in Fort Stockton: check in with the sheriff—he knows everything that is going on in his county; go by our drug contractor's office and visit with the therapist regarding Mary J.; go by the county clerk's office and finish this collateral request out of the Northern District; and conduct home inspections on Bob S. and Joe R. Talk about time management—the boss will love this! Sheriff B. is in a great mood, and he says all my people have been behaving themselves. Over coffee I advise him John D. will be getting out on parole—for the second time—and will be coming back home to Fort Stockton. That didn't make his day. At the drug treatment facility the contractor gives me a good report on Mary J. She's keeping all her appointments and has not submitted any dirty UAs. Her participation in treatment is good, and her mother has also attended a couple of counseling sessions. Great report!

The county clerk was busy, but she did have the judgments I had called ahead about—that was a quick and easy collateral, not like the last one that took two hours to find an old judgment. These people in Fort Stockton are great to work with; they really know how to help you. Man I love this job!

Well, there's Bob S.'s house. I think I'll drive past and around the block—just in case. Everything looks cool, and his car is in front, so he should be home.

Bob was surprised to see me, advising it was his day off since the day before he had pulled a double on the rig he works. Oil field work is steady, but the cold weather is hard, and it shows on Bob's face. The wife seems to be doing well, and the house is neat and clean. Things look solid, but I know better than to start bragging. This offender has a history of drug violations, which presents certain risk control issues. Risk control issues never go away!

At Joe R.'s no one comes to the door, but I thought I heard someone inside. I leave my card, drive around the block, and call Joe on the cellular phone. It amazes me how sneaky I can get when I have to. Sure enough, Joe's girlfriend answers the phone and advises Joe is still at work. Work is 15 miles out of town at a ranch, so I'll try to catch him first thing in the morning.

I'm running a little ahead of schedule, so I'll stop by and see Mary J. She should be home from work; if she's not, her mother will be, and she'll let me know how her daughter is really doing. The supervision issues here are enforcing court-ordered sanctions and drug treatment. Sure enough, Mary J. is there and seems to be doing really well. She gives me her community service hours documentation and discusses her progress in the drug treatment program. Her mother is obviously very satisfied with her daughter's progress and is a good supervision resource to me.

Before I check into the motel, I call the office on the cellular to check my voice mail. David S. called to advise he bonded out of jail. I call him back and set up an appointment for him to come in on Thursday. We'll staff him at that time. I'm glad now that I brought the laptop—I can catch up on some chronos. Since I lucked out and saw all the people I needed to, I won't need to go out tonight—it's getting too cold out here in West Texas anyway. What a day—win a few, lose a few. Gosh, I love this job!

The next morning comes early, and I catch breakfast before I hit the road. I figure I'll work my way back to the office and try to catch Joe R. at the ranch before he gets busy. I'm positive his girlfriend told him I was by the house, so he should be expecting me. I'm not quite comfortable with this offender because he does have some violence in his background. Therefore, officer safety and risk control are the primary supervision issues I am addressing. Wouldn't you know it, he locked the main gate on me—but what he doesn't know is the rancher previously gave me a key to the gate. As I drive up to the ranch headquarters, I can see my man out by the horse corral. He seems surprised to see me. We visit, and he convinces me he is making a "good hand." I try not to be too obvious, but I'm looking for any signs of contraband or a weapon. Ranch hands and rifles seem to go hand in hand—no pun intended. Nothing is obvious, although Joe just seems to be nervous. As I drive back down the road to the main gate, I call the Border Patrol sector headquarters and check in with the duty agent. Joe is clean as far as they know, but they agree to drive by in the next few days. They'll let me know. The agent advised they have received recent intelligence of illegal aliens working in the area where Joe works.

Well, I'm almost home, and it's a beautiful day. In fact, it looks like it will warm up. The only pressing issue I know of is the staffing on David S. You know what, I really do love this job!

Source: The author, Richard V. Russell, was supervising U.S. probation officer for the Western District of Texas. He is now retired and resides in Midland, Texas. Reprinted with permission.

Working with Female Offenders

Most supervision techniques and treatment programs have been developed to serve characteristic offenders. In terms of gender, male offenders have always outnumbered female offenders by a ratio of 3:1. Thus supervision and treatment have been adapted to men's backgrounds, risk level, and individual needs. What this means is that though some of these strategies work for women, others require a deeper understanding of finer gender distinctions to formulate an approach that works with this third. It is worth noting that the gender differences addressed in this section do not apply universally but are intended as general guidelines for working with most women under correctional supervision.

Although female probationers originate from all walks of life, many have typical backgrounds. Women under community supervision have typically entered the criminal justice system because of a crime they committed alongside a male partner (boyfriend, husband, or brother) or else if acting alone, out of financial need. The typical female probationer has not completed high school and lacks skills for employment above the minimum wage. Three out of four women have dependent children. The low wages and reality of children mean that many women are living below the poverty line with little perceived means and opportunity to change their situation. There is a disproportionate number of women who have been physically or sexually abused and/or neglected as children. The abuse oftentimes continues into adulthood through male partners and is sometimes passed on to children as women remain in a submissive and dependent role. Although more women than in the past may act in leadership crime roles, far more of them serve in secondary, traditional roles (Alarid et al., 1996). Early experiences of abuse and disempowerment later affects a woman's self-esteem, emotional and mental states, and rate of substance abuse, all of which are linked as various pathways to crime (Alarid & Cromwell, 2006). Because many women define themselves by their relationships rather than by their careers, they tend to seek partners who will provide them with what they feel they deserve.

This link between early experiences and criminality is noteworthy because ordinarily women typically are more at risk of harming themselves than of harming others. All else being equal, women generally pose less risk than men do to the community at large. This is partially due to the way that risk is currently defined by classification instruments.

Practitioners who have worked with both sexes have noted that women under supervision seem more open to sharing their feelings and thoughts than men, in part because women value relationships and the establishment of rapport to further them. Men under supervision, on the other hand, value independence and tend to withhold information (not always intentionally) because they have been socialized not to share their problems with others (Festervan, 2003). As a result these gender differences can contribute to a view of female offenders as having more needs than men, when in fact women are just more open about them.

Festervan (2003), who operates a woman's residential community facility, recommends that female offenders address prior sexual and drug abuse in an environment they perceive as safe from sexual harassment, one not framed only in terms of sexualized interactions with men. This entails nonconfrontational therapy modalities best supervised by female staff and separated from male offenders. Although Festervan believes that men can be effective officers, anyone who works with female offenders must be well-versed in issues such as pregnancy, parenting and childcare, domestic violence, sexual abuse, mental health, educational opportunities, and substance abuse. Supervising such a woman involves an ability to empathize with her past while simultaneously aiding her in changing her victim mentality to becoming more responsible and empowered.

Evaluation of Neighborhood-Based vs. Traditional Community Supervision

Recall that in neighborhood-based supervision (NBS) probation officers conduct supervision and implement a case plan by being more visible and having a strong community presence. The elements of NBS include assignment of offenders according to zip code or type of offense (or both), development of community partnerships with police and treatment providers, and faith-based initiatives. Cases are assigned to officers according to geographic beats in communities that are ideal for using geographic information systems (GIS) technology (see Box 5.5).

NBS sites started in Boston; Phoenix; Tucson; Dallas/Ft. Worth; Waco, Texas; and Spokane, Washington. Preliminary evaluations of these sites compared probationers supervised in an NBS program, which had smaller caseloads, with those supervised using traditional probation. An evaluation of one site indicated that probationers supervised in an NBS program perceived receiving more support from their probation officers in finding employment and in connecting to treatment providers than did probationers supervised according to traditional caseloads (Lutze, Smith, & Lovrich, 2004). NBS officers experienced more autonomy and a closer connection with police and community than did traditional probation officers, although relationships with treatment service providers were similar for both groups. NBS probationers were more likely to be cited for technical violations than were traditional probationers, yet both groups committed a similar number of new crimes while under supervision. Overall recidivism rates between the two groups were not significantly different (Lutze, Smith, & Lovrich, 2004). Evaluations of other sites are needed to obtain a more complete picture of NBS.

BOX 5.5 TECHNOLOGY IN CORRECTIONS

Using Geographic Information System Technology in Probation and Parole Supervision

Geographic information system (GIS) mapping uses special computer software to visually diagram locations in a neighborhood or entire city of individuals and/or events. GIS mapping enables a probation or parole agency to obtain a full picture of who is on probation and where probationers live. By "parsing" and "geocoding" the data, probation supervisors have detailed information to use when assigning new cases to their officers. Available data includes the number of police calls for service, the number and location of orders of protection, and access to treatment venues from probationers' residences. An officer who supervises an entire caseload of offenders in the same area can achieve a higher level of field surveillance than an officer who must drive all over a city. GIS technology can also overlay information on bus routes, employer locations, locations of alcohol establishments, and schools to determine feasibility of probationer success and how travel time can be minimized when probationers move from one location to another. This technology gives probation officers more details about their jurisdiction or the "beat" in which their clients live, and information can be shared with police departments, who already use GIS to locate suspects and investigate new crimes.

GIS technology is also helpful for supervisors when assigning new clients to a caseload. A supervisor can examine where an offender lives and assign offenders in the same neighborhood to the same officer, such as in neighborhood-based supervision. In this way, officers can supervise their caseload in a small area of town, where they are more likely to visit them in the neighborhood rather than driving haphazardly all over town. Using GIS mapping, routes from one house to the next can be planned for a series of home visits. The possibilities of GIS applications for corrections are still being discovered and linked to other agencies within the broader criminal justice system.

Sources: Keith Harries. 2003. Using geographic analysis in probation and parole. *National Institute of Justice Journal* 249: 32–33; Jaishankar Karuppannan. 2005. Mapping and corrections: Management of offenders with geographic information systems. *Corrections Compendium* 30(1): 7–9, 31–33.

SUPERVISION OUTSIDE THE STATE

Interstate Compact
An agreement signed by all states and U.S. territories that allows for the supervision of parolees and probationers across state lines.

Prior to 1937 a probationer or parolee could not be supervised outside the state in which he or she was convicted, even though many transient offenders were arrested and convicted far away from home. As a result, an offender often could not be provided with supervision in the very place that would offer the best chance for success on probation or parole. A group of states entered into a statutory agreement wherein they would supervise probationers and parolees for each other. Known as the **Interstate Compact**, the agreement was originally signed by 25 states in 1937. By 1951 the Interstate Compact had been ratified by all the states as well as by Puerto Rico and the Virgin Islands.

The Interstate Compact on Juveniles was established in 1955 to provide for return of juvenile runaways, escapees, and absconders as well as for cooperative supervision of juvenile probationers and parolees. A survey of field staff and interstate compact administrators found that 15,000 youths in the United States were being supervised via interstate compact but that one third of all requests submitted by a sending state were denied by a receiving state (Linke & Krauth, 2000).

sending state
Under the interstate compact, the state of conviction.

receiving state
Under the interstate compact, the state that undertakes the supervision.

The compacts identify a **sending state** (the state of conviction) and a **receiving state** (the state that undertakes the supervision). The receiving state informs the sending state of a probationer's progress on a quarterly basis, but the sending state retains ultimate authority to modify the conditions of probation, to revoke probation, and to terminate probation. It is also generally held that the sending state alone has authority to determine upon what basis a violator may be returned. The reasons for return cannot be challenged by the receiving state.

An offender must meet certain residence requirements of the receiving state. Ordinarily the probationer or parolee must be a resident of the receiving state, have relatives there, or have employment there. The receiving state agrees to provide "courtesy supervision" at the same level that it gives to its own cases.

The three main problems with interstate compacts were liability, monitoring compliance, and slow processing speed. Because probation supervision styles varied from state to state, each state had different thresholds and policies for when a probationer was considered in violation. For example, one state might consider a probationer to be in violation even though another state wished to continue supervision. In addition, some states were asked to accept far more interstate compact supervision cases than they sent out. At times some states sent their most noncompliant cases elsewhere, so that this form of supervision used other states as "dumping grounds." Finally, the process of obtaining approval was slow, and some offenders relocated prior to being approved for supervision. Interstate compacts were largely unorganized and inconsistent in their approaches (Linke & Krauth, 2000). Because of these ongoing problems, the National Institute of Corrections (NIC) determined that the best resolution was to provide a new way to administer interstate compacts (National Institute of Corrections & Council of State Governments, 2002).

The Interstate Compact for Adult Offender Supervision

Interstate Compact for Adult Offender Supervision
A formalized decree granting authority to a commission to create and enforce rules for member states for the supervision of offenders in other states.

The result of the NIC study was to create an **Interstate Compact for Adult Offender Supervision** in 2000. This revised compact developed an interstate commission composed of one representative commissioner from each participating state. The commission is a national organization empowered to create and enforce the same rules for all states, collect national statistics, coordinate training and education, and notify victims about public safety. The commission conducts annual meetings to modify rules and to deal with conflicts among states as needed.

In addition to the commission, each state has its own council composed of a compact administrator and at least one person from each branch of government (legislative, judicial, and executive). The compact administrator is charged with administering and managing all interstate compacts for his or her own state (National Institute of Corrections & Council of State Governments, 2002). With this new structure and oversight commission, correctional administrators are hopeful that the problems with interstate compacts will be a thing of the past. As of 2004 all states except Virginia and Mississippi were members. There are reportedly as many as 250,000 offenders nationwide under interstate compact supervision.

Revocation and the Interstate Compact

Without going through extradition proceedings, a sending state may enter a receiving state to take custody of a probationer or parolee who has violated the terms of release. The probationer waives extradition prior to leaving the sending state, so the sending state can retake a person being supervised in another state simply by having its officer present appropriate credentials and proving the identity of the person to be retaken. The probation violator is usually incarcerated in the receiving state at the expense of the sending state.

The receiving state is obligated to surrender a probationer unless a criminal charge is pending against the individual in the receiving state. In such a case, the probationer cannot be retaken without the receiving state's consent until he or she is discharged from prosecution or from any imprisonment for such offense. The effect is that the sending state cannot retake the probationer into custody until all local charges are disposed of.

A national organization called the Parole and Probation Compact Administrators' Association (PPCAA) was formed so that interstate compact officers could exchange information and solve challenges that arise. PPCAA meets twice per year to address issues as they occur so that all state policies are consistently enforced.

SUMMARY

- A valid classification is important to assess offender risk and identify treatment needs, which in turn lead to developing a case plan and an appropriate level of supervision.

- Techniques of evidence-based practices in community corrections include risk and needs assessments, case planning, motivational interviewing, cognitive-behavioral treatment, and principles of correctional intervention.

- Merely observing the conditions of release or managing not to be arrested for a new offense does not indicate that an offender has been rehabilitated. The personality, training, and experience of a supervisory officer determine an outcome just as much as an offender's motivation.

- Implementing a case plan is achieved through monitoring and treatment. Monitoring is through contact and surveillance, their forms depending on the level of supervision.

- A treatment plan consists in removing or reducing barriers that could result in recidivism as well as assisting an offender in positive behavioral change, which might involve placement in a treatment program. Adequate supervision must focus on all phases of offenders' lives, including family issues and relations with the community in which they live and work.

- Working with female offenders requires knowing about the potential pathways to crime invoked by domestic violence, sexual and physical abuse, mental illness, lack of educational opportunities and skills, and substance abuse problems. Supervising women entails empathizing with their pasts while simultaneously aiding them in changing their victim mentality to become more responsible and empowered.

- Neighborhood-based supervision (NBS) of probation seeks to make probation a more respected and more visible part of the corrections system, changing its operation and accountability. The effectiveness of NBS rests in part on an officer being able to secure the assistance and cooperation of community agencies and individuals within his or her beat.

- Interstate compacts are written agreements between two agencies that allow probationers and parolees to be supervised in another state than the place of conviction.

DISCUSSION QUESTIONS

1. Argue for the use of neighborhood-based supervision of probation over traditional methods. In what situations might NBS be most useful?

2. How does officer assessment of client needs in education, employment, treatment, etc. help develop a program plan? How much should a client be expected to do while under supervision?

3. Discuss the use of various risk prediction scales. How might risk assessment best be used in community supervision?

4. Discuss the concept of caseload and workload computation. Why might workload be a better method of allocating probation or parole officer resources?

5. How might interstate compact supervision be *more helpful* for an offender than local supervision? How might interstate supervision be *more difficult* for an offender?

WEBSITES, VIDEOS, AND PODCASTS

Websites

Center for Evidence-Based Practices, University of California–Irvine
http://ucicorrections.seweb.uci.edu

General Information About Risk and Needs Assessments
http://www.riskandneeds.com

Information on Case Management and Risk Assessment
http://www.justiceconcepts.com

Empirical Validation of the Arizona Risk/Needs Assessment
http://www.ncic.org/library/018821

Applying EBP to Offender Supervision
http://www.nicic.org/library/020095

"Thinking for a Change" Lesson Plans—An Example of a Cognitive-Behavioral Program
http://www.nicic.org/library/016672

Changing Offender Behavior System
http://www.changecompanies.net

A Research Study of Assessments and Conditional Releases in Canada
http://www.csc-scc.gc.ca/text/rsrch/reports/r133/r133-eng.shtml

Motivational Interviewing
http://www.motivationalinterviewing.org

Evidence-Based Practices That Work in Florida
http://www.dc.state.fl.us/pub/recidivismWSIPP/index.html

The Special Needs of Women in the Justice System
www.gainscenter.samhsa.gov

Videos/Podcasts

Role-playing Scenarios on Video: Two PO/Offender Contact Sessions (24 minutes)
http://www.nicic.org/library/022005

Female Offenders
http://www.corrections.com/system/podcast/file/120/CSOSA123.mp3__audio_mpeg_Object_.mp3

The podcast interviews Ashley McSwain, executive director of Our Place D.C., and Dr. Willa Butler of Court Services and Offender Supervision Agency, discussing how both organizations are meeting the unique needs of female offenders.

Introduction to Monroe County, Indiana, Adult Community Corrections

http://www.youtube.com/watch?v=HJnHy9BFKhk

Part 1 discusses the Department's mission, cost savings, and public perceptions of community corrections services (5:25 minutes).

Community Alternative Supervision in Monroe County, Indiana, Adult Community Corrections

http://www.youtube.com/watch?v=w5pIo9P9o5o&feature=related

Part 2 discusses specific programs at different levels in the county, such as community service, Level 1 work release, Level 2–3 electronic monitoring, Level 4 curfew of GPS, and Level 5 daily reporting. Shows how an ankle device is placed on an offender (9 minutes).

CASE STUDY EXERCISES

Classification and Supervision in Probation and Parole

There are two new clients in your caseload. Below is the information you have received on each person. Using the Risk and Needs Classification Instrument (Figure 5.1 in this chapter), complete the following:

1. Assess the risks posed by the offender and select an appropriate supervision assignment based on the risk score.
2. Score the "needs" level of the client.
3. If you're able to interview the offender, use the Sample Assessment Interview starting on page 115 of this chapter and complete the 55 questions. If an interview is not possible, consider the factors that have placed the client at risk and which factors are related to the offense.
4. Choose the top three to four problems to develop goals that the client should strive to achieve and action items of what the client needs to do to reach each goal. Then complete the "program plan" part of the assignment.

CASE A: Thomas User, Possession of Methamphetamine

Thomas User, age 20, has been placed on probation for possession of methamphetamine and Ecstasy. There were no known victims in the current offense. Police reports indicate that Mr. User was stopped by a police cruiser because he had been standing on the same corner for hours. An outer pat search revealed that he had eight tablets confirmed by drug testing to be Ecstasy and that he had enough methamphetamine for up to 12 hits.

Mr. User has two previous misdemeanor convictions as a juvenile, one for possession of paint huffing material and one as a minor in possession of alcoholic beverages. He has one misdemeanor conviction as an adult for menacing in the second degree.

Mr. User has remained in the same rental house with two roommates for the last three years—the roommates seem neutral influences at this point. He has been employed at one fast-food restaurant for seven months out of the last 12 months. The rest of the time Mr. User says he sold and used drugs. He drinks alcohol "recreationally on occasion," but alcohol does not seem to be related to his offense. He has a drug habit that is related to his arrest, but he has not yet been assessed for drug treatment. It is unclear how motivated he is to attend a treatment program.

Mr. User has an IQ of 68, which defines him as developmentally disabled, but he has no signs of mental illness. He is a high school dropout, having only completed the tenth grade. He does not have his GED. He reports himself in good physical health and has mentioned he has been sexually abused in the past by a former boyfriend, for which he wants to be tested for HIV. You notice that he seems underweight, and he has two teeth missing.

Mr. User is single and not in any relationship right now, although he shares his living expenses with his two roommates. He reports that he has fathered one child, but he does not know the whereabouts of the child or the mother. The child is approximately three years of age, and there is no claim by the mother for child support.

CASE B: Maria Diaz, Identity Theft

Maria Diaz has been placed under community supervision for identity theft. She pleaded guilty to stealing the identities of 14 different victims from her employer's protected database, opening up accounts in their names and charging merchandise in small amounts, averaging $500 per victim, stealing an estimated grand total of around $7,000 in merchandise. She says that she has had significant financial difficulties and has filed for bankruptcy. Ms. Diaz is 25 years of age, divorced, and has no known juvenile arrest or adjudication history. As an adult, she had one prior forgery charge for which she was originally placed on probation (which was revoked for technical violations), and assigned to a halfway house for nine months, where she successfully completed her supervision.

Ms. Diaz has a high school diploma, and she has a transient job history. Moving from one minimum wage job to another, her employed time in the last year is estimated to be 50%. She was ordered to pay $7,000 in restitution for her current offense. She has not yet made any payments toward her restitution. Her divorce was finalized one year ago, and her ex-husband is nine months behind on child support payments. Because of her financial situation, she currently lives with her boyfriend, who is allegedly an undocumented immigrant from Mexico. She says that he "is unpredictable . . . I never know if he'll be home at night or if he'll call and want me to bail him out of jail."

Because of her boyfriend's unstable situation, Ms. Diaz reports moving back and forth between her sister's house and her boyfriend's address, having lived at two different addresses in the past year. She has one dependent child living with her who is 10 years old. Mother and daughter both report good medical health, and there is no evidence indicating otherwise. There is also no evidence that alcohol or drug use was related to the current offense, and Ms. Diaz has never attended drug treatment. Her motivation to start restitution payments is low and her attitude is a bit problematic, but it is hoped that Ms. Diaz' resistance will change with motivational interviewing and job training. There is no evidence of developmental disability, sexual dysfunction, or emotional problems, and Ms. Diaz does not report being on any medications for mental or physical problems.

SAMPLE ASSESSMENT INSTRUMENT

Column One: Questions to Ask Client has suggested questions to elicit attitude information about the offense, the offender's background, and about present plans and problems. The average interview takes about forty-five minutes.

Use a natural, open conversational style of interviewing that is comfortable for both you and the probationer. If the probationer presents some important or interesting information requiring follow-up, feel free to do so before returning to the structured sequence.

If the information needed to score the items is not obtained from the open-ended questions, one or two follow-up questions are provided for each item.

For some items "a" and "b" questions are included. If the "b" question is asterisked (*), always ask it unless the answer to the "a" question makes the "b" questions meaningless (e.g., "no" to question 10a). If question "b" is not asterisked, ask it if the needed information was not elicited from question "a".

If provided questions fail to elicit the needed information, continue to inquire with increasingly direct questions unless you see the word –stop-. "**Stop**" means to discontinue inquiry (except to repeat or clarify a misunderstood question).

Column Two: The Client's Response
Choose only one multiple choice response that best represents what the client is saying.

Column Three: Special Instructions or Notes for this Question
Examples are provided in Column 3 or special notes for the interviewing officer that pertain to this question, as to how to score.

QUESTIONS	CLIENT RESPONSE	SPECIAL NOTES

1a. How did you get involved in this offense?
1b. (if denied) What did the police say that you did?
	1. Motivation for committing the offense:
	   a. Emotional motivation (e.g. anger, sex offense, etc)
	   b. Material (monetary) motivation
	   c. Both emotional and material motivation
		1. a.
		  –Using drugs
		  –Assault (not for robbery)
		b.
		  –Prostitution
		  –Car theft
		  –Selling drugs
		c.
		stealing from parents for revenge or peer acceptance

2a. How did you decide to commit the offense?
2b. Could you tell me more about the circumstances that led up to the offense?
	2. Acceptance of responsibility for current offense
	   a. Admits committing the offense and doesn't attempt excuses.
	   b. Admits committing the offense but emphasizes excuses (influence by friends, drinking, etc)
	   c. Denies committing the offense
		2. a. explains circumstances but takes responsibility
		b. blames circumstances doesn't take responsibility
		c. probationers who deny any significant aspect of the offense are scored "c" (probationer admits he helped to jimmy car window but denies responsibility for removing valuables because friends removed them).

3a. Looking back at the offense, what is your general feeling about it? –STOP–

3. Expression of guilt about current offense:
   a. No prior offenses (skip 5,6,7,8)
   b. Mainly misdemeanor
   c. No constant pattern
   d. Mainly felonies

3. a. Probationer must feel some personal shame and regret (not just to impress officer)
   b. "I feel bad because now I have a record"; "people are disappointed in me"; "I know it was wrong"
   c. Using drugs or sexual activities between consenting adults

4a. what prior offenses have you been convicted of?
4b. Were you ever in trouble as a juvenile? (list below)

4. Offense and severity
   a. No prior (skip 5,6,7,8)
   b. Mainly misdemeanor
   c. No constant pattern
   d. Mainly felonies

4-8 include juvenile and serious traffic offenses (drunk driving) don't count dismissals

4. Use only prior offenses
   a. Should not be used if probationer has more than two serious felonies
   b. Over 50% of probationer's offenses are felonies

5a. Have you ever been armed or hurt someone during these offenses?
5b. Did you ever threaten anyone?

5–8 Use current and prior offense factors to score 5-8

6a. How did you decide to commit these offenses? 6b. Did you plan these offenses beforehand?

6. Offenses were generally
   a. Planned
   b. no consistent pattern
   c. impulsive

6. Officer's judgement based on all factors
   a. Exhibitionist who drives around in a car looking for a girl to whom to expose himself
   b. Person who decides to commit and offense, then drinks to build courage
   c. Exhibitionist who is driving to work, suddenly sees a girl and pulls over and exposes himself
   d. Person who gets drunk and into a bar fight

7. Were you drinking or on drugs when you committed this offense?

7. Percent of offenses committed while drinking or on drugs.
   a. never
   b. 50% or less
   c. over 50%

Count offenses where there any chemical use regardless of whether person was intoxicated or not.

8. Did you do the offense alone or with others?

8. Offenses were generally committed
   a. alone
   b. no consistent pattern
   c. With Accomplices

Offense	(Item 4) Fel./Misd.	(Item 5) Assaultive	Circumstance of Offense	(Item 6) Planned?	(Item 7) Chemicals?	(Item 8) Accomplices?

School and Vocational Adjustment: Now, I'd like to find out some things about your background. Let's begin with school. How did you like school?

9. What was your favorite subject in school? –STOP-

9. Favorite subject
   a. vocational
   b. Academic
   c. Gym
   d. no favorite

9.
   a. Business Course
   b. Music or Art

10a. Did you have a favorite teacher in high school?
10b. what did you like about him/her?

10. Attitude toward teachers
   a. no favorite
   b. teacher chosen because of certain qualities that the probationer admired
   c. teacher chosen because of close personal relationship with the teacher

10. a. "She would help kids"
    b. "she would help me"

11a. How far did you go in school?
11b. Did you have any problems with school work? (if didn't graduate why not?)

11. Probationer's school performance
   a. no problems
   b. learning problems
   c. lack of interest, behavior or other problems

11. a. Don't use for probationer who didn't complete high school.
    b. for probationer whose learning problems result from a lack of capacity. If probationer has both lack of capacity and behavioral problems, score b. Lack of capacity take precedence when scoring.

12. Now, I'd like to know about your work history. What kind of jobs have you had?

12. Primary vocation
   a. unskilled labor
   b. Semiskilled labor
   c. skilled labor or white collar
   d. no employment history (homemaker skip to 13 &14)
   e. student or recent graduate (skip 13&14)

12. Average person could do job without training. Probationer's been in the job market for over 6 months but has no employment history.
   a. Job requires some training or experience.
   b. for homemaker, use prior vocational history if any. If none check "d" and skip 13 &14.
   c. Probationer was recently a student and hasn't had opportunity to establish employment pattern (skip 13 & 14).

13a. How long did you work on your most recent job?

13b. How long between that job and your previous job? (start w/ most recent and work backwards until pattern emerges).

13. Percent of working life where probationer was employed fulltime:
   a. over 90%
   b. over 50%–90%
   c. 50% or less

13. "Working life… ie time period society would expect one to be working, subtract time in school.

14a. What was your reason for leaving your most recent job?

14b. Have you had any trouble getting jobs?

14. Primary vocational problem
   a. none
   b. problems due to lack of skills or capacity
   c. attitude or other problems

14. a. Don't use "a" if working less that 90%
   b. "Because of my drinking problem.

(Item 12) (Start with most recent) Jobs & Job Responsibilities	(Item 13a) Duration	(Item 14a) Reason for Leaving
(Item 13b) Unemployment Interval		
(Item 13b) Unemployment Interval		
(Item 13b) Unemployment Interval		

15a. where do you live now?
15b. Have you moved around much? (deal with time after age 18)

15. Living stability background:
  a. essentially stable living arrangements
  b. Some unstable periods
  c. essentially unstable living arrangements

15. Consider what is stable for the probationer's age group.

16a. Have you had any trouble supporting yourself or received welfare? 16b. (If applicable) How did you support yourself when you were unemployed?

16. History of being self-supporting:
  a. Probationer has usually been self supporting
  b. probationer has had several periods where he/she wasn't self supporting.
  c. has essentially not been self supporting

16. Illegal activities and welfare are not counted as self-supporting. For probationer who has not had the opportunity to support him/herself (homemaker or living with relative) estimate the likelihood of his/her being able to support her/himself.

17a. How do (did) you get along with your father?
17b. How do you feel about your father?

17. Present feelings toward father:
  a. Close
  b. Mixed or neutral
  c. hostile

17. **a.** In multi-father families, use the person whom the probationer identifies as father
  b. "we get along" (without implication of closeness)

18a. If you did something wrong as a teenager, how did your father handle it?
18b. What kind of discipline did he use?

18. Type of discipline father used (during teen years)
  a. verbal or privilege withdrawal
  b. permissive (let do as he/she pleased)
  c. physical

18. **a.** If the probationer didn't live with father or father figure during at least part of teenage years, do not rate item 18.
  b. "He always left it to mom"

19a. How do (did) you get along with your mother?
19b. How do you feel about your mother?

19. Present feelings toward father:
  a. Close
  b. Mixed or neutral
  c. hostile

19. **a.** In multi-mother families, use the person whom the probationer identifies as mother.
  b. "we get along" (without implication of closeness

20a. If you did something wrong as a teenager, how did your mother handle it?
20b. What kind of discipline did she use?

20. Type of discipline father used (during teen years)
  a. verbal or privilege withdrawal
  b. permissive (let do as he/she pleased)
  c. physical

20. **a.** If the probationer didn't live with mother or mother figure during at least part of teenage years, do not rate item 18.
  b. "He always left it to dad"

21a. were you ever abused by either of your parents?
21b. did either of them ever go overboard on the punishment? -STOP-

21. Was probationer ever physically abused by a biological, step or adoptive parent?
  a. yes
  b. no

21. Item 21 should be based on facts described and not whether the client felt abused
  a. cuts on face, severe body bruises, sexual abuse, locked in closet or starved for unusual amount of time.

22a. how would your parent's have described you as a child (before you were a teenager)?
22b. did both of your parents see you the same way?

22. Parental view of probationer:
  a. good child
  b. problem child
  c. parents differed

22a. no special problem "like anybody else"
  b. "my parents were always complaining about me" seen as "strange kid"

23. how would you describe yourself as a child?

23. As a child, probationer describes self as:
   a. good child (normal or average)
   b. problem child

23. Accept what the probationer says even his/her behavior doesn't match his/her perception (ex from item 22 apply here).

24a. how do you get along with your brothers and sisters?
24b. how do you feel about them?

24. General feelings toward siblings:
   a. Close
   b. Neutral or mixed
   c. hostile
   d. no siblings

24a. Include half-siblings; exclude step-siblings.
   b. "like some, not others."

25. would you describe your early childhood as happy or unhappy? -STOP-

25. General attitude toward childhood
   a. happy
   b. not happy

25. Accept the probationer view.

26. If you could change anything about your childhood, what would you change?

26. Satisfaction with childhood
   a. basically satisfied
   b. dissatisfied with material aspect
   c. Dissatisfied with self, family or emotional climate.

26. "I should've gone to school."

27. Can you describe your father's personality? (if the answer is un-clear, ask probationer to describe another person he/she knows well).

27. Probationer's description of personality
   a. multi-facedted
   b. Superficial (ex. "good" "nice" "bad" etc)

27. The focus of this item is the complexity with which the probationer views people. The ability to describe attributes, or explain the reasons for behavior, is being measured. "Superficial" indicated a lack of capacity to perceive depth of personality and not just an evasion of the question. One or two complex statements are sufficient for an "a" score.
   a. – "ambitious and honest"
      –"sensitive to others"
      –"dad was strict because that is the way he was brought up"
   b. –"no good drunk" (with no further explanation)
      –"kind"
      –"don't know"

28a. what are your friends like?
28b. have any of them been in trouble with the law?

28. Probationer's associated are:
   a. essentially non-criminal
   b. Mixed
   c. Mostly criminal

28. Don't count marijuana use (alone) as criminal
   a. don't use "a" if probationer committed offense with accomplices

29a. how do you get along with your friends?
29b. how do they act toward you?

29. In interaction with friends probationer is:
   a. used by others
   b. withdrawn
   c. other problems
   d. normal

29. This item should be based on officer's judgment of the quality of the probationer's interactions. If the officer is used by friends even though the probationer thinks he/she get along "ok" check choice "a".

30a. do you have a closest friend?

30b. what do you like best about him/her?
-STOP-

30. Description of probationer's relationship with his/her closest friend:
  a. talk or help each other
  b. do things together (less emphasis on talking or sharing feelings)
  c. has none

30. a. –"we do things for each other"
    –"we're like brothers"
  b. –"he's a hunter too"

31. are you satisfied with the way you get along with people?

31. Satisfaction with interpersonal relationships:
  a. feels satisfied
  b. feels dissatisfied

31. Accept the probationer's statement.

32. In general, do you tend to trust or to mistrust people? –STOP-

32. General outlook toward others:
  a. basically trusting
  b. mixed or complex view
  c. basically mistrusting

32. A complex view of people (trust some situations and not in others)
  – "I trust people too much."
  – "It takes a while to get to know them."

33a. Can you tell me about your relationships with women (men)?

33b. Do you generally go out with a lot of women/men or date the same person for long periods?

33. Probationer's opposite sex relationship pattern generally is:
  a. long term or serious relationships (over six months)
  b. short and long term relationships
  c. short term less emotionally involved relationships, or little dating experience

33. short term relationships with no solid commitments to persons of the opposite sex

34. In your relationship with your wife/girlfriend (husband/boyfriend), who tends to make the decisions?

34. In opposite sex interactions, probationer generally:
  a. dominates
  b. is average or adequate
  c. is non assertive or dominated

34. Officer's judgment: Do not accept the probationer's response without exploring his/her relationships or seeing how some specific decisions are made (who decides what to do or with whom to socialize; who controls the money).

35. Do you consider yourself to be a nervous (or anxious) person? -STOP-

35. Does probationer view self as a nervous person?
  a. yes
  b. no

35. Accept the probationer's statement
  a. –"I worry a lot"
    –"I'm hyperactive."

36a. What kinds of things get you depressed?

36b. What do you do when you're feeling depressed? (If denies, find out how he/she keeps from getting depressed.)

36. What does probationer do when feeling depressed?
  a. seeks someone to talk to. Or tries to figure it out
  b. seeks an activity to distract self
  c. drinks or uses drugs
  d. isolates self

36. "Forget about them"
  –"watch TV" D
  –"I pray"
  –"I go to sleep"

37a. Have you ever thought seriously about hurting or killing yourself?

37b. (If probationer says yes to above) Have you ever tried it?

37. Self-destructive behavior
  a. never seriously contemplated suicide
  b. has had definite thoughts of suicide
  c. has attempted it

37. requires overt action that resulted in self-harm or clear intent toward suicide.

38a. What do you do when you are feeling angry with people?

38b. Have you ever hurt anybody when you were angry?

38. In handling anger, probationer
  a. is physically aggressive
  b. avoids expression to others or has trouble expressing anger appropriately
  c. Responds appropriately

38. **a.** Based on all sources of reliable information and not just on probationer's statement: Physically aggressive problems should take precedence in scoring. IF probationer says, "I Leave," find out if/how he/she deals with the anger later.
  b. "I break things"

39a. Can you describe your personality?

39b. What do you like and what do you dislike about yourself?
-STOP-

39. In describing self, probationer
  a. emphasized strength
  b. Emphasizes in adequacy (probationer tends to downgrade self)
  c. can't describe self

39. **a.** If the probationer gives both positive and negative statements about himself/herself, choose the one emphasized most. If the positive and negative have equal emphasis, choose the first response given.
  b. Choice "c" is designed to identify the probationer who is incapable of showing insight or complexity into himself/herself; "I'm okay"; "I'm nice"; "I get into too much trouble"; etc.

40. (No question asked. Rate your impression of probationer's openness in discussing feelings.)

40. openness in discussing feelings
  a. discusses as openly as able
  b. is evasive or superficial

40. **a.** If the officer felt that the probationer was fairly straightforward in talking about his/her feelings.
  b. If the officer thought the probationer was evasive or superficial.

41. Aside from your legal problems, what is the biggest problem in your life right now?
-STOP-

41. What does the probationer view as his/her most important problem area right now?
  a. Personal
  b. Relationships
  c. Vocational-Educational (including employment)
  d. Financial
  e. no big problems presently (score item 42 as "a")

41. **a.** Probationer names several important problems -drinking or drugs -"Get my head together"
  b. -"get things straightened out with my fiancée"
  -"try to get along better with my parents"

42. How do you expect this problem to work out?

42. Attitude toward solving problems:
  a. optimistic; expects to succeed (include 41e)
  b. Unclear
  c. Pessimistic; expects to fail

42. **a.** "OK because I've got a better paying job"
  b. "OK I hope"
  "I'll be okay if I get a better paying job."
  c. Probationer is pessimistic about outcome or can't figure out a solution.

43a. What goals do you have for the future?
43b. What are your plans for achieving your goals?
-STOP-

43. Future Plans
  a. Short term goals (most of which can be fulfilled within 6 months)
  b. unrealistic goals
  c. realistic, long term goals (well developed beyond 6 months)

43. a. −"Just live day to day." Poorly developed goals with no plans for achieving them.
  b. −Strange, way-out, or impossible to achieve goals.
  c. Probationer is able to (1) set a goal within the realm of possibility and (2) list the steps necessary to achieve the goal.

44. (no question asked. Rate the item based on follow-through on jobs, education, training programs, treatment programs, etc., based on all sources.)

44. Probationer usually sticks with, or completes, things he/she begins.
  a. yes
  b. no

44. Compare to the average probationer.

45a. How will being on probation affect your life?
45b. What do you expect to get from being on probation?
-STOP-

45. Probationer's general expectations about supervision
  a. no effect
  b. monetary, counseling, or program help
  c. hopes supervision will keep him/her out of trouble
  d. negative expectations
  e. mixed or unclear expectations

46. Age of earliest court appearance:
  a. 14 or younger
  b. 15–17
  c. 18–22
  d. 23 or older

46. Include juvenile offenses and serious traffic offenses (drunk driving, hit and run). Including divorce, custody proceedings, etc.

47. Number of prior offenses:
  a. None
  b. 1–3
  c. 4–7
  d. 8 or more

47. Exclude the probationer's present offense when rating this item. Include juvenile and serious traffic offenses.

48. Number of commitments to state or federal correctional institutions:
  a. None
  b. 1
  c. 2 or more

48. Include juvenile commitments.

49. Time spent under probation or parole supervision:
  a. None
  b. 1 year or less
  c. Over 1 year; up to 3 years
  d. Over 3 years

49. Include juvenile supervision.
  a. Use "a" for new probationer.

50. (Circle all applicable choices.)
   a. Frequent headaches, back or stomach problems
   b. Serious head injuries
   c. Prior psychiatric hospitalization
   d. Outpatient psychotherapy
   e. None of the above

51. Highest grade completed:
   a. 9th or below
   b. 10th to 12th
   c. High school graduate (exclude GED)
   d. Some post-high school training leading toward a degree

52. Did probationer ever receive special education or remedial help in school?
   a. Yes
   b. No

53. Probationer was raised primarily by:
   a. Intact biological family
   b. Other

54. Did either parent have a history of (circle all applicable choices):
   a. Being on welfare
   b. Criminal behavior
   c. Psychiatric hospitalization
   d. Suicide attempts
   e. Drinking problems
   f. None of the above

55. Have siblings (including half and step siblings) ever been arrested?
   a. None
   b. Some
   c. Most
   d. Not applicable

50. a. vague complaints not diagnosed by a physician.
   b. Skull fractures/head injuries that required treatment (beyond X-ray)
   c. Professional inpatient or outpatient drug/alcohol treatment.

52. Include special programs for learning deficiencies (rather than behavior problems). Do not include English as a Second Language.

53. Choice "a" requires both natural parents in an intact home until probationer reached about 16 years of age.

54. Includes step and adoptive parents.

Prioritizing Strengths and Problems

Instructions: After you have conducted your interview, examine all the areas in the first column of this table below. Choose three areas that are your client's top strengths and three areas that are the priority problem areas that are most directly related to legal trouble

Area	Rank Order Top 3 Areas that Are Strengths/Positive Resource	Rank order Top 3–4 Problem Areas Related to Crime
Education/Learning		
Mental Health		
Employment Record		
Vocational Skills		
Financial Management		
Residential Stability		
Family History		
Interpersonal Skills		
Companions/Peers		
Intimate Marital Relationships		
Drugs & Alcohol		
Plans & Goals		
Physical Health		

DEVELOP THE CLIENT'S PROGRAM PLAN

Problem Statement: Using the 3-4 problems from the table above, re-state each problem area as a specific statement as to WHY or HOW that area is a problem for THAT client. *You will have one problem statement for each problem area identified in above Table.*

Long-Range Goal: For each problem statement, develop one long range goal that the client will strive to achieve. Incorporate how the client's strengths can be a part of those goals.

Probationer Action Item to Meet Goal: Develop 2-3 step-by-step action items (like a roadmap) for the probationer to achieve by certain dates to reach each long-term goal. Include dates or deadlines by which the client needs to complete each item.

Officer Action Item to Meet Goal: Think of at least one thing a supervision officer needs to do to help the client achieve his or her long-term goal for each of the problem areas.

Problem Statement #1:

_____

Long-range Goal for Problem #1:

_____

_____

Probationer Action Item A to Meet Goal 1:

_____

_____

_____

_____

Probationer Action item B to Meet Goal 1:

_____

_____

_____

_____

Probationer Action item C to Meet Goal 1:

_____

_____

_____

_____

Officer Action Plan to Help Client Reach Goal 1:

_____

_____

_____

Problem Statement #2:

_____

Long-range Goal for Problem #2:

_____

_____

Probationer Action Item A to Meet Goal 2:

_____

_____

_____

_____

Probationer Action item B to Meet Goal 2:

_____

_____

_____

_____

Probationer Action item C to Meet Goal 2:

_____

_____

_____

_____

Officer Action Plan to Help Client Reach Goal 2:

_____

_____

_____

Problem Statement #3:

_____

Long-range Goal for Problem #3:

_____

_____

Probationer Action Item A to Meet Goal 3:

_____

_____

_____

_____

Probationer Action item B to Meet Goal 3:

_____

_____

_____

_____

Probationer Action item C to Meet Goal 3:

_____

_____

_____

_____

Officer Action Plan to Help Client Reach Goal 3:

_____

_____

_____

Problem Statement #4:

_____

Long-range Goal for Problem #4:

_____

_____

Probationer Action Item A to Meet Goal 4:

_____

_____

_____

_____

Probationer Action item B to Meet Goal 4:

_____

_____

_____

_____

Probationer Action item C to Meet Goal 4:

_____

_____

_____

_____

Officer Action Plan to Help Client Reach Goal 4:

_____

_____

_____

Signed/Dated,

_____   _____
Client   Supervising Officer

6

Community Supervision for Offenders with Special Needs

CHAPTER LEARNING OBJECTIVES

1. Understand how intensive supervision differs from regular probation or parole supervision.
2. Identify various treatment options for drug-addicted offenders, such as drug court and therapeutic communities.
3. Analyze the issues inherent in the supervision and treatment of offenders with mental illness.

4. Describe the characteristics of a mental health court and a veterans court.
5. List the specific strategies that are used for supervising and treating sex offenders in the community.
6. Identify strategies that are most effective for working with offenders who are active gang members.

Public defender Chela Guzman-Wiegert stood with her client before Judge Porter during a weekly session of veterans court in Minneapolis, Minn to address the mental health needs of military veterans.

CHAPTER OUTLINE

KEY TERMS

intensive supervision probation/
    parole
relapse
Antabuse

drug courts
retention rates
mental health courts
therapeutic community

penile plethysmograph
child safety zones

About one in five military service members who return from Iraq and Afghanistan have some level of post-traumatic stress disorder (PTSD) or major depression as a result of their experience overseas. Less than half of those affected will ever seek mental health treatment or counseling, due in part to the stigma that mental illness has. Untreated PTSD in young people with specialized knowledge, skills, and abilities is likely to lead to violent outbursts, substance abuse, and eventually arrest.

Take Jonathan Wheeler's case. Mr. Wheeler was deployed to Fallujah and became part of a special Marine unit that identified "high-value" Iraqi casualties in an active war zone. Like most members of his unit, he routinely used alcohol and marijuana. However, he failed a drug test, which sent him to the brig (military detention) for 30 days. Detention in the brig disqualified Mr. Wheeler from receiving future Veterans Administration (VA) benefits.

Within a year after he was discharged and returned home, Mr. Wheeler had such intense panic attacks that he was unable to work. For the next five years, his behavior became worse rather than better. He drank alcohol, used drugs, and exhibited violent behavior in front of his wife and two children before an arrest landed him in jail facing a possible conviction. A few months after the arrest, he agreed to go to counseling, where he was diagnosed with PTSD and possible injury to the brain. Cases like Mr. Wheeler's can now be handled in an alternative court called veterans court, which allows military service members a diversionary alternative to criminal conviction if they comply with required counseling and medication and agree to permanently stop alcohol and drug use. Mr. Wheeler is now 31 years old and has been clean and sober for three months. If all goes well, he intends to volunteer as a peer mentor in Veterans Court and to reapply for VA benefits, given his new situation (Mador, 2010).

INTENSIVE SUPERVISION AND SPECIALIZED CASELOADS

Standard probation techniques provide sufficient monitoring for most sentenced offenders, but there are some offenders who have different needs or who need a more intensive form of monitoring and treatment. **Intensive supervision**

intensive supervision probation/parole
A form of probation that stresses intensive monitoring, close supervision, and offender control.

probation/parole (ISP) is an enhanced form of supervision that subjects offenders to closer surveillance, more conditions to follow, and more treatment exposure than are regular probationers and parolees. The use of ISP began in California in the 1950s under an assumption that increased contact would improve rehabilitation efforts and provide a viable alternative to incarceration. ISP was not really used all that much until the 1980s, when it reemerged by using smaller caseload sizes to keep tighter control on probationers and parolees. Essentially, probation and parole reemerged with increased supervision without much attention to treatment. Although smaller caseloads certainly provided increased surveillance and control, officers detected more technical violations, and this led to a higher revocation rate. The lack of treatment did not necessarily promote a safer community. The lesson learned from the 1980s and 1990s was that intensive treatment was as important as intensive supervision (Steiner, 2004).

Important changes were introduced to save ISP from extinction, many of which emerged from evidence-based practices. First, high-risk offenders were chosen for close supervision with intensive cognitive-behavioral treatment in order to significantly lower recidivism. Second, change was treated as a process, and offenders were allowed a certain degree of noncompliance to complete a program. Third, direct contact with an offender in the form of personal visits and phone contact increases the chances of program completion (Hanley, 2002). The important measure is not rate of program failure for technical violations but rate of rearrest for new crimes. High-risk offenders who were exposed to appropriate services to address criminogenic needs had fewer new crimes and rearrests (Bonta, Wallace-Capretta, & Rooney, 2000; Hanley, 2002; Paparozzi & Gendreau, 2005).

ISP is referred to today as *specialized caseloads*. The use of specialized caseloads means that a supervising officer becomes an expert in working with a particular subpopulation of offenders based on a particular criminogenic need or type of offense. About 10%–15% of probationers and parolees are eligible for inclusion in a specialized caseload. The specialized caseloads we discuss in this chapter consist of offenders who are addicted to drugs and alcohol, offenders with a mental illness, offenders convicted of a sex offense, and offenders who are gang members.

Offenders on specialized caseloads must meet frequently with their supervision officer to discuss their progress.

© Mikae Karlsson/Alamy

OFFENDERS WHO ARE ADDICTED TO DRUGS AND ALCOHOL

A majority of offenders serving community correction sentences has problems with drugs or alcohol, or their crime was in some way drug-related. For example, one third of new prison admissions are for drug charges, mostly for possession of a controlled substance (Levin, 2011). A nationwide survey of more than 2,000 probationers under active supervision found nearly half of them admitted to being under the influence of drugs or alcohol during the commission of their crime. For a number of others, substance abuse contributed indirectly to the crime(s) that led to their conviction (Mumola & Bonczar, 1998). This group includes those whose probation or parole was revoked due to their continued use of drugs while under supervision (Levin, 2011).

According to Steiner (2004), obstacles that probation and parole officers face in the supervision of offenders with substance abuse problems include:

- assigning quality drug treatment programs to trained staff;
- ability to refer clients to a community-based program (due to lack of space availability);
- limited ability to keep clients in mandatory treatment; and
- relapse after intensive treatment ends (events, thought patterns, or stressful situations can trigger substance use)

Because of these challenges, a supervision style called a *treatment retention model* was proposed for parole officers. The model recommends that treatment begin for offenders while they are incarcerated and that, when they are released from prison, a cognitive-behavioral relapse prevention program retain offenders in treatment throughout the reentry and parole period (Steiner, 2004). When offenders with substance abuse problems begin to **relapse** (return to drug use) while under supervision, Steiner argues for graduated sanctions tailored to a treatment plan rather than mere revocation to prison. In this section, we discuss general supervision and treatment strategies that probation and parole officers use with clients who have a problem with drugs or alcohol.

relapse
When an offender with a substance abuse problem returns to using alcohol or drugs.

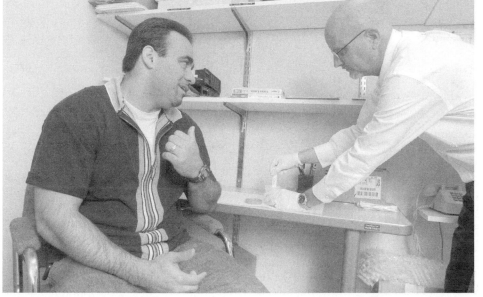

Drug and alcohol testing is common while on probation supervision.

Prescription Medications That Decreases Cravings

One supervision tool consists of monitoring a prescription medication that helps offenders stay away from drugs or alcohol. For example, alcoholics take **Antabuse**, a prescription medication that negatively reacts with their system if they ingest alcohol. Clients on Antabuse must take this medication every two to three days under the watchful eyes of staff, who administer the medication in community clinics or in day reporting centers. Medications such as Methadone or Buprenorphine are administered to clients with addictions to heroin or other opiate-based drugs. Naltrexone is an opiate antagonist that blocks opiate access to brain receptors. These substances must be used over a long period of time to decrease severe drug dependency.

Drug Courts

Drug courts are a proactive way for a court judge, prosecutor, and defense attorney to work with a treatment provider in monitoring and treating people with substance abuse problems. The idea of drug courts began in 1989 in Dade County, Florida, under an assumption that outpatient treatment interventions with first-time drug offenders or low-level drug users were more likely to curb future drug use than punishment without treatment. A second assumption was that the sooner a treatment intervention began after arrest, the less time an offender might spend in jail in a negative environment where drug use could continue (Alonso, 2009).

The drug court concept is much different from traditional criminal courts. The judge, prosecutor, defense attorney, and probation officer all work together with a treatment provider to allow more informal and direct interaction. The entire team monitors the progress of each client via staffing and court hearings every two weeks. Promoting the idea of a drug court from within the criminal justice system is sometimes difficult insofar as attorneys trained in traditional courtroom practices may resist change, as Judge Alonso's *Field Notes* essay attests (see Box 6.1).

BOX 6.1   FIELD NOTES

What were the challenges and rewards you faced introducing the concept of drug courts?

As a judge handling criminal cases, I was frustrated at the large number of probationers testing positive for alcohol and illegal drugs. While working on my Masters at the National Judicial College, I shared my frustration with one of my professors. He introduced me to drug courts and their existence in many cities. That year, I returned home and began implementing the rudimentary steps of drug courts following the ten key components. Since this was a new concept in our jurisdiction, I was met with incredible resistance from probation officers, defense attorneys, and the district attorney's office. Even our legislators informed me that this was a rehabilitative program not supported by the public. The public, they said, supported the "tough on crime, lock them up and throw away the key" concept.

Judge Al Alonso, Retired
Bexar County Court No. 1,
San Antonio, Texas

My first obstacle was the opposition of our ten probation officers who had been trained on being "tough." In a traditional court, if a defendant tested positive for illegal drugs, in most cases, they recommended revocation and incarceration. If a judge ordered treatment instead of jail, the judge was considered weak and ineffective. One of the probation officers even asked to be transferred out of my court.

Our district attorney's office would not agree to pre-trial diversion and did not buy into the non-adversarial approach of drug courts. The DA advised me their prosecutors were not "social workers." And the attorneys, who were trained in law school to be advocates for the adversarial approach, also had a difficult time representing a client within a team approach fostered by the

(Continues)

BOX 6.1   FIELD NOTES (*Continued*)

What were the challenges and rewards you faced introducing the concept of drug courts?

drug court program. All the members in the drug court team—probation officer, treatment therapist, drug court coordinator, defense attorney, prosecutor—work together toward supporting defendants (drug court participants) in their recovery.

After studying the drug court program and reading the research, I knew drug court was the best program we had in our criminal justice system in addressing non-violent drug abusers and alcoholics. I realized the answer to all resistance was to educate all members on drug courts, including our county elected officials and state legislators.

In 2002, I obtained a U.S. Department of Justice grant. The grant provided for drug court training for a ten-member team, plus one state legislator. We were the

first court in the county to be certified by the National Drug Court Institute, a major step in beginning to turn back the resistance. Slowly, attitudes began to change. The next challenge was communication with the program participants. Team members had to learn the technique of "motivational interviewing," a non-confrontational, non-argument, sympathetic approach. Each participant is treated with fairness, dignity, and respect. Some change of personnel took place.

Today, we have four drug courts. In my 40-year professional career, board certified in criminal law, and 15 years as a judge, this is the criminal justice program that changes lives, saves money, and lowers crime. It is the most satisfying work I have done in my legal career.

Drug courts have expanded to DWI courts, juvenile courts, and tribal reservations, which all share distinct commonalities. Phases are used to reward good behavior and predictable sanctions are administered if clients fail to undergo treatment or miss court dates. Clients who relapse might have to repeat certain segments of a program, and repeated relapses can mean short-term incarceration. Thus judges intervene before a pattern of technical violations occurs, as with regular probation, and a court collaborates with drug treatment specialists. With any addiction, relapse is to be expected, but participants are also responsible for preventing relapse from becoming a pattern.

Drug courts are specifically for nonviolent drug offenders with at least moderate substance usage. The offenders may be misdemeanants or felons, and they must voluntarily agree to participate. An initial substance abuse assessment determines eligibility for program participation (Listwan et al., 2003). About half of drug courts are preadjudication, which means that upon successful completion of a drug court program, charges are dismissed. Post-adjudication drug courts usually mean that following a plea of guilty the sentence remains, but the defendant stays out of jail. If preadjudication offenders withdraw or are terminated from a program without successful completion, they are charged and tried for the original offense and sentenced accordingly.

Drug court treatment is one year in length and typically begins with an intensive two weeks of inpatient treatment. Treatment involves detoxification through acupuncture, drug testing through urine screenings, and group and individual counseling. Clients are also referred to Narcotics Anonymous and Alcoholics Anonymous (Alonso, 2009). As a client progresses through a program, the levels gradually taper to day treatment and then to outpatient treatment, which latter is the most common status. Most clients relapse during treatment, but a continual pattern of drug use is not acceptable and results in program failure. Drug court completion rates for those who successfully finish a one-year program vary from 29%–43% (Taxman & Bouffard, 2003).

GENDER-RESPONSIVE STRATEGIES   Treatment approaches for substance abuse should vary depending on why clients abuse substances in the first place. As Bloom and

McDiarmid (2000) note, "Men in recovery tend to emphasize the problems caused by the consequences of drug use, and women more often report the 'stressors' leading to drug use" (p. 15). Research shows that women use drugs to cope with traumatic situations, such as domestic violence, mental illness, sexual abuse, and physical abuse. In this manner, women are likely to self-medicate alone and need to be drawn out of the despair they feel. Women also use substances to maintain a relationship with a significant other who also uses them (Dannerbeck, Sundet, & Lloyd, 2002; Guydish et al., 2011).

Men who participate in drug court tend to abuse alcohol or marijuana. They use these in a more social and public context than women do, which involves establishing or maintaining a reputation or gaining a sense of control. Men have better completion rates, perhaps because drug courts have been modeled to better address their needs, patterns, and reasons for drinking (Dannerbeck, Sundet, & Lloyd, 2002). As a result, gender-specific drug court programs have evolved for men and women.

Programs for women can be directed more specifically at traumatic significant relationships, parenting issues, and domestic violence. Supervision of female probationers should therefore be relational, in that they engage any children and spouse in a recovery process. Programs that use an "empowerment model of skill building to develop competencies that enable women to achieve independence" are ideal strategies for female offenders (Bloom & McDiarmid, 2000, p. 13).

EVALUATING DRUG COURTS   Drug courts reportedly saved money over traditional court processing in Multnomah County, Oregon, when the costs for arrest, booking, court time, treatment, jail time, and probation were totaled for 120 people, some of whom went through drug court and some of whom did not. When these people were tracked to determine recidivism, the drug court participants were less likely to be rearrested than those in the control group. The cost of obtaining drug court treatment was $5,928 per year per offender, whereas it cost $7,369 for traditional processing of one drug offender for one year (Carey & Figgin, 2004). Other researchers disagree that drug courts save money. Although drug court clients did indeed spend less time behind bars prior to court disposition, they spent twice as long in jail for noncompliance of drug court sanctions than did a randomized control group that was eligible but did not go through drug court (Gottfredson, Najaka, & Kearley, 2003; Gottfredson, Kearley, Najaka, & Rocha, 2007).

The best method of testing effectiveness is random assignment either to drug court or to regular supervision (whether to probation or prison). Sites at which this has been done found that drug courts had a positive effect on reducing recidivism. The control group was rearrested at nearly three times the rate of the drug court participants (Gottfredson & Exum, 2002), and the difference between the two groups remained apparent two years later (Gottfredson, Najaka, & Kearley, 2003). After three years, the judicial hearings and drug testing had a direct effect on reducing future crime and return to drug use: Participants who had more judicial contact and who felt they received fair treatment, even if they didn't like the outcome, were more likely to follow a contract and less likely to commit crime and return to drug use than did offenders who had less or no judicial contact (Gottfredson, Kearley, Najaka, & Rocha, 2007).

A nationwide study of 95 drug courts (17,000 graduates) over a two-year period revealed an average rearrest rate of 16.5% after the first 12 months following graduation, and 27.5% after 24 months (Roman, Townsend, & Bhati, 2003). Recidivism rates varied widely among the different program participants, making comparison across programs difficult. Programs serving felony offenders and offenders who had a more severe drug problem had higher recidivism rates than did programs that treated only misdemeanor clients. Access to other community services, program size, police practices, prosecutor decisions, program duration, and violation policies affected the recidivism rate as well. Researchers caution against the use of recidivism as the sole measure of program success, and also against making too many comparisons across programs that should not be compared.

Two consistent conclusions were drawn when comparing program participants. First, when drug court graduates were compared with drug offenders who went to prison without treatment, the former were rearrested at significantly lower rates over a three-year period (Galloway & Drapela, 2006; von Zielbauer, 2003). A second conclusion indicates a difference in recidivism by gender, finding that women had lower rearrest rates than men did. Also, Caucasian individuals had lower recidivism rates than did minority drug court participants (Roman, Townsend, & Bhati, 2003). These findings might be due to drug court participant behavior, the justice system response, or a combination of both factors. The drug court model does seem most applicable to offenders who are motivated to change (Listwan et al., 2003).

Therapeutic Communities

When outpatient treatment is not enough, offenders on probation or parole who have more severe addictions require an inpatient residential treatment facility, such as a residential drug treatment center or therapeutic community. **Therapeutic communities** (TCs) focus on long-term treatment of alcoholism and drug addiction and abstinence from substances for criminal offenders. This section addresses TCs in the community. TCs are generally better suited for long-term polydrug addictions (addiction to more than one kind of drug for an extensive period of time), whereas drug courts are geared toward moderate forms of addiction. Helping an individual through change is a process that entails stumbling blocks. Thus a typical TC provides six to nine months of residential drug and alcohol treatment, with a period of aftercare as an offender transitions from a therapeutic environment to dealing with the stressors of daily life. Table 6.1 summarizes the differences between therapeutic communities and drug courts.

therapeutic community
A type of residential community facility specifically targeted for drug offenders, offenders who are alcoholics, and/or drug addicts who are amenable to treatment.

THE THERAPEUTIC COMMUNITY ENVIRONMENT TC candidates are thoroughly screened for suitability and readiness for treatment. If accepted, offenders with a substance abuse problem must be motivated to adhere to all rules and participate in all activities required by a TC program. A TC environment is considered a supportive surrogate family, except that physical fighting and sexual relations are not allowed. Each day in a TC is highly structured and disciplined. Clients have daily cleaning chores within the facility and hours of peer group sessions in which the attitudes and behavior of each resident are confronted. The goal of these sessions is to tear down the defense mechanisms and excuses that addicts adopt when using drugs as a response to a desire or stressor. The sessions attempt to resocialize clients to new thoughts, attitudes, and behavioral choices in all areas of their lives (with family, friends, work, leisure time, spirituality, and so forth). Other types of counseling focus on self-worth, self-discipline, and respect for authority. There is little idle time, for even free personal time is used for some type of intellectual or creative self-improvement.

The TC is also the only type of program that is largely peer-operated and peer-enforced. Although there might be a free-world staff contact person, TC rules are enforced by residents and a group is run by them, who earn various leadership roles based on a level's hierarchy. Clients who graduate from a program are transferred to outpatient treatment while still remaining on probation or parole, depending on

TABLE 6.1   Comparing Therapeutic Communities and Drug Courts

Characteristic	Therapeutic Community	Drug Court
Initial point of intervention	Post-adjudication only	Pre-adjudication or post-adjudication
Type of program	Residential/inpatient	Nonresidential/outpatient
Where located	Community or prison	Community only
Average length of stay	32 weeks	45 weeks
Voluntary	Yes	Yes
Estimated percent of waking hours devoted to treatment and self-improvement	100%	20%–25%
People involved in defendant's progress	TC counselor, TC former addicts, TC peers in program	Judge, prosecutor, public defender, probation officer/case manager, treatment provider
Who imposes rewards and sanctions	TC participants/peers (confrontational)	Judge (nonadversarial collaborative)
Treatment and monitoring forms	Group, confrontation, individual counseling, community meetings, drug testing, shaming, extra chores	Group counseling, individual counseling, drug testing, acupuncture, community service, case management visits
Weekly cost	$569–$708	$34–$146
Episode cost (entire length of stay)	$14,818–$32,361	$2,486–$4,888

Source: Michael T. French, Ioana Popovici, and Lauren Tapsell. 2008. The economic costs of substance abuse treatment: Updated estimates and cost bands for program assessment and reimbursement. Journal of Substance Abuse Treatment 35(4): 462–469.

their initial status. Abel Salinas, manager of a community-based, residential substance abuse treatment facility, provides insight into the rewards and challenges of working with probationers who have substance abuse problems (see Box 6.2).

CHALLENGES OF THE TC   One of largest challenges for TCs to overcome is a low program completion rate. Treatment programs should expect failures and relapses, but during the first 30 days between 25%–85% of new residents drop out.Efforts

BOX 6.2   FIELD NOTES

When working with offenders who have difficulties with substance abuse, what are the most rewarding long-term and short-term aspects? What are the greatest challenges and how do you and your staff attempt to overcome them?

There are many rewarding aspects that result from working with substance abusers. However, the single most rewarding aspect that I can see is the improvement in the quality of life for, not just the offender who successfully completes treatment, but

Courtesy of Leanne Fiftal Alarid

Abel Salinas
Manager, Substance Abuse Treatment Facility

for the immediate and extended family as well. Too many times, children and spouses suffer the residual effect of a drug user's inability to maintain employment, effectively communicate problems to their significant others, and serve as role models to children who seek the support and guidance of adult users. Children who witness this learned behavior often times fall into the same lifestyle as their using parents, and the cycle continues.

(Continues)

BOX 6.2 **FIELD NOTES** (*Continued*)

By helping to repair one person, the domino effect of ruined lives and extreme hardships for families can be stopped or broken, and in some situations, even reversed. Seeing a former offender who spent time in the drug and alcohol treatment facility at a local grocery store, while putting gas in their car, or at a movie theater, and having them tell you that they have removed themselves from their drug-using lifestyle and are well on their way to improving their family relationships and employment status is nothing short of gratifying.

A very rewarding short-term aspect are those offenders who come into the program who, although not entirely excited to be here, nonetheless appear to have their stress level lowered somewhat by their new structured and therapeutic environment. This is often the complete opposite of the chaotic and deceitful environment that they've left, where the threat of violence, arrest, and looking over their shoulder is the norm.

The single greatest challenge in residential services can be described as the *career criminal* vs. the *drug abuser*. The drug abuser readily admits a problem, wants help, understands the negative consequences of their drug abuse, but still feels a strong desire to use drugs. This is where the treatment staff, probation officers, and security personnel intervene to assist the individual, using cognitive behavioral therapy and motivational interviewing techniques.

On the other hand, the career criminal does not admit a problem, does not want help for a drug problem, does not understand the negative consequences of their drug abuse or drug dealing, does not have any desire to stop their anti-social behavior, and sees treatment as only a way of avoiding a lengthy jail or prison term. Their only desire is to get back into the community and neighborhoods and continue their lifestyle. This clash of attitudes and beliefs between the career criminal and drug abuser is probably one of the most challenging aspects to deal with in residential services. Although the career criminal, in my opinion, represents only a small minority of the entire population, their manipulation of well-intentioned residents, staff, and counselors can have a detrimental impact on many of the residents.

We try our best to overcome this constant push and pull by singling out the career criminals and offering them more intensive treatment, while paying special attention to their criminogenic needs. Good quality communication between security staff, counselors, and probation officers keeps us on our toes and lessens the chances of falling for the manipulative ways of the career criminal.

---

are needed either to improve **retention rates** (perhaps by redefining *success* and *failure*) or to better screen applicants' motivation to participate. For the first 30 days new residents need to be more thoroughly educated about the treatment process, and they might need confidence building before being confronted in group therapy.

A second challenge concerns the use of shaming and humiliation with clients who misbehave or fail to participate. Examples include "PT" (extra chores or duties), wearing a dunce cap or a sign (stating the infraction) around the facility for a specified period of time, or shaving one's head. Some of the methods of punishment for disobedience have been criticized for their ineffectiveness in changing behavior.

retention rates
The combined total of the successful completers and those actively enrolled compared to the total number admitted to drug court.

TYPES AND USES OF THERAPEUTIC COMMUNITIES A **community-based** TC is designed for clients who have often failed in other community programs (for example, a halfway house, probation, or parole) because of either alcohol abuse or illegal substance addiction. Residential drug and alcohol treatment programs are also used as diversion from prison. For example, Florida has an 18-month Drug Punishment Program, which includes six months in a secure facility, then three months in a community facility followed by nine months of intensive supervision probation.

Another similar program for nonviolent probationers exists in Dallas, Texas. This facility provides 200 of its 300 beds for clients in the first six months of the program. Then clients with adequate support systems enter a six-month aftercare program in which they live at home and report to a probation officer. The remaining

community-based therapeutic community
A therapeutic community designed for those who have failed in other programs because of either alcohol abuse or illegal substance addiction.

100 beds are reserved for clients who do not have strong support systems and need an additional three months to make a successful transition through the "live-in, work-out" program. This is important because transition from residential living to community living is seen as a prime opportunity for relapse. Probation officers work with treatment facility staff to review clients' progress (Barthwell et al., 1995, pp. 39–47).

Sometimes TC programs are used as a transition step for clients who graduate from prison-based therapeutic communities or other types of drug treatment programs while behind bars. For example, women in California with drug problems could attend a drug treatment program and then, upon their release, be transferred to a residential program in the community to grapple with issues of relapse and possible temptations.

EVALUATIONS OF THERAPEUTIC COMMUNITIES Offenders who participate in community-based residential treatment programs are often in the last program available before jail or prison (Perez, 2009). The pressure to succeed can cause significant stress, and clients are also at high risk for relapse and recidivism because making the transition from a structured environment directly to their home in the community, even when under probation and parole supervision, poses challenges (Sung, 2011). For example, offenders with a long criminal history, high rate of unemployment, and educational underachievement find the transition most difficult.

Overall evaluations of residential treatment have found that it reduces future criminal behavior and future drug use, particularly for those who are engaged in the treatment—that is, accepting of program norms and protocols (Sung, 2011). For those who complete it, residential drug treatment is more effective than outpatient treatment (Levin, 2011). Participants who did not complete treatment were left vulnerable to relapse (Prendergast, Wellisch, & Wong, 1996), which is fairly common for drug offenders. Box 6.3 discusses a program called *HOPE* aimed at drug offenders who resist drug tests and treatment while under community supervision.

BOX 6.3 **COMMUNITY CORRECTIONS UP CLOSE**

HOPE for Offenders Who Resist Drug Testing

Under traditional community supervision, offenders receive advance notice that they must provide a drug test and get ample time to take it. This also allows them to schedule their drug use around the test, even to avoid it altogether. Offenders who use drugs while under supervision also tend to miss scheduled appointments, which results in a long time before an officer can schedule a court date to determine whether revocation is appropriate. A program called *HOPE*, which stands for Hawaii's Opportunity Probation with Enforcement, seeks to increase compliance and to reduce the costs incurred by revocation. HOPE is a variation of the drug court concept in that offenders enter HOPE only if they have violated probation by missing a drug test or failing to undergo treatment. A formal warning is delivered immediately in open court by a judge, and offenders are issued a color code (e.g., blue, red, green, etc.). Every day, they must call a hotline to learn the color assigned for that day. If their color has been chosen, they have until 2:00 PM that same day to provide a urine sample. Failure to drug test results in a few days in jail, with probation resuming upon release. In such a case, probation is *not* revoked but *modified* by an officer to allow the judge to issue a bench warrant to authorize an arrest and jail booking for two to three days. With each incident of noncompliance, jail days increase. As behavior improves, drug tests become less frequent. Evaluations of offenders in HOPE indicate this modification works to reduce missed drug tests and skipped appointments, and in turn reduces drug use. HOPE offenders have also committed fewer new crimes when compared to other high-risk probationers under traditional supervision.

Source: http://www.nij.gov/topics/corrections/community/drug-offenders/hawaii-hope.htm

SUPERVISING OFFENDERS WHO ARE MENTALLY ILL

A disproportionately large number of people with mental health issues come to the attention of the criminal justice system. Due to the deinstitutionalization of the mentally ill and the lack of community mental health providers to serve clients without health insurance, indigent people with mental illnesses have limited resources to avoid drawing attention to themselves. As a result, jails and prisons have become the largest mental health institutions in the country. Yet correctional institutions are stressful and overcrowded places that in turn exacerbate mental conditions (Slate & Johnson, 2008). Also, the cost of confining an inmate with a severe mental illness to special housing is 2.5 times greater than for an inmate not on psychotropic medication. It is for this reason that most offenders with mental illness qualify for community correctional supervision.

It is estimated that about 16% of all probationers have general mental health needs and between 5%–10% of parolees have serious mental illnesses that require medication and therapy (Slate et al., 2003). The Council of State Governments (2008, p. 2) reported that "nearly two-thirds of boys and three-quarters of girls detained in juvenile facilities were found to have at least one psychiatric disorder, with approximately 25 percent of these juveniles experiencing disorders so severe that their ability to function was significantly impaired." Although a small number of offenders with mental illnesses needs to be separated from the rest of society, incarceration is overly stressful and not the best situation for stabilizing the majority of mentally ill individuals, who are better served in the community.

Supervising offenders with mental illnesses poses a special challenge because most correctional supervision officers do not have training in mental health or in psychiatric disorders. *Having a base level of knowledge about various forms of mental illness and the laws pertaining to the treatment of mental illness is very important when working with offenders.* Here are some of the basics: Most people with severe mental illnesses are *not* violent or dangerous; they simply need help getting to a psychiatrist, becoming stabilized on medication, and meeting their basic needs for safety, food, and permanent housing. The long-term challenge is to convince offenders with mental illness to remain on medication even when they report feeling better. People with severe mental disorders who go off their medications may eventually find themselves in jail or on probation because they eventually draw attention to themselves. Some self-medicate with illegal drugs or turn to criminal activities to support a habit and are turned away from a resource-depleted mental health system. There are also some severely mentally ill people who are not stabilized on medication and who may act out in deviant ways, though they are not necessarily violent or dangerous (Slate et al., 2003). In this section we discuss community-based responses to offenders with mental illnesses, including mental health courts, veterans courts, specialized caseloads, outpatient treatment, and residential treatment.

Mental Health Courts

Many of the people suffering from mental illnesses who come to the attention of the criminal justice system are appropriate candidates for a diversion program, from which they can obtain linkages to medication and counseling services. Mental health courts began in 1997 for this purpose. Like drug courts discussed in the previous section, **mental health courts** use a team problem-solving approach, in lieu of traditional case processing, to supervise and treat mentally ill offenders in the community. Participants are initially identified during the jail booking process through mental health screening or assessment. For example, a jail diversion coordinator

mental health courts
A diversion program for mentally ill defendants in which the judge, prosecutor, and probation officer play a proactive role and monitor the progress of clients through weekly visits to the courtroom.

Offenders with mental illness receive counseling and medication monitoring by a service provider who in turn communicates client progress with the community supervision officer.

© Barry Lewis/Alamy

receives an instant message when a client with certain criteria is booked in jail. Within 24 hours, the diversion coordinator notifies the courts that an eligible diversion case should be considered. Eligibility criteria are long-term Axis I disorders that as defined by the current version of the *Diagnostic and Statistical Manual of Mental Disorders*, have affected daily functioning, such as schizophrenia, anxiety or obsessive-compulsive disorder, bipolar disorder, and severe depression. Participants must be competent and able to voluntarily participate on their own. The eligible Axis I disorders do not include substance abuse as a *primary* diagnosis. However, even though an Axis I disorder must be an offender's primary problem, substance abuse is frequently a *secondary* diagnosis. Offenders with a mental illness who also have a substance abuse problem—a large proportion of this population—are treated simultaneously for both conditions.

Another way of identifying appropriateness for the diversion program bypasses the preapproval of a prosecutor, relying instead on mental health specialists along with a jail medical screener to make a group decision that is then presented to a court for final approval. Once a judge agrees, the group creates a transition plan while an eligible offender stabilizes on medications in jail, separated from the regular jail inmate population.

Once a participant is accepted into a mental health court program, a mental health court team forms, comprised of a judge, prosecutor, defense attorney, mental health providers, and a pretrial services officer with specialized training in mental health (Slate & Johnson, 2008). Defense attorneys assist offenders who are unable to fully understand their circumstances because of their psychiatric disorder and possible chemical dependence. The same team members meet with each participant twice a month in a *status hearing* to discuss progress in the program. The status hearing takes place in a courtroom whose daily docket is specifically for mental health court clients. Prior to each status hearing, team members "staff" each individual situation, which means they meet as a group without a participant present to update and share information. Each team comes to a decision on which actions to take at the next status hearing—whether to increase or decrease medication, treatment exposure, and sanctions, to graduate a participant to the next level, or to in some way reward him or her with a gift certificate. Specially trained probation officers have *specialized caseloads*, which are smaller caseloads that use a special case management style specific to the needs and challenges that people with mental illnesses face.

The more successful mental health courts have a solid community partnership with an availability of services addressing homelessness, transportation needs, and medication stability. Outcome evaluations of various courts have found that participants in mental health courts received less new charges and arrests and, as a result, fewer new jail bookings and days in jail than did nonparticipants with a mental illness. Participation in mental health courts also increased the rate at which clients received services compared to those who were court-ordered through a traditional process to undergo treatment (Council of State Governments, 2008).

Veterans Courts

At the beginning of this chapter we discussed Jonathan Wheeler's brush with the law following his return from Iraq. It is estimated that 20% of returning military service personnel suffer from some level of post-traumatic stress disorder (PTSD) or major depression, yet few of those affected ever seek mental health treatment or counseling. PTSD is a type of mental illness that frequently causes memory loss, blackouts, and a reliving of horrific scenes that can lead to panic attacks, anger, depression, and substance abuse. The negative effects of PTSD can be reduced with prescribed medication and sobriety from alcohol and illegal drugs. Although not all persons with PTSD come in contact with the criminal justice system, it was recently acknowledged by the Department of Veterans Affairs (VA) that an option needs to be provided for treatment and close supervision of such cases to ensure stability with medication and satisfaction of basic needs for food, clothing, and shelter. The earliest veterans courts were opened in 2004 in Anchorage, Alaska, and in 2008 in Buffalo, New York (Berenson, 2010). They have since expanded to over 22 jurisdictions in the U.S., particularly in areas with a disproportionately high number of vets. For example, San Antonio, Texas, is home to over 160,000 veterans, of whom 11,000 (less than 7%) have experienced combat. A court was established in this city in 2011.

Most veterans courts require, first, that an individual has been honorably discharged from the military, which is also a prerequisite for obtaining the VA benefits that help fund these courts. Although veterans can obtain help through the VA at any time provided their mental illness or traumatic brain injury is directly connected to combat, a veterans court intervenes once a misdemeanor has been committed. Veterans court participants agree to undergo weekly drug testing and treatment through the VA Health Care Network, as needed for their individual situation (Russell, 2009). Some courts also assign a court-approved mentor to provide a participant with a positive support system and to help him or her with resolving problems. As with all treatment courts, veterans court also employs a system of incentives for compliance and sanctions for noncompliance. Once conditions are met, an offense is expunged from an individual's criminal record. Early evaluations of participants have shown a low recidivism rate (Russell, 2009).

FACT OR FICTION?

Criminals cannot be rehabilitated.
Fiction.
Fact: Rehabilitation works with many (though not all) offenders, but rehabilitation programs must be implemented for a proper length of time and use cognitive-behavioral methods specific to problems related to criminal behavior.

Specialized Mental Health Probation Caseloads

Another response to supervising offenders with mental illness is by means of a specially trained caseload officer specializing in mental health issues (Castillo & Alarid, 2011). When traditional probation caseloads were compared with specialized caseloads, 90 supervisors drawn from a nationwide sample of 25 probation departments reported training in mental health issues and a reduced caseload number as the two biggest differences (Skeem, Emke-Francis, & Louden, 2006). Such training gave probation officers a more empathetic understanding of various mental imbalances, enabling them to recognize mental deterioration before a situation reached the point of no return. Training also helped officers to understand psychological resistance and to learn how to gain the trust and compliance necessary to work with this population. Specialized caseload size was less than half that for traditional probation—averaging 48 clients compared with 130—allowing officers on specialized caseloads a style of case management with an enhanced focus on both treatment and supervision (Skeem, Emke-Francis, & Louden, 2006).

Maintaining a positive working relationship with treatment providers was important for these specialized probation officers. The two greatest challenges found in working with mentally ill probationers were coordinating treatment and ensuring compliance with medication and counseling sessions. Mentally ill individuals tend to behave in a noncompliant manner more often than do probationers in traditional caseloads. Consequently problem-solving strategies and court appearances were used much more often than revocation to address noncompliance. It is recommended that community officers who work with offenders with mental illnesses be:

> patient and flexible, have a basic knowledge of mental health disorders, and be particularly skilled in firm yet non-confrontational communication strategies . . . monitoring compliance with any medication regimen and detecting signs that may indicate that the defendant is a danger to others or disoriented . . . pay attention to signs of withdrawal (such as poor hygiene, disorganization within a household or drastic changes in physical appearance) . . . [and] establish a collateral network that includes treatment providers and individuals who are in daily contact with the defendant and thus in the best position to observe early signs of deteriorating and/or dangerous behavior (Administrative Office of the U.S. Courts, 2007, chapter V, p. 17).

Outpatient Community Treatment

The strongest predictors of recidivism for offenders with mental illness have been found to be prior criminal history, previous substance abuse problems, and resistance to psychotropic medication compliance (Swanson et al., 2001). Outpatient community treatment allows mentally impaired offenders who are stabilized on medication and no longer a danger to themselves or others a chance to avoid the harmful incarcerative environment while improving independent functioning and continuing an ongoing treatment regimen. Outpatient community treatment appears most successful when services begin with residential treatment. It is believed that offenders with mental illnesses who were released from jail and who then used aftercare services thereby lessened their likelihood of future arrests (Swanson et al., 2001; Ventura, Cassel, Jacoby, & Huang, 1998).

Based on this discussion, we recommend that mental health services be strongly connected with criminal justice agencies. Examples of programs with such criminal justice collaborations are those in Milwaukee, Wisconsin, and Multnomah County, Oregon. Further, it is necessary to continually educate workers in criminal justice about mental health issues, such as through a standardized training curriculum for probation and parole officers. A model program in New York incorporates elements of crisis intervention and recognizes signs of mental disorder (Slate et al., 2004).

COMMUNITY-BASED RESIDENTIAL FACILITIES FOR MENTALLY ILL OFFENDERS   An inpatient residential facility is an alternative to a jail setting for offenders who need more structure and treatment intervention but are not yet ready to be released to outpatient services, probation, or parole. After undergoing cognitive-behavioral treatment and stabilizing on medication, mentally ill offenders are transferred to probation within three to four months. These separate treatment programs are seen as more effective than jail in reducing felony recidivism (Braddock, Lehman, & Maclean, 2002).

SUPERVISING SEX OFFENDERS

The term *sex offense* refers to sexual acts against a victim's will, and includes a wide range of behaviors ranging from exposing oneself in a public place (a misdemeanor) to rape (a felony). Some sex offenders are aggressive and violent, while others are passive and use more subtle techniques to gain compliance from their victims. In any case, sexual acts against children are included in the definition because it is assumed that children are unable to give consent. Sex offenders are a heterogeneous group, and some target children whereas others exclusively victimize adults. Child molesters are more likely to have been victimized as children by someone else, while offenders convicted of sexual assault evince anger management problems and chemical dependency (Alexander, 2010). In any case, whether child molester, incest offender or rapist, a perpetrator is more likely to groom victims with whom he or she is already familiar (Harris, 2004).

People might be surprised to find out that even though 60% of all convicted sex offenders are under conditional supervision in their community (Jenuwine, Simmons, & Swies, 2003), typically the period of supervision is significantly longer than it is for other types of offenders. Sex offenders generally have lower recidivism rates than other types of offenders but they are strongly feared and regarded with enormous disdain by the public. Public contempt than and political pressures have caused more laws to be passed that regulate sex offenders perhaps any other type of offender, with the exception of death row prisoners. These laws include mandatory treatment, polygraphs, increased supervision, public notification, and the possibility of civil commitment and/or chemical castration.

Probation and parole officers in sex offender units are specially trained in the area of sex offenses and in recognizing secrecy and deceit, which frequently characterize crimes against children. Payne and DeMichele (2008) discuss how to work with sex offenders without compromising an officer's own mental health. One way is to separate such persons from what they have done. Working with sex offenders does not mean condoning their behavior. The mark of a true professional is an ability to supervise and willingness to talk with a person who has behaved badly, along with a capacity to view the behaviors as well as the individual in a nonjudgmental way, yet without being manipulated or conned.

Sex Offender Treatment

Sex offenders are typically court-mandated to undergo intensive treatment specific to the type of sex offense. Sex offender treatment programs use multiple regimens that include cognitive-behavioral therapy to address thinking errors and victim

FACT OR FICTION?

Sex offenders are eligible for community supervision.

Fact: Over half of all sex offenders are supervised in a community. People who have committed just about every type of crime end up under community supervision—either coming out of prison on parole or as an alternative to prison—including sex offenders, who comprise a wide variety of personalities and commit a range of crime types.

minimization, polygraph tests to detect deception, and aversive conditioning to alter inappropriate sexual interests. Aggressive rapists require an entirely different treatment approach than do more passive pedophiles. The assumption about inappropriate sexual behaviors is that there is no "cure" in the medical sense, but offenders can learn how to control their urges and replace them with appropriate behaviors.

Decisions in court cases have raised interesting legal issues involving treatment programs for sex offenders. One consideration is that sex offender treatment requires offenders to admit their guilt. If the crime is denied, then the offender will not be allowed to participate in treatment. Failure to participate in a treatment program is a violation of probation or parole and a legitimate reason for revocation. A Connecticut appellate court noted that an offender must be informed in advance that denial of guilt will ultimately result in revocation (*State v. Faraday*, 2002).

Another issue that has surfaced during sex offender treatment is that an offender must acknowledge all prior sex offenses. In *McKune v. Lile* (2002), the U.S. Supreme Court held that a sex offender treatment program did not violate the Fifth Amendment's privilege against self-incrimination when it required that offenders acknowledge past crimes, insofar as doing so was the beginning of rehabilitation and acceptance of responsibility for their actions. According to the Supreme Court, acknowledging past crimes even if the state offers no immunity and could then potentially prosecute for them is different from the right to invoke Fifth Amendment protection in the face of criminal prosecution by the state.

POLYGRAPH TESTS Polygraph tests have been recognized as a tool to reduce the secrecy and deceit that sex offenders typically use with their victims and with supervising probation officers. Many sex offenders are motivated by gaining power over their victims in a calculating way that minimizes detection. As a result, some jurisdictions require that sex offenders, when initially placed under community supervision, submit to a baseline polygraph examination that explores previous sexual behaviors and current deviant thoughts. Polygraphed sex offenders "reported many more victims [especially male victims], far less history of being sexually abused themselves, and a much higher incidence of having offended as juveniles" than did the nonpolygraphed sex offender group (Hindman & Peters, 2001, p. 10). If used properly, the baseline test can then be shared with treatment providers to measure treatment progress as well as with law enforcement, if necessary, to compare against any later polygraph tests given throughout a period of probation.

penile plethysmograph
A device that measures erectile responses in male sex offenders to determine level of sexual arousal to various types of stimuli. This device is used for assessment and treatment purposes.

PENILE PLETHYSMOGRAPH A **penile plethysmograph** is used as treatment to identify the gender and ages of victims to whom a sex offender is attracted. This device also tracks how treatment is progressing and whether a different approach needs to be used. A sex offender may not contest a penile plethysmograph as a probation or parole condition. The Seventh Circuit Court of Appeals upheld submission to a penile plethysmograph as a parole condition for a Michigan inmate convicted in federal court of kidnapping and allegedly molesting a six-year-old boy before attempting to drown him (*Walrath v. Getty*, 1995). The offender in this case objected to the condition, saying that it was fundamentally unfair and therefore denied him due process. His parole was revoked. On appeal, the Seventh Circuit ruled that "the Commission may impose or modify other conditions of parole so long as they are reasonably related to the nature of the circumstances of the offense and the history and characteristics of the parolee."

Therapy can be supplemented with prescribed hormones called medro oxyprogesterone acetate, otherwise known as Depo-Provera. Depo-Provera changes male hormone levels to decrease sexual urges and increase responsiveness to treatment.

These medications are also known as antiandrogens or selective serotonin reuptake inhibitors because they change the hormone balance in the brain to help decrease sexual urges (Harris, 2004; Payne & DeMichele, 2008).

Containment Supervision Approach

Supervising sex offenders in the community involves more frequent contacts and more frequent searches than with other offenders. This is because the majority of sex offenses are planned acts committed when opportunities arise. A "containment approach" is recommended, with the following guidelines (English et al., 1996):

- two to four face-to-face contacts between officer and probationer per month;
- two probationer home-and-computer searches per month;
- thorough mental health evaluation;
- weekly cognitive-behavioral group therapy and individual counseling;
- regular staffings with treatment provider and polygraph examiner; and
- sharing of information on a regular basis between probation officers and treatment providers.

A risk assessment that is specific to sex offenders is called a *Static 99*, which identifies factors related to the likelihood of future sexual offending (see Table 6.2). Sex offenders who are most at risk of recidivism are increasingly monitored using global positioning systems (GPS) technology to quell public concerns. Currently 44 states authorize the use of GPS or electronic monitoring of sex offenders; 10 of these states require lifetime monitoring of the highest-risk sex offenders (Armstrong & Freeman, 2009). We discuss how GPS technology works in more detail in chapter 9.

Sex offenders must provide blood and saliva samples to create a DNA (deoxyribonucleic acid) bank. This condition was initially challenged as violating parolees' right against unreasonable searches and seizures. The Tenth Circuit Court of Appeals upheld the ruling because of the significance of DNA evidence in solving sex offenses, the minimal intrusion on an inmate's right to privacy, and a parolee's diminished constitutional rights (*Boling v. Romer,* 1996). Other special conditions required of sex offenders might include prohibition of any pornography, restricting Internet access to certain chat rooms and websites, prohibition of patronizing sex-oriented businesses, and exclusion from **child safety zones** (McKay, 2002). Monitoring a parolee's home computer and limiting Internet sites is discussed in Box 6.4.

child safety zone
A condition of probation or parole whereby the offender is not allowed within a certain range of places where children typically congregate such as schools, day care centers, and playgrounds.

TABLE 6.2   Risk Factors Related to Sex Offending

Slow-Changing Risk Factors	Sudden Risk Factors Requiring Immediate Attention
Deviant sexual arousal	Sexual preoccupation
Loneliness	Emotional collapse
Impulsivity	Lack of social support systems
Intimacy conflicts and deficits	Victim access
Pro-rape/pro-molester attitudes	Use of drugs or alcohol
Ineffective problem solving	Noncompliance with supervision

Source: Roger Pimentel and Jon Muller. 2010. The containment approach to managing defendants charged with sex offenses. *Federal Probation* 74(2): 24–26.

BOX 6.4   TECHNOLOGY IN CORRECTIONS

How Are Internet Activities of Sex Offenders Monitored?

With the increase in wireless capabilities in public places and across entire cities, access to the Internet is widespread, and it is virtually impossible to prohibit use as part of probation or parole conditions. Officers have instead allowed offenders to use the Internet, but courts have upheld the right of officers to examine and control the type of Internet sites offenders visit. Officers with specialized caseloads of offenders for whom the Internet should be monitored can obtain free software called *Field Search* that allows them to visit an offender's home and conduct a search of a computer hard drive for URLs linked to unauthorized sites (for example, pornography sites for offenders convicted of a sexual offense). The software is so thorough that it detects deleted web addresses visited during a specific period of time—either since an officer's last visit or since the hard

drive was first installed. It can be set to detect websites, images, videos, zipped files, browser histories, cookies, and password-protected files on any type of computer. Even those addresses deleted by so-called wiping software that claims to erase websites off a computer can be detected, and date- and time-stamped as to the last time a file or image was opened. When unauthorized addresses are detected, an offender takes a polygraph test to corroborate the findings. The results of the software scan together with a failed polygraph test can be used as evidence for an officer to request a change in the terms of supervision or to terminate the supervision altogether.

National Law Enforcement and Corrections Technology Center. 2009. Field Search. *TechBeat* (Winter). Accessed May 15, 2011: http://www.justnet.org

Sex Offender Registration Laws

Sex offender registration statutes stemming from Megan's Law in 1996 assist police in investigating sex crimes and allow the public to know identities and locations of convicted sex offenders in their area. Registration is required through the Dru Sjodin National Sex Offender Public Website (http://www.nsopw.gov), operated by the U.S. Department of Justice. By law all sex offenders on probation and parole are required to register, with each state varying on how long sex offenders remain on the registry.

Washington was the first state to actively require registration of all sex offenders in 1990. California actually enacted the first registration statute in 1947, but it wasn't used much and didn't catch the nation's attention quite like Washington's statute did (Tewksbury, 2002). When states began developing their databases, the information reported was inconsistent. The Adam Walsh Child Protection and Safety Act of 2006 created a national sex offender registry that includes name, address, date of birth, convictions, fingerprints, place of employment, age and gender of victims, completion of sex offender treatment, and a recent photo.

The database organizes sex offenders into three risk tiers. Tier 1 offenders are considered the lowest risk because they are responsive to treatment and are employed. Tier 1 offenders must include a photo depending on the state and require an offender to update information once per year. Tier 2 offenders are considered moderate risk and must update their whereabouts every six months. Tier 3 offenders are considered at highest risk of committing another sexual offense either because they have refused treatment, they have denied their offense, or they lack remorse for their victims. As a result Tier 3 offenders must update their whereabouts every three months, and some states require that offenders remain on the registry for the rest of their lives. Failure to register and update information is a felony.

There are about 728,000 convicted sex offenders throughout the United States, of whom 100,000 are estimated to be still missing from the registry (Wolf, 2011).

States that fail to comply with federal regulations risk losing federal funding, but many states say that it costs them *more* money to comply than the funding they would lose by not tracking sex offenders according to federal regulations. In the federal system, any federal sex offense that occurred after 1998 or any military conviction for a sex crime after 1997 must be registered (Administrative Office of the United States Courts, 2003). Moreover, registered offenders are not just adults. In Texas, for example, 8.5% of all sex offenders were juveniles, most of whom were considered higher risks than many of the adults due to having committed more sex crimes total and more sex crimes of an aggravated nature (Craun & Kernsmith, 2006).

When legally challenged, the U.S. Supreme Court said that the public posting of a sex offender registry does not violate the due process clause of the Fourteenth Amendment (*Connecticut Department of Public Safety et al. v. Doe,* 2003). Connecticut law required sex offenders to register for 10 years, but those convicted of sexually violent offenses must register for life. The offender in this case alleged that this law was unfair because he was no longer "currently sexually dangerous," and therefore the law violated his due process rights. The Court disagreed, ruling that the law is constitutional, even if no prior opportunity is given to prove that the defendant is not dangerous. Cases have also argued unsuccessfully that registration violates an offender's right to privacy, saying that disclosure of information serves a public safety function that supersedes an offender's right to privacy.

In another case, also decided that same year, the Court said that a sex offender registration and notification law does not violate the ex post facto clause of the Constitution (*Smith v. Doe,* 2003). In this case, the Alaska Sex Offender Registration Act was retroactive, meaning it applied to offenders who were convicted *before* the law was passed. Defendants challenged its constitutionality, saying its retroactive application violated the ex post facto clause of the Constitution. The Court upheld the Alaska law, saying that the Alaska Offender Act *regulates* rather than punishes; therefore, its retroactive application does not violate the ex post facto clause. This is a significant decision because some states (such as Missouri) have retroactively applied the law to sex offenses going back as far as 1979. Critics of this decision contend that registries have had a significant negative impact on sex offenders' ability to find a place to live, work, and reintegrate back into the community.

Community Notification Laws

Community notification statutes make information about sex offenders available upon request to individuals, or else they authorize or require probation and parole departments, law enforcement agencies, or prosecutor offices to disseminate information about released offenders to the community at large. Notification statutes are a secondary way of informing the public of who is a sex offender, under an assumption that the registration process overlooks some offenders. As with the registry there are three tiers of risk, with each tier having its own set of notification procedures (see Table 6.3 for a sampling of states).

Sex offenders are believed to pose different levels of risk to a community, depending on the nature and prevalence of their crimes as well as their choices of victims. The third tier permits or requires proactive dissemination (knocking on doors, flyers, and so on), whereas the other lower tiers permit information dissemination only in response to individuals who seek out that information. Notifying a community about the presence of sex offenders is fraught with disparity, making this practice problematic (Shaffer & Miethe, 2011).

TABLE 6.3 Principal Features of Selected Sex Offender Notification Statutes

State	Year Statute Went Into Effect	How Long Offenders Remain Subject to Notification	Notification Mandatory or Discretionary	Notification Proactive or Only in Response to Request	Sex Offenses Covered by Statute	Implementing Agency	Immunity Explicitly Provided to Implementers	Who May Be Notified	Retroactivity	Information That May Be Disseminated
Alaska	1994	*for life:* 2 or more convictions *15 years:* 1 conviction	mandatory by administrative regulation	upon request	all offenses	State Dept. of Public Safety	provided	anyone	retroactive	limited by statute
Connecticut	1996	10 years after end of probation or parole	discretionary	proactive	selected offenses	probation	not provided	anyone	not retroactive	unrestricted
Louisiana	1992	10 years after release	mandatory	proactive	all offenses	offenders supervised by probation	provided	limited by statute	retroactive to June 1992	limited by statute
New Jersey	1994	indefinitely, but may petition for relief 15 years after release	mandatory	proactive	selected offenses	prosecutor and police	provided	people likely to encounter offender	retroactive	not specified
Oregon	1993, 1995	for life; may petition for waiver after 10 years	varies[1]	proactive and upon request	selected offenses	probation and police	not provided	anyone	retroactive	unrestricted
Tennessee	1995	10 years minimum; then may petition for relief	discretionary	proactive	all offenses	Tennessee Bureau of Investigation	provided	not specified	retroactive	"relevant" information
Washington	1990	for life, 15 years, or 10 years, depending on seriousness of offense	discretionary	proactive and upon request	all offenses	police	provided	not specified	retroactive	not specified

[1]Mandatory if under supervision; discretionary if not.

Source: Peter Finn, Sex Offender Community Notification. Washington, DC: U.S. Department of Justice, February 1997, p. 4.

One study examined whether community notification of sex offenders reduced recidivism and whether the program aided law enforcement in offender apprehension. The study used a treatment group and a matched control group, finding that after 54 months there was no statistically significant difference between the two groups as to rate of arrest. However, the offenders who participated in the notification program were arrested more quickly than were members of the control group (Finn, 1997).

Zevitz and Farkas (2000) investigated the impact of community notification on the workloads of Wisconsin probation and parole officers who supervise sex offenders. Because Wisconsin is a state that has authorized proactive information dissemination, the researchers found that much effort went into working with the community itself. Overall results indicated that sex offender supervision takes an extraordinary amount of training, time, and resources to find suitable housing, conduct home and employment visits, and monitor sex offenders to satisfy rising community expectations.

Sex offender registration and community notification laws are thus put in place to regulate sex offenders and to increase public safety, particularly to protect children. How have these policies affected the community? When parents are notified of a high-risk sex offender in their neighborhood, they report taking action to ensure that their own children receive more protection against sexual victimization (Bandy, 2011). However, studies have consistently found that most citizens do not report taking protective measures when they have been notified of a high-risk sex offender in their neighborhood (Anderson & Sample, 2008; Bandy, 2011). In fact, citizens reported feeling more *fearful* rather than safer with knowledge of where an offender lived (Beck & Travis, 2004). These policies still seem to concentrate on strangers (a condition that, in reality, characterizes *only 7% of all sex offenses against children*) and draw attention away from the more than nine out of ten perpetrators who are related to or already known to children (Alexander, 2010).

STRATEGIES FOR SUPERVISING KNOWN GANG MEMBERS

Most gang members are young offenders, either juveniles between 12 and 17 years or young adults in their early to mid-twenties. Gang members pose a challenge for probation and parole officers. While under supervision, gang members are significantly more likely than nongang members to be rearrested for drug and violent crimes (Olson, Dooley, & Kane, 2004). Gang members have more extensive criminal histories and associate with other people who have themselves been involved in criminal activity. This situation creates a high propensity for recidivism, making it necessary to assign active gang members to intensive supervision caseloads. A number of different strategies are used in the intensive supervision of such probationers and parolees in the federal system.

Creating Profiles for Officer Use

An information clearinghouse such as the Sacramento Intelligence Unit (SIU) has detailed information on gang history, activity, and interpretation of tattoos and gestures. SIU staff prepares profiles of gang members for community supervision officers just before an offender is released from prison. Nearly 4,000 profiles at SIU are compiled annually for this purpose and can be used in any jurisdiction (Administrative Office of the U.S. Courts, 2006).

FACT or **FICTION?**

Sex offenders are more likely to kill their victims than are other types of offenders.

Fiction.

Fact: Only 3% of sex crimes result in homicide. When sex offenders commit murder, the victim is more often an adult than a child.

Information Exchange with Law Enforcement

Probation officers should routinely interact with local law enforcement as a secondary source of information gathering and education. Some officers attend workshops and are members of gang task forces to further specialize and keep current as new groups emerge and as codes and signs change.

Mentoring At-Risk Youth

Officers in one federal district in Massachusetts visit local high schools and juvenile detention centers to present a drug education program to educate at-risk youth on the legal consequences of criminal conviction. Young offenders are also provided with mentors, some of whom are former offenders who have succeeded in the reentry process (Administrative Office of the U.S. Courts, 2006).

Checking the Chat Rooms

Gang members are savvy users of technology with their own cell phones, Blackberrys, personal websites, and Facebook walls. Probation and parole officers must keep current within the online community, including through social networks with discussion boards and chat rooms, to determine information about gang activity, parties, and drugs (Bennish, 2008).

SUMMARY

- ISP programs are most effective if they operate with close supervision and cognitive-behavioral treatment intervention.

- Drug court is a type of diversion program that integrates substance abuse treatment with a coordinated and ongoing interactive team that includes judges, prosecutors, and probation officers.

- Mental health courts and veterans courts are organizationally similar to other problem-solving courts except that they work with offenders who are mentally ill and/or are veterans, and they link to a variety of community service providers.

- Therapeutic communities use peer support and cognitive-behavioral interventions to help individuals overcome addiction to drugs and to prevent relapse episodes so they can maintain a life of sobriety.

- Sex offenders are a heterogenous group that engages in a wide variety of deceptive and manipulative behaviors to lure chosen victims.

- All sex offenders need intensive specialized treatment and intensive supervision (a containment approach), but some molesters need medications to control their hormonal balance.

- Supervision includes ongoing home visits, Internet restrictions, restrictions on residency and leisure time, monitoring of offenders' associations, collaboration with treatment providers, and engagement of polygraph experts.

- Sex offender registration and community notification statutes are for the regulation of sex offenders and for public safety—not for punishment.

- Gang members pose a special challenge to probation and parole officers in that they are more likely to be rearrested for violent crimes and are feared by the public.

DISCUSSION QUESTIONS

1. How does intensive supervision differ from regular probation or parole supervision?

2. Are drug courts a good idea for higher level drug dealers?

3. How many chances should drug-addicted offenders in drug court be given (i.e., how much leeway and for which types of offenses) before they are considered to have "failed" the program? Would your response be different for drug-addicted offenders in a therapeutic community?

4. Is a therapeutic community more or less effective for achieving sobriety than a drug court? Why?

5. What are the issues concerning the treatment of offenders with mental illness?

6. Should mental health courts be expanded for juveniles with mental illness? Why or why not?

7. What specific strategies are most effective for working with sex offenders in a community?

8. Does community notification of sex offenders increase public safety? Why or why not?

9. Is requiring sex offenders to register good public policy? Why or why not?

10. What specific strategies are most effective for working with offenders who are active gang members?

11. What types of offenders could benefit from specialized caseloads, other than the ones mentioned in this chapter?

WEBSITES, VIDEOS, AND PODCASTS

Websites

Juvenile ISP Programs
http://www.nicic.gov/library/018875

SAMHSA's National Registry of Evidence-Based Programs and Practices
http://nrepp.samhsa.gov/

New Jersey Adult Drug Courts
http://www.judiciary.state.nj.us/criminal/crdrgct.htm

Florida Drug Courts
http://www.flcourts.org/gen_public/family/drug_court/index.shtml

The CMHS National GAINS Center
www.gainscenter.samhsa.gov

Judge David L. Bazelon Center for Mental Health Law
http://www.bazelon.org

Policy on Mental Health Courts
http://www.youthlaw.org/policy/advocacy/juvenile_mental_health_court_initiative/

The Criminal Justice/Mental Health Consensus Project
www.consensusproject.org

Shared Services: Defendants with Mental Illnesses
http://dpca.state.ny.us/shared_mentally_ill.htm

National Center for Post-Traumatic Stress Disorder, U.S. Department of Veterans Affairs
http://www.ptsd.va.gov

Sex Offender Risk and Needs Assessment (Canada)
http://www.csc-scc.gc.ca/text/pblct/forum/e091/e091g-eng.shtml

Dru Sjodin National Sex Offender Public Website
http://www.nsopw.gov

Association for the Treatment of Sexual Abusers
http://www.atsa.com

Center for Sex Offender Management
http://www.csom.org

Training Curriculum for Supervising Sex Offenders in the Community
http://www.nicic.org/library/017636

Videos/Podcasts

Drug Court: Personal Story
http://www.youtube.com/watch?v=Cf1pRLwCP4o

This video is a look at the drug court graduates and staff from across New York State through history, statistics, and personal stories.

Drug Court and NADCP
http://www.youtube.com/watch?v=MyWXPsESJ2A

This video reviews the logic behind drug courts and describes the National Association of Drug Court Professionals.

Mental Health Court: Part 1, 2, 3

> http://www.youtube.com/watch?v=tPAopiYqDds
> http://www.youtube.com/watch?v=0vfu60kOSOk&feature=related
> http://www.youtube.com/watch?v=kd4-CU6M-YE&feature=related

This three-part series discusses various aspects of mental health courts. It comprises an educational video series.

Mental Health Care for Offenders

> http://www.correc tions.com/system/podcast/file/35/media_20041019.mp3

This podcast is about services and programs for offenders with mental health issues.

CASE STUDY EXERCISES

Which supervision conditions are pertinent to these sex offenders?

The specific conditions pertaining to sex offenders have received attention in recent years. For each case below, which additional conditions should be imposed on the offender in terms of his or her offense, and what challenges of community supervision does each case present?

Assume that conditions for sex offenders include one or more of the following:

- No contact with any minor child (including offender's minor children) if victim of sexual crime was a minor, or no contact with minors at all even if the victim was of adult age.
- Contact with minor children approved only if parole officer approves another supervising adult to be present at time of contact.
- No possession of sexually explicit material—written, audio, or visual.
- If the offense involved the use of the Internet or a computer, cannot have a personal computer and cannot work where access to Internet is allowed, or in some jurisdictions can have no computer access at all even if offense did not involve computer usage.
- Notification to neighbors and employers of offender's sexual offense history and supervision status.
- Mandatory participation in sexual offender treatment or aftercare programs.
- Mandatory routine polygraph exams as part of treatment or supervision.
- If offense involved filming or pictures of victims, no camera or video equipment access allowed.
- Cannot work in any employment that would allow access to children or victim-aged groups; cannot be self-employed.
- Cannot live within a certain distance of schools, playgrounds, public parks, or other places where minors congregate.

CASE A: Parolee Steven, Sexual Assault of a Minor

Steven is serving a 5- to 15-year sentence for Sexual Assault of a Minor. He has served seven and one-half years of his sentence, which is five years beyond the minimum time to be served. Because he has three prior convictions for similar offenses, he does not have to be released until he has served 10 years of his sentence. Steven spent time in prison for two of the three prior offenses against minors. Each time he was released, he successfully completed the release period of parole supervision. All of his victims have been his grandchildren; family members are strongly opposed to his release and fear he will commit similar acts upon release. Steven has completed a sexual offender treatment program during this incarceration; he always refused to participate in treatment during prior incarcerations. The prognosis by the treatment counselor is guarded but indicates that Steven has worked hard on learning his offending triggers and knows whom to avoid if released. He has not had any rule violations while incarcerated and has accounting skills. He will be released under the supervision of a parole officer to a community where none of his family reside and does not want contact with his family. He has been accepted into a halfway house program and plans on attending community-based sexual offender aftercare groups.

CASE B: Parolee Gloria, Lewd Sexual Conduct and Sexual Contact with a Minor

Gloria has been paroled after serving three years of her nine-year sentence for Lewd Sexual Conduct and Sexual Contact with a Minor. She was 27 years old at the time of the offense, and her victim was 16. Currently Gloria is 30 years old; her victim is now 19 years of age and enrolled as a full-time college student in another state. This is Gloria's first felony offense, and she has no history of offending behavior under community supervision. Gloria agreed to complete a sex offender treatment program during her incarceration but claimed during her counseling sessions that she and her victim loved each other and that sexual relations were consensual. Gloria still reports feelings for him, but the victim's family wishes to have no contact with Gloria. However, at this time no one knows how the victim feels about the relationship because his most recent contact information was unavailable when the field officer performed her investigations. The field officer did find out that Gloria's former employer would not accept her back in her former occupation as a registered nurse despite Gloria's statements that the institution would. Gloria wishes to parole back to the same house she lived in when arrested. She has one male child, aged 13, who has been staying with Gloria's mother over the last three years.

CASE C: Probationer Jonas, Indecent Sexual Behavior with a Minor

Jonas has been placed on probation for indecent sexual behavior with a five-year-old boy. This is his first felony offense, with two prior misdemeanor offenses as an adult—one count of indecent exposure and one count of misdemeanor theft. Jonas is now 20 years of age and lives with his maternal aunt, who was his guardian from when he was the age of 12 until he turned 18. Jonas has never been to prison.

Jonas suffered emotional and sexual abuse from his stepfather and mother for the first six years of his life, when he became known to Social Services investigating his case. This investigation resulted in his stepfather being charged with Indecency with a Child, and Jonas was placed in foster care. While in foster care over the next several years, Jonas was adjudicated numerous times for fire setting and cruelty to animals, for which he was finally sent to juvenile detention. While in detention at the age of 12, he tried to hurt himself and was removed to a padded cell for further assessment. Testing revealed that Jonas had attention deficit hyperactivity disorder and was prescribed Ritalin. He remained out of the system from the age of 12 until the age of 18, when he was arrested for indecent exposure.

His IQ was recently assessed using the Wechsler Abbreviated Scale of Intelligence (WASI test) and estimated to be 70 (verbal IQ was 72 and performance IQ 73). His current communicative and daily living skills are equivalent to that of an eight-year old boy, and his socialization domain is equivalent to that of a seven-year-old. He has a reduced capacity to learn new information and solve problems. He has a fourth-grade education and cannot read very well. He has not yet registered as a sex offender in the state. The PSIR recommended some form of cognitive-behavioral treatment.

7

Community Supervision Modification and Revocation

CHAPTER LEARNING OBJECTIVES

1. Identify how probation and parole conditions are modified and under what circumstances.
2. List options that probation and parole officers have available for resistant probationers before filing or reporting revocations to the court or parole board.

3. Analyze the rights probationers have during the revocation process and the differences with parolees.
4. Discuss the effectiveness of probation and parole separately, as a community sanction.

Lindsay Lohan, right, looks over at her attorney Shawn Chapman Holley during a July, 2011 court hearing to update the Judge on her progress on probation for drunk driving and misdemeanor theft. Lohan needs to complete 480 hours of community service within one year.

KEY TERMS

revocation	technical violations	preliminary hearing
early termination	absconder	final revocation hearing
law violations	due process	preponderance of evidence

Lindsay Lohan is no stranger to the corrections system, having been previously jailed three times and sent to drug rehabilitation twice. Lohan's latest brush with law includes being sentenced to 120 days in jail and 480 hours of community service for violating her probation. She was originally on probation for Driving While Intoxicated in 2007, and then most recently she violated her probation by stealing a necklace from a jewelry store (Dillon, 2011).

Jail combined with community service is an appropriate response when someone is not taking her probation seriously. Lohan, who can afford what she stole, likely committed the theft for the thrill of seeing whether she could get away with it. She reportedly doesn't mind her community service spent helping at a women's shelter and helping underprivileged kids.

INTRODUCTION

Probation and parole officer decision making is influenced not only by offender behavior but also by laws, agency policy, and even individual officer attributes. You learned from previous chapters how this discretion is guided by principles of rehabilitation and of social control for the good of the public. Placing an offender under community supervision implies that an offender's liberty is subject to compliance with specified rules and abiding by the law for a specified amount of time. In this chapter we discuss how, when and why a court (as in the case of probation) or a parole board (for parolees) would modify the length and terms of supervision. We begin with offenders who have fulfilled their payment obligations and have shown their ability to continue to abide by conditions. In such cases, shortening a term or easing restrictions can be used as a reward or applied after a minimum amount of time has been served.

Early Termination for Good Behavior

early termination
Termination of probation at any time during the probation period or after some time has been served.

Community supervision officers (CSOs) supervising probationers or parolees in some jurisdictions can apply on behalf of their clients for **early termination**. For example, probation officers can apply to the courts after a client has satisfactorily served one third of a probation term or two years, whichever is less. Although an officer initially recommends early termination, the authority to terminate early rests with a parole board for state parolees and with a judge for probationers. In federal court, a judge may

> terminate a term of probation previously ordered and discharge the defendant at any time in the case of a misdemeanor or an infraction or at any time after the expiration of one year of probation in the case of a felony, if it is satisfied that such action is warranted by the conduct of the defendant and the interest of justice (*Federal Rules of Criminal Procedure*, Title 18, Chapter 227, Article 3564).

Other rewards for good behavior can include a reduction of supervision level (thus reducing the number of contacts) or a reduction of curfew time. Positive recognition can include giving a probationer completion certificates, affirmation letters, or reference letters from his or her employer, school, or from a court (Carter & Ley, 2001). All of these incentives are discretionary, and a probation supervisor or judge reviews the behavioral record of a probationer before granting or rejecting a request.

In cases of deferred adjudication probation or suspended sentence in which a finding of guilt is deferred but an offender still must complete conditions, if the deferred adjudication period is successful, charges are dismissed and the finding of guilt is never made. Note that in some states a prior deferred adjudication probation can be used as a "prior" to increase a sentence if an offender commits another crime in the future.

The rate of successful termination of local- and state-level probation varies greatly by jurisdiction, due to a lack of uniform law as to when a probation revocation must be filed. A national average estimates that between 60–70% of state probationers (Nieto, 2003) and 49–57% of parolees successfully complete supervision. At the federal level the rate of success is higher, with over 80% of federal probationers terminating probation successfully with no violations (see Figure 7.1).

FIGURE 7.1   Federal Probation Outcomes

Source: U.S. Department of Justice. 2008. *Compendium of Federal Justice Statistics, 2004*. Washington, DC: U.S. Department of Justice.

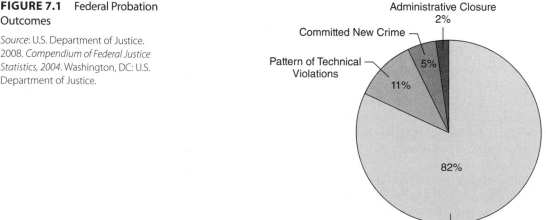

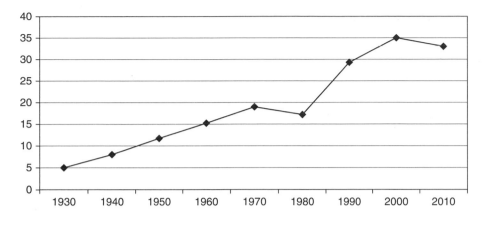

FIGURE 7.2 Percentage Who Enter State Prison Because of Parole Revocation: 1930 to Present

Sources for 1990 and beyond:

Robyn L. Cohen. 1995. *Probation and Parole Violators in State Prison, 1991.* Washington, DC: Bureau of Justice Statistics;

Joan Petersilia. 2000b. When prisoners return to the community: Political, economic, and social consequences. In *Sentencing and Corrections: Issues for the 21st Century* [paper 9 from the Executive Sessions on Sentencing and Corrections]. Washington, DC: U.S. Department of Justice.

Heather C. West, William J. Sabol, and Sarah J. Greenman. 2010. *Prisoners in 2009.* Washington, DC: Bureau of Justice Statistics.

Conversely, a resistant offender is someone either not making sufficient progress or involved in new criminal behavior. Violations or serious misbehavior can cause a period of supervision to be extended, additional conditions imposed, or a community supervision revoked. When considering modifying or revoking probation, the courts assess the risk an offender poses to a community, whether the change will increase compliance, and whether the change will better serve the needs of the offender at the present time. When prison is invoked, either by a judge who resentences offenders to prison or by a parole board that returns parolees back to prison, bed space is needed to make room. Figure 7.2 shows how revocations of parole have increased over time until they peaked at 35% of all prison admissions in 2000 and have just begun to decrease in the last few years. The increased rate is likely influenced by increased intensity of supervision along with lower tolerance for revocations (Grattet, Lin, & Petersilia, 2011; White, Mellow, Englander, & Ruffinengo, 2011). Of those who were returned to prison, only about 20% of federal and 25% of state prisoners under post-release supervision were returned because they committed a new crime (Glaze & Bonczar, 2008).

TYPES OF VIOLATIONS

Revocation of community supervision is generally triggered in two ways: law violations and technical violations. A **law violation** occurs if an offender commits another misdemeanor or felony crime. By contrast, a **technical violation** is a pattern of infractions that breaches a condition of probation or parole. Revocation for law violations occurred at a rate of about 6% of all federal probationers and about 15% of all federal parolees. Technical violations occurred by an additional 13% of probationers and 28% of parolees (U.S. Department of Justice, 2005a).

Law Violations

When considering all revocations as a whole, about 6–10% of all probation revocations are new crimes and 90% are rule violations. For parolees, the story is quite different; new crimes comprise a whopping 60–70% of all parole revocations. In misdemeanor and drug use or possession probation cases, most jurisdictions simply revoke probation instead of prosecuting an offender for a new crime. Revocation for a new crime is a more convenient option that achieves the same result, which is a modification of conditions or else incarceration and removal from society. Parolees are incarcerated

revocation
The process of hearings that results when the probationer is noncompliant with the current level of probation. Results of a revocation are either modifying probation conditions to a more intensive supervision level, or the complete elimination of probation and sentence to a residential community facility, jail, or prison.

law violations
Violations of probation or parole conditions that involve the commission of a crime.

technical violations
Multiple violations that breach one or more noncriminal conditions of probation.

for new crimes. Even if an offender is guilty of a new crime, however, revocation is not automatic. Instead it is left to the discretion of a court or parole board.

Even if evidence for a new offense doesn't meet "guilty beyond a reasonable doubt," the standard of proof for revocation is only "preponderance of the evidence"—a lower standard of proof that *is sufficient to revoke*, though not sufficient enough to be added to one's criminal record. If more evidence surfaces later such that an offender is tried for the crime that led to revocation, that is not considered double jeopardy because revocation is merely an administrative and not a criminal proceeding, even if it results in incarceration.

Technical Violations

Violations of supervision conditions come under the category of technical violations, meaning they do not constitute criminal acts but rather are a pattern of rule violations of orders from a court or parole board. Unlike new crimes, which are clearer as to when a revocation should be filed, technical violations allow for more officer discretion and a tendency for inconsistent responses between officers and jurisdictions. As a result, technical violation revocations can be used for reasons unrelated to public safety, such as by officers reducing their workload. Officers with higher caseloads of offenders were more likely to support revocations sooner than were officers with lower caseload sizes (Kerbs, Jones, & Jolley, 2009). This finding may be a tolerance issue—a reaction to job stress as a result of being overworked.

Research studies of revocation motions filed provide information on the most common types of technical violations along with the differences between parole and probation revocation rates (see Table 7.1).

A comparison of two probation jurisdictions in Table 7.1 shows large differences between "failing to report" and "absconding," likely due to definitions of no-shows

TABLE 7.1   Revocation Reasons Among Parole vs. Probation Violators

Reason for Revocation	National (Parole)	California (Parole)	National (Probation)	Illinois (Probation)
Arrest/conviction for new offense	70%	60%	16%	10%
Drug-related violations				
Positive test for drug use	8%	12%	27%	22%
Possession of drug(s)	7%	9%	N/R	N/R
Failure to report for drug testing	2%	5%	10%	34%
Failure to complete alcohol/drug treatment	2%	1%	20%	9%
Absconders	22%	27%	19%	3%
Other technical violations	18%	21%	9%	23%

Detail for parolees adds to more than 100% because some inmates have had more than one violation of parole. N/R= Data for drug possession was not reported.

Data adapted from: Timothy A. Hughes, Doris James Wilson, and Allen J. Beck. 2001. *Trends in State Parole, 1990–2000.* Washington, DC: U.S. Department of Justice, Bureau of Justice Statistics, p. 14; Peggy B. Burke. 1997. *Policy-driven responses to probation and parole violations.* Washington, DC: U.S. Department of Justice, National Institute of Corrections.

M. Kevin Gray, Monique Fields, and Sheila Royo Maxwell. 2001. Examining probation violations: Who, what and when. *Crime and Delinquency* 47(4): 537–557.

and policies for reporting these. As a general rule, probation is not revoked for occasional violation of technical conditions but for an ongoing pattern of infractions after other options have been tried such as verbal warnings, written reprimand, increasing reporting requirements, increasing rate of drug tests, and adding home visits. Because incarceration results in high costs, revocation should be a last resort in handling offenders with a pattern of technical violations. Filing and/or granting a revocation is a subjective judgment, so the types of technical violations and overall revocation rates vary greatly by jurisdiction. Extralegal factors such as individual demographics were more influential for technical violations than for criminal violations (Grattet, Lin, & Petersilia, 2011; Steen & Opsal 207).

Absconding from Community Supervision

One of the more serious, and surprisingly frequent, types of technical violations is that of absconding. Some jurisdictions list absconding from supervision by parolees as a new criminal offense. An **absconder** is defined as an offender under community supervision who, without prior permission, escapes or flees the jurisdiction he or she is required to stay within. Official nationwide estimates have reported that 12% of all parolees and about 18% of probationers abscond from supervision (Glaze & Bonczar, 2008) (Levin, 2008a). The absconding rate of clients at restitution centers was even higher (26%). Absconders had more extensive felony criminal histories, longer periods of supervision, and were subject to more stringent conditions than did offenders who terminated successfully (Mayzer & Gray, 2000).

absconder
An offender under community supervision who, without prior permission, escapes or flees the jurisdiction he or she is required to stay within.

WHY DO OFFENDERS LEAVE?   Offenders who abscond are uncertain about what their CSO will do once he or she discovers a violation, and that uncertainty translates into fear of losing their freedom. Most absconders leave out of fear; they do not trust or understand the system well enough to predict the outcome of their actions. In highly charged emotional states, offenders drop all responsibilities and release building pressures to escape without thinking about the serious consequences. Ironically, any violations that trigger an escape are usually less serious than an escape charge

A community supervision officer conducts a home visit to check on an absconded probationer.

© Modesto Bee/ZUMA Press

BOX 7.1   TECHNOLOGY IN CORRECTIONS

Finding Fugitives on the Internet Through *Fuginet*

In the past when a state trooper pulled over a vehicle for speeding, as long as the car registration and insurance were valid, the car was not reported stolen, and there were no visible signs that other crimes were being committed in the officer's presence, issuing a warning or a traffic ticket was the only choice. Because warrant data was not centralized with other counties within a state or between states, many people with outstanding warrants were let go.

Fuginet software provides a more efficient way for state and local law enforcement to apprehend fugitives within their own state once a warrant is issued. The database is updated daily by parole officers and can be accessed via a secure login on the Internet, so that information takes less time to be processed and conveys more detail about each offender: parole address, family information, and vehicle information and photos. Fuginet also includes facial recognition software that compares composite drawings of unidentified suspects with similar images in a database. It is anticipated that parole absconders will be arrested faster than before and that this database can also be used to help solve open investigations.

Source: National Law Enforcement and Corrections Technology Center. 2002. Fuginet'ing Parole Violators. *TechBeat* (Winter). Retrieved from: http://www.justnet.org

---

itself, which affects an offender for the remainder of a sentence and shadows any future convictions. For such persons reasons for absconding range from drug use to financial difficulty to needing to leave a state to visit a dying relative. A typical absconder is not in danger of committing any crimes while on escape but, on the contrary, is interested in laying low.

A smaller category of absconders includes individuals who understand the system too well. These individuals, who constitute a very small percentage of all absconders, have committed one or more serious crimes while under community supervision. If their recent criminal behavior is serious enough, they know they may never get out of prison again, so they take a chance on living out of prison until they are caught. This type of absconder is more likely to appear on a wanted list and may be a threat to community safety.

LOCATING AND APPREHENDING FUGITIVES   Because of the large number of absconders every year and the fact that most are not dangerous, most states take a passive approach to locating and apprehending fugitives. When an offender absconds from supervision, a warrant is filed with local, state, or national crime information systems. Ironically, many absconders never leave their state and can later be located by searching public utility records or through a routine traffic stop. More recently, locating fugitives has been made easier by law enforcement working with parole officers in the use of *Fuginet* (see Box 7.1).

IN-HOUSE ADMINISTRATIVE OPTIONS BEFORE FILING A REVOCATION

Administrative interventions are in-house approaches that take place when an offender shows initial signs of resistance or when technical violations first start. A CSO, in conjunction with a supervisor's advice or approval, is encouraged to use in-house options prior to filing a formal revocation. Through administrative interventions, an officer attempts to gain compliance from a resistant offender and uses oral or written reprimands, staffings, motivational interviewing techniques, or directives (Taylor & Martin, 2006). Administrative interventions are limited because initial conditions are set by courts or parole boards. A probation officer's job is merely to ensure that

TABLE 7.2 Probation Violation Decision Guidelines

Decision-Making Level	Probation Violation Type*	Possible Responses to Probationer
Probation Officer	Failure to report Making false statements Violating curfew Changing residence/jobs w/o permission Failure to pay restitution Failure to perform community service Drug use/positive drug test	Verbal warning/reprimand Case Staffing Home visit + 7-day curfew Loss of travel Community service: 1–8 hrs. Increase reporting Increase drug testing Probationer sign waiver
Supervisor Staffing	Failure to test for drugs or take Antabuse Failure to participate in drug treatment Possession of contraband Failing to register as a sex offender Repeated curfew violations Second positive drug test Repeated failure to report	Drug treatment Increase supervision level Community service: 20–40 hrs. Curfew (up to 30 days) Curfew (up to 30 days) Drug treatment Increase supervision level
Court Hearing	Third positive drug test Possession of weapons Absconding after 60 days Denying access to searches Committing new offense Threatening victim Deliberate pattern of noncompliance	Residential treatment Boot camp Electronic monitoring Intensive probation Jail or prison Day reporting center Extension of probation

* Response also depends on level of risk probationer poses.

Source: Madeline M. Carter (Ed.). 2001. *Responding to Parole and Probation Violations: A Handbook to Guide Local Policy Development.* Prepared for the National Institute of Corrections, U.S. Department of Justice (Washington, DC), pp. 54, 75.

these conditions are followed. However, the distinction between a judicial *condition* and a probation officer's *directive* is unclear (Barklage, Miller, & Bonham, 2006).

Various guidelines have been formulated to aid officers in available response options with resistant offenders. Offering more in-house options and decision matrices for minor technical violations will likely reduce revocation filings and incarceration responses (Kerbs, Jones, & Jolley, 2009). An example of these guidelines is found in Table 7.2. Note that response depends on severity of violation, an offender's predefined risk level defined by a risk and needs assessment, and assaultive history. Once a response range has been determined, with or without a second opinion from a supervisor, CSOs can choose from a variety of responses, depending on what they feel is appropriate for each particular case.

Some probation agencies have an offender sign a waiver that he or she agrees to modified sanctions in lieu of going to court and thus waives the right to a court hearing. This waiver is kept on file to show a court the avenues tried before a probation officer requested a formal revocation proceeding. According to Jones and Kerbs (2007), most officers preferred to use in-house intervention techniques with probationers who made little to no effort to find employment, who failed to report, did not appear for community service work, or upon the first positive alco-sensor test, indicating an offender has ingested a substance with alcohol. Supervisory strategies to reduce occurrence of technical violations include a sound assessment and case plan, as discussed in chapter 5 (Sachwald, Eley, & Taxman, 2006), intervention by a specially trained "technical violation" unit officer, reduction in the number of cases each officer supervises (Hill, 2006), and the use of out-of-custody hearings (Andrews & Janes, 2006).

REVOCATION PROCEDURES

When in-house strategies have been exhausted yet are still not being followed by an offender, a CSO recommends revocation. Revocation procedures are governed by a combination of constitutional rules, state law, and agency policy. Revocation proceedings begin with a violation report prepared by a supervision officer when enough information has been collected in chronological notes to document a pattern of technical violations or when a new crime has been discovered. In Box 7.2

BOX 7.2   **FIELD NOTES**

How Are Parole Violators and Parole Absconders Supervised?

When the officer suspects that a parolee has absconded or violated supervision, the parole officer first visits the last known residence. If there is no response at the parolee's home, then the officer reviews the local county jail bookings to determine if the parolee was arrested. Provided the parolee is not in local custody, the parole officer searches the state and national crime information centers. Then the officer calls local hospitals to determine if the offender was admitted for an illness or injury. Finally, the officer will call the local morgue and verify that the offender is not dead in the parolee's county of residence. After the parole officer has exhausted all possibilities, he or she completes a violation report and requests that a warrant be issued.

Fugitive or absconder violations are time intensive for officers. When a parolee is arrested for a new offense, another series of investigations begins. First, the officer must determine if anyone was killed or injured and if the offender in custody? If the parolee is in custody, this may explain why the offender could not be found and could not report. Please keep in mind that while the parole officer is dealing with one parolee, there are still 80 to 85 other parolees still on supervision that demand the officer's attention.

The parole officer will also deal with non-filed assaults. This is when the victim does not, will not or cannot go to the police and file a police report against the

Courtesy of Leanne Fiftal Alarid

Ralph Garza
Warrant Analyst, Texas Department of Criminal Justice, Parole Division

parolee. The parole officer attempts to gather as much evidence as possible without coercion, so that if a warrant is later issued against the parolee for the assault, then the evidence presented by the victim could result in a parole revocation for that offender.

Parolees with criminal charges are monitored by reviewing their upcoming court dates and cases. The officer will examine the parolee's case and note any changes or comments in an offender information database. If charges are pending against the parolee, then any parole hearings are held in abeyance until the pending charges are adjudicated. The Warrant Section of the Texas Parole Division issues approximately 150 warrants a day. That is 3,000 per month or 36,000 annually. A parolee with a warrant is not automatically returned to prison. Those offenders that either have a parole hearing or waive their hearing may be continued on supervision, transferred to an intermediate punishment facility, or revoked.

Given the overcrowding in county jails and prison units, the parole officer must exercise every possible means to keep the parolee reporting and out of jail through a series of graduated sanctions. The graduated sanctions most often utilized are: warnings/admonishments, increased control, increased monitoring/programming, and modifying the special conditions pending approval by a parole panel. Warnings and admonishments consist of compliance counseling,

(Continues)

BOX 7.1　FIELD NOTES (*Continued*)

How Are Parole Violators and Parole Absconders Supervised?

written reprimands, and case conferences. Compliance counseling is providing guidance to the releasee to follow the rules of supervision. It is meant as a first level non-threatening sanction. A case conference means a meeting occurs between the parolee, parole officer, and unit supervisor to discuss the violations.

The next level of sanctions is for the officer to reclassify the parolee at a higher supervision level for increased control. For example, if the parolee is on minimum supervision, the parolee requires a home visit every six months. If the parolee has not reported on time or has not attended his substance abuse treatment, the officer can increase to "intensive" where the parolee will receive a home visit every month until compliance is attained. Another increase control device is having the parolee report to the District Resource Center (similar to a day reporting center), which means now the offender has to find a ride, arrive on time, and participate in substance abuse meetings for two hours. The third level involves getting the parole panel to modify the conditions. If all else fails, the last stop is back to prison.

Ralph Garza discusses the steps that CSOs go through to file a warrant and a revocation. He stresses that offenders are given multiple chances and that incarceration is used only as a last resort after all other graduated sanctions have been tried.

Predefined agency policy determines whether offenders will be picked up off the streets and have to wait in jail for their revocation hearing or whether they may remain free until their hearing. Arrest for a technical violation or arrest for a new crime does not automatically mean that supervision will be revoked—it just means that an officer can incarcerate an offender and request that a court conduct a revocation hearing. Federal law contains the following provision for federal probationers:

> If there is reason to believe that a probationer or a person on supervised release has violated a condition of his probation or release, he may be arrested, and upon arrest, shall be taken without unnecessary delay before the court having jurisdiction over him. A probation officer may make such an arrest wherever the probationer or releasee is found, and may make the arrest without a warrant (Federal Criminal Code and Rules, 2004).

Information is collected in a variety of ways, such as via searches, home visits, collateral contacts, and drug tests. Box 7.3 discusses the issue of whether search warrants are required by probation and parole officers.

BOX 7.3　COMMUNITY CORRECTIONS UP CLOSE

When Do Community Supervision Officers Need a Warrant to Search?

In chapter 4 you learned that the exclusionary rule does not apply to pre-sentence investigation reports, insofar as evidence obtained or seized illegally by police in violation of the Fourth Amendment (though it cannot be used to convict) may still be included in a report because the conviction has already been decided. In the case of parolees (*Pennsylvania Board of Probation and Parole v. Scott,* 1998) and probationers *(State v. Pizel,* 1999), the court ruled that the exclusionary rule does not apply to parole or probation revocation hearings. The court ruled so because probation and parole officers do not need a warrant to conduct a legal search. As part of community supervision, probationers and parolees must allow officers to search their cars or places of residence without a search warrant. This warrantless condition has been upheld for revocation hearings in which the burden of proof is lower than in criminal court prosecutions. An offender's "consent" to warrantless searches based on reasonable suspicion that said offender has committed a parole violation is specified in the conditions of release that he or she must agree to and sign.

Warrants and Citations

A violation process is depicted in Figure 7.3 as a series of decision points. After a CSO discovers a violation and investigates, agency policy defines whether an offender is arrested immediately or is issued a citation or summons to appear at a revocation hearing and kept under supervision When an arrest warrant is issued, a parolee is detained in a county jail until the revocation hearing. Although the process and options are the same, the decision as to whether to revoke parole resides with a parole board and with a judge to revoke probation.

FIGURE 7.3   The Revocation Process

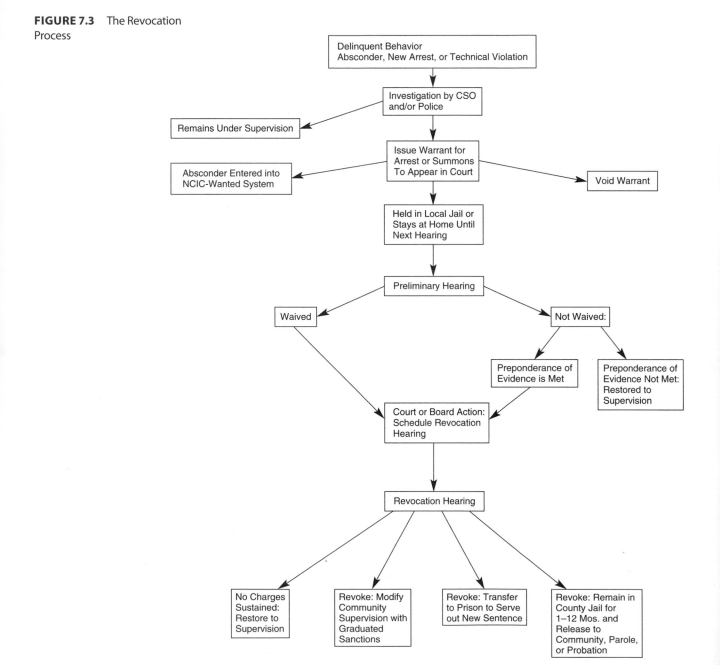

Adapted from: New York State Division of Paroles Office of Policy Analysis and Information. 1993. Overview of the parole revocation process in New York in *Reclaiming Offender Accountability: Intermediate Sanctions for Probation and Parole Violators,* Edward E. Rhine (Ed.). Laurel, MD: American Correctional Association, 41.

Courtesy of Raymond Alarid, Jr./Leanne F. Alarid

A probation officer with arrest powers locates one of her clients, and will bring him to jail to await a probation violation hearing.

The time it takes to revoke varies by jurisdiction according to case backlog and whether an offender openly admits the allegations. The time from violation detection by an officer to disposition by a parole board or a court ranged from 44 to 64 days (Burke, 1997). The federal system requires that revocation hearings be held within 90 days from the time an offender is taken into custody (U.S. Parole Commission, 2006). Most violators (82%) enter the jail-booking process by a warrant, but that means that a jail bed is occupied until a hearing process ends. In order to save jail space for individuals who are a true threat to public safety, more jurisdictions are turning to citations in place of automatic warrants for violators waiting for revocation hearings. If a violation was violent or if an offender might abscond, then he or she must wait behind bars until a revocation hearing. For most offenders who violate, a citation allows them to continue working to support dependents while at the same time preparing for a possible jail or prison term. Another distinct advantage of citations is that they save jail space for others.

Two-Stage Process

As depicted in Figure 7.3, offenders are entitled to a two-stage hearing consisting of a **preliminary hearing** and a **final revocation hearing**. A preliminary or *show cause* hearing is a recorded hearing to determine whether a preponderance of the evidence exists to believe a violation has occurred. If a preponderance of the

FACT OR FICTION?

When probationers and parolees are revoked for breaking the rules, it means that parole and probation don't work.

Fiction.

Fact: A revocation decision due to technical violations is complicated by an offender's situation, which rules are broken and why, agency policy on technical violations, officer discretion, and judicial discretion, and has little to do with the overall effectiveness of community supervision.

preliminary hearing
An inquiry conducted to determine if there is probable cause to believe that the offender committed a probation or parole violation.

final revocation hearing
A due process hearing that must be conducted before probation or parole can be revoked.

evidence exists, a revocation hearing is scheduled and later held separately. If a standard of proof is not met, charges are dismissed. Many jurisdictions, in an effort to speed up the process, allow offenders to waive a preliminary hearing. This is known in the federal system as an *expedited* revocation, which accounts for almost half of all revocations (Hoffman & Beck, 2005). An expedited revocation requires a parole violator to admit wrongdoing and waive a right to a revocation hearing before the U.S. Parole Commission, and does not allow a right to appeal a revocation decision.

Although most revocation decisions are discretionary, some jurisdictions explicitly mandate automatic revocation and resentencing for some behaviors. In the federal system, instances of mandatory revocation include: (1) commission of any crime of violence or facilitation of sexual contact against a child under the age of 16; (2) possession of a firearm; (3) possession of a controlled substance or positive drug test; and (4) refusal to comply with drug testing.

In discretionary matters, offenders who wish to contest accusations or to retain a right to appeal must wait in jail for a formal revocation hearing. Two studies indicate that discretionary revocation decisions are difficult to predict. Hoffman and Beck (2005) compared the outcomes of cases in which offenders agreed to expedite revocation with case outcomes *for the same charge* of offenders who waited for a formal hearing. About 38.5% of offenders who waited for a formal revocation received the same decision as expeditors, whereas 31% received a more lenient decision and 30% received a harsher decision.

In a second example in another jurisdiction, 42% of offenders whose case went in front of a judge had their probation conditions modified or extended by a court for noncompliance, and 54% went to some sort of intermediate residential facility, jail, or prison (Stickels, 2007).

Revocation will not always result in imprisonment, but additional conditions or stricter supervision will be imposed. Table 7.3 shows the number of months of imprisonment that federal offenders must serve if revoked. Regardless of severity or type of revocation, offenders originally convicted of a Class A felony are distinguished only by their original criminal history score determined at sentencing. For offenders originally convicted of all other types of offenses, essentially three violation grades or levels of severity of revocation behavior determine amount of time served. Grade A violations are new crimes while Grade B and Grade C violations are technical violations. For example, let's say Nadine was originally convicted of Possession of a Controlled Substance and her original criminal history category defined by her prior record was II. Nadine was sentenced to probation. While on probation she committed a series of technical violations (positive drug tests) defined as Grade B technical violations. According to Table 7.3, Nadine must serve between six and twelve months, as long as the number of months in the table does not exceed her original sentence length.

TABLE 7.3   Number of Imprisonment Months for Federal Revocations

Grade of Violation	ORIGINAL CRIMINAL HISTORY CATEGORY AT INITIAL SENTENCING					
	I	II	III	IV	V	VI
Class A Felony Superv.	24–30	27–33	30–37	37–46	46–57	51–63
Class B Felony or Below						
Grade A Violation	12–18	15–21	18–24	24–30	30–37	33–41
Grade B Violation	4–10	6–12	8–14	12–18	18–24	21–27
Grade C Violation	3–9	4–10	5–11	6–12	7–13	8–14

Source: U.S. Bureau of Prisons. 2008. *Guidelines Manual* (November 1, 2008). Section 7B1.4, p. 488.

An example of a state that has mandatory probation revocation rules is Michigan. In Michigan, mandatory revocation is imposed on juveniles who have been "waived" to adult probation supervision and who subsequently commit a new misdemeanor or felony crime while under supervision. In such a case, the new crime runs concurrent with the original offense—that is, the length of supervision for the new charge cannot exceed the term left of the original charge, but probation must be revoked (Michigan Judicial Institute, 2003).

LEGAL ISSUES REGARDING REVOCATION HEARINGS

A probation or parole revocation is an *administrative hearing* that is closer to a civil proceeding because it is seen as an extension of an existing sentence (*Hampton v. State*, 2001). As such, neither is governed by the same rules as in formal criminal trials. Given that legal rights at time of revocation are virtually identical, the rights afforded in probation revocation proceedings are extended to parole revocations and vice versa. The result of a probation revocation hearing is not a conviction but a finding of either revoked or continued probation (*Soliz v. State*, 1961), and the same is true for parole.

Rights Entitled to Offenders

During a revocation proceeding, offenders are entitled to certain rights prior to revocation of probation. These rights were granted by the U.S. Supreme Court to parolees (*Morrissey v. Brewer*, 1972) and probationers (*Gagnon v. Scarpelli*, 1973), arguably the two most important parole and probation cases ever decided. Gerald Scarpelli was on probation for a felony when he was arrested for burglary. He admitted involvement in the burglary but later claimed his admission was coerced and therefore invalid. His probation was revoked without a hearing and without a lawyer present. After serving three years of his sentence, Scarpelli sought release, saying that his **due process** rights were violated because he did not obtain a right to a hearing and a right to a lawyer during the hearing. The court extended the same due process rights to probationers that parolees were afforded one year earlier in *Morrissey v. Brewer*. Both probationers and parolees were entitled to the following due process rights before and during revocation hearings:

> **due process**
> Laws must be applied in a fair and equal manner. Fundamental fairness.

1. written notice of alleged probation violation;
2. disclosure of the evidence of violation;
3. an opportunity to be heard in person and to present evidence and witnesses;
4. a right to confront and cross-examine adverse witnesses;
5. a right to judgment by a detached and neutral hearing body; and
6. a written statement of reasons for revoking probation, including evidence used in arriving at that decision.

Rights Limited to Offenders

In revocation proceedings an offender is not constitutionally entitled to a jury (*People v. Price*, 1960) nor to a speedy trial. In some states, however, the law provides for a jury hearing in juvenile cases. A probationer or parolee is not entitled to the Fifth Amendment privilege against self-incrimination (*Perry v. State*, 2001). Remaining silent at a revocation hearing might prejudice the outcome against a defendant, but testifying at a revocation hearing can be used as evidence at a later criminal trial unless a probationer (or parolee) has been given immunity for what he or she says at the revocation.

Probationers are generally not entitled to a court-appointed lawyer during revocation proceedings unless they appear incapable of speaking for themselves

(Gagnon v. Scarpelli, 1973). Given the fact that inarticulate people must voice their need for counsel in order to obtain legal assistance, indigence is used as a proxy, with some states routinely providing counsel to indigent probationers in revocation proceedings.

Level of Proof and Evidence Required

preponderance of the evidence
A level of proof used in a probation revocation administrative hearing, in which the judge decides based on which side presents more convincing evidence and its probable truth or accuracy, and not necessarily on the amount of evidence.

Most courts require that evidence be collected to satisfy **preponderance of the evidence** as the standard for revocation (*United States v. McCormick,* 1995), which is evidence that convinces a judge that a probationer violated the terms of his or her probation. If the state presents proof of a condition violation, a probationer has the burden of presenting evidence to meet and/or overcome prima facie proof (*State v. Graham,* 2001). Preponderance of the evidence is approximately the same amount of evidence as that required to make an arrest (probable cause). However, one court case (*Benton v. State,* 2003) said that arrest for a crime by itself is not enough to revoke probation, but probation may be revoked for an "indictment" by a grand jury (*Newsom v. State,* 2004) or for a conviction by a judge or jury. Interestingly, parole revocation is permissible even if charges are later dismissed (*Reyes v. Tate,* 2001). So it seems that whether a lower burden of proof than preponderance of the evidence (such as reasonable grounds or reasonable suspicion) would suffice for revocation is being addressed by lower courts, but this has yet to be addressed by the U.S. Supreme Court.

The testimony of a CSO is crucial at a revocation proceeding. Whether such testimony—unsupported by any other evidence—is sufficient to revoke varies by state. For example, a probationer's admission to a probation officer was sufficient to support a revocation and eliminates the need on the part of the government to present proof of violation (*Fields v. State,* 2002).

Most states admit hearsay evidence during revocation, but some do not. Reliable hearsay evidence (statements offered by a witness based upon what someone else has told the witness and not upon personal knowledge or observation) may be admitted in a parole (or probation) revocation hearing *(Belk v. Purkett,* 1994). A yes answer to any of the three questions below signifies that hearsay is reliable and therefore may be admitted as evidence in a revocation proceeding:

1. Is the information corroborated by a parolee's own statements or other testimony at a hearing?
2. Does the information fit within one of the many exceptions to the hearsay rule?
3. Does the information have other substantial indicia of reliability?

Other Revocation Situations

Other situations include whether offenders can be revoked for not fulfilling financial commitments, juvenile probation revocations, and credit for time served on probation or parole.

REVOCATION FOR AN INABILITY TO PAY?   Violating an offender for failure to keep current on payments largely depends on whether the behavior was willful and intentional. For example, a probationer can be revoked for refusal to pay monthly fees, restitution, or fines. An indigent probationer cannot be revoked if he or she is unable to pay a fine or restitution, provided that probationer was not somehow responsible for failure to pay (*Bearden v. Georgia,* 1983). The probationer, however, has the burden of showing that the inability to pay was not willful. In other words, a defendant has to show effort and desire to fulfill financial obligations (*State v. Gropper,* 1995).

On the other hand, the courts will allow revocation, even in cases in which an offender is not at fault (i.e., there is no willful violation), if it can be shown that not revoking is a risk to public safety. For example, offenders under community supervision for predatory sex offenses were not able to complete mandatory sex offender treatment programs because none were available in their community. After finding no better alternatives, the court supported incarceration over allowing these offenders to remain in the community without treatment (*People v. Colabello,* 1997).

JUVENILE PROBATION REVOCATION   In the federal system, the United States Code differentiates between juveniles age 17 and younger (18 U.S.C., sec. 5037(c)(1)) and juveniles between the ages of 18 and 21 (18 U.S.C., sec. 5037(c)(2)). In either case, a juvenile may not be sentenced to a prison term longer than an adult would be for the same offense (*United States v. RLC,* 1992). The revocation options depend on the age of a juvenile at the time of sentencing for an original offense, not the age of a juvenile at time of revocation.

TIME ON PROBATION OR PAROLE IS USUALLY NOT CREDITED IF REVOKED   If probation is revoked and an offender goes to prison, most courts have ruled that time served on probation or parole is *not* credited toward a sentence in the same way that incarceration time in jail or prison would be (*Bruggeman v. State,* 1996). However, a federal court and now a Florida statute permit a court options to credit none, some, or all time spent under supervised release toward a sentence (*United States v. Pettus,* 2002; *Summers v. State,* 2002). Generally a parolee whose parole has been revoked may be paroled again, but the revoked parolee must remain in prison for a specified time before becoming eligible for another parole.

As long as an offender abides by the terms of parole (or probation), he or she will minimally receive credit on a sentence as straight time—that is, without the benefit of good time credits. In other states a parolee may receive reductions for good behavior while on parole.

CHARACTERISTICS OF OFFENDERS WHO VIOLATE DURING SUPERVISION

As we have seen so far, violations during probation or parole supervision are influenced primarily by offender behavior, officer discretion, and agency policy. This section discusses *who* is more likely to violate and *why*. Table 7.4 shows offender characteristics of federal probation revocations and Table 7.5 shows similar characteristics of state parolees returned to prison for their revocation. According to Table 7.4, female offenders over the age of 30 and those with no prior adult or juvenile convictions were more likely to succeed (Sabol et al., 2000).

Also, offenders who possessed skills that allowed them to maintain employment, those who were high school graduates, and those who lived with their spouse and/or children were less likely to become recidivists. Conventional ties and positive social support from friends and family significantly contribute to success. On the other hand, being young, being unmarried, having previous convictions, and lacking emotional maturity contributed to higher failure rates.

Of the parole violators who returned to state prison (most with a new sentence), more than 95% were men, over half were African-American, and most were young or middle-aged (between 25 and 39 years of age). An inverse relationship exists between prior criminal history and parole outcome: the lower the number of previous arrests, the greater the likelihood of parole success (Hughes, Wilson, & Beck, 2001; Solomon, 2006). Finally, the most serious offense for violators was a violent crime in 34% of cases, a property crime for 33% of violators, a drug crime in 23% of cases, and a public order crime in 13% of cases (see Table 7.5).

TABLE 7.4   Characteristics of Federal Probationers Terminating Supervision

Characteristic	Number of probation terminations	PERCENT TERMINATING SUPERVISION WITH:			
		Successful completion	Committed new crime	Technical violation	Admin. closure
Gender					
Male	10,781	81.2%	5.9%	10.9%	2.0%
Female	4,915	84.6%	4.3%	9.5%	1.5%
Race					
White	10,598	84.0%	5.3%	9.0%	1.7%
African-American	3,935	78.1%	6.1%	13.6%	2.2%
American Indian	428	64.7%	4.9%	28.3%	2.1%
Asian/Pacific Islander	492	92.5%	2.6%	4.2%	0.6%
Ethnicity					
Hispanic	2,818	80.8%	8.3%	9.9%	1.0%
Non-Hispanic	12,602	82.6%	4.8%	10.6%	2.0%
Age					
16–18 years	114	67.5%	7.9%	22.8%	1.8%
19–20 years	567	61.6%	11.3%	26.0%	1.1%
21–30 years	4,762	76.3%	7.4%	14.7%	1.5%
31–40 years	4,105	82.5%	6.0%	10.2%	1.3%
41 and over	6,166	89.0%	2.9%	5.8%	2.5%
Education					
Less than High School	3,642	76.2%	7.9%	14.2%	1.6%
High School Graduate	5,254	81.4%	5.1%	11.8%	1.6%
Some College	3,538	86.8%	3.8%	7.5%	2.0%
College Graduate	1,878	92.9%	1.9%	2.9%	2.3%
Drug Abuse					
None	12,664	92.6%	2.4%	3.7%	1.3%
Drug history	1,691	84.5%	1.4%	9.0%	2.5%
GROUP TOTAL	15,721	82.3%	5.4%	10.5%	1.8%

Note: Each termination was counted separately. Technical violations and terminations for new crimes are shown only if supervision terminated with incarceration or removal from active supervision for reason of a violation. The data exclude corporate offenders.

(a) Technical violations range widely from drug use, escape, quitting a job without permission, not reporting, and other probation conditions

Source: U.S. Department of Justice. 2008. *Compendium of Federal Justice Statistics, 2004.* Washington, DC: U.S. Department of Justice.

Measuring Recidivism

Countless published studies have measured probationer and parolee recidivism rates in the United States. As we discussed in chapter 1, the rate of success largely depends on the definition of success and failure used by researchers, such as law violations only or new crimes and technical violations:

1. how recidivism is defined (i.e., by rearrest, conviction, parole revocation, return to prison, or other return to criminal behavior);
2. duration of time that subjects were studied (the longer the period of time subjects were followed—for example, up to three years—the better); and
3. size of sample studied (a larger sample, or one that samples from more than one area of the country, is more generalizable).

While on probation, the rearrest rate varied from 12%–65%, and the conviction rate fluctuated between 16%–35%. The revocation rate, which for most studies

TABLE 7.5   Who Are the Parolees Who Get Sent Back to State Prison?

Characteristic	All 50 States	California	New York	Texas
Gender				
Male	95.3%	92.9%	96.7%	94.6%
Female	4.7	7.1	3.3	5.4
Race/Hispanic origin				
White non-Hispanic	27.5	30.8	11.1	23.1
Black non-Hispanic	51.8	33.4	54.2	50.3
Hispanic	18.3	31.9	33.1	26.0
Other	2.4	3.9	1.6	0.6
Age at prison release				
18–24	9.4	8.8	8.6	6.1
25–29	20.8	19.8	19.8	19.1
30–34	24.1	25.5	26.0	23.3
35–39	20.3	22.9	20.3	21.1
40–44	13.9	12.8	13.3	15.5
45–54	9.3	8.0	10.2	12.3
55 or older	2.0	2.0	1.8	2.5
Most serious offense*				
Violent	33.7	24.4	40.9	33.3
Property	30.1	25.3	15.6	36.8
Drug	23.1	27.1	33.6	21.3
Public order	12.9	22.9	9.4	8.6
Number of prior incarcerations				
1	42.3	28.9	52.9	44.1
2	14.0	12.6	12.6	14.1
3 to 5	26.3	27.1	26.7	28.4
6 or more	17.3	30.7	7.8	13.5

Source: Timothy A. Hughes, Doris James Wilson, and Allen J. Beck. 2001. *Trends in State Parole, 1990–2000.* Washington, DC: U.S. Department of Justice, 14.

included both technical violations and new crimes, varied from 14%–60% (Morgan, 1994). The various recidivism rates are likely more indicative of diverse decision-making style and behavior of probation officers, judges, and police officers than of actual differences in a probationer's return to criminal behavior.

Time to Revocation

Most rearrests of parolees occur within the first three months after release from prison (Grattet, Lin, & Petersilia, 2011). Gray et al. (2001) concurred when they found that about 30% of all probation violators were also terminated within the first three months of supervision, mostly with technical violations. Probationers who committed a new crime seemed to violate later in the probationary period, but they were also more likely to be unemployed, to have a prior criminal history, to be on probation for an assaultive offense, and to have a pattern of technical violations. Once the first 90 days tapers off, the likelihood of revocations decreases dramatically.

FIGURE 7.4 Results of a
Recidivism Study

Source: Patrick A. Langan and Mark
Cunniff. 1992. *Recidivism of felons on
probation, 1986–1989.* Washington,
DC: U.S. Department of Justice,
Bureau of Justice Statistics.

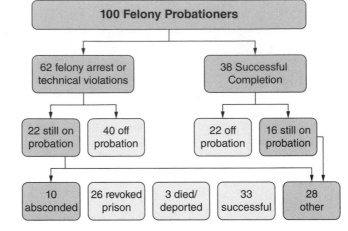

Figure 7.4 provides results of a recidivism study of a large felony probationer sample of 79,000 offenders in 17 states within three years of starting supervision. About 43% were rearrested for a felony within three years on probation. Within the rearrested group, 46% of probationers sent to prison or jail absconded within the three years. Furthermore, 71% either completed their probation or were still on probation (Langan & Cuniff, 1992).

Original Offense of Conviction and Recidivism

A three-year study of nearly 300,000 prisoners released in 15 different states found that 67.5% were rearrested for a new offense and over half were returned to prison within the study period (Langan & Levin, 2002). With the exception of robbers, property offenders (burglars, larcenists, and other thieves) had higher rates of re-arrest than offenders convicted of violent crimes. In a different study of offenders returning to the federal system between 1986–1997, offenders convicted of violent crimes (for example, robbery) were more likely to return to federal prison within three years than was any other offender type. About 32% of violent offenders returned to prison, as opposed to only 13% of drug offenders (Sabol et al., 2000).

Some of these differences stem from the different patterns of offending behavior that criminals exhibit. Some criminals begin their "career" at an earlier age, accrue more arrests, and sustain criminal behavior for a long time before decelerating their rate of offending. These criminals are termed *repeat* or *habitual* offenders. Other criminals, such as murderers, do not have criminal careers per se, but they commit a serious offense for which they are caught and serve time. These criminals are much less likely to recidivate.

We pointed out in the beginning of this chapter that probationers committed significantly fewer new crimes than parolees. As you can see in Figure 7.5, revocation rates varied by type of offense originally committed and by type of community supervision (probation vs. mandatory supervision). This table shows that probationers were more likely to complete supervision successfully than were parolees (both on discretionary parole and under mandatory parole supervision), no matter of which type of crime they had been convicted. Also, parolees who were convicted of property, drug, and public order crimes were more likely to succeed than were offenders who went to prison for violent crimes, weapons, or immigration offenses (see Figure 7.5).

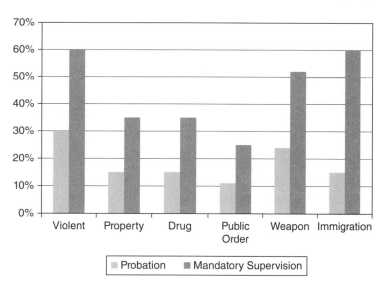

FIGURE 7.5 Probation vs. Parole: Federal Revocations (Both Technical and New Crime) Separated by Original Conviction

Why Have Revocation Rates Increased?

With the increase in rate of violations in recent years, research has been undertaken to discover the underlying causes of parole and probation revocations. One reason involves a shift in the way offenders are monitored, changing from a treatment approach to one of control. With more emphasis placed on control and punishment, the threshold level is lowered for behavior tolerated before revocation occurs (White, Mellow, Englander, & Ruffinengo, 2011). Second, an increase in the average number of offenders that each officer supervises causes more stress and offers less face-to-face contact. Officers spend less quality time with offenders and more time on rule enforcement and paperwork. A third reason is that parolees and probationers alike have more parole conditions imposed and thus more ways to violate. An increased number of conditions means that offenders experience more pressure to perform and to try to meet all those conditions. Fourth, with advances in drug testing technology, more drug use is now detected. Finally, with increased use of electronic monitoring in parole and probation, more hardened offenders tend to be placed in a community so as to avoid institutional overcrowding.

An increase in revocation rates puts pressure on a number of other components in the criminal justice system. For example, parole and probation officers must devote more of their time to revocation paperwork and less time to supervising other offenders in their caseload who are functioning satisfactorily. Furthermore, while probation and parole revocators are awaiting hearings, revocation drains court resources, parole board resources, and county jail bed space.

Alternatives to Incarceration for Technical Violations

Revocation for technical violations when probationers don't follow the rules is an extremely costly option for taxpayers. Many states recognize this and are responding with other options for probation violators. For example, Delaware's Probation Reform Law not only shortened a term of probation to no longer than two years, but technical violators could be placed on work release or in probation violation centers for up to five days per violation, not to exceed 10 days per calendar year

(Sentencing Accountability Commission & the Statistical Analysis Center, 2005). Michigan, Kentucky, and New Jersey created technical violator programs that are residential halfway house-style programs where offenders can be sent for intensive programming for up to 90 days. Most offenders are referred to these programs by probation and parole officers. An evaluation of New Jersey's "Halfway Back" intermediate sanction therapeutic program matched technical violators who were referred and completed the program with eligible technical violators that did not go through the program. While the Halfway Back residents had slightly fewer new arrests over 18 months than the comparison group, the two groups did not significantly differ in amount of time that elapsed until their first arrest. The program's biggest strength was that it saved $1.3 million in incarceration costs that would have been incurred for every 100 technical violators who had gone to jail as a response to revocation (White et al., 2011).

The future of community supervision entails examining patterns of behavior that reliably indicate when a parolee has become too much of a public safety risk to remain in a community. Prediction research into the causes of recidivism and subsequent revocation would be invaluable in equipping a parole officer with the tools necessary for supervision. Recall our earlier discussion of classification and risk and needs assessment instruments in chapter 5. It is interesting to note that many of the same variables that initially classify offenders also can predict post-release behavior on parole, which might lead us to a deeper understanding of why some offenders succeed and some do not (Williams, McShane, & Dolny, 2000a).

SUMMARY

- A decision to revoke for noncompliance is initially recommended by a supervision officer but is empowered at judicial discretion for probationers and at parole board discretion for parolees.

- Violations include new crimes and technical violations of conditions.

- Time served in a community is not credited as jail or prison time if supervision is revoked.

- Probationers and parolees must be given due process rights, including notice of charges, right to confront witnesses, and right to present evidence in their favor.

- Offenders do not have a constitutional right to an attorney, but one is provided if competency is an issue. There is typically no right to appeal a revocation, but about half of the states, by law or agency policy, allow parolees this option.

- The increase in the revocation rate is due to a shift in the way offenders are monitored; greater emphasis is placed on control and punishment, and less time is spent on treatment and reentry concerns (due to a higher caseload per officer).

DISCUSSION QUESTIONS

1. Should early termination of probation be given as a good behavior incentive or should probationers serve their entire term regardless of behavior? What are the advantages and disadvantages of each approach?

2. If you were a CSO and your client refused to report or check in, how many times (or how long) would it take before you filed a revocation with the courts?

3. If you were a CSO and your client could not find a job, what steps would you take to help this person? At what point would you consider taking him or

her back to court to request a modification in conditions or revocation for not having a job? Defend your answer.

4. If you were a CSO and your client admitted to using drugs and said that her drug test would come back positive, what would you do?

5. How do motivational interviewing techniques factor into unresponsive client behavior?

6. Which type of technical violation do you perceive as the worst kind, and why?

7. In a decision to revoke probation, what are implications for the probationer, the probation officer, and the community? Are these the same or different with a parolee?

8. Do the revocation procedures in place now provide due process for offenders? What, if anything, might be lacking?

9. Is the "preponderance of the evidence" standard of proof too low, and should a different standard be used for revocation? If so, should the new standard require more or less evidence?

10. How does revocation contribute to jail crowding? What alternatives could be tried to remedy this problem?

11. If you were an offender under post-prison parole supervision accused of a series of technical violations (three times that you didn't report and one positive urine screening for cocaine) for which you were guilty, would you request expedited revocation procedures or a hearing? Justify your answer.

WEBSITES, VIDEOS, AND PODCASTS

Websites

Probation Revocation Rights in Missouri
    http://doc.mo.gov/documents/prob/Red%20book.pdf

U.S. Parole Commission Rules and Procedures Manual
    http://www.usdoj.gov/uspc/rules_procedures/rulesmanual.htm

Georgia Parole Conditions
    http://oldweb.pap.state.ga.us/parole_conditions.htm

Iowa Code for Parole Revocations
    http://www.legis.state.ia.us/IACODE/2003/908

Videos/Podcasts

Violation of Probation in Florida
    http://www.youtube.com/watch?v=Z_hnUY3ikQQ

Attorney Deidra Sibley, of Allen & Arcadier in Melbourne, Florida, discusses violation of probation.

Probation Violation Hearing
    http://www.youtube.com/watch?v=CXWMflWmA7o

Mark Provenza, former Lorain City Law Director, at a probation violation hearing with Judge Patrick Carroll at Lakewood Municipal Court.

Modification and Termination

In the following two cases, list the violations of supervision that are applicable. What decision would you make in each case? Your choices are: (1) modification and retention under community supervision; (2) modification with some other graduated sanction; or (3) revocation and return to jail or prison. Pick one response for each case and fully justify your decision.

CASE A: Probationer Conner, Possession of an Explosive Device

Probationer Conner is under supervision for Possession of an Explosive Device, which was an undetonated homemade bomb. Mr. Conner has three years of college education (major in physics) and reportedly has an IQ of 125. Given his particularly eccentric behavior during pretrial, the special conditions of his supervision require that he obtain a comprehensive mental health diagnosis. Shortly after Mr. Conner's supervision term begins, he tests positive for marijuana use. When confronted by his probation officer, he admits to using marijuana. However, he states that he uses marijuana to self-medicate because it helps calm him, and he feels that he would commit violent acts if he were to cease its use. At this point Mr. Conner is not undergoing substance abuse treatment nor has he been court-ordered to do so. The probation officer reminds Mr. Conner of a condition of supervision that he neither use nor possess illegal drugs and advises him that his use of illegal substances cannot be allowed, adding that the sentencing court would be advised of any violation.

The probation officer immediately refers Mr. Conner for a psychiatric evaluation to determine whether he would benefit from psychotropic medication. The psychiatrist diagnoses him with Bipolar Affective Disorder, Type II, and prescribes Depakote, which takes up to two weeks to take effect. However, this medication requires regular lab work to evaluate its effectiveness. Mr. Conner fails to attend his next appointment with the psychiatrist, so you are unsure as to whether he is taking his Depakote medication regularly. Results of a urine specimen taken from him a week after his evaluation by the psychiatrist reveal trace amounts of Depakote but also that Mr. Conner has used both marijuana and methamphetamine. What should you as the probation officer do next?

CASE B: Parolee York, Aggravated Assault

Parolee York was convicted and sent to prison for two years for aggravated assault. She has a history of violent behavior and anger management issues. She has no known drug nor alcohol problems and until recently was a dishwasher at Joe's Pancake House. She has been under parole supervision with you for the last five months and for a time was reporting regularly. Special conditions of Ms. York's supervision require she complete anger management classes by the end of her term, which is supposed to end in seven months if all goes well. Anger management treatment takes three months, and the program has a waiting list of clients who are court-ordered to attend treatment. Ms. York had repeatedly stated she would undergo an anger management assessment but just never has. When you call to verify employment at the restaurant, her employer says that she quit coming three weeks ago and has been replaced by another dishwasher.

Now two weeks have gone by since you called Joe's Pancake House and still no sign of Ms. York. She won't return your phone calls. She missed her regular appointment with you this afternoon. You called the jail to see whether she had been picked up, but police have had no contact with her. What should you do next?

PART III

Enhancements and Graduated Sanctions

With the push toward decreasing jail and prison populations, intermediate community sanctions for offenders are becoming more popular for those for whom regular probation may be too lenient, but jail and prison is not an option. Chapter 8 considers residential sanctions, in which offenders must live away from home and inside a facility within the community while completing their sentence. Residential programs include halfway houses, work release, and correctional boot camps. Chapter 9 explores nonresidential community corrections programs in which the offender resides at home while participating in the program under a strict set of rules and curfews. Nonresidential programs include house arrest, electronic monitoring, and day reporting centers.

Finally, Chapter 10 discusses sanctions tied to restorative justice and economic sources. Restorative justice is a philosophy that underscores the need for offenders to acknowledge their crime and agree to repair the harm done to their victims and to the surrounding community. Forms of restorative justice include victim-offender mediation, family group conferencing, reparation boards, and sentencing circles. Community service, restitution, and fines are economic sanctions that can be used as tools to accomplish objectives in appropriate cases.

8

Residential Community Supervision Programs

CHAPTER LEARNING OBJECTIVES

1. Describe the purpose of residential community correctional facilities.
2. Discuss the effectiveness of residential community correctional programs for medium- and high-risk offenders.
3. Compare and contrast halfway houses, shock incarceration, and work release programs.

This is the inside of a brand new residential community corrections facility in which the rooms are grouped around the central communal area. Clients can leave the facility for work or with prior permission.

KEY TERMS

intermediate sanctions
residential community correctional
facilities

halfway house
restitution center
work release

work ethic camp
shock incarceration
boot camp

Former chief financial officer Andrew Fastow served four years, eight months on a six-year sentence in a federal prison in Louisiana for his leadership role in the Enron fraud. He became eligible for a six-month stay at a federal community correctional facility in Houston, where he was released at the end of 2011. The infamous Enron fraud was discovered back in 2003 when the company hid its losses from investors over a number of years. Fastow agreed to testify against fellow Enron executives Kenneth Lay and Jeffrey Skilling for a reduced prison term. Fastow was also able to shorten his prison sentence slightly if he completed a drug and alcohol abuse class (Stempel, Hays, & Wallace, 2011).

INTRODUCTION

Regular probation supervision is adequate for misdemeanor offenders and for felony offenders who pose a minimum or even a medium risk. However, offenders who are eligible for community supervision but who may not require 24-hour supervision like that provided by jail or prison are ideal candidates for intermediate sanctions. We introduced the term **intermediate sanctions** in chapter 1 as a community-based sentence that provides more freedom than prison but less freedom than traditional probation. There are both residential and nonresidential options. This chapter addresses residential programs that require offenders to live in a facility but allow them to remain in the community, where they have access to more treatment services. Sometimes a sentence to a residential facility is preceded by a short stay in jail for a few weeks or months. Though they are known by multiple names, the three residential programs discussed here are: (1) halfway houses; (2) work release programs; and (3) correctional boot camps.

intermediate sanctions
A spectrum of community supervision strategies that vary greatly in terms of their supervision level and treatment capacity, ranging from diversion to short-term duration in a residential community facility.

HALFWAY HOUSES

halfway house
The oldest and most common type of community residential facility for probationers or parolees who require a more structured setting than would be available if living independently.

residential community corrections facilities
A sanction in the community in which the convicted offender lives at the facility and must be employed, but can leave the facility for a limited purpose and duration if pre-approved. Examples include halfway houses, pre-release centers, restitution centers, drug treatment facilities, and work release centers.

Halfway houses are residential facilities for probationers and parolees who require a more structured setting than would be available from living independently. Halfway houses are staffed 24 hours a day, seven days a week for various types of offenders and are also known as *community corrections centers (CCCs)* or **residential community correctional facilities (RCCFs)**. The term *halfway house* was the original term used because of the two groups of clients accepted: the halfway out's and the halfway in's. Of the group that is *halfway out* of prison, offenders are either:

a) *pre-parole/pre-release:* Prisoners who are eligible for minimum-custody prison and who anticipate receiving parole within the next year; *or*

b) *parolees:* Offenders who pose a greater risk and need assistance in making the transition from prison to community.

The second group consists of those who are *halfway in* prison and includes either:

a) high-risk/high-need probationers; *or*

b) probation and parole violators given graduated sanctions.

Because of their diversity, it is therefore difficult to estimate the number of halfway houses. As of the last known nationwide count of local facilities in 2003, there are 628 facilities housing nearly 19,500 offenders. Of this number, over 90% of facilities are privately owned and operated, and less than 10% are operated by the Department of Corrections. The number of inmates living in RCCFs at the present writing represents 4.4% of the total inmate population in the U.S., at an average cost per day of around $43 per offender. Alaska, Iowa, Montana, and Wyoming are the most avid users of RCCFs, which house about 14% of their total inmate populations. In the federal system, there are over 8,000 federal inmates in CCCs (Sabol & Couture, 2008).

History of Halfway Houses

The concept of the halfway house has been traced back to the early 1800s in England and Ireland. In the United States, the halfway house originated in 1816, at a time when most penitentiaries still practiced a Pennsylvania-style system of solitude and complete silence. Prisoners were locked in their cells all day and were not allowed to interact with each other for fear they would "contaminate" each other. Interaction would take away from the penance that prisoners were thought to have to seek for full reformation (Keller & Alper, 1970).

Following a tumultuous riot in a Pennsylvania prison, a commission was appointed to examine the problems with the prison system. One commission recommendation was to create temporary shelters to help prisoners get back on their feet as they transitioned back to the community. This proposal was not adopted by the legislature because of strong feelings that prisoners, even after release from prison, should not be allowed to interact.

As penitentiaries transformed from the solitude of the Pennsylvania system to the silent interaction of the Auburn, or "congregate" system, prisoners were allowed to work outside of their cells. State support for halfway houses was still lacking, so private, nonprofit organizations opened halfway houses for the first time to provide a place for prisoners to live after release from prison.

For example, in 1845 the Isaac T. Hopper Home opened for male prisoners in New York City. In 1864 the Temporary Asylum for Discharged Female Prisoners opened in the Boston area. The Boston halfway house for women received less opposition than did facilities for men. This difference was due to an underlying belief that, unlike male prisoners, female prisoners did not associate for the purpose of conversing about criminal activity. Female prisoners were believed to contribute to their own rehabilitation (Wells, 1997). At that time, halfway houses merely offered food and shelter to ex-prisoners and did not provide treatment services.

By the end of the nineteenth century, private halfway houses opened in eight other states. Criminal justice officials, such as law enforcement officers and corrections administrators, remained opposed to halfway houses, and funds for them dwindled; with the Great Depression of the 1930s, many were forced to close. Only one halfway house, Pittsburgh's The Parting of the Ways, remained open (Keller & Alper, 1970).

In the 1950s, private halfway houses were viewed in a new light. Concern about crime and high parole revocation rates prompted halfway houses to assume a role beyond offering food and shelter. They provided transition services to prisoners, becoming involved in both treatment and correctional supervision. In addition to being less expensive than prison, halfway houses protected the community insofar as residents were more closely monitored than were traditional parolees.

In the 1960s halfway houses became more visible when Congress appropriated funds for the first time to open federal-level halfway houses. The Safe Streets Act of 1968 established a source of funding for halfway house expansion throughout the 1970s. A meeting of a newly formed group called the International Halfway House Association was held in Chicago in 1964. This private nonprofit policy organization, which later changed its name to the International Community Corrections Association, currently seeks to improve community corrections policy all over the world. The organization, serving a 1,000 individual members, now represents 250 private corrections agencies operating approximately 1,500 programs (International Community Corrections Association, 2011).

Private halfway houses have since found a permanent niche in the corrections market providing alternatives to imprisonment and creating an outlet for prison crowding control. In the last few years, for example, many females in California's prisoner population have been transferred to private community correctional facilities following court mandates to decrease the number of prisoners (Schultz, 2007).

Each halfway house is unique in structure, treatment programs offered, and type of clients it serves. Private halfway houses can choose which clients they wish to accept on a contractual basis. Their prison case manager or probation officer refers offenders who are eligible for placement. The government pays a facility a specified amount per day per offender, and the offender is expected to assist in the per diem payment. In a hypothetical example, if it costs $43 per day per offender to operate a residential halfway house, the state Department of Corrections pays the halfway house about $32 per day per offender, and each client is charged about 25% of the cost, or $11 per day. Each facility has a different per day cost, depending on how many in-house programs are offered. For instance, Crosspoint is a center in San Antonio that has a contract with the Bureau of Prisons to accept federal clients at $65 per day (Settles, 2004).

Program Components

Most RCCFs and CCCs do not have surrounding property fences nor any locks on the doors. Residents, who may leave a facility at any time to work at a verified job, must obey the following rules:

- live in one's facility;
- be employed (or be working part time and going to school);

- keep current on rent (offender is charged per daily stay to subsidize cost to taxpayers); and
- be preapproved to leave one's facility for reasons other than work.

Leaving one's facility other than for work, school, rehabilitation, or medical attention depends on good behavior and is limited to a certain duration, purpose, and curfew. When not at work, residents maintain their facility through assigned chores and perform court-ordered community service, as well as attend any classes or counseling sessions that their case manager mandates. Most halfway houses require residents to submit to regular drug testing and breathalyzers.

LEVELS SYSTEM: A FORM OF BEHAVIOR MODIFICATION   Increased freedom for residents must be earned and is based on good behavior, amount of time spent in the program, and their financial situation. Most halfway house programs offer some kind of behavior modification program called a *levels system,* in which the bottom level is the most restricted; the top level grants more freedom away from the halfway house and more privileges.

For example, in a five-level system new residents start on Level 5, in which a hold is placed on them (they cannot leave the facility) until their case manager has completed the intake process. Once intake is complete, residents move to Level 4, in which they remain until they obtain a job and catch up on their rent. Level 4 residents are allowed passes to attend treatment (Alcoholics Anonymous and Narcotics Anonymous) and are given one four-hour pass per week to attend church (outside of leaving for work). Each level has its own curfew, which is not applicable to residents who work evenings or nights. In addition to treatment and church passes, Level 3 residents may take one daytime pass of no longer than eight hours, with a curfew of 10:00 P.M. Level 2 residents have Level 3 privileges but with a later curfew of 11:59 P.M.

At Level 1, residents must be caught up on all restitution, community service, and rent. They must have $200 in savings. Level 1 residents have a weekday curfew of 11:59 P.M. but can take weekend passes, from Friday to Sunday, to visit preapproved friends and family. Level 1 residents can own an insured car and have driving privileges, whereas all other residents must depend on someone else for a ride or must take a bus. All residents, regardless of their level, must produce receipts and verification that an approved destination was visited. Passes are allowed to visit a verified address of a family member or for four hours at a time to see a movie or to go shopping. Some programs require residents to spend a certain number of days (e.g., two weeks) on each level before advancing to the next level.

TRANSITIONING OUT   Upon program completion of the residential phase, released clients are assigned to either a probation or parole officer in an appropriate jurisdiction. Some RCCFs have "aftercare" programs in which successful residential clients move out of the halfway house to live at home but continue to return periodically for drug testing, to attend group treatment, and to visit an RCCF nonresidential case manager who functions just like a probation or parole officer.

Residents who successfully completed an RCCF program have reported experiencing a greater internal locus of control. Released clients have found that RCCFs assisted them with readjustment from prison, finding a better job, and abstaining from drugs and alcohol while allowing them to financially assist their families and to develop closer family relations than when in prison.

Worker Perspectives and Role Orientation

Two types of staff work at a halfway house. One group is primarily involved in activities that are security-oriented, whereas case managers and counselors take care of treatment and rehabilitation. The job of a halfway house case manager has been described as similar to that of a probation and parole officer, in the sense that the counselor must be able to administer rehabilitation and punishment. Leanne Alarid worked at a halfway house in Denver, Colorado. She describes her job responsibilities working in both types of positions:

> I began working as a member of the client management staff, involved in security and physical accountability for over 80 males and females. In this capacity, I conducted population counts, searched people and belongings for contraband, signed clients in and out of the facility, dispensed medications and Antabuse, and conducted breathalyzers and urine screenings. When an opportunity to work as a case manager became available, I transferred within the facility from the security-oriented job to one oriented around treatment. In this position, I became occupied with treatment, programming, and revocation issues for 20 to 24 individuals. A case manager had duties very similar to a pre-release officer or a parole/probation officer in that I assessed my client's needs and risks and I devised individual program plans to meet each of their needs. I assisted my clients with adjustment problems they experienced while in the program, and I supervised their progress. I also taught drug and alcohol treatment classes for new clients, and I prepared pre-release plans and attended monthly parole board hearings.

Another perspective on working in a halfway house comes from Melodye Lehnerer (1992), who describes the different roles she played during her two-year experience conducting ethnographic research from one halfway house. Lehnerer began as a volunteer, moved to "peripheral member" status, and then became an "active member" as an assistant caseworker. As membership involvement increased, role conflict arose between staff affinity and identification as a researcher. The caseworker role required that Lehnerer be too much of a "social control agent," so she quit case management and started teaching general equivalency diploma (GED) classes and life skills to clients. As a teacher and staff member, she explains how clients viewed her differently as "staff" than as a volunteer:

> Quite often residents would approach me after class and apologize for their or someone else's behavior. It was their way of teaching me how the game was played. Given the context, staff members and residents were protagonists [sic]. That was just the way it had to be. . . . [I]n the classroom setting there existed a preexisting relationship based upon power differences. (p. 156)

Lehnerer reports that residents maintained a code of secrecy from staff. She also stresses the mutual distrust between residents and staff, and how information control was a valuable resource used by both parties: "Lack of trust was directly linked to staff beliefs that residents were concealing information and resident beliefs that staff were using information to further discredit them" (p. 228).

PUNISHMENT AND TREATMENT ROLE ORIENTATIONS Workers may experience role conflict, which is a clash between punishment and treatment goals. Alarid explains:

> When I moved from being involved in security issues and running facility operations to case management, I experienced more role conflict. The case manager

role had two opposing sides: treatment and reprimand. The most effective case managers were the ones who could balance the two sides and who believed in both. However, some counselors were lopsided in that they invested heavily in treatment issues but could not bring themselves to put someone in jail who posed a liability risk to the community. No one ever likes sending someone back to prison, but you have to be willing to switch hats pretty readily from helping someone out one day and having to revoke them the next. Because of this difficulty, the burnout rate among staff is fairly high. The most valuable thing I learned through all this was, above all, to treat people with fairness, consistency, and respect.

RCCFs for Female Offenders

Most female offenders have been convicted of misdemeanors or felonies that constitute either nonviolent property or drug crimes. Examples of typical offenses committed by women include theft, fraud, shoplifting, prostitution, and possession of a controlled substance. Since most female felons do not pose a threat to the community, they do not require prison sentences and are ideal candidates for community placement. One type of placement developed especially for women arrested for prostitution is a Women's Recovery Center in Minnesota (see Box 8.1).

Given that female offenders also have problems with drugs and/or alcohol, and that many are mothers of at least one child under the age of 18, residential community correctional facilities that address gender-specific issues have grown. There are more than 65 residential treatment programs and another 70 programs

BOX 8.1   COMMUNITY CORRECTIONS UP CLOSE

Dealing with the Root Causes of Prostitution

"I had been through so much abuse that I honestly believed that I was not worth anything, and it really didn't matter if I got high because nobody gave a damn anyways."—Sheila Ayala, graduate of the Magdalene Program (Neff, 2006).

In Nashville, Tennessee, Reverend Becca Stevens started "Magdalene" as a grassroots nonprofit outreach program for women involved in prostitution (Neff, 2006). Ramsey County in St. Paul, Minnesota, opened a 12-bed program called the "Women's Recovery Center" with funding from the Minnesota legislature (Nelson, 2004). Both centers are a diversion option at the front end or a postrelease option for female prisoners who have a genuine desire to get out of prostitution. Both programs address the root causes of prostitution, which are childhood and young adult physical and sexual abuse, drug dependency, and mental health issues resulting from abuse, including post-traumatic stress, depression, and low self-esteem. Women in the two programs learn to understand how sexuality formed a large part of their identity and how drug use masked a painful past. For example, Clemmie is

a Magdalene client who reported that since she was six years old, her mother allowed other adult men to molest her sister and her. "At that time [as a teenager], we got introduced with an older guy that had told me about how I can make money off of selling my body, and it was like 'off to the races' because I know I can do this. . . . I already know what the mens want." A program resident learns the difference between unequal male-female relationships (such as that of an abusive pimp who feeds her drug habit), in comparison with relating to others in a more equal way. Most important, she discovers self-worth and sobriety, which along with learning about opportunities for housing, legitimate employment, and health care teach her how to build a stable life to regain full parental rights of her children. The St. Paul program reports an 80% success rate; the Tennessee program success rate is unknown (Neff, 2006; Nelson, 2004).

Sources: Neff, Tom. 2006. *Chances: The women of Magdalene.* Video: The Documentary Channel; Nelson, William F. 2004. Prostitution: A community solution alternative. *Corrections Today* (October): 88–91.

resembling halfway houses for women to live with their children while they are serving a residential community sentence. Studies indicate that children of offenders suffer emotionally, developmentally, and economically when their parents go to prison. Children of incarcerated parents stand a greater chance of following in the footsteps of their parents by becoming involved in the juvenile justice system at an early age. Because the mother is still the primary caregiver in the majority of families, the effect of incarcerating mothers who have dependent children is pronounced (Mumola, 2000). The question then becomes: How can female offenders be punished or sanctioned without punishing their children?

JOHN CRAINE HOUSE   The John Craine House, located in Indianapolis, Indiana, is designed specifically for female offenders convicted of misdemeanors or nonviolent felony offenses who are caretakers of preschool-aged children. The program teaches the women to be emotionally and economically independent as a preventive intervention for their children (Barton & Justice, 2000). As only one of six programs in the country, Craine House holds a maximum of six adults and eight children at one time and serves 10 to 17 women and about 20 children each year.

Craine House resembles a halfway house in the sense that women pay for part of the program cost through an expectation of employment. Staff assess the needs of each woman and formulate an individualized treatment plan. However, this facility seems to provide much more individualized and specialized attention than do typical halfway houses, not only for offenders' needs but also for their children, described as follows:

> [Craine House provides] parenting skills, substance abuse treatment, job seeking skills, educational and/or job placement in the community, personal budgeting, nutrition information, and advocacy as indicated by individualized assessments. The program arranges for day care for the children at nearby locations to enable the women to work in the community. The program is staffed around the clock by counselors and family living specialists. . . . Basic goals for the Craine House program are to provide a safe, structured environment; promote the preservation of mother–child relationships; enhance the offenders' abilities to maintain economic and emotional independence while leading responsible, law-abiding lives; and prevent the neglect, abuse and potential delinquency of the offenders' children. (Barton & Justice, 2000, pp. 7–8)

Because of the high level of services offered, services cost Craine House $80 per person per day. The disadvantage is that this costs more than incarceration. However, considering that the facility also provides prevention programs for the children, the cost may be money well spent in the long run. The average length of stay in the program is five months (six-and-a-half months for those who complete the program and two months for noncompleters). Recidivism is measured by whether the women appear in court on a new charge after successfully leaving the program. Out of the 500 women who have been through the program, the recidivism rate is 20%. The long-term effects of Craine House as a prevention mechanism for the children who have participated would be worthwhile to measure.

Evaluations of RCCFs

Halfway house programs in one jurisdiction cannot always be generalized to other areas because wide variation exists in the quality of programs and in the types of offenders admitted. In the most effective programs, trained and qualified staff use cognitive-behavioral treatments and target interventions to high-risk (as opposed to low-risk) offenders (Lowenkamp et al., 2010).

Programs have been evaluated by examining their success or failure rates as well as by comparing recidivism rates of halfway house residents with a matched offender sample. Given that most RCCFs emphasize working and paying rent, clearly stable employment and substance abuse counseling are keys to successful program completion along with keeping current on restitution and child support (Cox, 2009). RCCFs whose clients were younger, used drugs and alcohol, had more extensive prior criminal histories, lacked employment and educational skills, and had fewer community ties were found more likely to fail than are ones serving individuals without substance abuse problems and with a less extensive criminal history (Hartmann, Friday, & Minor, 1994).

How beneficial is it to have high-risk offenders in residential community corrections programs? Data from 7,306 RCCF clients were compared with 5,801 parolees to analyze success rates and recidivism rates of low-risk versus high-risk clients. A risk score was calculated based on criminal history and demographic data, and scores separated low-risk and high-risk individuals in both the treatment and control groups (Lowenkamp & Latessa, 2005). For both *low-risk* groups, parolees had lower recidivism rates than RCCF clients. However, for high-risk individuals in both groups, high-risk RCCF clients were more successful than high-risk parolees. The researchers concluded that RCCFs are more effective with high-risk offenders than with low-risk offenders (Lowenkamp & Latessa, 2005). Research in that same jurisdiction found that high-risk youths were better served in an RCCF using cognitive-behavioral treatment interventions and trained staff than they were in less structured community-based supervision conditions (Lowenkamp et al., 2010).

WORK RELEASE PROGRAMS

work release
A program in which offenders who reside in a facility (a community facility, jail, or prison) are released into the community only to work or attend education classes or both.

Work release may be considered both a type of institutional corrections and a community corrections program, given that offenders reside in a facility (a community facility, jail, or prison) but are released into the community for a short duration every day to work, attend education classes, or both. Work release controls institutional crowding and simultaneously provides an offender with an opportunity to find and retain employment, which is the most important factor in reintegration success and in reducing recidivism. The first documented use of work release was in Vermont in the early 1900s, with work release legislation first introduced in the state of Washington in 1913. The federal system and all states have authorized work release programs since the mid-1970s, primarily for minimum-security inmates who are within six to nine months of being released from a jail or a prison (Mawhorr, 1997).

Inmate selection for work release programs are at the discretion of jail or prison administrators in 37 states and of judges in 11 states. Many states do not clearly define offender eligibility. Of the states that specify, work release eligibility varies greatly, from misdemeanants and those serving county jail time all the way to prisoners who qualify for minimum custody and who have good behavior and have served a certain percentage of time on their sentence (Daly, Brooks, & Leon, 2009). Statutes also typically limit violent and sex offenders from participating in work release. We discuss both jail-based and community-based work release next as a form of pre-release program in an offender's preparation for release into the community.

Jail-/Prison-Based Work Release

The traditional use of work release is much more restrictive than a halfway house environment because offenders in the former case are not allowed to leave a facility for any other reason than work and school. This type of release is for a specified purpose and for a specific duration.

The definition of work release varies greatly, however. A strict definition of work release can include defendants or convicted offenders who spend a portion of their time in jail and a portion of their time *working* in the community. If a broader definition is used, work release can include traditional work release, weekender programs, and some pretrial programs.

Statistics indicate that for jails nationwide, 7,369 offenders were on traditional work release. If the broader definition is used, an additional 10,473 offenders on a weekender program and 11,148 on some sort of other pretrial supervision might be added (Sabol & Minton, 2008). These numbers can also be substantiated by other state Department of Corrections websites. Some states, like Ohio and Washington, are avid users of work release for between 20–23% of prisoners (Daly, Brooks, & Leon, 2009).

A weekend jail program entails reporting to jail only on weekends (e.g., reporting in by 7:00 P.M. Friday and staying until Sunday at 7:00 P.M.) but living and working regularly during the week. Work release participants are employed in public works and community service projects in eight states, but most states allow clients on work release to hold regular jobs in private businesses. Earnings of work release inmates are collected by a jail or prison agency. Box 8.2 discusses the use of iris recognition to better ensure that the correct offenders exit jail each day for work release.

The two basic types of traditional work release, which are unsupervised and supervised, are:

- An offender on unsupervised work release would, for example, be incarcerated in jail from 6:00 P.M. until 6:30 A.M., whereby every morning the offender is released out the door to catch a bus to go to work. After leaving work at 5:00 P.M., the offender has 60 minutes to return to jail each evening. Offenders in this program must submit paycheck stubs and/or documentation of hours worked to account for their time.

BOX 8.2   TECHNOLOGY IN COMMUNITY CORRECTIONS

"The Eyes Have It": Iris Recognition for Work Releasees

Given the daily releases and reentries of work release inmates from jail, it is possible that staff could mistakenly authorize the reentry of a different person or, worse yet, allow the release of a wrong person. As a result some jails, such as the Pinal County jail have turned to iris recognition technology to reduce identification errors, especially when people have a similar look or share the same name. Unlike fingerprints, which can fade or change over one's life as a result of injuries or scarring, the iris tissue remains the same. Today's technology allows five times the number of comparison points using iris scanning instead of fingerprints, making iris recognition technology more accurate. Furthermore, on a single individual the left iris is different from the right, making the combination of the two irises unique. The iris image is initially captured on a high-resolution digital camera and stored in a database. The area where work releasees enter and leave a jail is equipped with an iris scanner that checks via infrared light whether a particular inmate can leave, recording both exit and entry times. There may soon be a national iris database, so identity information could be checked across states or against other facilities within a state.

Source: Kamp, Chase. 2011. PCSO unveils new iris-scanning ID technology. *Today Publications,* May 23, 2011. http://nfcnews.com/2011/05/24/arizona-sheriffs-office-acquires-new-iris-recognition-devices

- An offender on supervised work release would also spend the same number of hours in jail but would leave with a group in a county-owned van to go to a temporary or permanent work site for the day. The group would be accompanied by at least one deputy officer and would return together in the evening.

For both unsupervised and supervised work release, offenders who leave a work site or do not return on time will have a warrant issued for their arrest.

Work release can also be a useful sentence for first-time offenders, particularly if the offender already has a job or is already going to school at the time the crime is committed. In these specific cases, a judge orders that offenders must reside in jail but be allowed to continue working to pay restitution or to attend school (for example, high school or college classes). This option is sometimes used when restitution centers or halfway houses are not available in an area. Work release can also be an option for physically disabled or mentally disabled offenders if program staff help them seek gainful employment, a goal significantly more difficult than for the average offender (Mawhorr, 1997).

The available evidence for work release programs is scant. Of the five known studies evaluating work release from a prison setting since 1974, four found that participating in work release reduced recidivism compared with prisoners who were eligible but did not participate (Drake, 2007; Jeffrey & Woolpert, 1974; LeClair & Guarino-Ghezzi, 1991; Turner & Petersilia, 1996b). The fifth study, which used random assignment of treatment and control groups, found no difference in recidivism (Waldo & Chiricos, 1977). Washington state continues to use work release facilities regularly for about one fifth of all offenders exiting prison. A follow-up study reported that, compared to prison that costs $22,838 per person for one year, work release recovers 16% of that cost through charging offenders room and board, and the rate of recidivism for new crimes is 2.8% lower (Drake, 2007).

Community-Based Work Release: Restitution Centers

restitution center
A type of residential community facility specifically targeted for property or first-time offenders who owe victim restitution or community service.

Restitution centers are a type of residential community correctional facilites specifically targeted for work-capable offenders who owe victim restitution or community service, are eligible for minimum custody, and have six months or less until their earliest release date (Drake, 2007). In a work release facility, the emphasis is on gainful employment and payment of rent, child support, restitution, and other court-ordered fees. The center collects from offenders all money earned and dispenses a portion for agency subsistence (rent and food), transportation, victim restitution payments, and child-support payments, giving the offender a small amount of pocket money. The remainder is saved in an individual account until release.

Restitution centers provide some treatment but the focus for offenders is on stable employment and paying back the victim. Some programs will release an offender when restitution is paid in full. As a result, some jurisdictions such as Florida, Texas, and Washington consider work release *a type of RCCF* or pre-release center (Levin, 2008). Many work release facilities are coed, and a small number are exclusively for women (Festervan, 2003).

TEXAS RESTITUTION AND TRANSITIONAL TREATMENT CENTERS   Restitution centers are operated by the county for probationers, whereas Transitional Treatment Centers serve parolees and probationers who are released from a residential substance abuse facility. During their stay in either a restitution center or in a transitional treatment center,

Clearing roadside weeds is one of many forms of community service.

© AP Photo/Matt York

residents remain employed and develop restitution plans; the centers offer GED, life skills, cognitive restructuring curriculums, and individual and family counseling as needed. Residents may also be required to work at community service projects on weekends and during evening hours. They normally remain at a center until their restitution is completed. About eight out of 10 clients remain employed by the time they complete the program (Levin, 2008). The average cost of a restitution placement costs taxpayers $60 per day, with an additional $10 to $25 a day paid by each offender. Across the state, restitution center clients pay over $4.5 million toward court fees, fines, and victim restitution. In addition, they contribute community service hours that equal approximately $600,000 in labor costs if they were paid for that labor (Levin, 2008). One internal evaluation of various centers around the state reported that 18.4% of clients were revoked to prison over a two-year period (Texas Department of Criminal Justice, 1999), compared with felony probationers who averaged a 30% prison revocation rate (Texas Legislative Budget Board, 2005).

FLORIDA WORK RELEASE CENTERS   In Florida, state prisoners who are minimum-custody inmates are eligible for work release when they have ten months remaining on their sentence. Inmates usually find a minimum-wage job within one month despite not having any help from anyone within the work release agency. The client is not allowed out of the facility unless he or she is going to look for work or going to an existing job. Once employed, about 75% of a client's paycheck is deducted for various expenses—45% for facility room/board, 10% for restitution, 10% for child support (if applicable), and 10% for savings. The remainder is provided as an allowance every two weeks (Berk, 2008). Staff monitor employment closely, visiting on site weekly. Berk found that work release inmates had higher employment rates and earned about $400 more per quarter for the first year than a comparison group that did not participate in a work release program. He (2008) concludes:

> For prison programs, the bottom line is the recidivism effect. I find that work release participation does lower recidivism but that individuals who commit

income-generating crimes [such as robbery, burglary, and drug dealing] are responsible for this change. Ex-offenders who commit non-income motivated crimes have improved employment outcomes after work release participation, but their probability of returning to prison does not change. (p. 24)

Work Ethic Camps

work ethic camp
A 120-day alternative to prison that teaches job skills and decision making using a cognitive–behavioral approach, followed by intensive supervision probation.

A **work ethic camp** is a 120-day prison-alternative residential program based on a cognitive–behavioral treatment approach. One program in Nebraska allows inmates to be eligible once they have completed a 90-day intake and assessment period (Siedschlaw & Wiersma, 2005). Once participants have completed the 120-day program, they are released on intensive supervision probation. The work ethic camp is considered a minimum-custody facility, and though it costs nearly $44 per day per person, the duration of the stay is about half that of the cost to incarcerate, which translates into a cost savings. The higher program cost is due to the assistance the program offers in developing job-readiness skills, decision-making skills, and life skills such as money management. A work ethic camp is similar to a halfway house in that it combines work and treatment.

COMBINED WORK RELEASE AND THERAPEUTIC COMMUNITY   Another program that combines work release with treatment through the therapeutic community concept (discussed in chapter 6) is the CREST program. Clients entering the program from prison must first progress through a significant amount of drug and alcohol education, counseling, and confrontation before they are eligible for the work release phase in the community. Evaluation data indicated that CREST participants have significantly lower relapse and lower recidivism rates than a comparison group (Nielsen, Scarpitti, & Inciardi, 1996). More recently, a study of nearly 20,000 Irish prisoners who participated in combined work and treatment programs (life skills, substance abuse treatment, and other therapeutic services) were significantly less likely to return to prison as a result of program participation (Baumer, Donnell, & Hughes, 2009).

SHOCK INCARCERATION

shock incarceration
A brief period of incarceration followed by a term of supervised probation. Also called shock probation, shock parole, intermittent imprisonment, or split sentence.

Shock incarceration refers to a brief period of imprisonment that precedes a term of supervised probation in the hope that the harsh reality of prison will deter future criminal activity. A variety of shock incarceration formats are used that go by a number of names—shock probation, intermittent incarceration, split sentence, and boot camp. The programs vary somewhat in design and organization, but all feature a short jail term followed by supervised release. The target population is young offenders with no previous incarceration in adult prisons. An estimated 10% of all adults on probation received a split sentence consisting of some combination of incarceration and probation (Glaze, Bonczar & Zhang, 2010).

In shock probation, an offender is sentenced to imprisonment for a short time (the shock) and then released on probation. It is hoped that incarceration will be so distasteful that the offender will fear returning and will thereafter avoid criminal behavior. Short incarceration periods are praised for making an unforgettable initial experience without enabling full immersion in an institutional subculture. Another type of shock incarceration is correctional boot camp programs.

Courtesy Leanne Fiftal Alarid

Boot camp attempts to break down offenders and then to retrain them to respect authority, increase self-control, and act responsibly.

Correctional Boot Camps

The idea of **boot camp** programs for offenders first began in 1983 in Georgia, whereby correctional programs borrowed the military concept of breaking existing habits and thought patterns and rebuilding offenders to be more disciplined through intensive physical training, hard labor, drill and ceremony, and rigid structure. This concept multiplied as the most common form of shock incarceration throughout the 1990s. Boot camp programs exist inside state prisons or as stand-alone community facilities:

boot camp
A form of shock incarceration that involves a military-style regimen designed to instill discipline in young offenders.

- *Inside Prison Walls*. Participants are chosen from a prison population by correctional administrators. The boot camp is within prison walls, but boot camp participants remain separate from the general population for the program duration. Offenders are paroled upon graduation from boot camp. Time served is significantly less than with a regular prison sentence.
- *Stand-Alone Community Facilities*. Offenders at time of sentencing are chosen by judges to participate in a facility administered by a county. Following boot camp, offenders graduate to intensive supervision probation or regular probation.

Regardless of whether the boot camp program is inside prison walls or in a stand-alone facility, it operates the same. Correctional boot camp participants live in "barracks," wear military-style fatigues, use military titles, and address their drill instructors by "sir" or "ma'am." Each "platoon" of 45–60 individuals is responsible for the actions of every individual, and many boot camps use group rewards and punishments to encourage participants to work together. The drill instructors attempt to break down old habits and attitudes of the recruits and build them back up into respectful young men and women. Eligible candidates, who volunteer to participate, are young first-time felony offenders who are able to meet minimum physical requirements. Programs typically last 90 to 180 days before graduation. Box 8.3 tells the story of a boot camp participant named Mr. John from his teacher's perspective.

The successful correctional boot camps also provide therapeutic and educational activities, such as drug and alcohol education, individual or group counseling, vocational training, anger management, and academic education, which together comprise almost half a day. Of the juvenile boot camp programs studied, counseling was the most effective component. Programs that provided counseling had lower recidivism rates than boot camp programs without this component (Wilson, MacKenzie, & Mitchell, 2005). Ronald Moscicki (1996), superintendent

BOX 8.3　COMMUNITY CORRECTIONS UP CLOSE

Would Getting "Out of the Life" Have Saved Mr. John?

Despite the troubled and violent lives students at the Harris County Boot Camp have led, the story of Derrick John still seems to catch them off guard. I drag it out and use it to get their attention just once during the few weeks that I will be their teacher. I wait for the precise moment when I feel it will be most effective—sometimes at the beginning of our time together, sometimes at the end. Most of the time, however, I tell the story when I am feeling overwhelmed by the task in front of me.

He was a nice guy with a great smile, I always start. An attractive, lean young man, 6-foot-3 or taller, I often told him he should go to Hollywood when he got out of Boot Camp. I actually looked forward to seeing him in class. This is not always true of the students I teach. While it's easy to like the students, almost all are tough and drain on any teacher caring enough to look into their eyes. Even the smart, easy learners have needs for attention that are so deep they draw energy from you. They have holes in their young lives that have made them hard and violent or else depressed and despairing.

Simple autobiographies the students write their first class take days for me to read because of the harsh existence most have had. And that's just the parts of their lives they are willing to write down. Even joking, these students have affectations that show they are covering up, trying for a resilience to bounce back from family cycles that have led them to crime.

For a while, Mr. John was one of those same draining students who spent the first half of his tenure at Boot Camp with a chip on his shoulder. "Why do we have to do this? I don't understand that," he'd say, without really ever listening or trying to understand in the first place. When his mood was even darker, he'd just lay low and try not to call attention to himself. Those quiet students who try hard to go unnoticed are often the most troubled, I have found. On those quiet days, I worried the most about Mr. John, feeling like he was still fuming, boiling deep inside his youthful outward appearance.

Then, for whatever reason, a light went on inside Mr. John when he was about halfway through the program. I see this reaction to Boot Camp often. The program teaches discipline and respect, and the students seem to catch on at some point. Either that happens, or they realize they are here for the long haul and should take advantage of the county's services. Whichever is the case, an education immediately reduces their chances of returning to the criminal justice system.

Mr. John started caring, and then he started learning. He finished assignments quickly and made scores higher than I even expected of him. But halfway is often too late for some probationers, especially those who quit school as early as Mr. John. Time and his Boot Camp days were running out. Every day his schoolwork improved. He became an ideal student, working hard and offering me a respect he had never shown before. I began to joke about having him stay in the program long enough to get his G.E.D. We call it "recycling," and it means more time at Boot Camp for probationers. It's the thing they dread the most. "If I could just keep you another three months, Mr. John," I'd say, "I could help you finish this G.E.D." "I think I'll just have to talk someone into getting you recycled." It would make him crazy when I would say this. No one wanted to be recycled. Everyone wanted to go home, even those whose home life had led them to Boot Camp.

Dodging Recycling

No one ever jokes about recycling, either. It's much too serious a subject to the probationers. I was only half joking, though. I would have loved to have kept Mr. John in Boot Camp and still think about the difference it would have made had he stayed there for another three months.

His beaming smile would fade for a moment at my attempt at humor. "You wouldn't do that to me," he'd start. "Would you?" Something in my returned look would tell him I wasn't serious, and his smile would reappear before I even needed to reassure him. Of course, I could never have him recycled at that point. He was now the picture of a perfect student. I knew, however, he had started working too late to finish his G.E.D. in Boot Camp. I emphasized the importance of continuing his education now that he was on the right track. He could still get his G.E.D. in a few more months with the help of the continuing education program at the Harris County Adult Probation Department. He just had to take more of the responsibility on himself.

Finally, one Wednesday, as is always the case with graduations at Boot Camp, he left the program along with the other 45 members of his barracks. He marched for the crowd of parents and visitors and listened to the graduation speech of hope for the future—now with cleaned slates and new, healthier habits and minds. He was so nervous, like all the probationers are on this day, that he shook my hand quickly with little notice as to whose hand it was. He never let his eyes meet mine, although I tried to

(Continues)

| BOX 8.3 | COMMUNITY CORRECTIONS UP CLOSE (*Continued*) |

Would Getting "Out of the Life" Have Saved Mr. John?

impress him with one last remark. "Keep at it, Mr. John. You've come too far to stop," I said.

Nine days later, his last essay still in my briefcase, Mr. John was shot and killed by a police officer after a robbery. He had fallen back in with a peer group that had waited for him back home and outside the secure barbed wire fence of the Boot Camp. At 17 years old, Mr. John never even had a life. With little or no parenting and an unsuccessful school experience, he never had a chance. When he entered Boot Camp, he may have looked like a hardened street thug, but when he left, he looked like the boy he still was.

Story's Impact

I don't know what part of Mr. John's story reaches my other students first. Maybe they see their own vulnerability to death. Maybe they were shocked by his youth. Maybe they are just frustrated that I use him as an example of my desire to keep them out of trouble and into education.

I can't keep them alive just by keeping them locked up, which is what I wish I had done with Mr. John. I know that wouldn't be a life. I know also that if they return to their former habits and former friends, things are going to happen to them anyway. Sooner or later. Prison or death.

I run across Mr. John's math workbook when I'm searching other files. Occasionally, I see an essay he wrote tucked in with other students' school papers. Maybe I run into the newspaper article about his death. I keep all these remembrances intentionally. It always surprises me for that minute; stuns me with reality.

I see his smile and picture his long legs stretching from his desk at the back of the classroom. And his eyes; I can still see the boy that would never live long enough to be a man. I want to be reminded of Mr. John. That's why I keep his schoolwork. I also want my other students to be reminded. I want them to realize that this same probationer could be any one of them. I tell them that I can't have it happen again. The story of Mr. John has broken my heart, and it will never harden to such blows. With this, I'm telling them that I care. I want them to try. I want them out of trouble and into a happy life that does not include violence and death.

Question: What can be done, if anything, to change the life path of individuals who are going in the wrong direction?

Source: Hensley, Denise Bray. 1995. One boy's life. *Houston Chronicle* (September 17). Reprinted with author permission.

---

of a boot camp program in New York, believes that treatment is actually the hardest part:

> Boot camps often seem to begin with the assumption, "If it ain't rough, it ain't right." Most people think that "rough" is sweaty drills, "in your face," and bulging muscles. They never associate "rough" with inmates sitting in a circle in white shirts and ties, with counselors and drill instructors leading a treatment group or academic classes, teaching inmates how to read and write. . . . In truth, the military part is the easiest because it is constant repetition. . . . (pp. 287–288)

Table 8.1 shows a daily schedule that begins at 5:30 a.m. and is full of hard labor, drills, and confidence-building rope courses along with educational classes and an early bedtime.

For many offenders, such as Hank, age 23, boot camp was a wake-up call. Hank was sentenced to prison for 18 months and was selected for boot camp with the promise of getting out in four months. He remarks:

> You don't see anything like this in regular jail. My family tells me how much I've changed. I lost 25 pounds, learned to control my impulses, and learned to not drink. The program and classes are all supportive. I never expected to learn about wellness and parenting. I have a 2-year-old son and another one

TABLE 8.1 Daily Schedule for Offenders in New York Shock Incarceration Facilities

TIME	SCHEDULE
A.M.	
5:30	Wake up and standing count
5:45–6:30	Calisthenics and drill
6:30–7:00	Run
7:00–8:00	Mandatory breakfast and cleanup
8:15	Standing count and company formation
8:30–11:55	Work and school schedules
P.M.	
12:00–12:30	Mandatory lunch and standing count
12:30–3:30	Afternoon work and school schedule
3:30–4:00	Shower
4:00–4:45	Network community meeting
4:45–5:45	Mandatory dinner, prepare for evening
6:00–9:00	School, group counseling, drug counseling, pre-release counseling, decision-making classes
8:00	Count while in programs
9:15–9:30	Squad bay, prepare for bed
9:30	Standing count, lights out

Source: National Institute of Justice. 1994. *Program focus shock incarceration in New York.* Washington, DC: U.S. Department of Justice, National Institute of Justice (August).

just 3 months old. I want to go home and do the right thing. I wanted to quit many times; for a while, every day I thought, "This is the day I quit and get out of here." The staff made me realize that I need to stick it out "one day at a time." I learned how to talk to other people, staff, and other inmates. . . . I was always a follower who got into trouble easily. I learned how to say "no" to my impulses. The first week I hated the DIs [drill instructors] . . . [but] they taught me respect. When I think of it, that was missing in my life. Today, when I leave here, I can hold my head high and be proud of my completion of the program. I also know I need a support system to keep myself from getting into negative situations. (as quoted in Ransom & Mastorilli, 1993, pp. 317–318)

Wayne, 18 years old and convicted of assault and battery, was a perfect candidate for boot camp. Not only does Wayne have a problem controlling his temper, but he also has a drinking problem. He talks about the positive changes as a result of boot camp:

This was a heck of an experience. I've been in several programs and halfway houses, and this is the best program I've ever seen. . . . The 12-step classes are outstanding. They teach you how to stay sober. In addition, they teach you how to be responsible for yourself. This is, mentally, a tough program. When I first got here, I thought this place was crazy, a bunch of cops yelling. I did not know what to expect. I thought about quitting often. I've been impulsive and

| BOX 8.4 | WOULD OFFENDERS CHOOSE THE MILITARY OVER PRISON? |

Military recruits are finally coming home from Iraq and Afghanistan. The last 10 years of military activity in the Middle East has increased the likelihood by 20% that soldiers may develop symptoms of post-traumatic stress disorder, and a small chance that they may never return with over 6,000 American casualties. Despite these numbers, a survey of inmates in a minimum security prison found that six out of 10 people favored spending 8 years in the military over 8 years in prison if given a choice on day for day with no time off for good behavior. The military option was less popular as an alternative to parole, which received the nod by 43%. The main reason for favoring the military option was that it would provide training and a better option over the lack of opportunities in prison. Prisoners with less formal education and a longer criminal history tended to support the military option. A solid 30% of prisoners would not consider the military over prison, even if only 4 years out of 8 would have to be served, primarily due to (at the time of the survey), our country actively deploying troops (Frana and Schroeder, 2008).

Source: Frana, John F. & Schroeder, Ryan D. 2008. Alternatives to incarceration. *Justice Policy Journal* 5(2): 5–25.

did what I wanted to do. One day, I was tired and when a DI was yelling at me, I told him I would not give him the pleasure of seeing me quit. I've learned to respect the DI. I can talk to the DI. They're not cops, the enemy. They made me responsible for myself. They taught me to care. . . . When I leave here Friday, I've already got plans to go to A.A. [Alcoholics Anonymous] meetings. . . . There is no negativity here like regular jail. I've tried to think about something negative . . . nope, nothing. Now don't get me wrong. I hate this place. . . . However, I love what the program has done for me. I never had plans or goals in my life. I've learned to suck it up and drive on. Open my ears and shut my mouth, otherwise, you are in the front leaning push-up position a lot. I have not found myself in that position in about a month; that's progress. (Ransom & Mastorilli, 1993, pp. 313–314)

It seems, then, that boot camp, despite its denial of television and cigarettes and its requirement of rigorous physical engagement, has provided positive experiences to help offenders and so has increased its legitimacy above that of prison (Franke, Bierie, & MacKenzie, 2010). See Box 8.4 for what offenders thought about joining the U.S. military as an alternative to prison.

Criticisms of Boot Camps

Boot camps have their share of critics. A primary concern is that these stand-alone community-based facilities widen the net, choosing offenders who otherwise would have received a *lesser* sentence (probation) had boot camp not been available. In net widening, costs increase because offenders who should be on probation undergo a more expensive program. Another concern is that the confrontational style of military-style boot camps, characterized by coercion, stress, and leadership styles likely to reduce self-esteem, can have potentially negative outcomes by increasing the potential for violence and encouraging an abuse of power. Such factors can make boot camps targets for civil lawsuits. For example, one boot camp closed in Tampa after a 14-year-old boy died as a result of a videotaped beating by boot camp staff (Associated Press, 2006). Other camps in at least four other states have closed, citing possible abuses and high recidivism rates (Milligan, 2001).

FACT OR FICTION?

Most correctional boot camps have closed because they did not significantly lower recidivism enough to justify the increased cost.

Fact: Many boot camp programs limited eligibility to young offenders who otherwise would have received probation. Although attitudes changed in the short-term, behavior did not, and boot camps increased institutional populations and costs above that of prisons

Evaluations of Boot Camp Programs

There are over 30 known evaluations of boot camp programs. The vast majority of boot camp research has shown that although attitudes of graduates were more positively adjusted in the short-term, such attitude changes did not directly translate into long-term reduced recidivism. Only five or six out of thirty studies showed significant recidivism reduction of boot camp graduates compared to offender groups (Duwe & Kerschner, 2010). The most successful programs offered a treatment component of at least three hours per day mixed with discipline and were characterized by voluntary participation, selection from prison-bound offenders, and longer program duration. Finally, aftercare, or a period of transition after an intense boot camp experience, was important for learning retention (Kurlychek & Kempinen, 2006). The drills, labor, and discipline of the boot camp experience, by themselves, are not enough to reduce recidivism. Not surprisingly, programs that allowed prison administrators, rather than judges, to select participants were more likely to alleviate prison crowding, insofar as the former officials selected offenders who were already in prison.

Interest in boot camps has diminished such that by 2000, due to years of net widening and lack of counseling and educational components to significantly reduce recidivism, one third of them had closed, with 51 programs remaining in operation at a cost per day of $58 per offender (Parent, 2003). Today fewer than 40 programs remain open in the United States, and their future remains uncertain.

SUMMARY

- RCCF offenders posed a higher risk and had more treatment needs than traditional probationers but less risk than people incarcerated in prison.

- Halfway houses remain a valuable residential community program for reentry of offenders coming out of prison. Overall evaluations of halfway houses show that benefits outweigh the costs, particularly for high-risk offenders.

- In allowing their children to live with them, residential programs for female offenders, aid them in learning better parenting skills and in maintaining close relationships, which in turn prevents recidivism.

- Work release and restitution centers focus offenders on working to pay back victims and learning how to maintain employment. Work release, through offender subsistence payments, helps curb program costs to taxpayers by about 20%.

- Boot camps as a type of shock incarceration program vary in the degree of treatment programs offered. Voluntary participation, selection from a prison population, and intensive aftercare provisions are important elements of the boot camp experience. But because recidivism rates for most boot camps are no different from those for prisoners, the popularity of boot camps has declined in recent years.

DISCUSSION QUESTIONS

1. How are halfway houses similar to and different from work release?

2. What would working in a halfway house be like? What are some of the problems you might face?

3. Should programs like the John Craine House be expanded?

4. Discuss the positive and negative aspects associated with correctional boot camps.

WEBSITES, VIDEOS, AND PODCASTS

Websites

University of Cincinnati Research Studies: Halfway Houses
www.uc.edu/ccjr/research.html

John P. Craine House
http://www.crainehouse.org

Ohio Community Corrections Association
http://www.occaonline.org/links.asp

Factsheet: Juvenile Boot Camps
http://www.nmha.org/go/boot-camps

Videos/Podcasts

California Department of Corrections and Rehabilitation Videos
http://www.youtube.com/user/CACorrections#p/u/31/yI-A6Gq5Gmk

This five-minute video shows an example of a Women's Residential Multiservice Center in California.

Michigan Halfway House
http://www.youtube.com/watch?v=1o27_MvD1og

Brighton Hospital is a leader in drug and alcohol treatment and counseling services that began in the 1950s in Michigan. The clinic's rehabilitation treatment programs include an adult halfway house.

Cleveland Judge Nancy McDonnell speaks about a community-based correctional facility.
http://www.youtube.com/watch?v=OXR1mEzAIc8

This eight-minute video features a community-based corrections facility that opened in 2011 in Cuyahoga County, Ohio.

Cognitive-Behavioral Therapy for Addicts
http://www.youtube.com/watch?v=9zMVFSpJYM8

This video showcases Inside Out—a cognitive-based therapy (CBT) program for substance abuse treatment.

CASE STUDY EXERCISE

Site Visit to One Community-Based Residential Correctional Program

Visit one community-based correctional program, and use this visit to conduct your own case study. Your visit may be done individually or with a small group. You will likely need to clear the visit ahead of time with your instructor, who may suggest a facility with which he or she has some connection. If this is a group exercise, members can be assigned to each focus on a small section of the paper or presentation. There are four sections, and questions are presented so that each member can ask a few questions during the site visit. Write a paper or make a presentation to include one or more of the following areas:

Section 1: Program Description

- What are the goals of this program?
- What tools or techniques are used to meet these goals?
- What is the capacity (how many clients can be treated at one time)?
- How many contact hours/treatment hours are part of this program?

Section 2: Clients

- Who are the clients being served?
- What does the typical client look like (gender, age, education, and so on)?
- What are the client's perspectives of the treatment program?

Section 3: Staff

- What is the client-to-staff ratio?
- What are the staff backgrounds and qualifications?
- What are the perspectives of the staff about working there (or about program effectiveness)?

Section 4: Evaluation

- How many clients finish the program, and how many drop out or do not complete it?
- What are the reasons for not completing the program?
- What is the daily (or yearly) cost per client served?
- Have any clients been tracked after they leave the program? What were the results?

Nonresidential Graduated Sanctions

CHAPTER LEARNING OBJECTIVES

1. Describe the conditions under which offenders are court-mandated to house arrest.
2. Compare how electronic monitoring has progressed from radio frequency to global positioning systems.
3. Explain the importance of correctional technology as a tool, but not as a replacement, for community supervision.
4. Identify how day reporting centers are unique from other community supervision programs.

© AP Images/Dayton Daily News, Ty Greenlees

The Sobrietor is a breath-testing device used to aid in the supervision of convicted drunk drivers.

CHAPTER OUTLINE

KEY TERMS

house arrest

electronic monitoring

home-based electronic monitoring

remote location monitoring

real-time access

global positioning system

active GPS

passive GPS

exclusion zones

inclusion zones

day reporting centers

At age 22, Jeffrey Woods had already served time in two different jails for drug addiction. He wasn't a dangerous person; he was just on the wrong path. When he was sentenced to a day reporting center, Woods viewed it as an opportunity to make significant changes—and he did. He began by attending all-day classes on drug addiction, relapse prevention, and legitimate employment sustainment. He earned his GED, found a job, and has remained clean from all drugs. He is confident and grateful for the chance to avoid jail. His success was recognized when he was recently invited to speak at the day reporting center's graduation ceremony (Sloan, 2011).

Positive behavioral modification is important for encouraging continued success, as in Jeffrey Woods' case. What other ways could correctional programs recognize and reward positive behavior?

INTRODUCTION

This chapter examines community-based sanctions that offenders participate in while living at home. These programs can be sentences by themselves, or they can be combined with other sanctions such as probation, as a phase of aftercare, following a period of time spent in a residential facility, or following confinement in jail and prison. Types of nonresidential programs to be discussed include house arrest, electronic monitoring, and day reporting centers.

HOUSE ARREST

house arrest
A community-based sanction in which offenders serve their sentence at home. Offenders have curfews and may not leave their home except for employment and correctional treatment purposes. Also called home detention or home confinement.

House arrest is an intermediate sanction designed to confine pretrial detainees or convicted offenders to their homes during the hours when they are not at work, attending a treatment program, or visiting a supervising officer. Defendants who cannot afford bail and who do not qualify for release on personal recognizance may be considered for house arrest. For convicted offenders, house arrest is a condition of probation and is frequently coupled with a home-based voice verification device.

Purposes of Home Detention

House arrest is otherwise known as home detention or home confinement; it is neither a new concept nor a U.S. innovation. Galileo (1564–1642) was placed under house arrest by church authorities for his heretical assertion that the earth revolved around the sun. House arrest programs have proliferated since the 1990s in the United States as an alternative to incarceration for pretrial detainees and as a means of easing jail overcrowding while ensuring appearance in court. House arrest is also a more restrictive form of probation for convicted offenders insofar as it strictly limits time spent outside the home.

> Staples and Decker (2010, p. 7) explain how house arrest technology works:

> Offenders sign a three page 17-point contract. . . . Clients must develop a daily schedule of approved activities . . . [consisting of] weekly face-to-face meetings with their house arrest officer. . . [and] also meet with collateral contacts and make unannounced on-site visits to places of employment and residences. . . . A Mitsubishi® Electronic Monitoring system device . . . functions to verify compliance . . . by recording the offender's voice, taking his or her picture, and collecting breath samples. . . through a straw inserted into the home monitoring unit. The photograph is displayed on a computer screen in the house arrest office next to a reference photo previously entered into the system. . . . If a client does not respond to phone calls, they have 2 hours to call the house arrest officer or show up in person.

Through their interviews of people under house arrest, Staples and Decker (2010) observed rigid and repressive conditions that seemed to ignore differences among individuals and increased participants' anxiety over something going wrong. They suggest that discipline should "be productive and not simply repressive" (p. 17).

COMMUNITY CONTROLLEES IN FLORIDA   *Community controllees* are required to maintain employment and to participate in self-improvement programs, such as a general equivalency diploma (GED) program to obtain a high school diploma, drug and alcohol counseling, or other "life skills" programs. Many are required to perform community service as well. When they are not participating in work, self-help programs, or community service, they must be at home. Florida community control officer caseloads are limited by statute to 20 offenders, and the officers work weekends and holidays. They are required to make a minimum of 28 contacts per month with each offender for a period not to exceed 24 months. Officers' schedules vary from day to day, resulting in regular but random visits with offenders. If an offender is not where he or she should be at any particular time, a violation of community control is reported to the court. Some house arrest programs randomly call offenders, and a computer verifies an offender's unique voice electronically. If the voice is that of another person or a tape-recorded voice of the offender, the computer will register an unauthorized absence. Too many unauthorized absences can result in a technical violation of probation and time in jail.

House Arrest Criticisms and Opportunities

A few criticisms are directed at house arrest. First, some argue that staying at home for most people does not seem to be a punishment or a negative experience. This might be true if an offender were not scrutinized so closely, did not receive such frequent visits, and were not awakened in the middle of the night to take a photo. In most jurisdictions, the courts have indeed recognized that home confinement is *not* the same as jail or prison confinement and that therefore time spent in home confinement awaiting trial as a pretrial detainee cannot be counted as time served toward a conviction, in the way that jail time serves for other pretrial detainees (*People v. Ramos*, 1990). In some jurisdictions, however, home detention is considered a part of probation, and time spent is counted. As with probation, if house arrest is revoked, time served in home confinement does not count toward the sentence or toward time served.

Another criticism is that the intrusiveness of house arrest violates a pretrial detainee's constitutional right to privacy in the home, especially one occupied by other family members who are not under supervision. To get around this, house arrest for pretrial defendants is *voluntary*; offenders sign a contract that they understand the conditions and if they do not agree, they are resentenced to another sanctioning option. A *convicted* offender's privacy rights, however, are not considered by law to be violated by the use of house arrest and/or electronic monitoring.

A potential risk with house arrest is that offenders can still commit crimes from their residences. For example, pretrial detainees and probationers have been arrested for selling drugs out of their homes. Because customers went to the house of detainees who thus never left home, no house arrest violations were recorded. If it were not for suspicious neighbors calling the police, such probationers might have been able to continue selling drugs without getting caught for some time. Although this is a very real risk, the main purpose of house arrest is to reduce offender movement while being monitored; it does not function to deter crime or to reduce recidivism.

Another challenge of house arrest is that domestic violence incidents can erupt. Because offenders are home all the time and cannot leave their house to "cool off," some take out their frustrations on family members. Several community control officers report that it is not unusual for house arrestees to request that they be sent to prison instead of continuing under house arrest.

Considerable self-discipline is required to comply with house arrest. Although many offenders are impulsive by nature and may be unable to sustain required behavior for long periods, *for the right persons* with stable employment and supportive families, house arrest allows them to keep working and to support their families without incarceration. Given that house arrest is an enhancement of probation or parole and entails more conditions than routine supervision, offenders under house arrest are highly likely to be revoked for a technical violation. Today most house arrest programs are paired with some form of electronic monitoring, so let's examine this correctional technology.

ELECTRONIC MONITORING: RADIO FREQUENCY AND GLOBAL POSITIONING SYSTEMS

Imagine this scenario: George was paroled from prison on condition that for the first year he wear an electronic device that fits snugly around his ankle. The ankle device is waterproof and shockproof, and George must wear the device even while

---

FACT OR FICTION?

House arrest, electronic monitoring, and global positioning systems all have basically the same monitoring capabilities.

Fiction.

Fact: These technologies have very different monitoring capabilities and limitations—some more advanced than others. House arrest and radio frequency monitoring are generally less sophisticated than global positioning systems and devices that monitor alcohol use.

showering and sleeping. A transmitter inside George's ankle bracelet emits a continuous signal to his personal receiver, which is attached to the phone lines at his residence. This receiver only transmits to George's ankle device. If the signal is lost for any reason—say, if George moves 500 feet beyond his device—then the transmitter is unable to communicate with the receiver, and the receiver automatically calls in to a centralized computer. The computer checks to see whether the absence of a signal is authorized or unauthorized. The absence is authorized if George has received prior permission from his parole officer, for example, to go out looking for a job or is at work during his scheduled hours. If the absence is unauthorized, his parole officer is automatically notified. George has a curfew, and he still must visit his parole officer, who checks the device to make sure George has not tried to tamper with it or remove it in any way. George must get permission prior to going anywhere, so he has to plan everything in advance.

George's sanction consists of a **home-based electronic monitoring** system, which operates from radio frequencies through phone lines. **Electronic monitoring** (EM) is a correctional technology used in intensive supervision probation, specialized parole, day reporting centers, and house arrest—typically between one and six months. EM can also be applied to pretrial releasees—that is, on defendants who have not yet been convicted but require an elevated level of supervision while out on bond or under pretrial supervision (see Figure 9.1). In the federal system, pretrial releasees have been monitored for up to nine months (Camp, Camp, & May, 2003).

home-based electronic monitoring
An intermittent or continuous radio frequency signal transmitted through a land line telephone or wireless unit into a receiver that determines whether the offender is or is not at home.

electronic monitoring
A correctional technology used as a tool in intensive supervision probation, parole, day reporting, or home confinement, using a radio frequency or satellite technology to track offender whereabouts using a transmitter and receiver.

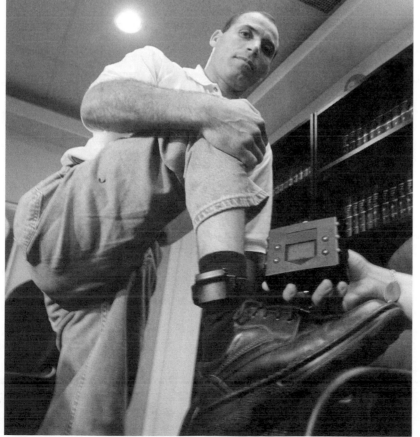

© AP Images/CP, Tom Hanson

Ankle monitoring devices can transmit either to home-based receivers using radio frequencies or via global positioning satellite system to a receiver carried around the waist.

FIGURE 9.1   How Electronic Monitoring is Used

Source: American Probation and Parole Association. Accessed: http://www.appa-net.org/publications&resources/pubs/electronic_monitoring.pdf.

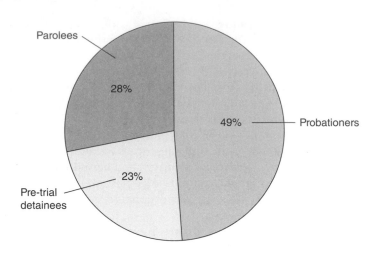

History of Radio Frequency Electronic Monitoring

Tracking objects using radio frequency signals has been possible since the 1920s when the U.S. Army monitored airplanes and large ships. Biologists used this technology to track animals, and the first electronic monitoring of humans dates back to the early 1960s when EM was used for checking changes in oxygen levels, body temperature and other vital signs (Klein-Saffran, 1995). Robert Schwitzgebel at the University of California developed and patented electronic monitoring technology in 1964 to record a parolee's location using a one-way transmitter. When patients were deinstitutionalized from mental hospitals, some were monitored using EM, but the technology was still quite limited to measuring physiological changes rather than actual location.

In the mid-1970s a two-way transmission system was developed, which led to an idea of the use of EM around the ankle. New Mexico judge Jack Love saw a picture of a wrist transmitter in a 1977 Spiderman comic book and persuaded a computer salesman to develop the device. The wrist device was first tried in 1983 on offenders convicted of driving under the influence (DUI) and of white-collar crimes at a time when cell phones were not the norm (Vollum & Hale, 2002). When a probation office called a house, offenders verified their whereabouts by inserting the wrist device into a receiver that sat next to the telephone. These early units were called home-based radio frequency electronic monitoring systems because they verified whether an offender was at home.

PROBLEMS OF EARLY HOMEBOUND EM   Early electronic monitoring programs required that offenders had a landline telephone—something critics asserted discriminated against indigent offenders who could not afford landline service. A second drawback was that passive EM was only able to track whether an offender was within a certain number of feet of the receiver connected to his or her telephone. Home-bound EM systems were not able to track where offenders went once they left their home. The earliest wrist systems were not customized to each offender, and more than one wrist system could be used on the same monitoring system. Thus there was no guarantee that a probation office was actually communicating with the correct person (Greek, 2002). Certain areas such as bathtubs could not receive transmissions, which would ultimately cause false alarms. (See Box 9.1 for the latest updates on home-based systems.)

BOX 9.1   TECHNOLOGY IN CORRECTIONS

Advances in Electronic Monitoring

Voice verification monitoring

Monitoring occurs throughout the day and/or night by means of a special pager or random calls made to particular locations at specific times to verify an offender's presence. When the pager beeps, the offender must immediately call the probation or parole office. Through voice and photo verification—that is, checking the voice on the phone against official voice and photo templates created at the probation office—the computer determines a positive match. The computer also records the phone number from which a call originated (Staples & Decker, 2010).

Group monitoring

Individual home-based systems still exist, but now there are ways that a single receiver can monitor up to 75 clients at one time. This makes it possible for community facilities such as halfway houses and group homes to detect the presence or absence of clients within a 300-foot range, which prevents temporary unauthorized absences and allows facilities to better detect a "walk-away" or escape (BI Inc., 2009).

Remote location monitoring systems

Handheld portable receiving devices can intercept an offender's transmitter signals to enable officers to randomly drive by a residence or workplace to verify the location of an offender without stopping to see him or her in person (Gowen, 2001).

Sources: BI Inc. 2009. BI products and services. Retrieved at: http://www.bi.com; Gowen, Darren. 2001. Remote location monitoring—A supervision strategy to enhance risk control. *Federal Probation 65*(2): 38–41.

Global Positioning Systems

The most sophisticated technology for monitoring offenders in the community is a **global positioning system** (GPS). A GPS uses 24 military satellites that orbit the earth and 5 ground control stations to pinpoint locations anywhere in the world using data coordinates. A one-piece transmitter and GPS receiver containing a microprocessor is worn by an offender. The GPS portable receiver replaces the receiver that was plugged into the landline phone on home-bound systems. The transmitter and receiver serve as a medium between the satellite and the central control unit that monitors offender locations (Armstrong & Freeman, 2009).

The way the receiver records data and how often the data are transmitted determines the type of GPS system. In a **passive GPS system**, the tracking point data is temporarily stored throughout the day and downloaded at night through a landline phone while the offender is sleeping. Although major violations are instantaneously reported, most location information can be delayed up to 12 hours. Agencies that use GPS tend to use passive GPS systems because they cost half as much to operate as the more advanced active GPS systems (Pattavina, 2009).

Active GPS systems transmit data through wireless networks used by cell phones. Active systems are also known as real-time units because data can be transmitted with a short lag time. The offender's transmitter emits a radio frequency signal from once per minute to once every 10 minutes. A phone continuously calls a reporting station to update the offender's location, which establishes a track point that can be visually seen on a computer or wireless PDA. Some companies provide monitoring centers whereas other companies provide officers with web-based capabilities to view on their own. The more frequently the computer reports a tracking point, the more time must be spent examining the data over each 24-hour period. GPS equipment can be leased for around $8 per day for a real-time unit, compared to $4 per day for passive GPS. When the cost of supervision is added to equipment charges, the total cost is between $11 and $20 per day (Ych, 2010).

remote location monitoring
When a supervising officer uses a hand-held remote receiver to wirelessly verify an offender's physical location.

global positioning system
A system that uses 24 military satellites orbiting the earth to pinpoint the offender's exact location intermittently or at all times.

passive GPS
A GPS system that temporarily stores location data that is downloaded through a landline phone once every 24 hours or at specific times when the offender is home.

active GPS
A real-time GPS system that transmits data through wireless networks continuously at a rate of once or twice per minute. A phone line continually calls a reporting station to update the offender's location, which is tracked by a computer.

exclusion zones
Exact locations the offender
is prohibited from being in
or near.

inclusion zones
Exact locations, such as
employment, school, or an
appointment, where the
offender is required to be at a
certain time.

HOW DO THE ZONES WORK?   The microprocessor inside the receiver also allows a probation officer to use software to program **exclusion zones** and/or **inclusion zones** (Gowen, 2001). Thus an offender on probation for an offense related to his compulsive gambling habit would not be allowed to enter any casino without the device sounding an unauthorized area alarm. Another exclusion zone could be the residence and workplace of an identified victim. In contrast, an inclusion zone allows an officer to program an offender's work schedule, special appointments, and other events so the computer can verify a location as it is reached. If necessary, an officer is alerted if an offender enters an exclusion zone, as in the case of an assaultive offender who has gone near his or her victim.

Each offender, according to his or her crime and work schedule, has personally defined restricted areas and persons that constitute when a violation is committed. In each GPS system, notification methods are different. In some systems, all alerts are transmitted from in-house monitoring centers to a supervising officer's pagers; it is the responsibility of the officer to check each alert to determine what happened. Reasons for alerts vary widely, and it is not always initially apparent why an alert has occurred. Serious alerts result if an offender enters an exclusion zone, enters an inclusion zone at a time other than what the schedule dictates, or attempts to tamper with or remove a unit. Other reasons for a registered alert could be battery failure or technical failure, such as when through no fault of an offender a signal is blocked and cannot be received. One study reported that *each offender* averages approximately three to four alerts every month (Armstrong & Freeman, 2009). If an officer is supervising 20 offenders, that averages to two alerts per day. Which system registers more false alarms—an active or passive GPS—is open to question. One study in Florida found passive GPS to register three times more false alarms than did active systems (Levin, 2008b), whereas active and passive systems in Arizona seemed to register similar numbers and type of alerts (Armstrong & Freeman, 2009). One concern about a high number of alerts, particularly those for equipment failure, is the reliability and shortcomings of equipment. With a high number of alerts, there may be a tendency for officers to become complacent over time, as if a boy were "crying wolf."

Authorities can potentially use EM and GPS to solve crimes by tracing an offender's whereabouts. In a boat theft case in Tampa, police were able to prove that a suspect was at the scene of a crime at the exact time the theft was committed. The suspect was on EM for felony grand theft (Kalfrin, 2008). As a bonus, some units even allow officers to text message or leave a voice message directly on the receiver worn by an offender. Examples of different GPS companies include:

- VeriTracks by Satellite Tracking of People, LLC, Houston, TX;
- SMART (Satellite Monitoring and Remote Tracking) Ware by Pro Tech Monitoring Inc., Odessa, FL;
- Exacutrac by BI, Inc., Boulder, CO;
- iSecuretrac Corporation, Omaha, NE; and
- G4S Justice Services, LLC, Atlanta, GA.

FOR WHAT TYPE OF OFFENDER IS GPS INTENDED?   GPS is authorized in nearly every state in the U.S., but most states mandate its use for sex offenders. Of these, 10 states require that high-risk sex offenders be monitored for *life* via GPS or EM (Armstrong & Freeman, 2009). Another five states allow GPS for a wider variety of offenses—both sexual and nonsexual—although only for the term under supervision. The type of technology used, whether EM or GPS, depends solely on a client's offense and risk level (see Table 9.1).

TABLE 9.1   Electronic Monitoring Techniques for Various Offender Risk Levels

Risk Level	Type of System	Contact Frequency	Verification
Low	Remote pager	Random/infrequent	Phone call/pager
Low/Medium	Home-based system	Programmed or random	Phone call/pager & voice verification
Medium/High	Hybrid (pager and home-based system)	Frequent/random	Phone call/voice verification
High	GPS/satellite	Continuous	GPS signals Emitted exclusion/inclusion zones Video camera at home

Source: Adapted from Darren Gowen. 2001. Remote location monitoring—A supervision strategy to enhance risk control. *Federal Probation 65(2)*: 39.

LIMITATIONS OF GPS   Drawbacks to GPS technology include loss of GPS signal, short battery lives, and cost. Despite advances in technology, in more remote areas where cell phone service is weak or unavailable, radio frequency EM is a more reliable option. Even in urban areas, receivers have trouble picking up signals from satellites in some locations (for example, in a basement of a high-rise office building or between buildings). In addition, in cell phone "dead spots" an offender's receiver is unable to make the repeated cell phone calls to a central station with updates (Turner et al., 2007).

GPS is not completely foolproof. For instance, a motivated offender with specialized tools could cut through an ankle device. Although equipment reliability and data access do not differ among vendors, the primary difference is cost (Blackwell, Payne, & Prevost, 2011). As the cost of using GPS decreases and as cell phone service improves in rural areas, the number of offenders supervised using satellites will increase in the future. Box 9.2 discusses the issue of surgically implanted microchips under the skin of offenders under correctional supervision.

With technological advances in computers and satellites, the potential for offender tracking is limitless. Box 9.3 examines how electronic monitoring can be combined with less invasive methods to measure alcohol levels of DUI offenders.

BOX 9.2   TECHNOLOGY IN CORRECTIONS

Are Surgically Implanted Microchips a Violation of Offender Privacy?

British ministers are considering surgically implanting microchips beneath the skin of offenders supervised in the community. The chips are the same ones that are used to track pets, cattle, luggage, and cars. "The tags, injected into the back of the arm with a hypodermic needle, consist of a toughened glass capsule holding a computer chip, a copper antenna and a capacitor that transmits data stored on the chip when prompted by an electromagnetic reader" (Brady, 2008, p. 1). The tags are reportedly beginning to be used with humans in limited conditions, such as tracking

gang members within jails, entry into secure locations, or voluntary usage by customers of exclusive nightclubs (Brady, 2008). The courts have not yet ruled on whether this practice is too invasive or violates privacy under community supervision.

Source: Brady, Brian. Prisoners to be chipped like dogs. *The Independent*, January 13, 2008. Retrieved from: http://www.independent.co.uk/news/uk/politics/prisoners-to-be-chipped-like-dogs-769977.html

BOX 9.3 TECHNOLOGY IN CORRECTIONS

Methods to Measure Blood-Alcohol Content

Only about 10% of all offenders who used alcohol at the time of their offense have been actually ordered to abstain from alcohol while on probation or parole. When the use of alcohol or drugs is revoked for clients, the courts accept testing results solely from urinalysis screenings. When a urine sample is collected from an offender, a staff member of the same sex is typically present to observe the procedure. The sample must be preserved in a cool environment, so logistically it is not realistic to conduct urine tests that often. For the client who is ordered not to drink alcohol, other less invasive methods have been devised to test blood-alcohol content (BAC) levels in the body on a more routine basis. One company has developed a system called SCRAM (Secure Continuous Remote Alcohol Monitoring) and another a device called the Sobrietor. SCRAM combines EM with the use of transdermal technology to measure ethanol levels through perspiration. Measurements can occur randomly or continuously, and, as with EM and GPS, ethanol readings can be communicated via a smart modem to a central monitoring station. The BI Sobrietor is a handheld remote device that detects alcohol in the breath through a sample as an individual verifies his or her voice (Reuell 2008). The unit calibrates to the voice of the person being tested and is compared to a baseline voiceprint already on file.

An ignition interlock system is a different method for testing DUI offenders, now mandatory in some states. Ignition interlocks are installed in vehicles through the ignition system and require a driver to submit to a breathalyzer before the car will start. Some require the driver to periodically blow into the interlock while driving. Although an ignition interlock will disable a car if alcohol is detected, other systems can measure alcohol levels when an offender is not driving. One concern with all of these systems is whether the correct offender is being tested. Combining the ignition interlock with image transmission and voice verification has improved the validity of the test. In any case, an offender's picture is taken or voice is recorded at the same time he or she submits to a test.

By modifying a glucose monitoring device, tissue spectroscopy is the latest new technological development in measuring BAC levels. This technique "measures a person's BAC [on the inner forearm] through a sensor pad that detects light reflected from capillaries in the middle layers of the skin. The amount of infrared light wavelengths reflected through the skin is affected by alcohol consumption" (Levin, 2008b, p. 6). Tissue spectroscopy is currently being developed for commercial use.

Sources: Levin, Marc A. 2008b. Five technological solutions for Texas' correctional and law enforcement challenges. *Texas Public Policy Foundation Policy Perspective* (June). Retrieved from: http://www.texaspolicy.com; Reuell, Peter. 2008. High-tech device knows when you're not sober. *The Metrowest Daily News*, February 10, 2008. Retrieved from: http://www.metrowestdailynews.com/multimedia/

HOW DO PEOPLE FEEL ABOUT EM/GPS? Electronic monitoring has had its share of critics, from those concerned that its widespread use has resulted in net widening to those with ethical concerns that private companies are profiting from correctional supervision technology (Lilly, 2006; Nellis, 2006). For the most part, as technology has become more precise in tracking an offender's whereabouts, the general public has become more confident in and supportive of its use for offenders.

Although supporting the use of electronic monitoring as a tool for increased field supervision and visits, probation officers have also observed that increased contact means more paperwork. One officer said:

> They're getting seen at least weekly. Sometimes, you know, if people are not compliant or doing what they're supposed to be doing, they're being seen maybe twice a week. . . . There's a lot of requirements by the court . . . [They get] assessments, and get treatment, and get evaluations, and attend meetings . . . [and] everything has to be verified. Like grocery shopping, we need to know where they are going. It has to be the closest store. We need to see their receipts the following time. . . . If they got a window [of free time], you're responsible for where they're supposed to be. (Martin, Hanrahan, & Travers, 2008, p. 9)

Officers also have said that because of regulations, there is a high probability of violations. The trend now in EM is to use graduated sanctions for technical violators and reserve jail time as a last resort.

Offenders sanctioned by EM preferred it as an alternative to jail in every case, although they reported experiences such as limitations on spontaneity, loss of control and of freedom, the suffering of shame, and family problems from constantly being at home. EM was viewed as both less controlling than jail and as a second chance sanction, allowing offenders to remain productive in the community (Martin, Hanrahan, & Bowers, 2009; Payne & Gainey, 2004). Offenders have raised legal and constitutional issues regarding electronic monitoring, but the courts have consistently rejected these or were not ready to review them (*U.S. v. Balon,* 2004). EM and GPS have so far passed constitutional muster and become an often-used alternative to imprisonment.

Empirical Evaluations of EM and GPS

Completion rates of convicted nonviolent federal offenders are quite high at 89%. Most pretrial detainees complete federal EM and GPS programs, but the rate is lower at 77%. The four reasons pretrial drug offenders and supervision violators were most likely to fail were (1) unauthorized leave of absence (but later return); (2) flight/absconding (whereabouts unknown); (3) arrest for a new crime; and (4) tampering with EM equipment (Gowen, 2000). Program completion rates decreased after 180 days, so six months seems a typical threshold for how long offenders should be under close scrutiny (Cotter & De Lint, 2009).

Two experiments that compared EM offenders with those under regular community supervision found recidivism rates to be relatively similar. Empirical evaluations support the notion that EM technology makes a difference in how offenders act *while under supervision*, compared to similar offenders on traditional probation or parole. Florida offenders ($n = 75,661$ total) placed under one of two types of electronic monitoring (home-based and GPS monitoring) were separated into groups by type of sentence (for example, EM as a probation violation sanction, EM as a post-prison sentence, or a direct sentence to EM) and measured while under supervision. Offenders on EM were more likely to complete the terms of supervision and were less likely to commit technical violations and new crimes than those in a comparison group (Padgett, Bales, & Blomberg, 2006). Padgett and her colleagues suggest that EM is effective in monitoring serious offenders. In addition, home-based EM was as effective as GPS in significantly reducing the likelihood of technical violation, of committing new crimes, and of absconding while under supervision. Using the assumptions of this study, a cost-benefit analysis determined that EM yielded between 6–12 times more benefits through crime reduction than the costs of having parolees and probationers on EM during correctional supervision (Yeh, 2010).

A California study of high-risk sex offenders found that GPS parolees had about the same rate of recidivism as other high-risk sex offenders under traditional parole supervision (Turner et al., 2007). Regarding long-term effects, the use of EM reduces recidivism rates for parolees up to three years after supervision has ended (Marklund & Holmberg, 2009).

GENDER DIFFERENCES   It seems that gender and family conditions play a significant role in the outcome of EM sentences. Men who lived with a significant other while on EM reported receiving positive family support and help with dependent children, but female offenders reported that significant others were a source of stress and conflict impacting their success on EM. The female offenders perceived little support from their partners in child care. The lack of freedom to leave home because of EM affected women's primary caretaker role of dependent children (Maidment, 2002). In terms of offenders spending much more time at home, some situations improve whereas other situations worsen.

Success with EM and GPS depends on identifying the type of individual, home, and work situation that creates an ideal environment for completion without causing risk to the public. EM and GPS offer tremendous potential for community supervision, although some caution that perceived expectations of GPS are perhaps greater than its performance capabilities at this time (Armstrong & Freeman, 2009). In a work in progress in which researchers interviewed officers, "agents consistently said that GPS monitoring cannot stop sex offending behavior . . . [and it is still unclear] whether GPS creates a false sense of security" (Turner et al., 2007, p. 19). We predict that GPS technology will become more reliable and less expensive in the future, making EM the method of choice for community-based supervision. There will be, however, a threshold at which we have to decide as a society how much invasion of privacy we are willing to accept for that accuracy.

DAY REPORTING CENTERS

day reporting centers
Nonresidential programs typically used for defendants on pretrial release, for convicted offenders on probation or parole, or as an increased sanction for probation or parole violators. Services are provided in one central location, and offenders must check in daily.

Day reporting centers (DRCs) are a three-phase outpatient program in which offenders report daily for treatment programs, itinerary, and random drug testing. The centers offer all resources and educational programs in one place. The staff to offender ratio is low, with about one staff member to every fourteen clients served (Craddock, 2009). DRCs are also open extended hours to accommodate offenders who work days and evenings. Some jurisdictions (for example, Nebraska and Indiana) use day reporting for defendants on pretrial release (Kim et al., 2007, 2008), and other states (such as North Carolina and New Jersey) use DRCs as a reentry mechanism for prisoners out on parole (Craddock, 2009) or as an increased sanction for probation or parole violators.

"Day centres" have been popular in England and Wales since the 1970s and began to appear in the United States in 1985. Juveniles were already exposed to day treatment centers established in the United States, so the concept was applied to adults. Connecticut and Massachusetts were among the first states to adopt day reporting centers with a goal of reducing jail or prison crowding and providing a closer level of supervision than traditional probation or parole. *Most DRC programs exist in states that do not have intensive probation supervision as a sentencing option.* Many DRCs accept high-risk offenders such as sex offenders, stalkers, mentally ill offenders, developmentally disabled offenders, probation/parole violators, and graduates of therapeutic communities. A large DRC center might process up to 2,000 offenders per day whereas smaller centers have a daily capacity of between 40–85 offenders.

A typical experience at a day reporting center means reporting *every day* and being there from 9:00 A.M. to 5:00 P.M. Take, for example, Sandra's case. Sandra violated her parole due to continued drug use while on parole for fraud. Eligible for a day reporting center (DRC) as a graduated sanction, she was offered this option over jail. For the next three weeks she must report daily to the DRC, where she provides a daily itinerary, attends relapse prevention twice a week, and is drug-tested every third day. When she is not at the center, Sandra must remain at home and answer computer-generated random telephone calls several times during the day and occasionally at night. She must make advance arrangements to leave home to go to a

Day reporting centers provide structured group sessions that supervised offenders attend on a weekly basis.

© Nicole S. Young/iStockphoto

store or on any errands. DRC case managers stop by unannounced at her home later in the week and find her not there. Although she arrives home 20 minutes later, she remains in Phase 1 for an extra week as a consequence of her actions. In the second phase, she can start looking for a part-time job, but Sandra continues to be involved in structured classes and community service and receives computer-generated calls.

After 60 days of good behavior in Phase 2, Sandra begins Phase 3, which requires relapse prevention classes and counseling once a week and reporting to the DRC only once a week. By the time offenders reach Level 3, they must either be employed full time, be going to school full time, or engaged in a combination of both. Assuming that no major violations have occurred, after two more months in Phase 3, Sandra is transferred from the DRC caseload back to her former parole officer for monthly meetings and continued relapse prevention until the end of her sentence (Kim et al., 2008). For probationers and parolees who do not take their supervision conditions seriously, other DRCs serve to provide enforcement or "muscle" without sending these people to jail or prison.

Treatment-Oriented Versus Supervision-Oriented DRCs

The common theory behind DRCs is that offenders will stay out of trouble if they are occupied, especially with activities that improve their chances for a more normal life—for example, by obtaining a GED or finding a job. DRCs all have a requirement of daily itinerary, attendance, and program phases (Kim et al., 2007). Because of the wide variety of clients whom DRCs around the country serve, they also differ in their program goals. Some DRCs are more treatment-oriented and others more supervision-oriented (Craddock, 2009).

Treatment-oriented DRCs provide a wide range of services, all on an outpatient basis. The most common services are job-seeking skills and job placement, drug abuse education and treatment, psychological counseling, life skills training, and GED education classes and literacy. Other services provided by a smaller number of DRCs include parenting, anger management, vocational training, and transportation assistance. Once employed, offenders are still required to attend treatment programs at night or on weekends. Craddock (2009) noted that DRCs that focus on criminogenic needs outlined by risk assessment instruments help increase program completion rates and reduce recidivism. She found that "employment programming is the only component that predicts completion" (p. 130). Her findings also suggest that housing assistance be incorporated for parolees coming out of prison.

Supervision-oriented DRCs ensure that clients are abiding by the rules, enforce accountability through itineraries, and keep clients busy so they do not have the time or opportunity to engage in criminal activity. Itineraries are important for two reasons. First, clients learn (some for the first time) how to plan their days in advance. Second, DRCs can monitor where clients are when random phone calls are placed via computer. DRCs are authorized to give out Antabuse, a prescription medication prescribed for alcoholics that prevents the use of alcohol. Urine screenings and alco-sensor tests ensure that clients have not been using drugs. Another characteristic of DRCs is that many clients are under 24-hour electronic monitoring. As clients remain longer in the program under supervision, DRCs may be able to give them more freedom by removing electronic monitoring devices. Many DRCs use a combination of supervision and treatment approaches.

DRCs are nonresidential versions of halfway houses in terms of providing similar services, except that DRC offenders live at home. Like most halfway houses, most DRCs are private facilities that contract out to state and local entities. Further, contact between program staff and offenders in DRCs is for longer time periods than under intensive supervision probation (ISP). ISP programs include more field visits (in which an officer goes to a home or job site to visit an offender), but DRCs are actually more structured through EM, phone contact, and in-facility time because offenders go to the center (Kim et al., 2007).

Sentences to DRCs range from 40 days to 12 months, with an average of six months' duration. DRCs are more costly than traditional probation/parole, and even more expensive than ISP. However, DRCs cost less than residential treatment or incarceration. Much of the treatment program costs are absorbed by the DRC itself or by another agency. In one out of every four DRCs, offenders pay for their own drug treatment.

Evaluations of DRCs

Keep in mind that DRCs serve high-risk clients who have a lot of responsibility in this program. Also remember that program success is greatly influenced by local policy and practitioner decisions. Rearrest rates, by comparison, are more influenced by actual offender behavior.

COMPLETION RATES   DRC programs seem notorious for lower completion rates compared to those of other community-based programs. Termination rates averaged 50% within four to six months and ranged from 14% to 86%, higher for service-oriented programs than for supervision-oriented DRCs. Failure rates were also higher for programs longer than six months in duration (Craddock, 2009). High failure rates resulted because of the level of supervision intensity and the type of offender admitted to the program. Whereas work release programs accepted lower-risk offenders, DRCs tended to accept probation and parole violators and other types of higher-risk clients (Parent, 1995). As stated earlier, DRCs that focus on criminogenic needs, specifically employment and transitional housing, help increase program completion rates (Craddock, 2009).

Perhaps evaluation of DRCs is more a matter of who the clients are and whom they are compared against than of their completion rates. DRC programs seem to fare well as a reentry program for prisoners, especially when compared with prisoners who are freed under no supervision and compared with parolees under traditional parole. Even after controlling for demographics and prior criminal history, prisoners released with no supervision had a greater volume of arrests and were arrested faster than DRC clients (Ostermann, 2009).

DOES TIME SPENT IN THE DRC MAKE A DIFFERENCE? The Illinois Criminal Justice Authority tracked a treatment group of pretrial detainees who had participated in a DRC for 70 or more days, comparing it with a group that had been eligible for the DRC but had participated for 10 days or less without dropping out of the program. Members of these two groups were tracked for three years in terms of their rearrest and reincarceration rates. The group spending more time in the DRC (the 70-day and over group) was not only rearrested and reincarcerated at significantly lower rates than the control group but remained free for an average of 122 days longer (Martin, Lurigio, & Olson, 2003).

However, researchers in Indiana and Utah found that offenders who were placed in a DRC for longer than 120 days were significantly less likely to complete the program than those who had spent 120 days or less in the DRC (Roy & Grimes, 2002). So it seems that though longer is better, the ideal period of time spent in a DRC is more than 70 days but no longer than 120 days.

PREDICTORS OF DRC FAILURE The Illinois Criminal Justice Authority was also interested in factors that predicted who would be rearrested and who would remain crime free. The researchers found that previous criminal history (more prior arrests), youth, and less time spent in a DRC program were the most significant predictors of rearrest following release from a DRC (Martin, Lurigio, & Olson, 2003). Similar results in terms of age and criminal history were found elsewhere (Craddock, 2009; Roy & Grimes, 2002). In addition, employment was the main component that predicted program completion and reduced the likelihood of rearrest and reincarceration (Craddock, 2009; Kim et al., 2007).

In sum, there is no one right way to operate a DRC or any of the programs discussed in this chapter. Each program has different goals and different kinds of clients. The key is to specifically define the goals of a program (for example, to reduce institutional crowding, to allow a graduated sanction for probationers, and the like) and then measure whether it achieves those goals and contributes to an improved quality of life for society at large, for offenders, and for victims. We discuss these improvements further in the next chapter.

SUMMARY

- House arrest by itself provides cost savings but does not deter criminal misconduct. The level of monitoring is minimal unless house arrest is combined with electronic monitoring.

- Technological advances in electronic monitoring include the use of computers and satellites to monitor offenders in the community. No matter what type of electronic monitoring system is currently used, all offenders must minimally wear an ankle monitoring device, which they cannot tamper or remove without sounding an alarm to a central control station.

- Day reporting centers typically accept convicted offenders or pretrial detainees who require a higher level of supervision than do clients under electronic monitoring or house arrest. Day reporting centers also provide all services in one place and are the most costly type of nonresidential intermediate sanction, although they still cost less than jail or prison.

- All forms of nonresidential programs are more effective when goals are clarified and when target

offender populations are more accurately defined to best meet offender needs without unduly compromising public safety.

DISCUSSION QUESTIONS

1. Which of the intermediate sanctions discussed in this chapter are probation or parole enhancements, and which sanctions are true alternatives to prison?

2. How does electronic monitoring support house arrest? What ethical and social criticisms are associated with EM?

3. How do electronic monitoring devices work? What are some of the technical problems associated with them?

4. Do day reporting centers accomplish their objectives?

 ## WEBSITES, VIDEOS, AND PODCASTS

Websites

Tracking Sex Offenders using Electronic Monitoring
http://www.theiacp.org/tabid/299/Default.aspx?id=1054&v=1

Electronic Monitoring of Offenders in Washington, D.C.
http://www.csosa.gov/supervision/accountability/monitoring.aspx

Electronic Monitoring of Offenders in Michigan
http://www.michigan.gov/corrections/0,1607,7-119-1435-5032--,00.html

Effectiveness of Electronic Monitoring Research Report
http://www.criminologycenter.fsu.edu/p/pdf/EM%20Evaluation%20Final%20Report%20for%20NIJ.pdf

Davidson County Day Reporting Center Evaluation
http://www.nicic.gov/library/period173

Evaluation of Maricopa County (Arizona) Day Reporting Center
http://www.nhtsa.dot.gov/people/injury/alcohol/repeatoffenders/eval_dayreport.html

Videos/Podcasts

Drug Testing Technology in Corrections
http://www.corrections.com/system/podcast/file/9/media_20040624.mp3

A podcast detailing drug testing technology and its effectiveness.

Day Reporting Centers
http://www.youtube.com/watch?v=IYde4_38Q3Y

This video is about the DRC in Georgia and how it is effective.

House Arrest and GPS/Electronic Monitoring System
http://www.youtube.com/watch?v=vznM3y8n9DA

An in-depth look at how house arrest works using GPS monitoring bracelets.

CASE STUDY EXERCISES

Intermediate Community Programs

Considering the circumstances provided in the following cases, you are the judge, and you must decide to which form of intensive supervision community program (any residential program from chapter 8 or nonresidential supervision from the options in chapter 9) to send an offender . . . Jail is not an option, and you must assume that more is needed beyond traditional probation or parole. After you have made your decision, defend your answer.

CASE A

John is a 29-year-old man who has been twice convicted of fraud by forging checks. His first conviction resulted in a sentence of five years on probation with an order to make restitution in the amount of $2,720. John made three payments of $230 each before absconding supervision. He turned up again after six months and was reinstated on probation by the court after he promised to faithfully fulfill the terms of his supervision and to complete his restitution obligation. During his supervised release, he was in violation of probation conditions regularly and never completed his restitution payments. The current case involves John passing a forged check at a local grocery store in the amount of $624. Due to his previous failure and noncompletion of probation, the court is concerned that he is not capable of following court-ordered probation conditions, yet it does not want to commit him to state prison or to a jail term because his offense is nonviolent. John has a wife and two small children and is their only source of support. He has a high school diploma, he is not mentally ill or disabled, and he is currently employed as a house painter.

CASE B

Ricardo is a 23-year-old identified gang member of the Mexican Mafia, a Latino gang with roots in California. He has a history of criminal offenses including shoplifting, one motor vehicle theft, and three DUIs. Ricardo is not assaultive, but the group in which he is a member has been known to participate in assault and other violent acts. His file does not indicate his rank in the gang, but it shows he has been a confirmed member for at least six years. His current offense is larceny involving theft from his former employer, a local carpet-laying company. The PSI report concludes that Ricardo needs more structure than can be gained from probation or intensive supervision, but it does not recommend a prison sentence due to his current nonviolent offense. The PSIR reports that Ricardo needs to learn discipline, good work habits, and respect for the rights of others, and is concerned about his attitude toward authority.

10

Economic and Restorative Justice Reparations

CHAPTER LEARNING OBJECTIVES

1. Examine how restorative principles and practices differ from traditional criminal justice practices.

2. Explain the forms that restorative justice takes, including victim-offender mediation, victim impact classes, family group conferencing, and circle sentencing.

3. Discuss the economic/monetary sanctions used in both restorative and traditional criminal justice systems to include restitution, community service, fines, fees, and forfeiture.

During a follow up mediation session in a Tulalip Tribal Elder court, a young first time defendant listens to the victim talk about the impact that criminal trespassing had on him.

CHAPTER OUTLINE

KEY TERMS

community justice
restorative justice
reintegrative shaming
stigmatization

restitution
community service
fine
victim compensation fund

forfeiture
day fines
fee

Tommy is 16 and lives on a tribal reservation. He enjoys taking other people's cars without permission and driving them fast and furious. Even at night it is not hard for people to identify Tommy because it is such a small community; everyone knows each other. While joyriding in another vehicle, Tommy crashed into an uninsured parked car and into a police car. This case went through a circle sentencing session, described as follows:

> In the circle, the victim talked about the emotional shock of seeing what had happened to his car and his costs to repair it. Then, an elder leader of the First Nations community where the circle sentencing session was being held (and an uncle of the offender) expressed his disappointment and anger with the boy. The elder observed that this incident, along with several prior offenses by the boy, had brought shame to his family. . . . After the elder finished, a feather (the "talking piece") was passed to the next person in the circle, a young man who spoke about the contributions the offender made to the community, the kindness he had shown toward elders, and his willingness to help others with home repairs. . . . The police officer, whose vehicle had also been damaged . . . proposed to the judge that in lieu of statutorily required jail time for the offense, the offender be allowed to meet with him on a regular basis for counseling and community service. After asking the victim and the prosecutor if either had any objections, the judge accepted this proposal. The judge also ordered restitution to the victim and asked the young adult who had spoken on the offender's behalf to serve as a mentor for the offender. After a prayer in which the entire group held hands, the circle disbanded and everyone retreated to the kitchen area of the community center for refreshments.

Why might circle sentencing work better in smaller communities than in urban areas?

INTRODUCTION

When an offender is punished for a crime, the public may feel short-term satisfaction and the victim may find some closure, but many might still be left wondering how the punishment will actually affect the offender's future attitude and behavior. In a traditional criminal justice system, the state acts on behalf of victims to punish an offender. It should be no surprise that even following offender sentencing, victims can still feel angry, unsupported, more socially isolated, and more distrustful of a system that was designed to punish on their behalf. Many come to realize that government-sanctioned retribution achieves a form of justice or revenge but does not necessarily heal. Traditional criminal justice strategies and the "get tough" movement may not be as effective as we once thought in dealing with the harm, social isolation, and destruction of community trust that result when crimes are committed. Separating predatory and violent offenders from the general public is necessary, but incarceration is not a magic bullet for most offenders, the majority of whom will be released one day. Incarcerating more people for longer periods of time does not necessarily make our communities safer.

The concept of **community justice** entails using community stakeholders to control and reduce crime and to rebuild community relationships through community policing, community courts, and restorative justice. Examples of community stakeholders can be found in Figure 10.1. Although some authors use the terms *community justice* and *restorative justice* interchangeably, community justice is actually a broader concept that describes a philosophy encompassing the whole criminal justice system (police, courts, and corrections), whereas restorative justice is concerned with alternative dispute resolution and contains a corrections component (Karp & Clear, 2002).

In chapter 1 we introduced the concept of **restorative justice** as a sentencing philosophy and practice that emphasized an offender taking responsibility to repair the harm done to a victim and surrounding community. Restorative

community justice
A philosophy of using the community to control and reduce crime through community policing, community courts, restorative justice, and broken-windows probation.

restorative justice
Various sentencing philosophies and practices that emphasize the offender taking responsibility to repair the harm done to the victim and to the surrounding community. Includes forms of victim offender mediation, reparation panels, circle sentencing, and monetary sanctions.

FIGURE 10.1 Community Stockholders

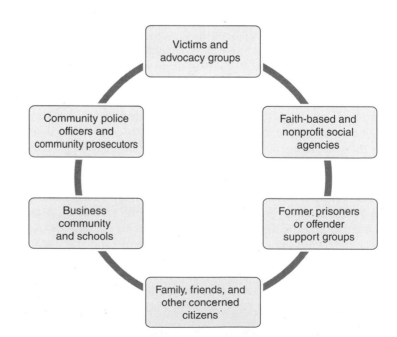

justice is more victim-centered than traditional methods of criminal justice, involving the victim and the community throughout the entire process of justice (Karp & Clear, 2002). It is practiced worldwide in both juvenile and adult systems, and the form it takes is largely dependent on cultural factors. The form that restorative justice has taken in the United States is termed *Western* in comparison with aboriginal, which refers to that practiced by indigenous peoples in countries such as Canada, New Zealand, and Australia (Cameron, 2006). Canada recognizes both forms insofar as Western restorative justice speaks to the dominant Canadian majority and aboriginal initiatives honor the traditional values and legal principles of the aboriginal people. In the U.S., Western restorative justice is community-based and combines mainstream American criminal justice with the indigenous justice practiced by Native Americans long before European settlers colonized North America (see Table 10.1). Let's begin by discussing restorative justice principles and comparing them with traditional criminal justice sentencing practices.

RESTORATIVE JUSTICE PRINCIPLES

Restorative justice, with roots in a variety of faith traditions, moves from a philosophy of vengeance and retribution to one of healing, reconciliation, and forgiveness. In contrast to mainstream criminal justice that focuses on punishment of the offender, restorative justice focuses on victim, offender, and community throughout the whole process of restoring justice.

Restorative justice can be applied to community-based sanctions or to prisoner reentry. The theory behind it is John Braithwaite's (1989) **reintegrative shaming**, which assumes that after a crime is committed social bonds are weakened and must

reintegrative shaming
After a crime is committed, the social bonds are weakened and must be repaired in order for the offender to move on and change future behavior.

TABLE 10.1   Roots of Restorative Justice in the U.S.

MAINSTREAM AMERICAN JUSTICE	INDIGENOUS NATIVE AMERICAN JUSTICE
Imported from Anglo-American models	Indigenous, shared views of the community and victims*
Written codified laws, rules, procedures*	Unwritten/oral customs, traditions, practices
Crime is a violation of the state	Crime is a violation of one person by another
Justice is administered*	Justice is part of the life process*
Offender is focal point; privilege against self-incrimination	Victim is focal point*; offender is obligated to verbalize accountability
Adversarial (fact-finding) process; victim and offender have no contact	Communal*; victim and offender are involved in the whole process and decide action jointly
Conflict settled in court; focus on establishing guilt and blame	Conflict settled through mediation and repairing relationships*
Public defender or lawyer representation*	Extended family member representation
Retributive and deterrence	Restorative or holistic; connects everyone involved*
Incarceration, so criminal can pay debt to society	Community service, restitution, reconciliation*
Criminals who break the law deserve to be punished	Criminal acts are a part of human error, which requires correctional intervention by the community*
Church and state are separated	Spiritual realm is cohesive with justice*
Stigma is difficult to remove	Forgiveness is possible and encouraged

Note: *Applies to restorative justice

be repaired in order for an offender to move on and change future behavior. The principle of reintegrative shaming allows the victim and the community to disapprove of a form of criminal behavior, while also relying on them to later forgive the offender. Reintegrative shaming is seen as more humane and more effective in the long run than the use of **stigmatization**. Stigmatization only serves to further outcast an offender and prevents him or her from becoming a fully functioning and productive societal member (Braithwaite, 1989).

stigmatization
The characterization of person as disgraceful.

Rather than focusing on deficits, restorative justice attempts to strengthen community life by drawing on the participation of the victim, the victim's social support network, the offender, the offender's social support network, and the community. Restorative justice asks: What or who was harmed? Who is responsible for the harm done? What needs to happen to repair the harm? All forms of restorative justice have the following commonalities:

1. One or more sessions are held in the community, with the goal first to provide the victim (and/or the victim's social support network) with an opportunity to communicate how the crime affected him or her physically, emotionally, financially, and socially.
2. The second goal is to develop a reparative plan, accepted by both the victim and the offender, in which the offender will repair the harm caused.
3. Victim and offender participation is voluntary, and conditions of each meeting are defined with respect to all parties.
4. The parties rely on community partners and volunteers, such as Mothers Against Drunk Driving, Parents of Murdered Children, battered women's shelters, mediators, community prosecutors, school-based officers, and various faith-based organizations.
5. Offenders must accept full responsibility for their criminal behavior. This means admitting guilt and being willing to comply with restoration agreements.
6. Although restorative justice efforts can take place within jails and prisons (for example, via victim impact panels), most forms are community-based as alternatives to traditional court processing or as a part of diversion.

Using these six common principles and through dialogue and open communication, it is determined who is responsible, how harm can be repaired, and how the victim can be provided closure and healing. The four restorative justice methods discussed consist of victim-offender mediation, reparation boards, family group conferencing, and sentencing circles. Restitution and community service are restorative in nature and are also discussed later in the chapter.

Victim-Offender Mediation

Victim-offender mediation (VOM) has existed since the early 1980s in the United States, and there are thousands of programs around the world (Bazemore & Umbreit, 2001; Umbreit, Coates, & Vos, 2001). This type of mediation is different from that traditionally found in civil courts because in the former there is no dispute about liability. The various phases of VOM are depicted in Figure 10.2. A mediator first meets with offender and victim separately to discern each party's willingness to cooperate. Assuming that both parties volunteer, the mediator is present in the same room with them (and if the offender is a juvenile, the parents are invited). After the facts of the offense are described, the focus is on repairing the harm done to the victim, which is quite emotional for both sides. Shaming

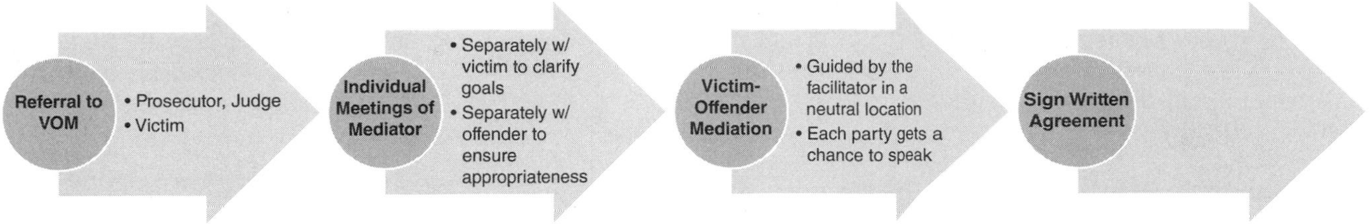

FIGURE 10.2 The Victim-Offender Mediation Process

plays a part in releasing the hurt, the anger, and the resentment that the victim feels (Kenney & Clairmont, 2009). The parties, in one or more sessions, reach a mutually desirable written agreement that is later filed with the courts.

The primary reasons victims choose to participate are to seek restitution or re-payment, to oversee punishment, and to share their grief with offenders. The ability of the mediator and the face-to-face format are key variables in victims' satisfaction. Victims who participate in VOMs report satisfaction with case outcomes and less fear of being revictimized. They were also more likely to receive restitution payments than with traditional court cases. Researchers concluded that VOM "is at least as viable an option for recidivism reduction as traditional approaches. And in a good number of instances, youth going through mediation programs are actually faring better" (Umbreit, Coates, & Vos, 2001, p. 32).

After six months of observing sessions involving victims, juvenile offenders, and their parents, researchers found a distinct difference between reactions of mothers and fathers. Although fathers were generally silent and did not appear to express any apprehension about their children's misbehavior, "mothers enter restorative conferences with their cultural scripts intact; they are presumed responsible for their children's behavior. . . . Many offenders' mothers have said to me after a con-ference, 'I felt like everyone thought I was a bad mother' or 'I want to prove I'm a good mother'" (Cook, 2006, p. 115). There was a marked difference in the partici-pation of parents. All the mothers were actively involved, but only half of the con-ferences were attended by fathers; many of the latter seemed uninvolved or even uninterested.

There are some downsides of VOM. First, there is concern that victims' per-spectives have been given too much "free reign whereas offenders have more lim-ited room to maneuver . . . it lends credence to claims that offenders' perspectives are not sufficiently addressed by RJ" (Kenney & Clairmont, 2009, p. 303). Solu-tions to this problem include a strong facilitator who can manage emotions on both sides and allow a more balanced view so as not to undermine the restorative part of VOM. Second, there is no strong evidence that VOM reduces offender re-cidivism. Between 40% to 60% of victims refused to participate because they ei-ther didn't want to take time for a perceived trivial offense, they feared meeting the offender, or they desired traditional punishment for the offender (Umbreit, Coates, & Vos, 2001).

Reparation Boards

Otherwise known as youth panels or community diversion boards, panels consist-ing of members from the community have existed as part of the juvenile justice system since the 1920s (Bazemore & Umbreit, 2001). Community reparation boards function as mediators between the court and an offender and may or may not

Community reparation boards, similar to the one pictured here, reviews each offender's case in an attempt to help them in the reentry process.

involve a victim. The board does not decide guilt or innocence; rather, it meets post-conviction with offender and victim separately (or together if the victim wishes) to clarify how an offender will repair the harm caused and to identify strategies for reducing future offending (Karp & Clear, 2002). Each board has a chair who manages the session, with sanctions decided by the board rather than by a judge. Local volunteers and members of faith-based organizations agree to mentor or to assist in supervision of an offender's reparation through a volunteer reparations board. Board members typically receive some training prior to serving, and the vast majority of them serve voluntarily. The board reports back to the court monthly or quarterly on an offender's progress or lack thereof. Should an offender fail to comply with the sanctions, the board makes a recommendation to the court (Bazemore & Umbreit, 2001). Of all forms of restorative justice, this method seems to involve more community than victim participation.

Family Group Conferencing

Family group conferencing is used when victim and offender come from the same family or close-knit group. Family group conferencing assumes that, even in a domestic or family violence situation, family (and extended family) should remain a major part of the decision and that the state's authority to control family matters is secondary. The goal of conferencing is to strengthen and empower families—not to tear them apart. Unlike VOM, which most directly involves just a victim and offender, family group conferencing involves supporters of all ages of both victim and offender. A larger group of people means there is typically a facilitator and some type of security staff present. The group meets in a location of the family's choice at a specific time to be determined in advance. The conference begins, in a similar fashion as VOM, with the facts of the case. After the offender admits to the charges, each member is given a chance to speak within the group. There may be some time provided for the offender and his or her supporters to discuss solutions before reconvening in the larger group. Other times, the negotiations take place out in the open with the victim present.

Family group conferencing in the United States is typically used in juvenile cases or when victim and offender are part of the same family (except for child abuse or neglect cases, which are dealt with through child protective services). School resource officers or police officers organize and facilitate family meetings at school or at a community resource center after school (Bazemore & Umbreit, 2001). One study of family group conferencing for juvenile delinquents discovered that many eligible cases (for example, shoplifting and runaway) were *not* selected, for various reasons. In many of the shoplifting cases, retail stores refused to participate, and in the runaway cases, the juvenile was more often the victim rather than the one at fault (Walker, 2002). Like every other form of restorative justice, family group conferencing has required that juveniles take responsibility for their actions and that the victim participates. In Walker's study, 16% of the youths selected denied criminal involvement and were excluded for that reason. For youths who participated in a conference, most sanctions consisted of a "symbolic" apology, community service, offender counseling, or some combination of the three. Recidivism did not significantly differ overall between juveniles who participated and juveniles who did not. When juveniles were divided by their adjudication offense (violent versus nonviolent), those who participated in conferences for nonviolent offenses were less likely to be adjudicated compared with a matched juvenile group that did not participate in conferences.

Sentencing Circles

A sentencing circle was described in Tommy's case at the beginning of this chapter. Sentencing circles are based most closely on tribal justice and the use of reintegrative shaming by more parties than a victim or a single mediator. A sentencing circle group consists of the offender, the victim, family, friends, and coworkers of the offender and the victim, social service personnel, juvenile justice personnel, and interested community members, all of whom gather simultaneously in a circle. The purpose of a sentencing circle is for a group to arrive at a consensus of what should be done to achieve justice in a particular situation. A "talking piece" such as a stick or feather is used to keep some sort of order, such that the person holding the talking piece is the only one authorized to speak. The talking piece is passed around the circle until everyone who wants an opportunity to state his or her opinion or to offer advice can do so.

Of all four forms of restorative justice, sentencing circles involve the largest number of participants and therefore require the most organization. They may be followed by other circles that attempt to further heal and/or to support crime victims who have experienced trauma, pain, or loss. Circles may be most effective in smaller communities in which people tend to know each other and when offending behavior intersects with dysfunctional relationships. However, they should be used sparingly with offenders convicted of minor crimes (Bazemore & Umbreit, 2001).

Effectiveness of Restorative Justice Methods

Measures of restorative justice include victim satisfaction with the outcome or process, payment of restitution, and cost savings. Restorative justice is most welcomed by victims of property crimes because they are more likely to be compensated for property losses. In traditional criminal justice, the victim is rarely

FACT OR FICTION?

The victims feel dissatisfied and do not receive justice when their perpetrator does not go to jail.

Fiction.

Fact: Victims who decide to participate in restorative justice options report feeling satisfied with the outcomes. Victims are more likely to receive closure on their cases when they've engaged in dialogue with their offenders.

compensated. When given a choice, 75% of respondents to a study conducted in Minnesota indicated they would rather be compensated for a property crime than demand incarceration for the offender (Umbreit, 1999). At this time, however, restorative justice as the sole sanction is less likely to be endorsed by victims of violent crimes, who typically desire additional offender sanctions. Also, when victim and offender know each other well, such as when both are from the same family, it can be difficult for family members who may want to support both sides (Daly & Stubbs, 2006).

Some victims' groups have criticized certain restorative justice initiatives for still being centered around offenders. Victims may be surprised to learn that reintegrative shaming is used rather than retribution and stigmatization. Another reported problem is that some victims are not able to communicate or advocate on their own behalf, so restorative justice exerts too much pressure on them. "The greatest challenge victims pose to restorative justice is indifference. Restorative processes depend, case by case, on victims' active participation, in a role more emotionally demanding than that of complaining witness in a conventional criminal prosecution—which is itself a role avoided by many, perhaps most victims" (Smith, 2001, p. 5).

Evaluations of restorative justice techniques involving juvenile offenders indicate reduced recidivism of program participants, compared with juveniles going through traditional courts for similar offenses. However, restorative justice techniques for adult offenders in Canada and New Zealand were less successful in recidivism reduction (Aos, Miller, & Drake, 2006).

Restorative justice sanctions are primarily economic in nature (paying back losses) and labor-intensive (bettering the community). Economic sanctions such as restitution, community service, and fines, used in both restorative and traditional justice systems, are discussed next.

RESTITUTION

restitution
Court-ordered payment by the offender to the victim to cover tangible losses that occurred during or following the crime.

Crime victims in the U.S. suffer tangible losses of over $105 billion every year. Part of that loss is returned or restored by the very people who caused the harm in the first place. **Restitution** consists of court-ordered payment by an offender to a victim (or a victim's family) to cover tangible losses that occurred during or following a crime. Restitution typically refers to money, but it can also encompass an offender working for a victim without pay to provide direct services. The money or services offered by an offender helps a victim financially. Restitution is also designed to be an act of atonement for a criminal (see Figure 10.3 for the benefits of restitution).

Restitution in History

Restitution has a long history around the world. The Old Testament specified a fivefold restitution for stealing and then killing an ox and a fourfold restitution for stealing and killing a sheep. Double restitution was mandated for stealing (Exodus 21). Leviticus stipulated that restitution plus an additional fifth be made by robbers (Leviticus 6). The Code of Hammurabi, developed between 1792 and 1750 B.C.E., mandated a thirtyfold restitution if the victim was a "god" or a "palace" and a tenfold restitution if the victim was a "villein" (a low-status laborer). British philosopher Jeremy Bentham (1748–1833) prescribed restitution as an essential means of making a punishment fit a crime.

FIGURE 10.3 Benefits of Restitution in Restorative Justice

Restitution was an important custom in the mid-1800s when Quaker prison reformer Elizabeth Fry viewed repaying a victim as a step toward offender rehabilitation.

The authority of courts to grant restitution in the U.S. originates from federal statutes. From 1925 to 1982, restitution could only be imposed as a condition of probation, and it was strictly discretionary. Thus if an offender went to prison, incarceration was used as punishment in lieu of restitution. Stephen Schafer believed that the criminal justice system had become too centered on the offender and the state's interests, to the point that the crime victim was lost in the process. As the victim rights movement in the 1980s gained momentum, judges had to provide reasons for not ordering restitution in cases with tangible losses and an identified victim. In the 1990s, Congress passed a series of three acts to increase the offenses for which restitution could be collected:

<u>1992</u>	Mandatory provision for courts to impose restitution for back child support;
<u>1994</u>	Violence Against Women Act passed to mandate restitution in cases of sexual abuse, sexual exploitation of children, domestic violence, and telemarketing fraud; and
<u>1996</u>	Mandatory Victims' Restitution Act passed to require that restitution be imposed for violent crimes and Title 18 property offenses, and as a sentencing option in juvenile delinquency cases (Office for Victims of Crime, 2002).

As a result of these acts, victims were more likely to receive judgments in criminal and civil cases. The remaining problem was enforcing the court order so that victims could collect their restitution. Victims received very little information about how to collect restitution through traditional criminal and civil courts. Through restorative justice and presentence efforts, restitution is enforced and collected at greater rates than in the past.

Losses Eligible for Compensation

States have broadened the types of losses eligible for compensation as well as the parties eligible to receive restitution. For example, restitution is available for the purpose of lost income as a result of physical injury or time in court, medical expenses, transportation to and from the courthouse, necessary child care during litigation, expenses involving the investigation and prosecution of the case, counseling sessions, sexual assault exams, human immunodeficiency virus (HIV) testing, occupational and rehabilitative therapy, moving expenses, case-related travel and meal expenses, and burial expenses. Restitution may be ordered for psychological counseling in cases in which a victim has suffered physical injury (*United States v. Laney,* 1999). Restitution is limited to the replacement value of direct or actual losses as a result of a crime and cannot be ordered for losses defined as indirect or consequential, such as victims' attorney fees.

Eligible parties may include a victim or a victim's family (in cases of homicide). Eligible organizations that may receive restitution include those that provided medical care, shelter, or counseling to a victim. Many states authorize the collection of interest on the unpaid restitution amount, varying from between 6% to 10% per year (Office for the Victims of Crime, 2002).

Victims typically apply for restitution through the prosecutor's office. To receive restitution, a victim must press charges and agree to testify if necessary. Restitution is declared a victim right in 19 state constitutions (AK, AZ, CA, CT, ID, IL, LA, MI, MO, MT, NM, NC, OK, OR, RI, SC, TN, TX, and WI), even when the offender has been incarcerated. Despite the mandatory policy, victims are more likely to be reimbursed if the offender is sentenced to a community sanction so that he or she can work to pay the victim back. In other states where restitution is defined as offender rehabilitation, restitution is forfeited if the offender goes to prison.

Problems Associated with Restitution

Restitution remains underutilized in both misdemeanor and felony cases. Nationally, courts have ordered restitution in only 10% of felony convictions and 22% of misdemeanors. For felony crimes, restitution has been ordered in one out of four property offenses but in only 15% of all violent offenses (Durose & Langan, 2007). Restitution has been more often required for probationers than for people sentenced to prison, most likely because people on probation have the means to pay restitution whereas prisoners usually do not. Even though restitution may not often be court-ordered even when it is mandatory by law, a Pennsylvania study of 170,260 restitution-eligible cases determined that restitution was ordered for the appropriate offenders and that "the odds of receiving an order of restitution were significantly greater for property than person crimes, for offenders with no or low prior records, for female offenders, and for White offenders" (Ruback, Ruth, & Shaffer, 2005, p. 332).

One barrier to obtaining restitution is a victim's lack of participation in the justice process and lack of knowledge that restitution is available. Many victims fail to request restitution or have not retained documentation showing their losses. Three other problems associated with restitution are indigence of the defendant, determining the restitution amount, and collecting restitution.

INDIGENT OFFENDERS   If a defendant is indigent and cannot pay, courts generally cannot cite that defendant for contempt or send him or her to prison. However, indigence at the time of sentencing does not entitle an offender to immunity from restitution; restitution is more dependent on an offender's future ability to pay (*United States v. Bachsian,* 1993). If a defendant is able to pay but refuses, then incarceration is valid. In the federal system, if an incarcerated prisoner must pay restitution and has the ability to pay, parole release can be contingent upon him or her first paying off the entire restitution amount while incarcerated (U.S. Parole Commission, 2003). There are other standards in some state jurisdictions. For example, an Indiana court ruled that the decision to incarcerate a probationer for failure to pay depends solely on the type of probationary sentence. If restitution is ordered as a *suspended* probationary sentence, a defendant could be imprisoned for being unable to pay. If restitution is ordered as part of an *executed* probationary sentence, a defendant cannot be imprisoned for failure to pay (*Wooden v. State,* 2001).

Declaring bankruptcy no longer excuses offenders from paying restitution. A federal statute declared that restitution orders are not dischargeable in Chapter 13 bankruptcies (11 U.S.C.A., sec 1328(a)(3)). A Texas Criminal Appeals court extended this same line of reasoning to Chapter 7 bankruptcy cases (*Cabla v. State,* 1999).

DETERMINING THE RESTITUTION AMOUNT   In restorative justice cases, restitution amounts are determined at a victim-offender mediation session. In traditional criminal or civil cases, the court sets restitution amounts according to harm caused to a victim and a defendant's ability to pay based on full disclosure of assets and liabilities. Probation officers who complete presentence investigation (PSI) reports can suggest a restitution amount to a judge. To accurately determine a restitution amount, probation officers consider:

- whether restitution is discretionary or mandatory (usually defined by offense of conviction);
- the victims of the offense of conviction;
- the harms to the victim that are directly caused by the offense of conviction;
- the harms and costs that qualify for restitution; and
- the effect of a plea agreement on the restitution amount (Goodwin, 2001).

An offender's financial resources, existing financial obligations, and ability to pay are considered as well as whether or not a victim was insured or was partially at fault. A defendant usually has an opportunity prior to sentencing to challenge a victim's claims or the amount of restitution recommended in the PSI.

Because it is often difficult to accurately establish a fair restitution amount, the government has the burden to prove, based on preponderance of the evidence, that a victim did suffer the harm for which he or she is requesting restitution from an offender (Goodwin, 2001). The amount of restitution must be based on expenses a victim incurred by the time of sentencing and can be based only on the offense for which an offender was actually convicted.

Collecting Restitution

Collecting restitution is the responsibility of probation officers, day reporting centers, and restitution centers. The entity responsible for collecting restitution acts as both finance officer and collection agent by determining the weekly or monthly installment payment schedule and making sure the victim receives the money. Only about one third to one half of felony offenders had paid restitution in full by the time they completed their sentence (Ruback & Bergstrom, 2006). Offenders who get too far behind on payments or who are able to pay but refuse to do so might be reassigned to a formal collection agency.

FACT OR FICTION?

Victims are more likely to receive restitution payments if their offender is given a community corrections sentence than if the offender is sentenced to jail or prison.

Fact: Restitution payments are more likely to be enforced when an offender is employed at a regular job, which occurs during a community corrections sentence.

BOX 10.1   COMMUNITY CORRECTIONS UP CLOSE

Can Restitution Be Collected *Before* Sentencing?

Given that offenders sentenced to prison have no incentive to make restitution payments and that some offenders would rather go to jail to avoid making payments, the restitution burden is largely left to parole officers who become collection agents. The officers attempt to garnish wages to collect as much restitution as possible from an offender before a sentence expires.

Having become wiser, the federal justice system has changed the way it administers restitution with a more effective method. Once an offender decides to plead guilty, federal plea agreements now require defendants to complete a financial affidavit listing all assets and liabilities, including real estate, vehicles, mutual funds, and any other personal property valued over a certain amount. The financial litigation unit runs a credit report and conducts a search for assets to complete its investigation. Then the defendant is required to pay restitution with those assets, all *before* sentencing. Having a defendant pay before sentencing gives a prosecutor leverage with the plea agreement. If the defendant has completed restitution payments in full or at least attempted to make good, the prosecutor can make a deal with the defendant for a more lenient sentence, giving him or her an incentive. If the defendant does not pay, sentencing will be harsher and an attempt will be made to collect restitution through the backdoor—as many jurisdictions do now. The collection of presentence restitution has resulted in receipts of $5.25 million in one year.

Source: Stottmann, Jonathan O. 2007. Presentence restitution: When opportunity knocks. *News and Views 32 (19):* September 10.

Three ways that have been used to increase restitution collection rates are by notifying an offender through letters and phone calls, restorative justice techniques, and presentence efforts. Notification letters seemed to work for employed probationers who wished to avoid prison but had less effect on offenders who were already in prison. Some systems will not release an offender from parole early until all restitution has been satisfied. Box 10.1 discusses what the federal government has been doing recently to collect restitution *before* sentencing.

But what if an offender is a juvenile? Victim-offender mediation (VOM) requires that victim agree to meet with offender, and restitution is made a large part of the incentive for victim participation. Restorative justice sessions increased restitution collection rates compared with youth who did not participate (Umbreit & Coates, 1993).

Even after prison time has been served, it seems that being transferred to a restitution center for employment was more effective for an offender making restitution payments and for recidivism reduction after a sentence ends.

COMMUNITY SERVICE

community service
Unpaid labor for the public to compensate society for harm done by the offense of conviction.

Community service has been called "the most underused intermediate sanction in the United States" (Tonry, 1998, p. 89). **Community service** is defined as unpaid service to the public to compensate society for harm done by an offender. Community service is typically ordered by a judge as part of probation; the place of work is chosen by either a judge or a supervising officer. Community service might consist of working for a tax-supported or nonprofit agency such as a hospital, public park, or library, or for a poverty or public works program. The most frequent type of community service work is picking up roadside litter, doing landscape maintenance, removing graffiti, and painting buildings. Some work assignments have trucks or vans that transport work crews to a site where they are supervised for the day, but most assignments require an offender to take the initiative and report to complete a service order.

History of Community Service

Community service first began in the United States as an organized program in 1966 in Alameda County, California. This initiative was created as a substitute for paying fines for low-income female traffic offenders. The women worked without pay in lieu of their fine and avoided jail for fine nonpayment. Because of the positive attention this program received, hundreds of community service programs were established in the 1970s for juveniles and nonviolent adults. In the U.S., community service developed as an alternative to fines or as an additional condition of probation (Tonry, 1999a).

THE ENGLISH MODEL   Community service suffices in England and Wales as an acceptable alternative to prison for crimes considered minor, such as petty theft or drug possession. Special community service officers administer the sanction. The English model became popular in other areas of Europe, such as Scotland, Switzerland, and the Netherlands. The United States did not follow the English model, believing instead that community service was not punitive enough to substitute for prison. It is not uncommon to see U.S. judges order between 100 and 1,000 hours of community service in addition to other probation conditions (Tonry, 1999a). This difference in national perceptions of community service demonstrates that, in comparison with most other countries in the world, community corrections sanctions in the U.S. are more punitive (and are not just reflected in long prison sentences).

Purpose of Community Service

Like monetary restitution, community service is both punitive and rehabilitative. It is punitive in that an offender's time and freedom are partially restricted until the work is completed. It is rehabilitative in the sense that it allows offenders to do something constructive, to increase their self-esteem, to reduce their isolation from society, and to benefit society through their efforts. In comparison with restitution, community service requires neither an identifiable victim nor a victim cooperative in the prosecution process.

Further, community service provides an alternative sanction for indigent offenders who are unable to afford significant monetary sanctions and for those whose financial resources are so great that monetary restitution has no punitive or rehabilitative effect. Community service is a good example of a restorative justice program, and it can also be used to divert offenders from having a formal conviction on their record.

Prevalence of Community Service

According to Table 10.2, community service was used as part of probation sentences for 9% of misdemeanants and 20% of felony probationers nationwide (Kyckelhahn & Cohen, 2007). This nationwide estimate appears to differ widely by region. For example, community service is commonly used in states like Texas in 76% of drug and property offenses as a condition of probation.

Although community service is used as a jail alternative, it is rarely or ever used as a sole sanction (Caputo, 2005). The number of hours of community service varies depending on the nature and seriousness of an offense. For example, Texas assigns

TABLE 10.2   Probationers Who Were Ordered to Community Service, Restitution, and Treatment

Most serious conviction/offense	Number of defendants	PERCENT WHOSE SENTENCE TO PROBATION INCLUDED—		
		Community service	Restitution	Treatment
All offenses	7,834	19%	12%	26%
Felonies	6,649	20%	10%	29%
Violent offenses	741	26	15	20
Property offenses	1,813	22	26	9
Drug offenses	3,384	18	1	45
Public-order offenses	693	23	10	13
Misdemeanors	1,186	9%	22%	7%

Note: Data represent felony defendants in the 75 largest counties in 2004. Total for felonies includes cases that could not be classified into one of the four felony offense categories. A defendant may have received more than one type of probation condition. Not all defendants sentenced to probation received probation conditions. Detail may not add to total because of rounding.

Source: Kyckelhahn, Tracey & Cohen, Thomas H. 2007. *Felony defendants in large urban counties, 2004.* Washington, DC: Bureau of Justice Statistics, Table 29. Retrieved from: http://www.ojp.usdoj.gov/bjs/stssent.htm#scps

the following community service hours for probation (Texas Code of Criminal Procedure, Art. 42.12, Sec. 22(a)(1)):

PUNISHMENT RANGE	MAXIMUM HOURS	MINIMUM HOURS
First-degree felony	1,000	320
Second-degree felony	800	240
Third-degree felony	600	160
State jail felony	400	120
Class A misdemeanor	200	80
Class B misdemeanor	100	24

Community service orders ranged from 20 to 600 hours, with the average number of hours at 230 for felons and 60 for misdemeanants. In most jurisdictions, an offender's employment status must be considered in determining the community service schedule. Because employed offenders must be able to work and retain gainful employment, they are limited to 16 hours of community service per week. Unemployed offenders can perform up to 32 community service hours per week (Caputo, 2005). Offenders in some jurisdictions may be able to perform community service in lieu of a fine or, with judicial permission, in lieu of incarceration. In Texas, eight hours of community service is equivalent to one day of jail confinement, regardless of the offense committed (Caputo, 2005).

Effectiveness of Community Service

Many nonprofit organizations, such as churches, homeless shelters, libraries, and the U.S. Forest Service, have benefited from the labor provided by offenders. Community service can turn into an opportunity, as in Carl's case featured in Box 10.2. Completion rates vary from 50% to a high of 85%, depending on how community service is enforced. A main reason offenders do not complete community service orders is a lack of enforcement on completing hours before a probation sentence is

BOX 10.2 COMMUNITY CORRECTIONS UP CLOSE

Carl's Community Service

Carl was a mail carrier for the U.S. Postal Service. He thought he was doing his customers a favor by throwing away all third-class mail in a dumpster because he deemed it a nuisance. One day he was caught, and an investigation led to his being fired and prosecuted for a federal misdemeanor. He was ordered to pay restitution and to perform 300 hours of community service. Carl was one quarter short of obtaining a B.A. degree in mathematics, according to the PSI report. The community service probation officer assigned Carl to work a seven-hour shift once a week at an elementary school for 42 weeks. He was initially assigned to playground and lunchroom duties, but his mathematics knowledge and leadership qualities were so impressive that he became a third-grade math tutor to three boys, even meeting with the boys' parents. All three boys improved their math grades and overall classroom performance. At the end of his community service, Carl was offered a job as a teacher's aide. Although he turned down the offer, Carl felt he had touched the lives of a few kids and had received much more in return. Because of the success of Carl's placement, the courts have expanded community service to four other schools.

Carl's case is one example of the many federal offenders who must complete community service. The success of community service programs depends on good agency relationships among probation departments, outside community agencies, and offender placements. Community service saves money, provides work for nonprofit agencies, and offers new opportunities to individuals like Carl.

---

served. Rarely are probationers extended on probation because they fail to complete community service hours (Caputo, 2005).

Community service has enjoyed wide public support even though it has only been empirically evaluated by a few researchers. For example, Bouffard & Muftic (2007) compared 200 DUI misdemeanants sentenced to community service to another group of similar offenders assessed a monetary fine. Offenders who completed community service had a recidivism rate similar to that of the monetary fine group. Despite a lack of cost-benefit analysis and considering only a 50% successful completion of community service compared to over 90% of offenders who paid a fine, the researchers continued to believe that community service offers more benefit than fines (Bouffard & Muftic, 2007).

More recently, Killias and colleagues conducted an experiment to randomly assign 116 traffic offenders in Switzerland to community service and 106 offenders to electronic monitoring. Reconviction rates were higher in the community service group (31%) compared to the electronic monitoring group (21%). Social integration was measurably better with the electronic monitoring group as well, favoring electronic monitoring methods over community service as a sole community sanction, although it was difficult to determine the amount of supervision the community service program provided in this instance (Killias, Gillieron, Kissling, & Villettaz, 2010).

As the search continues for less costly and more effective methods of dealing with offenders, community service has the potential to be a growing trend in U.S. corrections. One difficult problem with evaluating and expanding community service programs is that most do not have clear goals and objectives. In expanding their use, the following considerations must be delineated:

- Is the purpose of community service to reduce recidivism, to divert offenders, or both?
- Should community service be used instead of or in addition to other sanctions?

- Should community service be expanded for prison-bound offenders?
- How is the value of community service work calculated compared to days in jail or fine amounts?

There are no easy answers to these questions. The potential for use of community service with careful supervision and program administration without further increasing community risk is promising.

FINES

The English jurist Jeremy Bentham (1748–1832) once said, "A fine is a license paid in arrears." In other words, instead of buying beforehand permission to engage in a certain activity, an offender, if caught, pays a fine later. In modern times, a **fine** is defined as a judge-imposed monetary sanction whose amount depends on the severity of offense. The modern fine is directed at the consumers of a certain illegal activity and not at the indigent (O'Malley, 2008). Generally there are fixed fines and variable or day fines.

The first type is a fixed monetary amount that is referred to in the field and in this text as a *fine* proper. Ninety percent of fines go to victim/witness assistance programs or to a general **victim compensation fund**, which is a state fund that compensates victims of violent crime for losses not covered by restitution (Ruback & Bergstrom, 2006). A fine is viewed as a punishment, with failure to pay grounds for revocation or issuance of a warrant.

A fine can be imposed as a sole penalty, as in the case of traffic offenses, or accompanied by probation, an intermediate sanction, or incarceration. Fines have been used in European criminal justice systems as a primary sanction. For example, in Germany more than 80% of all crimes committed by adults are punished by a fine as the only penalty. Compared to many other countries, fines in the United States have generally been underused and their collection not well enforced.

fine
A fixed monetary sanction defined by statute and imposed by a judge, depending on the seriousness of the crime.

victim compensation fund
A state fund that dispenses compensation to victims of violent crime and is paid for by offenders who are convicted.

Monthly payments of fines or fees are expected from the offender while on probation.

© Dmitry Oshchepkov/iStockphoto

Prevalence of Fines

Fines are used in only 25% of all state felony cases and in 13% of federal cases (Durose & Langan, 2004). When they are used, they are in addition to a probation sentence. In the federal system, fines are used as a stand-alone or sole means of punishment in nearly one third of misdemeanor offenses but less than 1% of federal felony cases (U.S. Department of Justice, 2005a).

Fines are routinely imposed as the primary sanction for organizational or corporate defendants in cases of corporate or white-collar crime. According to the *Federal Sentencing Guidelines Manual* (2008, p. 510):

> The base fine is determined in one of three ways: (1) by the amount based on the offense [seriousness] level . . . (2) by the pecuniary gain to the organization from the offense; and (3) by the pecuniary loss caused by the organization, to the extent that the loss was caused intentionally, knowingly or recklessly.

Whichever loss is deemed the greatest of these three types is the one selected. This helps to ensure that organizations seek to detect and report such gains in the future and/or prevent intentional losses from happening again. Organizational fines using these guidelines typically range from $5,000 up to $72 million (*Federal Sentencing Guidelines Manual*, 2008).

When a fine is imposed in individual-level federal felony cases, they have ranged from $28 to as much as $10,000, with an average of $1,000 (Vigorita, 2002). Fines are assessed for offenders who are eligible for a community sentence and have an ability to pay. State-level judges rarely have information on a defendant's ability to pay, so eligibility rests largely on offense severity and prior criminal record. Employed offenders are more likely to be assessed fines than unemployed offenders. Judges reluctant to use fines point out that offenders tend to be poor and may have no means other than additional criminal activity to obtain the funds to pay their fines. Fixed fines may overly burden a poor person but be less consequential to an affluent offender. When a financial penalty is too high, however, offenders are significantly more likely to revoke their probation (Ruback & Bergstrom, 2006). In addition, the Seventh Circuit Court of Appeals held that the federal district court was not authorized to order a defendant to pay fines to private charities because fines are paid to the government, not to private parties (*United States v. Wolff*, 1996).

Revoking Probation for Fine Nonpayment

O'Malley (2008) stressed that the modern fine is technically not aimed at indigent people and is not translatable into jail time. A substantial number of probationers do not satisfy their entire financial obligation. What happens if a defendant does *not* pay the whole fine? A defendant can avoid paying a fine, in part or in full, if he or she is demonstrably unable to pay. The U.S. Supreme Court held that probation cannot be revoked solely because of an offender's inability to pay a fine or restitution, because revocation based on indigence violates the equal protection clause of the Fourteenth Amendment (*Bearden v. Georgia*, 1983). The Court distinguished, however, between indigence (inability) and unwillingness (refusal) to pay. Unwillingness to pay court-ordered restitution or fines despite a probationer's ability to do so may result in revocation. Statutes in most states and the federal system allow a flexible payment schedule if a defendant is unable to pay an entire fine immediately, modifying a sentence to reduce the fine and in some cases rescinding the fine and imposing an alternative sanction.

The federal system mandates that federal prisoners shall not be released on parole or mandatory release until a fine is paid in full (U.S. Parole Commission, 2003). In contrast, many fines remain unpaid in the state system. As a result, the American Bar Association and researchers have issued recommendations over the years that include (1) clearer payment instructions for offenders; (2) positive motivation to encourage payments in full; (3) designation of a central officer or public official to collect fines; and (4) authorization of that official either to file a court order holding an offender in contempt of court or to file a civil lawsuit against that offender for the remaining fine balance (Ruback et al., 2006).

INCREASING PAYMENTS OF FINES AND RESTITUTION   One of the drawbacks of imposing any type of financial obligation is the court response if offenders fail to follow through. Traditionally that response has been "jail therapy" (that is, incarceration). How then do we increase the numbers of probationers who make payments of fines and restitution *without* increasing incarceration rates? *Project MUSTER* (Must Earn Restitution) was an experiment for low-risk, work-capable probationers who were court-ordered to pay but who missed three months or more of payments or were 60% or more in arrears of the total amount (Weisburd, Einat, & Kowalski, 2008). Selected probationers were assigned at random to one of three groups: (1) no change in supervision; (2) served with a violation of probation and an upcoming court date; or (3) the MUSTER group. Those in the MUSTER group served with a violation notice like those in Group 2, received employment training, and were ordered to complete an additional 15 hours of community service *per each week* that payments were missed. After six months, the researchers found that probationers in Groups 2 and 3 were more likely to make court-ordered payments than those in the "do nothing" Group 1. One third of MUSTER probationers, compared to 13 percent of Group 1, paid in full. Over 60% of MUSTER probationers (compared to 35% of the first group) paid at least half the obligation. It seems that the mere threat of probation violation was enough of a motivation to increase payment in full, although undertaking extra community service did not contribute to paying fines and restitution (Weisburd, Einat, & Kowalski, 2008).

Day Fines

Using fixed fines in criminal sentencing presents difficulties due to offenders' socio-economic differences. For this reason, a pilot program began on Staten Island, New York, to use fines in a different way, based on a system practiced in many European countries. **Day fines**, otherwise known as structured fines, are court fines figured as multiples of an offender's daily income. For example, a school custodian and a stockbroker, both convicted of the same offense with the same criminal history and identical risk factors, would pay different amounts because they earn different amounts of money. The stockbroker, who makes an annual income of $100,000 per year, would pay more than the custodian, who makes $25,000 per year. Based on a day fine of 10%, the stockbroker would be fined $10,000 and the custodian would pay $2,500. In a day fine system, offenders would be fined the same multiple or percentage of income, determined by their crime and prior history. In this way, day fines would provide the same degree of financial hardship to each offender. Using the previous example in a tariff or conventional fine situation, the stockbroker and the custodian might have received fines of the same amount. Despite a good idea in theory, day fines have not caught on in practice. Instead, judges can reduce fixed fines for indigent defendants.

day fines
Fines that are calculated by multiplying a percentage of the offender's daily wage by the number of predefined punishment units (the number of punishment units depend on the seriousness of the crime).

FEES AND COURT COSTS

Differentiated from a fine, a **fee** is a court-imposed reimbursement that an offender pays directly to the courts for administration of the criminal justice system. Fees are also known as *court costs* in other regions of the country. The two terms have the same meaning, so we will use *fees* in this text. Fees are the government's attempt to recover from individual offenders the expenses incurred in the investigation and prosecution of a defendant's case. One thing is clear: Acquitted defendants do not pay fees. The lower courts are divided, however, on the legal costs for convicted offenders. Although some jurisdictions have fixed court costs, others are variable depending on ability to pay. Though all courts have authority on what a probationer must pay, most trial courts do not assess court costs to prisoners because few have any authority over parole conditions, unless a parole board is statutorily authorized to require repayment (some are, but most are not). A sample fee schedule is provided in Table 10.3.

Probation user fees are also imposed for probationers, especially if they are under a court structure and if the jurisdiction is fee-dependent. For example, because a significant percentage of probation budgets rely on probation user fees, there is legitimate concern as to whether probationers who are compliant in making their payments are ever released from supervision early—or whether they are carried on the caseload because of the money they provide.

A fee is not considered punitive and is therefore subject to different legal standards for nonpayment than a fine. Even though probationers with fines were ordered to pay lower fees than probationers without fines, it is likely that fees would

fee
A monetary amount imposed by the court to assist in administering the criminal justice system by the offender's repayment of debt accrued by the investigation, prosecution, and supervision of the case.

TABLE 10.3   Sample Probationer Fee Schedule and Fines

FEES/COURT COSTS	
$200–$1,000	Court operations (depending on complexity of investigations and hearings)
$5 per sample	Provide a DNA sample
$1,000–$5,000	Repayment of attorney's fees or appointed defense counsel for defendants who were later found *not* to be indigent

FEES FOR COMMUNITY SUPERVISION PROGRAMS	
$60 per month	Probation
$10 per month	Radio frequency electronic monitoring
$25 per month	Global positioning system electronic monitoring
$250	Community service administration fee
$25	Traffic offense fee
$400 per month	Residential Community Corrections Facility (work release or halfway house)
$8 per test	Drug and/or alcohol tests (urinalysis)
$75	Diagnostic testing (mental illness, substance abuse, etc.)
No charge	Inpatient substance abuse treatment
$40–$75 per month	Outpatient treatment (assuming once per week)

FINES	
$200–$10,000	General State Victim Compensation Fund Assessed by statute

still compete with other financial obligations such as monthly household bills, fines, victim restitution, and payment for court-ordered treatment. Courts have held that it is unacceptable to require an indigent defendant to pay court costs. Perhaps this is why Illinois probationers in higher income brackets were more likely to be ordered to pay probation fees than probationers in lower income brackets (Olson & Ranker, 2001). Of the 55% of probationers who were ordered to pay, nearly three fourths conformed.

Offenders in rural areas were more likely to be assessed partial fees than offenders in urban areas. This may be due to the ideology of courts in rural areas that all offenders contribute something to the greater whole, as opposed to caseloads in urban areas that are larger, giving officials less time to enforce their collection. Perhaps rural jurisdictions rely more heavily on reimbursement if they have a lower available tax base from which to draw (Ruback & Bergstrom, 2006)

To what degree does probation serve as a collection agency? Requiring probation or parole officers to collect fees reduces officers to collection agents and diminishes the counseling role of their work (Olson & Ranker, 2001). Effective collection techniques are important for restitution, fines, fees, and forfeitures. Recommendations to increase the likelihood of full payment include:

- a convenient location to make payments (collections departments, probation departments, mail, electronic);
- a wide variety of payment methods (credit cards, debit cards, cash, money orders, electronic transfers);
- discounts for early payment; and
- surcharges and overdue payment reminder notices for late payment.

FORFEITURES

forfeiture
A government seizure of property that was illegally obtained, was acquired with resources that were illegally obtained, or was used in connection with an illegal activity.

When material items are acquired through profit directly resulting from illegal activities, those items are subject to seizure by police and are resold, with those proceeds donated according to state law. This is called **forfeiture** because the government takes away any property used in connection with an illegal activity—namely, from drug trafficking and distribution (Ruback & Bergstrom, 2006). Although any property may be seized, homes and cars are the most typical items, as part of either a criminal or civil action.

In a criminal case, forfeiture occurs after a conviction. But in a civil case, forfeiture can occur when proof by a preponderance of evidence is met. *Preponderance of evidence* is a lower standard of proof than the threshold of *beyond a reasonable doubt* required in criminal court. The purpose of forfeiture is to make certain that offenders do not keep illegal property and make a profit, and to discourage criminals from using houses and businesses to conduct criminal transactions. Unlike a traditional fixed fine, forfeiture is not considered a punishment by the Supreme Court. However, a forfeiture is limited in that it must not be "grossly disproportionate to the gravity of the defendant's offense [or else] the forfeiture would violate the excessive fines clause" of the Eighth Amendment (Ruback & Bergstrom, 2006, p. 257). The authors estimate that 40,000 forfeitures occur every year, 80% of which are civil and the remaining 20% from criminal cases. Perhaps the most well-known forfeiture in recent times was the $17 billion worth of property seized following Bernie Madoff's 2009 conviction and subsequent 150-year sentence to federal prison for securities fraud, investment fraud, money laundering, and lying to the Securities and Exchange Commission.

SUMMARY

- Community justice is a philosophy of using the community—through community policing, community courts, and neighborhood-based probation—to control and reduce crime.

- Once a crime has been committed, restorative justice emphasizes an offender taking responsibility to repair the harm done to victim and surrounding community.

- Restorative justice is more victim-centered than traditional methods of criminal justice, involving the victim and the community throughout an entire process of justice.

- Restorative justice programs rely heavily on community partners and volunteers to carry out mediation, reparation boards, face-to-face meetings with victims, and victim impact classes. Present patterns in the use

- of restitution vary widely, although observers predict greater emphasis on restitution in the future, particularly in conjunction with other sentences.

- Community service also holds promise, but at present its provision is not well enforced.

- The use of fixed fines is still perceived as either too lenient or too problematic for impoverished offenders sinking deeper into poverty as a result.

- Fees are a monthly payment by an offender that helps curb the cost of community supervision.

- Forfeitures are material items or property acquired from criminal activities that are seized by police, inspected for contraband, and resold at regulated auctions.

- Collection rates of the various economic sanctions remain fairly low at present.

DISCUSSION QUESTIONS

1. How is restorative justice different from traditional justice approaches?

2. How do monetary restitution and community service differ? How are they alike?

3. How can restitution be used for juveniles who are too young to legally work full time?

4. Is it fair to require that probationers pay court costs but not parolees? Why or why not?

5. Why is the collection of fines treated differently from the collection of fees? Should they be treated the same if they are not paid in full?

6. Why do you think the day fine notion has *not* caught on in American criminal justice?

WEBSITES, VIDEOS, AND PODCASTS

Websites

Restorative justice resources
   http://restorativejustice.org

The Center of Restorative Justice and Peacemaking, University of Minnesota
   http://www.cehd.umn.edu/ssw/rjp/

The Center for Restorative Justice, Simon Fraser University, Canada
   http://www.sfu.ca/crj

Restorative Justice Ministry Network of North America
   http://www.rjmn.net

Bridges to Life: Faith-Based Restorative Justice Program
   http://www.bridgestolife.org

National Center for Victims of Crime
   http://www.ncvc.org/ncvc/main.aspx

The purpose of economic sanctions
http://www.econlib.org/library/Enc/Sanctions.html

Video/Podcasts

Bridges to Life Restorative Justice Program, PBS Video
http://www.youtube.com/
watch?v=Z8HZmD9VckY

A video about the Bridges to Life program aired on PBS.

Why Restorative Justice Works, Part 1 and 2
http://www.youtube.com/watch?v=yAbn6hhMBLs&
feature=related
http://www.youtube.com/watch?v=nAw2ZfsikGc&
feature=related

CASE STUDY EXERCISES

Restorative Justice

In each of the following scenarios, assume that you are a prosecutor or judge and wish to refer a case to one of the four available restorative justice options. Which restorative justice option is best suited to each case, and why?

CASE A: Cross Burning at a Southern Baptist Church

An 18-year-old male with no prior record has been convicted of a "hate" crime. He, with two juveniles (ages 15 and 16), burned a cross in the yard of a church and painted derogatory racial messages on its front door. Most of the church congregation is African-American; the offenders are white, and the 18-year-old is reportedly affiliated with a white supremacist organization. The offender states that he began his involvement with the organization only recently and committed the offense as part of his initiation. The church members are divided on what should be done—half are willing to discuss the issue with the boys while the other half want to press criminal charges. What should the pastor do?

CASE B: Accidental Fire

Two boys from the neighborhood are Anthony and Bernardo, both age 11. They play nearly every day after school at one of the two boys' houses. They can usually find something to do like catching frogs or fishing, or they find other neighborhood kids to start a flag football game. The two boys are bored one day and start snooping around Bernardo's father's workshop. They come across some flammable liquids and matches, which they take out behind the workshop to look at closer, near the next door neighbor's fence. Some of the starter fluid accidentally spills out, and a fire starts on the dried grass. The boys run back to the workshop to find something to put out the fire, but within minutes the fire spreads to the wooden fence and is licking at the house next door. A neighbor across the street sees smoke and calls the fire department. A corner of the neighbor's siding starts to burn before a fire truck arrives to put out the fire, resulting in about $600 in damages on the house. The neighbor is willing to forgo pressing criminal charges for now, until some restorative justice options can be discussed.

CASE C: Bethany's Bruise

From outward appearances, the Franklins seem like most normal families. Both parents work, the three kids go to school, and the family dog, a German shepherd, stays home. The Franklins keep to themselves after the parents arrive home from work, usually by 7:00 P.M. The kids are usually alone between 4:00 and 7:00 P.M. Sometimes the neighbors can hear shouting, slamming doors, and loud music blaring from the Franklin home after school, but they assume that with three teenagers inside, that is to be expected. Seeing that Bethany Franklin has a bruised arm, a teacher at school notices handprints on where it appears that Bethany was grabbed. When the teacher asks Bethany what happened, the girl says that it's nothing. A few weeks later, the teacher notices a cut below Bethany's eye and immediately calls Social Services. A Social Service investigation results in interviewing the parents, who deny any wrongdoing. Bethany refuses to reveal how she keeps getting bruises and cuts. The older brother suggests that Bethany probably hurt herself intentionally. However, the younger brother admitted that he saw the older brother grab his sister's arm and twist it. Upon further questioning, the younger brother said this was not the first time he had seen his sister get hurt and proceeded to tell about more incidents involving the older brother. What type of restorative justice response is best in this situation?

PART IV

Special Issues in Community Corrections

The four chapters in this section discuss specialty issues that are paramount to community corrections: challenges offenders face in reentry to the community from prison, the career pathways of community supervision officers, juvenile offenders, and collateral consequences that follow a felony conviction.

Chapter 11 pays particular attention to issues involved in the preparation for prisoner reentry, as well as what a parole board hearing is like. Chapter 12 examines the shortage of probation personnel and pays particular attention to how officers are selected and trained, along with nuances in supervision, such as legal issues and privatization. Chapter 13 discusses in detail legal issues and community corrections programs for juvenile delinquent status offenders and dependent and neglected children who come to the attention of the juvenile justice system.

The final chapter in the text examines civil disabilities that felony offenders experience even after they have completed serving their sentence that disallows them from full participation in activities such as voting in a public election, holding a public office, being employed in certain occupations, owning a firearm, among others. Chapter 14 also investigates the mechanisms by which convicted offenders may be able to restore some or all of these civil rights.

11

Preparing for Prisoner Reentry: Discretionary Parole and Mandatory Release

CHAPTER LEARNING OBJECTIVES

1. Examine the preparations needed for reentry while an offender is still incarcerated.
2. Discuss how reentry affects a prisoner, a victim, a community, and a prisoner's family.

3. Explain the discretionary parole process of how prisoners become eligible for release.
4. Describe a typical parole board hearing, including legal issues in parole board decisions.

Nearly 600,000 prisoners are released every year just like these two men, who are getting out on mandatory release after each having served 10 years.

CHAPTER OUTLINE

Issues in Reentry
Prisoner Perspectives on Getting Out
The Prisoner's Family
Justice Reinvestment in Disadvantaged
    Communities
Community-Based Reentry Initiatives

Eligibility for Parole
Time Sheets and Eligibility Dates
Prerelease Preparation Within an Institution

The Parole Board and Releasing Authority
The Parole Hearing
Parole Hearing Attendees
Parole Risk Assessment
The Parole Board Decision

Legal Issues in Parole Hearings
No Due Process Protections
Use of Hearsay, DNA, and No Right to an Attorney

Summary

KEY TERMS

desistance
reentry
Justice Reinvestment
continuity of care
reentry courts

minimum eligibility date
maximum eligibility date
good time
parole eligibility date
prerelease facility

prerelease plan
parole board
victim impact statement
salient factor score
full board review

People who end up in prison are a diverse group, all of whom face different challenges when they are released—even famous music artists like Earl Simmons, better known as DMX. Simmons' troubles began in 2009 when he provided medical clinic staff a fake name and social security number. After suspicions were raised about Simmons' possible involvement in animal abuse, police searched his home and found malnourished dogs living there and remains of other dogs that had been burned to death, all well as guns, ammunition, and drug paraphernalia. A judge sentenced Simmons to 90 days in jail and 18 months of probation, which he was scheduled to complete in November 2010. Weeks before he was to complete probation, Simmons was arrested at an Arizona nightclub for using cocaine and alcohol, driving on a suspended license, and failing to report to probation. In December 2010 Simmons was sentenced to the Department of Corrections for one year, with an opportunity for early release for good behavior. In a recent interview from prison, Simmons says that he didn't do anything to warrant going to jail, but he has since learned that he needs to break his old ties, leave Arizona, and start over in a new location. He reportedly also completed a gospel album.

INTRODUCTION

Of the offenders released every year from prison, 80% remain under some form of community supervision while 20% will have served their entire sentence behind bars. In either case, a substantial number of people must make a major life transition without having a concrete plan of employment, savings, and living arrangements. This chapter discusses how prisoners become eligible for release, what parole board hearings are like, and the challenges that newly released prisoners face during reentry. **Reentry** is defined as any activity or program dedicated to preparing and integrating parolees back into a community as law-abiding citizens and using a

reentry
The process of preparing and integrating parolees into the community as law-abiding citizens using a collaborative approach with parole officers and treatment providers.

desistance
A life course change process from behaving in a dysfunctional and criminal way to replacing old behaviors with new thinking patterns, habits and law-abiding behaviors.

collaborative approach with parole officers, treatment providers, and citizens. The goal of community reentry is crime **desistance**, by which prisoners change dysfunctional and criminal behaviors into new habits that keep them out of the criminal justice system (Bahr et al., 2005).

ISSUES IN REENTRY

Not only do returning prisoners face daily situations very different from life behind bars but their very identities as to how they define themselves must change, so that over time others see them differently. O'Brien (2001, p. 61) explains:

> An ex-offender not only has to construct a new self based on the personal desire to create a non-criminal life, but also has to deal in some way with others' expectations. Such expectations are often derived from ignorance, outdated notions, or judgmental preconceptions. The person who is trying to harmonize self and role, therefore, has the added difficulty of remolding and reformulating others' expectations of him or her self.

As ex-offenders begin to realize how others view them, they must be prepared to redeem and heal themselves, shed the prisoner role, resist the stigma associated with being a felon, and assume new responsibilities and roles of parent, spouse, family member, worker, and neighbor, among others (Opsal, 2011). Box 11.1 examines

BOX 11.1   COMMUNITY CORRECTIONS UP CLOSE

What Might It Be Like to Transition from Prison to the Community?

Imagine that you've just gotten out of prison after spending three years of your life locked up in a boring routine you grew accustomed to. Now that you're out you want to celebrate, get back with your old friends, and try to catch up on the time you lost. After all, there's a lot of catching up to do. The people and situations you remember seem different, however. When you return to your neighborhood, you realize that the people who were doing well have moved on and all you see there now are those not doing so well. They'll be glad to lend you a couple of bucks or get you drunk so you can celebrate. But those were the people in the situation that aided and abetted your getting into this mess to begin with. What now? You burned your bridges with your brothers, who won't talk to you. Your mother will let you stay with her only until you can get on your feet again, but you don't know how long her support will last. You have a daughter who has been living with her (her grandmother); she is now five years old and doesn't even know you. You desperately want to connect with her but don't feel confident you have the skills to make the first move. You also feel guilty for not being able to repay your mom for raising your two sons and are

afraid you'll never be able to pay her back. Although you feel a huge sense of urgency, at the time same time fear and depression have set in, and you wonder whether leaving prison early was a mistake.

Like most people who relocate to a new state, offenders need to obtain identification cards, change their address, locate housing, and find a job. If relocation isn't stressful enough, think of the additional challenges of finding a job when you have only a high school education or GED, of having to explain a transient (or nonexistent) employment record, and of bearing the stigma of admitting your felony record. Many people who relocate know when they are moving, whereas often offenders in prison do not know their exact release date very far in advance, which presents an obstacle to plan for anything other than "Who's coming to pick me up?" Other difficulties include overcoming a drug or alcohol addiction, managing stress and anger, and avoiding temptations that lead to the beginnings of bad habits. Most offenders who do not make the transition fall short within the first six months after they leave prison. The reentry process therefore starts while prisoners are incarcerated and attempts to bridge this crucial phase.

what it is like to get out of prison so you can better understand some of the needs and challenges former prisoners face in coming back to the larger community.

As Box 11.1 illustrates, a number of challenges stand between an offender and successful reentry. First, recently released offenders, though likely indigent, still need an identification card, clothes, and bus pass; up to one third also need medication for a physical and/or psychological condition (LaVigne, 2006). They may not be eligible for certain benefits so that their prerelease institution needs to assist them in applying to various programs, which can take a few months for approval.

Second, it is often necessary to actually make appointments for ex-offenders rather than simply handing them a list of referrals. Given federal regulations against openly sharing medical records coupled with the fact that most offenders do not leave prison with medical records in hand, some releasees experience a dangerous lag between the time when their medications run out and when they are able to see a doctor to obtain prescription refills. Because some ex-offenders lack the initiative or education to find a service provider right for their situation, they are more likely to follow through if they are expected to appear for a prescheduled appointment.

Third, parolees and other recently released offenders have other survival needs to meet, such as finding and maintaining stable employment, finding suitable housing, and staying clean of illegal drugs. They also require transportation to find employment, to go to work, and to attend treatment sessions. Their health care can be overlooked in light of all the other responsibilities that need their attention (Hammett, Roberts, and Kennedy, 2001). In addition to education and employment services, female parolees also have reported needs for protection from abusive relationships in the community, child advocacy, and assistance with family reunification (Richie, 2001). Even after incarceration for as little as two months, female releasees experienced shifts in family structure, such as from separation, divorce, and changing location of dependent children (Arditti and Few, 2006).

Parole officers understood their role in referring parolees on the basis of their needs to community agencies and in assisting ex-prisoners with successful community reentry (Seiter, 2002). When asked to ascertain the most important features of successful reentry programs, steady employment was mentioned by parole officers as the key element, followed by ex-prisoners remaining drug free, having positive social support systems, and experiencing plenty of structure through daily activities (Seiter, 2002).

Prisoner Perspectives on Getting Out

Craig Hemmens and his research team interviewed 775 newly released inmates (over a few minutes to a few hours) as they waited for their bus to take them back to their hometowns. Hemmens (1998) found that older releasees and ones who had served shorter sentences reported less apprehension about reentry. Ex-prisoners who had served sentences of three years or less conveyed significantly less apprehension about successful reentry compared with those who had served sentences of four years or more. Because this study was cross-sectional, none of the prisoners were subsequently tracked to determine whether they did succeed. Prisoners generally have good intentions and plan on staying out of prison upon release. Many releasees do attempt to live a legitimate life by finding employment, but they experience a great deal of stress and of being objects of disdain during their transition period.

One such individual was Robert Grooms (1982), who wrote about the perils of release from prison and why, despite all the advantages he had over most other former convicts upon release, he did not make a success. When he was released, Grooms experienced problems finding a job, found he had nothing in common with old friends, and felt uncomfortable around "square-johns." He wrote:

I had another problem common among recently released prisoners. I wanted to make up all at once for lost time. I wanted the things that others my age had worked years to achieve, and I wanted them right away (p. 543).

Grooms could not "sit still" and he did not want to be alone, so he began to hang around places at which he felt comfortable. He found himself talking with ex-convicts in taverns about what they had in common: crime, the prison experience, and violence. Grooms concluded:

When he is released, a prisoner is in a real sense cast out into a totally alien society. Overnight he is expected to discard months and years of self-survival tactics, to change his values, to readjust to situations and circumstances that he had long forgotten, and to accept responsibility. More important, he has to overcome, in a society that rejects him, his lack of self-worth; he has to become accepted where he is not wanted. Is it any wonder that so many newly released prisoners feel out of their natural environment, that many first-time, petty offenders leave prison and find someone weak to prey on, or that the recidivism rate is so high (p. 545)?

Ex-prisoner apprehension is in part a reaction to social alienation, lack of support, and lack of preparation for release into an environment that requires taking on immediate responsibilities, such as paying rent, looking for employment, sustaining a job, and abiding by supervision conditions. Figure 11.1 depicts a map of the number of legal barriers that each state has imposed upon ex-felons. (We discuss these barriers in detail in Chapter 14.) Notice that states vary widely on how restrictive they can be, with the number of restrictions ranging from 10 up to 48. Too many pressures like these can lead to self-sabotage in some cases. On the bright side, even marginal employment opportunities can serve for offenders over age 26 as a turning point in desisting from crime (Uggen, 2000).

FIGURE 11.1 Number of Legal Barriers During Prisoner Reentry

Source: Legal Action Center. 2011. After prison: Roadblocks to reentry. Available from: http://www.lac.org/roadblocks-to-reentry/main.php?view=national#

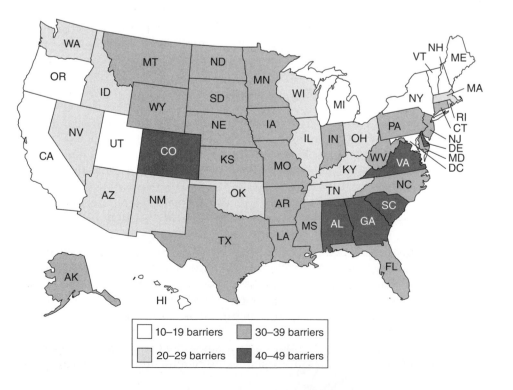

The Prisoner's Family

Reentry not only affects ex-prisoners, but it is also a vulnerable time for their families, potential employers, any victims, and surrounding community. A prisoner's family has suffered during the period of incarceration from the stigma of having a loved one behind bars. More than 1.5 million children under age 18 have at least one parent who is currently incarcerated. A significant number of prisoners' children is raised by extended family members such as grandparents, aunts, or sisters. As years go by, prisoners with long sentences tend to receive less family financial support and fewer face-to-face visits and letters. Even when ex-prisoners are released into a community, only between 24–54% have someone to meet them at the prison or to pick them up at a bus station to take them home (Seiter & Kadela, 2003; LaVigne, 2006). If an ex-prisoner had been supporting dependents prior to arrest, years of financial and emotional neglect will have changed these relationships. For offenders' families, reentry means that these ties must be reestablished or mended.

Yet with all these difficulties, families remain supportive when prisoners are released, helping them find job and places to live. From a lifespan perspective, families can effect a change in ex-prisoner behavior away from drug use and other dysfunctional habits to healthier, socially acceptable lifestyles. Friends have been found to be less supportive than families because of the formers' tendency to influence an offender to return to unproductive and illegal behavior (Bahr et al., 2005). About 80% of prisoners lived with one or more family members upon release. As Bahr and colleagues observed, family support was found to be instrumental in overall offender success and reduction of recidivism (LaVigne, 2006). An example of a New York reentry program using a family case management technique is PARTNER, which stands for *Parolees and Relatives Toward Newly Enhanced Relationships*. A team consists of a family case manager from La Bodega, a New York parole officer, an offender, and that offender's family. The case manager visits the offender's family and conducts a needs assessment prior to the offender's release. PARTNER is a model program of how communities and government agencies can work together to enhance prisoner reentry (Lehman et al., 2002).

Justice Reinvestment in Disadvantaged Communities

We know that the locations where parolees reside are *not* evenly spread within a community. Rather, a larger number of parolees originates from disadvantaged and economically impoverished areas that have a high amount of unemployment, open drug use, and community instability and disorganization. As more and more prisoners return to the same communities, these actually become *less cohesive and more unstable*, with a potential to become more criminogenic (Seiter & Kadela, 2003).

One positive idea used to help disadvantaged communities and to encourage states to save money on incarceration expenses is called **Justice Reinvestment** (Tucker & Cadora, 2003). States that indicate (and can later show evidence) they will reduce their prison populations receive federal funding to be used for employment programs, libraries, schools, and public housing in high crime neighborhoods. By opening a community-based clinic for basic mental and physical health needs conveniently located near ex-offenders' homes, the Justice Reinvestment program is a way to establish **continuity of care**. Data must show measurable declines in prison population without indicating subsequent increases in public safety problems (Clear, 2011).

Similarly to the Justice Reinvestment program, reentry can encompass restorative justice and civic community service using a model of civic engagement,

Justice Reinvestment
Federal funding available for employment programs, libraries, schools, and social services in disadvantaged neighborhoods if states can show evidence that they have reduced their prison populations with no increase in the crime rate or increased safety issues.

continuity of care
Ensuring that a newly released prisoner has access to receiving necessary mental health medication and medical services in the community as were provided in jail or prison.

provided a community is willing to accept an offender's return (Bazemore & Stinchcomb, 2004). Other experts argue that reentry encompasses more than community acceptance:

> The reentry philosophy is based on the belief that police, courts, institutions, and community corrections all have a role in creating significant, long-term rehabilitative change for offenders. This philosophy assumes that criminal justice agencies cannot create long-lasting change for offenders without the inclusion of the family, community-based service providers, and the faith community (Wilkinson, Rhine, & Henderson-Hurley, 2005, p. 160).

This means that reentry is based on more than just criminal justice and to be truly successful must overlap with workforce development, family or social policy, and health policy. This is why the federal government began various community-based reentry initiatives with funding from the Department of Justice, the Department of Labor, and the Department of Health and Human Services.

Community-Based Reentry Initiatives

Successful reentry includes prerelease planning, community referrals, quick access to benefit programs, and continuity of care between that received at the institution and in the new community situation (Hammett, Roberts, & Kennedy, 2001). Programs that support the reentry of criminal offenders have increased over time, particularly with respect to housing, job placement, mentoring services, and faith-based initiatives (Wilkinson and Rhine 2005). Reentry partnerships have formed with faith-based organizations and grassroots community groups in neighborhoods that receive a disproportionate number of ex-prisoners returning to the streets (Robinson & Travis, 2000). Reentry partnerships do not necessarily entail more resources—they merely involve using existing resources in a smarter and more holistic way by collaborating with other agencies in criminal justice and in the larger community. Let's examine a few of these as examples.

reentry courts
A collaborative, team-based program that aims to improve the link between parole supervision and treatment providers to help recent parolees become stabilized.

REENTRY COURTS **Reentry courts** are a collaborative, team-based program that occurs after prison with the aim of improving the link between parole supervision and treatment providers. Reentry court programs initially identify and begin to work with offenders prior to release. After release, an offender has structured court appointments with a reentry team, which coordinates job training, housing, substance abuse treatment, and transportation. Reentry courts are similar to drug courts in that they use judges, court hearings, and graduated sanctions and incentives to reward positive behavior and predictably punish negative behavior. They operate on contracts that keep offenders law abiding for fear of returning to prison (Robinson & Travis, 2000). Two examples are discussed below.

A Colorado reentry court has the goal of reintegrating parolees under mandatory release who have a dual diagnosis of mental illness and a substance abuse problem. A parolee initially meets with an administrative law judge within 14 days of leaving prison. The judge, together with the offender, the parole officer, and the mental health treatment provider establishes monthly goals, and this group meets every month for one year to revisit these reentry goals (Robinson & Travis, 2000).

Another reentry court in East Harlem targeted nonviolent felons who had at least two convictions. The program had three phases, which one third of participants had successfully completed; the other two thirds were in an earlier stage of the program. Initial evaluations of 45 participants found that 22% were convicted of committing a new crime while under a one-year supervision by the

© AP Images/John Harrell

The Plainfield Reentry Facility in Indiana provides jobs to inmates such as working in a deli and customer service skills that offenders need to successfully integrate back into society.

reentry court. When the 45 participants were compared with a matched group of 90 parolees who did not attend reentry court, the two groups showed similar recidivism rates (Farole, 2003). Even though these sample sizes are too small to make any general statements about reentry courts, researchers need to better understand factors that promote success after prison. Preliminary analyses of a reentry preparation program called Project Greenlight compared participants with a matched group of parolees and found that Greenlight participants performed no better than regular parolees (Wilson & Davis, 2006). Until more is learned about why ex-prisoners return to prison, an increased attention to the need of prisoners for substantial assistance with reentry has certainly been a step in the right direction.

DAY REPORTING AND/OR DISTRICT RESOURCE CENTERS   Nonresidential programs for parolees released to a community are known as either day reporting centers or district resource centers (DRCs). Both types of DRCs are similar in that they offer services for the first six months for parolees recently released. While a parolee is looking for a job during the day, classes are offered at night. The focus is on three main areas: substance abuse counseling, anger management, and cognitive-behavioral approaches. In addition, employment assistance classes are offered to help parolees obtain a job.

ELIGIBILITY FOR PAROLE

The first step in the reentry process is that an offender be eligible for parole consideration. Those permanently ineligible for release include offenders on death row, offenders serving life *without* parole, and some habitual offenders sentenced under statutes such as "three strikes and you're out."

Time Sheets and Eligibility Dates

For the remainder of inmates (those with mandatory or discretionary releases), a computer keeps track of all good time earned and number of days served to determine minimum and maximum eligibility dates. The **minimum eligibility date** is the shortest amount of time defined by statute, minus good time earned, that must be served before an offender can go before a parole board. In some states, such as Nebraska, parole boards are required to see offenders once per year even if the minimum eligibility date has not yet been met (Proctor, 1999). The **maximum eligibility date** is the longest amount of time that can be served before an offender must, by law, be released (whereupon an offender has "maxed out" his or her sentence).

Good time (or "gain time") was originally introduced as an incentive by prison authorities for institutional good conduct. Good time reduces the period of sentence an inmate must serve before parole eligibility. Now good time is automatically granted (in states that offer it) unless an inmate commits a disciplinary infraction. That is, good time is lost for misbehavior in prison rather than awarded for good behavior. Good-time credits vary greatly from state to state, ranging from five days per month to as many as 45 days per month. In recent years large amounts of good time have been temporarily awarded by correctional authorities (for example, 120 days for every month served) to reduce prison overcrowding and avoid lawsuits. When jail and prison crowding subsides, good time is decreased to the regular amount.

Typically a case manager at each prison institution submits good time earned (or in some cases submits good time lost for misbehavior) to a parole board or division within the Department of Corrections that prepares status or time sheets. Offenders receive an updated time sheet every six months to one year so they know when to expect their first parole hearing.

Prisoners generally become eligible for release upon completion of their minimum sentence. The manner in which a **parole eligibility date** is established varies from state to state. Mandatory minimum states require that between 50%–85% of an entire sentence be served before a prisoner first becomes eligible. Other discretionary parole states require a prisoner to have served one third of an imposed sentence to be eligible for consideration for early parole. However, most statutes allow further reductions in an eligibility date through credit for time served in jail before sentencing and good-time credits. Federal law provides mandatory parole when an offender has served two thirds of a term of five years or longer, unless he or she has amassed serious disciplinary infractions in prison or there is a high probability of recidivism (U.S. Parole Commission, 2006).

Some states credit good time to an offender upon arrival in prison and calculate eligibility date by subtracting credited good time from the maximum sentence. A prisoner who is serving a 15-year sentence and receiving standard good time of 20 days per month (i.e., 50 days' credit on his or her sentence for each 30 days served) would thus be eligible for parole consideration after 40 months. As a first parole eligibility date approaches, institutional case managers (also called institutional parole officers in some states) prepare an individualized prerelease plan for a parole board.

Prerelease Preparation within the Institution

Some prisoners are fortunate to be transferred to a prerelease program within the criminal justice system in preparation for their release. A **prerelease facility** is a minimum-security residential program that houses prisoners who have earned this privilege through good institutional conduct and are within two years of their release date. Prerelease facilities provide increased opportunities for job readiness, education, housing assistance, and furloughs. Faith-based volunteer programs (e.g., *Welcome Back* programs) educate offenders about networks of social support agencies that can assist with the release process in their locale. Texas uses "state jails" specifically for offenders who are within two years of release.

Halfway houses and work release are also types of residential prerelease facilities used prior to parole. Richards and Jones (1997) interviewed 30 men who were released from prison and transferred to a halfway house as a form of graduated release. One prisoner explained the pressures of getting behind in rent upon his arrival at the halfway house:

> You leave the penitentiary on a Tuesday, you come here [to the halfway house], and you're broke for the whole week or two till they send your money from the penitentiary. What kind of shit is that? Ya know, I mean a man come home from the penitentiary they don't even give you gate money. They give you $5 [and] bus fare. . . . I owe for [bed] sheets, owe for bus tokens, I owe for my rent. You're automatically 2 weeks behind in rent, see what I'm saying. . . . I didn't ask to come here and be put in the hole by your all program. Ya all know that when I come here it would take a while for me to find a job (pp. 13–14).

One of the issues likely to affect offender success rates is financial pressure, which builds not only from daily living expenses but also from having to set aside money for paying court costs, fees, victim restitution, and back child support that accumulated while behind bars. Despite this some states, such as Washington, believe in the importance of work release and prerelease centers, sending between 30%–40% of all prisoners there before parole release. This rate is considered quite high compared with most other states surveyed (Austin, 2001; Fehr, 2004).

Prison institutions prepare a **prerelease plan** while an offender is still incarcerated. This includes a summary of institutional conduct and program participation as well as plans for housing and employment upon release. Some states employ case hearing officers to interview each prisoner, prepare a case summary, and report directly to a parole board with their recommendation. Other states submit case summaries and written reports along with a case file. Preparing some form of prerelease plan in advance of a scheduled parole hearing has three main advantages:

1. A prerelease plan increases an offender's chances of parole because it solidifies living arrangements and work opportunities.
2. A prerelease plan saves time during a parole board hearing.
3. Ties to a community will likely increase an offender's success on parole and make it less likely that this offender will return to crime.

An institutional case manager interviews a prisoner to document exactly where he or she will be living and the names of any household members. A different (local) field parole officer interviews household members to ensure that an address is valid and checks whether it is an acceptable place for an offender to live. Positive family relations increase a likelihood of parole. Offenders are discouraged from paroling to themselves, which means living and supporting oneself without any assistance. Because most offenders at time of release from prison do not have the money required for rent and utility deposits, the vast majority must parole to an existing household of a friend or relative. In an effort to assist in community reintegration, paroling employable offenders to a halfway house or community residential center is helpful.

An institutional case manager documents the amount of money an ex-prisoner has in savings and any job leads or specific employment plans he or she has. According to Petersilia (2000b), most offenders leave prison without any savings and with

prerelease plan
A case management summary of institutional conduct and program participation, as well as plans for housing and employment upon release, that is submitted to the parole board in cases of discretionary parole or to the parole officer in cases of automatic release.

few solid job prospects. The case manager then summarizes any programs an offender has attended or completed (e.g., general equivalency diploma courses) while in prison and lists all disciplinary infractions (write-ups) received during the entire period of incarceration.

Essentially the case manager brings together official data (e.g., current conviction, current age, amount of time served for current conviction, number of prior prison incarcerations, number and type of prior convictions) and data about an offender's education level, employment history, and substance abuse history. All of the information is scored in a systematic way, and a report is provided to a parole board for a parole hearing. This report is prepared according to predefined state parole guidelines and is used by a parole board much like a probation officer's presentence investigation report by a judge at time of sentencing. Time is saved during the hearing because the parole board does not have to search through offender files (many of which are fairly thick) to find the factors that measure the risk level an offender will pose when released.

THE PAROLE BOARD AND RELEASING AUTHORITY

parole board
An administrative body empowered to decide whether inmates shall be conditionally released from prison before the completion of their sentence, to revoke parole, and to discharge from parole those who have satisfactorily completed their terms.

The prison releasing authority is a group of individuals that have authority to release prisoners prior to completion of their sentence. Traditionally this group has been known as a **parole board**, but as determinate sentencing replaced indeterminate sentencing in 16 states, the name attached to this group has varied by state. This text uses the more traditional term of *parole board* to apply to any prison releasing authority, regardless of its sentencing framework, for two reasons: (1) most states have a mixed sentencing structure with elements of both determinate and indeterminate sentencing; and (2) *even in states with determinate sentencing structures,* 75% still retain a releasing authority group with discretionary release (Kinnevy & Caplan, 2008).

Parole boards have four basic functions:

1. to decide when individual prisoners should be released;
2. to determine any special conditions of parole supervision;
3. to successfully discharge a parolee when conditions have been met; and
4. to determine whether parole privileges should be revoked if conditions are violated.

Some parole boards have additional functions, such as granting furloughs, reviewing pardons and executive clemency decisions made by a governor, restoring civil rights to ex-offenders, and granting reprieves in death sentence cases. Each state establishes the extent of its own parole board's authority.

Although most parole boards are independent entities, they are appointed by a governor or director of the Department of Corrections for a term that ranges from three to seven years (average of 4.8 years). Only two states (Ohio and Wisconsin) have appointed members for life. The size of the group ranges from three to 19 members, with an average of seven board members. The chair of the board and all board members in 28 states are full-time salaried employees, and the rest are part-time employees paid per diem (Paparozzi & Caplan, 2009).

A gubernatorial appointment must be confirmed by a legislature. Parole board members must possess integrity, intelligence, and good judgment to command respect and public confidence. Board members should have sufficiently broad academic training and experience to be qualified for professional practice in fields such as criminology, education, psychology, law, social work, and sociology. Each member must have the capacity and desire to learn and understand legal processes, the dynamics of human behavior, and the cultural conditions contributing to crime. Ideally parole board members have previous professional expertise that has given them intimate knowledge of the situations and problems confronting offenders—that is, of the human experience (Paparozzi & Caplan, 2009).

The Parole Hearing

Once prisoner eligibility for release has been determined, an offender is scheduled for a parole hearing date. Parole board members have access to an entire offender case file with a summary report completed by the institutional case manager. As previously mentioned, some hearing examiners scrutinize only a case file without interviewing an offender, whereas other parole boards have access to both a case file and an offender in person. In the federal system a sentencing judge, an assistant U.S. attorney, and a defense attorney can all make written recommendations to a parole board. Federal prisoners can later request a copy of their parole hearing recording under the Freedom of Information Act (U.S. Parole Commission, 2006).

Parole board hearings serve many purposes, which include:

1. to resolve inconsistencies in available information directly from an offender, a victim, or other parties;
2. to review institutional program participation and institutional conduct to better understand behavior while confined and indications of change;
3. to consider an offender's motivation for parole; and
4. to consider input from a victim and other interested parties.

Parole board hearings are tape-recorded and conducted in one of three ways: in person, by video teleconference, or the board views a hard-copy paper file without meeting the person. Face-to-face parole board hearings are the most common of the three and take place at the prison in which an eligible prisoner is located. Hearings in person allow a prisoner to be in the same room with a parole board. Some boards conduct parole release hearings using videoconference technology (see Box 11.2), which has greatly reduced a need to travel to each prison while allowing an opportunity to

BOX 11.2 TECHNOLOGY IN CORRECTIONS

Federal Parole Hearings Videoconference

The Parole Commission used to travel to more than 60 facilities all over the United States to conduct parole release and revocation hearings face-to-face. Prisoners facing parole release hearings met with the Commission in a prerelease facility. Prisoners facing revocation hearings traveled by airplane from a local jail to a central transfer facility in Oklahoma or to a detention center in Philadelphia within a 90-day period. Following their revocation hearing, they would again travel to wherever the Commission felt was best to place them.

Using videoconferencing, Parole Commission members can remain in Maryland while prisoners can visibly and audibly interact with them from any federal facility in the United States. The technology was initially tried with parole release hearings. The Commission found that

"video and audio transmissions are clear and the hearings are seldom interrupted by technical difficulties . . . [and] the prisoner's ability to effectively participate in the hearing has not been diminished" (U.S. Department of Justice, 2005, p. 19262). Videoconferencing saves travel time and money for Commission members as well as the travel time, money, and risk involved in transferring prisoners. The practice has been so successful with parole release hearings that it was extended to revocation hearings.

U.S. Department of Justice. 2005. 28 CFR Part 2: Paroling, recommitting, and supervising federal prisoners: Prisoners serving sentences under the U.S and D.C. Codes. *Federal Register* 70 (70), April 13, 2005, p. 19262.

A parole board asks questions to determine a prisoner's readiness for early community release.

Courtesy of Leanne Fiftal Alarid

ask and answer questions. File review parole hearings offer no face-to-face contact with a prisoner, and a board makes a decision based only on documents submitted by prison officials.

A video or face-to-face parole hearing is attended by one to three board members (or *hearing examiners*) who represent an entire board (West-Smith, Pogrebin, & Poole, 2000). In a face-to-face hearing, one hearing examiner thoroughly reviews the file and leads with most questions. If other members are present, they review the file less thoroughly and ask supplemental questions from a different angle or ask follow-up questions to those of the leading parole board member. At least two signatures are required to parole a person convicted of a nonviolent crime (West-Smith, Pogrebin, & Poole, 2000), but most states average three required signatures (Kinnevy & Caplan, 2008).

Parole Hearing Attendees

Parole boards consider input from other sources to assist them in making their decision. Each state varies as to who can attend a hearing and how that information must be conveyed (whether in person, through written correspondence, by telephone, or videotaped). Some states allow an offender's family at parole hearings, but most do not permit legal representation for an offender. Prosecutors, law enforcement, and victims directly involved in an offender's case are invited to make a statement. Relatives or potential employers may write letters or submit a videotaped statement for use at a hearing. The federal system limits each offender to one representative to make a statement on his or her behalf (U.S. Parole Commission, 2006). Box 11.3 illustrates the specific process of the parole board in the state of Oklahoma.

Written correspondence through a victim impact statement is the most common form of correspondence accepted from victims. A **victim impact statement** addresses how a crime has taken a toll physically, emotionally, financially, and/or psychologically on a victim and a victim's family. Many victim impact statements cite how the victim continues to experience psychological, physical, and/or financial difficulties as a direct result of the actions of the offender (Bernat, Parsonage, & Helfgott, 1994). States such as Alabama specify that impact statements be confidential because of concern that prisoners might attempt to further

victim impact statement
A written account by the victim(s) as to how the crime has taken a toll physically, emotionally, financially, or psychologically on the victim and the victim's family. Victim impact statements are considered by many states at time of sentencing and at parole board hearings.

BOX 11.3   COMMUNITY CORRECTIONS UP CLOSE

The Parole Process in Oklahoma

A five-member parole board in Oklahoma meets quarterly to decide on approximately 800 cases, or about 3,200 cases per year. Half of all cases are decided on the basis of offenders' files alone, while the remainder involve a face-to-face meeting with an offender at a single prison over a four-day period (about 100 face-to-face cases per day). An initial Stage 1 meeting with an offender averages about five minutes, and family supporters may attend at the same time. Three out of five parole board members must vote in favor of moving a case to a Stage 2 hearing. If a case at Stage 1 does not receive a requisite number of votes, a parole date is automatically deferred.

All Stage 2 hearings take place about one month after Stage 1 hearings. During Stage 2 parole opponents are invited to attend, such as a victim, a victim's family, and the district attorney who prosecuted a case. Again a hearing at Stage 2 must obtain a voting majority by the board. As in Stage 1, if a Stage 2 process does not receive the requisite votes, a case is deferred until later.

In the third and final stage in the process, each board recommendation is reviewed by a governor. A governor's signature is the final step in a two-month process. Of the 3,200 cases that go up for parole, an estimated 1,000 are granted each year.

Source: Tribune Media Services. 2003. *Parole Board: Oklahoma.* [DVD—47 minutes]. Ordered through http://www.bio.com

---

harm their victim(s) for opposing that offender's release. Other states, such as Arizona and Oklahoma, are more proactive, because they allow victims to veto (refuse) a parole release decision if they had requested notification of a hearing but were not given a chance to contribute their opinion (Bernat, Parsonage, & Helfgott, 1994).

Parole Risk Assessment

Given concerns about discrepant decision making in the 1970s, there was a movement toward the use of objective guidelines in a release decision. Parole decisions were made more transparent and parole authorities were held accountable for their decisions through the use of parole guidelines, which also made such decisions more rational and consistent. Researchers soon found that parole decisions could be quantitatively predicted by using age, offense seriousness, and prior institutional commitments to predict a risk of recidivism. The **Salient Factor Score** (SFS) was developed for use by the Federal Parole Commission that assigned a numerical score to each variable thought to predict risk of committing a future crime. The higher the score, the less likely the probability of recidivism.

Over 80% of releasing authorities now use some type of decision-making instrument or risk assessment that includes numeric scoring. Although some risk assessments have been developed in house by a state's Department of Corrections, other states have taken to using valid tools sold by private companies, such as the Level of Service Inventory-Revised (which is also used in the supervision of offenders), the COMPAS, and the Static-99 for sex offenders (Kinnevy & Caplan, 2008). Although no prediction device is 100% accurate, risk-prediction instruments that contain variables statistically related to reduction of criminal behavior can predict different probabilities of recidivism with a small number of known variables.

In an age of evidence-based practices, researchers are fine-tuning parole risk-prediction instruments according to other characteristics, such as gender. Because female parolees have always shown lower recidivism rates than male parolees according to traditional instruments, a model was developed to more accurately

FACT or **FICTION?**

Victims have no influence on a parole board's decision to release.

Fiction.
Fact: Victims who appear in person at parole hearings to contest release are most persuasive, but even victims who send letters are significantly more effective in convincing a parole board to deny release than are those who take no action (Morgan & Smith, 2005).

salient factor score
The parole guidelines developed and used by the U.S. Parole Commission for making parole release decisions. Served as the model for parole guidelines developed in many other jurisdictions.

predict success and failure rates for female parolees. Researchers found that age at first arrest, age at release, release status (i.e., new release or parole violator), and number of prior arrests most accurately predicted parole failure of women (McShane, Williams, & Dolny, 2002). Other generalizations about success on parole can be found in Box 11.4.

The Parole Board Decision

The top three factors that releasing authorities indicate make an impact on their releasing decisions are crime severity, crime type, and offender criminal history. A victim's input has the next degree of impact, followed by inputs from an offender's family and from a district attorney (Kinnevy & Caplan, 2008). In their aim to maximize both public safety and offender rehabilitation, parole boards also base their decision on a number of criteria, including an offender's:

- probability of recidivism;
- risk to community safety;

Box 11.4   COMMUNITY CORRECTIONS UP CLOSE

Evidence-Based Findings About Risk and Post-Prison Release Success

There is such an abundance of prediction instruments and discussion on prisoner risk that it sometimes is difficult to determine key factors in the likelihood of recidivism after release from prison. All evidence points to eight central risk factors, of which the more match an offender, the more likely he or she will return to crime in the future:

1. *criminal identity*—attitudes and beliefs are supportive of crime;
2. *antisocial personality disorder*—lack of concern for others or for rules, blaming others, irritable, aggressive;
3. *early and persistent involvement in law-breaking behavior* (conviction record, number of incarcerations, number of parole or probation revocations);
4. *significant others or close associates are antisocial;*
5. *lack of nurturing and supportive relationships;*
6. *alcohol and/or drug abuse;*
7. *low levels of performance in school and employment* (education level, reading ability, work history); and
8. *lack of interest in legitimate leisure, hobbies, and recreational pursuits.*

Surprisingly, the risk factors that are less often linked to whether an offender will recidivate but that are still a main focus of many parole boards are seriousness or type of current offense, whether an offense is a sex crime, offender age, gender, and presence of mental illness.

Some risk factors, like one's past criminal record, cannot be changed. However, most major risk factors *can be altered*

by an offender, and confinement is an ideal time to begin the change process. The three best ways that a prisoner can prepare for success on the outside while still confined are:

1. to complete meaningful treatment interventions before release—that is, to change thinking patterns, take responsibility for actions, and stop blaming everyone else;
2. to maintain contact with positive and supportive family members via mail, phone, or in-person visits; and
3. to develop a solid prerelease plan, which includes living arrangements and job leads.

After a prisoner is released, factors shown to reduce recidivism while on parole are:

- cognitive-behavioral treatment programs for high-risk offenders;
- concentrated treatment services combined with parole supervision over the first few weeks of release (e.g., day reporting center);
- strong employment ties and assistance in finding employment;
- stable relationships with significant family members;
- assistance in obtaining identification, clothing, and medication; and
- mentors available at time of release.

Source: National Research Council. 2008. *Parole, desistance from crime, and community integration*. Washington, DC: National Academies Press.

- conduct and program participation while in confinement; and
- sufficiency of release plan.

A parole board makes a decision on each case based on three possible options: to grant parole, to deny parole, or to defer to a later date. A decision to *grant* parole results in scheduling a conditional release before an expiration of a maximum term of imprisonment. Release decisions require the vote of two out of three board members to grant parole for that region. Crimes of a violent or sexual nature can require a **full board review**—that is, that all members of a parole board review a case. If so, all board members meet with the chair at a central office for a few days out of every month. A violent or sex offender is paroled if the full board decides by a majority or quorum vote that he or she should be released. In Colorado a quorum is defined as four of seven members who recommend release (West-Smith, Pogrebin, & Poole, 2000).

A parole *denial* results in continued imprisonment. In the federal system, a denial of parole on a sentence less than seven years in length allows an offender to automatically go before a board again in 18 months. A sentence longer than seven years delays the next parole board hearing for another two years (U.S. Parole Commission, 2006). See Box 11.5 for further discussion of how a parole board fares in its decisions to release compared with mandatory parolees who do not go up before a parole board.

full board review
The statutory requirement that all members of the parole board review and vote on the early release from prison of individuals who have committed felony crimes, usually of a violent or sexual nature. Some states require this type of review on every discretionary release.

BOX 11.5   HOW DO PAROLE BOARDS PERFORM?

Comparing Parolees Released by a Parole Board With Those Released Under Mandatory Supervision

Hughes and colleagues (2001) were interested in comparing the performance of parolees on mandatory release with those released by a parole board. Unconditional releases were not part of the sample. Over a 10-year period, the rates of success of discretionary parolees varied between 50%–56%, whereas mandatory parolees were successful only 24%–33% of the time. They concluded: "In every year between 1990 and 1999, state prisoners released by a parole board had higher success rates than those released through mandatory parole" (p. 11).

A more recent study measured recidivism by rearrest over a two-year period, using a sample of 30,624 prisoners released from 15 states (Solomon, 2006). The sample was divided into three groups: unconditional (no supervision), mandatory supervised release, and discretionary parole release. The unconditional releasees served the most time behind bars and more of them had previously been arrested for violent offenses than either of the other two groups, suggesting that they were significantly more disconnected from community ties than were supervised parolees. Despite this difference, mandatory supervised releasees and unconditional releasees recidivated at the same rate—61% and 62%, respectively, over the two-year period. A slightly lower rate—54%—of those released on discretionary parole by a parole board recidivated.

Even when technical violators were removed from the data, those committing new crimes did not change under the three types of supervision because most rearrests were for new crimes rather than for technical violations. Although technical violators are taken into custody, official statistics do not record them as *arrests*. In interpreting the overall recidivism findings among the three groups, Solomon (2006, pp. 31–32) says:

> Clearly there is a value judgment being made here, in characterizing a four-percentage point difference as "relatively small," differing "only slightly." . . . Because parole boards take into account factors such as a prisoner's attitude and motivation level, institutional conduct, preparedness for release and connections to the community . . . I would expect this group to be substantially, rather than marginally, less likely to recidivate. The suggestion here is that lower rearrest rates may be largely due to who is selected for discretionary release rather than discretionary supervision itself, which is not systematically different than mandatory supervision across states.

A release *deferral* means that a parole board has delayed its final decision (to grant or deny parole) until a later time, somewhere between six months and a year. The most common reason for deferrals is that an offender has not yet completed an in-prison treatment program related to his or her offense. For example, a sex offender in some states must complete sex offender treatment before being considered for release, whereas a chronic drug user might have to complete an in-prison substance abuse program. The problem is not that an offender won't complete a program but rather that space available for treatment is limited and an offender must wait for an opening, which many times doesn't occur until after his or her minimum release eligibility date has already passed. The second most common reason for deferrals is administrative delay, such as paperwork is not in order or has not been completed by the Department of Corrections, a victim has not yet provided input (in the 17 states that require a victim impact statement before a board can make a decision), or an offender is at another facility and not available for interview at a scheduled time (Kinnevy & Caplan, 2008).

LEGAL ISSUES IN PAROLE HEARINGS

Prisoners seeking parole have been sentenced to prison and are seeking early privileged release. Insofar as parole is a privilege and not a right, one of the most surprising aspects of the parole process is an inability to challenge parole board decisions. Courts have provided some procedural protections and have articulated criteria for parole conditions and returning parolees to prison. Below are some key court cases in the parole process.

No Due Process Protections

In *Menechino v. Oswald* (1971), a prisoner argued that the New York State Board of Parole's denial of parole was illegal because he had not received a right to counsel, a right to cross-examine witnesses, a right to produce favorable witnesses, and the specification of the grounds upon which the denial decision was based. The court ruled that due process was *not* an issue in parole because parole is a privilege and not a right.

A short time after the *Menechino* case, the U.S. Supreme Court directly addressed the issue of due process in parole release decision making. In *Greenholtz v. Inmates of the Nebraska Penal and Correctional Complex* (1979), prisoners who had been denied parole brought a class action suit against the Nebraska Board of Parole. The U.S. Supreme Court emphasized that parole boards have broad discretion in their decision making, even if this is at times imperfect. Prisoners were afforded a parole hearing and when parole was denied, they were informed how each fell short of qualifying for parole. The Court ruled that this was enough to satisfy due process because "there is a . . . difference between losing what one has and not getting what one wants" (*Greenholtz v. Inmates of the Nebraska Penal and Correctional Complex*, 1979, pp. 9–10). *Greenholtz* required reasonable notice of a parole hearing date (one month before a hearing is reasonable), an initial hearing wherein a prisoner is allowed to present a case, and, if parole is denied, written reasons for denial.

Use of Hearsay, DNA, and No Right to an Attorney

There are some interesting rulings about what types of information can be used during parole board hearings. For example, hearsay evidence may be used in parole release decisions (*Goldberg v. Beeler*, 1999). Parole boards have even been known to deny parole if DNA evidence informally sent by law enforcement or by a crime victim matches a parole candidate with an earlier crime for which he or she was never prosecuted (Johnson & Willing, 2008). DNA evidence does not convict or add time to a sentence for such crimes but just allows a parole board to deny early release for crimes for which an offender was convicted. At the same time, a parole board may not deny parole for false, insufficient, or capricious reasons (*Tucker v. Alabama Board of Pardons and Paroles*, 2000), so there seems to be a fine distinction as to what kinds of information are allowed to become part of a decision.

Prisoners seeking parole do not have a right to be represented by counsel. Although a lawyer is welcome to attend in support of a prisoner, that lawyer may not represent nor speak on behalf of the prisoner during a parole hearing (*Franciosi v. Michigan Parole Board*, 2000). The same court one year earlier also ruled that providing a statement of reasons for denial of parole is not required (*Glover v. Michigan Parole Board*, 1999). Even if a parole board changes its mind about its decision, no due process rights are necessary, provided a prisoner has not actually been released from an institution (*Jago v. Van Curen*, 1981). Admitting guilt or refusing to admit participation in a crime can be used in some jurisdictions as a reason to deny release (*In re Ecklund*, 1999; *Silmon v. Travis*, 2000). Unlike sentencing, parole board decisions are not subject to judicial review if made in accordance with statutory guidelines (*Ramahlo v. Travis*, 2002).

In conclusion, challenges that newly released prisoners confront are the same today as they have been for decades. The new issue facing society is to what degree we are going to support community-based transition programs so that prisoners do not repeat their criminal cycle? For example, to what degree are appropriate employers going to hire someone with a criminal background? In terms of discretionary parole decisions, the trend continues of replacing subjective assessments with quantitative risk assessments that social scientists show reduce propensity to commit future crime. Parole boards certainly have the potential to assume an important role in the release of prisoners, providing that members have the appropriate education, training, and experience for the job (Paparozzi & Guy, 2009). Until parole board membership is valued as a paid professional position that is merit-based rather than a political appointment, quantitative risk assessment will slowly become the method of choice in the prediction of future criminal behavior instead of relying on the political nature and subjective judgment of board members.

SUMMARY

- Reentry programs include those that take place in a prison setting as well as community-based programs that follow up on the transition process.

- Reentry initiatives include reentry courts and collaborations between parole agencies and grassroots community organizations or other criminal justice agencies.

- Issues in reentry affect not only a parolee but his or her family, victim, and community.

- A parolee faces issues related to finding stable employment, locating suitable housing, and reestablishing contact with his or her family. Because most releasees are also under supervision, they face pressure to be careful with whom they associate and to check in with their parole officer.

- There are three types of release from prison—release without any supervision, release under a short period of mandatory supervision by a parole officer, and release under discretionary parole.

- Parole boards have power to decide whether to release prisoners serving sentences with an eligibility for discretionary parole.

- Parole boards determine when revocation of parole and return to prison are necessary.

- Because discretionary parole is defined as a privilege rather than a right, courts have allowed minimal, if any, due process.

DISCUSSION QUESTIONS

1. What issues do prisoners face in preparing for their reentry into a community?

2. How does prisoner reentry potentially affect a victim and/or a victim's family?

3. What issues exist with respect to prisoner reentry and the impact on his or her family?

4. If you were a victim of a violent crime, would you take time to write an impact statement or attend a parole board hearing, knowing the offender would also be there? Why or why not?

5. What are the primary qualifications of a good parole board member? Why are these qualities important?

6. Why are good public relations between a parole board and its outside community necessary?

7. If you were a parole board member, what factors would you consider in attempting to arrive at a fair and just decision? Why?

8. If you were a prisoner, which method of release from prison would you prefer—discretionary or mandatory/automatic? Why?

WEBSITES, VIDEOS, AND PODCASTS

Websites

National Reentry Resource Center
http://www.nationalreentryresourcecenter.org/

The Reentry Policy Council
http://www.reentrypolicy.org

Reentry National Media Outreach Campaign
http://www.reentrymediaoutreach.org

Council of State Government Chart of Reentry Housing Options for Individuals Released From Prison
http://tools.reentrypolicy.org/housing

U.S. Parole Commission
http://www.usdoj.gov/uspc/

Missouri Office of Victim Services: Parole Hearings
http://www.doc.missouri.gov/victims/
victimparolehearings.htm

Ohio Parole Board
http://www.drc.state.oh.us/web/parboard.htm

Texas Parole Release Guidelines
http://www.tdcj.state.tx.us/bpp/new_parole_
guidelines/new_parole_guidelines.html

Videos/Podcasts

Housing and Health at Reentry
http://www.youtube.com/watch?v=Jd3sHnzwMWQ

This 63-minute video is sponsored by the National Reentry Resource Center.

Mentoring Offenders in the Community at Reentry: A Panel Discussion
http://www.youtube.com/watch?v=biuWGlo_39I

This 70-minute video is sponsored by the National Reentry Resource Center.

Reentry of Inmates with Mental Illness
http://www.corrections.com/system/podcast/
file/21/media_20031022.mp3

The podcast discusses mental illnesses amid prison populations and how agencies can plan for the release of prisoners with mental illness.

Reentry Programming
http://www.corrections.com/system/podcast/
file/50/media_20050728.mp3

This podcast reviews supervision of adults on parole and probation.

Reentry and Work
http://www.corrections.com/system/podcast/
file/48/media_20050419.mp3

A podcast discussion of offender reentry programs in the U.S.

State Penitentiary Reintegration: Innovator's Focus
http://www.youtube.com/watch?v=LNLIAuO3pQg

A 17-minute video by Ashland Institute about unconditional prison release.

CASE STUDY EXERCISE

Preparing for Prisoner Reentry

Various systems are used to make release decisions about incarcerated offenders. In states in which sentences are indeterminate, a paroling authority often must make a decision to release an offender and decide when that release should occur. Sentencing laws might determine when an offender is eligible for release, but he or she is not granted a release until a parole authority approves.

In the following cases, a paroling authority must determine whether to release an offender to a community. Factors considered often involve probability of recidivism, victim impact, community impact, conduct of offender in an institution, and release plan offered. Consider these cases and determine whether an offender's release has merit.

CASE A

Joseph, age 28, is serving up to 20 years for two counts of armed robbery. He has already served the mandatory minimum of five years and is being considered for release for the first time. Joseph served a previous sentence for burglary and successfully completed a release period before he committed the current crimes. The victims in both robberies were elderly gas station attendants, and very small amounts of money were obtained from the robberies. The victims remain fearful of the offender, and both indicate that their lives were significantly affected by the experience. Neither victim ever returned to work out of fear of similar future events. While incarcerated Joseph has completed substance abuse treatment for his cocaine dependence, meeting treatment summary calls for his attendance in facility Cocaine Anonymous meetings. He attends such meetings about half of the time they are offered. He has also completed an anger management program, has been assigned to several inmate jobs, and has had no rule violations while incarcerated. Joseph would like to have transitioned to a work release facility, but due to a waiting list he was not able enter its program prior to being considered for release. His community plan is to return to the same community where he committed his crimes, live with his elderly aunt, seek work as a construction laborer, and attend community substance abuse aftercare. He would be under the supervision of a parole officer upon his release, if granted.

CASE B

Fred is a 39-year-old individual serving 14 years for possession with intent to sell a controlled substance. This is his second prison term, having served a six-year sentence for sale of heroin in the 1990s. He was paroled on the first offense after four years and successfully completed parole supervision. However, he was arrested on the current charge within two months of being released from parole supervision. Law enforcement officials reported that he had been under surveillance for several months before the arrest and was suspected of dealing drugs during most of the period under parole supervision. While under supervision, he reported regularly to his parole officer and worked steadily at a job in a warehouse owned by his brother-in-law. There were no known law violations during the period of supervision. Fred's institutional adjustment has been excellent. He attended drug counseling and is a member of the prison Narcotics Anonymous group. He attained his GED certificate and reports that he wants to attend community college when released. He will work for his brother-in-law again when released and live with his sister and her husband until he can afford to rent an apartment. The sheriff in the county in which he would live has protested his parole release, stating that Fred is a manipulative and devious individual who maintains a façade of cooperation and honest living while continuing to sell drugs. Fred has served five years of his current fourteen-year sentence. Institutional counselors recommend his release at this time.

CASE C

Marie is a 55-year-old female who has served 30 years of a 20 years-to-life sentence for murder. She was convicted of killing her two young children (ages two and four years). She reported that her live-in boyfriend would not agree to stay with her as long as she had children. She chose to kill the children to maintain that relationship. She has maintained a near-perfect prison record and is considered by authorities a model inmate. She reports great remorse for her actions. The prison chaplain has counseled her for many years and states that she has been "born again" and "forgiven" for her crimes and sins. Marie works as a chaplain's assistant in the institution and is well thought of by both prisoners and prison officials alike. If paroled, she will work for Prison Ministries in her hometown and will be provided with a place to stay by her employers.

12

Career Pathways in Community Corrections

CHAPTER LEARNING OBJECTIVES

1. Understand how community corrections staff are selected and trained.
2. Identify the types of knowledge, skills, and abilities that staff need to work with offenders in community-based corrections.
3. Analyze important issues for department orientation, such as firearms' policies and stress reduction.
4. Discuss the growth and criticism of private probation agencies and treatment providers.

San Diego County Probation officer handcuffed a probationer in her own home during a multi-agency targeted drug sweep and warrant arrest, where the two waited for police to complete the arrest.

KEY TERMS

preservice training
Peace Officer State Training
in-service training
role ambiguity

role conflict
negligence
absolute immunity
qualified immunity

private probation
private service provider
Section 1983

Kenneth Dupree worked as a parole officer in Philadelphia until 2010. One year after leaving his job, he was officially charged by the state attorney general's office with two counts of bribery, official oppression, and obstruction. Parolees whom Dupree had supervised reported to law enforcement that Dupree had solicited and accepted cash bribes with an understanding that he ignore positive drug tests, among other parolee violations. Dupree also coercively tried to get parolees to do him favors, as in an instance of asking a parolee to steal Corian countertop slabs worth a total of $30,000 from the man's place of employment. A grand jury heard evidence in the case, but Dupree has not yet been convicted (Medina, 2011).

Why is upstanding behavior and ethics so important when supervising offenders?

INTRODUCTION

People are initially attracted to probation and parole careers because of dual desires to help people and to protect the community, but ultimately it's helping others that motivates new trainees to stay in the profession (Deering, 2010). As you've learned, community supervision officers generally engage in four main functions:

1. Enforce supervision conditions by means of monitoring with home visits, employment checks, and meetings with offenders;
2. Refer offenders to drug and alcohol treatment, anger management programs, parenting classes, and other community-based services according to their individual needs;

3. Conduct investigations and write reports regarding any significant violations, sharing applicable information with law enforcement personnel; and
4. Work with crime victims and the community to meet restitution payments and community service, if applicable.

In implementing these functions, Carl Klockars (1972) developed a classic typology of probation supervision officers that designated four basic types: law enforcer, time-server, therapeutic agent, and synthetic officer. Box 12.1 illustrates the variance of the four styles according to supervision officers' professional beliefs about crime causation, the kind of training they received, and each department's orientation. Orientation to system goals considered important (rehabilitation, deterrence, reentry, monitoring, etc.) affects the strategies officers use to ensure that offenders fulfill conditions of supervision. However, such orientation does not necessarily affect the amount of time spent in treatment and supervision activities (Payne & DeMichele, 2011). This is because orientations are not rigid and opposing in nature but, rather, are flexible, applicable to offenders on a case-by-case basis (Ward & Kupchik, 2010). Furthermore, in supervising juvenile delinquents, officers over the age of 40 tended to hold less punitive attitudes than younger officers (Ward & Kupchik, 2010).

Officers oriented toward law enforcement perceived that "keeping a pulse on their caseload"—knowing what their parolees were doing—through face-to-face interactions and monitoring was more important than handling the increased paperwork resulting from using computerized tracking records.

The agents generally strove toward a very traditional law enforcement role, where they did not need to assess danger or risk or criminal activity by anything more than their own developed intuition and personal investigative skills (Lynch, 1998, p. 855).

BOX 12.1　COMMUNITY CORRECTIONS UP CLOSE

Carl Klockars' Typology of Work Styles

Law enforcers stress the legal authority and enforcement aspects of their job, conveying that firmness and obeying the laws are essential. Of prime importance to such officers are the court orders, authority, and decision-making power.

Time-servers have similar philosophies as law enforcers but manifest little aspiration to improve their skills or change their ways. Their conduct on the job is that of abiding by the rules and meeting minimal job responsibilities, but they do not strive to excel. They uphold rules and regulations but do not examine these. They do not "make the rules—they just work there."

Therapeutic agents see their role as administering a form of treatment, introducing a probationer or parolee to a better way of life, and motivating constructive patterns of behavior. They give guidance and support to those unable to solve their problems by themselves, providing their clients with an opportunity to work through their ambivalent feelings. The philosophy of the therapeutic agent includes respecting clients, demonstrating concern, and helping individuals perceive the degree to which their old ways of behaving have been problematic.

Synthetic officers are distinguished by the recognition of a balance in their roles between treatment and law enforcement components. Thus they frequently encounter role conflict in combining an authoritarian or judgmental model with a therapeutic one. This type of forward-looking officer is most likely to engage in evidence-based practices.

1. Which working style tends to produce a higher revocation rate compared with other ones?
2. With which style will officers tend to take more time and engage in longer client sessions?
3. How does the working style of an officer affect the success or failure of an offender?

Source: Carl B. Klockars, Jr. 1972. A theory of probation supervision. *Journal of Criminal Law, Criminology and Police Science* 63(4): 550–557.

Most officers may be characterized as more like synthetic officers, who are a combination of law enforcers and therapeutic agents (Steiner, 2004). Such officers apply punishment and treatment on a case-by-case basis and are involved in evidence-based practices—that is, holding offenders accountable for their behavior while being engaged in problem solving. As you read this chapter, think about how these varied roles and working styles are influenced by officer beliefs, selection, and training.

SELECTION AND APPOINTMENT OF PROBATION OFFICERS

Initial selection of probation or parole officers is similar to that of other public employees. In addition to holding a baccalaureate degree, probation and parole officers are also prohibited from having any felony convictions and must undergo a criminal background check. Most states also require parole and probation officers to be American citizens. Officers are appointed, selected on merit, or chosen by some combination of the two.

Appointment System

Jurisdictions that appoint probation officers are run by a judicial selection committee that appoints its chief probation officer. The chief probation officer can hire assistant probation officers. There are more than 4,000 U.S. probation officers in 94 judicial districts, supervising offenders under mandatory supervised release and those on military parole.

Merit System

Merit, or civil service, systems were developed to remove public employees from political patronage. In a merit system, applicants who meet minimum employment standards are required to pass a competitive exam. Those who score above a specified minimum grade are placed on a ranked list. Candidates are selected from the list according to their order of rank. In some systems applicants are also graded on the basis of their education and employment history. The merit system is used in some states to determine promotions and is required in four states (Delaware, Indiana, Rhode Island, and Wisconsin). Elements of both appointment and merit systems are also used. Applicants are initially screened through a merit exam, and candidates are selected by an agency through a process similar to that of an appointment system.

OFFICER QUALIFICATIONS, TRAINING, AND SALARY

What does it take to be a good probation or parole officer? A female parole officer named Jane who made a career out of community correctional work remarked:

> We have to be able to recognize volatile situations; and you have to be able to know how to handle those situations using your communication skills. I have been involved in situations that could have easily turned volatile, but my manner, my demeanor, my communication skills, and the manner in which I dealt with these individuals has made a very big difference in the way they have responded to me (Ireland & Berg, 2008, p. 483).

BOX 12.2   FIELD NOTES

What types of knowledge, skills, and abilities do you believe are important for students to acquire before looking for a job [or develop shortly after being hired] as a probation officer?

The most important knowledge, skills, and abilities that I believe are important for students to acquire before looking for a job involve the use of practical work techniques. Although the theoretical aspects learned as a student are important, one must understand critical thinking and professional interpersonal relationships. The ability to identify and analyze information and observations swiftly to determine the validity of a judgment is a skill used on a daily basis. Students must learn to condition their mind to set aside assumptions, mindsets, and biases, and evaluate evidence to substantiate which hypothesis of a question has the least amount of inconsistencies.

Furthermore, working professionally with others is a skill that must be acquired when entering the field. When working in a group, individual creativity, uniqueness, and autonomous thinking are still important; however, you must learn to collaborate in order to obtain and maintain the cohesiveness of the structure to accomplish the goal.

Knowing how to work with different offenders is important. You must learn to identify problems by focusing on the risk and needs of each individual. Understanding social learning, social bonding, mental disorders,

Courtesy of Leanne Fiftal Alarid

Eladio D. Castillo, *M.S.*
Former Adult Probation Officer

substance abuse, finances, and criminal tendencies will facilitate your decision on how much time you should spend on the individual, whether in treatment or socioeconomic assistance. Whatever the problem(s) may be, you must learn to identify it at the initial appointment or early in the probation term to avoid potential noncompliance.

Also, time and stress management are important skills one must acquire. As is the case in many jobs, the number of offenders on a probation officer's caseload is often more than policy recommends. Nonetheless, you must learn to manage your time to accomplish specific tasks, projects, or goals. Time management depends on the individual, and you must learn to prioritize activities. You will feel the weight of stress over time, but adapting and coping with the stress is key.

Lastly, understanding and communicating in a secondary language is an asset. Executives consider secondary languages when hiring, and some agencies even provide incentive pay. When working with offenders, you can use their primary language, if it is not English, to better communicate and understand them. If the offenders feel comfortable with you, their compliance increases from my experience. Although a secondary language is not required, it would be beneficial to acquire the skill, not only for probation, but in any of your future aspirations.

In Box 12.2 Eladio Castillo provides more tips on desirable knowledge, skills, and abilities for supervising offenders in a community. Generally individuals should possess basic knowledge about human behavior as well as good oral and written communication skills to be able to interview offenders, provide testimony to judges, sympathize with victims, and correspond with offenders' employers and family members. Relationship building and establishing rapport is key. Knowing how to treat people fairly, consistently, firmly, and with respect is of utmost importance, especially when in the presence of an offender's family or employer (Ireland & Berg, 2008). It is helpful for officers to be knowledgeable about different cultures and to be good managers of time.

Education and Experience

Traditionally probation officers were recruited out of social work and psychology fields. As the emphasis of probation changed from treatment to public safety and control, a preference emerged for officers with degrees in criminal justice and criminology. Most adult probation and parole officers must have a minimum of a

BOX 12.3   COMMUNITY CORRECTIONS UP CLOSE

Sample Job Advertisement

U.S. PROBATION OFFICER

A career position for pre-sentence and investigation/supervision officer in U.S. Probation. Minimum requirements: BS/BA social sciences and at least 3 yrs related experience. Computer skills required. MA/MS preferred. Under age 37 (OPM Reg. SCRF842.803A)

Starting salary $55K. Send cover letter, resume and AO78 application (available at www.ohsp.uscourts.gov)

PAROLE/PROBATION OFFICER

Wages: $17.81–$28.32 /hr (depends on grade)
Union: United Auto Workers

Job Description: Employee of this position follows the policies, procedures, Directors Office Memorandums (DOMs), and guiding principles of the Department of Corrections to provide background information to the courts on offenders convicted in Circuit Court and to supervise those convicted.

Minimum Education: Possession of a bachelor's degree in criminal justice, correctional administration, criminology, psychology, social work, counseling and guidance, child development, sociology, school social work, social work administration, education psychology, family relations, human services, or theology.

Minimum Experience:
  PPO 9: None required.
  PPO 10: One year of professional experience working with adult offenders equivalent to a Parole/Probation Officer 9.
  PPO 11: Two years of professional experience working with adult offenders equivalent to a Parole/Probation Officer, including one year equivalent to a PPO 10.

Special Requirements: Possession of a valid driver's license and the availability of an automobile for business. Possession of a cell phone listed in the name of the employee. Residence is required in the area where employed. Passing a criminal background check and substance abuse test.

How to Apply: Interested applicants must submit a cover letter, resume, copy of official college transcript and Reference Authorization form. All required forms must be submitted at the time of application for further consideration. Application materials must be postmarked by the deadline date.

Source: http://www.careerbuilder.com Retrieved on August 15, 2011.

---

baccalaureate degree, and at least 86% of states hiring juvenile probation officers require that they possess a degree (Reddington & Kreisel, 2003). As you can see from the sample job posting in Box 12.3, knowledge of crime causation and criminal law is important. It is advantageous for applicants who work with juveniles to have knowledge of developmental and adolescent psychology and juvenile criminal justice. In addition to educational requirements, some jurisdictions also require psychological evaluation, weapons' qualification, and drug screening.

Adult Basic Training

Once an officer has been selected and hired, he or she begins training. **Preservice training** provides the basic knowledge, skills, and abilities that newly hired officers need before they begin working independently. Combined probation and parole departments require an average of 208 hours of preservice training before officers assume their duties. However, probation and parole offices that are separate require significantly less training for probation officers (84 hours on average) than for parole officers (182 hours). Preservice training requirements range from 0 hours for probation officers in West Virginia to 600 hours for parole and probation officers in North Dakota (Camp, Camp, & May, 2003). Table 12.1 lists a typical training curriculum

preservice training
Fundamental knowledge and/or skills for a newly hired officer in preparation for working independently.

TABLE 12.1   Probation/Parole Officer Basic Training Program Course Topics and Hours

I.	ORIENTATION ORGANIZATION, POLICY, AND PROCEDURES: 12 Hours		
	300	Division of Community Corrections Employee	4
	301	Overview of Community Corrections	3
	306	Community Corrections Administration	1
	307	Targeting Offender Needs	4
		Total	12
II.	LEGAL CONSIDERATIONS: 20 Hours		
	302	Introduction to the Legal System	2
	303	Legalities of the Pre-Sentence/Diagnostic Investigations	4
	304	Probation Law: Part I—Violations, Sanctions, Hearings	4
	304	Probation Law: Part II—Arrest, Search, Seizure	6
	315	Parole Law	2
	317	Processing New Parole Cases	2
		Total	20
III.	OFFICER-PROBATIONER/PAROLEE RELATIONS: 28 Hours		
	320	Understanding Offender Behavior	4
	324	Counseling Methodologies: Part IA (CBI)	2
	324	Counseling Methodologies: Part IB (Nonverbal/Verbal Intervention)	2
	324	Counseling Methodologies: Part II—Gangs	4
	325	Crisis Interventions and Domestic Disputes	4
	330	Counseling Substance Abuse Cases	2
	331	Interview Techniques	4
	336	Offender Supervision	6
		Total	28
IV.	PROBATIONER/PAROLEE MANAGEMENT: 32 Hours		
	311	Case Management	6
	313	Unlawful Workplace Harassment	2
	318	Parole Violations and Revocations	4
	326	Community Resource Management	2
	327	Processing Probation Cases: Part I/II	16
	329	Closing Cases	2
		Total	32
V.	DEFENSIVE PROTECTION: 30 Hours		
	328	Arrest Procedures	8
	333	Controls, Restraints, Defensive Techniques	18
	334	Personal Protection	4
		Total	30
VI.	COURTROOM PREPARATION AND DEMEANOR: 8 Hours		
	305	Public Speaking	2
	314	Moot Court	4
	332	Role of the Probation/Parole Witness	2
		Total	8

(Continues)

TABLE 12.1   Probation/Parole Officer Basic Training Program Course Topics and Hours (*Continued*)

VII.	OTHER: 30 Hours	
312	Drug Identification	4
335	Basic Life Support	8
337	Employee Wellness	4
338	Professional Ethics	2
339	Personal Conduct	6
000	Review and Testing	6
	Total	30
	Course Total	**160**

Source: North Carolina Department of Correction Office of Staff Training. www.doc.state.nc.us/OSDT/Forms/Syllabus_PPO.DOC

for probation and parole officers in North Carolina that provides 160 hours of basic training.

In many states in which probation and parole officers carry firearms, they must complete **Peace Officer State Training** (POST). POST topics encompass strategies of case supervision, record keeping, legal liability, professional ethics, arrest and detention procedures, firearms' handling, defense tactics, and stress reduction. During the training process, POST instructors use metaphors and stories from their own field experiences that greatly influence how new recruits perceive the organizational culture. POST trainers thus shape the attitudes and values of probation and parole officer subculture, which together affect officer work role orientation (Crank, 1996).

Peace Officer State Training
Specialized and standardized training that officers are required to complete before they may carry a firearm on the job.

Juvenile Preservice Training

For supervision of juveniles, the American Correctional Association recommends juvenile probation officers receive 40 hours of preservice training, whereas the American Bar Association suggests 80 hours of preservice training with an additional 48 hours within the first six months. Reddington and Kreisel conducted a nationwide survey to determine trends in juvenile probation officer training. They found that 20 states certified juvenile probation officer positions requiring an average of 100 hours of preservice training. Most other states mandated orientation training in which an officer does not go through an academy but strictly learns on the job, with between 8–200 hours of training required within the first year of employment. Compared with adult probation officers, who average 125 training hours, juvenile probation officers average just over 77 hours (Reddington & Kreisel, 2000, 2003). The main reason for this difference is that there are no national training standards for juvenile probation officers.

In-Service Training

In-service training consists of continuing education training that occurs annually for seasoned officers following their first year of employment. This allows officers to keep current with new laws and new developments in the field or to repeat important topics from initial training. Training topics can include evidence-based practice principles, cognitive-behavioral treatment principles, empathy training, motivational interviewing, and supervision techniques with special needs offenders. In empathy training, probation officers become sensitized to what juvenile probationers endure during arrest and detention (Rainey, 2002). In motivational interviewing officers

in-service training
Periodic continuing education training for seasoned officers.

learn reflective listening skills, how to better understand their client's perspective, how to elicit a client to open up, and how to respond when a client becomes resistant (Hartzler & Espinosa, 2011).

The American Correctional Association recommends that seasoned officers receive 40 hours of annual training. Meeting 40 training hours annually appears to be the most common requirement for adult probation and parole departments, with an average ranging between 33 hours for probation officers and 42 hours for parole officers (Camp, Camp, & May, 2003). For officers supervising juveniles, only 30 states require annual training—a median of 30 hours per year (Reddington & Kreisel, 2000).

Officer Salary

Based on positions advertised nationwide in 2011 (www.payscale.com), an entry-level probation officer or correctional treatment specialist with less than one year of experience can expect a median salary of $33,000. With five to nine years of experience, the median salary for the same job is $38,000; with 10 to19 years, the salary is $44,000, and with 20 years or more on the job, the salary rises to $56,000. Another salary website reported overall average for probation and parole officers as $46,000 (www.indeed.com/salary/). Probation officers in urban areas working for local government agencies tended to earn higher salaries than when a department was situated in a state government.

Another general trend is that parole officers in stand-alone departments had a higher starting salary. They also earned higher salaries over their career than did parole or probation officers in combined departments. The differences in salary could be due to fewer turnovers of probation officers in stand-alone departments, or from earning better raises over time than those provided by combined departments.

Probation and parole administrators earned considerably more than did field officers. The average salary for parole administrators was $161,435 and for probation administrators $101,109. In combined departments probation and parole administrators earned an average of $84,442 (Camp, Camp, & May, 2003). As officers' job expectations have risen, so has the amount of training and salaries. One example of increased responsibility is an authorization to carry weapons.

FIREARMS' POLICIES FOR PROBATION AND PAROLE OFFICERS

One of the strongest indicators of a department's philosophy is its stance on firearms. One study found that as the percentage of armed officers increases, the more enforcement-oriented the department (Roscoe et al., 2007). In the federal system, 85 out of 94 judicial districts allow federal probation officers to carry firearms of .40 caliber and above. At the state and county levels, officers in 35 adult probation jurisdictions and in 40 adult parole jurisdictions carry firearms (see Table 12.2). Although these numbers might seem as if most officers carry a weapon, only about half of all firearm-carrying jurisdictions in the adult system are *mandatory*. The other half of jurisdictions have authorized firearms, but their use is either voluntary or the policy is limited only to the small number of officers who supervise specialized caseloads or who make evening home visits (Nieto, 1996).

In comparison with those officers supervising adults, the vast majority of juvenile officers do not carry firearms. In the juvenile system, 13 states allow officers

© AP Images/Rick Rycroft

A trainee takes aim at a simulated gunman projected onto a screen of the Firearms Training System (FATS). FATS helps officers who carry guns make better decisions during confrontations.

firearms, two give officers the option, and two states narrow firearms only to certain counties or to officers who supervise serious juvenile offenders. The firearms' policy of the Eastern District of Missouri states that "officers should avoid the use of a firearm except in self-defense or in defense of a fellow probation officer. The officer may not use a firearm unless the officer believes he/she, or a fellow officer, is in imminent danger of death or serious bodily injury and there is no means of a safe retreat" (Scharr, 2001, p. 47). This firearms' policy, as written, does not allow a probation officer to use a firearm to come to the aid of any other third party. Federal officers receive two weeks of firearm training that requires qualifying with at least 80% accuracy and passing a written exam.

TABLE 12.2   Firearms' Policies for Probation and Parole Officers

	PROBATION		PAROLE	
Firearms' Policy	**Adult**	**Juvenile**	**Adult**	**Juvenile**
Officers Not Armed Statewide	17	40	12	43
Mandatory Arming Statewide	17	4	25	3
County Specific	6	5	2	2
Optional Choice	9	2	9	2
Job Specific (Intensive)	3	2	4	1

Source: American Probation and Parole Association. 2006. *APPA Adult and Juvenile Probation and Parole National Firearm Survey 2005–2006*. Lexington, KY: APPA. Accessed. http://www.appa-net.org/information%20 clearing%20house/survey.htm

Arguments in Support of Carrying Firearms

Most officers, particularly those who made late-night home visits and specialized units who supervised gang members and violent offenders, reported feeling safer when carrying a firearm. Officers who favored firearms while on duty tended to be younger men more likely to practice law-and-order case management strategies than to take casework or treatment-oriented approaches. Guns seem to satisfy a psychological need for safety independent of an actual threat (Roscoe et al., 2007). An interesting viewpoint came from female parole officers who noted that in a male-dominated occupation emphasizing safety, security, and physical prowess, female parole officers acquired more respect from male parole agents by making a decision to *carry* a weapon even if they never intended to use it (Ireland & Berg, 2008). However, not all female officers feel the same. In Box 12.4 juvenile probation officer Teressa Price provides her professional opinion about carrying a firearm on the job.

BOX 12.4   FIELD NOTES

Did carrying a firearm change the way you approached community supervision of juveniles? If so, how? Do you think the policy is a good idea?

As a juvenile probation officer (JPO), I feel it is important that I am equipped with everything necessary to maintain my safety, as well as the safety of those around me. I was a JPO for eight months before becoming certified to carry a firearm. For those eight months, I was stationed at a local high school and was required to visit the homes of juveniles on my caseload on a weekly basis from 6 PM to 10 PM. I had to be out after dark, wearing a visible vest with "Probation Officer" in big letters on the back. Anyone could spot me easily and all I had was mace and a baton, not enough to protect myself from a kid with a gun.

I received my certification on a Friday and began carrying my firearm the following Tuesday. I would not say that it necessarily changed how I supervised the juveniles on my caseload, but it did change my comfort level in that I knew that I had the training and ability to react in the unfortunate situation that anyone, not just a juvenile, should open fire either at the school or in the community.

Detaining juveniles, sending them to placements, and boot camps or treatment centers, along with placing them on electronic monitoring sometimes are a part of supervising juveniles. All of the above things came at a monetary cost to the parents who, often times, could not afford the burden of paying child support to a placement for their

Teressa Price
Former Juvenile Probation Officer

Courtesy of Leanne Fiftal Alarid

child resulting in the government garnishing their wages. And I was the one making the decision to recommend these things to the court. All it would take is one upset juvenile, or parent for that matter, to get their hands on a firearm and see me as a target.

With violence among juveniles increasing, I believe it is a good policy that juvenile probation officers have all the equipment necessary to protect them. If someone opens fire randomly, or at me specifically, I would not be able to do much with a can of mace. With being stationed at a school, it is especially important because I, along with the school resource officer, would also have the ability to protect the students and faculty of the school. While I would not say that school shootings are the norm, I would say that these things do happen occasionally. Juveniles are receiving charges for bringing a weapon on school property—anything from a small baseball bat to an AK-47. In the crucial minutes it would take for someone to call 911 and the police to respond, many could be wounded or dead. School probation officers and school resource officers could respond immediately to the threat whether that threat is another student, or an intruder in the school.

I know that juvenile probation officers carrying firearms is a controversial subject and that not everyone agrees that it is a necessary part of supervising children in the community. I, however, am grateful to have every protection possible, along with the knowledge and training on how and when to use it in the event that I need it.

Arguments Against Carrying Firearms

Jurisdictions in which probation is under the judicial branch have tended to oppose the carrying of firearms, contending that doing so is a function under the executive branch of powers and not appropriate for employees of the judicial branch. The New Jersey Supreme Court upheld this, ruling that judicial officers performing an executive branch function unconstitutionally violated the separation of powers (*Williams v. State of New Jersey*, 2006) and might conflict with rehabilitation objectives and traditional casework strategies (Small & Torres, 2001).

Officers opposed to carrying a firearm question whether a threat is real or perceived. Such opponents argue that not every probation officer needs to carry a deadly weapon, especially if that officer supervises misdemeanants or juveniles. Rita explains that carrying weapons can change how situations are handled:

> When I was first a parole agent, we did not carry weapons. When I left, it was an option [*pause*]; it was also a part of my decision to leave. I did not feel that carrying a weapon was good for the job. We had not done that; you learned to talk your way through things; you learned to look at things differently [*pause*] in order to resolve your problems. I was not for weapons, although I was comfortable with them. [*thoughtful pause*] . . . When I came back, it was mandatory to carry a weapon. It was required. I became comfortable with it. I've never had to use it for protection or because I was in fear (Ireland & Berg, 2008, p. 484).

Probation officers who carried a firearm experienced *more incidents of confrontation* than did officers not carrying a firearm. This might have been due either to a higher volatility of an offender or the way in which an officer handled a situation— or both. Furthermore, if a probationer or parolee is carrying a weapon, an armed officer's safety is at greater risk compared with that of an unarmed officer (Scharr, 2001).

Officer confrontations have greatly decreased as officers pay more attention to safety issues by conducting home visits in pairs, wearing body armor, and training in self-defense techniques. Of the serious incidents that have occurred, over half occurred in the field, and only 28% occurred in a probation office. The three most common incidents were threats, animal attacks, and other situations defined as dangerous (Small & Torres, 2001).

From a more practical viewpoint, carrying firearms entails ongoing liability and training costs. One jurisdiction in which adult probation officers did carry firearms later prohibited all officers from carrying weapons. The moratorium resulted from concern about the department's ability to pay for proper training within its budget (Chasnoff, 2006). Some jurisdictions favor a policy of carrying firearms but simply can't afford to implement it. Other options should be provided that include use of chemical agents, stun guns, pressure points' training, and field visits by two officers.

As probation and parole officers increasingly carry firearms on the job, they are also considered a type of law enforcement officer, particularly if they have completed peace officer training. Should officers be authorized to carry weapons, decisions must be made as to actual need, proper training, liability issues, and selection procedures that minimally include physical and psychological examinations. All officers who choose to carry a firearm receive training, such as via an interactive video called *Firearms Training System* (see Box 12.5).

BOX 12.5   TECHNOLOGY IN CORRECTIONS

Interactive Firearms Video Training

The Firearms Training System (or FATS) consists of the use of interactive video technology to enhance the training in firearms of any peace officer, including probation, parole, and pretrial services officers. In FATS training, which is different from shooting at traditional fixed targets, a video image projected onto a screen is connected to a computer, speakers, and firearm replicas that spray a harmless liquid peppermint when a trigger is pulled. Each unique scenario requires trainees to choose which action to take. After a variety of scenarios, trainees discuss and justify their actions to an instructor.

An evaluation found that 32% of probation officers reported that FATS training altered their conception "to a great extent" of a firearm's value for self-defense, and another 34% said their understanding changed "to some extent." The training helped clarify the meaning of the

firearms' policy as well as the moral and liability issues that accompany the use of potentially deadly force. Scharr concluded:

> After the training, officers clearly indicated they were surprised at how quickly a critical incident could occur, how likely it is that they will be perceived as law enforcement officers during a critical incident, how difficult it can be to work in teams and communicate during a critical incident. . . . This suggests that the training was effective in heightening officer awareness of danger and the necessity for continued training in mental preparedness and self-defense proficiency (p. 49).

Source: Timothy M. Scharr. 2001. Interactive video training for firearms safety. *Federal Probation* 65(2): 45–51.

With this training also comes more liability and responsibility, making a decision to carry firearms very much an individual choice that should be carefully considered. We recommend that applicants find out in advance what kind of firearms' policy exists (mandatory, optional, none, and so forth) and determine what is warranted in accord with their basic values.

STRESSORS ENCOUNTERED IN PROBATION AND PAROLE

Probation and parole supervision is centered around managing people rather than on processing information. Building professional relationships and "achieving successful outcomes with offenders who have managed to make changes in their life" (Annison, Eadie, & Knight, 2008, p. 266) is an art, and when officers can impact the lives of their clients for the better they are rewarded with a great deal of satisfaction. As one federal probation officer observed, "If you can help someone lead a stable and productive life, then it is worth all the effort. You can't explain the rewards of helping someone else. To see someone make it through that system and lead a productive life is a reward" (Quinn, 2002, p. 265).

Jobs that are people-centered also tend to demand higher levels of risk-taking and result in greater burnout than do jobs that are data-oriented. This is in part because caring officers "often connect emotionally (whether in a positive or negative way) with our clients or the victims, and this can in turn cause us emotional turmoil" (Catanese, 2010, p. 37). Further, the emotional attachment to the job that comes from working with clients is different from connecting with the working conditions of one's department. Client-centered employees who do not feel a positive emotional connection or sense of belonging were more likely to leave, and organizational factors were found to contribute more to employee turnover than did the nature of the work itself (Lee, Phelps, & Beto, 2009). Although most jobs are stressful to some degree, situations that place unreasonable demands on one or that take a person outside his or her comfort zone can exacerbate stress. This section seeks to inform readers realistically about community corrections supervision so that those interested in this profession are more fully aware of the demands this line of work presents. Studies of officer stress certainly apply to any position involving community corrections supervision.

Sources of Stress

How do officers manage the pressures of maintaining a caseload, what with its work of supervising clients' contacts and drug tests and of filing reports within a specific time period? Researchers have uncovered the following sources of stress for community supervision officers (Drapel & Lutze, 2009; Slate, Johnson, & Wells, 2000; Wells, Colbert, & Slate, 2006):

- excessive paperwork;
- lack of time to accomplish the job due to high caseloads;
- lack of promotional opportunities;
- role ambiguity;
- role conflict (treatment vs. punishment);
- perceived court leniency on offenders;
- failure to recognize accomplishments;
- administrative policies; and
- fear of being sued.

Sometimes feeling overly stressed can simply mean that a job is not a good fit for a person. In criminal justice, submitting written documentation is an important part of taking legal responsibility for the supervision of another person. Federal officers in particular spend a lot of time documenting matters on every client they supervise, which accounts for complaints of what some officers refer to as "excessive paperwork" (Slate & Johnson, 2008). Time spent on such paperwork coupled with heavy caseloads have led to feelings of not having enough time for the actual work of supervision.

In fact, caseloads that were too high were a major source of job discontent. Although caseload sizes averaged 140 offenders, they ranged widely between a low of 30 to nearly 4,000 individuals for one officer to supervise. As caseload size increased, officers were less tolerant of technical violations and more likely to write a court report to support a violation (Kerbs, Jones, & Jolley, 2009). To the extent that writing a report entails more work, this finding may seem counterintuitive, but it is possible that officers hope to receive a temporary reprieve by way of a replacement with a different client. Experts have consistently recommended that caseload sizes be reduced to an appropriate level to allow officers meaningful contact with offenders while also reducing their stress and turnover (Drapela & Lutze, 2009; Ireland & Berg, 2008).

ROLE AMBIGUITY   **Role ambiguity** refers to the fact that community supervision officers have discretion and can choose whether or not to exercise it. The degree of independent decision making that community correctional officers have has been equated with that of a police lieutenant (Ireland & Berg, 2008). People accustomed only to following the lead of others and uncomfortable making their own decisions can experience a sense of uneasiness with this kind of authority. This is why setting boundaries, using common sense, and behaving ethically and consistently are so important. Further, "professionals may become too involved with their work, not setting proper boundaries with individuals on their caseload. They may find themselves staying at work longer or not being able to separate work from their personal

role ambiguity
The discretion that exists in the role of the probation and parole officer to treat clients fairly and consistently and according to individual circumstances.

An important part of learning the job as a probation or parole officer is proper search techniques.

© Modesto Bee/ZUMA Press

lives" (Catanese, 2010, p. 37). Time management is especially important when officers must conduct home visits in the field.

role conflict
The two functions of a probation and parole officer, that of enforcing the rules and laws, and providing support and reintegration, that are sometimes contradictory and difficult to reconcile.

ROLE CONFLICT   Role conflict, a common source of stress, can arise from competing responsibilities. For officers must be empathetic, understanding, and objective enough to help offenders who have broken the law. At the same time, they must be able to revoke or terminate clients who do not follow the conditions of their supervision (as we will discuss in the next chapter).

Finally, supervising offenders can all too often mean ignoring basic principles of behavior modification: to reward positive behavior and to discourage negative behavior. Officers in community corrections supervision frequently take action on negative behavior while downplaying positive or prosocial behavior. Such practices are enough to make a behavioral psychologist shudder and might explain, at least in part, why so many offenders "fail" under supervision. A policy of rewarding offenders for positive behavior can help officers feel good as well.

Alleviating the Fear of Being Sued: Types of Immunity

Given the large amount of discretion officers have, the fear of being named in a civil lawsuit is a concern for some (Drapela & Lutze, 2009). One way to decrease stress is for officers to know the general limits of the law regarding actions and inactions on the job. First, it is important for officers to minimize risk by keeping track of the people they are supervising and responding professionally to inappropriate behaviors. No matter how accomplished and competent an officer is, a probationer or parolee can at times injure or victimize the general public. What happens if a victim feels an injury could have been prevented if only an officer had "properly supervised" the client?

negligence
The failure of an officer to do what a reasonably prudent person would have done in like or similar circumstances.

Given that it is impossible for officers to control the actions of their clients at all times, the best they can do is to follow departmental policy, follow the orders of a court or a parole board, and justify their actions with accurate paperwork. **Negligence** is a failure to do that which a reasonably prudent person would do in similar circumstances. For example, if an officer finds out through credible sources that one of her probationers is planning to commit a crime and therefore is in a position to prevent it but fails do so, she is likely negligent. An officer can be held liable (or responsible) if the negligence was gross or willful. Though such terms depend on the meaning assigned by a judge or jury, gross or willful negligence generally means that a person must have intentionally or maliciously failed to act (del Carmen et al., 2001).

Because probation and parole officers are government officials (as are police, judges, and prosecutors), they are entitled to different types of legal protection so that they are comfortable exercising discretion without fear of being personally sued over the actions of clients under their supervision. The type of immunity that officers have depends on what *function* they are performing (Drapela & Lutze, 2009).

ABSOLUTE IMMUNITY FOR QUASI-JUDICIAL FUNCTIONS   **Absolute immunity** protects government officials from any legal action unless they engage in acts that are intentionally and maliciously wrong. Absolute immunity provides the highest level of protection for anyone who officially acts in a legislative, quasi-judicial, or prosecutorial function. For example, parole board officials have absolute immunity in decisions to grant, deny, or revoke parole (*King v. Simpson,* 1999). Probation and parole officers have absolute immunity only when they are acting in a quasi-judicial function, such as in the preparation and submission of a presentence investigation report, even if there are errors later found in the report (*Spaulding v. Nielsen,* 1979). Recall that every defendant has an opportunity to review and make changes to any errors in his or her PSI before it is submitted to a judge. State statutes, however, must define PSI reports as a quasi-judicial function—otherwise a probation officer is eligible for a lower level of protection called *qualified immunity.* Another important thing to remember is that even though absolute immunity protects individuals from being sued (even if there was harm caused), it does not protect them from being tried in criminal court if criminal behavior occurred.

> **absolute immunity**
> Protection from legal action or liability unless workers engage in discretion that is intentionally and maliciously wrong.

QUALIFIED IMMUNITY FOR ADMINISTRATIVE FUNCTIONS   Compared with absolute immunity, qualified immunity is much more narrow and is limited to compliance with agency policy for employees in the executive branch or workers performing administrative functions, such as offender monitoring and supervision. In **qualified immunity**, workers are not liable for wrongdoing when their actions are found to be "objectively reasonable" and within the scope of agency directives and/or policies at that time, given limited information. The legal standard of being "objectively reasonable" is ironically quite subjective. Given that most functions of probation and parole officers are administrative, such officers have qualified immunity even when involved in a disciplinary or probation revocation hearing, which is considerably different from a court hearing whose outcome results in conviction.

> **qualified immunity**
> Protection from liability in decisions or actions that are "objectively reasonable."

Community supervision officer functions are defined differently from jurisdiction to jurisdiction. In New York, for example, parole officers have only qualified immunity when recommending an issuance of a revocation warrant. This is because under New York law issuing a revocation warrant is considered an investigatory, not a prosecutorial, function (*Best v. State,* 1999). In another state the same activity—initiating a parole revocation proceeding and presenting a case during parole revocation hearings—was identified as a quasi-judicial function and was therefore subject to absolute immunity. The biggest problem arises when there is an *absence* of policy for various activities, such as for neighborhood-based supervision activities like those integrated with police substations in which probation officers build relationships with agency leaders and work toward solving problems endemic to a community (Drapela & Lutze, 2009). Despite fears of lawsuits, the reality is that officers who do their job well and follow agency policy are protected by qualified immunity. In cases in which no policy exists for a particular activity, policy needs to be drafted and officer training must occur.

Despite these potential stressors, many people find community corrections very rewarding and have spent their entire career in this field. Catanese's (2010) recommendation is to "maintain a light and humorous work environment ... steer clear of negative people and form relationships with colleagues who have positive attitudes ... surround themselves with others who are not in the same profession . . . [and] avoid negative coping skills such as alcohol consumption, risky behaviors, or isolation" (p. 38).

PRIVATE PROBATION

private probation
An agency that is owned and operated by a private business or nonprofit organization, and contracts with the state, local, or federal government to supervise clients convicted of a misdemeanor.

private service provider
Any for-profit or non-profit private organization that contracts with county-level or state-level government to provide probation supervision, independent probation treatment services, or both probation supervision and treatment.

As state and local governments look to trim costs in their budgets, they have increasingly turned to private companies for a wide array of services, from drug testing to electronic monitoring. **Private probation** agencies contract with local or state government to provide misdemeanor probation supervision. According to Alarid and Schloss (2009), private probation refers to the supervision side, but it is frequently the case that a private probation company will also provide treatment services, so a more generic term for a private probation company is a **private service provider**. Such a provider is "any for profit or non-profit private organization that contracts with county-level or state-level government to provide probation supervision, independent probation treatment services, or both probation supervision and treatment under one roof" (Alarid & Schloss, 2009, p. 5).

The privatization debate is centered on two main arguments. The first assumes that continued growth in the correctional system ensures survival of private agencies that depend on outside referrals and fees collected from offenders. The second suggests that because government cannot adequately function as effectively as private companies, services for lower-risk individuals must be redistributed out of necessity, so that the government can refocus its efforts on higher risk clients (Garland, 2001).

Private nonprofit entities have been involved in community supervision of offenders for quite a long time—since the 1800s, in fact. The Salvation Army has a long history of providing such services. Over time state codes and statutes were formulated to permit the provision of private agencies for ancillary treatment services to state and local probationers, such as for mental health, driving-while-intoxicated classes, drug treatment, and anger management (see Figure 12.1). Also, private agencies were to provide direct probation supervision. Because of a limited number of staff available to supervise a growing number of probationers, states are increasingly contracting with private probation agencies to assist with supervision.

At least 18 states currently use the private sector for some form of supervision. Ten states grant private agencies sole responsibility for supervising misdemeanor and low-risk clients, relying on a state agency to focus on felony probationers (Schloss & Alarid, 2007). In the 10 states that rely on the private sector for misdemeanor supervision, it is estimated that over 300,000 probationers are being supervised by private agencies, which is three times the number of offenders in private jails and prisons. This number does not include the thousands of probationers who are court-ordered to attend outpatient treatment centers (many of which are private) and the thousands of offenders in residential community correction facilities.

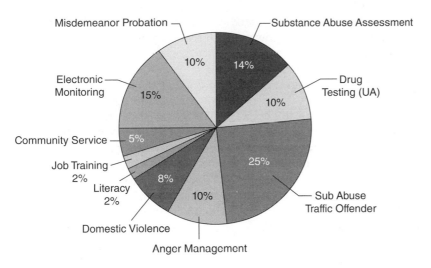

FIGURE 12.1 Correctional Services Contracted to Private Providers

A privatized probation system would allow states to choose from a variety of contractors, who would compete on the basis of cost for services provided, outcomes such as victim restitution collection, recidivism reduction, and low technical violation revocation rates (which in theory would reduce the need to use jail beds and thereby save the government money). There would be financial consequences such as fining private providers for not providing an agreed-upon level of services (Hucklesby, 2011). Some private contractors engage in no face-to-face contact with any low-level probationers but rather assist a state in monitoring community service compliance via phone calls, mail, and case paperwork. As a result, one state probation office was able to concentrate its efforts on the supervision of high-risk cases (Bosco, 1998). One such private company providing misdemeanor probation services is Providence Community Corrections, which operates in Florida, Georgia, South Carolina, Tennessee, and Washington. Providence Community Corrections is a subsidiary of Providence Service Corporation, which provides substance abuse treatment and is involved with drug courts and adult community corrections (see www.provcorp.com).

Statutes Authorizing Private Probation

The American Legislative Exchange Council (ALEC) has developed model legislation related to probation privatization. Regulating the private sector has generally been slow, with some jurisdictions operating in a grey area of unclear or nonexistent standards concerning the awarding of contracts to private providers, staff hiring requirements, and curricula for outpatient treatment services (Schloss & Alarid, 2007). Statutes examined by Schloss and Alarid (2007) in seven states that authorized private probation (Alabama, Arkansas, Florida, Georgia, Missouri, Utah, and Tennessee) found that most required agencies to sign a formal contract with the government outlining the scope of services to be provided, the responsibilities of the contractor, and the obligations of the court. For example, private agencies in Missouri wishing to provide services must make application with a circuit judge, prove financial ability to operate a probation office, and provide liability insurance. However, Missouri has few standardized guidelines for private agency approval other than that an agency cannot be related in any way to a judge. Once agencies are approved for a three-year term, there are no requirements to provide verification of fees collected.

Criticism of Probation Privatization

Critics of privatization argue that the need to provide effective correctional services is at odds with the business agenda of profit-making. Private sector supervision of probation is viewed as intruding upon and competing with government's traditional, core responsibility to carry out punishment in a fair manner (Bosco, 1998). Furthermore, the private sector is usually not equipped to be a full-service organization and thus might only be able to take on low-risk offenders who require little if any monitoring. Private-sector services offer no uniform method of monitoring probation conditions or of ensuring that victim restitution is collected (Leznoff, 1998).

Also, state statutes stipulate a range of requirements for hiring officers as employees. Some states, such as Georgia, provide specific requirements for ongoing training and education of private probation officers. Georgia requires officers to have completed two years of college, have no felony convictions, and to be a minimum age of 21. Other states have no educational or training requirements for hiring individuals who wish to become private probation officers (Schloss & Alarid, 2007). Thus there is concern that employees in private companies, compared with those in the public sector, receive less training, have less opportunity for career advancement, and show higher staff turnover (Hucklesby, 2011).

Another concern relates to a lack of standardization for agencies that wish to become probation program providers. Some states have no requirement that providers demonstrate such qualifications as licensing and experience. This is particularly disconcerting given that the U.S. Supreme Court ruled in the case of a private prison that the same level of qualified immunity protection should *not* be provided to employees of private correctional companies as to government employees (*Richardson v. McKnight*, 1997). This is because private companies can include into their contracts those conditions under which they will indemnify employees found liable for their actions on the job. In *Correctional Services Corp vs. Malesko* (2001), the Supreme Court ruled that in such a **Section 1983** case the harmed individual must sue the person responsible for the harm, but that a private company is *not* considered a person. Therefore a private company cannot be sued under Section 1983, and a plaintiff must go after individuals deemed to be responsible. These two U.S. Supreme Court decisions indicate that individual employees working for private companies are by far the least protected individuals in the criminal justice system, especially if a company has not fully outlined an indemnification clause.

Ethical questions arise if private probation agencies are also treatment providers and require their ancillary services as part of probation supervision. Schloss and Alarid (2007) argue for more stringent and standardized requirements for the supervision of offenders by private probation agencies, believing that Georgia, Utah, Colorado, and Tennessee provide good examples in this endeavor.

ATTORNEY VIEWS ON PRIVATIZATION   Recommendation of community supervision as a sanction is partly dependent upon the perception of courtroom attorneys—that is, whether they accept probation as a viable alternative. During a case screening process, prosecutors decide whether sufficient evidence exists to charge a defendant with a crime. If enough evidence exists, prosecutors also decide the level or severity of an offense. They are in a unique position to assess defendant eligibility for probation and/or to connect defendants with private probation agencies. Because of this,

Section 1983
A federal lawsuit alleging that a government official violated one or more of an individual's civil rights afforded them in the U.S. Constitution.

prosecutors and defense attorneys were surveyed on the use of private treatment providers. Private agency accountability to courts was of primary concern for prosecutors, whereas defense attorneys were more concerned about treatment costs for their clients (Alarid & Schloss, 2009).

In contrast with traditional probation in which a court orders a client to report to his or her probation officer after sentencing, private service providers station a representative in court to make initial contact with a client upon sentencing. In this way an offender's initial appointment and intake are completed immediately after sentencing rather than following the seven- to fourteen-day time period it takes to start traditional probation. Court attorneys generally supported having a private representative present in court (Alarid & Schloss, 2009). Attorneys also believed that qualifications for offering supervision and treatment services were important, such as utilizing identical curricula statewide, in order that treatment offered by private providers would be uniform.

SUMMARY

- Probation or parole officers are selected by appointment, by merit, or by a combination of the two. In most states necessary qualifications include U.S. citizenship, being at least 21 years of age, possessing a baccalaureate degree, passing a drug test, and not having a felony record.

- Issues continually evolving are provisions for preservice and in-service training and the effect of firearms' policies on probation and parole supervision.

- Applicants should find out about the firearms' policy of the department to which they are applying and also determine whether carrying a firearm is suitable to them, insofar as this is very much an individual decision.

- The future of probation supervision aims to give line-level officers more decision-making opportunity and responsibility, which in turn will likely decrease job stress and burnout.

- Workers in corrections enjoy absolute immunity when acting in a quasi-judicial or prosecutorial function but have only qualified immunity when performing administrative or other discretionary functions.

- Private service providers (PSPs) are growing in number and seem to be accepted by court attorneys who work with PSP representatives.

- Some private community corrections organizations have the potential to effectively supervise low-risk clients, but requirements range widely by jurisdiction.

DISCUSSION QUESTIONS

1. What type of knowledge, skills, and abilities are necessary for a community supervision officer to possess?

2. Why are college degrees required for probation and parole officers but not necessarily for entry-level police officers? What advantages might a college education provide in the field of community correctional supervision?

3. Do probation officers receive enough training for the responsibilities they have? Why or why not?

4. What are the advantages and disadvantages regarding probation and parole officers carrying firearms?

5. Would you carry a weapon on the job? Why or why not? If so, explain under what conditions you would carry it.

6. Out of the possible sources of stress identified, which ones can be controlled by an officer and which ones are inevitable to the job? Discuss innovative ways that work-related stress can be effectively managed.

7. How can probation and parole officers minimize the chances that they will lose a civil lawsuit if they are ever sued?

8. Do you agree or disagree with the following statement: Private probation supervision and treatment services should be expanded.

9. Which limitations or controls would you place on private probation agencies? Why?

WEBSITES, VIDEOS, AND PODCASTS

Websites

Career Planning Resources for Probation, Parole, and Correctional Treatment Workers
http://www.career-planning-education.com/law-criminal-justice/probation-officers.htm#outlook

Pennsylvania Practice Improvement Collaborative
http://www.ireta.org/pic/parole_probation_training.htm

Pennsylvania (Carbon County) Adult Probation and Parole Officer Firearms' Policy
http://www.pabulletin.com/secure/data/vol31/31-14/584.html

Judicial Correction Services, Inc.
http://judicialservices.com/

Videos/Podcasts

Working in the Corrections Field
http://www.corrections.com/system/podcast/file/72/media_20050506.mp3

This podcast discusses how to find work as a corrections officer. It also gives an overview of various unions in the corrections field.

Officer Stress
http://www.corrections.com/system/podcast/file/38/media_20050602.mp3

This podcast interviews a former officer. The discussion focuses on the stress of working in the field of criminal justice and corrections.

CASE STUDY EXERCISE

Decisions of a Community Corrections Administrator

In these scenarios you are a community correctional administrator tasked with making policy changes, changes in the way things are done and, if need be, personnel adjustments. You also have control over a budget and how allocated money is spent.

CASE A: Adjusting Probation Caseloads

Charles is chief probation officer in Pleasant County, a position he has held for 10 years. Prior to becoming chief, he served as a middle manager in the same department for six years and as a probation officer for 10 years. The county has 4,500 probationers total, of which 1,500 are on probation for a felony and 3,000 are misdemeanants. Of the 1,500 felony offenders, 275 are defined as *specialized cases*. Of the 3,000 misdemeanants, 1,500 are Class A and the other half are Class B and Class C.

If all positions are full, the county can support a total of 30 probation officers (15 felony and 15 misdemeanor officers), two middle managers (one supervising all officers with misdemeanor cases and another supervising all officers with felony cases), and a chief probation officer. All probation officers currently conduct pre-sentence investigations and write reports on a rotating basis. Right now cases are assigned based only on whether they are a felony or a misdemeanor, and a new client is given to the officer handling the least amount of cases.

There is currently a hiring freeze due to economic difficulties and budget shortfalls facing Pleasant County for at least two more years, but this could last longer. As a result, if a probation officer leaves there is no replacement, and clients on his or her caseload are divided among existing officers. Currently Charles has two middle managers, 13 misdemeanor officers, and 14 felony officers, so he is down by three positions. The morale in his department has been decreasing due to remaining officers doing more work for the same amount of pay, so Charles must act fast. He is considering a number of options:

Option 1: Move four of the misdemeanor officers over to felony caseloads, so there will be 18 felony officers and nine misdemeanor officers. All officers still rotate on the PSIs.

Option 2: Move five of the misdemeanor officers over to felony caseloads, so there will be 19 felony officers and eight misdemeanor officers. One of those felony officers will be assigned to write all felony pre-sentence investigation reports for the county and not do any supervision.

Option 3: Keep caseload numbers the same (100 for felony and 200 for misdemeanor), and geographically separate offenders by zip code so it is easier for an officer to visit clients in a smaller area.

Option 4: Have smaller felony caseload sizes for specialized types like sex offenders, offenders with mental illnesses, etc. (e.g., 55 for specialized felony caseloads and 100 for general felony caseloads).

Option 5: Allow Class B and Class C misdemeanants electronic check-in and mail-in options (this affects 1,500 offenders), so only one officer has to supervise Class B and Class C while seven officers supervise Class A misdemeanants at 214 offenders each).

Which options should Charles select and why? You may choose as many as you think are cumulatively effective. Is there another option that might be better than the ones listed, without hiring new staff?

CASE B: Responding to a Civil Lawsuit

Simon is a federal prisoner with a documented heart condition who was transferred to your halfway house. You are the halfway house manager of a private facility that contracts with the federal government. You decide to give authorization to allow Simon to use the staff elevator instead of the stairs so he will not overexert himself. You communicated your decision in writing and at a recent staff meeting to all employees, so everyone knows. One night two months later a brand new employee begins working the evening shift. Everyone else has gone home except another senior staff member who is occupied with another client. The new employee catches Simon trying to use the staff elevator. Simon tries to convince the new employee that he has been approved to use it, but the employee thinks this is another con job by someone trying to pull one over on her, and instead of verifying authorization with the senior staff member she makes Simon use the stairs. At the top of the stairs Simon goes into cardiac arrest, and an ambulance is called. He suffers a heart attack but lives due to the fast-acting new employee. Alas, Simon sues the new employee, you, and your facility in a **Section 1983** case, asserting that the new employee is at fault for denying access and that you, the administrator, are at fault for not conveying the necessary information to train her appropriately. The facility overall is at fault because the event occurred inside it, Simon contends.

Can your facility be sued? For what? Can you be sued as an administrator? For what? Can the new employee be sued? For what? How would the courts likely rule on this one?

Juvenile Justice, Probation, and Parole

When a juvenile commits a new crime while on probation or parole, a warrant is issued for arrest until an investigation is completed.

© Bonnie Kamin/PhotoEdit

CHAPTER OUTLINE

KEY TERMS

parens patriae
mens rea
juvenile delinquency
conduct in need of supervision
     (CINS)

transfer of jurisdiction
concurrent jurisdiction
statutory exclusion
judicial waiver
intake

delinquency petition
adjudication
disposition
youth courts
school-based probation

School districts in Texas, California, and Maryland that receive state funding based on the number of students who attend class can actually lose money because of absentee students. For every student who misses one day of school, a district in Anaheim, California, loses $35. Some states have increased the penalty for habitual truancy. For example, "failure to attend school" is a Class C misdemeanor in Texas that can result in up to $500 in fines. Truancy is such a pervasive problem that in some larger cities, a judge has been designated solely to deal with all such cases (Brezosky, 2010).

As a diversionary alternative to juvenile hall and payment of fines, some districts are turning to handheld global positioning system (GPS) devices to track youths who repeatedly skip school. The new program requires truant students to carry a GPS device and to enter a code at key times during the day to track their exact location, such as going to and from home and school during lunch and just before an 8:00 PM curfew. Such youths receive an automated wake-up call and an adult "coach" calls them three times per week for progress reports. School district officials report that they have received grant funding to help pay for each GPS device, which costs between $300–$400 to purchase, with an operational cost of $8 per day. So far programs like these have resulted in absentee rates declining from 23% to 5% (Carpenter, 2011).

INTRODUCTION

The juvenile justice system becomes involved when juveniles engage in behaviors that violate family codes/civil law (status offenses) or violate criminal law (delinquency). It also becomes involved when juveniles need to be protected from abuse or neglect by their parents (dependent children). Sometimes a juvenile has a history of all three situations.

In the last decade, many state and county juvenile justice systems have decreased their use of detention, particularly removing misdemeanants and status offenders from detention. While cracking down on staff abuse of juveniles in detention, such systems have committed to serving youths in the least restrictive environment possible. With secure facilities costing an average of nearly $280 per day for one juvenile and mounting evidence that community corrections options are more effective, these latter have become the preferred choice for most offenses involving juveniles (Levin, 2010). This has meant more alternatives to detention, better methods of screening youths for risk, and increased community-based services, more created in the last few years than ever before.

These responses have decreased the rate of juvenile delinquency overall since the 1990s. Yet juvenile arrests still account for 17% of all violent crimes and 26% of all property crimes (when added in with adults) each year in the U.S. (Snyder, 2008). Delinquency concerns center around how to handle juveniles who violate laws, particularly those who commit serious and violent felony crimes. Answers do not come easily, partially because there are philosophical differences regarding juvenile offending. On the one hand is a recognition that many status offenses and delinquent acts originate from abusive families, unhealthy peer groups, school failure, life in high-crime areas, and other deeply rooted social problems and failures of social control (see Figure 13.1). On the basis of the concept of **parens patriae**, the juvenile justice system seeks to do what is best for a child's welfare and safety. On the other hand, the theory of just deserts advocates societal protection and the accountability of youth offenders based on the seriousness of an act committed and the harm done to a victim and outlying community. First we examine how the juvenile justice system compares with the adult criminal justice system.

parens patriae
Latin term meaning that the government acts as a "substitute parent" and allows the courts to intervene in cases in which it is in the child's best interest that a guardian be appointed for children who, through no fault of their own, have been neglected and/or are dependent.

FIGURE 13.1   Risk Factors Connected With Juvenile Delinquency

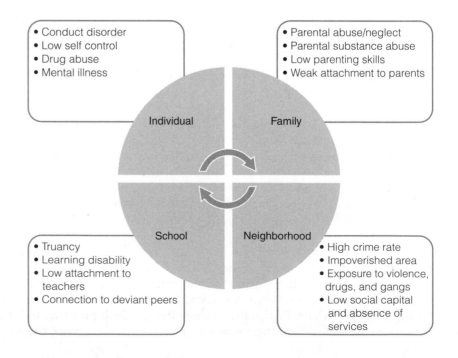

JUVENILE JUSTICE AND ADULT CRIMINAL JUSTICE SYSTEMS COMPARED

Despite a growing similarity between juvenile and adult criminal proceedings, some differences persist, the most notable being the role of a juvenile court judge. First, a juvenile court judge takes a more active part in proceedings. He or she is expected to act as a wise parent rather than as an impartial arbiter, which latter is a judge's role in adult criminal cases. A juvenile court judge may initiate questioning of an alleged offender, cross-examine witnesses, bring up a juvenile's background, and actively admonish or counsel him or her. Similarly, juvenile intake officers and judges have significantly more discretion than their counterparts have with adults, whether in a decision to dismiss a case with a warning, to divert it by informal probation, or to choose from a wide array of graduated sanctions. Juvenile justice personnel work in the best interest of a child rather than by a rigid set of rules or sentencing guidelines.

A third difference between juvenile and adult justice is in the severity of punishment imposed. For instance, juveniles spend limited time in institutions because they are released upon reaching a maximum age specified by state law. In contrast, adult criminals can be made to spend life in prison, a sanction that cannot be administered to juveniles unless they are tried as adults through a waiver or certification process. The differences between adult and juvenile proceedings are summarized below (del Carmen & Trulson, 2005):

Adult Proceedings	Juvenile Proceedings
1. Arrested	1. Taken into custody by police
2. Charged	2. Prosecutor petitions court
3. Accused of crime under the criminal penal code	3. Violation under the juvenile code or family code (civil)
4. Trial	4. Adjudication
5. Formal, public trial	5. Quasi-civil and private hearing
6. Right for case to heard by either a judge or jury	6. No right to a jury (although some states do provide a jury if requested)
7. Sentenced if found guilty	7. Disposition hearing to develop plan of action
8. Community-correctional options	8. Community-based placements, residential facilities, gender-specific services, family counseling
9. Incarcerated in a state or federal prison	9. Secure facility as last resort
10. Serves sentence for definite term or release determined by parole board	10. Youth detention authorities determine release or upon reaching age of majority
11. Released on parole, if eligible	11. Released for aftercare

In reality the above differences are more terminological than substantive and are, therefore, more symbolic than real. They have minimal impact on process because the procedures are similar regardless of the term used. For example, adults who are arrested and juveniles who are taken into custody are deprived of liberty and are under control of the criminal justice system. Because both processes lead to hearings, neither is there much difference between an adult suspect being charged and a prosecutor petitioning a court for a juvenile to be adjudicated. Sentencing and disposition both subject an offender to lawfully prescribed sanctions, including incarceration. Whether an adult is on parole or a juvenile is in aftercare, the degree of supervision and the results of violation are similar.

Jurisdiction of Juvenile Courts

The types of cases that proceed to juvenile courts are defined by state law. Jurisdiction, or an authority to try cases in juvenile courts, varies from state to state. Such jurisdiction is usually based on the *age* of an offender and the *act* committed.

mens rea
Latin term meaning "guilty mind" that addresses level of mental intent to commit a crime.

BASED ON AGE   Criminal liability is based on the concept of ***mens rea***, which is a Latin term for "a guilty mind" (Garner, 2009, p. 1006). Without intent, an act is generally not considered criminal. A guilty mind implies that an actor knows what he or she is doing; therefore, an act is punishable because the actor intended an injury to occur. Children under a certain age, however, are presumed by law to be unaware of the full consequences of their actions. Absent *mens rea*, they should not and cannot be punished like adults.

During the latter part of the eighteenth century, children younger than seven years old were deemed incapable of *mens rea* and exempt from criminal liability. Those above seven years of age could be prosecuted and sentenced to prison or given the death penalty if found guilty. No state in the United States at present punishes juveniles so severely at such a young age, but the minimum age that juveniles come under the jurisdiction of juvenile courts varies from state to state.

In present-day juvenile cases, there is an upper and lower age limit, as determined by state law. Wide variations exist among states—from a youngest age of six years when a juvenile enters the juvenile justice system to an oldest age of 24. For most states the juvenile age group over which they have original jurisdiction ranges from 10–17 years (see Figure 13.2). Juveniles younger than the minimum age who

FIGURE 13.2   Oldest Age in Which Juvenile Court Has Original Jurisdiction

Source: H. N. Snyder, and M. Sickmund. 2006. *National Report Services Bulletin: Juveniles in Court.* Washington, DC: Office of Juvenile Justice and Delinquency Prevention, p. 103.

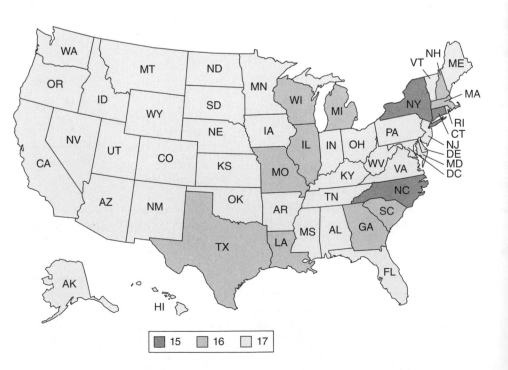

commit criminal acts are usually processed informally by police or placed in the care of state social welfare services. Offenders older than the maximum age are processed as adult criminals. The minimum and maximum ages refer to the age at which an act was committed, not when an offender was caught or tried in court.

BASED ON ACTS COMMITTED   Juvenile cases that trigger court intervention are of three types: **juvenile delinquency, conduct in need of supervision (CINS)**, and juveniles as victims. About six in ten of all juvenile justice cases are delinquency proceedings, which center upon criminal actions committed by juveniles that would also be considered criminal if committed by adults. Another two in ten cases are for conduct in need of supervision, which includes status offenses that would not be illegal if committed by an adult. The remaining two in ten cases concern child victims of abuse or neglect (Roberts, 2004).

Each state, by law, determines which acts come under each category. In general, juvenile delinquents are those who commit acts that are punishable under a state's penal code. Examples are murder, robbery, burglary, and any act considered criminal in a particular state. Every year juvenile courts in the United States handle an estimated 1.7 million juvenile delinquency cases (Knoll & Sickmund, 2010). Most delinquency cases (85%) have been referred by law enforcement agencies. The percentage of boys and girls adjudicated for each type of offense is presented in Table 13.1, which indicates that about 73% of all delinquency cases that come to a court's attention involve boys, while about 27% involve girls.

In contrast, CINS—also known in some jurisdictions as CHINS (children in need of supervision), MINS (minors in need of supervision), or JINS (juveniles in need of supervision)—are juveniles who commit status offenses that would *not* be punishable if committed by adults. These include truancy, running away from home, tobacco use, inhalant abuse, curfew violation, and underage drinking (Snyder & Sickmund, 2006). The most common status offense for girls is running away, which is tied to parental abuse or neglect. Law enforcement agencies refer fewer CINS cases to court than they do delinquency cases—just over half of all CINS cases have been referred to juvenile courts by police. The rest have reached the courts through reports from social services agencies, victims, probation officers, county attorneys, schools, or parents (Snyder & Sickmund, 2006).

Waiver to Adult Court

For the most serious and violent juvenile cases, all states have provisions for a **transfer of jurisdiction** from juvenile courts to adult courts. Transfer, also known as a *waiver* or *certification*, can be waived in three ways (Adams & Addie, 2010):

- **Statutory exclusion.** State legislative statutes automatically exclude certain juvenile offenders from juvenile court jurisdiction and require their cases be filed directly with criminal courts.

juvenile delinquency
Acts committed by juveniles that are punishable as crimes under a state's penal code.

conduct In need of supervision (CINS)
Acts committed by juveniles that would not have been punishable if committed by adults; status offenses.

transfer of jurisdiction
The transfer of a juvenile from juvenile court to adult court for trial.

statutory exclusion
The automatic exclusion of certain juvenile offenders from juvenile court jurisdiction by state statute, requiring the case to be filed directly with the adult criminal court.

TABLE 13.1   Delinquency and Gender Differences

Most Serious Offense	Girls	Boys
Total delinquency	27%	73%
Person	30%	70%
Property	27%	73%
Drugs	18%	82%
Public order	28%	72%

Source: C. Knoll , and M. Sickmund. 2010. *Delinquency cases in juvenile court, 2007.* Washington, DC: OJJDP.

judicial waiver
Transferring a juvenile case from a juvenile court to an adult court.

concurrent jurisdiction
Original jurisdiction for certain juvenile cases is shared by both criminal and juvenile courts, with the prosecutor having discretion to file such cases in either court.

- **Judicial waiver.** Authority to transfer a case to criminal court is given to a juvenile court judge, who certifies, remands, or binds over for criminal prosecution.
- **Concurrent jurisdiction.** Original jurisdiction is shared by both criminal and juvenile courts, in either of which a prosecutor has discretion to file. This process is also known in some states as prosecutorial waiver, prosecutor discretion, or direct file.

A court hearing must be held if a prosecutor requests certification, and ultimately judges rule on the decision. Most states allow that decision to be appealed.

Statutory exclusion has outpaced judicial waivers as the most commonly used transfer decision, insofar as prosecuting violent offenses against a person is mandatory. Other states allow a discretionary waiver as appropriate to the situation. Most waiver decisions follow an intake decision, or an initial decision to formally file a case before a court. Once transferred, a juvenile ceases being a juvenile and becomes an adult in the eyes of the law, including for the purposes of trial proceedings and sentencing.

Out of every 1,000 petitioned delinquency cases, only nine cases were judicially waived (Adams & Addie, 2010). Of the 8,500 cases waived in 2007, 48% were for violent crimes of person, 27% for property crimes, 13% for drugs, and 11% for public order crimes (Adams & Addie, 2010). A decision to transfer is, in theory, based on a juvenile's severity of offense, prior record, prior responses to supervision or treatment in the juvenile justice system, and level of dangerousness he or she might pose in the future. Wide variation on waivers exists among states, resulting in inconsistency. For example, although some juveniles did fit the transfer criteria, many certified juveniles presented no history of violent convictions, and 3 out of 10 offenders had no previous criminal record whatsoever.

Not all waived juveniles end up doing prison time. In fact, about half of waived cases are supervised on adult probation or in a community-based facility, which is comparable to what juveniles would have received in the juvenile justice system (Butts & Mears, 2001). The other half of waived juveniles (n = 4,095) who are found guilty are sentenced to confinement. Of the youths under age 18 in an adult prison, 51% are in maximum security, 38% are in medium security, and 11% are in minimum custody (U.S. Department of Justice, Bureau of Justice Statistics, 2003). One study found that incarcerating juveniles with adults increases the juveniles' rate of violence and later recidivism. Although waivers are indeed a symbol of "get tough" policies, the reality is that few youths are truly a public safety threat and most youths will age out of crime anyway (Butts & Mears, 2001).

AN OVERVIEW OF THE JUVENILE JUSTICE PROCESS

We have discussed general differences between juvenile justice and the adult criminal justice systems thus far. The civil or quasi-civil process of juvenile justice casts a wider net than that of the adult system. Juvenile behavior that sets the justice process in motion can come to attention by way of the general public, probation officers, victims, parents, neighbors, school authorities, and/or the police. Most state statutes encourage police officers to release juveniles to a parent or guardian. In practice, police officer decisions include release, warning, referral to a community agency for services, referral to a *citizen hearing board,* and referral to court intake. Figure 13.3 details the three stages of the juvenile justice process: intake, adjudication, and disposition.

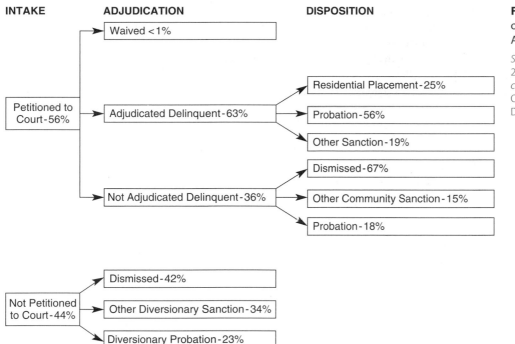

INTAKE   ADJUDICATION   DISPOSITION

FIGURE 13.3   Case Flow of Delinquency Cases After Arrest

Source: C. Knoll and M. Sickmund. 2010. *Delinquency cases in juvenile court, 2007.* Washington, DC: Office of Juvenile Justice and Delinquency Prevention, p. 4.

Intake

A juvenile taken into custody by police usually goes through an **intake** process—a case screening process that determines whether that juvenile should proceed further through the juvenile justice system or whether alternatives are more suitable. Intake officers are experts in crisis intervention, in gathering information, and in assessing risk and needs. Considered one of the most crucial points in the juvenile justice system, intake involves a probation officer interview of a youth and his or her parents or guardians. To determine potential causes of delinquency, intake questions pertain not only to a pending incident but also to juvenile home life, school problems, peers, mental health, drug abuse, and physical health. An intake officer can decide whether:

- a warning would suffice and a juvenile should be released to parents;
- an outside referral should be made to social services or drug court;
- a case qualifies for diversion;
- a case should go forward to the adjudication stage (i.e., whether enough evidence is present); and
- a case is serious enough to consider filing a petition to waive to adult court.

If a case is to be handled formally, a **delinquency petition** is filed to request either an adjudicatory hearing (in which a case proceeds through juvenile courts) or a waiver hearing (in which a case is further screened to see whether it should proceed through adult courts). If a case is to be handled informally through diversion, a petition will not be filed. Intake officers can decide whether to counsel parents and child and just close a case, even against a police officer's recommendation for formal adjudication.

Slightly less than half of all juvenile cases were either dismissed or diverted from the system at intake (Knoll & Sickmund, 2010). Cases were dismissed at intake because of lack of evidence. The diverted cases were documented in a written

intake
The process whereby a juvenile is screened to determine if the case should proceed further in the juvenile justice system or whether other alternatives are better suited for the juvenile.

delinquency petition
A petition that is filed to request a hearing to declare a youth as "delinquent".

agreement known as a consent decree. Juvenile diversion works identically to adult diversion and includes a period of supervision with such conditions as school attendance, community service, drug counseling, curfew, and restitution, if applicable. Diverted cases that were successfully completed resulted in later dismissal (Knoll & Sickmund, 2010).

Intake is considered highly subjective, involving very little collateral investigation or checking of sources. The intake process has been criticized for its lack of formal guidelines and a possibility of inconsistency from one intake officer to another (Lindner, 2008). As a result, prosecutors have replaced probation officers in some jurisdictions in an attempt to correct such inconsistency.

Intake can also involve detention screening, crisis intervention, and other procedures if mandated by a court. A juvenile may be detained by police but only up to 24 hours (Snyder & Sickmund, 2006). Federal law stipulates that juveniles be separated from adult offenders by "sight and sound." This assures that juveniles are detained in facilities separate from those used for adults. The U.S. Supreme Court has held that preventive detention of juveniles, due to a likelihood that they will commit other offenses, is constitutional (*Schall v. Martin*, 1984).

If an intake officer decides to refer a case to court, the prosecutor petitions the court for the juvenile in question to be adjudicated. A summons is issued directing the juvenile to appear before the court at a specified time and place for an initial appearance on the petition. An arraignment is then held, and the juvenile is given an opportunity to admit or deny the allegations.

Adjudication

adjudication
Juvenile justice equivalent of a trial in adult criminal cases.

Adjudication is the processing of a juvenile case through the juvenile courts, which are also known as family court or as probate court. Proceedings are less formal, and a judge takes a more active part in the hearing—including asking questions of juveniles, their parents or guardians, and witnesses. Although there are lawyers and rules of evidence, juveniles do not have a right to a jury trial or to bail. This is because the purpose of an adjudication hearing is to establish responsibility for a criminal act. About 64% of cases that go to family court are adjudicated delinquent, which is the same as a finding of guilt. The other 36% of cases *not* adjudicated delinquent will be dismissed unless a youth and his or her parents can be convinced to voluntarily take part in a sanction (Knoll & Sickmund, 2010). Table 13.2 illustrates the "big picture" outcomes of actual number of cases that were adjudicated in juvenile court versus cases that were not adjudicated.

TABLE 13.2   Case Outcomes of Adjudicated vs. Nonadjudicated Cases in Juvenile Court, 2007

Case Outcome	Adjudicated	Not Adjudicated	Total Juvenile Court Cases
Placement	148,603	0	148,603
Probation	327,425	234,194	561,619
Fines, restitution, community service	110,207	302,908	413,115
Dismissed after a warning or counseling	0	534,260	534,260
Waived to adult court	0	8,467	8,467
TOTAL	586,234	1,079,829	1,666,064

Source: M. Sickmund, A. Sladky, and W. Kang. 2010. Easy access to juvenile court statistics: 1985–2007. Available online: http://ojjdp.ncjrs.gov/ojstatbb/ezajcs/

YOUTH COURTS Most states have established **youth courts** to respond to youths who have no prior record and who have been involved in delinquency, such as vandalism or graffiti defacement, theft, disorderly conduct, assault, possession of marijuana, and minor possession of alcohol. The philosophy behind teen courts is to tap into the primary group of influence for young kids—other peers. The thinking here is that youths who have made bad choices are more likely to listen to other youths than to their parents or to other people they view as authority figures. Youth volunteers act as a panel or as jurors, usually under the supervision of an adult coordinator or adult judge (Butts & Buck, 2000). The National Youth Court Association reported that youth courts are most often tied to juvenile courts (42%) or sponsored by a school (36%) or by a private community agency (22%). Through these leadership roles, the teen court concept also allows prosocial youths an opportunity to become involved as positive mentors in their community and to learn about legal principles and their application.

> **youth courts**
> Community-based programs in which youth sentence their peers for minor delinquent and status offenses. Also known as teen, peer, and student courts.

Youth courts are a good example of restorative justice because many of their creative sentences involve a youth offender taking responsibility for his or her behavior and redressing harm to a victim and community. The most frequent dispositions given in youth court are community service, written apology or essay, and restitution. Some youths are sentenced to serve as jurors for other peers who come before a youth court, while others are engaged in victim offender mediation (Butts & Buck, 2000). The effectiveness of teen courts remains unclear, for most evaluations have not included a comparison group. The National Youth Court Association is the central clearinghouse of information related to programs and studies of youth courts (see www.youthcourt.net).

Disposition

If a juvenile is found to have engaged in conduct alleged in a petition, the **disposition** stage follows. For less serious misdemeanors and nonviolent felonies, a juvenile court judge wields greater discretion than do judges in adult criminal trials. Rehabilitation is an integral part of juvenile corrections, so a judge typically has a wide choice of available dispositions, including oral reprimand, probation, drug court, mental health court, and community service. Although most youths are still able to live at home on probation, some youths with too many problems at home or who show evidence of parental abuse or neglect require residential placement in a community-based facility.

> **disposition**
> Juvenile justice equivalent of sentencing in adult cases.

BLENDED SENTENCES Some states allow an opportunity for judges to impose both juvenile and adult correctional sanctions. In states such as Colorado, Massachusetts, Rhode Island, South Carolina, and Texas, a sanction starts under juvenile jurisdiction but when a juvenile comes of age, the case is transferred to the adult system. For example, if a 16-year-old female juvenile is sentenced to probation, she begins supervision under a juvenile probation officer. Upon reaching her 17th birthday (in some states the age is 18 years), her case is transferred to adult probation.

Other states (Arkansas, Connecticut, Iowa, Kansas, Minnesota, Missouri, Montana, and Virginia) allow for imposition of both juvenile and adult sanctions but suspend the adult sanction unless a juvenile violates the juvenile sanction. Blended sentencing laws thus create a middle ground between traditional juvenile and adult sanctions, but they also narrow the gap between juvenile and adult punishments. Currently, 21 states have some form of blended sentencing laws with limits for certain juvenile offenders (Snyder & Sickmund, 2006).

The U.S. Supreme Court decided that juveniles could no longer be sentenced to life without parole for non-homicide offenses that they committed when they were under the age of 18 (*Graham v. Florida* 2010 *Sullivan v. Florida*, 2010). The court based

A juvenile appears before a juvenile judge at a disposition hearing in which he received six months' probation and 80 hours of community service for shoplifting.

© Billy E. Barnes/PhotoEdit

its decision on the fact that a life without parole sentence does not allow any opportunity for release despite the fact that a juvenile will mature and change over time. The court agreed that a life without parole sentence for juvenile non-homicidal offenses is cruel and unusual punishment. The decision in this case seems to indicate that the court has re-emphasized once again that juveniles need to be treated and punished *differently* than adults, even for crimes when juveniles are charged as adults. In Terrence Graham's case, he and three friends attempted to rob a store and were charged with armed burglary with assault. Graham originally was sentenced to serve one year in the county jail followed by two years probation. Graham's probation officer filed a revocation when Graham was arrested for a new offense while on probation (burglary and attempted robbery). Other major U.S. Supreme Court cases that have affected juveniles over the last 45 years are summarized in Table 13.3.

RESIDENTIAL PLACEMENTS FOR JUVENILES

For more serious offenses, some states invoke determinate sentencing laws that require confinement in a secure institution for a minimum number of years (such as 1–10 years for a third-degree felony, 2–10 years for a second-degree felony, 3–10 years for a first-degree felony, and 10–40 years for a capital felony). Although most adjudicated delinquency cases have resulted in formal probation, about 25% of youths have been placed in residential settings such as (in order of most to least secure): training school, detention, reception or diagnostic center, inpatient drug treatment, boys' or girls' ranch, shelter, and private group home (Hockenberry, 2011; Sickmund, 2010). Table 13.4 compares the percentage of each type of facility that confines its residents, uses mechanical restraints on juveniles, locks juveniles in their rooms for four or more hours, and allows unauthorized departures. A considerable number of group homes, shelters, and wilderness camps are not secure facilities, and youths who decide not to comply with such programs can walk away.

Very few delinquents end up in a secure locked facility, such as a large training school or detention, which is designated for youths who have committed a felony

TABLE 13.3 Major United States Supreme Court Decisions in Juvenile Justice

Cases That Recognize Constitutional Rights for Juveniles	Cases That Limit Constitutional Rights for Juveniles
Kent v. United States (383 U.S. 541 [1966]) Juveniles must be given due process rights when transferred from juvenile to adult court. These rights consist of a hearing, counsel representation, access to court records, and a statement of reasons in support of a waiver order.	*McKeiver v. Pennsylvania* (403 U.S. 528 [1971]) Juveniles have no constitutional right to trial by jury even in juvenile delinquency cases in which a juvenile faces possible incarceration.
In re Gault (387 U.S. 1 [1967]) Juveniles must be given four due process rights in adjudication proceedings that can result in confinement in an institution in which their freedom would be curtailed. These rights consist of notice of charges, counsel (appointed if juvenile is indigent), ability to confront and cross-examine witnesses, and privilege against self-incrimination.	*Davis v. Alaska* (415 U.S. 308 [1974]) Despite confidentiality laws, the fact that a juvenile is on probation may be elicited by an opposing lawyer in a cross-examination of a juvenile witness.
In re Winship (397 U.S. 358 [1970]) Proof beyond a reasonable doubt, not simply by a preponderance of the evidence, is required in juvenile adjudication hearings in cases in which an act would have been a crime if committed by an adult.	*Smith v. Daily Mail Publishing Co.* (443 U.S. 97 [1979]) A state law making it a crime to publish the name of a juvenile charged with a crime is unconstitutional because it violates the First Amendment right to freedom of the press.
Breed v. Jones (421 U.S. 517 [1975]) Juveniles are entitled to a constitutional right against double jeopardy in juvenile proceedings.	*Schall v. Martin* (467 U.S. 253 [1984]) Preventive detention of juveniles is constitutional.
Roper v. Simmons (543 U.S. 551 [2005]) It is unconstitutional to execute juveniles who committed their crime before the age of 18.	*Fare v. Michael C.* (442 U.S. 707 [1985]) A request by a juvenile to see his probation officer is not equivalent to asking for a lawyer. Moreover, there is no probation officer-client privilege, meaning that any information a juvenile gives to a probation officer may be divulged in court even if the information were given by the juvenile in confidence.
Graham v. Florida (08-7412) and *Sullivan v. Florida* (08-7621) 560 U.S. __ [2010] Juveniles may not be sentenced to life without the possibility of parole for a nonhomicide they committed while under the age of 18 because such punishment is cruel and unusual.	*New Jersey v. T.L.O* (469 U.S. 325 [1985]) Public school officials need reasonable grounds to search students; they do not need a warrant or probable cause.

offense and are a danger to a community. This risk would explain why such a facility most often uses isolation, mechanical restraints and other confinement measures. About 70% of residential facilities are publicly operated settings in which youths from 15–17 years old have been placed by the courts. Some youths are being temporarily held in detention centers until their cases are adjudicated and disposed. The reality is that many of these youths pose little threat to a community, and alternatives can be provided.

Group Homes

Group homes, home-like settings with sitting areas, a kitchen, and bedrooms, are considered among the least restrictive residential placements for youths unable to live with their own families (Deitch, 2009). There are typically 10–20 youths of

TABLE 13.4   Characteristics of Residential Facilities for Juveniles (percentages reflect facilities that reportedly engaged in a particular practice if necessary [N = 2,458])

Type of Facility	Locked Youth in Isolation for 4 + Hours	Other Confinement Features (other than locked sleeping rooms)	Used Mechanical Restraints	Had Unauthorized Youth Departures
Training school (n = 210)	51%	93%	69%	6%
Detention (n = 734)	45%	96%	42%	3%
Reception/diagnostic center (n = 64)	31%	75%	52%	10%
Residential treatment center (n = 847)	10%	46%	16%	29%
Wilderness camp/ ranch (n = 85)	6%	26%	20%	38%
Shelter (n = 167)	4%	30%	4%	37%
Group home (n = 661)	1%	13%	2%	39%
TOTAL FACIL TIES (N = 2,458)	**21%**	**53%**	**23%**	**22%**

Source: S. Hockenberry, M. Sickmund, and A. Sladky. 2011. *Juvenile residential facility census, 2008: Selected findings.* Washington, DC: Office of Juvenile Justice and Delinquency Prevention.

the same sex between the ages of 12–17 living together under 24-hour supervision. They attend school together, participate in weekly family counseling and in community activities like field trips, and are assigned to an individual counselor. Most group homes are privately owned and operated by contracting out to state and county government. They cost $115 per day per person, compared to $162 for a secure placement (Deitch, 2009).

Given that secure institutions are located in remote areas of a state and that the larger ones tend to be less safe, the current trend has been to decrease the percentage of youths living in such large facilities. The alternative is to employ a continuum of sanctions using smaller community-based facilities and other community options, such as probation and those depicted in Figure 13.4.

JUVENILE PROBATION

As with adults, probation is the disposition most often used by judges when formally adjudicating juvenile delinquency cases. Juvenile probation can be formal or informal. **Formal probation** takes place through court action after an adjudication hearing in which a juvenile is found to have committed a delinquent act. Informal probation occurs when a juvenile voluntarily (or with prior consent from his or her parents) agrees to be placed on probation even prior to adjudication. If he or she adheres to the conditions imposed, charges are dropped and nothing appears in the juvenile's record.

Nearly six in ten delinquency cases receive some form of probation. Over the last two decades, the number of formal probation cases increased to 327,400 juveniles while the number of informal probation cases decreased to 173,100, reflecting a trend toward formal juvenile case processing, primarily for property offenses (Livsey, 2010). The gender split of youths on probation is 75% male and 25% female, with youths aged 14–16 accounting for the largest share of probationers.

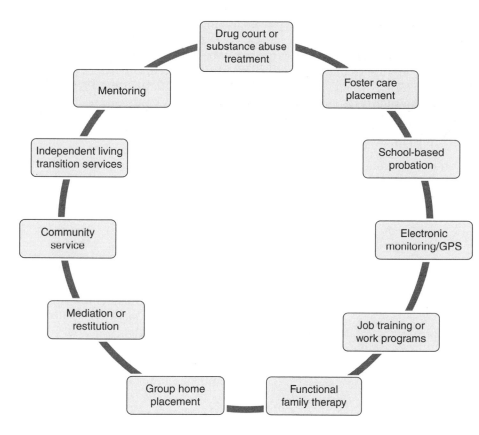

FIGURE 13.4   Community Correctional Program Options for Juveniles

Conditions of Probation

Juvenile court judges have considerable discretion when imposing probation conditions because very few states specify which conditions should be imposed. Instead, setting conditions is left to the sound discretion of a juvenile court, usually upon recommendation of a probation officer acting as a wise parent. Typically conditions include provisions designed to control as well as to rehabilitate a juvenile. These dual goals make the imposition of conditions more challenging for a court but at the same time assure wide discretion, in that just about any condition of probation can be justified as rehabilitative and as contributory to behavior control.

Juvenile probation conditions are either mandatory or discretionary. Mandatory conditions are nearly identical to conditions for adults, with an addition of curfew and mandatory school attendance. If a juvenile is unable to live at home, he or she is placed in a foster home, group home, or other residential setting. Discretionary conditions have included therapy effective for families (functional family therapy), individual cognitive-behavioral therapy, drug treatment, and gender-specific services that are different for girls than for boys.

Change as an Integral Process

Changing attitudes and behaviors is a difficult and sometimes painstaking process, but this is an integral part of growing from a youth into an adult. Encouraging the maturation process is the essence of juvenile probation and its most effective tool for rehabilitation. An important part of change consists of a realization that it is a process involving

FACT OR **FICTION?**

Probation is thought of mainly as a supervision condition for diverted or adjudicated juveniles.

Fact: Probation is the most common form of supervision for diverted or adjudicated juveniles.

some minor victories and also some setbacks. Change is not like a light switch that can be turned on and off at will; rather, it occurs over time. A frequently asked question about the change process is whether change can be forced or whether its undertaking is completely up to each individual. If change is self-induced, when does it occur and how do people know when they've changed? Box 13.1 addresses these very important questions from a former director of a boys' ranch for at-risk youths.

Juvenile Probation Officers as "Superheroes"

The job of a juvenile probation officer is often more demanding than that of an adult probation officer. Playing multiple roles of hard-nosed cop, confessor, teacher, problem solver, crisis manager, and community resource specialist, this officer has

---

BOX 13.1   FIELD NOTES

Question: When you worked as a program director at a boys' ranch, when did youth offenders begin to make changes in their lives and who was instrumental in that process?

In juvenile corrections success is measured by the future behaviors of the youth. As program director my charges were urban youth who were knockin' on prisons' door due to repeated offenses and probation violations. To succeed I needed to learn how to create the conditions where most of the boys would make the decision to change and how to make that happen as early as possible.

To help learn what worked I conducted an exit interview with every boy that successfully finished the program and tracked recidivism. The most significant discovery was boys that changed could always discuss when they made the decision! They could easily talk about what was happening at the time, who was helpful to them in deciding to make the change, and how they went about it. These decisions were usually made alone, thinking about their situation and deciding to try a technique taught in a skills group on anger management, problem solving or assertiveness. The usual time frame for making the decision was 3 to 5 months. There were some 30-day wonders and some hardheads at 9 to 10 months, but they were not the norm.

After hearing about their decision to change, my focus in the interview shifted to asking if there was anything we could have done to get them to make the decision earlier. The short answer is that resistance to change varies widely between individuals. When asked if the reason for such a late decision was "on us" or "on you," the latter was the case. The usual answer was, "It was on me because I wasn't ready to change."

Courtesy of Leanne Fiftal Alarid

Mark Masterson, M.Ed., NCC
Director of Corrections, Sedgwick County, Kansas

The interviews helped me realize that reducing resistance to change first requires feeling safe in your environment. That doesn't happen fast in a juvenile offender facility. For this reason I sequenced programming to include cognitive skills curricula on problem solving, anger management and refusal skills during the first three months. It worked well and was like "planting seeds" to grow when the time was right.

Decisions to change ingrained antisocial thinking, attitudes and behaviors are hard work and most likely to be made during times of pain and frustration. Each setback or crisis translates into an opportunity for self-reflection and supportive intervention. Interestingly, not a single youth reported making the decision during a scheduled counseling session. For this reason all direct care staff needed to be trained to watch for and effectively use these moments and to be included as members of the treatment teams.

The conditions for change are ripe when the youth is "tired of being tired" of the risks and consequences of their behavior and they decide to reach out to a staff member they feel cares about them. I found maximizing these opportunities was the key for youth to make a decision to change in less time. Staff members that are able to connect with youth and make themselves available at these times are critical to the change process. Many times when told of their helpfulness, the staff member did not realize the significance of the moment for the youth. It was their usual practice of doing their jobs, having a caring attitude, being approachable and then available to the youth that separated the most effective staff from the rest. This became a cornerstone of our training program and helped improve youth success and reduce recidivism.

a difficult job made even more challenging by changing system philosophies, programs that won't accept particular youths, and an increasingly high-risk clientele.

In his book *Screwing the System and Making It Work*, Mark Jacobs (1990) observed the drama and genuine passion that juvenile probation officers exhibited in their jobs as advocates for youths who had never had anyone else stand up for them. Jacobs describes such barriers as unsupportive parents and sometimes the narrow criteria of the system itself, with its agencies often screening out the very youths who most needed help. The paperwork situation is frustrating, along with the inordinate amount of time spent in court appearances, investigations, and furnishing necessary documentation, all of which take away from counseling and helping functions. Despite these drawbacks, juvenile probation officers remained optimistic, believing that change is possible. Validated by Jacobs as modern-day "superheroes," these officers display a noteworthy creativity and sacrifice in their jobs despite systemic barriers (Jacobs, 1990). A juvenile probation officer who prioritizes rehabilitation as part of system accountability is the last hope for a juvenile (Ward & Kupchik, 2009).

It is therefore recommended that, when developing individualized case plans, probation officers consider equally the juvenile offender, the victim, and the community. This standard further requires that a probation officer, in conjunction with a juvenile and his or her family, assesses medical needs, individual capacity to benefit from a program, transportation availability, and availability of a community placement.

Intensive Supervision Probation

Intensive supervision probation (ISP) is defined as a program of intensive surveillance of and contact with an offender aimed at reducing criminal conduct by limiting opportunities to engage in it. ISP is for serious and/or chronic offenders who would otherwise be committed to a correctional facility but are eligible for community placement. Strategies vary from one state to another, but there are some common features in intensive supervision of juveniles:

- unannounced visits at home, school, known hangouts, and job sites;
- collateral contact of family members, friends, teachers, and neighbors; and
- curfew enforcement.

intensive supervision probation
A form of probation that stresses intensive monitoring, close supervision, and offender control.

Historically, this program was called "Operation Night Light" in many jurisdictions because it involved juvenile probation officers and police officers who traveled together making evening home visits of probationers. The partnership involved each officer stepping out of his or her traditional role to take a collaborative interest in the juvenile's progress (Alarid, Sims, & Ruiz, 2011a). Intensive supervision can include an in-home, evidence-based family counseling approach such as functional family therapy, family crisis counseling, or family system intervention. Family counseling that occurs at least twice per week for 15 weeks seems more effective, especially with higher-risk juveniles 14 years and younger (Lipsey, Howell, & Tidd, 2002).

School-Based Probation

A comparatively new but increasingly popular concept in juvenile probation supervision is **school-based probation**. As we discussed at the beginning of this chapter, truancy is a serious problem in primary and secondary education that is also linked to delinquency. In school-based probation supervision, juvenile probation officers have their offices right in a school building and are likely to also get access to student attendance records, grades, and progress reports, which is information

school-based probation
A type of probation where probation officers move out of traditional district offices into middle, junior high, and high school buildings and supervise their caseloads right in the schools.

School-based probation officers have partnered with school resource officers to reduce truancy and keep a closer eye on kids already on probation.

unavailable to most traditional juvenile probation officers. Juvenile probation has thus partnered with schools and campus police to enforce probation conditions and prevent future delinquency (Alarid, Sims, & Ruiz, 2011b). Benefits of school-based probation include:

- *More contact.* More direct contact with probationers—in some cases daily contact—can lead to better relationships and more awareness of school, home, and peer problems.
- *Direct observation.* Direct observation of probationers' interactions with other youths can lead to more effective and immediate responses to problems.
- *Increased school success.* Juveniles supervised by school-based probation officers can have more incentive to attend school regularly and to try hard, increasing their overall chances of succeeding as students.
- *Reduced misbehavior at school.* (Griffin & Torbet, 2002).

Alarid and her colleagues (2011b) found that strong leadership, information sharing, and involvement of parents were three contributors to program success.

Legal Issues in Juvenile Probation

The only case ever to be decided by the U.S. Supreme Court on juvenile probation supervision is *Fare v. Michael C.* (1985). This important California case helps to define the relationship between a probation officer and a probationer during probation supervision. Michael C., a juvenile, was taken into police custody because he was suspected of having committed a murder. He was advised of his *Miranda v. Arizona* (1966) rights. When asked whether he wanted to waive his right to have an attorney present during questioning, he responded by asking for his probation officer. He was informed by police that his probation officer would be contacted later but that he could talk to them if he wanted.

Michael C. agreed to talk to police and during questioning made statements and drew sketches that incriminated himself. When charged with murder in juvenile court, he moved to suppress the incriminating evidence, alleging it was obtained in violation of his *Miranda* rights. He said that his request to see his probation officer was, in effect, equivalent to asking for a lawyer. However, the evidence was admitted at trial, and Michael C. was convicted.

On appeal the U.S. Supreme Court affirmed the conviction, holding that the request by a juvenile probationer during police questioning to see his probation officer, after having received the *Miranda* warnings, is not equivalent to asking for a lawyer and is not considered an assertion of the right to remain silent. Evidence voluntarily given by the juvenile probationer after asking to see his probation officer is therefore admissible in court in a subsequent criminal trial.

The *Michael C.* case is significant because the Supreme Court laid out two principles that help define the supervisory role of a juvenile probation officer. First, the Court stated that confidentiality of communication between a probation officer and a juvenile probationer is not equivalent to lawyer-client privilege. This means that information given by a probationer to a probation officer may be disclosed in court, unlike the information given to a lawyer by a client that cannot be revealed to anyone unless the right to confidentiality is waived by both client and lawyer. Said the Court:

> A probation officer is not in the same posture [as a lawyer] with regard to either the accused or the system of justice as a whole. Often he is not trained in the law, and so is not in a position to advise the accused as to his legal rights. Neither is he a trained advocate, skilled in the representation of the interests of his client before police and courts. He does not assume the power to act on behalf of his client by virtue of his status as advisor, nor are the communications of the accused to the probation officer shielded by the lawyer-client privilege.

Second, the *Fare v. Michael C.* case is also significant because the Court emphasized that a probation officer's loyalty and first obligation are to the state, despite any obligation owed to a probationer. The Court said:

> Moreover, the probation officer is the employee of the State which seeks to prosecute the alleged offender. He is a peace officer, and as such is allied, to a greater or lesser extent, with his fellow peace officers. He owes an obligation to the State notwithstanding the obligation he may also owe the juvenile under his supervision. In most cases, the probation officer is duty bound to report wrongdoing by the juvenile when it comes to his attention, even if by communication from the juvenile himself.

This statement defines where a probation officer's loyalty lies. Professionalism requires that an officer's loyalty must be with the state and not with a probationer, regardless of the sympathy that officer might have for the juvenile.

JUVENILE PAROLE/AFTERCARE

Juveniles who are confined in a state institution are released on aftercare, which is the equivalent of parole. Juvenile aftercare dates back to the 18th century when youths were released to "masters" for additional training (Gordon, 2003, p. 5). Today's youths are released to their families and monitored by a court. There are currently 100,000 youths who transition out of secure placements every year. Many lack the necessary developmental skills to obtain a job or to survive independently when they are released. Instead, they return to "families struggling with domestic violence, substance abuse, unresolved mental health disabilities, and extremely low income. Many youths return to neighborhoods with few supportive programs, high crime rates, poverty, and poorly performing schools" (Youth Reentry Task Force of the Juvenile Justice and Delinquency Prevention Coalition, 2009, p. 9). Many recently released youths who have not completed school face unemployment and homelessness.

A release decision is left to the discretion of institutional officials, with the exception of a few states that have juvenile parole boards. If released on aftercare, a juvenile is supervised after he or she reaches the age of majority—generally 18 years of age. In some jurisdictions juvenile officers supervise both juvenile probationers and parolees. The conditions of probation and parole are the same in many jurisdictions, the most common being not committing violations of the law, getting gainful employment, meeting curfew, submitting to electronic monitoring and drug testing, reporting regularly, and allowing home visits. Juvenile aftercare presents many challenges including: "(1) a lack of communication between institutional staff and aftercare staff during the transitional period, (2) the inability to identify appropriate service providers for youth, (3) large caseload sizes for aftercare workers, and (4) selection of inappropriate youth for aftercare" (Gordon, 2003, p. 4).

To overcome these challenges, Congress passed the Chafee Foster Care Independence Act, which provides monetary assistance to states to develop programs and provide vouchers to former foster care youths between the ages of 16 and 21. The act, administered through the U.S. Department of Health and Human Services, attempts to help at-risk foster care youths to achieve self-sufficiency as adults. This act affects 30,000 foster care youths, out of the nearly half a million youths currently in foster homes, who emancipate every year (Youth Reentry Task Force of the Juvenile Justice and Delinquency Prevention Coalition, 2009).

For youths coming from secure correctional institutions, housing, mental health care, and employment are chief concerns. Youths who received mental health care within their first three months after release were significantly less likely to recidivate than were delinquents who did not receive such services (Bouffard & Bergseth, 2008). Task forces call for a federal policy to strengthen funding for reentry to assist vulnerable youths with the integration process of finding appropriate housing, continuing to receive medical and mental health services, and benefitting from some sort of transition mentoring (Youth Reentry Task Force of the Juvenile Justice and Delinquency Prevention Coalition, 2009).

Juvenile Parole Boards and Parole Officers

Most release decisions are made by a committee at an institution or else a youth is released when he or she ages out of the juvenile justice system. Only five states have a separate juvenile parole board (California, Colorado, New Jersey, South Carolina, and Utah), whose memberships vary from five to nine members. Some members serve full time, others part time; most are appointed by a governor while others are elected; some are paid, others unpaid (Frendle, 2004).

Juvenile parole officers have duties and responsibilities similar to those of adult parole officers. For example, a parole officer (State of New Hampshire, Human Resources, 2006):

- conducts predispositional and other investigations as directed by a court or juvenile parole board of juvenile delinquents and/or children in need of services;
- prepares written reports and recommendations for a court or juvenile parole board, including reporting alleged violations of conditional release and juvenile parole;
- supervises juveniles in order to ensure compliance with the terms of conditional release, juvenile parole, or other conditions set forth by a court or juvenile parole board;

- takes into custody juveniles who violate conditional release or juvenile parole and prepares case information for prosecution before a court or juvenile parole board;
- coordinates with court officials, law enforcement agencies, community-based agencies, state agencies, family members, and the public to assist a court in making dispositional determinations on matters of juvenile delinquency and children in need of services;
- provides family-centered intervention to families and caretakers to help maintain a family unit;
- coordinates suitable out-of-home care to meet specific needs of a juvenile and family, including facilitating transportation; and
- manages cases to ensure that case plans are carried out and that court and administrative reviews under state and federal laws are completed in a timely manner.

Probation and parole officers use both confrontational and client-centered approaches with juveniles. Confrontational strategies were used more frequently with younger clients and included informing youths of potential consequences ahead of time in order to obtain compliance. Rapport, motivational interviewing, and the art of persuasion were used as well to decrease revocation (Schwalbe & Maschi, 2011).

Revocation of Juvenile Probation or Parole

The revocation rate of delinquent youths is quite high. Between one-third up to one-half commit a new offense while under supervision, and more are revoked for technical violations (Schwalbe & Maschi, 2011). The revocation process works the same way as it does for adults (discussed in chapter 7). Most delinquents have committed an offense similar to a misdemeanor or a status offense, for which probation is the maximum sanction. If probation is revoked, however, a juvenile can then be classified as a delinquent because of violation of a court order. Revocation for delinquent offenses categorized as felonies can result in a juvenile being sent to an institution for juveniles. Revocation of a blended sentence can result in imposition of a sentence that continues into adulthood.

THE FUTURE OF JUVENILE JUSTICE

The juvenile justice system is over 100 years old, and in that time it has undergone a huge transformation into the system we have today. Although the future of juvenile court as a separate entity from the adult criminal justice system is still debated, the juvenile system we have now is more balanced with elements of both rehabilitation and punishment. There are a wider range of community-based and graduated sanctions than in the past. There are diversion options such as drug courts and mental health courts to keep children out of the juvenile system, yet options exist for youths who are better served in the adult system. The use of assessment tools is important for the prevention of and early intervention in youths with substance abuse and mental health problems. An emphasis on restorative justice is ideal for facilitating a stronger family unit and increasing institutions of social control through schools, peer groups, and communities. Evidence-based practices and use of technology to increase data gathering and information sharing have filtered into juvenile agencies. The most effective programs for juvenile offenders appear to be community-based, small residential facilities that offer individual cognitive-behavioral therapy as well as family counseling, quality education classes, and aftercare support (Zavlek, 2005). With the implantation of evidence-based practices in juvenile corrections, we believe the future of juvenile justice looks bright.

SUMMARY

- Juvenile justice in the United States is heavily influenced by *parens patriae* and the concept of diminished *mens rea*.

- Juvenile courts are an American creation that have jurisdiction based on age and acts committed. Minimum and maximum ages for juveniles vary from state to state.

- Juvenile delinquency refers to acts that, if committed by adults, are punishable under a state's penal code; conduct in need of supervision comprises acts committed by juveniles that, if committed by adults, would not be punishable at all.

- After a juvenile is taken into custody, the processing sequence for juveniles consists of intake, adjudication, and disposition.

- Juveniles may be transferred for trial from a juvenile court to an adult court. Once transferred to an adult court, a juvenile is tried and punished like an adult. Juveniles are allowed parole as an option for all non-homicide offenses and cannot be sentenced to death for homicide.

- Probation is the disposition that judges use most often in delinquency cases.

- Juvenile probation through schools is a mechanism by which youths can be effectively supervised.

- No conclusive data or study establishes that juvenile probation or parole is more effective than other approaches to corrections.

DISCUSSION QUESTIONS

1. How does *parens patriae* influence the way juvenile offenders are processed?

2. Do you think the juvenile justice system should become more like the adult criminal justice system? If so, for which types of offenses? If not, why not?

3. Provide examples illustrating the main difference between juvenile delinquency and conduct in need of supervision. Can both apply to a juvenile?

4. In the traditional juvenile justice system, do the intake, adjudication, and disposition stages unfairly label children as delinquent?

5. Do you think that youth court should be expanded to include crimes other than vandalism, theft, disorderly conduct, assault, possession of marijuana, and minor in possession of alcohol? If so, what other crimes and why?

6. Pick one effective method of supervising a juvenile in a community and discuss the characteristics of the program, concluding with why you believe it to be effective.

7. Is school-based probation an effective means of supervision? Why or why not?

8. What did the Court say in the case of *Fare v. Michael C.*? Why is that case important for probation officers?

9. In the juvenile justice cases that have been decided by the U.S. Supreme Court, what general trend or direction is noteworthy?

10. If you could change anything about the juvenile justice system, what would it be and how would your change make an improvement?

WEBSITES, VIDEOS, AND PODCASTS

Websites

The National Youth Court Association
   http://www.youthcourt.net/

American Bar Association Juvenile Justice Center
   http://www.abanet.org/dch/committee.
   cfm?com=CR200000

National Council on Crime and Delinquency
   http://www.nccd-crc.org/

National Youth Gang Center
   http://www.iir.com/nygc

South Dakota Juvenile Aftercare
http://doc.sd.gov

Texas Youth Commission
http://www.tyc.state.tx.us

Videos/Podcasts

Juvenile Delinquency Court Orientation
http://www.youtube.com/watch?v=rRXKIZTKJ-w

This 13-minute video provides an educational overview of a delinquency court in California.

Inside Juvenile Detention: Court Day
http://www.youtube.com/watch?v=diXmUvZb_eg

This eight-minute video shows a real juvenile justice court hearing to determine the best placement for two brothers.

Addressing the Needs of Juvenile Status Offenders and Their Families
http://www.youtube.com/watch?v=1wh1TKc_I2Q

This two-hour educational video is sponsored by the Office of Juvenile Justice and Delinquency Prevention, the American Bar Association Commission on Youth at Risk, and the Department of Health and Human Services Families/Youth Services Bureau.

Trying Children as Adults Panel, Florida (1 hour, 50 minutes)
http://www.mainsailcom.com/ABA/

Girls in the Correction System
http://www.corrections.com/system/podcast/file/16/media_20050201.mp3

This is a podcast of an interview with the CEO of Girl Inc. about girls in the correctional system.

Juvenile Reentry
http://www.corrections.com/system/podcast/file/47/media_20030717.mp3

A podcast discussion about the juvenile offender and reentry programs

San Diego County Probation Department Video 1–3
http://www.youtube.com/watch?v=ZSLTeyfcQWs&feature=related
http://www.youtube.com/watch?v=Q3WFV2Vlmkc&feature=related
http://www.youtube.com/watch?v=qFk51TkAJGQ&feature=related

This is a series of three videos that examines probation and the juvenile court system in San Diego County.

CASE STUDY EXERCISE

Juvenile Justice, Probation, and Parole

You are a juvenile probation officer attempting to decide what to do about each of the court referrals before you in order to make recommendations to a judge. Should a case be dismissed? Should a case be diverted to another program (e.g., to teen court)? Should a case be adjudicated? If so, should a case be adjudicated within the juvenile justice system, or should the case be waived to adult court?

CASE A

Brian is a 13-year-old male who has come to the attention of a court for an offense of vandalism. He and a friend "tagged" a school building with graffiti and broke several windows in the school gymnasium. The school principal estimated the total damage and cleanup costs to be approximately $1,300. Brian resides with both natural parents and two younger siblings. The family income is $65,000 annually. Brian admits to the offense but refuses to identify his co-offender to authorities. The family has agreed to pay complete restitution. Brian has no prior juvenile record although he has been disciplined several times in school in the past year for minor violations of school rules. His grades, which were formerly A's and B's, have fallen off to C's and D's.

CASE B

Quint is a 17-year-old male who has been referred to a court for aggravated robbery. He is accused of robbing a convenience store and assaulting the clerk. He is a high school dropout with a lengthy history of arrests including robbery, burglary, car theft, and larceny. Quint was adjudicated delinquent for burglary 10 months before the current offense and placed on probation. His probation officer reports that he has been uncooperative and hostile toward supervision. He lives off and on with his mother and three younger siblings. His mother reports that she has little control over his behavior and that he spends many nights away from home. She suspects that he is using drugs.

CASE C

Carlos is a 15-year-old male who was referred to a court for truancy. He has missed 34 school days in the past 90 days and is failing in all his classes. His parents report that they send him to school every day, but he never stays. Even when they take him to the front door of the school, he leaves immediately after they do. Carlos is of average intelligence and relates well to his peers. He has no other involvement with illegal activity, and until this past school year he did well in school, attending regularly. His parents have no explanation for the change in his behavior.

CASE D

Cathy is a 14-year-old female who has been referred to a court for running away. Her parents report she is a chronic runaway, having left home on more than 10 occasions since age 12. She is in the seventh grade. She has been held back twice and is thus two grade levels behind her peers. Cathy was diagnosed with Attention Deficit Disorder at age seven. She is currently taking Ritalin under a physician's supervision. Her parents have attempted to get help for Cathy on many occasions, but nothing seems to be effective. She has been referred once for shoplifting, three times for truancy, and three times previously for running away.

Collateral Consequences of Felony Convictions and Restoration of Rights

CHAPTER LEARNING OBJECTIVES

1. Identify why civil and political rights are important.
2. Describe examples of civil rights that are lost as a result of felony conviction.
3. Justify the rationale behind granting a pardon.
4. Explain the various ways in which civil rights may be restored.

Job applications that ask about prior convictions create a tough situation for felons who are court-ordered to find employment. How are the needs of employers to screen applicants balanced with a desire for felons to become productive societal members?

Have you been convicted of a crime in the past ten years other than misdemeanors and summary offenses?

Yes ☐   No ☐

If yes, explain circumstances and disposition of matter below.

CHAPTER OUTLINE

KEY TERMS

civil rights
political rights
outlawry
attainder
good moral character
moral turpitude

public offices
surety bond
pardon
conditional pardon
certificate of rehabilitation

automatic restoration of rights
certificate of discharge
expungement
sealing of records
restricted access

Receiving a presidential pardon is difficult these days, and it is anyone's guess what distinguishes a successful application from one that is turned down. So far since he took office, President Obama has granted only 17 pardons while he has denied nearly 800 applications, along with a denial of nearly 2,000 sentence commutations. Randy Dyer was one of the lucky ones who was granted a pardon for a 1975 conviction for distributing drugs to the U.S. from Mexico. He and his wife Karla gathered references from about 100 people who attested to Mr. Dyer's upstanding moral character, even though an application had required only three people to sign affidavits on the applicant's behalf. It is likely that the 35 years that Mr. Dyer spent changing the lives of countless prisoners as a preacher at a correctional facility had something to do with it. Now all his civil rights have been restored, but his conviction still remains on record. People who are denied a pardon can reapply at a later date (Delaney, 2011).

INTRODUCTION

I really get kind of peeved when people say "give back to the community" because I'm not a part of the community anymore as far as I can see it . . . [the] community doesn't want a damn thing to do with me, why should I go back and give anything to do with the community?

—Paul, former offender (as cited in Uggen, Manza, & Behrens, 2004, p. 280)

You are no doubt aware that conviction of a crime results in a direct penalty such as a fine, probation, community-based sanction, or even confinement. However, this chapter discusses the less known collateral, or indirect, consequences of a felony conviction. Distinctions between direct and collateral consequences of conviction are summarized in Table 14.1.

Collateral consequences of conviction include both civil and political disqualification or deprivation. *Black's Law Dictionary* defines **civil rights** as "individual rights of personal liberty guaranteed by the Bill of Rights and by the 13th, 14th, 15th, and 19th Amendments, as well as by legislation such as the Voting Rights Act" (Garner, 2009, p. 263). Civil rights are enjoyed by all people—citizens, aliens, legal residents, and undocumented immigrants—within the borders of the United States. Such rights include freedom of speech, freedom of the press, freedom from discrimination, and freedom of assembly. **Political rights** entail "the right to participate in the establishment or administration of government, such as the right to vote or the right to hold public office" (Garner, 2009, p. 1348). Political rights are limited to citizens.

civil rights
Rights that belong to a person by virtue of citizenship.

political rights
Rights related to the participation in the establishment, support, or management of government.

Background of Civil Disabilities

Collateral consequences of conviction have roots in ancient Greek and Roman as well as English civilizations. Historically the purposes of civil penalties were to register social disapproval and to disallow family members from inheriting any property of guilty offenders (Damaska, 1968). The Greeks called such a disability *infamy,* a word that found its way into Anglo-American criminal law in the term *infamous crimes.* Infamous crimes carried severe penalties as well as additional sanctions of outlawry and attainder. **Outlawry** considered offenders outside the protection of the law and, in effect, established open season on them for any citizen to hunt down and kill. These *outlaws* lost all civil rights and forfeited all property to the Crown through **attainder**, defined in common law as "the act of extinguishing a person's civil rights when that person is sentenced to death or declared an outlaw for committing a felony or treason" (Garner, 2009, p. 137). Outlawry and attainder were justified insofar as offenders were considered to have declared war on society by committing an infamous crime, and therefore a community had a right to retaliation and retribution.

outlawry
In old Anglo-Saxon law, the process by which a criminal was declared an outlaw and placed outside the protection and aid of the law.

attainder
At common law, the extinction of civil rights and capacities that occurred when a person received a sentence of death or outlawry for treason or another felony. The person's estate was forfeited to the Crown.

TABLE 14.1   Direct and Collateral Consequences of Conviction

Direct Consequences of Conviction	Collateral Consequences
Criminal penalties, as specified in a state or federal penal code	Civil consequences, as specified in various state or federal laws or by administrative agencies, local agencies, or private employers
Includes fines, community service, probation, intermediate sanctions, or incarceration	Includes loss of right to vote, disqualification for jury service, loss of good moral character, and so on
Lasts only during a sentence	Lasts during a sentence and possibly for years after a sentence is completed or for life
Time served cannot be restored	Can be restored by legislation, court decision, or agency decision

Much of U.S. common law heritage was borrowed from the English, with the exception of outlawry, bills of attainder, and forfeiture of all property. Outlawry as a form of punishment is not allowed in the United States by virtue of Article l of the Constitution, which forbids "bills of attainder." In comparison with English society, the framers of the U.S. Constitution relaxed civil punishments. For example, instead of entailing a loss of all property, forfeiture now refers to property or assets gained or used directly from a crime.

good moral character
The totality of virtues that form the basis of one's reputation in the community.

moral turpitude
An act of vileness, or socially offensive behavior, that is contrary to justice, honesty, or the public's accepted moral standards.

Many collateral consequences flow from an assumption that a convicted offender lacks **"good moral character,"** and therefore fails to satisfy requirements to vote, to be a credible witness, to obtain and retain many occupational licenses, to hold public office, and to be a member of certain professions. A criminal act involving **moral turpitude** is defined as "conduct that is contrary to justice, honesty, or morality" (Garner, 2009, p. 1030). In some cases state laws assume a loss of good moral character only if a criminal act involves moral turpitude, but most states use such a designation if a person is convicted of any criminal act or at least of a felony. This chapter discusses collateral consequences of conviction and how rights lost may be restored.

CIVIL DISABILITIES TODAY

There are good reasons for removing some civil rights from offenders. Some argue that this is necessary in order to maintain public confidence in government operations, such as running for public office, serving as a notary public, establishing witness credibility on the stand, and enforcing juror restrictions. A second reason is to narrow government benefits to the law abiding, cutting off those who break the law in the areas of welfare, pensions, student financial aid, and federal employment opportunities and disallowing naturalization privileges to aliens who break the law (Buckler & Travis, 2003). Such cutbacks further separate people socioeconomically. More recently certain rights have been denied offenders on grounds of increasing public safety and protecting children from harm. These abrogations involve firearm restrictions, sex offender registration, and loss of parental rights.

How Rights Are Lost

FACT OR **FICTION?**

Although former felons might have problems finding a job, a loss of other civil rights is not that significant to worry about.

Fiction.

Fact: Up to twenty different civil rights can be lost permanently that affect an individual's credibility, narrowing government benefits that help reentry and housing eligibility, and possibly resulting in further losses. Although some rights lost make sense, others have little to do with a conviction and go beyond a need for public safety.

Civil rights can be lost through judicial discretion, licensing agencies, or by statute. For example, a judge may decide that an offender should lose a certain civil right related to an offense committed, such as by denying welfare benefits to a person convicted of conspiracy to defraud the government. Licensing agencies may decide to deny a license to an individual who commits a felony offense. Moreover, private employers are not expected to hire a convicted felon and can later terminate an individual if it is discovered that he or she refused to disclose this information.

Each state determines which civil and political rights are lost, when they are lost, and for how long a limitation remains in effect. In some states a conviction must be followed by incarceration for a specified period before civil rights are lost. In others a right is lost simply from a felony conviction. Some rights are permanently lost and cannot be restored; others are automatically restored upon completion of a sentence or may be restored by action of an executive or court. The American Bar Association is currently creating databases to determine the specific limitation of rights for adults and juveniles by state. (Websites for these databases can be found at the end of this chapter.)

CIVIL AND POLITICAL RIGHTS COMMONLY AFFECTED BY FELONY CONVICTION

Figure 14.1 shows the civil and political rights restricted or removed following conviction of a felony crime. Note that though some of these rights are federal losses that apply across the board, most are left up to each individual state to decide. Also, some rights' restrictions are specific to drug offenses or sex offenses but do not necessarily apply to crimes of violence or property crimes. This section discusses eight of the most commonly restricted rights, concerning voting, employment, firearms, government benefits, parenting, the courts, public office, and sex offenders.

Loss of Right to Vote

Voting is considered a basic right within a democratic society, yet about 5.3 million citizens are not allowed to vote because of a felony conviction (Sentencing Project,

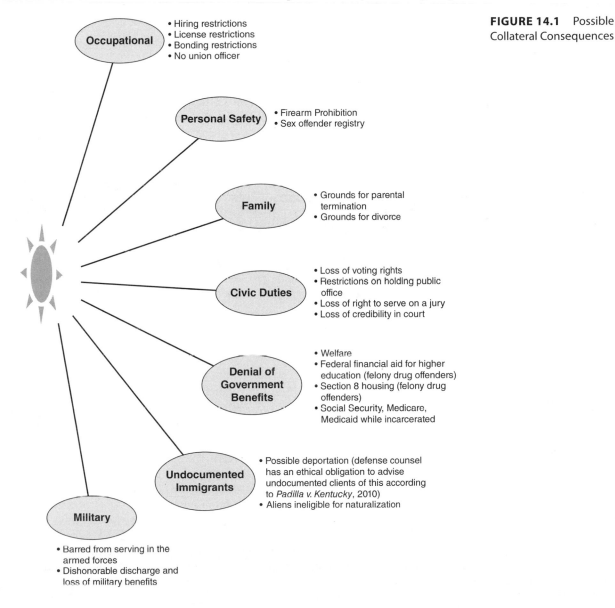

FIGURE 14.1   Possible Collateral Consequences

Occupational
- Hiring restrictions
- License restrictions
- Bonding restrictions
- No union officer

Personal Safety
- Firearm Prohibition
- Sex offender registry

Family
- Grounds for parental termination
- Grounds for divorce

Civic Duties
- Loss of voting rights
- Restrictions on holding public office
- Loss of right to serve on a jury
- Loss of credibility in court

Denial of Government Benefits
- Welfare
- Federal financial aid for higher education (felony drug offenders)
- Section 8 housing (felony drug offenders)
- Social Security, Medicare, Medicaid while incarcerated

Undocumented Immigrants
- Possible deportation (defense counsel has an ethical obligation to advise undocumented clients of this according to *Padilla v. Kentucky*, 2010)
- Aliens ineligible for naturalization

Military
- Barred from serving in the armed forces
- Dishonorable discharge and loss of military benefits

2011). In the 1970s the U.S. Supreme Court held that it is constitutional for a state to deprive ex-felons of the right to vote, thus giving states a lot of authority, if they so desire, to disenfranchise offenders (*Richardson v. Ramirez,* 1974). The impact of not being able to vote (also called *felony disenfranchisement*) is quite significant, for about half of persons not allowed to vote have successfully completed their sentences. The Sentencing Project (2011) also found that:

- about 13% of African-American men are disenfranchised, at rate seven times the national average; and
- four states deny the right to vote to all ex-offenders who have completed their sentences.

At this time only Maine and Vermont allow prisoners to vote through the mail, and some permit probationers and parolees to vote. A majority of states prohibits felons from voting while they are on parole (35 states) or probation (30 states), but increasingly more states allow the restoration of voting rights after a sentence is complete. Table 14.2 shows current voting restrictions for felons in the U.S.

In the last decade, it appears that public sentiment on the issue of felony disfranchisement is turning. Seventeen states have made changes to laws that would either allow more ex-felons to vote or would make the process for felons to have their voting rights restored less cumbersome. For example, Louisiana enacted a bill requiring the Department of Public Safety and Corrections to provide felons with voter registration applications when they leave prison. Only a small number of states (Iowa, Kansas) have further restricted felons' voting rights in the last decade.

TABLE 14.2   Voting Restrictions

No Restrictions	Cannot Vote While Incarcerated	Cannot Vote While Incarcerated or on Parole	Cannot Vote Until Completion of Sentence	Lifetime Bar That Can Be Lifted
Maine	Hawaii	Alaska	Arizona	Alabama
Vermont	Indiana	California	Arkansas	Delaware
	Illinois	Colorado	Florida	Iowa
	Massachusetts	Connecticut	Georgia	Kentucky
	Michigan	New York	Idaho	Maryland
	Montana	Wisconsin	Kansas	Mississippi
	New Hampshire		Louisiana	Tennessee
	North Dakota		Minnesota	Virginia
	Ohio		Missouri	Washington
	Oregon		Nebraska	Wyoming
	South Dakota		Nevada	
	Utah		New Jersey	
			New Mexico	
			North Carolina	
			Oklahoma	
			Pennsylvania	
			Rhode Island	
			South Carolina	
			Texas	
			West Virginia	

Source: Sentencing Project. 2011. *Felony Disenfranchisement Laws in the United States*. Retrieved from http://www.sentencingproject.org/doc/publications/fd_bs_fdlawsinusMar11.pdf

Loss of Employment-Related Rights

You have learned in this text that stable employment is a primary way for offenders to reduce their risk of reoffending, yet many current restrictions decrease offender opportunities for jobs. Employment of former convicts raises issues of broad restrictions on occupational licenses, limitations in public and private employment, and restriction on an individual's capacity to be bonded. Without even counting the common application question—Have you ever been convicted of a felony?—licensing restrictions alone make future job prospects for former felons very limiting. For this reason, in the licensing section the argument stands that the limitations in place now are perhaps too restrictive and need to be reexamined.

PRIVATE EMPLOYMENT   A job applicant with a criminal record faces almost insurmountable barriers to private employment. This is because job applicants with a felony conviction are not protected from discrimination by private employers in the hiring process. With more employers conducting background investigations prior to a job offer, Internet companies that perform such checks can provide employers with a right to know about an applicant's history so as to avoid lawsuits for negligence in the hiring process. While this gives some employers an opportunity to consider for employment those applicants with a criminal past, others seem to use a criminal record as a reason for not hiring. Companies required to conduct background checks have been found to be more reluctant to hire former offenders than were companies in which a check was optional (Stoll & Bushway, 2008). When asked, 60% of all employers were reluctant to hire anyone with a criminal record, regardless of offense (Holzer, 1996). For this reason, states like Florida and Hawaii permit employers to consider convictions only after a conditional offer of employment has been made (Haw. Rev. Stat., Section 378–2.5).

Some business and trade organizations and private employers provide jobs to convicted offenders. The Solution To Employment Problems (STEP) program of the National Association of Manufacturers is one such effort. In this program, employers provide equipment and instructors to train offenders while they are in prison and then guarantee them jobs upon their release. However, in the absence of laws specifically prohibiting such bias, private employers may discriminate on the basis of prior conviction, claiming risk and lack of good moral character as justifications.

PUBLIC EMPLOYMENT   Paid employment within a federal, state, or local governmental agency constitutes public *employment* because the pay or salary comes from public coffers. Public *office* refers to government positions that involve policy making. Thus a janitor in the office of a police chief is a public employee but not a public officer because he or she does not have policy-making responsibilities. On the other hand, a police chief is both a public officer and a public employee.

Most state statutes permit public employment of people convicted of a felony. A felony conviction may not be sole grounds for denial of public employment unless an offense bears a direct relationship to a position sought. In addition, a small number of states apply a direct relationship test to consider other factors such as rehabilitation, time lapse since offense, offender's age at time of conviction, and the nature and seriousness of an offense. No statutory restrictions are placed on the public employment of convicted people in the District of Columbia, Maine, Utah, and Vermont.

OCCUPATIONAL LICENSE LIMITATIONS   Federal, state, and local governments throughout the United States restrict entry to more than 800 occupations and professions through licensing requirements (see Table 14.3 for examples). The number of occupations that require licenses has doubled in the last 30 years.

TABLE 14.3 Examples of Occupations or Fields That Require a License

Accountant/CPA	Acupuncturist	Aircraft Dispatcher/Mechanic/Pilot
Alarm Systems	Alcohol Server	Appraiser, Real Estate
Architect	Asbestos Removal	Athletic Trainer
Attorney/Lawyer	Auctioneer	Audiologist
Banking	Barber/Hairdresser	Boiler Operator
Building Codes	Bus Driver, School	Charter Boat Operator
Child Care Provider	Chiropractor	Collection Agency Operator
Commercial Fisher	Commercial Vehicle Operator	Concert Promoter
Contractor	Cosmetologist	Counselor/Therapist
Customs Broker	Dentist/Dental Hygienist	Dietitian/Nutritionist
Electrician	Electrology	Emergency Medical Technician
Engineer	Explosives Handler	Forester
Freon Technician	Funeral Director/Services	Geologist
Hearing Aid Dealer	Home Inspector	Insurance Occupations
Investment Broker/Dealer	Land Surveyor	Law Examiner
Locksmith	Long-Term Health Care	Massage
Medical Examiner	Midwife	Mortician
Naturopath	Nursing (LPN, RN)	Occupational Therapist
Optician	Optometrist	Osteopath
Painter	Paramedic	Pastoral Counselor
Pesticide Applicator	Pharmacist/Technician	Physical Therapy
Physician/Surgeon	Plumber	Podiatrist
Psychologist	Real Estate	Refrigeration
Residential Builder	Respiratory Care	Sanitarian Examiner
Security Guard	Social Worker	Speech-Language Pathologist
Tattooing	Taxidermist	Teacher
Therapeutic Recreation	Veterinarian	Water Systems Operator

Sources: Illinois Department of Professional Regulation (http://www.dpr.state.il.us/); North Carolina Secretary of State Occupational Boards (http://www.secretary.state.nc.us/blio/occboards.asp); South Carolina Department of Labor, Licensing, and Regulation (http://www.llr.state.sc.us/pol.asp); Washington State Department of Licensing (http://www.dol.wa.gov).

State licensing boards have denied ex-convicts an occupational license if a conviction was related to an occupation or if it was too recent. For example, an offender who has served time for robbery may be denied a license to be a bank teller but not to be a land surveyor. For some occupations, such as attorney, any felony conviction is cause for suspension or revocation of an existing certification or may disqualify an applicant from obtaining a license. Other occupations require that a license be issued only to *people of good moral character,* which can exclude convicted individuals. The exact provisions of licensing statutes vary from state to state, from occupation to occupation, and even within occupations.

Increasingly more occupations are restricted, and a disqualification might not have anything to do with a crime or how long ago it occurred. One source found that private companies are even more restrictive than are most state licensing departments. For example, one private company regulates 16 different occupations considered "security-related" (e.g., armed guards, locksmiths, alarm system staff), and

the Private Security Bureau checks the criminal backgrounds of applicants. But unlike virtually every other such agency, the bureau doesn't then evaluate whether applicants' past behavior has any relevance to their current work, how

Former felons convicted of drug offenses can be denied from living in public housing and from receiving other forms of government assistance, especially individuals who have not completed a drug rehabilitation program.

long ago the crime occurred or whether they have tried to rehabilitate themselves. Instead, applicants with a record sullied by most crimes above a traffic ticket are automatically rejected (Dexheimer, 2007, p. 1).

It seems that in this case, 20 years must pass after a conviction for an applicant to become eligible again. A criminal record that disqualifies can be for a felony conviction, a misdemeanor conviction, or for only certain types of crimes. A lack of uniformity in the laws and practices of states and localities makes it difficult for people with criminal records to determine where they are allowed to apply their training and skills, whether they have acquired these in or out of prison. This largely explains why former convicts are not able to achieve the same levels of upward economic mobility as their nonincarcerated counterparts (Pew Charitable Trusts, 2010).

LOSS OF GOOD MORAL CHARACTER   Many occupational licenses require that a licensee possess *good moral character*. It is assumed that a person convicted of a criminal offense is not of good moral character. The obstacles created by provisions for and assumptions about good moral character are all the more formidable because a convicted person has a difficult time proving or restoring his or her good moral character. Moreover, few procedures for restoring civil rights erase a conviction for or adjudication of delinquency, and therefore *good moral character* is seldom, if ever, restored. As a practical matter, licenses are refused or revoked according to the various meanings that licensing agencies ascribe to such terms. In general, however, a licensing agency regards a conviction as conclusive evidence of bad character, and the courts have not changed this long-standing practice.

LOSS OF CAPACITY TO BE BONDED   Jobs in which employees handle money or merchandise can require an employee to be bonded. For example, banks, warehouses, truck-driving companies, collection agencies, bookkeepers, ticket takers, and vendors might require a bond before an employee is allowed to work. A bond protects an employer or company from losses caused by dishonest employees. A bonded employee is known as a principal. He or she signs a contractual agreement and pays a fee to obtain a simple bond. A **surety bond** is signed by a principal and by one or more third parties, known as sureties, who promise to pay money in the event that the assured—the party in whose favor a bond is written—suffers damage because that principal fails to perform as agreed. A decision to write or deny a bond rests with an insurance company, which carefully investigates all people who request bonds and refuses to bond people it considers poor risks. A person with a felony criminal record is considered a poor risk by a company issuing a bond.

> **surety bond**
> A certificate signed by the principal and a third party, promising to pay in the event the assured suffers damages or losses because the employee fails to perform as agreed.

The McLaughlin Company, through the Employment and Training Administration of the U.S. Department of Labor, offers fidelity bonding coverage for job applicants. The coverage is available to people who cannot obtain suitable employment because they have police, credit, or other records that preclude their coverage by conventional commercial bonds. Ex-offenders are eligible for such bonds if they are qualified and suitable for a job but are not commercially bondable under ordinary circumstances. An applicant applies for this bond through a state employment office. The bond becomes effective when the applicant begins work after the manager of a local employment service office or other authorized representative of a state agency has certified the bond. Unfortunately, few ex-offenders take advantage of this program and instead refrain from applying for jobs that require bonding. Because employers and prospective employees seem to lack information about this bonding available through state employment agencies, we highlight this option in Box 14.1.

Loss of Right to Own or Possess a Firearm

For some individuals, loss of the right to own a firearm is the most restrictive of all civil disabilities incurred by conviction. Federal law prohibits convicted felons from possessing, shipping, transporting, or receiving any firearms or ammunition (18 U.S.C., sec. 921(a)(20)). It also prohibits possession of guns by anybody convicted in any court of domestic violence, which is a misdemeanor crime (18 U.S.C. sec. 922(g)(9)). According to Buckler and Travis (2003), 37 states restrict both firearm possession and ownership for people convicted of a felony crime, and seven additional states restrict the mere possession of any firearms by felons. Twenty-one states allow firearm restrictions to be restored (12 upon passage of time from completion of sentence and nine following restoration of rights proceedings). Seven states have no such firearms restrictions whatsoever for those convicted of a felony (Massachusetts, Missouri, New York, Ohio, Pennsylvania, Tennessee, and Vermont.)

The issue of loss of the right to own a firearm has been litigated in a number of cases. In *Beecham v. United States* (1994), the U.S. Supreme Court held that "federal felons remain subject to the federal firearms disability until their civil rights are restored through a federal, not a state, procedure." This means that "federal felons who have had their civil rights restored by state law or procedure nonetheless are still prohibited by federal law from possessing firearms."

In another case, a defendant was charged with possessing a .25 caliber semiautomatic handgun in 1997 after having been convicted of a felony in 1972 for second degree burglary. In 1975 the Alabama Board of Pardons and Paroles had granted the defendant a certificate to restore "all his civil and political rights" although that certificate did not expressly name which rights those were. The court reversed the weapons conviction

BOX 14.1	**COMMUNITY CORRECTIONS UP CLOSE**

How Can At-Risk Job Applicants Become Bonded?

Commercially purchased bond insurance serves to protect an employer against employee dishonesty or for loss of money or property as a result of theft, forgery, larceny, or embezzlement. Insurance companies refuse coverage to persons considered *at risk,* such as former offenders, recovering substance abusers, people who have declared bankruptcy, those with poor credit scores, persons with dishonorable discharges from the military, and employees who have behaved with questionable credibility or honesty. As a result, such applicants at risk are routinely denied employment because they cannot be bonded.

The U.S. Department of Labor (USDOL) created the Federal Bonding Program in 1966 as an incentive for employers to hire employees at risk. The bonds issued by the Federal Bonding Program have been:

> designed to reimburse the employer for any loss due to employee theft of money or property with no deductible amount to become the employer's liability (i.e., 100% bond insurance coverage). . . . Bond issuance can apply to any job at any employer in any State, and covers any employee dishonesty committed on or away from the employer's work facility. Any full or part-time employee paid wages (with Federal taxes

automatically deducted from pay) can be bonded, including persons hired by "temp agencies." However, self-employed persons cannot be covered by these Fidelity Bonds.

Most public or private companies must be preapproved or "certified" to use Fidelity Bonds. Once certified:

- Bonds are issued free of charge effective the day that an applicant is scheduled to start work, and they are self-terminating after six months.
- Bond insurance ranges from $5,000 to $25,000 coverage for an initial six-month period, with no deductible.
- When an initial six-month bond coverage expires, continued coverage can be purchased by an employer if a worker has demonstrated job honesty during that time period.

At-risk job applicants seeking bonding services should call 1.877.872.5627 for the nearest workforce office and should contact a state bonding coordinator for the appropriate state of residence.

Source: U.S. Department of Labor. 2009. *The Federal Bonding Program.* Retrieved from: http://www.bonds4jobs.com/index.html

---

when it decided that a certificate restoring "all civil and political rights without reservation" *permitted* the defendant to carry a firearm (*U.S. v. Fowler*, 1999).

A Massachusetts defendant received a certificate restoring his civil and political rights, but this same certificate allowed (by Massachusetts law) him to possess rifles and shotguns while restricting him from carrying any handguns. The defendant was arrested for the possession of six shotguns in violation of federal firearm law. The U.S. Supreme Court held that the *possession of firearm* clause in a certificate to restore civil rights is an all or nothing clause, in that when a certificate bars only one type of firearm, it bars all types of firearms as far as the federal firearm statute is concerned. Thus even though Massachusetts state law had permitted the defendant to possess rifles, his restriction of handguns invoked the *unless clause* insofar as a handgun is a type of firearm. Therefore the defendant was not allowed to possess any firearm—a rifle, a shotgun, or a handgun (*Caron v. U.S.*, 1998). In effect, the Court ruled that federal law prevails over state law in case of a conflict concerning firearms regulation.

Loss of Government Benefits for Drug Offenders

If an offender is incarcerated, government payments for social security, unemployment, and welfare are temporarily stopped and Medicaid and Medicare benefits are stopped temporarily until release (the loss of which doesn't affect most offenders with a community-based sentence). An offender must reapply upon release to get these benefits reinstated. Offenders convicted of drug offenses lose Supplemental Security Income (SSI) and Social Security Disability (SSDI) if their disability is alcohol or drug dependence, according to Public Law 104-121.

DENIAL OF HIGHER EDUCATION FINANCIAL AID   College students who are convicted of any state-level or federal-level drug offense (misdemeanor or felony) *while receiving federal financial aid for school* are ineligible to receive future financial aid. The law does not require a student to report previous convictions years before receiving financial aid. At least 24 states also disqualify students so convicted from state-level aid because receiving such is contingent upon federal eligibility. The period of financial aid denial is one year for a student's first offense of possession of a controlled substance, two years for a second offense, and indefinitely for a third drug-related offense. Financial aid denial becomes indefinite after a second offense for sales of a controlled substance. Even the Internal Revenue Service has become involved by refusing to allow a tax credit claim for tuition during a conviction year. Students who become ineligible for financial aid can have their aid reinstated sooner if they complete an approved drug rehabilitation treatment program, according to Section 483 of the 1998 Amendment to the Higher Education Act, found at 20 U.S.C., section 1091 (r). However, about 15 states are choosing to ignore this amendment's provision for reinstatement altogether. Visit http://www.raiseyourvoice.com/statereport/fallingthrough.pdf to see where your state falls on the issue.

DENIAL OF WELFARE   Withholding welfare benefits is the most recent form of collateral consequence for convicted *drug* offenders. When the government overhauled the welfare system with its Welfare Reform Act, the former Aid to Families with Dependent Children (AFDC) program was replaced with a one called *Temporary Assistance for Needy Families*. The federal act denied food stamps and welfare benefits to anyone convicted of the possession or sale of controlled substances but allowed states to modify the ban as they saw fit. Thirteen states opted out of the ban entirely (thus allowing welfare for drug offenders) so that children of offenders are not negatively impacted. About half of all states have modified the ban to require drug treatment or have placed a time limit on the ban, and 11 states deny welfare benefits altogether to convicted drug offenders.

DENIAL OF PUBLIC HOUSING   The U.S. Department of Housing and Urban Development (HUD) can prohibit the public housing occupancy of any individual who uses drugs or infringes on the health, safety, or right to peaceful enjoyment of such premises. HUD policy bans individuals for three years who have been evicted for "drug-related criminal activity" (which does not even require a conviction). HUD has placed a lifetime ban on two different offenders: first, sex offenders who must register for the rest of their lives in a sex offender database and, second, individuals who manufacture methamphetamine on public housing property. Aside from these restrictions, HUD allows public housing agencies in each state to set their own admission and termination policies as they see fit. As a result, it has become commonplace for public housing agencies to exclude people with all felony convictions, which was not the intent of the original policy. In June of 2011, HUD issued a statement that public housing agencies should, when making screening decisions, consider evidence of rehabilitation and counseling as indication of future positive behavior. Furthermore, evicted occupants and/or those convicted of a drug offense can be readmitted into public housing if they submit proof of completion of drug court or of a supervised drug rehabilitation program (24 CFR 960.204; 24 CFR 966.4; 24 CFR 982.553).

Loss of Parental Rights

About 1.5 million children under age 18 have at least one parent serving time in prison. Of the 48 states that terminate parental rights of felony offenders, 18 states may terminate such rights due to long-term prison confinement, "which deprives the child of a normal home life or produces negative effects on the parent-child relationship" (Buckler & Travis, 2003, p. 442). Most states (37) can terminate parental rights for a serious felony conviction against one or more children in a household, which includes murder/manslaughter or felonious assault/battery. If it can be shown to a court that a continuation of a convicted parent's relationship with a child poses a threat to that child's well-being, such a conviction can result in a termination of parental rights (Buckler & Travis, 2003).

Losses in Court

To sustain the integrity of the court system, two common rights that are limited for felons are the right to serve on a jury and the ability to be viewed as a credible witness in any future court proceedings.

RIGHT TO SERVE ON A JURY   The exclusion of convicted people from jury service has its origin in common law. The federal rule is that citizens are not competent to serve on a federal grand or petit (trial) jury if they have been convicted of a crime punishable by imprisonment for more than one year and if their civil rights have not been restored (28 U.S.C. sec. 1865). Felons are deprived of the right to serve on a jury except in four states (Alaska, Illinois, Maine, and Missouri). Eleven states and the District of Columbia permit felons to serve on juries after they complete their sentences. On the other hand, other states suspend the right only until an offender is released from incarceration or after a passage of time (Buckler & Travis, 2003). The right to serve on a jury may be restored through a pardon or expungement in most states, except eight that offer no restoration mechanisms for this right.

LOSS OF CREDIBILITY AS A WITNESS   Absolute disqualification to be a witness in court applies to people convicted of perjury (telling a lie under oath) or of subornation of perjury (inducing another person to take a false oath). The justification of absolute disqualification for those convicted of perjury is that such people cannot be trusted to give truthful testimony. The usual situation, however, is that a person convicted of a crime other than perjury or **subornation of perjury** is permitted to testify. However, the fact of any previous conviction can be used to discredit a witness's testimony, with a court or jury allowed to take this record into account. A witness asked whether he or she has been convicted of a felony or other crime must answer truthfully. Opposing counsel may then argue, and usually does, that because a witness is a convicted offender, his or her testimony should not be believed. Whether a witness who is an ex-offender is entitled to full credibility or no credibility at all is up to a judge or jury to decide.

Loss of the Right to Hold Public Office

Elective as well as some appointive positions in federal, state, and municipal governments are generally regarded as **public offices.** A public office does not have to carry any compensation, such as membership on a school board or a municipal council. Federal statutes and the U.S. Constitution contain provisions that exclude some offenders from holding certain positions in the government of the United States.

public offices
Elective positions in federal, state, and municipal governments as well as appointive positions.

Congress may bar ex-felons from holding any nonconstitutional public office for offenses that include falsifying, destroying, or removing public records or documents, receiving compensation in matters affecting the government, rebellion, and treason.

A total of 40 jurisdictions limit or restrict felons from holding public office. Twelve states restrict the right to hold public office after a felony conviction, unless the convicted person receives a pardon. Fifteen states return the right to hold public office after discharge from probation, parole, or prison. Four states restrict this right until a mandatory period of time has elapsed following completion of a felon's sentence, ranging from three to 15 years. Nine states permanently restrict this right, not allowing any means of restoration (Buckler & Travis, 2003).

Effects of a Conviction for a Felony Sex Offense

Sex offenders face an enormous number of limitations that affect their civil liberties and integration with society well after conviction. As we learned in chapter 6, sex offenders are required to register with local law enforcement, and a community may be notified of their whereabouts while they are under supervision, depending on their tier level. These limitations have made it extremely difficult for sex offenders to move on with their lives, and these policies can potentially violate their rights to privacy after their supervision has ended (Mercado, Alvarez, & Levenson, 2008; Tewksbury, 2005). Ironically, the invasiveness of such policies upon offenders, all in the interest of public safety, has not significantly altered the self-protective behavior of citizens, though there is some evidence the public has taken measures to protect children from high-risk sex offenders residing nearby (Bandy, 2011). Critics of policies regulating sex offenders argue that these are founded on faulty assumptions about sex offending, such as that sex offenders prey only on children and are strangers to their victims (Tewksbury, 2011). In fact, sex offenders vary widely in their behavior toward and choice of victims, to whom many of them are related or at least acquainted with in some way. In the following sections we discuss two more restrictions of sex offenders: residency restrictions and possible civil commitments.

RESIDENCY RESTRICTIONS   Residency restrictions prohibit sex offenders from living within 500–2,500 feet of areas in which children are likely to be present. Prohibited areas in which population is more dense and disorganized are also more prohibitive of sex offenders than are rural areas (Socia, 2011). Residential locations permitted sex offenders are not always convenient distances to work, treatment services, and family support—elements necessary to reduce recidivism. In addition, sex offenders required to register for life are unable to live in public housing, which reduces their housing options even further. In Ohio, locations of 1,095 sex offenders were spatially mapped in relation to the 345 schools in the area. Researchers found that 45% of sex offenders in their sample were living within 1,000 feet of school property (Grubesic, Mack, & Murray, 2007). In this particular county, half of all residents lived within 1,000 feet of a school, so adhering to policy reduced housing choices by 50%. In more densely populated counties, the percentage is likely higher.

Restricting where sex offenders live has not been shown to decrease recidivism and offense opportunity (Zandbergen, Levenson, & Hart, 2010). What seems more effective with sex offenders than these restriction and notification policies is opportunities for treatment completion and a positive social support system—both of which have decreased recidivism.

INVOLUNTARY CIVIL COMMITMENT OF SEXUAL PREDATORS   Convicted sex offenders are also subject to possible involuntary civil confinement following incarceration if they pose a continual and dangerous threat to public safety related to a lack of control over their own behavior and have a severe mental illness or disorder that requires treatment. If their mental illness is linked to a continual threat to others, offenders can be held against their will. Because involuntary commitment is a civil statute, a commitment decision does not constitute double jeopardy (*Seling v. Young*, 2001). The attorney general's office in each state screens cases, but a lack of written guidelines affords authorities wide discretion as to who should be committed.

The Adam Walsh Child Protection and Safety Act requires offenders with any history of sex offenses to be screened prior to release to determine whether they are sexually dangerous. If they are deemed such, they remain in custody of the federal or state prison system until a court hearing is held to determine whether by "clear and convincing evidence" they should be civilly committed or released. A commitment process is private and confidential. However, Mansnerus (2003) was allowed to attend six hearings with special permission. She reports:

> The hearings are roughly modeled on commitments for the mentally ill, but with a key difference. In a regular civil commitment, the focus is on the patient's current state of mind; crimes committed long ago are usually not considered relevant. In the hearings at Kearney, however, criminal records are considered critical evidence of the patient's thoughts, behaviors and possibility of committing future crimes . . . almost any information about him is admissible . . . like hearsay evidence, evaluations written years ago by the police or psychiatrists, statements to therapists and the patient's own writings (p. 2).

In *Kansas v. Hendricks* (1997), the Supreme Court decided that a Kansas statute that permits a potentially indefinite commitment of sexually violent predators is constitutional. The Kansas Sexually Violent Predator Act authorizes a civil commitment of people likely to engage in predatory acts of sexual violence due to a mental or personality disorder. Defendant Hendricks had an extensive history of sexually molesting children and was scheduled for release from prison. But the state filed a petition to commit him under this act. The Court held that the Kansas law did not violate the prohibition against double jeopardy.

However, five years later in *Kansas v. Crane* (2002), the Supreme Court held that civil commitment of a dangerous sex offender is not permitted without proof of serious difficulty in controlling behavior. It added, however, that total inability to control behavior is not required. Rather, the state must show that an offender has difficulty controlling that behavior and that the lack of control is related to a serious mental illness. Taken together, the *Hendricks* and *Crane* cases determined that civil commitments of dangerous sex offenders are constitutional, but the state must prove prior to such commitments that these offenders are unable to control their behavior (del Carmen, Ritter, & Witt, 2005, p. 321).

The next section discusses ways to overcome the collateral consequences of felony convictions.

RESTORING RIGHTS THROUGH A PARDON

A **pardon**, designed to mitigate collateral disabilities as an act of forgiveness or mercy, is defined as "the act or an instance of officially nullifying punishment or other legal consequences of a crime" (Garner, 2009, p. 1144). Courts differ on the issue of a pardon's legal effect. Some jurisdictions hold that a pardon wipes out a crime as though it never happened; thus, an offender is a "new person." Other

pardon
An executive act of clemency that serves to mitigate or set aside punishment for a crime.

jurisdictions hold that, for some purposes, a pardon does not wipe out the fact of a conviction. Under this last view, the recipient of a pardon is regarded not as a new person but as a convicted criminal. This happens, for example, when a pardoned criminal takes the stand as a witness in a trial. His or her testimony might be impeached and credibility diminished because of the previous conviction even though a pardon has been granted. Again, states differ on how the results of a pardon are viewed.

The Power to Pardon

Historically in England insofar as any crime was considered an offense against the king, the power to pardon belonged to the king and was an act of personal forgiveness. Given that crimes are now viewed as a wrong against the government, Article II, Section 2 of the U.S. Constitution gives the president the power to pardon or commute in all federal cases except impeachment. The purpose of a pardon is primarily to correct judicial error. For federal pardons, the Office of the Pardon Attorney in the Department of Justice receives applications from all over the country. The pardon attorney, responsible for making recommendations to the president, recommends that federal offenders wait at least five years after they have completed their sentence to apply.

In most states today, the power to pardon state felony cases belongs to the governor, acting alone or in conjunction with some official or board of pardons. The power to pardon, which belongs to a state official, it extends only to offenses against the state and not usually to violations of municipal ordinances. In some states, a pardon can be given at any time after a person is charged or indicted while in others it can be granted only after conviction. Other states forbid a pardon until a certain length of sentence has been served or until a specific number of years of successful parole has been completed.

Kinds of Pardons

Pardons are either absolute (full) or conditional. An absolute pardon freely and unconditionally absolves an individual from the legal consequences of his or her conviction. Because no conditions whatsoever are attached (*Biddle v. Perovich*, 1927), an absolute pardon does not require that an offender accept or reject it. Also, once delivered, it cannot be revoked, and it restores citizenship rights. By contrast, a **conditional pardon** does not take effect until certain conditions are met or until after an occurrence of a specified event. For example, a public officer who commits an offense while in office and is convicted might be pardoned if he or she shows remorse, apologizes to the public, and resigns from public office. A conditional pardon generally does not restore full civil rights of an offender unless express language to that effect is stated in its proclamation. This type of pardon can be revoked for violation of the conditions imposed. An offender might opt to serve out his or her sentence rather than accept conditions deemed onerous attached to the pardon. Some courts prohibit the right of a governor to revoke a conditional pardon without a determination that a person pardoned has violated conditions.

conditional pardon
A pardon that becomes operative when the grantee has performed some specific act(s) or that becomes void when some specific act(s) transpires.

Procedure for Obtaining a Pardon

The procedure for obtaining a pardon is fixed by statute or by regulations of a pardoning authority. Generally a convicted offender must apply for a pardon, and time must elapse after release from confinement or discharge on parole before he or she may apply. Upon application, an offender is required to notify certain people, typically the prosecuting attorney, the sheriff, and the court of conviction. Posting (i.e., publication of a public notice) may be required. There might be limitations on repeated application for pardon, such as a minimum time interval. In most cases a pardoning authority conducts an investigation. A public hearing on an application might be held in some states.

Legal Effects of a Pardon

An absolute pardon restores most, but not all, civil rights lost upon conviction. For federal offenses, one publication notes that "a presidential pardon restores civil rights lost as a result of a federal conviction, including the rights to vote, to serve on a jury, and to hold public office, and generally relieves other disabilities that attach solely by reason of the commission or conviction of the pardoned offense" (Federal Statutes Imposing Collateral Consequences Upon Conviction, 2000, p. 13). For federal offenders, the Supreme Court has held that only federal law can nullify the effect of a federal conviction through pardon, expungement, or restoration of civil rights (*Beecham v. United States*, 1994).

There are two points of view on the issue of whether a pardon eradicates guilt. The classic view, which represents the minority position today, was expressed by the U.S. Supreme Court over a century ago:

> A pardon reaches both the punishment prescribed for the offense and the guilt of the offender; and when the pardon is full, it releases the punishment and blots out the existence of the guilt, so that in the eyes of the law the offender is as innocent as if he had never committed the offense (*Ex parte Garland*, 1867).

The opposite and majority view states that a pardon is an implied expression of guilt and that a conviction is not obliterated (*Burdick v. United States*, 1915). Each state determines which view it upholds. State law, a court decision, or a state pardoning authority defines the procedures and determines the effects of a pardon for state felony convictions. Such determinations are binding only in that state. For example, a pardon given in one state may be used to increase the punishment of a subsequent offense in that state (*State v. Walker*, 1983) but not in other states. An absolute pardon usually restores eligibility for future public office but will not restore a person to any public office he or she held at the time of conviction. By contrast, a conditional pardon usually does not restore rights or remove disqualifications for office (*Ex parte Lefors*, 1957). Generally a conviction for which a witness has been conditionally pardoned can nonetheless be used for witness impeachment in some courts.

Effects of a Pardon on Occupational Licensing

A pardon does not automatically restore an occupational license revoked as a result of a criminal conviction. Although loss of a professional license is a penalty, some court decisions hold that proceedings to revoke a license are not penal in nature (*Marlo v. State Board of Medical Examiners*, 1952; *Murrill v. State Board of Accountancy*, 1950). A professional license lost through conviction is usually not restored by a pardon because licenses are issued by licensing authorities or boards that have their own power and are independent from a pardoning authority.

President Obama signs a pardon request for a federal prisoner. Hundreds of pardon applications are reviewed by a committee and only a small number make it to this stage.

© Martin H. Simon/Corbis

OTHER WAYS OF RESTORING RIGHTS

Restoration of rights can be done in two ways: by application or by automatic restoration. Most states provide for automatic restoration because it is easier to administer and is less discriminatory toward certain types of offenders. In Table 14.4 you will see how each state allows offenders to regain voting rights—some restorations of which are automatic and others that must be accepted through an application process.

Automatic Restoration

automatic restoration of rights
Reinstatement of some or all civil rights upon completion of sentence. The extent of restoration varies by state and by offense type.

certificate of discharge
Official written document signifying that an offender has completed his or her sentence.

Automatic restoration of rights upon completion of sentence is possible in 33 states. For example, a New Hampshire statute, which provides automatic restoration by virtue of a **certificate of discharge**, reads:

The order, certificate, or other instrument of discharge, given to a person sentenced for a felony upon his discharge after completion of service of his sentence

TABLE 14.4 Discretionary Restoration of the Vote After a Felony Conviction

State	Restored Upon Completion of Sentence	Restored After Additional Waiting Period	Restoration Discretionary
Alabama			Felony offenses involving moral turpitude must obtain executive restoration of rights or pardon
Arizona	First offenders only		Recidivists must obtain pardon or judicial restoration
Delaware		Five years, except for certain serious offenses	Pardon required for certain serious offenses
Florida		Five years for nonviolent offenders	Executive restoration of rights or pardon
Kentucky			Pardon
Maryland	First offenders only	Three years for recidivists	Pardon required if two or more violent felonies
Mississippi			Pardon or legislative restoration
Nebraska		Two years for all offenses	
Tennessee			Pardon or judicial restoration
Virginia			Executive restoration of rights or pardon
Wyoming		Five years for first-time nonviolent offenders	Executive restoration or pardon for violent offenders and recidivists

Source: Sentencing Project. 2011. *Felony Disenfranchisement Laws in the United States.* Retrieved from: http://www.sentencingproject.org/doc/publications/fd_bs_fdlawsinusMar11.pdf

or after service under probation or parole, shall state that the defendant's rights to vote and to hold any future public office of which he was deprived by this chapter are thereby restored and that he suffers no other disability by virtue of his conviction and sentence except as otherwise provided by this chapter (N.H. Rev. Stat. Ann., sec. 607-A:5).

The laws of other states that grant automatic restoration of rights are basically similar, but the provisions differ somewhat. The Illinois Unified Code of Corrections, for example, contains this language:

On completion of sentence of imprisonment or on a petition of a person not sentenced to imprisonment, all license rights and privileges granted under the authority of this State which have been revoked or suspended because of conviction of an offense shall be restored unless the authority having jurisdiction of such license rights finds after investigation and hearing that restoration is not in the public interest (Illinois Unified Code of Corrections, sec. 1005-5-5(d)).

Most courts consider the effect of automatic restoration of rights as equivalent to a pardon. A certificate of good conduct and/or an automatic restoration of rights retain(s) a conviction. Thus a conviction remains on record as a prior conviction for purposes of increasing a future sentence if an offender is ever convicted again of another offense. The ex-offender is not restored to eligibility to receive an occupational or professional license and still must report the conviction on job application forms.

CERTIFICATE OF REHABILITATION   States without an automatic restoration option require initiative on the part of an offender to remove the disabilities that follow a conviction. Typically, a **certificate of rehabilitation** is furnished upon completion of proceedings that specifies the rights that are restored. An ex-offender must possess one of these certificates to apply for a job or a license barred by virtue of a criminal conviction. Nonetheless, the certificates are not binding and do not prevent a prospective employer or a licensing agency from taking a conviction into account in deciding whether to give an offender a job or a license. This is because none of the methods and procedures for removing or reducing the collateral consequences of a criminal conviction restores good moral character to an ex-offender.

Expungement of Arrest and Conviction Records

Expungement erases or destroys a record and limits public availability to arrest records and conviction records. A distinction must be made between *arrest* records and court records that did *not lead to conviction* versus court records of *conviction*. Arrest records are defined and handled by law enforcement officers according to the number of police contacts resulting in an arrest, regardless of case outcome (e.g., dismissal, diversion, plea of guilty, trial, etc.). A record of conviction is one in which a defendant pleaded guilty or was found guilty and was formally sentenced by a court. Each state expunges arrest and conviction records differently, and some states use the term *sealing* of records when they are describing the action of expungement (by the definition above), so comparisons across states can be confusing.

Forty states allow people to expunge or seal *arrest* records, and if an applicant is successful at expunging, 30 of those same states also allow a denial that such arrest records exist. Fewer than half the states allow expungement for convictions, however. For felony offenses, one source reports that 21 states have expungement procedures (Legal Action Center, 2004, p. 6), while another source says that 26 states, the District of Columbia, Puerto Rico, and the Virgin Islands have such procedures (Bureau of Justice Statistics, 2004). However, in all but 10 of these states, even if a record is expunged its information is still accessible to law enforcement, courts, and other government agencies. The meaning of the word *expungement* can be misleading because some expungement statutes only remove a court decision but not evidence of a case itself. So if expungement is allowable, a defendant must specify the expungement of both arrest records and conviction records, or must first expunge a decision and then seal the rest of a record. Other states do not automatically remove the legal action from a public criminal record. Four states featured below provide examples of expungement statutes.

EXPUNGEMENT IN WASHINGTON   Washington's version of expungement is called *vacating a conviction*. Upon completion of sentence an applicant must wait from three years (for misdemeanors) up to 10 years (for Class B felonies). Vacating a record in Washington takes a conviction off the record and gives a person the right to deny having a criminal record; however, the arrest or other court records of a case remain without a finding of guilt. Once a conviction is vacated, it cannot be used as part of one's criminal history in any future conviction to determine a sentence. For all purposes, including responses to questions of employment and on housing applications, a person whose conviction has been vacated may state that he or she has never been convicted of that crime. An expunged conviction also results in a restoration of all civil rights, except for the right to own a firearm.

EXPUNGEMENT IN OHIO   After a period of three years for nonviolent first-time felonies and after one year for misdemeanors, offenders in Ohio pay a fee of $50 for their records to be considered for expungement. If a judge agrees to do so, at least

13 agencies must be notified, which makes it quite difficult to actually clear a person completely. Such expunged records include complaints, arrests, warrants, institutional commitments, photographs, fingerprints, judicial docket records, and presentence reports. In addition, offender records are sealed rather than destroyed, and state law permits sealed records still to be viewed by some employers, such as agencies that work with children or the elderly (Horn, 2000).

EXPUNGEMENT IN OREGON In Oregon an offender seeking expungement must pay an applicant fee of $80 and not be currently under any form of supervision. After a waiting period of one year from arrest and three years or more following any misdemeanor or Class C felony conviction, only one conviction may be expunged every ten years. Offenders whose cases are dismissed do not have to wait to apply for expungement. Traffic cases, Class B felonies, and Class A felonies are ineligible (Or. Rev. Stat. §137.225(1) through (12)).

EXPUNGEMENT IN NEW JERSEY In New Jersey a person may apply to expunge an *indictable offense* after 10 years, a *disorderly people offense* or a juvenile adjudication five years later, a municipal ordinance two years later, and a charge of juvenile possession of a controlled substance one year after a sentence is completely served. Types of offenses that cannot be expunged include murder, manslaughter, kidnapping, sexual assault, crimes against children, arson, perjury, robbery, motor vehicle offenses, sale or distribution of large quantities of drugs, and occupational crimes committed by people holding public office. Even after records are expunged, certain occupations involving fields such as law enforcement, the judicial branch, and corrections agencies still require applicants to report in detail information about any expunged arrests and/or convictions (Stewart Law Firm, 2000).

Sealing of Records

A more significant issue concerns the easy access to criminal records on the Internet. In some jurisdictions defendants who have had their conviction expunged complain that evidence of an offense still appears online (e.g., an offense appears with no decision or verdict, leaving employers to question its status). Extra steps might still need to be taken by a defendant to ensure that expunged information is not disclosed in public databases. In some states this requires an additional step known in some areas as *sealing* or a *petition for nondisclosure*. A **petition for nondisclosure** is a court order prohibiting public disclosure of a defendant's criminal history record. Other states call this **sealing of records**; it is an act or practice of officially preventing access to particular (especially juvenile) criminal records, in the absence of a court order (Garner, 2009, p. 1377). Sealing differs from expungement in that the latter erases a record, whereas in sealing specifically defined records are closed and can only be opened by a court order. Sealing of records usually applies to juvenile adjudications or to adult arrests or diversion *not* resulting in a conviction.

As with expungement, a sealing process must be initiated by an offender. An applicant must establish that his or her desire to seal these records outweighs the right of the public to access their information. Sealed records restrict public access to everyone (including the applicant who wants the records sealed), and such an applicant is not obligated to disclose any information to any employer, governmental agency, or official. Legally, an applicant who has his or her records sealed can say that no such records exist. Note that sealed records are retained and not physically destroyed. The only way sealed records can be examined is if the original applicant or a prosecutor files a court order to unseal them that is granted by a court, insofar as public interest outweighs the original justification to seal.

petition for nondisclosure
A court order prohibiting public disclosure of the defendant's criminal history record.

sealing of records
The legal concealment of a person's criminal (or juvenile) record such that it cannot be opened except by order of the court.

In some states with sealing statutes (e.g., Colorado), criminal records may be sealed only for crimes in which a person was not charged, a case was dismissed, or a defendant was acquitted. Sealing can include the following: fingerprint cards, arrest records, photos, an indictment, prosecutorial information, competency hearing transcript, a disposition, pretrial custody, correctional institution records while in custody, and any probation or parole records. No information involving a conviction may be sealed (Colorado Revised Statutes 1998, § 24-72-308).

It appears that in the state of Washington convictions must first be vacated, and then an applicant may apply to request that a record be sealed. Washington's sealing law was designed primarily to petition the courts to seal arrest or court records that have not led to a conviction. Record sealing is an option for dismissed cases but is more difficult to obtain for deferrals and convictions (Washington Law GR-15, Chapter 10.97.060).

Are Juvenile Records Confidential?

Youths who have been arrested, taken into custody, or been adjudicated as delinquents in juvenile court for a Class A or Class B misdemeanor or for any felony also have a juvenile record. Generally juvenile records can be made available nationwide to any law enforcement or court personnel at any time as well as to licensing agencies, employers, and educational institutions under certain circumstances and upon request. The fact that a juvenile is on probation is a matter of public record in most states. Court personnel can disclose such information, but because the details of juvenile probation in case files are confidential, nothing more can be disclosed (such as offense committed, conditions and length of probation, and treatment programs prescribed).

restricted access
Juvenile arrest, adjudication and disposition records are accessible to law enforcement or criminal justice personnel for a criminal justice-related purpose (hiring for potential employment at any law enforcement agency, investigation of a crime, sentencing for a future crime, etc.) but are not accessible to anyone else for any other purpose.

In Texas, for example, juvenile records are automatically eligible for **restricted access** when an individual turns 21 years old. Restricted access is important not only because employers are blocked from information but because an individual has a right to legally deny the existence of a juvenile record (i.e., any juvenile arrest, adjudication, or disposition prior to age 17). Juvenile crimes ineligible for restricted access include crimes of violence and offenses that have been waived to adult court. To become eligible for restricted access, there must be no deferred adjudications, convictions for felonies, or Class A or Class B misdemeanors between the ages of 17–21. When once juvenile records have been restricted a crime is committed after an individual's 21st birthday, these records are subsequently removed from restricted access and made available to potential employers again. Given that they are no longer restricted to criminal justice personnel, an individual must openly claim that he or she has a juvenile record if asked. Restricted access is different from having a record sealed. A juvenile record in Texas can be sealed only if an offense is eligible for sealing by law and a petition is filed in court to have that record sealed (Texas Juvenile Probation Commission & Texas Youth Commission, 2003).

The confidentiality of juvenile records, however, is not a constitutional right and may be lifted by state law or agency policy. Over the years, confidentiality has gradually diminished. Juvenile codes in most states allow names of juveniles involved in delinquency proceedings to be released to the media. In 16 states juvenile court records or proceedings (including probation records) are now public. The general rule, however, still is that in the absence of state law or an agency policy allowing disclosure, juvenile records are confidential.

Should Convicted Felons Be Less Stigmatized?

Society expects former offenders to have learned their lesson and to change their ways, becoming responsible and productive members of a community. Most people want former felons to stop committing crimes and to become taxpayers with conventional jobs. Yet our laws and restrictions do not fully permit ex-offenders to live where they want and to have a decent job for which they are qualified, and they are restricted from civic responsibilities. With all the limitations to which former felons are subjected, it is no wonder they face seemingly insurmountable challenges to becoming part of a community and gaining a sense of belonging.

The majority of people under correctional supervision certainly have an *intent* to remain out of trouble in the future. Even though those with the best of intentions do not always remain crime free, the likelihood of committing criminal behavior decreases over a person's lifetime as he or she ages. Crime desistance refers to a gradual process of establishing self-control and of resisting old habits even in the face of disappointing setbacks. The most vulnerable period of recidivism is within the first six months of offender release, but recidivism risk decreases with the passage of time. One study found that *after seven years, the risk of an ex-offender reoffending was nearly identical to that of a person who had never committed a crime* (Kurlychek, Brame, & Bushway, 2007). This is important to keep in mind when we consider lifetime bans of civil and political rights.

Yet the removal of civil disabilities remains an open question. On the one hand, rehabilitated ex-offenders have a right to start their lives over using the tools they have developed through treatment efforts. Conversely, the public has a right to know of a previous criminal record to protect itself against a recidivist offender. However, given that most offenders do not intend to recidivate, how can genuine desisters be distinguished from those at risk of public endangerment? When has an offender paid his or her debt to society? If our society were serious about reducing recidivism and allowing former offenders to move beyond their past, we would create *opportunities* for them to change, we would reinforce civic participation as part of reentry preparation, and we would revisit the collateral consequences that continue to marginalize former offenders to permanent outcast status (Uggen, Manza, & Behrens, 2004).

SUMMARY

- Collateral consequences, which take the form of civil disabilities, can deprive a person of civil and political rights and make finding or holding a job difficult.

- The types of civil disabilities resulting from conviction vary widely from one state to another and are governed by federal and state laws.

- Civil and political rights lost after conviction include the right to vote, to serve on a jury, to hold public office, to own and possess a firearm, to receive welfare benefits, and to exercise parental rights.

- Private and public employers can discriminate against offenders unless such is prohibited by law.

- All 50 states and the District of Columbia have sex offender registration laws; most states also have sex offender notification laws.

- In some states, sexual predators may be civilly committed.

- Pardon is an act of grace that is available for offenders, but it is hard to obtain.

- The effects of a pardon vary from one state to another. In some states it erases guilt; in others it does not.

- Expungement, if allowed, destroys a record and limits public availability. Offenders must apply to get records expunged and states vary widely on what records can be expunged and for what types of offenses.

- Sealing, if allowed for a particular offense, closes existing records and limits access except by court order. Sealing is not a right, but a privilege, so access can be lifted if state law allows.

DISCUSSION QUESTIONS

1. If you were an employer, would you hire a former felon who has been recently released on parole? What about hiring an offender who has finished parole and has stayed out of trouble for two years? Justify your answer.

2. Which civil and political rights, in your opinion, should be permanently prohibited from ALL offenders for the rest of their lives?

3. Which civil and political rights, in your opinion, do not make any sense to limit? If you feel that some civil and political rights should be limited according to offense, identify which should be limited to which type of offender.

4. Should residents be notified of the presence of a sex offender in a neighborhood? Discuss this issue from the perspective of residents and then from the perspective of an offender.

5. Which rights would you agree to restore to a property offender who has stayed out of trouble for five

years after completing her sentence? Under what conditions?

6. Should an ex-felon be allowed to own or possess a firearm? Would you ban all guns or would you make exceptions for hunting rifles?

7. Assume you are given a choice between expungement of and sealing of a conviction. Which would be more appropriate and why?

8. Which rights would you agree to restore to a sex offender who has stayed out of trouble for five years after completing his sentence? Under what conditions? Which rights would you not restore under any circumstances?

WEBSITES, VIDEOS, AND PODCASTS

Websites

Database of Collateral Consequences by State, Finalized December 2012

Sponsored by the American Bar Association Criminal Justice Section
http://isrweb.isr.temple.edu/projects/accproject/

Collateral Consequences Juveniles Face—Database by State

Sponsored by the American Bar Association Criminal Justice Section
http://www.beforeyouplea.com

The Sentencing Project, Resources on Voting Rights for Felons
http://www.sentencingproject.org/template/page.cfm?id=129

Federal Statutes Imposing Collateral Consequences Upon Conviction
http://www.usdoj.gov/pardon/collateral_consequences.pdf

National Sex Offender Public Website
http://www.nsopw.gov

State Sex Offender Registry Websites (Federal Bureau of Investigation)
http://www.fbi.gov/hq/cid/cac/registry.htm

Federal Office of the Pardon Attorney
http://www.usdoj.gov/pardon/readingroom.htm

Restoration of Rights for Ex-Felons

http://www.aclu.org/votingrights/exoffenders/index.html

Labor Market Information for Community Supervision Officers to Help Offenders Obtain Employment
http://nicic.gov/library/024136

Expungement and Sealing Laws in Various States
http://www.recordclearing.org/states.htm

Videos/Podcasts

The Continuing Cycle of Reincarceration
http://www.youtube.com/watch?v=4BSwEYyFu2E&feature=share.

Michelle Alexander, book author, discusses a wide variety of issues related to the cycle of incarceration, including racial discrimination, collateral consequences, shame, and stigma.

Finding Work
http://www.corrections.com/system/podcast/file/13/media_20050708.mp3

This podcast is about the issues of finding work by those who have criminal records.

Hiring People Under Community Supervision Program: Employers' Perspectives
http://www.corrections.com/system/podcast/file/118/CSOSA118_3_.mp3

This podcast is an employer's perspective about hiring ex-convicts.

CASE STUDY EXERCISES

Should Rights Lost Be Automatically Restored, or Should an Offender Apply for This Privilege?

This chapter presents controversial issues on the loss of rights as a result of conviction for a crime. States differ on which specific rights are lost upon conviction, the duration of the loss, and whether rights lost should automatically be restored after a sentence is served or restored only upon application by an ex-offender. There are no authoritative national answers to these hypothetical case studies because laws, court decisions, agency rules, and practices in the private sector vary. The aim here is to make the reader think about what he or she would do if given final decision on what the law, court, agency chief, or private employer should say or do in such cases. Each decision must be justified based on the reader's personal opinion instead of on what established law or practice says. In sum, disregard the law in these cases and simply give your well-considered opinion

CASE A: THE RIGHT TO VOTE

Assume that Citizen *Adams*, head of a prominent investing firm in your community for many years, was charged, tried, and convicted of defrauding investors in his company. Prior to that, *Adams* was an active citizen in civic and humanitarian activities as well as in political circles. He was a member of the Rotary Club and was president of that organization for five years. He is sentenced to 10 years in prison. Assuming your state has no law governing this issue: **(a)** Should Citizen *Adams* be allowed to vote while he is in prison? **(b)** If your answer is no, should *Adams* be allowed to vote after he gets out of prison and is back in the community? **(c)** If Citizen *Adams* were an ordinary member of the community, without any previous involvement or influence, would your answer be different?

CASE B: THE RIGHT TO HOLD PUBLIC OFFICE:

Councilwoman *Bufford*, currently a prominent member of your city council, was charged, tried, and convicted of sexually harassing her male secretary while she was in office. She was convicted because she threatened to fire this man if he did not engage in intimate relations with her. The secretary refused and was fired. Assume that such conduct by *Bufford* is criminal in your state. *Bufford* was placed on probation for two years, which she successfully served. She now wants to run for the same office, saying that she has "learned her lesson," is now married, and promises to be on her best behavior if elected. You are in her district and voted for her in previous elections. Questions: **(a)** Should *Bufford* be allowed to hold public office again? **(b)** Will you vote for *Bufford* again?

CASE C: THE RIGHT TO PUBLIC EMPLOYMENT

Cisneros served time in a city jail for one year because he was convicted of beating up his wife, which resulted in her confinement in a hospital for two days. He is now divorced from his wife and is jobless. He has served time in jail with good behavior and is applying for a job as a janitor at the community college where you are a student. Questions: **(a)** Are you in favor of hiring *Cisneros* for the job or not? **(b)** Assume that *Cisneros* in fact is a former professor in the community college and, after having served time for the same crime, is now reapplying for the same job as professor. Do you think he should be rehired as professor? **(c)** Assume that *Cisneros* is a professor and was convicted of reckless homicide of a student after he drove one evening on campus while drunk. Would your answer be the same or different?

CASE D: THE RIGHT TO AN OCCUPATIONAL LICENSE

Dr. *Davis*, a medical doctor in the community in which you reside, was convicted of shooting one of his neighbors after the two had a big fight. The fight ensued because *Davis* had carried on an affair with his neighbor's wife, which the neighbor later discovered. *Davis* was placed on probation for five years after a plea bargain to a charge of terroristic threats. Assume you are a legislator and are asked the following questions by reporters: **(a)** Should *Davis* be allowed to practice medicine while he is on probation? **(b)** Should *Davis* be denied an occupational license if after he violates the terms of his probation he then serves two years in prison for the offense?

CASE E: THE WISDOM OF A PRIVATE EMPLOYER

You are the owner of a big grocery store in town and run a successful business. One day an applicant comes to you and applies for any job he might obtain in your store. He says he did not finish high school and smoked marijuana in the past, but no longer uses now. He further tells you that he was confined in a state institution for juveniles when he was 16 years old because he took part in a robbery with the wrong crowd. He is now 20 years old, is no longer a part of that crowd, and has been clean from drugs for 6 months. As sole owner of the store, you have the final decision to hire or not to hire. **(a)** What will you do? **(b)** And why?

CASE F: THE RIGHT TO OWN A FIREARM

Mr. Tate is an avid hunter and a member of the local gun club. In his house *Tate* has all kinds of firearms, which he uses to hunt. One night he had a serious quarrel with one of his neighbors. In a fit of great anger, *Tate* went inside the house, pulled out one of his guns, and shot and seriously injured the neighbor. This was his first offense ever involving a firearm. *Tate* was convicted and sentenced to serve five years in a state prison. While in prison he was a model prisoner, and he was released on parole after only two years. Assume that both state and federal laws provide for *Tate* to be deprived of his right to own firearms. **(a)** Should he be allowed all his firearms back? If so, when? If not, why not? **(b)** What firearm restrictions would you place upon him?

CASE G: THE DECISION TO PARDON

Ferguson, one of your former classmates, while under the influence of drugs was convicted of rape, based mainly on the testimony of three witnesses who claimed to have been at the same fraternity party when the crime was committed. *Ferguson* is currently serving a 10-year sentence in a state prison. New DNA evidence now shows that *G* did not commit the rape and instead proves that somebody else at the party did it. The same three witnesses, however, say they stand by their court testimony and that for them nothing has changed. **(a)** Should *Ferguson* be pardoned as soon as possible by the governor (who is the only person authorized in the state to grant a pardon)? **(b)** If a pardon is given, should it restore *Ferguson's* good moral character and all other rights he lost as a result of conviction?

CASE H: THE DECISION TO SEAL

Jacobs is a juvenile who was 15 years old when she committed a burglary and received two years of juvenile probation which she completed. Before that, at age 14, she received deferred adjudication for the sale of drugs. She is now 18 years old and wants all her juvenile records permanently sealed. Assume you are the juvenile court judge before whom *Jacobs'* request is made. Assume further that your state law gives you, as judge, discretion to seal juvenile records. **(a)** Will you grant *J's* request? Why or why not? **(b)** If so, would you agree to seal just one or both offenses?

absconder   An offender under community supervision who, without prior permission, escapes or flees the jurisdiction he or she is required to stay within.

absolute immunity   Protection from legal action or liability unless workers engage in discretion that is intentionally and maliciously wrong.

active GPS   A real-time GPS system that transmits data through wireless networks continuously at a rate of once or twice per minute. A phone line continually calls a reporting station to update an offender's location, which is tracked by a computer.

adjudication   Juvenile justice equivalent of a trial in adult criminal cases.

Alexander Maconochie   A British naval captain who served as governor of the penal colony on Norfolk Island, off the coast of Australia. He instituted a system of early release that was the forerunner of modern parole. Maconochie is known as the *father of parole*.

amercement   A monetary penalty imposed arbitrarily at the discretion of a court for an offense.

antabuse   A prescription medication that causes someone to experience severe nausea and sickness if mixed or ingested with alcohol.

attainder   In common law, an extinction of civil rights and capacities that occurred when an offender received a sentence of death or outlawry for treason or another felony. The subject's estate was forfeited to the Crown.

automatic restoration of rights   Reinstatement of some or all civil rights upon completion of sentence. The extent of restoration varies by state and by offense type.

bail   Monetary payment deposited with a court to ensure a defendant's return for the next court date, in exchange for said defendant's release.

boot camp   A form of shock incarceration that involves a military-style regimen designed to instill discipline in young offenders.

brokerage of services   Supervision that involves identifying the needs of probationers or parolees and referring them to an appropriate community agency.

caseload   The number of individuals or cases for which one probation or parole officer is responsible.

casework   A community-supervision philosophy that allows an officer to create therapeutic relationships with clients through counseling and behavior modification, assisting them in living productively in a community.

certificate of discharge   Official written document signifying that an offender has completed his or her sentence.

certificate of rehabilitation   A certificate furnished upon completion of proceedings that specifies the rights have been restored.

child safety zone   A condition of probation or parole whereby the offender is not allowed within a certain range of places where children typically congregate such as schools, day care centers, and playgrounds.

chronos   A chronological account of detailed notes written by a probation or parole officer and organized by date, about any client contact and/or case information that becomes a permanent part of the offender's case file.

civil disenfranchisement   Loss of the right to vote by felony offenders.

civil rights   Rights that belong to a person by virtue of citizenship.

classification   A procedure consisting of assessing the risks posed by an offender, identifying the supervision issues, and selecting an appropriate supervision strategy.

clear conditions   Conditions that are sufficiently explicit so as to inform a reasonable person of the conduct that is required or prohibited.

clemency   An act of mercy by a governor or president to erase consequences of a criminal act, accusation, or conviction.

cognitive-behavioral therapy   A therapeutic intervention for helping a person to change that is a blend of two types of therapies—cognitive therapy of the mind and behavioral change of the body.

collateral consequences   Disabilities following a conviction that are not directly imposed by a sentencing court—such as loss of the right to vote, to serve on a jury, to practice certain occupations, or to own a firearm.

collateral contact   Verification of a probationer or parolee's situation and whereabouts by means of an officer's speaking with a third party who knows the offender personally (such as a family member, friend, or employer).

community corrections   A nonincarcerative sanction in which offenders serve all or a portion of their sentence in a community.

community corrections act   Formal written agreement between a state government and local entities that funds counties to implement and operate community corrections programs on a local level.

community justice   A philosophy of using community—through community policing, community courts, restorative justice, and broken-windows probation—to control and reduce crime.

community resource management team model (CRMT)   A supervision model in which probation or parole officers develop skills and linkages with community agencies in one or two areas only. Supervision under this model is a team effort, each officer utilizing his or her skills and linkages to assist an offender.

community service   Unpaid labor on behalf of the public to compensate society for harm done by an offense of conviction.

commutation   Shortening sentence length or changing a punishment to one that is less severe, as from a death sentence to life in prison without parole.

completion rates   Individuals who are favorably discharged from drug court as a percentage of the total number admitted but who are not still enrolled.

concurrent jurisdiction   Original jurisdiction for certain juvenile cases that is shared by both criminal and juvenile courts, with a prosecutor having discretion to file such cases in either court.

conditional pardon   A pardon that becomes operative when the grantee has performed some specific act(s) or that becomes void when some specific act(s) transpire(s).

conduct in need of supervision (CINS)   Acts committed by juveniles that would not be punishable if committed by adults; status offenses.

continuity of care   Ensuring that a newly released prisoner has access to receiving necessary mental health medication and medical services in the community as were provided in jail or prison.

conviction   A judgment of a court, based on a defendant's plea of guilty or *nolo contendere* and on the verdict of a judge or jury, that said defendant is guilty of the offense(s) with which he or she has been charged.

day fines   Fines calculated by multiplying a percentage of an offender's daily wage by the number of predefined punishment units (the number of which depends on the seriousness of a crime).

day reporting centers   Nonresidential programs typically used for defendants on pretrial release, for convicted offenders on probation or parole, or for probation or parole violators as an increased sanction. Services are provided in one central location, and offenders must check in daily.

deferred adjudication   An offering made by a court to a defendant during the pre-adjudication stage to allow said defendant to complete community supervision and/or a community-based treatment program. Successful completion of pre-adjudication supervision or program results in dropped charges and no formal conviction. Also known as *diversion*.

delegated release authority   Statutory authority that allows pretrial services officers to release a defendant before an initial court appearance in front of a judge.

delinquency petition   An intake officer's formal request to a juvenile court judge to hear a juvenile case in family court or probate court and determine whether the juvenile is to be declared delinquent.

determinate sentencing   A sentencing philosophy that focuses on consistency for a crime committed, specifying by statute or sentencing guidelines an exact amount or narrow range of time to be served in prison or in a community and mandating a minimum amount of time before an offender is eligible (if at all) for release. Also known as a *presumptive, fixed,* or *mandatory sentence.*

diminished constitutional rights   Constitutional rights enjoyed by an offender on parole that are not as highly protected by the courts as the rights of nonoffenders.

disclosure   The right of a defendant to read and refute information in a presentence investigation report prior to sentencing.

discretionary release   Conditional release because members of a parole board have decided that a prisoner has earned the privilege while still remaining under supervision of an indeterminate sentence.

disposition   Juvenile justice equivalent of sentencing in adult cases.

diversion   An alternative program to traditional criminal sentencing or juvenile justice adjudication that provides first-time offenders with a chance or addresses unique treatment needs, with a successful completion resulting in a dismissal of current charges. Also known as *deferred adjudication.*

drug courts   A diversion program for drug addicts in which a judge, prosecutor, and probation officer play proactive roles and monitor the progress of clients through weekly visits to a courtroom, using a process of graduated sanctions.

due process   A recognition that laws must be applied in a fair and equal manner. Fundamental fairness.

dynamic factors   Correlates of the likelihood of recidivism that can be changed through treatment and rehabilitation (drug and alcohol abuse, anger management, quality of family relationships, and so forth).

early termination   Termination of probation at any time during a probation period or after some time has been served.

electronic monitoring   A correctional technology tool in intensive supervision probation, parole, day reporting, or home confinement, using a radio frequency or satellite technology to track offender whereabouts via a transmitter and receiver.

evidence-based practices   Correctional programs and techniques shown through systematically evaluated research studies to be most effective with offenders.

exclusion zones   Exact locations an offender is prohibited from being in or near.

exclusionary rule   A rule of evidence enforcing the Fourth Amendment's prohibition against unreasonable search and seizure, whereby illegal police searches are not admissible in a court of law. The purpose is to deter police misconduct.

expungement of record   An erasure. Process by which a record of criminal conviction (or juvenile adjudication) is destroyed or sealed after expiration of time.

failure to appear   A situation in which a defendant does not attend a scheduled court hearing.

fee   A monetary amount imposed by a court to assist in administering the criminal justice system through an offender's repayment of the debt accrued by an investigation, prosecution, and supervision of a case.

field contact   An officer's personal visit to an offender's home or place of employment for the purpose of monitoring progress under supervision.

filing   A procedure under which an indictment is *laid on file* or held in abeyance with neither dismissal nor final judgment, in cases in which justice has not required an immediate sentence.

final revocation hearing   A due-process hearing that must be conducted before probation or parole can be revoked.

fine   A fixed monetary sanction defined by statute and imposed by a judge, depending on the seriousness of a crime.

forfeiture   A government seizure of property that has been illegally obtained, has been acquired with resources that were illegally obtained, or has been used in connection with an illegal activity.

full board review   A statutory requirement that all members of a parole board review and vote on an early release from prison of individuals who have committed felony crimes, usually of a violent or sexual nature. Some states require this type of review on every discretionary release.

full pardon   A pardon without any attached conditions.

global positioning system (GPS)   A system that uses 24 military satellites orbiting the earth to pinpoint an offender's exact location intermittently or at all times.

good moral character   The totality of virtues that form the basis of one's reputation in a community.

good time   Sentence reduction of a specified number of days each month for good conduct.

halfway house   The oldest and most common type of community residential facility for probationers or parolees who require a more structured setting than would be available if living independently.

hearsay evidence   Information offered as a truthful assertion that does not come from personal knowledge but from a third party.

home-based electronic monitoring   An intermittent or continuous radio-frequency signal transmitted through a landline telephone or wireless unit into a receiver that determines whether an offender is at home.

house arrest   A community-based sanction in which offenders serve their sentence at home. Offenders have curfews and may not leave their home except for employment and correctional treatment purposes. Also called *home detention* or *home confinement*.

inclusion zones   Exact locations, such as locus of employment, school, or appointment, where an offender is required to be at a certain time.

indeterminate sentence   A sentencing philosophy that encourages rehabilitation and incorporates a broad sentencing range in which discretionary release is determined by a parole board, based on an offender's remorse, insight into his or her mistakes, involvement in rehabilitation, and readiness to return to society.

in-service training   Periodic continuing education training for seasoned officers.

institutional corrections   An incarcerative sanction in which offenders serve their sentence away from a community in a jail or prison institution.

intake   A process whereby a juvenile is screened to determine whether a case should proceed further in the juvenile justice system or whether alternatives are better suited for said juvenile.

intensive supervision probation   A form of probation that stresses intensive monitoring, close supervision, and offender control.

intermediate sanctions   A spectrum of community supervision strategies that varies greatly in terms of supervision level and treatment capacity, ranging from diversion to short-term duration in a residential community facility.

interstate compact   An agreement signed by all states and U.S. territories that allows for the supervision of parolees and probationers across state lines.

interstate compact for adult offender supervision   A formalized decree granting authority to a commission to create and enforce rules of member states for the supervision of offenders in other states.

Irish system   Developed in Ireland by Sir Walter Crofton, a system that involved graduated levels of institutional control leading up to release under conditions similar to modern parole. American penitentiaries are partially based on the Irish system.

John Augustus   A Boston bootmaker who was the founder of probation in the United States.

judicial waiver just deserts   The concept that the goal of corrections should be to punish offenders because they deserve to be punished and that punishment should be commensurate with the seriousness of an offense.

justice model   A correctional practice based on the concept of just deserts and even-handed punishment. The justice model calls for fairness in criminal sentencing so that all people convicted of a similar offense receive a like sentence. This model of corrections relies on determinate sentencing and/or abolition of parole.

Justice Reinvestment   Federal funding available for employment programs, libraries, schools, and social services in disadvantaged neighborhoods if states can show evidence that they have reduced their prison populations with no increase in the crime rate or increased safety issues.

juvenile delinquency   Acts committed by juveniles that are punishable as crimes under a state's penal code.

law violations   Violations of probation or parole conditions that involve a commission of a crime.

liberty interest   Any interest recognized or protected by the due-process clauses of state or federal constitutions.

mandatory release   Conditional release to a community under a determinate sentence that is automatic at the expiration of a minimum term of sentence, minus any credited time off for good behavior.

marks system   A system of human motivation organized by Alexander Maconochie that granted credits for good behavior and hard work and took away marks for negative behavior. Convicts used the credits or marks to purchase either goods or time (a reduction in sentence).

maximum eligibility date   The longest amount of time that can be served before an inmate must be released by law.

medical model   The concept that, given proper care and treatment, criminals can be cured to become productive, law-abiding citizens. This approach suggests that people commit crimes because of influences beyond their control, such as poverty, injustice, and racism.

medical parole   The conditional release from prison to a community of a prisoner with a terminal illness who does not pose an undue risk to public safety.

mens rea   Latin term meaning "guilty mind" that addresses the level of mental intent to commit a crime.

mental health courts   A diversion program for mentally-ill defendants in which a judge, prosecutor, and probation officer play proactive roles and monitor the progress of clients through weekly visits to a courtroom.

minimum eligibility date   The shortest amount of time defined by statute, minus good-time earned, that must be served before an offender can go before a parole board.

moral turpitude   An act of vileness or socially offensive behavior that is contrary to justice, honesty, or the public's accepted moral standards.

motion to quash   An oral or written request that a court repeal, nullify, or overturn a decision, usually made during or after a trial.

motivational interviewing   A communication style in which a community-supervision officer creates a positive climate of sincerity and understanding that assists an offender in the process of change.

negligence   The failure of an officer to do what a reasonably prudent person would do in like circumstances.

neighborhood-based supervision   A supervision strategy that emphasizes public safety, accountability, partnerships with other community agencies, and beat supervision.

net widening   Using stiffer punishment or excessive control for offenders who would ordinarily be sentenced to a lesser sanction.

Norfolk Island   A notorious British "supermax" penal colony a thousand miles off the coast of Australia that housed the most incorrigible prisoners.

offender-based presentence report   A presentence investigative report that seeks to understand an offender and the circumstances of an offense and to evaluate said offender's potential as a law-abiding, productive citizen.

offense-based presentence report   A presentence investigative report that focuses primarily on an offense committed and an offender's culpability and prior criminal history.

outlawry   In old Anglo-Saxon law, the process by which a criminal was declared an outlaw and placed outside the protection and aid of the law.

pardon   An executive act of clemency that serves to mitigate or set aside punishment for a crime.

parens patriae   Latin term meaning that the government acts as a "substitute parent" and allows the courts to intervene in cases in which children, through no fault of their own, have been neglected and/or are dependent and in which it is in their best interest that a guardian be appointed for them.

parole   Early privileged release from a penal or correctional institution of a convicted offender, in the continual custody of the state, to serve the remainder of his or her sentence under supervision in a community.

parole board   An administrative body empowered to revoke parole, to discharge from parole those who have satisfactorily completed their terms, and to decide whether inmates shall be conditionally released from prison before completion of their sentence.

parole conditions   The rules under which a paroling authority releases an offender to community supervision.

parole d'honneur   French for *word of honor,* from which the English word *parole* is derived.

parole eligibility date   The point in a prisoner's sentence in which he or she becomes eligible for parole. If an offender is denied parole, a new parole eligibility date is scheduled in the future.

passive GPS   A GPS system that temporarily stores location data downloaded through a landline phone once every 24 hours or at specific times when an offender is home.

Peace Officer State Training   Specialized and standardized training that officers are required to complete before they may carry a firearm on a job.

penile plethysmograph   A device that measures erectile responses in male sex offenders to determine level of sexual arousal to various types of stimuli. This device is used for assessment and treatment purposes.

petition for nondisclosure   A court order prohibiting public disclosure of a defendant's criminal-history record.

political rights   Rights related to participation in the establishment, support, and management of government.

post-adjudication   The state in which a defendant has been sentenced by a court after having either pleaded guilty or been found guilty by a judge or jury. Being adjudicated is equivalent to a conviction.

post-sentence report   After a defendant has pleaded guilty and been sentenced, a report written by a probation officer in order to aid probation and parole officers in supervision, classification, and program plans.

pre-adjudication   The state in which a defendant has not yet pleaded guilty or been found guilty by a judge or jury. Said defendant is either in a pretrial stage or has been offered deferred adjudication.

preferred rights   Rights more highly protected than other constitutional rights.

preliminary hearing   An inquiry conducted to determine whether there is probable cause that an offender has committed a probation or parole violation.

preponderance of evidence   A level of proof used in a probation revocation administrative hearing by which a judge decides guilt, based on which side presents more convincing evidence and its probable truth or accuracy, and not necessarily on amount of evidence.

prerelease facility   A minimum-security prison that houses inmates who have earned such a privilege through good institutional conduct and who are nearing their release date.

prerelease plan   A case-management summary of offender institutional conduct and program participation as well as plans for housing and employment upon release, which is submitted to a parole board in cases of discretionary parole or to a parole officer in cases of automatic release.

prerelease program   A program in a minimum-security, community-based or institutional setting for offenders who have spent time in prison and are nearing release. Its focus includes transitioning, securing a job, and reestablishing family connections.

presentence investigation   An investigation undertaken by a probation officer for the purpose of gathering and analyzing information to complete a report for a court.

presentence investigation report (PSI)   A report submitted to a court before sentencing describing the nature of an offense, offender characteristics, criminal history, loss to victim, and sentencing recommendations.

preservice training   Fundamental knowledge and/or skills for a newly hired officer in preparation for working independently.

presumptive sentence   A statutorily determined sentence that offenders will presumably receive if convicted. Offenders convicted in a jurisdiction with presumptive sentences will be assessed this sentence unless mitigating or aggravating circumstances are found to exist.

presumptive sentencing grid   A narrow range of sentencing guidelines that judges are obligated to use. Any deviations must be provided in writing and may also be subject to appellate court review.

pretrial release   While preparing for the next scheduled court appearance following arrest, a defendant's release into a community as an alternative to detention.

pretrial supervision   Court-ordered correctional supervision of a defendant not yet convicted whereby said defendant participates in activities such as reporting, house arrest, and electronic monitoring to ensure appearance at the next court date.

principles of effective intervention   Eight treatment standards that, if practiced, have been shown to reduce recidivism below that of other methods and that constitute the theory behind evidence-based correctional practices.

prisoner reentry   Any activity or program conducted to prepare prisoners to return safely to a community and to live as law-abiding citizens.

private service provider   Any for-profit or nonprofit, private organization that contracts with county-level or state-level government to provide probation supervision, independent probation treatment services, or both probation supervision and treatment.

private probation   An agency owned and operated by a private business or nonprofit organization that contracts with state, local, or federal government to supervise clients convicted of a misdemeanor.

probation   Community supervision of a convicted offender in lieu of incarceration under conditions imposed by a court for a specified period, during which it retains authority to modify those conditions or to resentence said offender if he or she violates those conditions.

public employment   Paid employment at any level of government.

public office   An uncompensated government position, either elected or appointed.

qualified immunity   Protection from liability in decisions or actions that are "objectively reasonable."

real-time access   Instant and immediate access via a supervising officer's Internet connection to pinpoint an exact location of an offender using GPS monitoring with a 30-second delay (as opposed to other GPS devices that have a significantly longer delay before a location can be confirmed).

reasonable conditions   Probation conditions with which an offender can reasonably comply.

receiving state   Under the interstate compact, the state that undertakes a supervision.

recidivism   A return to criminal behavior, variously defined in one of three ways: rearrest; reconviction; or reincarceration.

recognizance   Originally a device of preventive justice that obliged people suspected of future misbehavior to give full assurance to the public via stipulation to a court that an apprehended offense would not recur. Recognizance was later used with convicted or arraigned offenders with conditions of release set.

reentry   A process of preparing and integrating parolees into a community as law-abiding citizens using a collaborative approach with parole officers and treatment providers.

reentry courts   A collaborative, team-based program that aims to improve the link between parole supervision and treatment providers to help recent parolees become stabilized.

reflective justice   A form of justice whereby each defendant's case is considered in total according to its subjectivities, harms, wrongs, and contexts, then measured against concepts such as oppression, freedom, dignity, and equality.

reintegrative shaming   A process that occurs after an offense has been committed whereby an offender initially experiences reproach from significant others and social disapproval from a community but then is later forgiven, welcomed back into society and provided an opportunity to start anew.

relapse   When an offender with a substance-abuse problem returns to abusing alcohol and/or drugs.

remote-location monitoring   When a supervising officer uses a handheld remote receiver to wirelessly verify an offender's physical location.

reprieve   Postponing or interrupting a sentence (for example, a prison term or an execution).

residential community corrections facilities   A community sanction in which a convicted offender lives at a corrections facility and must be employed, but can leave said facility for a limited purpose and duration if preapproved. Examples include halfway houses, prerelease centers, restitution centers, drug-treatment facilities, and work-release centers.

restitution   Court-ordered payment by an offender to a victim to cover tangible losses that occurred during or following a crime.

restitution center   A type of residential community facility specifically targeted for property or first-time offenders who owe victim restitution or community service.

restorative justice   Various sentencing philosophies and practices that emphasize an offender's taking of responsibility to repair harm done to a victim and to a surrounding community. Includes forms of victim-offender mediation, reparation panels, circle sentencing, and monetary sanctions.

retention rates   The combined total of successful program completers and active program enrollees compared to the total number admitted to drug court.

revocation   The process of hearings that results when a probationer is noncompliant with a current level of probation. Revocation results either in modifying probation conditions to a more intensive supervision level or a complete elimination of probation, with a sentence to a residential community facility, jail, or prison.

risk assessment   A procedure that provides a measure of an offender's propensity to commit further criminal activity and that indicates the level of officer intervention required.

role ambiguity   The discretion inherent in the role of a probation and parole officer to treat clients fairly, consistently, and according to individual circumstances.

role conflict   The two functions of a probation and parole officer that are sometimes contradictory and difficult to reconcile: (1) enforcing rules and laws; and (2) providing support and reintegration.

salient factor score   The parole guidelines developed and used by the U.S. Parole Commission for making parole release decisions. Has served as a model for parole guidelines developed in many other jurisdictions.

school-based probation   A type of probation wherein probation officers move out of traditional district offices into middle, junior high, and high school buildings, supervising their caseloads right in schools.

sealing of records   The legal concealment of a person's criminal (or juvenile) record such that it may not be opened except by order of a court.

Section 1983   A federal lawsuit alleging that a government official violated one or more of an individual's civil rights afforded them in the U.S. Constitution.

security for good behavior   A recognizance or bond given a court by a defendant before or after conviction, conditioned on his or her being "on good behavior" or on keeping the peace for a prescribed period.

sending state   Under the interstate compact, the U.S. state in which a conviction is based.

sentencing   The post-conviction stage, in which a defendant is brought before a court for formal judgment pronounced by a judge.

sentencing commission   A governing body that monitors the use of sentencing guidelines and departures from recommended sentences.

shock incarceration   A brief period of incarceration followed by a term of supervised probation. Also called *shock probation, shock parole, intermittent imprisonment,* or *split sentence.*

Sir Walter Crofton   An Irish prison reformer who established an early system of parole based on Alexander Maconochie's experiments with a mark system.

special conditions   Conditions tailored to fit the needs of an offender.

standard conditions   Conditions imposed on all offenders in all jurisdictions.

standard of proof   The level of proof, measured by strength of evidence, needed to render a decision in a court proceeding.

static factors   Correlates of the likelihood of recidivism that, once they are set, cannot be changed (such as age at first arrest, number of convictions, and so forth).

statutory exclusion   An automatic exclusion of certain juvenile offenders from juvenile court jurisdiction by state statute, requiring a case to be filed directly with an adult criminal court.

stigmatization   A process, in effect long after an offense has been committed, whereby an offender continues to experience social disapproval and bias and is never fully welcomed back into society nor provided an opportunity to start anew.

subornation of perjury   The criminal act of persuading another person to commit perjury.

supervision   The oversight that a probation or parole officer exercises over those in his or her custody.

surety   An individual who agrees to become responsible for the debt of a defendant or who answers for the performance of a defendant, should said defendant fail to attend the next court appearance.

surety bond   A certificate signed by a principal and a third party promising to pay in the event the assured suffers damages or losses because an employee fails to perform as agreed.

surveillance   A method of community monitoring that ascertains offender compliance through one or more of the following means: face-to-face home visits, curfew, electronic monitoring, phone verification, and drug testing.

suspended sentence   An order of a court after a verdict, finding, or plea of guilty that suspends or postpones an imposition or execution of sentence during a period of good behavior.

technical violations   Multiple violations that breach one or more noncriminal conditions of probation.

therapeutic community   A type of residential community facility specifically targeted to drug-addict and alcoholic offenders and/or drug addicts amenable to treatment.

ticket-of-leave   A license or permit given to a convict as a reward for good conduct that allowed him or her to go at large and work before expiration of sentence, subject to certain restrictions and revocable upon subsequent misconduct. A forerunner of parole.

transfer of jurisdiction   The transfer of a juvenile from juvenile court to adult court for trial.

transportation   The forced exile of convicted criminals. England transported convicted criminals to the American colonies until the Revolutionary War and afterwards to Australia.

unconditional release   A type of release from prison without correctional supervision because a full sentence has been served behind bars. Also known as *maxing out* or *killing your number.*

victim compensation fund   A state fund that dispenses compensation to victims of violent crime, paid for by convicted offenders.

victim impact statement   A written account by a victim as to how a crime has taken a toll physically, emotionally, financially, and/or psychologically on said victim and victim's family. Victim impact statements are considered by many states at the time of sentencing and at parole-board hearings.

widening the net   Sentencing an offender who should have received probation to a harsher, intermediate sanction only because such sanction is available, not because said offender requires more intensive supervision.

work ethic camp   A 120-day alternative to prison that teaches job skills and decision making using a cognitive-behavioral approach, followed by intensive supervision probation.

work release   A program in which offenders who reside in a facility (a community facility, jail, or prison) are released into a community solely to work or attend education classes, or both.

youth courts   Community-based programs in which youths sentence their peers for minor delinquent and status offenses. Also known as *teen, peer,* and *student courts.*

Zebulon R. Brockway   An American prison reformer who introduced modern correctional methods, including parole, to Elmira Reformatory in New York in 1876.

References

Adams, Devon B. 2002. *Summary of state sex offender registries, 2001*. Washington, DC: U.S. Department of Justice, Bureau of Justice Statistics.

Administrative Office of the U.S. Courts. 2003. *The supervision of federal defendants* [Monograph 111]. Washington, DC: Administrative Office of the U.S. Courts.

Administrative Office of the U.S. Courts. 2005a. *The pretrial services investigation and report* [Monograph 112]. Washington, DC: Administrative Office of the U.S. Courts.

Administrative Office of the U.S. Courts. 2005b. *The presentence investigation report for defendants sentenced under the Sentencing Reform Act of 1984* [Monograph 107]. Washington, DC: Administrative Office of the U.S. Courts.

Administrative Office of the U.S. Courts. 2006. Gang member supervision growing part of job for probation officers. *The Third Branch* 38(2): 1–3. Retrieved from: http://www.uscourts.gov/ttb/02-06/gangsupervision/index.html.

Administrative Office of the U.S. Courts. 2007. *The supervision of federal offenders* [Monograph 109]. Washington, DC: Administrative Office of the U.S. Courts.

Alarid, Leanne F., Velmer S. Burton, James W. Marquart, Francis T. Cullen, and Steven J. Cuvelier. 1996. Women's Roles in Serious Offenses: A Study of Adult Felons. *Justice Quarterly* Vol. 13(3): 431–454.

Alarid, Leanne F., and Paul Cromwell. 2006. *In her own words: Women offenders' views on crime and victimization*. Los Angeles, CA: Roxbury.

Alarid, Leanne F., Leslie A. Hernandez, and Christine S. Schloss. 2009. Utilization of community-based programs: Which sanctions do attorneys recommend?" *The Criminal Law Bulletin*, 45(5): 847–860.

Alarid, Leanne F., and Carlos D. Montemayor. 2010a. Attorney perspectives and decisions on the presentence investigation report: A research note. *Criminal Justice Policy Review* 21(1): 119–133.

Alarid, Leanne F., and Carlos D. Montemayor. 2010b. Legal and extralegal factors in attorney recommendations of pretrial diversion. *Criminal Justice Studies* 23(3): 239–252.

Alarid, Leanne F., and Christine S. Schloss. 2009. Attorney views on the use of private agencies for probation supervision and treatment. *International Journal of Offender Therapy and Comparative Criminology* 53(3): 278–291.

Alarid, Leanne F., Barbara A. Sims, and James Ruiz. 2011. Juvenile probation & police partnerships as loosely coupled systems: A qualitative analysis. *Youth Violence and Juvenile Justice* 9(1): 79–95.

Alarid, Leanne F., Barbara A. Sims, and James Ruiz (forthcoming). School-based juvenile probation and police partnerships for truancy reduction. *Journal of Knowledge and Best Practices in Juvenile Justice and Psychology*.

Albonetti, Celesta A., and John R. Hepburn. 1997. Probation revocation: A proportional hazards model of the conditioning effects of social disadvantage. *Social Problems* 441: 124–137.

Alexander, Melissa, Scott W. VanBenschoten, and Scott T. Walters. 2008. Motivational interviewing training in criminal justice: Development of a model plan. *Federal Probation* 72(2): 61–66.

Alexander, Ryan. 2010. Collaborative supervision strategies for sex offender community management. *Federal Probation* 74(2): 16–19.

Alonso, Alfonso. 2009. *Best practices for drug courts*. An unpublished Master's thesis. University of Nevada Reno.

Altschuler, David M. 1999. Trends and issues in the adultification of juvenile justice. In *Research to results: Effective community corrections*, edited by Patricia M. Harris. Lanham, MD: American Correctional Association, pp. 233–271.

American Friends Service Committee. 1971. *Struggle for justice*. New York: Hill and Wang.

American Probation and Parole Association. n.d. APPA position statement: Community justice. Retrieved from: http://www.appa-net.org/about%20appa/communityjustice_1.htm.

———. 1994. APPA position statement: Weapons. Retrieved from: http://www.appa-net.org/about%20appa/weapons.htm.

———. 2006. *APPA adult and juvenile probation and parole national firearm survey 2005–2006*. Lexington, KY: APPA. Retrieved from: http://www.appa-net.org/information%20clearing%20house/survey.htm.

Anderson, Amy L., and Lisa L. Sample. 2008. Public awareness and action resulting from sex offender notification laws. *Criminal Justice Policy Review* 19: 371–396.

Andrews, Don A., and James Bonta. 1998. *The psychology of criminal conduct*, 2nd ed. Cincinnati, OH: Anderson.

Andrews, Don A., James Bonta, and J. Stephen Wormith. 2006. The recent past and near future of risk and/or need assessment. *Crime and Delinquency* 52(1): 7–27.

Andrews, Sara, and Linda S. Janes. 2006. Four-point strategy reduces technical violations of probation in Connecticut. *Topics in Community Corrections: Effectively Managing Violations and Revocations*. Longmont, CO: National Institute of Corrections.

Annison, Jill, Tina Eadie, and Charlotte Knight. 2008. People first: Probation officer perspectives on probation work. *Probation Journal* 55(3): 259–271.

Aos, Steve, Marna Miller, and Elizabeth Drake. 2006. *Evidence-based adult corrections programs: What works and what does not*. Olympia, WA: Washington State Institute for Public Policy. Retrieved from: http://www.wsipp.wa.gov/rptfiles/06-01-1201.pdf

Arditti, Joyce A., and April L. Few. 2006. Mothers' reentry into family life following incarceration. *Criminal Justice Policy Review* 17(1): 103–123.

Armstrong, Gaylene, and Beth Freeman. 2009. *GPS monitoring of sex offenders in Maricopa county, Arizona.* Paper presented at the annual meeting of the Academy of Criminal Justice Sciences, Boston, MA.

Associated Press. 2006. The truth is out with second autopsy: Boy's boot-camp death now said to be result of beating. *The Kansas City Star,* March 17, A7.

Association of Paroling Authorities International. 2005. *Paroling Authorities Survey.* APAI: Association of Paroling Authorities International. Retrieved from: http://www. apaintl.org/documents/surveys/2005.pdf

Augustus, John. 1939. *First probation officer.* New York: National Probation Association.

———. 1972. *A report of the labors of John Augustus, for the last ten years, in aid of the unfortunate.* Montclair, NJ: Patterson Smith. (Originally published 1852)

Austin, James. 2001. Prisoner reentry: Current trends, practices, and issues. *Crime and Delinquency* 47(3): 314–334.

Bahr, Stephen J., Anita Harker Armstrong, Benjamin Guild Gibbs, Paul E. Harris, and James K. Fisher. 2005. The reentry process: How parolees adjust to release from prison. *Fathering* 3(3): 243–265.

Bandy, Rachel. 2011. Measuring the impact of sex offender notification on community adoption of protective behaviors. *Criminology and Public Policy* 10(2): 237–263.

Barklage, Heather, Dane Miller, and Gene Bonham. 2006. Probation conditions versus probation officer directives: Where the twain shall meet. *Federal Probation* 70(3): 37–41.

Barthwell, Andrea G., Peter Bokos, J. Bailey, Miriam Nisenbaum, Julien Devereux, and Edward C. Senay. 1995. Interventions/Wilmer: A continuum of care for substance abusers in the criminal justice system. *Journal of Psychoactive Drugs* 27(1): 39–47.

Barton, William, and Cheryl Justice. 2000. The John P. Craine House: A community residential program for female offenders and their children. Paper presented at the annual meeting of the American Society of Criminology, San Francisco, California, November 14–17.

Baumer, Eric P., Ian O'Donnell, and N. Hughes. 2009. The porous prison. *The Prison Journal* 89(1): 119–126.

Bazemore, Gordon, and Jeanne Stinchcomb. 2004. A civic engagement model of reentry: Involving community through service and restorative justice. *Federal Probation* 68(2): 14–24.

Bazemore, Gordon, and Mark Umbreit. 2001. A comparison of four restorative conferencing models. *Juvenile Justice Bulletin* (February). Washington, DC: U.S. Department of Justice, Office of Juvenile Justice and Delinquency Programs.

Beck, Allen J. 2000. *Prisoners in 1999.* Washington, DC: U.S. Department of Justice, Bureau of Justice Statistics.

Beck, V.S., and Lawrence F. Travis. 2004. Sex offender notification and fear of victimization. *Journal of Criminal Justice* 32(5): 455–463.

Bennish, Steve. 2008. Technology helps gangs go hi-tech. *Dayton Daily News,* February 18.

Benson, Michael L., Leanne F. Alarid, Velmer S. Burton, and Francis T. Cullen (forthcoming). Reintegration or stigmatization? Offenders' expectations of community reentry. *Journal of Criminal Justice.* http://www.sciencedirect.com/science/article/pii/S0047235211000596

Berenson, Steven. 2010. The movement toward veterans courts. *Clearinghouse Review: Journal of Poverty Law and Policy* 44: 37–42.

Berk, Jillian. 2008. Does work release work? Retrieved from: http://client.norc.org/jole/SOLEweb/8318.pdf

Bernat, Frances P., William Parsonage, and Jacqueline Helfgott. 1994. Victim impact laws and the parole process in the United States: Balancing victim and inmate rights and interests. *International Review of Victimology* 3(1/2): 121–133.

Berry, William W. 2009. Extraordinary and compelling: A re-examination of the justifications for compassionate release. *Maryland Law Review* 68(4): 115–141.

Beto, Dan Richard. 2000. Reinventing probation: A history of the national movement and the Texas initiative. *Criminal Justice Mandate* 8(1): 9–13.

Bexar County Diversion Program. 2006. Providing jail diversion for people with mental illness. *Psychiatric Services* 57(10): 1521–1523.

BI Inc. 2009. BI products and services. Retrieved from: http://www.bi.com

Blackwell, Brenda Sims, and Brian K. Payne. 2011. Measuring electronic monitoring tools: The influence of vendor type and vendor data. *American Journal of Criminal Justice* 36: 17–28.

Bloom, Barbara, and Anne McDiarmid. 2000. Gender-responsive supervision and programming for women offenders in the community. In *Topics in community corrections annual issue 2000: Responding to women in the community.* Longmont, CO: LIS, Inc. and National Institute of Corrections.

Bonczar, Thomas P. 1997. *Characteristics of adults on probation, 1995.* Washington, DC: U.S. Department of Justice.

Bonczar, Thomas P., and Lauren E. Glaze. 1999. *Probation and parole in the United States, 1998.* Washington, DC: U.S. Department of Justice, Bureau of Justice Statistics.

Bonta, James, S. Wallace-Capretta, and J. Rooney. 2000. A quasi-experimental evaluation of an intensive rehabilitation supervision program. *Criminal Justice and Behavior* 29(June): 312–329.

Bosco, Robert J. 1998. Connecticut probation's partnership with the private sector. In *Topics in community corrections: Annual issue 1998: Privatizing community supervision.* Longmont, CO: National Institute of Corrections, U.S. Department of Justice, pp. 8–12.

Bottcher, Jean, and Michael E. Ezell. 2005. Examining the effectiveness of boot camps: A randomized experiment with a long-term follow-up. *Journal of Research in Crime and Delinquency* 42(3): 309–332.

Bouffard, Jeffrey A., and K. J. Bergseth. 2008. The impact of reentry services on juvenile offenders' recidivism. *Youth Violence and Juvenile Justice* 6: 295–318.

Bouffard, Jeffrey, and Lisa R. Muftic. 2007. The effectiveness of community service sentences compared to traditional fines for low-level offenders. *The Prison Journal* 87(2): 171–194.

Brady, Brian. 2008. Prisoners to be chipped like dogs. *The Independent*, January 13. Retrieved from: http://www.independent.co.uk/news/uk/politics/prisoners-to-be-chipped-like-dogs-769977.html

Braithwaite, John. 1989. *Crime, shame, and reintegration.* Cambridge, NY: Cambridge University Press.

Brame, Robert, and Doris Layton MacKenzie. 1996. Shock incarceration and positive adjustment during community supervision: A multisite evaluation. In *Correctional boot camps: A tough intermediate sanction,* edited by Doris L. MacKenzie and Eugene E. Hebert. Washington, DC: U.S. Department of Justice.

Brezosky, Lynn. 2010. Valley JP creates a truancy ruckus. *San Antonio Express News*, August 8, Metro, 1B.

Brown, Kelly L. 2007. Effects of supervision philosophy on intensive probationers. *Justice Systems Journal* 4(1): 1–18.

Buckler, Kevin G., and Lawrence F. Travis. 2003. Reanalyzing the prevalence and social context of collateral consequence statutes. *Journal of Criminal Justice* 31: 435–453.

———. 1998. *Critical elements in the planning, development, and implementation of successful correctional options.* Washington, DC: U.S. Department of Justice, Bureau of Justice Assistance.

Bureau of Justice Statistics. 2006. *Felony defendants in large urban counties.* Washington, DC: U.S. Department of Justice.

Burke, Peggy B. 1995. *Abolishing parole: Why the emperor has no clothes.* Lexington, KY: American Probation and Parole Association, and California, MO: Association of Paroling Authorities, International.

———. 1997. *Policy-driven responses to probation and parole violations.* Washington, DC: U.S. Department of Justice, National Institute of Corrections (March).

Button, Deeanna M., Matthew DeMichele, and Brian K. Payne. 2009. Using electronic monitoring to supervise sex offenders: Legislative patterns and implications for community corrections officers. *Criminal Justice Policy Review* 20(4): 414–436.

Butts, Jeffrey A., and Janeen Buck. 2000. *Teen courts: A focus on research.* Washington, DC: Office of Juvenile Justice and Delinquency Prevention.

Butts, Jeffrey A., and Adele V. Harrell. 2003. Delinquents or criminals: Policy options for young offenders. Retrieved from: http://www.urban.org/

Butts, Jeffrey A., and Daniel P. Mears. 2001. Reviving juvenile justice in a get-tough era. *Youth and Society* 33(2): 169–198.

Byrne, James, and Jacob Stowell. 2007. The impact of the Federal Pretrial Services Act of 1982 on the release, supervision, and detention of pretrial defendants. *Federal Probation* 71(2): 31–38.

Cadigan, Timothy P. 2003. Average length of pretrial supervision. *News and Views* 28(23): 1–2.

Cadigan, Timothy P. 2007. Pretrial services in the federal system: Impact of the Pretrial Services Act of 1982. *Federal Probation* 71(2): 10–15.

Cameron, Angela. 2006. Stopping the violence: Canadian feminist debates on restorative justice and intimate violence. *Theoretical Criminology* 10(1): 49–66.

Camp, Camille Graham, and George M. Camp. 1999. *The corrections yearbook: 1999.* Middletown, CT: Criminal Justice Institute.

Camp, Camille Graham, George M. Camp, and Bob May. 2003. *The 2002 corrections yearbook: Adult corrections.* Middletown, CT: Criminal Justice Institute, Inc.

Caputo, Gail A. 2005. Community service in Texas: Results of a probation survey. *Corrections Compendium* 30(2): 8–9, 35–37.

Carey, S., and Michael Figgin. 2004. A detailed cost analysis in a mature drug court setting. *Journal of Contemporary Criminal Justice* 20(3): 315–334.

Carpenter, Eric. 2011. Kids who skip school are tracked by GPS. *The Orange County Register,* February 17, 2011. Available on-line at: http://www.ocregister.com/common/printer/view.php?db=ocregister&id=288730

Carter, Madeline M. (Ed.). 2001. *Responding to Parole and Probation Violations: A Handbook to Guide Local Policy Development.* Prepared for the National Institute of Corrections, U.S. Department of Justice (Washington, DC).

Carter, Madeline M., and Ann Ley. 2001. Making it work: Developing tools to carry out the policy. In *Responding to parole and probation violations: A handbook to guide local policy development,* edited by Madeline M. Carter. Washington, DC: National Institute of Corrections, U.S. Department of Justice.

Castillo, Eladio D. and Leanne F. Alarid. 2011. Factors associated with recidivism among offenders with mental illness. *International Journal of Offender Therapy and Comparative Criminology* 55(1): 98–117.

Catanese, Shiloh A. 2010. Traumatized by association: The risk of working sex crimes. *Federal Probation* 74(2): 36–38.

Center for Community Corrections. 1997. *A call for punishments that make sense.* Washington, DC: Bureau of Justice Assistance. Retrieved from: http://www.communitycorrectionsworks.org/art4web-ccc/pdfs%20of%20booklets/punishments.pdf

Chasnoff, Brian. 2006. Unarmed probation officers fret. *San Antonio Express News*, October 21, 1A.

Clark, Cherrie L., David W. Aziz, and Doris L. MacKenzie. 1994. *Shock incarceration in New York: Focus on treatment.* Washington, DC: National Institute of Justice (August).

Clark, John, and D. Alan Henry. 2003. *Pre trial services programming at the start of the 21st century: A survey of pretrial services programs.* Washington, DC: Bureau of Justice Assistance (July).

Clark, Michael D. 2005. Motivational interviewing for probation staff: Increasing the readiness to change. *Federal Probation* 69(2): 22–28.

Clear, Todd R. 2011. A private-sector , incentive-based model for justice reinvestment. *Criminology & Public Policy* 10(3): 585–608.

Clear, Todd, R., and Ronald Corbett. 1997. Community corrections of place. Retrieved from: http://www.corrections.com/njaca/Fact_Sheets/Fact_sheets_start.htm

Cohen, Neil P. 2005. *The law of probation and parole,* 2nd ed. St. Paul, MN: West Group. (2005 supplement).

Cohen, Thomas H., and Brian A. Reaves. 2006. *Felony defendants in large urban counties, 2002.* Washington, DC: U.S. Department of Justice.

Cook, Kimberly J. 2006. Doing difference and accountability in restorative conferences. *Theoretical Criminology* 10(1): 107–124.

Cooprider, Keith W., Rosemarie Gray, and John Dunne. 2003. Pretrial services in Lake County, Illinois: Patterns of change over time, 1986–2000. *Federal Probation* 67(3): 33–41.

Corbett, Ronald P. Jr. 2000. Juvenile probation on the eve of the next millennium. *Perspectives* (Fall): 22–30.

Cotter, Ryan, and Willem DeLint. 2009. GPS-electronic monitoring and contemporary penology: A case study of U.S. GPS-electronic monitoring programmes. *The Howard Journal of Criminal Justice* 48(1): 76–87.

Council of State Governments. 2008. *Mental health courts: A primer for policymakers and practitioners.* Washington, DC: Bureau of Justice Assistance.

Craddock, Amy. 2009. Drug reporting center completion. *Crime and Delinquency* 55(1): 105–133.

Crank, John. 1996. The construction of meaning during training for probation and parole. *Justice Quarterly* 13(2): 265–290.

Craun, Sarah W., and Poco D. Kernsmith. 2006. Juvenile sex offenders and sex offender registries. *Federal Probation* 70(3): 45–49.

Cullen, Francis T., John E. Eck, and Christopher T. Lowenkamp. 2002. Environmental corrections: A new paradigm for effective probation and parole supervision. *Federal Probation* 66(2): 28–37.

Cullen, Francis T., and Paul Gendreau. 2000. Assessing Correctional Rehabilitation: Policy, Practice, and Prospects. pp. 109–175 in J. Horney (ed.) *Criminal Justice 2000: Volume 3—Policies, Processes, and Decisions of the Criminal Justice System.* Washington, DC: U.S. Department of Justice, National Institute of Justice.

Czuchry, Michael, Tiffiny L. Sia, and Donald F. Dansereau. 2006. Improving early engagement and treatment readiness of probationers. *The Prison Journal* 86(1): 56–74.

Daly, Kathleen, and Julie Stubbs. 2006. Feminist engagement with restorative justice. *Theoretical Criminology* 10(1): 9–28.

Dannerbeck, A., Paul Sundet, and Kathy Lloyd. 2002. Drug courts: Gender differences and their implications for treatment strategies. *Corrections Compendium* 27(12): 1–9.

Davidson, Janet T., Richard Crawford, and Elizabeth Kerwood. 2008. Constructing an EBP post-conviction model of supervision in United States probation, district of Hawaii: A Case Study. *Federal Probation* 72(2): 22–28.

Davies, G., and K. Dedel. 2006. Violence risk screening in community corrections. *Criminology and Public Policy* 5(4): 743–770.

Deering, John. 2010. Attitudes and beliefs of trainee probation officers: A new breed? *Probation Journal: The Journal of Community and Criminal Justice* 57(1): 9–26.

Deitch, Michele. 2009. Keeping our kids at home: Expanding community-based facilities for adjudicated youth in Texas. *Texas Public Policy Foundation Policy Perspective* (May). Retrieved from: http://www.texaspolicy.com

Delaney, Arthur. 2011. Obama presidential pardons: The elusiveness of executive clemency. Huffington Post, June 3, 2011. Retrieved from: http://www.huffingtonpost.com/2011/06/03/obama-presidential-pardons_n_870431.html?view=screen

del Carmen, Rolando, Maldine Beth Barnhill, Gene Bonham, Lance Hignite, and Todd Jermstad. 2001. *Civil liabilities and other legal issues for probation/parole officers and supervisors,* 3rd ed. National Institute of Corrections: U.S. Department of Justice.

del Carmen, Rolando, Sue E. Ritter, and Betsy A. Witt. 2005. *Briefs of Leading Cases in Corrections,* 4th ed. Cincinnati, OH: Anderson.

del Carmen, Rolando, and Chad Trulson. 2005. *Juvenile Justice: The System, Process, and Law.* Belmont, CA: Wadsworth.

Dexheimer, Eric. 2007. Locked out of their livelihoods. *Austin American-Statesman,* February 18. Retrieved from: http://www.statesman.com.

Dillon, Nancy. 2011. Lindsay Lohan sentenced to 120 days in jail for probation violation. *New York Daily News,* April 22, 2011. Retrieved at: http://articles.nydailynews.com/2011–04–22/

DiMascio, William M. 1997. *Seeking justice: Crime and punishment in America.* New York: Edna McConnell Clark Foundation.

Drake, Elizabeth. 2007. *Does participation in Washington's work release facilities reduce recidivism?* Olympia, WA: Washington State Institute for Public Policy. Retrieved from: http://www.wsipp.wa.gov/rptfiles/07–11–1201.pdf

Drapela, Laurie A., and Faith E. Lutze. 2009. Innovation in community corrections and probation officers' fears of being sued. *Journal of Contemporary Criminal Justice* 25(4): 364–383.

Durose, Matthew R., and Langan, Patrick A. 2007. *Felony sentences in state courts, 2004.* Washington, DC: Bureau of Justice Statistics.

Eisenberg, Michael, Jason Bryl, and Tony Fabelo. 2009. *Validation of the Wisconsin Department of Corrections Risk Assessment Instrument.* New York: Council of State Governments. Available at: http://justicereinvestment.org/files/WIRiskValidationFinalJuly2009.pdf

Ely, John F. 1996. Inside-out: Halfway house staff management of punishment and empathy on the ambiguous boundary between prison and the outside [Unpublished Ph.D. dissertation]. University of California-Santa Barbara.

English, Kim, Suzanne Pullen, L. Jones, and M. Kruth. 1996. *Managing adult sex offenders: A containment approach.* Lexington, KY: American Probation and Parole Association.

Erickson, Rosemary J., Wayman Crow, Louis A. Zurcher, and Archie V. Connett. 1973. *Paroled but not free.* New York: Behavioral Publications.

Evjen, Victor H. 1975. The federal probation system: The struggle to achieve it and its first 25 years. *Federal Probation* 39(2): 3–15.

Farole, Donald. 2003. The Harlem parole reentry court evaluation: Implementation and preliminary impact. New York: Center for Court Innovation. Retrieved from: http://www.courtinnovation.org/_uploads/documents/harlemreentryeval.pdf.

Farrall, Stephen. 2003. J'accuse: Probation evaluation-research epistemologies, part one: The critique. *Criminal Justice* 32: 161–179.

Fehr, Larry M. 2004. Washington female offender reentry programs combine transitional services with residential parenting. *Corrections Today* (Oct): 82–84.

Festervan, Earlene. 2003. *Women probationers: Supervision and success.* Lanham, MD: American Correctional Association.

Finn, Peter. 1997. *Sex offender community notification.* Washington DC: National Institute of Justice.

Fischer, Brenda. 2003. "Doing good with a vengeance": A critical assessment of the practices, effects and implications of drug treatment courts in North America. *Criminal Justice* 3(3): 227–248.

Fogel, David. 1979. *. . . We are the living proof . . . The justice model for corrections,* 2nd ed. Cincinnati, OH: Anderson.

Forst, Brian. 1995. Prosecution and sentencing. In *Crime,* edited by James Q. Wilson and Joan Petersilia. San Francisco, CA: Institute for Contemporary Studies, pp. 363–386.

Foucault, Michel. 1977. *Discipline and punish.* New York: Pantheon Books.

Frana, John F., and Ryan D. Schroeder. 2008. Alternatives to incarceration. *Justice Policy Journal* 5(2): 5–25.

French, Michael T., Ioana Popovici, and Lauren Tapsell. 2008. The economic costs of substance abuse treatment: Updated estimates and cost bands for program assessment and reimbursement. *Journal of Substance Abuse Treatment* 35(4): 462–469.

Frendle, Julie Wesley. 2004. *An overview of juvenile parole boards in the United States.* Prepared for the New Mexico Sentencing Commission.

Galloway, Alyson L., and Laurie A. Drapela. 2006. Are effective drug courts an urban phenomenon? *International Journal of Offender Therapy and Comparative Criminology* 50(3): 280–293.

Garner, Bryan A. 2009. *Black's Law Dictionary,* 9th ed. St. Paul, MN: West Group.

Gendreau, Paul. 1996. The principles of effective intervention. In *Choosing correctional options that work: Defining the demand and evaluating the supply,* edited by A.T. Harland. Thousand Oaks, CA: Sage.

Gendreau, Paul. 1998. Keynote speech: What works in community corrections: Promising approaches in reducing criminal behavior. In *Successful community sanctions and services for special offenders,* edited by B. J. Auerbach and T. C. Castellano. Lanham, MD: American Correctional Association, pp. 59–74.

General Accounting Office: Harris, DC, Charles Michael Johnson, Barry J. Seltser, Douglas M. Sloane, David P. Alexander, Stuart M. Kaufman, Pamela V. Williams, Thelma Jones, George H. Quinn, Katherine M. Wheeler, Jena Sinkfield, Jan B. Montgomery, and Ann H. Finley. 1997. *Drug courts: Overview of growth, characteristics,* *and results.* Washington, D.C., United States General Accounting Office.

Glaze, Lauren E., and Thomas P. Bonczar. 2009. *Probation and Parole in the United States, 2008.* Washington, DC: Bureau of Justice Statistics, U.S. Department of Justice.

Glaze, Lauren E., and Thomas P. Bonczar. 2008. *Probation and Parole in the United States, 2007.* Washington, DC: Bureau of Justice Statistics, U.S. Department of Justice.

Glaze, Lauren E., Thomas P. Bonczar, and Fan Zhang. 2010. *Probation and Parole in the United States, 2009.* Washington, DC: Bureau of Justice Statistics, U.S. Department of Justice.

Glaze, Lauren E., and Seri Palla. 2005. *Probation and parole in the United States, 2004.* Washington, DC: Bureau of Justice Statistics, U.S. Department of Justice.

Golden, Lori S., Robert J. Gatchel, and Melissa A. Cahill. 2006. Evaluating the effectiveness of the National Institute of Corrections' 'thinking for a change' program among probationers. *Journal of Offender Rehabilitation* 43(2), 55–73.

Goodwin, Catharine M. 2001. Looking at the law: Update on selected restitution issues. *Federal Probation* 65(1): 54–62.

Gordon, Jill. 2003. Aftercare. In *Encyclopedia of Juvenile Justice,* edited by McShane, Marilyn D. and Frank P. Williams III. Thousand Oaks, CA: Sage Publications.

Gordon, Jill A., Christina M. Barnes, and Scott W. VanBenschoten. 2006. The dual treatment rack program: A descriptive assessment of a new in-house jail diversion program. *Federal Probation* 70(3): 9–17.

Gottfredson, Denise C., and M. Lyn Exum. 2002. The Baltimore city drug treatment court: One-year results from a randomized study. *Journal of Research in Crime and Delinquency* 39(3): 337–356.

Gottfredson, Denise C., Brook W. Kearley, Stacy S. Najaka, and Carlos M. Rocha. 2007. How drug treatment courts work: An analysis of mediators. *Journal of Research in Crime and Delinquency* 44(1): 3–35.

Gottfredson, Denise C., Stacy S. Najaka, and Brook Kearley. 2003. Effectiveness of drug treatment courts: Evidence from a randomized trial. *Criminology & Public Policy* 2(2): 171–196.

Gottfredson, Don, Michael Gottfredson, and James Garofalo. 1997. Time served in prison and parolee outcomes among parolee risk categories. *Journal of Criminal Justice* 5: 1–12.

Gowen, Darren. 2000. Overview of the federal home confinement 1988–1996. *Federal Probation* 64(2): 11–18.

———. 2001. Remote location monitoring—A supervision strategy to enhance risk control. *Federal Probation* 65(2): 38–41.

Grattet, Ryken, Jeffrey Lin, and Joan Petersilia. 2011. Supervision regimes, risk, and official reactions to parolee deviance. *Criminology* 49(2): 371–400.

Gray, M. Kevin, Monique Fields, and Sheila Royo Maxwell. 2001. Examining probation violations: Who, what and when. *Crime and Delinquency* 47(4): 537–557.

Greek, Cecil E. 2002. The cutting edge: Tracking probationers in space and time: The convergence of GIS and GPS systems. *Federal Probation* 66(1): 51–53.

Griffin, Patrick, and Patricia Torbet (Eds.). 2002. *Desktop guide to good juvenile probation practice*. Washington, DC: National Center for Juvenile Justice.

Grooms, Robert M. 1982. Recidivist. *Crime and Delinquency* 28: 541–545.

Grubesic, Tony H., Elizabeth Mack, and Alan T. Murray. 2007. Spatial analysis for evaluating the impact of Megan's law. *Social Science Computer Review* 25: 143–162.

Gulley, Neale. 2011. Nation's first veterans court counts its successes. *Reuters*, January 9, 2011. Retrieved from: http://www.reuters.com/assets/print?aid=ustre7082u020110109

Guydish, Joseph, Monica Chan, Alan Bostrom, Martha A. Jessup. Thomas B. Davis, and Cheryl Marsh. 2011. A randomized trial of probation case management for drug-involved women offenders. *Crime and Delinquency* 57(2): 167–198.

Hammett, Theodore M., Cheryl Roberts, and Sofia Kennedy. 2001. Health-related issues in prisoner reentry. *Crime and Delinquency* 47(3): 390–409.

Hanley, Dena. 2002. *Risk differentiation and intensive supervision: A meaningful union?* An unpublished doctoral dissertation, University of Cincinnati, Cincinnati, OH.

Hansen, Christopher. 2001. The cutting edge: A survey of technological innovation: Where have all the probation officers gone? *Federal Probation* 65(1): 51–53.

Hansen, Chris. 2008. Cognitive-behavioral interventions: Where they come from and what they do. *Federal Probation* 72(2): 43–49

Harries, Keith. 2003. Using geographic analysis in probation and parole. *National Institute of Justice Journal* 249: 32–33.

Harris, Danielle A. 2004. *A typological approach to exploring pathways for rapists, child molesters, and incest offenders*. An unpublished master's thesis. College Park: University of Maryland.

Harris, M. Kay. 1996. Key differences among community corrections acts in the United States: An overview. *The Prison Journal* 76(2): 192–238.

Hartman, David J., Paul C. Friday, and Kevin I. Minor. 1994. Residential probation: A seven year follow-up study of halfway house discharges. *Journal of Criminal Justice* 22(6): 503–515.

Hartney, Christopher, and Susan Marchionna. 2009. *Attitudes of US voters toward nonserious offenders and alternatives to incarceration*. Oakland, CA: NCCD. Available at: http://nccd-crc.issuelab.org/research/5/filter/title

Hartzler, Bryan, and Erin M. Espinosa. 2011. Moving criminal justice organizations toward adoption of evidence-based practice via advanced workshop training in motivational interviewing: A research note. *Criminal Justice Policy Review* 22(2): 235–253.

Haynes, Stacy Hoskins, Barry Ruback, and Gretchen R. Cusick. 2010. Courtroom workgroups and sentencing: The effects of similarity, proximity, and stability. *Crime and Delinquency* 56(1): 126–161.

Hemmens, Craig. 1998. Life in the joint and beyond: An examination of inmate attitudes and perceptions of prison, parole, and self at the time of release [Unpublished Ph.D. dissertation]. Sam Houston State University.

Hemmens, Craig, Kathryn Bennett, and Rolando del Carmen. 1998. The exclusionary rule does not apply to parole revocation hearings: An analysis of *Pennsylvania Board of Probation and Parole v. Scott*. *Criminal Law Bulletin* 35(4): 388–409.

Henry, Thomas. 2007. Reflections on the 25th anniversary of the pretrial services act. *Federal Probation* 71(2): 4–6.

Hensley, Denise Bray. 1995. One Boy's Life. *Houston Chronicle* (September 17).

Herman, Susan, and Cressida Wasserman. 2001. A role for victims in offender reentry. *Crime and Delinquency* 47(3): 428–445.

Hill, Brian J. 2006. Four-point strategy reduces technical violations of probation in Connecticut. *Topics in Community Corrections: Effectively Managing Violations and Revocations*. Longmont, CO: National Institute of Corrections.

Hindman, Jan, and James M. Peters. 2001. Polygraph testing leads to better understanding adult and juvenile sex offenders. *Federal Probation* 65(3): 8–15.

Hockenberry, Sarah, Melissa Sickmund, and Anthony Sladky. 2011. *Juvenile residential facility census, 2008: Selected findings*. Washington, DC: Office of Juvenile Justice and Delinquency Prevention.

Holsinger, Alex M., Arthur J. Lurigio, and Edward J. Latessa. 2001. Up to speed: Practitioners' guide to understanding the basis of assessing offender risk. *Federal Probation* 65(1): 46–50.

Holzer, Harry J. 1996. *What employers want: Job prospects for less-educated workers*. New York: Sage.

Homant, Robert J., and Mark A. DeMercurio. 2009. Intermediate sanctions in probation officers' sentencing recommendations: Consistency, net widening, and net repairing. *The Prison Journal* 89(4): 426–439.

Horn, Dan. 2000. Offenders find records hard to erase. *Cincinnati Enquirer,* December 18.

Hucklesby, Anthea. 2011. The working life of electronic monitoring officers. *Criminology & Criminal Justice* 11(1): 59–76.

Hudson, Barbara. 2006. Beyond white man's justice: Race, gender, and justice in late modernity. *Theoretical Criminology* 10(1): 29–47.

Hughes, John M. 2008. Results-based management in federal probation and pretrial services. *Federal Probation* 72(2), 4–14.

Hughes, Timothy A., Doris James Wilson, and Allen J. Beck. 2001. *Trends in state parole, 1990–2000*. Washington, DC: U.S. Department of Justice, Bureau of Justice Statistics.

International Community Corrections Association. 2009. Retrieved from: http://www.iccaweb.org/history.htm

Ireland, Connie, and Bruce Berg. 2008. Women in parole: Respect and rapport. *International Journal of Offender Therapy and Comparative Criminology* 52(4): 474–491.

Jacobs, Mark D. 1990. *Screwing the system and making it work: Juvenile justice in the no-fault society*. Chicago: University of Chicago Press.

Jeffrey, R., and S. Woolpert. 1974. Work furlough as an alternative to incarceration. *Journal of Criminology* 65(3), 405–415.

Jenuwine, Michael J., Ronald Simmons, and Edward Swies. 2003. Community supervision of sex offenders—Integrating probation and clinical treatment. *Federal Probation* 67(3): 20–27.

Johnson, Kevin, and Richard Willing. 2008. New DNA links used to deny parole. *USA Today*, February 7. Retrieved from: http://www.usatoday.com/news/nation/2008-02-07

Jones, Mark, and John J. Kerbs. 2007. Probation and parole officers and discretionary decision-making: Responses to technical and criminal violations. *Federal Probation* 71(1): 9–15.

Kalfrin, Valerie. 2008. Ankle device foils boat burglar's plan, police say. *The Tampa Tribune*, January 9.

Karp, David R., and Todd R. Clear. 2002. *What is community justice?* Thousand Oaks, CA: Pine Forge Press.

Karuppannan, Jaishankar. 2005. Mapping and corrections: Management of offenders with geographic information systems. *Corrections Compendium* 30(1): 7–9, 31–33.

Keller, Oliver J., and Benedict S. Alper. 1970. *Halfway houses: Community-centered correction and treatment.* Lexington, MA: D.C. Heath.

Kelly, Brian J. 2001. Supervising the cyber-criminal. *Federal Probation* 65(2): 8–10.

Kelly, Phaedra Athena O'Hara. 1999. The ideology of shame: An analysis of first amendment and eighth amendment challenges to scarlet-letter probation conditions. *North Carolina Law Review* 77(2): 783–864.

Kempinen, C.A., and Megan C. Kurlychek. 2003. An outcome evaluation of Pennsylvania's boot camp: Does rehabilitative programming within a disciplinary setting reduce recidivism? *Crime and Delinquency* 49(4): 581–602.

Kendig, Newton, Barbara Boyle, and Anthony Swetz. 1996. The Maryland Division of Correction medical-parole program: A four-year experience, 1991 to 1994. *AIDS & Public Policy Journal* 11(1): 21–27.

Kenney, J. Scott, and Don Clairmont. 2009. Using the victim role as both sword and shield: The interactional dynamics of restorative justice sessions. *Journal of Contemporary Ethnography* 38(3): 279–307.

Kerbs, John J., Mark Jones, and Jennifer M. Jolley. 2009. Discretionary decision making by probation and parole officers: The role of extralegal as predictors of responses to technical violations. *Journal of Contemporary Criminal Justice* 25(4): 424–441.

Kilgour, D., and S. Meade. 2004. Look what boot camps done for me: Teaching and learning at Lakeview Academy. *Journal of Correctional Education* 55: 170–185.

Killias, Martin, Gwladys Gillieron, Izumi Kissling, and Patrice Villettaz. 2010. Community service versus electronic monitoring-What works better? *British Journal of Criminology* 50: 1155–1170.

Kim, Dae-Young, Cassia Spohn, and Mark Foxall. 2007. An evaluation of the DRC in the context of Douglas County, Nebraska. *The Prison Journal* 87(4): 434–456.

Kim, Dae-Young, Hee-Jong Joo, and William P. McCarty. 2008. Risk assessment and classification of day reporting center clients. *Criminal Justice and Behavior* 35(6): 792–812.

Kinnevy, Susan C., and Joel M. Caplan. 2008. *Findings from the APAI international survey of releasing authorities.* Center for Research on youth and social policy. Retrieved from: http://www.apaintl.org/pdfs/final_apai_survey_10222008.pdf

Kittrie, Nicholas N., Elyce H. Zenoff, and Vincent A. Eng. 2002. *Sentencing, sanctions, and corrections: Federal and state law, policy, and practice,* 2nd ed. New York: Foundation Press.

Klein-Saffran, Jody. 1995. Electronic monitoring versus halfway houses: A study of federal offenders. *Alternatives to Incarceration* (Fall): 24–28.

Klockars, Carl B. Jr. 1972. A theory of probation supervision. *Journal of Criminal Law, Criminology and Police Science* 63(4): 550–557.

Knoll, Crystal, and Melissa Sickmund. 2010. *Delinquency cases in juvenile court, 2007.* Washington, DC: Office of Juvenile Justice and Delinquency Prevention.

Krauth, Barbara, and Larry Linke. 1999. *State organizational structures for delivering adult probation services.* Longmont, CO: LIS, Inc. for the National Institute of Corrections.

Kurlychek, Megan C., Robert Brame, and Shawn D. Bushway. 2007. Enduring risk? Old criminal records and predictions of future criminal involvement. *Crime and Delinquency* 53(1): 64–83.

Kyckelhahn, Tracey, and Thomas H. Cohen. 2007. *Felony Defendants in Large Urban Counties, 2004.* Washington, DC: Bureau of Justice Statistics, Table 29. Retrieved from: http://www.ojp.usdoj.gov/bjs/stssent.htm#scps

Langan, Patrick A., and Mark Cunniff. 1992. *Recidivism of felons on probation, 1986–1989.* Washington, DC: U.S. Department of Justice, Bureau of Justice Statistics (February).

Langan, Patrick A., and David J. Levin. 2002. *Recidivism of prisoners released in 1994.* Washington, DC: U.S. Department of Justice, Bureau of Justice Statistics (June).

Latessa, Edward J., Richard Lemke, Matthew Makarios, Paula Smith, and Christopher T. Lowenkamp. 2010. The creation and validation of the Ohio Risk Assessment System (ORAS). *Federal Probation* 74(1): 16–22.

Lattimore, Pamela K. 2006. Reentry, reintegration, rehabilitation, recidivism, and redemption. *The Criminologist* 31(3): 1–6.

La Vigne, Nancy G. 2006. Prisoner reentry: Taking stock and moving forward. *Austin/Travis County Reentry Roundtable Annual Community Forum.* The Urban Institute.

LeClair, D. P., and Susan Guarino-Ghezzi. 1991. Does incapacitation guarantee public safety? Lessons from the Massachusetts furlough and prerelease programs. *Justice Quarterly* 8(1): 9–36.

Lee, Renee C. 2011. A growing burden: As more elderly prisoners serve time, state officials struggle to pay their medical costs. *Houston Chronicle*, May 16, 2011. http://www.chron.com/disp/story.mpl/metropolitan/7566086.html

Lee, Won-Jae, James R. Phelps, and Dan R. Beto. 2009. Turnover intention among probation officers and direct care staff: A statewide study. *Federal Probation* 73(3): 28–39.

Lehman, Joseph, Trudy Gregorie Beatty, Dennis Maloney, Susan Russell, Anne Seymour, and Carol Shapiro.

2002. *The three r's of reentry.* Washington, DC: Justice Solutions.

Lehnerer, Melodye. 1992. Becoming involved: Field research at a halfway house for ex-offenders [Unpublished Ph.D. dissertation]. York University.

Levin, Marc A. 2008a. Work release: Con job or big payoff for Texas? *Texas Public Policy Foundation Policy Perspective* (April). Retrieved from: http://www.texaspolicy.com

———. 2008b. Five technological solutions for Texas' correctional and law enforcement challenges. *Texas Public Policy Foundation Policy Perspective* (June). Retrieved from: http://www.texaspolicy.com

———. 2010. In juvenile justice, less is often more. *Texas Public Policy Foundation Policy Perspective* (May 7). Retrieved from: http://www.texaspolicy.com

———. 2011. Breaking addiction without breaking the bank: Cost-effective strategies for Texas lawmakers to reduce substance abuse. *Texas Public Policy Foundation Policy Perspective* (April). Retrieved from: http://www.texaspolicy.com

Leznoff, JoAnne. 1998. Privatization of community supervision as a public safety issue. In *Topics in community corrections: Annual issue 1998: Privatizing community supervision.* Longmont, CO: National Institute of Corrections, U.S. Department of Justice, pp. 19–24.

Lilly, J. Robert. 2006. Issues behind empirical EM reports. *Criminology & Public Policy* 5(1): 93–102.

Lilly, J. Robert, Richard A, Ball, G. David Curry, and Richard Smith. 1992. The Pride, Inc., program: An evaluation of 5 years of electronic monitoring. *Federal Probation* (December): 42–47.

Lindner, Charles. 2007. Thacher, Augustus, and Hill: The path to statutory probation in the United States and England. *Federal Probation* 71(3): 36–41.

Lindner, Charles. 2008. Probation intake: Gatekeeper to the family court. *Federal Probation* 72(1): 48–53.

Lindner, Charles, and Margaret R. Savarese. 1984a. The evolution of probation: Early salaries, qualifications, and hiring practices. *Federal Probation* 48(1): 3–10.

———. 1984b. The evolution of probation: The historical contributions of the volunteer. *Federal Probation* 48(2): 3–10.

———. 1984c. The evolution of probation: University settlement and the beginning of statutory probation in New York City. *Federal Probation* 48(3): 3–12.

———. 1984d. The evolution of probation: University settlement and its pioneering role in probation work. *Federal Probation* 48(4): 3–13.

Linke, Larry, and Barbara Krauth. 2000. *Perspectives from the field on the interstate compact on juveniles: Findings from a national survey* [NIC-016491]. Longmont, CO: National Institute of Corrections.

Lipsey, Mark W., J. C. Howell, and S. T. Tidd. 2002. *A standardized program evaluation protocol for North Carolina's juvenile justice system programs.* Nashville, TN: Vanderbilt University, Center for Evaluation Research and Methodology.

Lipton, Douglas, Robert Martinson, and J. Wilks. 1975. *The effectiveness of correctional treatment.* New York: Praeger.

Listwan, Shelley Johnson, Jody L. Sundt, Alexander M. Holsinger, and Edward J. Latessa, 2003. The effect of drug court programming on recidivism: The Cincinnati experience. *Crime and Delinquency* 49(3): 389–411.

Little, Gregory L. 2005. Meta-analysis of moral recognition therapy: Recidivism results from probation and parole implementations. *Cognitive-Behavioral Treatment Review* 14(1/2): 14–16.

Livsey, Sarah. 2010. *Juvenile delinquency probation caseload, 2007.* Washington, DC: Office of Juvenile Justice and Delinquency Prevention.

Locke, Hubert G. 1998. Closing comments. In *Successful community sanctions and services for special offenders,* edited by B. J. Auerbach and T. C. Castellano. Lanham, MD: American Correctional Association, pp. 253–259.

Lowenkamp, Christopher T., and Kristin Bechtel. 2007. The predictive validity of the LSI-R on a sample of offenders drawn from the records of the Iowa Department of Corrections data management system. *Federal Probation* 71(3): 25–29.

Lowenkamp, Christopher T., Richard Lemke, and Edward Latessa. 2008. The development and validation of a pretrial screening tool. *Federal Probation* 72(3): 2–9.

Lowenkamp, Christopher T., and Edward J. Latessa. 2005. Increasing the effectiveness of correctional programming through the risk principle: Identifying offenders for residential placement. *Criminology & Public Policy* 4(2): 263–290.

Lubitz, Robin L., and Thomas W. Ross. 2001. Sentencing guidelines: Reflections on the future. In *Sentencing and corrections: Issues for the 21st century* (No. 10, June). Washington, DC: U.S. Department of Justice.

Lutze, Faith E., R. Peggy Smith, and Nicholas P. Lovrich. 2004. A practitioner-initiated research partnership: An evaluation of neighborhood based supervision in Spokane, Washington. An unpublished manuscript.

Lynch, Mona. 1998. Waste managers? The new penology, crime fighting, and parole agent identity. *Law and Society Review* 32(4): 839–869.

Mack, Julian W. 1909. The juvenile court. *Harvard Law Review* 23: 102–109.

MacKenzie, Doris L. 2000. Evidence-based corrections: Identifying what works. *Crime and Delinquency* 46(4): 457–472.

MacKenzie, Doris L., Angela R. Gover, Gaylene Styve Armstrong, and Ojmarrh Mitchell. 2001. A national study comparing the environments of boot camps with traditional facilities for juvenile offenders. *National Institute of Justice Research in Brief.* Washington, DC: U.S. Department of Justice.

Mador, Jessica. 2010. New veterans court aims to help soldiers struggling at home. *Minnesota Public Radio News,* March 22, 2010. Retrieved from: http://minnesota/publicradio.org/display/web/2010/03/22/veterans-court/

Maidment, MaDonna R. 2002. Toward a woman-centered approach to community-based corrections: A gendered analysis of electronic monitoring in eastern Canada. *Women and Criminal Justice* 13(4): 47–68.

Manchak, Sarah M., Jennifer L. Skeem, Kevin S. Douglas, and Maro Siranosian. 2009. Does gender moderate the predictive utility of the Level of Service Inventory-Revised (LSI-R) for serious violent offenders? *Criminal Justice and Behavior* 36(5): 425–442.

Mansnerus, Laura. 2003. Questions rise over imprisoning sex offenders past their terms. *New York Times,* November 17: 1–6. Retrieved from: http://www.nytimes.com

Marklund, F., and S. Holmberg. 2009. Effects of early release from prison using electronic tagging in Sweden. *Journal of Experimental Criminology* 5(1): 41–61.

Martin, Christine, Arthur J. Lurigio, and David E. Olson. 2003. An examination of rearrests and reincarcerations among discharged day reporting center clients. *Federal Probation* 67(1): 24–30.

Martin, Jamie S., Kate Hanrahan, and James H. Bowers. 2009. Offenders' perceptions of house arrest and electronic monitoring. *Journal of Offender Rehabilitation* 48(6): 547–570.

Martin, Jamie S., Kate Hanrahan, and Teah M. Travers. 2008. *Probation officers' assessment of electronic monitoring as an intermediate sanction.* Paper presented at the annual meeting of the Academy of Criminal Justice Sciences, March 11–15, 2008. Cincinnati, OH.

Martinson, Robert. 1974. What works? Questions and answers about prison reform. *Public Interest* 35(Spring): 22–35.

Maruna, Shadd, and Anna King. 2008. Selling the public on probation: Beyond the bib. *Probation Journal* 55(4): 337–351.

Maxfield, Michael G., and Terry L. Baumer. 1990. Home detention with electronic monitoring: Comparing pretrial and postconviction programs. *Crime and Delinquency* 36(4): 521–536.

Maxwell, Gabrielle, and Allison Morris. 1996. Research in family group conferences with young offenders in New Zealand. Pp. 88–110 in *Family group conferences: Perspectives on policy and practice,* edited by Joe Hudson, Allison Morris, Gabrielle Maxwell, and Burt Galaway. Monsey, NY: Criminal Justice Press.

Mawhorr, Tina L. 1997. Disabled offenders and work release: An exploratory examination. *Criminal Justice Review* 22(1): 34–48.

Mayzer, Roni, and M. Kevin Gray. 2000. Probation absconders. Paper presented at the annual American Society of Criminology meeting, San Francisco, California, November 15–18.

McDonald, Douglas, Judith Greene, and Charles Worzella. 1992. *Day fines in American courts: The Staten Island and Milwaukee experiments.* Washington, DC: U.S. Department of Justice, National Institute of Justice.

McKay, Brian. 2002. The state of sex offender probation supervision in Texas. *Federal Probation* 66(1): 16–20.

McManus, Patrick D., and Lynn Z. Barclay. 1994. *Community Corrections Act: Technical assistance manual.* College Park, MD: American Correctional Association.

McMenamin, Dan. 2011. Man who scaled millennium tower plans to appeal sentence of probation, community service, and restitution. *Bay City News,* February 1, 2011. Retrieved from: http://sfappeal.com/news/2011/02/man-who-scaled-millennium-tower-plans-to-appeal-sentence.php

McShane, Marilyn, Frank P. Williams, and H. Michael Dolny. 2002. Do standard risk prediction instruments apply to female parolees? *Women and Criminal Justice* 13(2/3): 163.

Medina, Regina. 2011. Parole officer accused of extorting bribes. *Philadelphia Daily News,* June 9, 2011. Available at: http://www.philly.com/philly/news/123586239.html

Mercado, Cynthia C., Shea Alvarez, and Jill S. Levenson. 2008. The impact of specialized sex offender legislation on community re-entry. *Sexual Abuse: A Journal of Research and Treatment* 20: 188–205.

Michigan Judicial Institute. 2003. Case review and probation revocation in designated case and automatic waiver proceedings. In *Juvenile Justice Benchbook* (Revised edition), pp. 457–467.

Milligan, Jessie. 2001. Blood, sweat, and fears. *Fort Worth Star Telegram Sunday Magazine,* March 18, 2001.

Minor, Kevin I., James B. Wells, and Crissy Sims. 2003. Recidivism among federal probationers: Predicting sentence violations. *Federal Probation* 67(1): 31–36.

Miyashiro, Carol M. 2008. Research 2 results (R2R): The pretrial services experience. *Federal Probation* 72(2): 80–86.

Moreland, D.W. 1941. History and prophecy: John Augustus and his successors. *National Probation Association Yearbook.* Presentation delivered at the 35th Annual Conference of the National Probation Association, Boston, Massachusetts, May 29, 1941.

Morgan, Kathryn D. 1994. Factors associated with probation outcome. *Journal of Criminal Justice* 22: 341–353.

———. 1995. Variables associated with successful probation outcome. *Journal of Offender Rehabilitation* 22(3/4): 141–153.

Morgan, Kathryn, and Brent L. Smith. 2005. Victims, punishment, and parole: The effect of victim participation on parole hearings. *Criminology & Public Policy* 4(2): 333–360.

Morgan, Kimberly. 2011. Snoop Dogg released from probation early. Long Beach Celebrity Examiner, May 28, 2011. Retrieved from: http://www.examiner.com/celebrity-in-long-beach/snoop-dogg-released-from-probation-early

Morris, Norval. 2002. *Maconochie's gentlemen: The story of Norfolk Island and the roots of modern prison reform.* New York: Oxford University Press.

Morris, Norval, and Michael Tonry. 1990. *Between prison and probation: Intermediate punishments in a rational sentencing system.* New York: Oxford University Press.

Moscicki, Ronald W. 1996. If you don't take responsibility, you take orders. In *Juvenile and adult boot camps,* edited by American Correctional Association. Lanham, MD: American Correctional Association.

Mumola, Christopher J. 2000. *Incarcerated parents and their children.* Washington, DC: U.S. Department of Justice, Bureau of Justice Statistics.

Mumola, Christopher J., with Thomas P. Bonczar. 1998. *Substance abuse and treatment of adults on probation, 1995.* Washington, DC: U.S. Department of Justice, Bureau of Justice Statistics.

National Institute of Corrections and the Council of State Governments. 2002. *Interstate compact for adult offender supervision: State officials guide.* Longmont, CO: National Institute of Corrections, U.S. Department of Justice.

National Law Enforcement and Corrections Technology Center. 2002. Fuginet'ing Parole Violators. *TechBeat* (Winter). Retrieved from: http://www.justnet.org

National Law Enforcement and Corrections Technology Center. 2009. Field search. *TechBeat* (Winter). Retrieved from: http://www.justnet.org

National Research Council. 2008. *Parole, desistance from crime, and community integration*. Washington, DC: National Academies Press.

Neff, Tom. 2006. *Chances: The women of Magdalene*. Video documentary, The Documentary Channel, February 26, 2006.

Nellis, Mike. 2006. Surveillance, rehabilitation, and electronic monitoring: Getting the issues clear. *Criminology & Public Policy* 5(1): 103–108.

Nelson, William F. 2004. Prostitution: A community solution alternative. *Corrections Today* (October): 88–91

Newville, Lanny L. 2001. Cyber crime and the courts: Investigating and supervising the information age offender. *Federal Probation* 65(2): 11–17.

New York State Division of Parole, Office of Policy Analysis and Information. 1993. Overview of the Parole Revocation Process in New York. In *Reclaiming Offender Accountability: Intermediate Sanctions for Probation and Parole Violators*, edited by Edward E. Rhine. Laurel, MD: American Correctional Association.

Nielsen, Amie L., Frank R. Scarpitti, and James Inciardi. 1996. Integrating the therapeutic community and work release for drug-involved offenders: The CREST program. *Journal of Substance Abuse Treatment* 13(4): 349–358.

Norman, Michael D., and Robert C. Wadman. 2000. Probation department sentencing recommendations in two Utah counties. *Federal Probation* 64(2): 47–51.

North Carolina Sentencing and Policy Advisory Commission. 1994. *Structured sentencing for felonies-training and reference manual*. Raleigh, NC: Author.

O'Brien, Patricia. 2001. *Making it in the free world: Women in transition from prison*. New York: State University of New York Press.

Office for the Victims of Crime. 2002. *Victims' rights and services*. Washington, DC: U.S. Department of Justice, Office for Victims of Crime.

Ogden, Thomas G., and Cary Horrocks. 2001. Pagers, digital, audio, and kiosk: Officer assistants. *Federal Probation* 65(2): 35–37.

Olson, David E., Brendan Dooley, and Candice M. Kane. 2004. The relationship between gang membership and inmate recidivism. *Illinois Criminal Justice Information Authority Research Bulletin* 2(12): 1–12.

Olson, David E., and Gerard F. Ranker. 2001. Crime does not pay, but criminals may: Factors influencing the imposition and collection of probation fees. *Justice Systems Journal* 22: 29–46.

O'Malley, Pat. 2008. Theorizing fines. *Punishment and Society* 11(1): 67–83.

Opsal, Tara D. 2011. Women disrupting a marginalized identity: Subverting the parolee identity through narrative. *Journal of Contemporary Ethnography* 40(2): 135–167.

Ostermann, Michael. 2009. An analysis of New Jersey's day reporting center and halfway back programs: Embracing the rehabilitative ideal through evidence-based practices. *Journal of Offender Rehabilitation* 48: 139–153.

Ostrom, Brian J., Matthew Kleiman, Fred Cheesman, Randall M. Hansen, and Neal B. Kauder. 2002. *Offender risk assessment in Virginia*. Williamsburg, VA: National Center for State Courts.

Outlaw, M.C., and R. Barry Ruback. 1999. Predictors and outcomes of victim restitution orders. *Justice Quarterly* 16: 847–869.

Padgett, Kathy G., William D. Bales, and Thomas G. Blomberg. 2006. Under surveillance: An empirical test of the effectiveness and consequences of electronic monitoring. *Criminology & Public Policy* 5(1): 61–92.

Panzarella, Robert. 2002. Theory and practice of probation on bail in the report of John Augustus. *Federal Probation* 66(3): 38–42.

Paparozzi, Mario A., and Joel M. Caplan. 2009. A profile of paroling authorities in America: The strange bedfellows of politics and professionalism. *The Prison Journal* 89(4): 401–425.

Paparozzi, Mario A., and Paul Gendreau. 2005. An intensive supervision program that worked: Service delivery, professional orientation, and organizational supportiveness. *The Prison Journal* 85(4): 445–466.

Paparozzi, Mario A., and Roger Guy. 2009. The giant that never woke: Parole authorities as the lynchpin to evidence-based practices and prisoner reentry. *Journal of Contemporary Criminal Justice* 25(4): 397–411.

Parent, Dale. 1995. Day reporting centers. In *Intermediate sanctions in overcrowded times*, edited by Michael Tonry and Kate Hamilton. Boston, MA: Northeastern University Press.

———. 2003. *Correctional boot camps: Lessons from a decade of research*. Washington, DC: National Institute of Justice.

Pattavina, April. 2009. The use of electronic monitoring as persuasive technology: Reconsidering the empirical evidence on the effectiveness of electronic monitoring. *Victims and Offenders* 4: 385–390.

Payne, Brian K., and Matthew DeMichele. 2008. Warning: Sex offenders need to be supervised in the community. *Federal Probation* 72(1): 37–42.

Payne, Brian K., and Matthew DeMichele. 2011. Probation philosophies and workload considerations. *American Journal of Criminal Justice* 36: 29–43.

Payne, Brian K., and Randy R. Gainey. 2002. The influence of demographic factors on the experience of house arrest. *Federal Probation* 66(3): 64–70.

———. 2004. The electronic monitoring of offenders released from jail or prison: Safety, control, and comparisons to the incarceration experience. *The Prison Journal* 84(4): 413–435.

Perez, Deanna M. 2009. Applying evidence-based practices to community corrections supervision: An evaluation of residential substance abuse treatment for high-risk probationers. *Journal of Contemporary Criminal Justice* 25(4): 442–458.

Petersilia, Joan. 2000a. Parole and prisoner reentry in the United States, part 1. *Perspectives* 24(Summer): 32–46.

———. 2000b. When prisoners return to the community: Political, economic, and social consequences. In *Sentencing and corrections: Issues for the 21st century* [paper 9 from the Executive Sessions on Sentencing and Corrections]. Washington DC: U.S. Department of Justice (November).

———. 2002. *Reforming probation and parole in the 21st century.* Lanham, MD: American Correctional Association.

———. 2003. *When prisoners come home.* New York: Oxford University Press.

Peterson, Liz Austin. 2009. A potential at ease: Harris County youth boot camp may replace rigorous drills with therapy. *Houston Chronicle,* January 28.

Pew Charitable Trusts. 2010. *Collateral costs: Incarceration's effect on economic mobility.* Washington, DC: Pew Charitable Trusts.

Phillips, Kirby. 2001. Reducing Alcohol-Related Crime Electronically. *Federal Probation* 65(2): 42–44.

Pimentel, Roger and Jon Muller. 2010. The containment approach to managing defendants charged with sex offenses. *Federal Probation* 74(2): 24–26.

Prendergast, Michael, Jean Wellisch, and Mamie Mee Wong. 1996. Residential treatment for women parolees following prison-based drug treatment: Treatment experiences, needs and service, outcomes. *The Prison Journal* 76(3): 253–274.

President's Commission on Law Enforcement and Administration of Justice. 1967. *The challenge of crime in a free society.* Washington, DC: U.S. Government Printing Office.

Proctor, Jon L. 1999. The new parole: An analysis of parole board decision making as a function of eligibility. *Journal of Crime and Justice* 22(2): 193–217.

Purkiss, Marcus, Misty Kiefer, Craig Hemmens, and Velmer S. Burton. 2003. Probation Officer Functions—A Statutory Analysis. *Federal Probation* 67(1): 12–23.

Quinn, Frederick. 2002. *The courthouse at Indian Creek.* Santa Ana, CA: Seven Locks Press.

Rainey, James. 2002. Probation cadets see job from behind bars. *Los Angeles Times,* February 8, p. A3.

Ransom, George, and Mary Ellen Mastorilli. 1993. The Massachusetts boot camp: Inmate anecdotes. *The Prison Journal* 73(3/4): 307–318.

Reddington, Frances P., and Betsy Wright Kreisel. 2000. Training juvenile probation officers: National trends and practice. *Federal Probation* 64(2): 28–32.

———. 2003. Basic fundamental skills training for juvenile probation officers: Results of a nationwide survey of curriculum content. *Federal Probation* 67(1): 41–45.

Reuell, Peter. 2008. High-tech device knows when you're not sober. *The Metrowest Daily News,* February 10. Retrieved from: http://www.metrowestdailynews.com/multimedia/

Rhine, Edward E. 2002. Why "what works" matters under the "broken windows" model of supervision. *Federal Probation* 66(2): 38–42.

Richards, Stephen C., and Richard S. Jones. 1997. Perpetual incarceration machine: Structural impediments to post-prison success. *Journal of Contemporary Criminal Justice* 13(1): 4–22.

Richie, Beth E. 2001. Challenges incarcerated women face as they return to their communities: Findings from life history interviews. *Crime and Delinquency* 47(3): 368–389.

Rikard, R.V., and Ed Rosenberg. 2007 Aging inmates: A convergence of trends in the American criminal justice system. *Journal of Correctional Health Care* 13(3): 150–162.

Roberts, Albert. 2004. *Juvenile Justice Sourcebook: Past, Present, and Future.* Oxford: Oxford University Press.

Robinson, Laurie, and Jeremy Travis. 2000. Managing prisoner reentry for public safety. *Federal Sentencing Reporter* 12(5) (March/April).

Roman, John, Wendy Townsend, and Avinash Singh Bhati. 2003. *Recidivism rates for drug court graduates: Nationally based estimates.* NCJ 201229. Washington, DC: U.S. Department of Justice.

Roscoe, Thomas, David E. Duffee, Craig Rivera, and Tony R. Smith. 2007. Arming probation officers: Correlates of the decision to arm at the departmental level. *Criminal Justice Studies* 20(1): 43–63.

Rotman, Edgardo. 1995. The failure of reform. In *The Oxford history of the prison,* edited by Norval Morris and David Rothman. New York: Oxford University Press, pp. 71–197.

Roy, Sudipto, and Jennifer N. Grimes. 2002. Adult offenders in a day reporting center—A preliminary study. *Federal Probation* 66(1): 44–50.

Ruback, R. Barry, and Mark H. Bergstrom. 2006. Economic sanctions in criminal justice: Purposes, effects, and implications. *Criminal Justice and Behavior* 33(2): 242–273.

Ruback, R. Barry, Stacy N. Hoskins, Alison C. Cares, and Ben Feldmeyer. 2006. Perception and payment of economic sanctions: A survey of offenders. *Federal Probation* 70(3): 27–31.

Ruback, R. Barry, Gretchen R. Ruth, and Jennifer N. Shaffer. 2005. Assessing the impact of statutory change: A statewide multilevel analysis of restitution orders in Pennsylvania. *Crime and Delinquency* 51(3): 318–342.

Ruddell, Rick, Brian Roy, and Sita Diehl. 2004. Diverting offenders with mental illness from jail: A tale of two states. *Corrections Compendium* 29(5): 1–5, 38–42.

Russell, Robert T. 2009. Veterans treatment court: A proactive approach. *New England Journal on Criminal and Civil Confinement* 35: 357–372.

Sabol, William J., and Heather Couture. 2008. *Prison inmates at midyear 2007.* Washington, DC: U.S. Department of Justice, Bureau of Justice Statistics.

Sabol, William J., and Todd D. Minton. 2008. *Jail inmates at midyear 2007.* Washington, DC: U.S. Department of Justice, Bureau of Justice Statistics.

Sachwald, Judith, Ernest Eley, and Faye S. Taxman. 2006. Four-point strategy reduces technical violations of probation in Connecticut. *Topics in Community Corrections: Effectively Managing Violations and Revocations.* Longmont, CO: National Institute of Corrections.

Samenow, Stanton E. 1984. *Inside the criminal mind.* New York: Times Books.

Sandhu, Harjit S., Richard A, Dodder, and Minu Mathur. 1993. House arrest: Success and failure rates in residential and nonresidential community-based programs. *Journal of Offender Rehabilitation* 19(1/2): 131–44.

Scharr, Timothy M. 2001. Interactive video training for firearms safety. *Federal Probation* 65(2): 45–51.

Schloss, Christine S., and Leanne F. Alarid. 2007. Standards in the privatization of probation services: A statutory analysis. *Criminal Justice Review* 32(3): 233–245.

Schultz, E.J. 2007. Female inmates: Jammed behind bars? Sacramento Bee, July 9. Retrieved from: http://www.november.org/stayinfo/breaking07/Jammed.html

Schwalbe, Craig S., and Tina Maschi. 2011. Confronting delinquency: Probation officers' use of coercion and client-centered tactics to foster youth compliance. *Crime and Delinquency* 57(5): 801–822.

Seiter, Richard P. 2002. Prisoner reentry and the role of parole officers. *Federal Probation* 66(3): 50–54.

Seiter, Richard P., and Karen R. Kadela. 2003. Prisoner reentry: What works, what does not, and what is promising. *Crime and Delinquency* 49(3): 360–388.

Sentencing Accountability Commission and the Statistical Analysis Center. 2005. First Year Assessment of the 2003 Probation Reform Law's Impact on the Administration of Justice in Delaware (Senate Bill 50 & 150). Retrieved from: http://www.state.de.us/budget/sac/publications/sb50.pdf.

Sentencing Project. 2011. *Felony Disenfranchisement Laws in the United States*. Retrieved from:http://www.sentencingproject.org/doc/publications/fd_bs_fdlawsinusMar11.pdf at the following website: http://www.sentencingproject.org/template/page.cfm?id=133

Settles, Tanya. 2004. *Financial management and strategic planning in a non-profit service organization: Crosspoint, Inc. of San Antonio*. Packard Foundation.

Shaffer, Deborah Koetzle, Bridget Kelly, and Joel D. Lieberman. 2011. An exemplar-based approach to risk assessment: Validating the risk management systems instrument. *Criminal Justice Policy Review* 22(2): 167–186.

Shaffer, Deborah Koetzle, and Terance D. Miethe. 2011. Are similar sex offenders treated similarly? A conjunctive analysis of disparities in community notification decisions. *Journal of Research in Crime and Delinquency* 48(3): 448–471.

Sickmund, Melissa, T.J. Sladky, and Wei Kang. 2008. *Census of juveniles in residential placement databook*. Washington, DC: Office of Juvenile Justice and Delinquency Prevention. Retrieved from: http://www.ojjdp.ncjrs.org/ojstatbb/cjrp/

Siedschlaw, Kurt D., and Beth A. Wiersma. 2005. Costs and outcomes of a work ethic camp: How do they compare to a traditional prison facility? *Corrections Compendium* 30(6): 1–5, 28–30.

Sims, Barbara, and Mark Jones. 1997. Predicting success or failure on probation: Factors associated with felony probation outcomes. *Crime and Delinquency* 43: 314–327.

Skeem, Jennifer L., Paula Emke-Francis, and Jennifer Eno Louden. 2006. Probation, mental health, and mandated treatment. *Criminal Justice and Behavior* 33(2): 158–184.

Slate, Risdon N. 2003. From the jailhouse to Capitol Hill: Impacting mental health court legislation and defining what constitutes a mental health court. *Crime and Delinquency* 49(1): 6–29.

Slate, Risdon N., Richard Feldman, Erik Roskes, and Migdalia Baerga. 2004. Training federal probation officers as mental health specialists. *Federal Probation* 68(3): 9–15.

Slate, Risdon N., and W. Wesley Johnson. 2008a. *The criminalization of mental illness: Crisis and opportunity in the justice system*. Durham, NC: Carolina Academic Press.

Slate, Risdon, and W. Wesley Johnson. 2008b. *A comparison of federal and state probation officer stress levels*. Paper presented at the annual meeting of the Academy of Criminal Justice Sciences, Cincinnati, OH.

Slate, Risdon N., W. Wesley Johnson, and Terry L. Wells. 2000. Up to speed: Probation officer stress: Is there an organizational solution? *Federal Probation* 64(1): 56–59.

Slate, Risdon N., Erik Roskes, Richard Feldman, and Migdalia Baerga. 2003. Doing justice for mental illness and society: Federal probation and pretrial service officers as mental health specialists. *Federal Probation* 67(3): 13–19.

Small, Shawn E., and Sam Torres. 2001. Arming probation officers: Enhancing public confidence and officer safety. *Federal Probation* 65(3): 24–28.

Smith, Michael E. 2001. What future for "public safety" and "restorative justice" in community corrections? *Sentencing and corrections: Issues for the 21st century* (No. 11, June). Washington, DC: U.S. Department of Justice.

Smith, Michael E., and Walter J. Dickey. 1999. Reforming sentencing and corrections for just punishment and public safety. *Sentencing and corrections: Issues for the 21st century* (No. 4). Washington, DC: U.S. Department of Justice.

Snyder, Howard. 2008. *Juvenile arrests 2006*. Washington, DC: Office of Juvenile Justice and Delinquency Prevention.

Snyder, Howard, and Melissa Sickmund. 2006. *Juvenile offenders and victims: 2006 national report*. Washington, DC: Office of Juvenile Justice and Delinquency Prevention.

Socia, Kelly. 2011. The policy implications of residence restrictions on sex offender housing in upstate NY. *Criminology and Public Policy* 10(2): 351–389.

Solis, Dianne. 2006. Convicts get help going straight to work. *Dallas Morning News*, September 24.

Solomon, Amy L. 2006. Does parole supervision work? Research findings and policy opportunities. *Perspectives* (Spring): 26–37. Retrieved from: http://www.urban.org/uploadedpdf/1000908_parole_supervision.pdf.

Stageberg, Paul, and Bonnie Wilson. 2005. *Recidivism among Iowa probationers*. Iowa Division of Criminal and Juvenile Justice Planning. Retrieved from: http://www.state.ia.us/government/dhr/cjjp/images/pdf/recidivism%20among%20Iowa%20probationers.pdf#.

Staples, William G., and Stephanie K. Decker. 2010. Between the home and institutional worlds: Tensions and contradictions in the practice of house arrest. *Critical Criminology* 18: 1–20.

State of New Hampshire, Human Resources. 2006. Retrieved from: http://nh.gov/hr/classpec_j/5462.htm.

State of Oregon, Department of Administrative Services, Juvenile Parole and Probation Officer. Retrieved from: http://www.hr.das.state.or.us/hrsd/class/6634.HTM.

Steen, Sara, and Tara Opsal. 2007. Punishment on the installment plan: Individual-level predictors of parole revocation in four states. *The Prison Journal* 87: 344–366.

Steiner, Benjamin. 2004. Treatment retention: A theory of post-release supervision for the substance-abusing offender. *Federal Probation* 68(3): 24 29.

Stempel, Johnathan, Kristen Hays, and John Wallace. 2011. Ex-Enron CFO moved to halfway house from prison. *Yahoo News/Reuters* May 19, 2011. Retrieved from: http://news/yahoo.com/s/nm/20110518/bs_nm/us_enron_fastow/

Stewart Law Firm. 2000. Expungement under the New Jersey Code of Criminal Justice. Retrieved from: http://home.pro-usa.net/rstewart/lexpunge.htm.

Stickels, John. 2007. A study of probation revocations for technical violations in Hays County, Texas, USA. *Probation Journal* 54(1): 52–61.

Stinchcomb, Jeanne B., and Daryl Hippensteel. 2001. Presentence investigation reports: A relevant justice model tool or a medical model relic? *Criminal Justice Policy Review* 12(2): 164–177.

Stoll, Michael A. and Shawn D. Bushway. 2008. The effect of criminal background checks on hiring ex-offenders. *Criminology and Public Policy* 7(3): 371–404.

Storm, John P. 1997. What United States probation officers do. *Federal Probation* 61(1): 13–18.

Stottmann, Jonathan O. 2007. Presentence restitution: When opportunity knocks. *News and Views* 32(19): September 10.

Sung, Hung-En. 2011. From diversion to reentry: Recidivism risks among graduates of an alternative to incarceration program. *Criminal Justice Policy Review* 22(2): 219–234.

Taxman, Faye. 2002. Supervision—Exploring the dimensions of effectiveness. *Federal Probation* 66(2): 14–27.

Taxman, Faye S. 2008. No illusions: Offender and organizational change in Maryland's proactive community supervision efforts. *Criminology and Public Policy* 7(2): 275–302.

Taxman, Faye S., and Jeffrey A. Bouffard. 2003. Drug treatment in the community—A case study of system integration issues. *Federal Probation* 67(2): 4–14.

Taylor, Scott and Ginger Martin. 2006. Four-point strategy reduces technical violations of probation in Connecticut. *Topics in Community Corrections: Effectively Managing Violations and Revocations*. Longmont, CO: National Institute of Corrections.

Tewksbury, Richard. 2002. Validity and utility of the Kentucky sex offender registry. *Federal Probation* 66(1): 21–26.

Tewksbury, Richard. 2005. Collateral consequences of sex offender registration. *Journal of Contemporary Criminal Justice* 21: 67–82.

Tewksbury, Richard. 2011. Policy implications of sex offender residence restriction laws. *Criminology and Public Policy* 10(2): 345–348.

Texas Department of Criminal Justice. 1999. Community corrections facilities outcome study. Retrieved from: http://webarchive.org/web/2000081165233/http://www.tdcj.state.tx.us/publications/cjad/ccfout~1.pdf

Texas Juvenile Probation Commission and Texas Youth Commission. 2003. *Texas juvenile justice system files and records.* (March). Austin, Texas: Texas Youth Commission.

Texas Legislative Budget Board. 2005. Statewide criminal justice recidivism and revocation rates. Retrieved from: http://www.lbb.state.tx.us/pubsafety_crimjustice/3_reports/recidivism_report_2005.pdf

Tonry, Michael. 1997. *Intermediate sanctions in sentencing guidelines.* Washington, DC: U.S. Department of Justice, National Institute of Justice (May).

Travis, Jeremy. 2000. But they all come back: Rethinking prisoner reentry, *Sentencing and corrections: Issues for the 21st century.* Washington, DC: U.S. Department of Justice.

Tucker, Susan B., and Eric Cadora. 2003. Ideas for an open society: Justice reinvestment. *Open Society Institute* 3(3): 1–8. Retrieved from: http://www.soros.org/resources/articles_publications/publications/ideas_20040106/ideas_reinvestment.pdf

Turner, Susan, Jesse Janneta, James Hess, Randy Myers, Rita Shah, Robert Werth, and Alyssa Whitby. 2007. *Implementation and early outcomes for the San Diego high risk sex offender GPS pilot program* (Working paper). Center for Evidence-Based Corrections, University of California, Irvine.

Turner, Susan, and Joan Petersilia. 1996. Work release in Washington: Effects on recidivism and correctional costs. *The Prison Journal* 76(2): 138–164.

Uggen, Christopher. 2000. Work as a turning point in the life course of criminals: A duration model of age, employment, and recidivism. *American Sociological Review* 65(4): 529–546.

Uggen, Christopher, Jeff Manza, and Angela Behrens. 2004. Less than the average citizen: Stigma, role transition, and the civic reintegration of convicted felons. Pp. 261–293 in *After crime and punishment: Pathways to offender reintegration*, edited by Shadd Maruna and Russ Immarigeon. Portland, OR: Willan.

Ulrich, Thomas E. 2002. Pretrial diversion in the federal court system. *Federal Probation* 66(3): 30–37.

Umbreit, Mark S. 1999. Restorative justice: What works. In *Research to results: Effective community corrections*, edited by Patricia M. Harris. Lanham, MD: American Correctional Association.

Umbreit, Mark S., Robert B. Coates, and Betty Vos. 2001. The impact of victim–offender mediation: Two decades of research. *Federal Probation* 65(3): 29–35.

U.S. Bureau of Prisons. 2008. *Guidelines Manual* (November 1, 2008). Section 7B1.4, p. 488.

U.S. Department of Justice. 2005. 28 CFR Part 2: Paroling, recommitting, and supervising federal prisoners: Prisoners serving sentences under the U.S and D.C. codes. *Federal Register* 70(70), April 13, 2005: 19262.

———. 2008. *Compendium of federal justice statistics, 2004.* Washington, DC: U.S. Department of Justice. Accessed at: http://www.ojp.usdoj.gov/bjs/pub/pdf/cfjs0407.pdf

U.S. Department of Justice, Bureau of Justice Statistics. 1995. *Correctional Populations in the United States 1994.* Washington, DC: U.S. Department of Justice.

U.S. Department of Justice, Bureau of Justice Statistics. 2003. *Census of state and federal correctional facilities, 2000.* Washington, DC: U.S. Department of Justice.

U.S. Department of Labor. 2006. *Occupational outlook handbook, 2006–07 edition*. Probation officers and correctional treatment specialists, Bureau of Labor Statistics. Retrieved from: http://www.bls.gov/oco/ocos265.htm

U.S. Department of Labor. 2009. *The Federal Bonding Program*. Retrieved from: http://www.bonds4jobs.com/index.html

U.S. Parole Commission. 2003. *Rules and procedures manual*. Washington, DC: U.S. Parole Commission. Retrieved from: http://www.usdoj.gov/uspc/rules_procedures/rulesmanual.htm

———. 2006. Answering your questions. Retrieved from: http://www.usdoj.gov/uspc/questionstxt.htm

U.S. Sentencing Commission. 2002a. *2001 Sourcebook of federal sentencing statistics*. Washington, DC: U.S. Sentencing Commission.

U.S. Sentencing Commission. 2010. *Federal Sentencing Guidelines Manual* Chapter 5, Part A, Updated November 1, 2010. Available at: http://www.ussc.gov/guidelines/2010guidelines/manual_pdf/Chapter5.pdf

VanBenschoten, Scott. 2008. Risk/needs assessment: Is this the best we can do? *Federal Probation* 72(2): 38–42.

Van Ness, Daniel, and Karen Strong. 1997. *Restoring justice*. Cincinnati, OH: Anderson.

VanNostrand, Marie, and Crime & Justice Institute. 2007. *Legal and evidence-based practices: Applications of legal principles, laws, and research to the field of pretrial services*. Washington, DC: National Institute of Corrections.

VanNostrand, Marie, and Gena Keebler. 2007. Our journey toward pretrial justice. *Federal Probation* 71(2): 20–25.

VERA Institute of Justice. 2010. *The continuing fiscal crisis in corrections: Setting a new course*. New York NY: VERA Institute of Justice.

Vigorita, Michael S. 2002. Fining practices in felony courts: An analysis of offender, offense, and systemic factors. *Corrections Compendium* 27(11): 1–5, 26.

Visher, Christy A., Nicole Smolter, and Daniel O'Connell. 2010. Workforce development program: A pilot study of its impact in the U.S. probation office, District of Delaware. *Federal Probation* 74(3): 16–21.

Vollum, Scott, and Chris Hale. 2002. Electronic monitoring: A research review. *Corrections Compendium* 27(7): 1–4, 23–27.

von Hirsch, Andrew. 1976. *Doing justice: The choice of punishments*. New York: Hill and Wang.

von Zielbauer, Paul. 2003. Court treatment system is found to help drug offenders stay clean. *New York Times, November 9.Health section*. Accessed at: www.nytimes.com.

Vose, Brenda, Francis T. Cullen, and Paula Smith. The empirical status of the level of service inventory. *Federal Probation* 72(3), 22–29.

Vose, Brenda, Christopher T. Lowenkamp, Paula Smith, and Francis T. Cullen. 2009. Gender and the predictive validity of the LSI-R: A study of parolees and probationers. *Journal of Contemporary Criminal Justice* 25(4): 459–471.

Waldo, Gordon P., and Theodore G. Chiricos. 1977. Work release and recidivism: An empirical evaluation of a social policy. *Evaluation Quarterly* 1(1): 87–108.

Walker, Donald R. 1988. *Penology for profit*. College Station, TX: Texas A&M University Press.

Walker, Lorenn. 2002. Conferencing: A new approach for juvenile justice in Honolulu. *Federal Probation* 66(1): 38–43.

Wallace, Jim. 2011. Lee County bail bondsman new electronic monitoring provider. *WALB News 10 Update*, April 13. Retrieved from: http://www.walb.com/story/14412108/lee-county-bail-bondsman-new-provider-electronic-monitoring-for-5-counties?redirected=true

Walsh, C. L., and S. H. Beck. 1990. Predictors of recidivism among halfway house residents. *American Journal of Criminal Justice* 15(1): 137–156.

Ward, Geoff, and Aaron Kupchik. 2009. Accountable to what? Professional orientations towards accountability-based juvenile justice. *Punishment and Society* 11(1): 85–109.

Ward, Geoff, and Aaron Kupchik. 2010. What drives juvenile probation officers? Relating organizational contexts, status characteristics, and personal convictions to treatment and punishment orientations. *Crime and Delinquency* 56(1): 35–69.

Weisburd, David, Tomer Einat, and Matt Kowalski. 2008. The miracle of the cells: An experimental study of interventions to increase payment of court-ordered financial obligations. *Criminology and Public Policy* 7(1): 9–36.

Wells, Terry, Sharla Colbert, and Risdon N. Slate. 2006. Gender matters: Differences in state probation officer stress. *Journal of Contemporary Criminal Justice* 22(1): 63–79.

West, Heather C., and William J. Sabol. 2008. *Prisoners in 2007*. Washington, DC: U.S. Department of Justice, Bureau of Justice Statistics.

West-Smith, Mary, Mark R. Pogrebin, and Eric D. Poole. 2000. Denial of parole: An inmate perspective. *Federal Probation* 64(2): 3–10.

White, Michael D., Jeff Mellow, Kristin Englander, and Marc Ruffinengo. 2011. Halfway back: An alternative to revocation for technical parole violators. *Criminal Justice Policy Review* 22(2): 140–166.

Wicharaya, Tamask. 1995. *Simple theory, hard reality: The impact of sentencing reforms on courts, prisons, and crime*. New York: State University of New York Press.

Wilkinson, Reginald A., and Edward E. Rhine. 2005. The international association of reentry: Mission and future. *Journal of Correctional Education* 56(2): 139–145.

Wilkinson, Reginald A., Edward E. Rhine, and Martha Henderson-Hurley. 2005. Reentry in Ohio corrections: A catalyst for change. *Journal of Correctional Education* 56(2): 158–172.

Williams, Frank P. III, Marilyn D. McShane, and H. Michael Dolny. 2000a. Developing a parole classification instrument for use as a management tool. *Corrections Management Quarterly* 4(4): 45–59.

———. 2000b. Predicting parole absconders. *The Prison Journal* 80(1): 24–38.

Williams, Frank P. III, Marilyn D. McShane, Lorraine Samuels, and H. Michael Dolny. 2000. The youngest adult parolees: Do they have different parole experiences? Paper presented at the annual meeting of the American Society of Criminology, San Francisco, California, November 14–17.

Wilson, David B., Doris L. MacKenzie, and Fawn Ngo Mitchell. 2005. Effects of Correctional Boot Camps on Offending. A Campbell Collaboration systematic review, available at: http://www.aic.gov/au/campbellcj/reviews/titles.html

Wilson, James A., and Robert C. Davis. 2006. Good intentions meet hard realities: An evaluation of the Project Greenlight reentry program. *Criminology & Public Policy* 5(2): 303–338.

Wines, Fredrick H. 1919. *Punishment and reformation: A study of the penitentiary system.* New York: T.Y. Crowell.

Wolf, Isaac. 2011. States balk at tighter sex offender rules. Scripps Howard News Service, June 30. Available at http://www.scrippsnews.com

Wolf, Thomas J. 1997. What United States pretrial services officers do. *Federal Probation* 61(1): 19–24.

Wright, Martin. 1996. *Justice for victims and offenders: A restorative response to crime,* 2nd ed. Winchester, England: Waterside Press.

Wright, Ronald. 1998. *Managing prison growth in North Carolina through structured sentencing.* Washington, DC: National Institute of Justice.

Yeh, Stuart S. 2010. Cost-benefit analysis of reducing crime through electronic monitoring of parolees and probationers. *Journal of Criminal Justice* 38: 1090–1096.

Youth Reentry Task Force of the Juvenile Justice and Delinquency Prevention Coalition. 2009. *Back on track: Supporting youth reentry from out-of-home placement to the community.* Washington, DC: Youth Reentry Task Force of the Juvenile Justice and Delinquency Prevention Coalition.

Zandbergen, Paul A., Jill S. Levenson, and Timothy C. Hart. 2010. Residential proximity to schools and daycares: An empirical analysis of sex offense recidivism. *Criminal Justice and Behavior* 37: 482–502.

Zavlek, Shelley. 2005. Planning community-based facilities for violent juvenile offenders as part of a system of graduated sanctions. *Juvenile Justice Bulletin.* Washington, DC: Office of Juvenile Justice and Delinquency Prevention. Available at: https://www.ncjrs.gov/pdffiles1/ojjdp/209326.pdf

Zevitz, Richard, and Mary Ann Farkas. 2000. The impact of sex-offender community notification on probation/parole in Wisconsin. *International Journal of Offender Therapy and Comparative Criminology* 44(1): 8–21.

CODES

California Interstate Compact on Juveniles, Cal. Welf. and Inst. Code, secs. 1300–1308 (West).

California Penal Code, sec. 1203, 4853 (West).

Colorado Revised Statutes 1998, sec. 24–72–308.

Community Corrections Act, Oregon Revised Statutes 423.505 (Oregon Laws 1995).

Federal Rules of Criminal Procedure, Art. 3564.

Federal Criminal Code and Rules, 2004. Belmont, CA: West.

Illinois Unified Code of Corrections, sec. 1005–5–5(d).

Indiana Juvenile Code Title 31, Article 6, Chapter 9, Section 31–6–9–4(a).

Model Penal Code, sec. 7.07 (5); sec. 301.2.

N.H. Rev. Stat. Ann. sec. 607–A:5.

New York Penal Law, sec. 65.00–1 (McKinney).

Texas Code of Criminal Procedure, Article 42.12, Sec. 7, Sec. 11(1), Sec. 20, Sec. 22(a)(1). (Vernon).

III. Unified Code of Corrections sec. 1005–6–5(2).

United States Codes, Title 10, U.S.C., sec. 504; Title 11, U.S.C.A., sec. 1328 (a)(3); Title 18 U.S.C. sec. 921 (a)(20); sec. 922g1; sec. 3561; sec. 3563(a)(2); sec. 3563 (b)(11); sec. 3583 (e)(3); sec. 3606; sec. 5037 (c)(1); sec. 5037 (c)(2); Title 28 U.S.C. sec. 235(a)(1)(B)(ii)(IV); sec. 1865 (b)(5); Title 29 U.S.C., sec. 405.

U.S. Constitution, Article 1.

Wis. Stat. Ann. sec. 57.078.

COURT CASES

Ballenger v. State, 436 S.E.2d 793 (Ga. App. 1993).

Bearden v. Georgia, 461 U.S. 660 (1983).

Beecham v. United States, 511 U.S. 368 (1994).

Belk v. Purkett, 15 F.3d 803 (8th Cir. 1994).

Benton v. State, 2003 WL 22220501, Ala. Crim. App. (2003).

Best v. State, 264 A.D.2d 404, 694 N.Y.S.2d 689 (2d Dep't 1999).

Biddle v. Perovich, 274 U.S. 480, 47 S. Ct. 664, 71 L. Ed. 1161 (1927).

Boling v. Romer, 101 F.3d 1336 (10th Cir. 1996).

Breed v. Jones, 421 U.S. 517 (1975).

Bruggeman v. State, 681 So.2d. 822 (1996).

Burdick v. United States, 236 U.S. 79, 59 L. Ed. 476 (1915).

Cabell v. Chavez-Salido (1982) 454 U.S. 432.

Cabla v. State, 6 S.W.3d 543 (Tex. Crim. App.1999).

Caron v. United States, 524 U.S. 308 (1998).

Commonwealth v. Chase, in Thacher's Criminal Cases, 267 (1831), recorded in vol. 11 of the Records of the Old Municipal Court of Boston, 199.

Commonwealth of Massachusetts v. Talbot, 444 Mass. 586, 830 N.E.2d 177 (2005).

Connecticut Department of Public Safety v. Doe, 538 U.S. 1 (2003).

Correctional Services Corp v. Malesko, 534 U.S. 61 (2001).

Davis v. Alaska, 415 U.S. 308 (1974).

Eddings v. Oklahoma, 455 U.S. 104 (1983).

Ex parte Garland, 71 U.S. 333, 18 L. Ed. 366 (1867).

Ex parte Lefors, 303 S.W.2d 394 (Tex. Crim. App. 1957).

Ex parte United States, 242 U.S. 27, 37 S. Ct. 72, 61 L. Ed. 129 (1916).

Fare v. Michael C., 442 U.S. 707 (1985).

Fields v. State, 2002 WL 126972, Ala. Crim. App. (2002).

Franciosi v. Michigan Parole Board, 461 Mich. 347 (2000).

Gagnon v. Scarpelli, 411 U.S. 778 (1973).

Glover v. Michigan Parole Board, 460 Mich. 511 (1999).

Goldberg v. Beeler, 82 F.Supp.2d 302 (1999).

Goldschmitt v. State, 490 So.2d 123 (Fla. Dist. Ct. App. 1986).

Graham v. Florida, 560 U.S. ___ (2010). (08–7412)

Greenholtz v. Inmates of the Nebraska Penal and Correctional Complex, 442 U.S. 1, 99 S. Ct. 2100, 2107, 60 L. Ed. 2d 668 (1979).
Griffin v. Wisconsin, 483 U.S. 868 (1987).

Hampton v. State, 786 A.2d 375 (R.I. 2001).
Hawkins v. Freeman, 166 F.3d 267 (1999).
Higdon v. United States, 627 F.2d 893 (9th Cir. 1980).

Inouye v. Kemna, 06–15474 (9th Cir. 2007), DC No. CV-04-00026-DAE
In re Bocchiaro, 49 F. Supp. 37 (W.D.N.Y. 1943).
In re Ecklund, 139 Wash. 2d 166 (1999).
In re Gault, 387 U.S. 1 (1967).
In re Winship, 397 U.S. 358 (1970).
Jago v. Van Curen, 454 U.S. 14 (1981).
Jones v. State, 916 S.W.2d 766 (Ark. App. 1996).

Kansas v. Crane, 534 U.S. 407 (2002).
Kansas v. Hendricks, 521 U.S. 346 (1997).
Kent v. United States, 383 U.S. 541 (1966).
King v. Simpson, 189 F.3d 283 (2d Cir. 1999).

Lay v. Louisiana Parole Board, 741 So.2d 80 (La. Ct. App. 1st Cir. 1999).

Marlo v. State Board of Medical Examiners, 112 Cal. App. 2d 276, 246 P.2d 69 (1952).
Matter of J.B.S., 696 S.W.2d 223 (Tex. App. 1985).
McKeiver v. Pennsylvania, 403 U.S. 528 (1971).
McKune v. Lile 536 U.S. 24 (2002), 224 F. 3d. 1175.
Menechino v. Oswald, 430 F.2d 403, 407 (2d Cir. 1970), cert. denied, 400 U.S. 1023, 91 S. Ct. 588, 27 L. Ed. 2d 635 (1971).
Miller v. District of Columbia, 294 A.2d 365 (D.C. App. 1972).
Miranda v. Arizona, 384 U.S. 436 (1966).
Morrissey v. Brewer, 408 U.S. 471 (1972).
Murrill v. State Board of Accountancy, 97 Cal. App. 2d 709, 218 P.2d 569 (1950).

Newsom v. State, 2004 WL 943861, Miss. Ct. App. (2004).
New Jersey v. T.L.O., 469 U.S. 325 (1985).

Padilla v. Kentucky, 130 S. Ct. 1473 (2010).
Pennsylvania Board of Probation and Parole v. Scott, 524 U.S. 357 (1998).
People v. Colabello, 948 P.2d 77 (Colo. App. 1997).
People v. Heckler, 16 Cal. Rptr. 2d 681, 13 C. A. 4th 1049 (1993).
People v. Meyer, 176 Ill. 2d 372, 680 N.E. 315 (1997).
People v. Price, 24 Ill. App. 2d. 364 (1960).
People v. Ramos, 48 CrL 1057 (Ill.S.Ct.) (1990).
People v. Sweeden, 116 Cal. App. 2d. 891 (1953).
Perry v. State, 778 So. 2d 1072 (Fla. Dist. Ct. App. 5th Dist. 2001).

Ramahlo v. Travis, 737 N.Y.S.2d 160 (3d Dep't 2002).
Reyes v. Tate, 91 Ohio St. 3d 84, 742 N.E.2d 132 (2001).
Richardson v. McKnight, 521 U.S. 399 (1997).
Richardson v. New York State Executive Department, 602 N.Y.S.2d 443 (1993).

Richardson v. Ramirez, 418 U.S. 24, 94 S. Ct. 2655, 41 L. Ed. 2d 551 (1974).
Rodriguez v. State, 378 So.2d 7 (Fla. Dist. Ct. App. 1979).
Roper v. Simmons, 543 U.S. 551 (2005).

Samson v. California, 547 U.S. 843 (2006).
Scarpa v. United States Board of Parole, 477 F.2d 278, 281 (5th Cir. 1972), vacated as moot; 414 U.S. 809, 94 S. Ct. 79, 38 L. Ed. 2d 44 (1973).
Schall v. Martin, 104 S. Ct. 2403 (1984).
Seling v. Young, 531 U.S. 250 (2001).
Silmon v. Travis, 95 N.Y.2d 470 (2000).
Smith v. Daily Mail Publishing Co., 443 U.S. 97 (1979).
Smith v. Doe, 538 U.S. 84 (2003).
Soliz v. State, 171 Tex. Crim. 376 (1961).
Spaulding v. Nielsen, 599 F.2d 728 (5th Cir. 1979).
Stanford v. Kentucky, 109 S.Ct. 2969 (1989).
State v. Bourrie, 190 Or. App. 572, 80 P.3d 505 (2003).
State v. Faraday, 69 Conn. App. 421 (2002).
State v. Graham, 30 P.3d 310 (Kan 2001).
State v. Gropper, 888 P.2d 12211 (Wash. App. 1995).
State v. Pizel, 987 P.2d 1288 (Utah Ct. App. 1999).
State v. Walker, 432 So.2d 1057 (La. Ct. App. 1983).
Sullivan v. Florida, 560 U.S. ___ (2010). (08–7621).
Summers v. State, 817 So. 2d 950 (Fla Dist. Ct. App. 2d Dist. 2002).

United States v. Allen, 13 F.3d 105 U.S. (4th Cir. December 1993).
United States v. Bachsian, 4 F.3d 288 (1993).
United States v. Balon, 384 F.3d 38 (2d Cir. 2004).
United States v. Booker, 125 S. Ct. 738, 160 LED 2d 621 (U.S. 2005).
United States v. Caron, 524 U.S. 308 (1998).
United States v. Fowler, U.S. (11th Cir. 1999).
United States v. Gordon, 4 F.3d 1567 U.S. (10th Cir. September 1993).
United States v. Knights, 534 U.S. 112 (2001).
United States v. Laney, 189 F.3d 954 (9th Cir. 1999).
United States v. Lockhart, 58 F.3d 86 (4th Cir. June 1995).
United States v. McCormick, 54 F.3d 214 U.S. (5th Cir. 1995).
United States v. Pettus, 303 F.3d 480 (2d Cir. 2002).
United States v. Rivera, 96 F.3rd 41 (2nd cir. September 1996).
United States v. RLC, 503 U.S. 291 (1992).
United States v. Salerno, 481 U.S. 739 (1987).
United States v. Thurlow, 44 F.3d 46 U.S. (1st Cir. 1995).
United States v. Turner, 44 F.3d 900 (10th Cir. 1995).
United States v. Washington, 11 F.3d 1510 U.S. (10th Cir. November 1993).
United States v. Wolff, 90 F.3d 191 (7th Cir. 1996).

Walrath v. Getty, 71 F.3d 679 (7th Cir. 1995).
Warner v. Orange County Department of Probation, 115 F3d 1068 (2nd Cir 1997).
Williams v. New York, 337 U.S. 241 (1949).
Williams v. Oklahoma, 358 U.S. 576 (1959).
Williams v. State of New Jersey, 2006 NJ Lexis 389, (2006).

Young v. Harper, 520 U.S. 143 (1997).

Case Index

Name Index

Subject Index